Partners in

POWER

◆

Also by Roger Morris

RICHARD MILHOUS NIXON:
The Rise of an American Politician

HAIG:
The General's Progress

UNCERTAIN GREATNESS:
Henry Kissinger and American Foreign Policy

DEVIL'S BUTCHER SHOP:
The New Mexico Prison Uprising

Partners in
POWER

The Clintons
and Their America

◆

Roger Morris

A John Macrae Book

HENRY HOLT AND COMPANY ◆ NEW YORK

Henry Holt and Company, Inc.
Publishers since 1866
115 West 18th Street
New York, New York 10011

Henry Holt® is a registered trademark
of Henry Holt and Company, Inc.

Published in Canada by Fitzhenry & Whiteside Ltd.,
195 Allstate Parkway, Markham, Ontario L3R 4T8.

Library of Congress Cataloging-in-Publication Data
Morris, Roger.
Partners in power : the Clintons and their America/Roger Morris. — 1st ed.
p.   cm.
"A John Macrae book"
Includes bibliographical references and index.
1. Clinton, Bill, 1946–   . 2. Clinton, Hillary Rodham.   3. Arkansas—Politics and
government—1951–   4. United States—Politics and government—1993–   I. Title.
E886.M67   1996   96-17112
973.929'092'2—dc20   CIP

ISBN 0-8050-2804-8

Henry Holt books are available for special
promotions and premiums. For details contact:
Director, Special Markets.

First Edition—1996

Designed by Victoria Hartman

Printed in the United States of America
All first editions are printed on acid-free paper.∞
1   3   5   7   9   10   8   6   4   2

In memory of Ida Cox Transue
1888–1962

and for
Coleman Hammer-Tomizuka

Contents

Prologue: *"Times When Hope Is Palpable"*   1

BOOK I

1 • Sikeston: *"Riding on a Smile"*   15

2 • Hope: *"Bright Little Orphan"*   24

3 • Hot Springs: *"The Power to Save"*   36

4 • Georgetown: *"They'll Know What I'm Doing Here"*   60

5 • Oxford: *"Every String He Could Think Of"*   79

6 • Park Ridge: *"She Had to Put Up with Him"*   107

7 • Wellesley: *"Tomorrow, When You Are the Establishment"*   124

8 • Yale I: *"She Saw Right Past the Charm"*   139

9 • Yale II: *"She Never Drew Her Identity from Him"*   153

10 • Fayetteville: *"An Aura of Inevitability"*   170

BOOK II
_____

11 • *Regnat Populus: "The People Rule"*   193

12 • Little Rock I: *"A Guy Who Supposedly
Has an IQ of a Zillion"*   216

13 • Washington I: *"A Slow-Motion Coup d'État"*   251

14 • Little Rock II: *"You'll See They Love You Again"*   268

15 • Washington II: *"A Little Too Much
Like What It Really Is"*   292

16 • Little Rock III: *"Best of the New Generation"*   308

17 • Washington III: *"A Culture of Complicity"*   335

18 • Little Rock IV: *"A Feller Could Live Off the Land"*   359

19 • Little Rock and Mena: *"A World Nearly Devoid of Rules"*   389

20 • Little Rock to Washington: *"We Saw in Them
What We Wanted to Believe"*   428

Afterword   467

Acknowledgments   470

Sources and Notes   472

Select Bibliography   501

Index   505

. . . the man who believes in nothing, and
therefore has space for everything, has a terrible
advantage over us. What passes as a kindly
tolerance in him is in reality a craven acceptance
of the world's worst crimes. He's an immobilist,
an apathist, and a militant passivist. . . .
And of course he's a dear sweet man.

—*John le Carré*

Partners in

POWER

◆

Prologue

"Times When Hope Is Palpable"

They wait patiently, quietly. In the gentle valleys of central Virginia, where the small frame houses hug the highway, some people stand on their porches, still in bathrobes, their coffee cups steaming in the chill morning air. Others press closer to the road. They hold little American flags and lift small children to their shoulders for a better view.

This is opposition country. Some towns and counties have voted overwhelmingly to reelect the Republican president, George Bush. Like the rest of the nation, the region has given nearly twenty percent of its votes to eccentric independent candidate Ross Perot. Everywhere there are hand-lettered signs scrawled on cardboard and even bed-sheets—pleas, warnings, benedictions: "Keep Your Promises," "Small Business & Agriculture Need Help," "AIDS Won't Wait," "Don't Forget Bosnia," "We Are Counting On You." Over Culpeper a small airplane trails a kind of ultimatum against the pale winter sky: "CUT SPENDING NOW OR ROSS WILL IN '97." A woman along Route 29 near Warrenton holds up a message of two words: "Grace, Compassion."

For the moment, votes and old allegiances seem not to matter. As the fifteen-bus caravan speeds by, the people on the porches and along the roadside cheer and wave, and many are weeping. "We need to give the man a chance," a schoolteacher from Madison County tells a reporter. "He's going to be a president for all the people," one longtime Republican says to a stranger, as if in a kind of reassurance.

Governor William Jefferson Clinton of Arkansas is on his way to Washington to become the forty-second president of the United States.

1

His own bus bears the license plate HOPE 1, after the small town where he was born in southwestern Arkansas. A reportedly prodigal young governor, what he calls a New Democrat from the New South, he is the first of his party to win the White House in a dozen years and, at forty-six, the third-youngest chief executive in American history. He is not alone, just as he has never been alone in an unswerving twenty-year political career since law school. At his side is the woman who has been there from the beginning, eighteen years as his wife. A year younger than the new president, Hillary Rodham Clinton brings her own vivid history to this moment. If the new president carries hope, so does she, the symbol of a matured liberation and equality of women. For now at least, on the eve of her husband's inauguration, she promises to become the most powerful and significant First Lady in American history.

In a theatrically choreographed entry into Washington on a January day described as "drenched in symbolism," the president-elect and his wife are retracing in 1993 the path taken to the capital in 1801 by the first Democratic president, Thomas Jefferson. Inside Clinton's bus, the secure communications of the modern presidency are already in place, the special electronic phones that allow him to be briefed in secret on developments a world away in Somalia or Bosnia. But outside, the procession is to evoke history, tradition, legitimacy. The drive has begun at Jefferson's picturesque eighteenth-century plantation at Monticello. On narrow old back-country highways, the buses wind north for 120 miles across the rolling countryside of the Old Dominion and down the corridors of Civil War drama, through Brandy Station, where the greatest cavalry clash in North America took place on the eve of Gettysburg, past Manassas, with the blood-soaked battlefields of Bull Run.

Yet nothing is more impressive than the simple, uncontrived eloquence of the people at the roadside. When the buses have passed, the crowds in the little valleys drift away only slowly and reluctantly. In the wake of the motorcade, there is an expectant quiet once again, as if they are still waiting.

◆　◆　◆

The Clintons arrive later that afternoon at the Lincoln Memorial in Washington for a televised pageant, replete with symphonic fanfare, a flyover of military jets, candlelit processions, and celebrity performances. The president-elect listens in rapt admiration as rock stars sing "We Are the World," and in tribute to his own musical instrument and his favorite performer, ten famous saxophonists render Elvis Presley's "Heartbreak Hotel." It is the first of four days of carefully scripted, Hollywood-produced ceremonies, climaxing in the inauguration itself. At one point, at a Capital Center extravaganza, Bill Clinton will weep at the tributes paid him by movie stars and vocalists and will be unable to resist mouthing the lyrics while singer Barbra Streisand performs a sentimental hit. "The television cameras drifted away from Streisand, as Clinton knew they must," wrote *Harper's* editor Lewis Lapham, "and discovered the tear-stained face of the new president devouring the words as if they were made of chocolate."

Beyond the elaborate staging, away from the scaffolding and cameras and microphones, there is the same spontaneous sense felt along the Virginia roadsides. On a mild Sunday afternoon a great throng has gathered around the memorial's reflecting pool, churning the wintry mud of the parkway, surging forward here and there to be nearer the show. For all its vastness and variety, the crowd is good-natured, strikingly polite. "Thousands of black faces, yellow faces, white faces" is the way one observer describes the scene. "No pushing, no shoving."

"Cynics don't buy this," records a diarist who has been attending inaugurals for sixty years, "but there are times when hope is palpable."

In Washington proper, there are more professed Democrats in the crowd. There seems more sheer relish for the victory of faction and party. After twelve years of Republican presidents and the visible prominence of their wealthy backers, many ordinary citizens have a new feeling of inclusion and power. "In the past, you had to be a fat cat to get to the inauguration," says one Clinton supporter, a young worker with two small children. "And now we're the fat cats."

Of the Democrats' own genuine "fat cats" there will no doubt. "The air in the nation's capital these days is rich with the smell of curried favors," writes a correspondent. More than two hundred large corporations and several prominent individual contributors have provided nearly $20 million in interest-free loans for the Hollywood-produced galas. Others with similar stakes in government policy have paid an added $2.5 million to underwrite public events.

Just as during the inaugurals of Ronald Reagan and George Bush, private and corporate jets are parked wing to wing on the tarmac at National Airport, chauffeured luxury cars jam the fashionable narrow brick streets of Georgetown, and many celebrants of the new administration are laden with diamonds and sable. "Democrats look just like Republicans," observes a society reporter. "The two parties are now stylistically inseparable."

Even the Democrats' relative racial diversity seems bounded by class.

"The explosion of black yuppies around the Clinton-Gore galas is truly a sight to behold, with lots of fur and limousines," writes black columnist Courtland Milloy, who is repelled by the display of ostentation in the offspring of a community still wracked by poverty and prejudice. "A sense of entitlement to privilege was not a Bush thing. It was a white thing," he adds. "For black people to think that real power will be relinquished just because a Democrat is in the White House is foolish."

The night after the Clinton buses arrive, there are four exclusive dinners, at $1,500 a ticket, for what the *Washington Post* calls the "new Washington royalty." Many of the invited guests have given or raised hundreds of thousands of dollars, even millions, for Clinton—and some have done the same for *both* the Democratic and Republican candidates. "These people worked very hard to elect Bill Clinton. We're all here to pat each other on the back," one Democratic politician explains. "These people—the big law firms, the associations, the big corporation lobbyists—are the permanent ruling class here," says Charles Lewis, director of a small Washington organization called the Center for Public Integrity. "And they are guys who always back both horses. . . . This week they'll kick in some more, because they realize that putting up $100,000 or so is chump change in relation to what they'll get back."

Though journalists are barred from such gatherings, cordoned off in hotel lobbies or across the street, a witness repeats what the president-elect has said to at least one gathering of his wealthy contributors. "You're my friends," Clinton assures them, "and I won't forget you." As he makes his rounds of the parties, outside each is a handful of picketers, other Democrats from a group known as the Pioneer Valley Pro-Democracy Campaign, residents of the Berkshire Mountains of New England. "The face in the White House is changing," says their spokesman, "but the people who pull the strings behind the scenes are still the same."

The Clinton campaign itself has been dominated by those who represent and serve the governing interests outright, by the old capital harlotry. Among many others, campaign director Mickey Kantor and Democratic Party chairman Ron Brown, both appointed to the new cabinet, have made careers and small fortunes as part of the legion of lobbyists epitomized by the influential law firms and powerful pressure groups arrayed along Washington's K Street. Scores more like them will make up the new administration.

So natural a part of the transfer from politics to government, the caste privileges of the ruling interests now rankle even political consultants like James Carville, a plainspoken political strategist from Louisiana whose advice has been crucial in Clinton's long struggle for nomination and election. Though his own fees are always paid by the same interests, he is reminded abruptly where power lies in Washington. The night before the inauguration Carville is furious when he is refused fifty musical-event tickets for his young campaign workers. "They claim they're for kids," he tells a reporter, "and when I ask for tickets, they say, 'Oh, well, you can have six.' Right. They have to give them to the K Street puke fund."

In part at Carville's guidance, Clinton has won his highest margins among voters under thirty—an age group that once supported Reagan and Bush—as well as from more traditional Democrats over sixty-five. Yet the president-elect's own generation, more than seventy million voters in their thirties and forties, have given strong support to Ross Perot and have divided almost evenly between Clinton and Bush. In the end, the winner has taken only 43 percent of the national vote. In the three-way race, with Perot's 19 percent also against Bush, it has been enough. Bill Clinton is a minority president. But *change* has won in a 62 percent landslide.

On the eve of his inauguration, polls show the remarkable public faith and hope running through the crowds in and around Washington. A large majority of Americans expect Clinton to make "substantial progress" in dealing with grave problems of the economy, health care, race relations, the environment, and education and, most of all, in making government itself serve the country's needs rather than the interests of the rich and powerful or the stagnant habits of bureaucracy. "Even Republicans," reports the *Wall Street Journal,* "sense that the nation is almost desperate for things to start working better."

On these evenings of glittering celebration before the inauguration, at the luxury hotels and private parties, desperation seems invisible, almost an abstraction. But only a few minutes from the White House, the eight homeless shelters of the nation's capital are always full. At Mt. Vernon Place, the line forms at 2:00 p.m. to reserve a bed for the night. Only blocks away from the seat of government, teeming public-health clinics are open late into the night to provide thousands of the sick and suffering with their only chance for medical care or prescriptions.

At nearby junior highs, pupils will be excused to attend Bill Clinton's inaugural parade and then will return to their studies past ominous signs warning them not to smuggle in weapons, drugs, or beepers. The partly squalid, partly besieged capital of the United States is scarcely alone in these proclamations of fear. This inaugural morning, students in over a quarter of all schools in urban America will go to class by passing through metal detectors. Sitting at their desks, walking the hallways or playgrounds, they are statistically more likely to die of gunshot wounds than were most of the men who served in the military in the nation's wars. Revolvers and automatic weapons are now a chief cause of death among America's young people. As the Clinton presidency begins, the lives of many of the country's children are ending.

Among the guests come to town for the inauguration is Gordon Bush, the mayor of East St. Louis. He has paid his own way because his city cannot afford his air ticket. With most of its citizens receiving some form of public assistance, East St. Louis has 50 percent unemployment, pandemic drug use, a crushing debt, low tax revenues, and the highest murder rate in the United States. The mayor is hopeful President Clinton will do something to help preschool children. "When kids are thirteen years old," he says, "it's too late."

For much of the country, it has been possible to view the ruin of the great cities—nonwhite, poor, violent—as something apart from their own lives. But the desperate conditions, like the hopes for the new president, are now nationwide. In the eleven weeks since the election, there has been a vivid symbol of a wider decline. In these seventy-seven days alone, while the economy reportedly grew by 3 percent, while business confidence was said to gain and stock and bond markets were preening, firms large and small announced the loss of over three hundred thousand jobs, most of which will never return. Beyond the violent writhing cities, the rot runs to the very marrow of the nation, eating into a middle class once thought secure and affecting every aspect of American life.

"I desperately want to make a difference," Clinton tells a group of his fellow governors at a Library of Congress luncheon on January 19. His earnestness and empathy have overcome early and apparently deep-seated public doubts about his character. Nearly half of those who voted for him tell exit polls afterward that they are still convinced he is a "liar." "But at least he wasn't Bush, who offered no hope of change," says one analyst, explaining the public sense of the lesser of political evils. "On the campaign trail, Clinton came into contact with people in real pain, fighting real struggles, and this transformed him," says an aide. "Their pain became his and so, temporarily, did their struggles. That's how the guy managed to convince us he was for real."

Now, on the last day before he takes the oath of office, there is a deepening sense of this new president's unique paradox—and danger. "He labors beneath the burdens of no real confidence in him on one hand and too much hope on the other," Steve Erickson reports for the *Los Angeles Weekly,* "a mix by which the spirit of the country becomes weirdly combustible."

Along the Mall, there is another milling crowd at a festival of special exhibits, including a Brooklyn artist's "American Town Hall Wall," an eight-foot structure covered with what a passerby remembers as "hundreds" of small paper notes provided for scribbled statements to the new president, "myriad messages of hope and despair." One well-dressed couple strolls by and reads many of the six-inch squares with visible dismay. "I didn't know," the man remarks to the woman, "that there were so many of *them.*" During the afternoon Hillary Rodham Clinton pays a visit to the wall. As Secret Service agents clear the way, she stops briefly by a table provided for writing messages. A woman with a small girl takes the future First Lady's hand, and says softly, "We need health and education, Mrs. Clinton. Health and education. And don't let anybody fool your husband." The next man at the table hands her one of the small squares of paper. On it is written simply, "Courage!"

◆　◆　◆

Inauguration day arrives bright and cloudless, a southern winter sun soon melting the glaze of frost off Pennsylvania Avenue. At Blair House, across the street from the White House, Clinton begins his rituals at six-thirty with the daily presidential briefing on world affairs. This inaugural morning a Bush aide soberly explains the "Football"— the omnipresent small box conveying thermonuclear-attack codes. The electronic card to unlock the ciphers will pass to Clinton's side as he takes the oath of office at noon and will remain with him until the last moment of his presidency. It is part of the new man's beguiling initiation into the cultivated mystique of foreign policy.

The morning is full of emotion. Attending an early service at a historic African American church, once a stop on the underground railroad for runaway slaves, Clinton hears the Reverend Gardner Taylor of Brooklyn's Concord Baptist Church deliver a moving sermon on what the minister calls "the grandeur and the grime" of contemporary America. As Scripture is recited, the president-elect rocks back and forth in his pew and wipes away tears. As soloists sing a succession of traditional gospel hymns, he weeps again. Bill Clinton is "all nerve endings," a member of his staff will say later, "the most empathetic person of all time."

Sitting there in the church is another figure who knows something about Bill Clinton's feelings, about the tortured emotional history they share so intimately. His mother, Virginia Kelley, has risen early in her suite at the Mayflower Hotel to perform her forty-five-minute ritual of applying makeup, "putting on my paint," as she calls it. She still sees in the new president the child she raised with an alcoholic, abusive stepfather. "When he's hurting," she will say of her Billy, "he's just a big, old gray-headed version of my little boy." Across and beneath the city, Washington's subway is already packed with people making their way to the inauguration. Once again the crowds are genial and uncomplaining. On a swaying Orange Line train out of the Virginia suburbs, young girls in the middle of a car begin to sing softly: "Kumbayah, my Lord, Kumbayah. Someone's praying, Lord, Kumbayah." The jammed passengers fall silent, look awkward for a moment, and then smile at one another.

At the same moment more than ten thousand police and agents from several different forces and jurisdictions are dispersed throughout Washington, waiting for both Clinton and the crowds. Unprecedented security measures have been taken. There will be everything from antiaircraft guns and rooftop marksmen to sealed manhole covers. Even the decorated, suddenly polite inaugural capital has lately experienced what officials call "an increase in random and violent crime." Armed teenagers have terrorized and robbed tourists at the Smithsonian Institution, and visitors have been assaulted inside other national museums.

The inauguration proceeds without incident. In an earnest if unremarkable speech—written by an old friend and then a team of ghostwriters but edited in the end, like all his other major addresses, by Hillary Clinton—the president speaks of the hopes that have put him in office. "The American people have summoned the change we celebrate today. You have raised your voices in an unmistakable chorus," he tells the vast throng spread from the ornate west front of the Capitol down Pennsylvania Avenue and off into the distance toward the familiar white obelisk of the Washington Monument. "There is nothing wrong with America," he assures them, "that cannot be cured by what is right with America."

After the ceremony one witness thinks it a "seam in the fabric of time," another the "melding of moment and persona." Clinton has paid formal tribute to George Bush for "his half century of service to

America." Behind the protocol, the loser himself is rancorous. For his flight home to Houston Bush has invited old friends and early supporters, not the journalists who customarily accompany a former president on this parting journey. It is "a reminder," reports the *Washington Post,* "of Bush's bitterness toward the media from his unsuccessful reelection campaign."

Back at the Capitol, meanwhile, Clinton is being honored at the traditional luncheon with leaders of Congress. In the obligatory exchange of remarks an English reporter sees him radiate "the deliberate, and perhaps calculated, charm we have come to know, and occasionally to suspect." But as senators and representatives drone on, Clinton seems to shed the mask and grow pensive, suddenly drawn, looking in a moment to one observer "very young and very scared." He has been president of the United States scarcely an hour. From around the country during the afternoon and evening there are already stories of people praying and lighting their own candles for the nation's new leader. "Now our emotional investment in Clinton is frightening," writes one correspondent. Another writer calls it "the country's most reckless leap of faith yet."

That night there are more than a dozen official and unofficial inaugural balls—for wealthy backers, environmentalists, animal-rights advocates, gays and lesbians, even for several hundred homeless people who are advised to wear their best "church clothes." President Clinton will again make the rounds of the parties, playing the saxophone he learned well as a boy in Hot Springs, Arkansas, hugging friends, and working the crowds with "an efficient geniality," as one writer describes him, "a blue-collar craftsman of the squeeze." His sixteen-car motorcade now includes two dozen bodyguards, the trailing Secret Service "war wagon" with its special platform and armor-piercing portable artillery, a van full of reporters, and the now inevitable military aide handcuffed to the Football.

Sooner or later, at most of the parties, they play the theme song of the new administration: "Don't stop thinkin' about Tomorrow . . . Yesterday's gone, Yesterday's gone." The song has been chosen almost casually early in the campaign by a Clinton aide in Little Rock, but nowhere will the words prove more poignant or ironic than at the Arkansas Ball at the Washington Convention Center, packed with some seven thousand from the president's home state, ardent "FOBs," Friends of Bill. They are exultant in their victory and, typically, fiercely proud of their state, a place often ignored or ridiculed by outsiders. "Everybody knows where Arkansas is now," says a woman from

Paragould. "It's a new era," announces another from Little Rock. The most prominent among them, about to assume important new roles as presidential appointees or else highly paid Washington lobbyists, have been celebrating for days—at what an Arkansas reporter calls an "elite" dinner for a hundred in the Georgetown mansion of *Washington Post* owner Katharine Graham, at a Blue Jean Ball with chicken donated by Arkansas's own Tyson Foods, at the Grand Hyatt, where an Arkansas driver's license is the ticket of admission and the featured performance is by Politics, the band of the president's exuberant half brother, Roger Clinton.

Though there is no sign of it this night, among the happy Arkansans are several whose tenure in the new presidency will soon be troubled or will even end tragically—the First Lady's law partner and closest friend, Vince Foster, her other law partners Webb Hubbell and Bill Kennedy, Little Rock businessman and Clinton financial adviser David Watkins, White House aides Bruce Lindsey and Patsy Thomasson. At the other balls and parties around Washington are still more ranking members of the new government who will be gone and disgraced within the next two years—Secretary of Agriculture Mike Espy, Deputy Secretary and later Secretary of the Treasury Roger Altman, along with a number of his aides, White House counsel Bernard Nussbaum, and others. They will share a common bane. They are all to be haunted less by what happens in the new administration over the coming months than by what has already happened in Arkansas over the past decade and more. And in that they are typical. The fate of the Clinton presidency will be its past.

◆   ◆   ◆

Only once and fleetingly in his inaugural address has the new president referred to what awaits him after the bus rides, the ceremonies, the balls. "To renew America we must revitalize our democracy," he says halfway through the speech. "This beautiful capital, like every capital since the dawn of civilization," he continues, "is often a place of intrigue and calculation. Powerful people maneuver for position and worry endlessly about who is in and who is out, who is up and who is down, forgetting those people whose toil and sweat sends us here and pays our way. . . . And so I say to all of us here, let us resolve to reform our politics, so that power and privilege no longer shout down the voice of the people. . . . Let us give this capital back to the people to whom it belongs." When the president speaks this last line, there is a ripple of applause he will never hear, behind the Lincoln Memorial reflecting pool, far from the inaugural platform.

Afterward no words in the many thousands spoken in observance and celebration will seem so important, so relevant to the struggle between Clinton's promises of change and the defeat—or the betrayal—of the hopes he embodies. Praising Clinton's clarity of vision, the *New York Times* nonetheless admonishes him about the Washington he now enters, "where the public interest gets ground into the midway dust of a circus of greed." He cannot confuse "mere assertion with real accomplishment," they warn, or display "a self-righteous streak and a quick temper." With the same portent, the London *Economist* cautions the new president about his own Democratic Party "at his back—positioned perhaps to stab him eventually. . . . Already crowding into the lobbies are the groups that elected Mr. Clinton with their money and votes, or both, and have come to collect." Even the official inaugural poem Clinton has commissioned from Maya Angelou is foreboding: ". . . face your distant destiny./But seek no haven in my shadow./I will give you no hiding place down here."

The ceremony ends. "Quietly, tentatively," as one person remembers, some of the people around the reflecting pool have begun to sing "The Star-Spangled Banner." They pause as the rest of the crowd melts away. Like the people along the Virginia roads after the buses passed, they are waiting, reluctant to leave.

But they will not find an answer there. It begins with an earlier story from a moonlit spring night nearly a half century before, along a curving highway in a remote corner of Missouri.

BOOK I

◆

· 1 ·

Sikeston

"Riding on a Smile"

They were local boys from the Missouri boot heel. John Lett and Chester Oldham were driving south toward Sikeston on a warm Saturday night when they heard the back tire blow on the big maroon sedan ahead of them on the curve. They watched wide-eyed as the Buick swerved wildly off the narrow pavement of old Highway 60, skidded on the soft shoulder, vaulted across the drainage ditch, then turned over twice with the muffled crunch of mud and steel. In moments it was over. The car came to rest upside down on the edge of an alfalfa field, its radio still offering country music in the sudden silence, its headlights still reaching out through the darkness.

Lett and Oldham pulled over and made their way toward the wreck, "scared to death" of what they'd find, Lett told his wife later. The doors were closed, the driver's window down, but the car was strangely empty. In the back seat was a case of bourbon, the bottles somehow unbroken. Nervously they began searching the dark field and the bank of the ditch. Others were stopping now, drawn by the accident, their flashlights darting in the country blackness. Somebody went for the state trooper in Sikeston.

"Finally we had to go into the ditch," Lett remembered. They waded and poked in the three feet of brackish water. At first one man thought he heard something up the road, "kind of a gurgle and a splash," he said later. But the sound seemed too far away. They continued looking near the overturned car with its ghostly lights and tinny music.

It was near midnight, May 17, 1946, and America was changing. Three months before, US diplomat George Kennan had sent his fateful "long telegram" from Moscow about generic Russian treachery, impressing on receptive officials in Washington the sinister threat of the Soviet Union. In March, not far up the road from Sikeston, in Fulton, Missouri, Winston Churchill had spoken much the same omen and fear in the famous "iron curtain" speech. Across the country, powerful interests were financing the great red-baiting campaigns that would bring to power the Congress that launched Joseph McCarthy and Richard Nixon, the Congress of Taft-Hartley, the Hollywood Ten, and the Hiss case. This same weekend in May the deadline was to expire on a nationwide railway walkout. Part of a vast wave of labor grievances that had built up during the war years, it was an opening struggle for economic democracy in the coming boom. In a few days, however, a defiant President Harry Truman would seize the railroads and break the strike, a historic act of his own instinctive aversion to deeper reform, his own accommodation to what he and other Democrats saw as the forces of the moment. It was the beginning of the postwar era in the United States.

In the darkness along Highway 60 in southeastern Missouri near the Arkansas line, they were searching for a man none of them knew. Some had glimpsed him as he passed their cars on the road a few minutes before, speeding by in his shiny 1942 Buick, "a nice-looking young fellow," one said later, "somebody in a hurry . . . a stranger who didn't know the road."

◆ ◆ ◆

His name was William Jefferson Blythe II, and in a sense his car came hurtling that night out of a different America, a country before the cold war and its anxious politics of fear and reaction.

The family called him W.J. to set him apart from his father and namesake, Willie, a lean, hawklike man who had married a thirteen-year-old girl named Lou in Tippah County, Mississippi, near the Tennessee border, and then had moved west across Arkansas in a covered wagon to settle on the hot, windy plain of north Texas. W.J. had been born there in 1918, the fourth of nine children. He grew up in a cramped four-room farmhouse of canvas and paper walls, without plumbing or electricity, pitched on forty acres of hard-scrabble cotton and scanty pasture near the Red River, halfway between Sherman and Denison.

They were never far from want, and with the depression they became one more story of the torment in rural America. By the early 1930s, the scorched farms of north Texas were dying, and Willie Blythe along with them, a slow, agonizing death from colon cancer. The oldest son still at home, W.J. rose at three in the morning to keep the farm going and worked eight hours every day after school at nearby Ashburn Dairy, bringing home a little extra milk or butter with his few dollars in pay. His sisters remembered that his bed was set in the front room of the farmhouse, near the door for his comings and goings, and that he scarcely slept in it. They could never afford a hospital or regular medical care for Willie. Toward the end, their father lay in the back of the little farmhouse, shaking and screaming with convulsions. W.J. would calmly take a crippled sister and others out of the house, then go back in to give the writhing man some morphine, and emerge a few minutes later to assure them everything was all right. "He was always smiling," one of them remembered, "always so easygoing no matter what was happening or what he felt inside."

For two years, as Willie suffered and died, they had held on to the homestead with an emergency loan through a New Deal farm program. But in the summer of 1936, two payments behind and with less than a hundred dollars due on the note, they lost it to the bank. W.J. watched as his mother became a hotel maid in Sherman, a destitute widow in her midforties—almost the same age at which her grandson would become president of the United States fifty-seven years later. "There wasn't nothin' wrong with the Blythes 'cept they was poor," a relative who lived with them said afterward. "Rag poor," another added.

But there was to be something more about W.J. than poverty and pain, more than the loyalty and sacrifice of a young man trying to save the farm and care for a broken family. In this son of tender feeling there was also a more self-seeking purpose and ambition. Out of the boy who gave with such innocent ease there came a man who used others easily and took advantage of their own innocence. "He wasn't ever going to be a farmer or least of all be poor or unimportant," said a sister. When they lost the farm, the family moved to a shabby apartment in Sherman. From there eighteen-year-old W.J. was soon gone, on the road selling auto parts in Oklahoma and beyond.

He had quit the old White Rock School after only the eighth grade, but he would seem more educated than he was. He now called himself Bill Blythe, relying on a quick, naturally glib intelligence and on the methodical sunniness that became with strangers a winning, lasting charm, and he found his calling as that legendary American figure of two centuries, the traveling man, the itinerant salesman—"the fellow that chats pleasantly while he's overcharging you," as one country humorist put it.

Yet Bill Blythe was so likable, so sincere, so smooth without ever seeming smooth that even the sale—or its wounds afterward—could seem unimportant. People remembered how he was always touching, patting friends and customers on the back, often holding both their shoulders as he spoke or, more important, listening intently. "He made you feel like you were the only one in the world," said a close friend and customer. "A gentle, conscientious, beautiful person," another called him. "He was a wonderful salesman, a perfect salesman," said a member of his family. "He was always eager to please. And he sold himself."

It began, and ended, with the territory. The traveling man took it as he found it, the easy sells and the hard, the spenders and the cheap, the competitors honest and corrupt. There was the business as the public saw or imagined it—and then there was the inside reality of the favored, the exclusive, the rigged. The traveling man discovered early those seamy secrets of the trade and, like his fellow salesmen, kept them as a kind of private possession, not for the ordinary world to know or use. The salesman's route was the end of a relentless food chain on the raw outskirts of American capitalism, at once free and easy and unforgiving. "When they start not smiling back, that's an earthquake," said a famous figure in the trade. "And then you get yourself a couple of spots on your hat and you're finished."

The good salesman never changed or openly challenged his brittle, perishable world; he talked and smiled his way through and around it. There was no hard or soft sell, only the smart or the stupid. Technique took over, became substance. He drawled with the good ole boys, spoke fluently with the city people, learned just enough about every product, every customer to talk with seeming authority, without threatening or losing them.

In the late 1930s and on into the early 1940s, Bill Blythe sold car-alignment equipment throughout the Midwest and middle South for the J. H. Pereue Equipment Company of Memphis, driving from dealer to dealer, big town to small, hotel to tourist court, often towing a tool of the trade, what one account called "a bulky wheel-alignment-and-balancing contraption." It was a white-collar life of company cars and ample pay, of "relentless good cheer," as another account described it, and of many people well-met, some of them becoming friends, though none too close or for too long. In the end, if he allowed himself to think about it, the traveling man was mostly alone, with the next sale, with the run. "There is no rock bottom to the life," Arthur Miller wrote about a kindred Willy Loman. "He don't put a bolt to a nut, he don't tell you the law or give you medicine. He's a man out there in the blue, riding on a smile and a shoeshine. . . . It comes with the territory."

◆　◆　◆

Then, too, as in the folklore, as in all the bawdy old jokes about traveling salesmen, there were women—especially for Bill Blythe.

Less than a year after his father died, W.J. drove across the state line into Oklahoma to marry, somewhat furtively, a girl he had known in Sherman, eighteen-year-old Adele Gash. For a while they were crowded together with another Blythe son and his wife in one of the tiny rooms of the old farmhouse. "I never lived with so little," she would say later. But when Adele went to visit an aunt in Dallas, W.J. didn't come for her as he had promised. "I knew it was over," she would say, "when I got this package from him with all my clothes." They were divorced at the end of 1936, and by then the new Bill Blythe was on the road. Still, he went back to Adele often after the divorce and, the following spring, fathered a baby boy by her, Henry Leon, born in January 1938. Adele and her sister soon moved with the baby to northern California and for a time lost touch with Bill completely. "He was a wonderful, good-looking ladies' man," Adele would tell her family. "He wanted so much to be liked. Everyone liked him."

At a Nevada, Missouri, roadhouse early in 1940, he met a pretty dark-haired seventeen-year-old named Wanetta Alexander. She was skipping choir practice on a lark from a nearby town across the line in dry Kansas. "I was just standing there by the jukebox when a handsome young man walked over and asked me to dance," she would say. "I said no, but then "Alexander's Ragtime Band" came on. He insisted, 'You *are* going to dance with me.' And I did." He was stocky then, just under five feet ten inches tall, weighing about 180 pounds, with blue eyes and dark brown hair combed straight back. Wanetta thought him "a living doll . . . good-looking, good clothes, smart, classy." Later that year they met often at the Netherlands Hotel in Kansas City, where Bill sometimes stayed for weeks while making his rounds in western Missouri and Kansas. "We'd . . . hit all the hotels, restaurants, and dance halls," she recalled. "He was wonderful, gorgeous, fun, and happy-go-lucky."

By the end of 1940 Wanetta was pregnant, and Bill Blythe had gone to northern California, supposedly to see Adele and his first child. "He played with the baby like he loved it, and he was just his old self," said a friend. But after a few days Bill had suddenly run off with Adele's pretty younger sister, Minnie Faye. "W.J. wanted to marry Faye because he got another girl pregnant and wanted to get out of it," one relative explained. "He was a traveling salesman, I'll tell you," said another witness. "He sold himself to the ladies."

Bill and Minnie Faye Gash were married on December 29, 1940, in Durant, Oklahoma. That, too, was soon over. "Faye was calling Adele back in California and saying she had to come home," a member of her family recounted, adding the familiar refrain about Bill Blythe the charmer, the irrepressible seducer. "But she almost always spoke highly of W.J., just like everybody else."

Under pressure from the Alexander family, his hasty marriage to Minnie Faye was annulled in Little Rock in April 1941, and in less than a week he was in a judge's chambers in the Jackson County courthouse in Kansas City, marrying Wanetta. He had hurried through the rain to be there, and arrived just minutes before the ceremony. Eight days later, he was on the road again while his new wife gave birth to a baby girl. They named her Sharron. "Sure am glad that you are all right," he said in a telegram to the hospital. "How is the baby? . . . I love you always. Love, W.J. Blythe."

He traveled with Wanetta and the baby about six months that summer and fall, driving through southern Missouri and Oklahoma in his trademark robin's-egg-blue Buick, feeding and diapering the infant in the back seat of the car. They settled for a time in Monroe, Louisiana, in an apartment she remembered as "a dump." But within six months Wanetta was gone, too, taking their baby back to Kansas City. "Bill was cheating on me," she said later. "I know there was a lady at one of the nightclubs."

Over the next year and a half following Pearl Harbor, Bill Blythe stayed on the road, a man in his midtwenties facing the expanding wartime draft even with a wife and child. "The war has about drove me crazy," he wrote Wanetta in the spring of 1942. "Tell everyone hello and kiss the baby for me." Over the following months he wrote her often, worrying about his job and his draft status, thinking about joining the Coast Guard. "I was very glad to here [sic] from you," he wrote her again in January 1943. "I am going to Calif. Maybe then if you still want to we can start all over again. Love, Bill."

Six months later, on a hot July night, he was out with a woman in Shreveport, Louisiana, when she suddenly fell ill. He took her to Tri-

State Hospital, and while she was being treated he noticed the pretty, personable student nurse on the evening shift. She was Virginia Dell Cassidy, from a small town in southwestern Arkansas. Then barely twenty, with large eyes, full red lips, and long raven hair, she had an easy laugh and an air of worldly exuberance that belied her age or origins. She was engaged at the time to a high school sweetheart but was immediately taken with Bill Blythe and his striking good looks. The salesman had started to leave the hospital but then hesitated, turned back, and walked up to the young nurse to ask about the ring she was wearing. Without hesitation she replied that it didn't mean a thing, surprised at her own response. They went out for a soda that evening and kissed good night. He rented an apartment in Shreveport and took a job selling cars. "Yes, she's lying right here beside me," he once said with disarming candor when her roommate called looking for her. Swept away, Virginia would later describe the courtship in words that took on the flavor of a country western ballad. She soon pressed him to marry. He had not told her—and never would tell her—about his current wife or his children or any of the others.

Though Blythe did his best to resist marriage, Virginia was not to be denied. It wasn't long before he hurriedly wrote to Wanetta, saying he had "met a nurse down in Louisiana," and wanted out of their marriage. The young mother in Kansas City agreed and filed papers immediately that summer. "He was my first and only love," Wanetta would say afterward. On April 13, 1944, a Missouri court granted the divorce, ordering the absent William J. Blythe to pay forty-two dollars a month in child support. But even then it was too late. On September 3, 1943, after their swift late-summer romance, Bill Blythe had committed bigamy by marrying Virginia Cassidy before a justice of the peace in Texarkana.

He joined the army and was sent abroad only five weeks after his marriage to Virginia. A mechanic in an auto-maintenance battalion, he served first in North Africa, then in the liberation of Rome and the bloody Italian campaign north to the Arno River. A niece in the Blythe family remembered writing him once during the war, asking for a leaf from Europe for a school project. "Sorry, there are no leaves on the trees. They're all shot off," he wrote her back. Faithfully, Blythe sold his GI-issue cigarettes at a profit and sent the proceeds back to Virginia, who had finished training and returned to live with her parents in Hope, Arkansas. She wrote him, she remembered, "every day."

He was discharged as a technician, third grade, in December 1945 with a commendation for his service. He went back once after the war to see Wanetta and their daughter, and she remembered him walking with a limp, even using a cane, though there would be no military records of his having been wounded. "The boy had been through hell," an employer would say later.

For reasons of sentiment and privacy, she remembered, Bill had his reunion with Virginia in Shreveport, and after a brief stay in Hope they soon moved to Chicago, where he had a job selling on the road for an Illinois equipment company. He planned to settle down there eventually and open his own business. Virginia became pregnant almost immediately. Her conception came at the beginning of the great postwar baby boom.

That winter he was still driving two hundred miles a day, coming back at night to their apartment near the Loop; his rural Arkansas wife walked about the great lakeshore city somewhat wide-eyed. In an echo of his own painful past, Virginia flew back to Texas in February to nurse his dying mother, but Lou Blythe was gone before Bill could get there himself.

They had bought a small bungalow in Forest Park, just west of downtown Chicago. The transaction was taking longer than expected. Her baby due in August, still suffering acute morning sickness, Virginia planned to go home to Hope to give them both a respite while their suburban house was vacated and cleaned.

On a last evening out together with friends at the Palmer House, they posed for a nightclub photographer. Later they sent relatives the portrait, inscribed, "All our love, Bill and Virginia." She is in dark lipstick and long false eyelashes, with bright nail polish, a corsage, and a cigarette, he in a natty tweed sport coat showing the white points of his pocket handkerchief, a full-faced young salesman of twenty-eight, giving that reassuring smile.

In mid-May the Forest Park home was ready, their furniture moved in. Bill was hurrying his Buick through the Missouri night to get her, carrying a case of bourbon for his father-in-law, down country roads he had traveled so much in another time.

◆   ◆   ◆

It was nearly two hours after the accident that they finally discovered the body lying face down in the shallow water several yards away from the wreck, out in the unsearched darkness near where one of them had first heard the faint sounds. He had been thrown clear or perhaps had crawled from the car. When they found him, handsome Bill Blythe's hands were still clutching the ditch grass, trying to pull himself up and out. Though barely injured, only a small blue bruise visible on his head, he had been stunned enough to drown in the ditch where he fell, a simple narrow drainage channel dug by the New Deal to reclaim swampland and rescue poor farmers much like his own family in Texas. He was still forty miles from the Arkansas line, more than three hundred miles from Hope.

Virginia mourned big Bill Blythe as the great love of her life. Family and friends, ex-wives and abandoned children all gave the martyred young salesman the benefit of their fonder memories, discreetly burying the rest.

The good-natured baby born three months later bearing Bill Blythe's name would become president of the United States. Much of the father is evident in the son he never knew. Equally important, the salesman's death meant that his talented little boy would grow up not in Chicago but in Arkansas, with quite another father, another heritage—and that, too, would shape a presidency.

In 1993 his own side of the family often wondered what the charming, stoic traveling man might have thought of it all. There were differing memories about Bill Blythe's political views. Some thought him a Roosevelt Democrat, others a business Republican. But then a good salesman's convictions had to fit the moment—or else were put aside. His real politics, after all, were the sale.

A relative visited Bill Blythe's grave the week his son was inaugurated in Washington. "It made me feel better," she said. "But, you know, you could just never tell about W.J. Not really."

·2·

Hope

"Bright Little Orphan"

They buried Bill Blythe at Rose Hill in Hope. Sheltered by ancient oaks and glistening magnolias, it was the oldest white cemetery in the small town, just across the road from where Virginia's father had a grocery store and not far from Julia Chester Hospital, where she would have their baby later that summer of 1946.

In its southern sun and shadows Hope had long been a place of passages. A few miles away ran the historic Southwest Trail through the Louisiana Purchase, winding to an end just short of the Texas line and what was once an international border with Spanish America. The nearby trailhead of Washington, Arkansas, had housed Davy Crockett and Sam Houston, as well as the blacksmith who tempered James Bowie's famous knife, the field headquarters for US invasion forces in the Mexican War, and an emergency Confederate capital of Arkansas, a gathering point of die-hard Southern fugitives from Union victories. The politics and politicians of the place were raucous and legendary though ever serious, from the antebellum Know-Nothings to Arkansas's leading secessionists. News of Abraham Lincoln's 1860 election "fell on our little community," recorded one resident, "with the awfulness of a death knell."

Soon after the Civil War the first national railroad through the region bypassed the trail. Stranded, the old towns passed their hovering history on to the newer settlement growing up around the tracks of the Cairo & Fulton and the Missouri Pacific, a site the railroad maps christened Hope. The region was populated by refugees from spent cotton fields of the Carolinas, Georgia, and Alabama, "Southerners goin' West," one writer called them. Hope and its Hempstead County would always have something of the flavor of the border it marked—not only the Spanish moss or plantations left behind to the south and east but the vast country beyond, "the wide-brimmed Stetsons and stockmen's boots that," as a visitor noted, "symbolize the nearness of grasslands extending to the Rio Grande."

The migrants homesteaded in the pasture and forest basin of the same meandering Red River that ran southwest to Bill Blythe's Sherman. In their relative isolation they seemed almost a separate ethnic group of native-born, inbred Anglo-Saxon whites. Then and later, they were set apart by the fervor of their evangelical Protestantism, a warm, often fierce attachment to family and locale, and fortitude—if not resignation—in the face of what they had come to in this obscure corner of one of America's most impoverished states. Only a handful were merchants or professionals. Most had been dirt farmers, clerks, ordinary laborers. They and their descendants seldom escaped their lot, part of a deeper, enduring inequity that was the mark of very rich, very poor Arkansas throughout the twentieth century.

In the 1920s a traveling salesman hoping to promote his latest hybrid seeds offered local farmers prizes for producing oversize fruit. Hope soon became the watermelon capital of Arkansas by force-feeding and pampering ordinary strains into specimens of nearly two hundred pounds. The contrived melons brought civic pride and publicity but proved bitter. By 1946 they had become a metaphor for the town's economy. When a wartime military installation and a proving ground were curtailed, Hope's seventy-five hundred people found themselves thrown back on the hinterland of marginal cotton or fruit farms and on a handful of tiny prewar local industries, a brickyard, a sawmill, furniture and crate factories, a handle plant.

Ironically, Hope's black community had been remarkably prosperous for a time, in stark contrast to African Americans in the Mississippi Delta and the rest of Arkansas. Pinched white settlers had brought few slaves to begin with. But the railways offered blacks steady jobs beyond sharecropping, and after 1900 Hope became a magnet for those workers and soon a showcase of generational progress, with black-owned businesses and African American professionals common on East Division Street and beyond. Even during the depression, the old brick downtown was more lively with traffic and shoppers than most of the rest of Arkansas was, and the new black elite shared in the relative prosperity. By the 1940s, however, with the railroads dying and big chains already breaking local enterprise, the moment ended. "A forgotten Hope," one account called it. Though blacks constituted forty percent of the town's population—a much higher percentage than they did statewide—by 1946 they were fading back into the traditional poverty of southeast Hope, what whites had begun again to call Niggertown.

♦ ♦ ♦

Hope drew much of its population from smaller towns. Virginia Cassidy was born in the nearby Ebenezer community near Bodcaw—a tiny Arkansas town. Her parents were third-generation Arkansans and typical of the struggling migration of often strong women and plodding men. Her mother, Edith Grisham Cassidy, insisted the family move into Hope to raise their only daughter and later became a practical nurse by doggedly poring over a correspondence course at her kitchen table. Her husband, Eldridge, went from job to job in a mill, the handle factory, and a liquor store, laboring for years as an iceman before borrowing the money from a local landowner to open his own country grocery near Rose Hill. By all accounts Virginia's parents earned little despite long hours and hard work.

Behind the doors of the Cassidy home there was a still uglier reality. Virginia remembered her father as kindly and easygoing, a laughing, storytelling man though often bent under the burden of their want. "I saw my father crying for the first time in my life when he couldn't get me a new dress for Easter Sunday," she recalled. Yet the deeper torment for both was the woman they lived with. She "met every day with anger," Virginia said of her mother, whose wrath was directed against her husband and daughter.

A heavyset, hauntingly beautiful woman with tight curly hair and piercing black eyes—"those eyes could bore in on you and almost disintegrate you with their heat," said her daughter—Edith Cassidy exacted her revenge in countless acts of cruelty. Virginia remembered vividly the frequent childhood spankings and whippings with a specially selected sharp branch that left her small legs bloodied. Almost every evening there were jealous tirades against her father. Possessive and bitter, Edith accused her easygoing husband of infidelity with women along his ice route and blamed him for the family's poverty as well. In her nightlong rages she often attacked Eldridge physically, though he remained passive, placating, taking the blows. The violence was to last more than a decade, Virginia would remember. The child who had suffered similar humiliation, who would lie awake in the darkness listening to the savagery from the next room, absorbed the hurt in her own way. By the age of twelve she had already learned how to carry her "dark secrets."

For all of that, Virginia Cassidy grew into an outwardly happy adolescent, determined to see the goodness in others and radiating an irrepressible, even flamboyant cheerfulness. By the 1940s she was in many ways typical of her time and place in rural Arkansas and yet, in her sheer ordinariness, somehow different—defiant, with the voluptuous sexuality and free, robust quality that had drawn Bill Blythe that hot night in Shreveport, "a proud, positively cocky woman," said someone who knew her.

In 1946, her husband suddenly gone and his child yet unborn, Virginia Cassidy had already decided to leave the infant with her parents and study in New Orleans for a year to earn credentials for higher-paying work as a nurse-anesthetist. During her pregnancy she worried often about how she would care for her child; the decision to leave home to secure a career came only after much soul-searching. Though there were visits back and forth, their separation formed one of the son's earliest, most poignant images. "I remember my mother crying and actually falling down on her knees by the railbed," he would recount, describing a scene at the New Orleans station when he was barely two. "And my grandmother was saying, 'She's doing this for you.' "

He was William Jefferson Blythe III, though just Billy in the family. He lived the first four years of his life in the Cassidys' two-story frame home on Hervey Street, where screen doors banged and dogs barked in the southern stillness, and his grandmother Edith, "Mawmaw," as he called her, still shrieked at her husband in the night. Though there was apparently none of the physical abuse she had inflicted on her daughter, the angry woman with the burning eyes was a dominant and domineering influence in his early childhood. During his mother's year in New Orleans and even after she returned, Edith Cassidy remained the controlling and indulgent surrogate who spared no expense in the care of her grandson. So completely did the older woman take over the care and training of the little boy that the daughter still found the practical work of parenting unfamiliar well after her son's birth. Even after four years of motherhood, the feisty and loving Virginia said she was "as green as a blackjack table."

In the late 1940s there was scant diversion in Hope for children or adults. "We spent the evenings at the show, ballgames, or watching the

Missouri Pacific passenger trains come through," said one native. From the beginning, Cassidy and Grisham relatives doted on Billy. "The bright little orphan," one account called him. When he was old enough to walk, the men took him with them, especially to Eldridge's wooden-countered grocery to observe the Southern commerce of poor whites selling to poorer blacks.

Long afterward Bill Clinton would reminisce about lessons of tolerance and fairness learned in the store, how his family extended credit to penniless black farmers hostage to the seasons. But racial tolerance was not evident in the rest of the family at the time. The store credit, after all, was part of a system whereby sharecroppers had access to cash for only a few weeks after the fall settlement.

Away from the grocery, Billy lived in a neighborhood, played, and went to school with white children only. Campaigning years later, he came across the single black figure he recognized from his Hope boyhood, the Cassidys' housecleaner, Odessa. "I remember rocking with her on her porch," he told a reporter. He did not know her last name.

What he recalled more readily were the men of the family talking to him, telling him their inexhaustible stories. Along with a grandfather and great-grandfather, there was his mother's favorite uncle, Oren "Buddy" Grisham, a profane, easy-drinking, likable man fond of his innumerable dirty jokes. Uncle Buddy had quit school after the fourth grade and become almost a caricature of the good ole Arkansas boy of homespun humor and authority. Some of the talk was political. The Cassidys were southern Democrats, bound to the traditional party all the more by the populism of the New Deal.

Arkansas boys were taught the rewards of preparedness, the saving virtues of "a good pocketknife, a true rifle, and a cold-nosed coonhound," said one who heard the stories. The ability to spin or elaborate tales was a prized gift. In the larger house just behind the Cassidys, one of Billy's playmates, Vincent Foster, had an impressive, magnetic father known as the Fascinator for the circles of children he enthralled.

"The Arkansas frontier encouraged the rejection of all authority and an every-man-for-himself attitude" is how one historian described the tenor of a people who felt relentlessly thwarted and cheated. The hero or protagonist of the local parables came away with a shrewd sense of the necessity of submitting to the odds, if not the basic immutability, of the larger order they confronted, the man-made political and economic world as well as the natural.

The Cassidys held out ambition and encouragement for Billy, telling him that by ability and hard work he could rise above the generational sense of Arkansas inferiority. "I was raised by people who deliberately tried to disabuse me of that idea," he would say, "from the time I was old enough to think." Such aspirations were never at odds with the knowing resignation and crafty concessions prescribed in local lore and wisdom. It was what a traveling salesman had to learn. In the end the smart fellow got ahead far more by mastering the system than by defying it. "There is a streak in the Arkansas character," Garry Wills would write, "that militates against expecting too much from life (and militates, as well, against political reform)."

On the eve of his presidency forty years later, the man who listened intently as a boy on Hervey Street and in the grocery—and who later spoke and thought in a subtly similar idiom as a state and national leader—would call his storytelling grandfather and uncle "the main male influences in my childhood." He remembered his great-uncle Buddy Grisham as "the wisest man I ever met."

◆　◆　◆

Yet there was another man of crucial influence in Hope, a figure who might have come straight out of one of those more cautionary tales.

Roger Clinton emerged from much the same Arkansas of privation and pain. He had grown up poor in Hot Springs in the 1920s and was himself an abused child. His father had been a parole officer and then a butcher in a family grocery, his mother the tyrannical and manipulative Mama Clinton in what many saw as a matriarchal oppression not so different from the Cassidys'. The youngest of five children, at once mistreated and excused, Roger would be known as Baby Boy into middle age and would remain in the shadow of an aggressive older brother, Raymond, whose "waiting hands," as one relative saw it later, inherited the mother's considerable power. Watching him come out of that family life, his friends thought Roger Clinton lost almost from the beginning in the bustling resort city. He peddled papers on a corner, never finishing high school. "Roger was just in the street too much," one of them said afterward. "He saw the rest of Hot Springs doing well, and he could never measure up."

Before the war he worked for a time for Raymond, who was already becoming a prosperous Buick dealer in Hot Springs. Then, in the early 1940s, in the beginning of a patronage that would shape a history far beyond that of the two men themselves, Raymond Clinton used his influence with General Motors to set Roger up in his own Buick agency in Hope. Though the younger son had never wanted to leave their hometown, he leaped at the chance to ape his imposing brother. At the new dealership in Hope Roger would proudly throw an expansive Christmas party for customers and friends, just like Raymond's annual celebration back in Hot Springs.

The young Buick dealer cut an impressive figure in the tiny railroad town. Personable, free-spending, a slim man with dark, wavy hair who was vainly impressed with his own good looks, Clinton stood out in dour Hope for his snappy clothes, the tailored sport coats, and two-toned shoes. His friends called him Dude. Above all, he was known as the life of the party, with a special charm and attraction for young women.

But beyond the smiles and the shoes there was a side to Roger Clinton that only a few ever saw clearly—his reckless drinking and insatiable gambling, a penchant for violence, a ready willingness to flout the law, not only to accept but to join and exploit the legendary local corruption that he had known firsthand in the wide-open town where he grew up. In his youth he had badly injured a Puerto Rican boy in a poolroom brawl in Hot Springs, and only Raymond's intervention had saved him from the consequences. The older brother rescued him again after Roger set up a rigged crap table in Hope and had the "audacity," as one person put it, to draw in a powerful city official among those he cheated.

When Hempstead County went dry during the war, Roger bribed local police officers and sheriffs to give him the liquor they seized in raids on local moonshiners. Serving high-proof whiskey at his own raucous private parties, he boasted to girlfriends about his source of supply. Roger's best friend, Gabe Crawford, a future patron of some importance, owned a string of drugstores in Arkansas. When he opened another in Hope in the late 1940s, he and Roger had brought down three bookies and some slot machines from Hot Springs to ensconce in the backroom of the new pharmacy. It seemed that some of the citizens of dowdy Hope had gotten it into their minds that it was time to look to Hot Springs as an example of what a "drugstore" could be.

The family grocery at Rose Hill, it turned out, had also offered something more than the credit for struggling black farmers, and Hervey Street was more than the ordinary childhood home, or "my log cabin," as Bill Clinton would call it when he became a politician. It wasn't long before Roger Clinton went behind Virginia's back to make it possible for customers from Hope to buy a bottle without having to drive the thirty-five miles to Texarkana. Nor was her father

the only bootlegger in the family. Townspeople remembered that between stints as a practical nurse, his stout and fierce wife, Edith, sold
whiskey herself out of the house on Hervey Street.

None of the freelance vice, however, seemed to make up for the
eventual failure of Roger Clinton's Buick agency. The Hope market
never met Raymond's expectations, even with the postwar demand for
new cars. But by the later 1940s Roger had begun to squander what
profits there were in reckless wholesaling and in carousing weekends
in San Antonio, literally taking money from the agency till on top of
his $10,000 salary, "stealing from himself," as a secretary at the busi-
ness put it. "He never grew up," said a relative. "It didn't matter to
Roger. He was just a kid at heart and not very serious."

In 1947 Roger Clinton was leaving his wife of nearly fourteen years,
and her family suspected that he was already involved with the lively
young Hope widow Virginia Blythe, that they were "shacking up together," as one of them said, even while Virginia's baby stayed with her
parents on Hervey Street. She had started seeing Clinton less than a
year after Bill Blythe's death, often staying at his Hope apartment or
spending the weekend with him in Hot Springs. He was in his midthir-
ties, more than ten years older than the vivacious, equally high-spirited
nurse, and she was captivated by his high life in the small town. The
parties were wild and frequent and on more than one occasion Virginia could be seen mounting a nightclub stage in Hot Springs to sing
along with the evening's act or on a counter at Gabe Crawford's apartment belting out her own special song, "I'm the Hempstead County
Idiot." It all made for the sort of gossip that flooded Hope, where
"everyone knew everyone else," according to a man who grew up
there after the war, "and if you misbehaved, your mama knew it before
you got home."

Their affair was stormy, punctuated by memorable fights over his
promiscuity. On one occasion Virginia had defiantly marched three-
year-old Billy along with her to Clinton's apartment, where the boy
watched as she methodically cleared out another woman's belongings,
hanging the lingerie on a clothesline outside for the scandalized
neighbors to see. But there were also acts of tenderness, Clinton twice
paying Virginia's airfare home from New Orleans to visit her son. After
her return to Hope, where she took up her work as an independent
nurse-anesthetist, she saw more and more of him, he less and less of
other women. "They sort of drifted together," said a friend.

For her part, Edith Cassidy was, as usual, unreconciled. Deploring
Roger Clinton, seeing her own increasingly dissolute daughter on the

verge of a marriage that would take away the grandson she had raised as her own second child, she told Virginia early in 1950 that she was going to seek legal custody of Billy. "The blackness inside her had finally taken over," thought her daughter, "and there was nothing left but the blackness itself." The moment ignited yet another searing quarrel in the Hervey Street bungalow, Virginia screaming and frantically clutching at her son, the grandmother unusually and frighteningly reticent and composed. Edith Cassidy would go so far as to consult a local lawyer, though she never filed the threatened custody action against her own daughter.

Roger Clinton and Virginia Blythe were married in June 1950 on a balmy Monday evening only days before the outbreak of the Korean War. Aptly, the ceremony took place away from Hope, at a parsonage near the Hot Springs racetrack they both frequented. Gabe Crawford and his wife, Virginia—Roger's niece—were with them. But there was no one else from either family: Billy was still watched over by his embittered grandmother, and the Clinton side frowned on the wedding because Roger had still been married when the Blythe widow began seeing him in Hope. Only much later would Virginia learn that her second husband was often derelict in court-ordered support payments to his former wife and two stepchildren, that his Buick wages had been garnished as early as the 1948 divorce filing, and that by 1952 he owed more than $2,200 in arrears, nearly a quarter of his yearly salary.

Clinton moved his new bride and her four-year-old into a white six-room wooden bungalow on a corner lot on East Thirteenth Street, a plain postwar tract house then on the outskirts of town. For an interval little seemed to change. They continued to leave Billy with her parents while they spent weekends drinking and gambling in Hot Springs. Soon after the move Virginia had made a point of sitting Billy down to tell him in some detail about his real father, how they had met that night at the hospital in Shreveport, what a charming and lovable man Bill Blythe had been, how he had been officially commended for his service in the war, how he died on a Missouri highway, coming back for them. As always, he had listened intently, then and afterward enthralled with the legend, and the sudden death, of his father. Yet Billy was also obviously happy to have another man to fill the void that always evoked so much vocal pity and memory around him. From the beginning, he had called Roger Clinton Daddy, and in school he would gladly accept and use the new name Billy Clinton, not only for appearances or to make it easier for him, but also to welcome his new father. Virginia remembered a space at the back of the new house they turned into a playroom, where Roger set up a Lionel electric train set for his stepson and the two played for long stretches. Like many mothers she had doubts about which of them enjoyed the toy more.

There had been similar moments with the stepchildren in his earlier marriage. "We had no problems and did all the good things," one of them remembered. But Roger Clinton was already drinking steadily in those years and had started to abuse his first wife, if not her children. In her divorce complaint, she had accused him of hitting her with his fists and even the heel of a shoe. Now, soon after the move to Thirteenth Street, the new marriage began to suffer even more his bouts of drunken quarreling and violence.

Enraged one day that Virginia and Billy were going to visit her dying Grisham grandmother, he screamed, brandished a gun she did not even know he had, and drunkenly fired a round into a wall. They fled across the street to a neighbor's house to call the Hope police, and five-year-old Billy watched as they arrested his new father. Raymond Clinton drove down to Hope that night as soon as he heard, expecting to make his importance known, as Virginia told the story afterward, and once again to rescue Roger from another drunken escapade. But the local police were protective of Virginia Cassidy, the hometown girl, and not so easily influenced. Roger spent the night in the Hope jail despite the insistent blustering of Raymond. It was a time they all remembered. "There was a bullet hole in the wall. It could have ricocheted, hit my mother, hit me," Bill Clinton said, recounting a still palpably frightening story forty years later. "I ran out of the room. I had to live with that bullet hole, look at it every day." In the week he and Virginia spent away from Roger after the frightening and dangerous incident, however, the mother would admonish her fearful little boy to speak to his new father the next time he saw him and to treat him respectfully.

The shooting was more "grist for the busy rumor mills of Hope," according to a later account. Years afterward, when the Clintons had become famous, most of the neighbors who had lived along Thirteenth remembered little about the details of Roger's drunken abuse except that it obviously continued after the incident with the gun and the arrest. In the tiny corner house there were frequent shouting arguments through the night, Roger screaming accusations of infidelity at his working wife—"his tantrums," she called them—much like the dusk-to-dawn ranting of Edith Cassidy against Eldridge. Some of the neighbors would recall "vividly," as they brought back the scene, the intense little boy with cowboy boots and hat, so often out in front of the white bungalow after those nightlong ordeals. He always seemed to be transporting himself in some imaginary and furious flight, "racing up and down the sidewalk on his tricycle . . . over and over," remembered Brack Schenk, who watched him out the window, "leaning over, . . . churning down the sidewalk as fast as it would go."

◆ ◆ ◆

The indulgent family, especially Edith, had taught Billy to read at three, and in the autumn of 1951 Virginia enrolled him in Miss Mary's kindergarten. Set in a proper neighborhood on East Second Street, a white frame home remodeled to mimic a country schoolhouse with bell and steeple, Miss Mary's was a mark of respectability in the town. There was a single big classroom and small recess yard where the prim middle-aged mistresses, spinster sisters Mary and Nanny Perkins, supervised the activities and socialization of five- and six-year-olds. Discipline was gentle though firm, patriotism a part of good behavior for the nearly forty students, all of them scrubbed, neatly if modestly dressed, and, of course, without exception white. Staring down at them was the inevitable print of Gilbert Stuart's George Washington. One of Billy's classmates first mistook it for a portrait of the rather regal Miss Mary herself, pearl-white hair pulled back severely from her lined, dignified face.

"It was accepted," said Joe Purvis, who was in Billy's class in 1951–52, "that 'the leaders of tomorrow's free world are on Miss Mary's playground today.' " To Miss Mary's pretentious school were sent the children of Hope's "better families," of the town's nascent postwar elite of middle- and upper-middle-class businessmen. In the school along with Billy was agreeable, sandy-haired Thomas F. McLarty III, little Mack, heir to one of the largest automobile leasing and dealership operations in the South. There was also the earnest, well-behaved Vincent Foster, whose father, the Fascinator, was becoming extraordinarily successful in Arkansas real estate. While the backyard of Billy's grandparents' home on Hervey Street was "scarcely deep or wide enough to accommodate a clothesline," according to one description, the adjoining lawn of the big Foster house "could handle a marching band."

Launched out of this sleepy, unlikely railroad town with its force-fed watermelons and fitful economy, these boyhood friends would go on to lucrative careers in Little Rock as corporate executives and lawyers, part of a very different world of wealth and power. It was a remarkable kindergarten class, though it would owe its later fame, if not much of its fortunes, to the curly-haired, cheerfully grinning Billy Clinton, who had a background, both visible and hidden, rather less auspicious than that of most of his classmates—and who tried terribly hard, they remembered, to make everything right.

Billy was intent on belonging. "He wanted to be everyone's friend. It upset him if someone in any group that he went into didn't seem to like him," said his classmate George Wright. "It would trouble him so much that he seemed to be asking himself, 'What have I got to do to make this person like me?' I can remember that from when I was six years old." A bit chunkier and taller than his peers, he seemed awkward, "not as coordinated as the rest of us," one recalled. But he used his size and sunny disposition—always "friendly and joyous," said another classmate—to intercede in any disputes. "A peacemaker," Joe Purvis remembered. "Unlike most little boys, he didn't like to see quarreling and fighting, and he would be the one who tried to break up a scuffle and smooth things over. He wanted everyone to be happy and have a good time." Billy Clinton was, "even at five years old, a natural politician," thought George Wright. "I can tell it still hurts," Wright would add decades after their time at Miss Mary's, "when people say derogatory things about him."

By 1953 Roger Clinton finally lost his Buick franchise through mismanagement and his own pilferage. Once again Raymond would fill the breach, eventually taking his brother back as parts manager in his own thriving dealership. Billy was due to enter the second grade when Roger Clinton suddenly announced to Virginia and him that they were moving to Hot Springs. Virginia was relieved, if not elated, thinking the distance would keep family and friends from learning the worst about her already tortured marriage. Though many in the small town knew the truth she tried so hard to hide, Virginia believed she could leave Hope with the family's reputation intact.

Over the years to come, Billy returned frequently to visit his mother's relatives in Hope, riding the Greyhound bus back and forth by himself to stay weekends with the Cassidys or others. He felt "surrounded by a great big loving family when he was down there," he once told Virginia. As a young man far away from Arkansas he told colorful stories about the town's miraculous watermelons. As a politician he irresistibly evoked the name of his birthplace: "I still believe in a place called Hope," he would say again and again in the years ahead.

· 3 ·

Hot Springs

"The Power to Save"

There was no town like it in America. The old spas had come and gone. A few, like fashionable Saratoga Springs in upstate New York or FDR's Warm Springs in Georgia, were well known. But none had been more broadly or colorfully patronized than picturesque Hot Springs, Arkansas—and none was so pervasively, hypocritically corrupt.

"Let each come here, for here alone exists the power to save," promised a civic poem. "Here tottering forms, but skin and bone, are rescued from the grave." Wedged between forested slopes, the stone and brick spas of Bathhouse Row dispensed the steaming flow of forty-seven thermal streams, percolating a million presumably medicinal gallons a day from the depths of looming Hot Springs Mountain. An enthralled visitor in the 1940s found "singing birds in every bush and happy smiles on happy faces . . . in this Scenic Spot of [the] Southland." Others judged it "an immense field for quackery," as a *Harper's* writer once noted, though the US government itself seemed to be taking the cure. Perched on the mountainside above Bathhouse Row stood the ten-story tower and adjoining wings of the huge five-hundred-bed Army and Navy General Hospital, a nineteenth-century relic rebuilt during the depression, and in the 1950s still occupied by casualties from World War II and Korea.

When Roger Clinton took his family there in 1953, the miniature city of twenty-five thousand was "a bit of a metropolis," said one account, "dropped among the green-clad Ouachita Mountains." Postwar medicine and drugs were already beginning to empty the baths, but throngs of health seekers still milled among the magnolias of the slightly worn spas—the wealthy and famous let off from their limousines onto Bathhouse Row alongside the abject, often crippled poor, headed for what the US Park Service advertised as its "free bathhouse for indigent persons." Visitors now came for the pulsing resort itself more than for the waters. Nightclubs billed the touring acts of the era, typically Xavier Cugat's Latin band, popular singers Patti Page or Georgia Gibbs, and familiar movie stars like Mickey Rooney. Souvenirs and celebrities, racetracks and shooting galleries, alligator and ostrich farms—there seemed something for every taste among the year-round swarm of visitors.

On the surface it was a tourist economy, though the town also enjoyed a thriving trade from farms and settlements in the verdant hills around it. Up winding streets from Central were the bungalows and English manor-style houses, the frame gingerbread and imitation Southern mansions of the local middle class, notably better-off than most of the rest of Arkansas. Set away in southeast Hot Springs were its five thousand African Americans, mainly spa attendants, maids, cooks, and waiters, with their own proud blocks of small brick homes, their own hotels, hospitals, schools, and, of course, bathhouse. Behind all this, however, there was still another Hot Springs, more integral than the baths, more discreet than its black quarter.

Native author Dee Brown once alluded to "the city's long-standing record of tolerance." For nearly a century the little city in the gorge was a fount of vice and official venality, gambling and prostitution, protection rackets and other graft that constituted a backroom criminal economy far larger than even the bustling open commerce along the Row. Celebrity gangsters of the 1920s declared the town neutral ground, and made The Springs, as everyone called it, their favorite resort. Al Capone was said to have permanent lease on Suite 443 in the stately old Arlington Hotel on Central, holding it even after he went to federal prison. By the 1950s, however, the corruption had gone well beyond slot machines or call girls, and local factions fought over the inevitable spoils. As in the rest of America, Hot Springs vice became largely corporate, with organized crime and business-government accomplices ultimately controlling the lucrative black market in casinos and more.

"Liquor flowed, the Oaklawn racetrack beckoned, and illegal gambling and brothels flourished under the averted eyes of local authorities," said one account of the years after Roger Clinton came back with his new family. "Everyone had a back room with game tables and decks of slot machines," recalled a resident who grew up with Bill Clinton. A Justice Department investigation in the early 1960s concluded that picture-postcard Hot Springs had "the largest illegal gambling operations" in the United States. "You name it," said William Harp, who reported for the town's *Sentinel-Record* during those years, "you could buy it here."

Among the regular purchases were politicians themselves, legendary for bribery, graft, and vote fraud. Prostitutes and madams publicly paid the authorities a monthly "pleasure tax"; they were routinely escorted by police to the Garland County courthouse to pay the prescribed kickbacks. In the 1930s it was five dollars per whore and ten for madames. Returning veterans in 1946 led a "GI revolt" against city hall, making one of their own, Sid McMath, mayor of Hot Springs and eventually governor of the state. In the classic Arkansas pattern, however, reform was fleeting, the old politics enduring. When a local madam eventually retired from the largest bordello in town, her graphic memoirs in the 1960s charted the cynical return to business as usual after a brief postwar reform. As if to make the point, the lady's colorful history would be banned from the local library. The era from the mid-1950s to the mid-1960s was the "hottest" in the colorful annals of Hot Springs, Virginia Clinton herself later recorded, concluding that her new town was simply "addicted" to its gambling and other vice.

"For all of Roger Clinton's life," Virginia would reflect, "Hot Springs had been . . . a place where gangsters were cool, and the rules were made to be bent, and money and power—however you got them—were the total measure of a man." It had all depended on the hypocrisy and in many ways the collusion of respectable Hot Springs, thick with churches and civic clubs—and on a wider state corruption enveloping the capitol in Little Rock, where Springs politicians routinely passed on bribes "to a number of state officials," as one participant remembered. Among Virginia Clinton's closest friends in Hot Springs would be a woman who, as she described her, "actually carried the brown bag full of money to the governor's office" during the heyday of the regime. "Everybody knew," said a lawyer raised there in the 1950s and 1960s. "Baptist Arkansas just looked the other way, and a lot of people did real well." The town where Bill Clinton was raised, concluded a European journalist, was "a rhinestone of corruption on the southern Bible Belt."

On closer view there was a deeper melancholy. Hot Springs long harbored large numbers of itinerant, impoverished elderly. Not far from the strollers on Bathhouse Row and the glamorous customers at the nightclubs, seedy women's hotels and dingy back corridors of boardinghouses were home to wandering, blank-faced widows. Pathetic small colonies of the mentally ill were tucked away in run-down motor courts on the edges of town. "The Springs always had that roughness and tackiness to it, a real sadness as well as shadiness," said a native looking back on the postwar years. "Always."

Inevitably the place took its toll on even the outwardly secure. Shirley Abbott records in her poetic memoir, *The Bookmaker's Daughter,* the larger impact on values. In the end, she thought like many others, the pervasive corruption of the Springs "deconstructs and demolishes the American dream of virtue and hard work crowned by success, as well as all the platitudes and cant about the democratic process and small-town American life."

Roger Clinton had known much of that reality from growing up on the streets of the resort. Though Roger himself "wasn't much interested in politics," according to a relative, his brother Roy, an affable "yellow dog Democrat," as one friend called him, was elected to the Arkansas legislature in the 1950s. Now a part of the Hot Springs Clinton clan, little Billy Clinton came to enjoy passing out campaign leaflets for the legislator and, when he later went into politics himself, returned with some ceremony to seek Uncle Roy's political advice along with his great-uncle Buddy's in Hope. But neither man was the genuine political force among the wider circle of relatives. In politics as in the family, the far greater influence behind the scenes was Raymond's—and it would be to big Uncle Raymond that Billy turned again and again in matters of real power and ambition, albeit far more discreetly than when he undertook his ritual journeys home for filial wisdom.

Raymond Clinton was a remarkable character. A large, handsome man, shrewd and domineering, he was the most ambitious of the Clinton sons. Virginia and others thought he shared the weaker Roger's taste for the high life of the Springs and for the town's furtive worship of money and power—though he was far more its master than its victim. As a young man working at a drugstore only a few doors from the infamous Southern Club, he often watched as Al Capone strode down the sidewalk with a pair of bodyguards in front, behind, and to each side. ("You couldn't miss him," Raymond once told an interviewer.) He had found a partner to put up capital for an automobile dealership franchise in the 1930s and then promptly ousted him to take over the business. Clinton Buick soon became "a gathering place for powerful, politically savvy men in Hot Springs," as one person put it, the "magnetic" owner chairing the group and making deals on the phone while Roger stood behind the parts counter in the back. Raymond went on from the booming dealership to invest in real estate, liquor stores, and other ventures, joining the requisite civic clubs and aspiring to local society along the way. "He wanted in," said a member of the family.

Like other Hot Springs businessmen, Raymond Clinton was widely known to make his fortune and gain his influence from much more than "out-front" business or investments. "He ran some slot machines that he had scattered throughout town," said former FBI agent and Garland County sheriff Clay White. There was also convincing evidence of the prominent car dealer's links to organized crime and to the still formidable Ku Klux Klan in Arkansas. Like much else in the Springs, his dual life and power were an open secret. Once when Raymond's house was evidently firebombed, neighbors in the affluent area had little doubt that the incident was a result of his shady ties. "A lot of us just knew that it was either the Klan or the mob, and maybe some combination—certainly something to do with Raymond's considerable dealings in the underworld," said a local physician who knew him well.

The Clinton patriarch seemed to accept the risks just as he savored his influence. The relationship between the two brothers was convoluted in that Raymond had filled or taken the same authoritarian role as Mama Clinton. Toward Roger's avid young stepson Billy, however, Raymond was doting and avuncular from the beginning, treating him as a favorite nephew and then protégé, caring for him and even protecting him amid the alcoholic abuse by Roger Clinton. "Roger was pretty careful not to mistreat Billy in front of the Clinton clan, especially Raymond," said a relative, "but I've seen and heard of times when big ole Raymond stepped in, quietly and not so quietly, to scoop up that boy." They all saw Billy respond with delight and affection. Later there might be differences of view between the educated young man and the reactionary patriarch. But there seemed no question of Bill Clinton's underlying warmth and considerable respect for his uncle's power, for the refuge Raymond provided and the role he fulfilled. "While governor," a statehouse reporter would note later, Bill Clinton "frequently referred to Raymond G. Clinton as the most commanding male presence in his life, on several occasions referring to him as a father figure." Years later, an elderly relative in Hot Springs would view the disarray in the Clinton White House and reflect poignantly, "He needs an Uncle Raymond, and he hasn't got him."

Some thought the powerful older man saw Bill's political aptitude early on, perhaps even imagined him as a successor, building on power Raymond had only begun to develop and always coveted. "Raymond had a use for everybody, including the folks he loved like Billy," said a woman who knew him well. His loyalties seemed no less self-serving or expedient outside the family. Virginia remembered his supporting one old friend for sheriff, then abandoning the man when his daughter was to marry into the more prominent family of a rival candidate. By the 1960s Raymond Clinton had powerful friends beyond Hot Springs as well. He was a generous patron of Arkansas's senior US senator, John McClellan, among other ranking Democratic politicians, while also an avid backer of then-staunch segregationist Governor George Wallace of Alabama, personally driving Wallace whenever he visited Arkansas. "He was definitely politically connected," a nephew would say. "If you wanted to get something done, Uncle Raymond was in a position to do it."

◆　◆　◆

Roger Clinton and his family lived first on a four-hundred-acre farm owned by Gabe Crawford some miles outside Hot Springs. In the alcoholic haze of failure in Hope, Roger had grasped at anything to put off returning to work for his older brother and bumptiously decided on farming. The Dude now dressed each morning in his two-toned shoes and sharply creased trousers to tend cattle and sheep. But the rigor of the place, the drafty old house with its outdoor privy and ceaseless chores, soon told. Explaining it to his wife as a new "opportunity," Roger took back the old job at Raymond's dealership, and they moved to another house Crawford had for sale, a spacious old two-story frame bungalow at the northern edge of Hot Springs only about a mile from the heart of town.

The green-trimmed Tudor-style home sat on a high terrace above Route 7, the narrow highway grandly named Park Avenue as it angled down toward the Arlington Hotel and Bathhouse Row. Inside, the setting seemed altogether fitting for their life and the Springs. Across from the living room, decorated in bright pink, were Bill's bedroom and next to it Virginia and Roger's room with a bay window and a game table at the foot of the bed. Upstairs, running the length of the house, was what Virginia remembered as a fabulous party room, with Mexican furniture, familiar prints of dogs playing cards, and a built-in bar, backed by a mirrored wall with a candy-striped awning. Duly impressed Virginia thought it all "just what the three of us needed." She would also think for years that Roger had bought the house for them from their friend Gabe Crawford with his profit-able drugstores and bookie operations and that her own earnings turned over to her husband were going toward house payments and equity. But like so much else then and later, the property had been secretly purchased instead by Raymond Clinton; Roger, his wife, and his stepson were only renters.

Virginia enrolled Billy in St. John's parochial school at first, reluc-tant to put him in the notorious public schools, whose teachers as late as the 1950s were still not required to have college degrees. Within two years, however, he was at the old red-brick public elementary school, Ramble, with its wooden floors and daily morning assemblies, where pupils trooped into the auditorium, as one remembered, "for pledge, prayer, and song." The prayer they took for granted. Here, as in Hope, Billy was surrounded by the state's white fundamentalist majority. More worldly Hot Springs contained only an occasional Jewish family and a handful of Catholics, with their rare parish school. When the integration crisis erupted in Little Rock in the late 1950s, dozens of white families in the capital sent their "refugee" children the fifty-five miles to the Springs's still rigidly segregated, quietly traditional south-ern schools.

To a succession of housekeepers, black and white, who cared for him after school while both parents worked, Billy was always an amena-ble, genial child. "So easy to please," remembered Earline White, who loved cooking for his robust appetite, "and didn't have foolish, child-ish ways." Another saw in the talkative yet deferential little boy the potential charisma of a tent revivalist. "Have you ever thought about it?" she once asked Virginia. "How he could lead people to Christ!" Though she seldom attended church herself, his mother had taken him to Sunday schools in both Hope and Hot Springs. When he was only eight, the earnest youngster began to show his own religious devo-tion, rising early every Sunday to bathe and dress himself in coat and tie and then walking alone the four blocks to the Park Place Baptist Church, one of the city's largest congregations. There he "professed his faith at an early age," said a friend who recalled the ritual coming forward, the laying on of hands, the submerging baptism in the special tank above the pulpit. To church Billy carried a Bible given him by the family and duly inscribed, "William Jefferson Blythe III."

His outward serenity and conciliatory manner impressed other chil-dren just as they had on Miss Mary's playground in Hope. "I never remember Bill having a fight with anyone," a classmate would echo.

Rose Crane, who lived nearby through much of their childhood, thought him "the most genuinely kind human being I've ever known." In the Park Avenue terrace house he would thicken into a soft chubbiness outgrown only in his teens. Rose saw that rotund boy of eleven or twelve in his ineffable delight and tenderness toward his little brother, Roger, Jr., born in 1956. She remembered how much, over the years, Billy Clinton wanted everyone, especially the younger children whom others left out, included in games or outings and how he got down on his knees to dance with her little sister because "she was too small and didn't have anybody for a partner" when they played their favorite Elvis Presley records.

Only the very striving itself seemed disagreeable. At St. John's he received low marks in deportment, the nuns recognizing his ability but trying to discourage him from jumping to his feet with the answer to every question before any other student could speak. For some time afterward, the family recalled, Virginia's son was so precocious, so assertive she actually had to take him out of school from time to time. "She had to curb it," one recalled. "It was just unseemly. Billy was such a handful." But Virginia Clinton was always far more proud than concerned. Little Bill would go to great lengths to avoid punishment, she remembered, because it was such an insult to his dignity. Boastfully she repeated the tale of her ten-year-old coming home from an errand with another child carrying a load they were supposed to share. "Mother, if you use this," he said in her story, pointing to his head and then holding out his empty hands, "you don't have to use these."

A sensual woman with her own self-conscious sense of glamour and worth, Virginia Clinton was in her thirties as Billy went through school in Hot Springs. She had herself used Raymond's influence to break into the town's clannish medical establishment and soon had a brisk practice contracting as a nurse-anesthetist. In the habit of sleeping in her heavy makeup because she was always on call, she changed it in a morning ritual that took ninety minutes before she later managed to reduce it to only forty-five. From a home behind the Park Avenue house, Rose Crane saw the thoroughly cosmetic Virginia Clinton, immaculate in a stiffly starched white nurse's uniform, set off with long dark hair, burnished penny loafers instead of ordinary nurse's shoes, and perfectly manicured, brightly lacquered fingernails.

She usually returned from her hospital shift by midafternoon. In warmer months she invariably changed into shorts and halter to tend her flowers. Afterward, sipping a tall drink, she stretched out on a chaise in the yard to cultivate her deep tan—with "dark bare limbs, stomach and cleavage showing, painted eyebrows, long wispy eyelashes, dark eyeliner, bright glossy lipstick, fingernails and toenails as vibrant as the flowers in my garden," as she later described herself—all to the inescapable notice of neighbors and passersby, not to mention her son and other youngsters. "She was always attractive," Crane would say, "always well-groomed and with a style." Out of the starched uniforms or gardening halters, Virginia was fond of lounging in tailored men's pajamas and fuzzy mules, chain-smoking Pall Mall cigarettes and delivering one-liners in a slightly husky voice to her son's duly impressed preteen and adolescent friends. "Real Hollywood," one of them remembered her. "She was a good-looking lady and hilarious . . . like a walking female Will Rogers."

As in their courtship, she and her husband were now very much a part of the livelier, seamier Hot Springs, driving around town in familiar black or white company convertibles from the Clinton Buick dealership. They frequented the Tower Club, the Belvedere, the Wagon Wheel, and the Southern Club, and she claimed that she was on hand for every show at the Vapors, always impressed by its chandeliers and red velvet drapery, and the backroom which contained a full complement of slot machines, crap tables, blackjack dealers, and roulette wheels.

By day they were also regular bettors at Oaklawn, the popular Springs racetrack with a tiny golf course on the infield. At one point Roger even bought a thoroughbred, though it produced no triumphs. During the season, Virginia routinely scheduled her cases as early as possible in order to arrive at the track by midday, and she was notorious for reading racing forms on duty at the hospital. For months on end she hurried away from her job, left Billy with a housekeeper or else as a latchkey child—in later years to take care of his baby brother—and appeared daily at the two-dollar window at Oaklawn.

She impressed many as possessing, beneath her garish image, an underlying seriousness, shrewdness, and strength—and a confidence beyond that of most women of the time. Family and neighbors were aware that as a nurse-anesthetist she made more money than her husband did and, in any case, was clearly the more responsible of the two. "Bill grew up with a woman as the real breadwinner in the household, as the real grown-up figure," one relative observed. "I saw Virginia Clinton," Rose Crane would say with the force of the impression still audible in her voice, "as a very *powerful* woman."

The bond between mother and older son was deeply forged and never simple. Family and friends in Hot Springs remembered how soon she had treated a very young Billy "just like an adult." "I had never had any trouble thinking of Bill as a grown-up," she said later. It struck his own peers, then and later, that he had almost no chores around the house—"was really spoiled in that way," said one—and that he was "on his own so much of the time," as another recalled.

The small boy readily became a staunch ally and companion—and later something more. "Even when he was growing up," the mother remembered, "Bill was father, brother, and son in this family."

In a kind of routine, Virginia would come home from the hospital or track, put on some coffee, and begin to talk to her son and his friends with her customary zest and earthiness about what she had seen or heard, commonly some outrage small or large among the local medical community, with whom she had running feuds. The talk was almost never political or social in the larger sense and rarely went beyond the personal or the petty. At only eight or nine, Billy had mostly listened, taking it in. Later he spoke up, sometimes argued. "In high school he would debate her tooth and nail," and "neither would give an inch," said a childhood friend, David Leopoulos. "There were some red faces and bulging veins. . . . I was never sure who won . . . was afraid to ask."

Like many other Hot Springs boys, he tried the slot machines in the back rooms, but "natural stinginess soon made him give up," according to one account. Along with his friends he called to tie up the customers' line of Maxine, a prominent local madam. "Mainly to hear her cuss," he described later. "We never heard a woman use language like that." The devout young Baptist was neither ignorant nor innocent of his profitably decadent town.

But when, as an adolescent, Bill first accompanied Virginia to her beloved racetrack or to the Vapors to hear the famous Jack Teagarden play the tenor saxophone that Bill himself was learning, he was visibly uncomfortable—and disparaging, if not reproachful. "The dumbest thing I ever did," he had muttered leaving Oaklawn after only one race. The moment Teagarden's performance was finished, Virginia remembered clearly, Bill had turned to her and pointedly asked to leave.

She thought Bill disgusted by the high life around him in this wide-open town, though, she would say, adding that "Bill's reactions to Hot Springs's excesses have also probably helped shape him." Yet the aversions that molded a future president were always closer to home as well. "He made it clear," thought one writer, "that parts of her lifestyle were not for him." Remaining the loyal, intimate son, he would also begin—slowly, subtly, carefully—to set himself apart from his family, much as he would remain in and of Arkansas while marrying and reaching beyond it.

◆   ◆   ◆

Roger Clinton's rampages worsened as his alcoholism progressed. Soon after the move he began to beat both his wife and his stepson. In their first years in the Springs, Virginia often took Billy with her to the hospital to sleep during her night calls or shifts rather than leave him at home alone with her sodden, volatile husband. Though Roger now more than once proposed to adopt the boy formally and her son now commonly went by the name Billy Clinton, she adamantly refused to share legal custody.

As a smaller child especially, he spent "probably the majority of his free time at the houses of his friends," his Hope classmate Joe Purvis remembered. On weekends in the early 1950s, while his mother and his stepfather gambled, drank, and fought, all with equal passion, Billy often fled back to Hope, taking the bus by himself on Friday evenings and returning Sunday afternoon. Even his grandmother's noisy house on Hervey Street became a refuge. Most of the time there was no escape of any kind. Virginia would recall vividly how she and her son used to wait together every evening in the kitchen at Park Avenue and invariably "tense up" as they heard Clinton drive in and walk from the car. They had been in Hot Springs only months when she first packed their bags in the midst of an eruption and hurried Billy away with her to stay at a friend's apartment house for some days. Forty years later the mother would remember how unusually "soundly" her young son slept next to her that first night away from a torturous home.

In public Roger Clinton still fell into drunken brawls, often defending his equally hard-drinking and abusive backroom friend Gabe Crawford, who tended to pick fights he could not finish. But increasingly the violence also burst open in jealous rage over Virginia. She had danced with another man one night at the Tower, and Roger "beat him to a pulp," as she described it. He was now "mad at me . . . most of the time," she recalled, and as his life became more chaotic his anger and rage toward his wife only deepened. Afterward she would admit to taunting her husband by flirting with other men on their rounds of the clubs and casinos, though his alcoholic's suffering and abuse, their motive force deep within himself alone, needed no outside provocation.

Roger and Virginia took their screaming and flailing from the nightclubs and streets back to the terrace above Park Avenue and to an awakened, terrified child. "On nights like that, our house was just bedlam from the time we got home until dawn's early light," Virginia remembered. At eight, nine, and ten years of age, Billy lay in his room listening to what his mother called Roger Clinton's "accusations of infidelity, pitiful rants," bitter nightlong quarrels with persistent violence and profanity. In a cruel pattern, the fights repeated what his mother had heard as a young girl in Hope and foreshadowed exchanges with his own wife in the governor's mansion in Little Rock. (Nearly forty years later, with unconscious irony, a Washington reporter would also use the word *bedlam* to describe the chaotic decision making within the Clinton White House.)

There was to be no respite. Around the same time in the mid-1950s, Billy went through yet another telling episode with his imposing grandmother. Not long after they left Hope, Edith had suffered a stroke. Even unconscious, she oppressed the local hospital in Hope with her shrieking and thrashing. A physician carelessly resorted to morphine to quiet her, and she was soon addicted. After her partial recovery from the stroke, the Cassidys moved into a small apartment near Park Avenue in Hot Springs to be close to their daughter. But Edith was now a full-blown drug addict. In desperation, Virginia arranged to have her committed to the Arkansas state asylum at Benton, only thirty miles from the Springs. "Oh, God, it was an awful place," the daughter wrote of an institution that authorities would still document as one of the worst in the nation under Bill Clinton's own administration decades later. There Edith Cassidy remained for several months. Virginia often took Billy to visit her on Sundays in 1955, the two women sparring endlessly. A seemingly benign white-haired figure with her burning eyes behind sedate rimless glasses, Edith alternately begged and connived to be let out of the state madhouse.

After her release, her morphine addiction seemed kept at bay only by what they all saw as her formidable will, and Edith was once again a forceful presence in her grandson's life. She was often at the Park Avenue house, ever reminding him of the martyred Bill Blythe and how much she hated Roger Clinton. Other children remembered her as constantly at pains to find a way to show a photograph or extoll the many virtues of "Bill's *real* father."

By the autumn of 1955 Virginia was pregnant again. Both she and her husband wanted to have a baby together, although she must have known that the prospect of a new child obviously would do nothing to relieve their plight. She had already begun to put aside money, "rat-holing some of my paycheck every week," for a divorce she still resisted because of its social stigma as well as the economic sacrifice. The night after Roger Cassidy Clinton was born in July 1956, his father went out carousing, leaving nine-year-old Billy alone. Lying in her hospital bed, Virginia phoned home to find her first son abandoned and was forced to call Raymond Clinton to go over and take care of him. It was to become a familiar pattern: Roger Clinton would disappear for days at a time—even passing out at a girlfriend's house the night his father died—and return with pathetically implausible excuses that became a family joke. Yet as Billy and the rest of the family understood, proud Virginia Clinton never questioned or snooped. The husband's frequent betrayals went on almost as routine, with a kind of immunity and with an inevitable message to the boys watching it all. "Women who run around trying to find their husbands doing this, that, or the other thing just kill me," Virginia would say near the end of her life in a remark many thought aimed at her famous daughter-in-law as much as at anyone else.

After the birth of little Roger, as they called him, there were several nights when she fled the house with both children, taking refuge in a nearby motel. Virginia found her own escape in the attentions of other men, including a friend from the track and her hairdresser (a future husband), Jeff Dwire, who would be convicted some years later of securities fraud. Roger was now drinking his whiskey from tumblers, managing to keep the job at the dealership while becoming more wanton than ever at home, even erupting in obscenities during a children's birthday party. He was given to kicking or slapping Virginia in public or throwing her to the floor of their bedroom, where he hit her with her own shoe.

And though the abused wife could not bring herself to confess it even in her often-florid memoir, both friends and medical sources close to the boys' pediatrician in Hot Springs recalled that Billy and little Roger were themselves beaten and brutalized far worse than anyone later admitted. Their injuries were treated more than once at their doctor's office and even at the hospital, friends recounted. "A member of my family doctored them for some pretty bad stuff—stitches and all that," said a Hot Springs attorney. Virginia staunchly saw to it that no records remained to embarrass them later. There were apparently heated discussions about reporting the incidents to the police—often in front of an injured Billy. Each time, Virginia Clinton prevailed on the doctor and nurses to hold back the shameful secret of the battered children, saying "she would handle it herself," as one witness remembered.

At least twice during the late 1950s the police were called to the Park Avenue house. On one of those nights tiny Roger wailed about the danger to Dado, as he called his mother, while Billy telephoned his mother's lawyer to summon the officers. Again Roger Clinton was arrested for brandishing a gun. On one occasion he drunkenly refused to dress for the police and was taken to the station in his underwear, and in April 1959 Virginia angrily filed for divorce but promptly gave in to Roger's pleading after he promised to change.

By his own account, Bill Clinton was fourteen when he first stood up to the violence himself. As a high school freshman in 1960 he weighed more than two hundred pounds and stood nearly six feet tall, already substantially heavier and even taller than his stepfather. Listening one evening to yet another fight reverberate from his parents' closed bedroom, he busted in. "I just broke down the door," he recalled. "Daddy, I've got something to say to you, and I want you to stand up. If you can't stand up, I'll help you," he told a mumbling Clinton slumped at the game table. "I don't want you to lay a hand on my mother in anger ever, ever again, or you'll have to deal with me." This time it was Virginia who called the police, and once more big Roger spent the night in jail.

"The Clintons had three things that most Hot Springs residents of the 1950s would love," Rose Crane recalled wistfully. "A Coca-Cola box that was regularly filled, a convertible, and a mother who routinely served chicken and dumplings with plenty of white meat and no bones." The admiring neighbor's typical memory reflected how carefully and completely—despite the screaming, despite the police coming and going in the night—they all concealed the horror within. Even a staggering Roger Clinton, with his slurred speech, could suddenly appear steady and coherent when his own family telephoned or happened by. At any rate, his wife did nothing to break the deception, cautioning her children to conceal the horror as a family disgrace. "My mother just put the best face on it she could," Clinton himself would tell a writer in 1992. "A lot of stuff was dealt with by silence."

But by all accounts it was the outgoing, apparently open young Billy Clinton who maintained the most impenetrable mask. "Now that I know what was really happening inside that place," said a friend, "I'm blown away with how he never let on, never let himself go. He covered up like a dog burying a bone real deep." Early on, the boy who would be president inhabited the divided world so characteristic of his later profession, the chasm between public and private realities. Like many other children of alcoholics, he learned "to lie automatically," as one observer put it, "without any sense of guilt." His was a home, as many looked back on it, in which much was concealed and many falsehoods were glibly, persuasively voiced and even believed.

By high school or perhaps junior high, young Bill had grown into a charmer who reflexively spoke what others wanted to hear—in the mode of his most intimate family transactions. "We can only guess now how he hated it all," said a close childhood friend—"the stepfather, probably also his mother, who let it happen and who the rest of the family was always saying was trash anyway, just the whole lying life he really had but always had to hide so well." Not until the 1992 presidential campaign would Bill Clinton speak publicly of the enduring torment of his childhood—not, that is, until advisers deemed a suitably expurgated version of the dysfunction and abuse to be a poignant, humanizing story and its telling an undeniable political asset.

It all seemed to reach a climax in the early 1960s when Virginia chanced to learn the "devastating" news that the Park Avenue house belonged to Raymond Clinton after all, and she resolved to leave as soon as she could afford to. For nearly two years she wavered over what she called her "frightening" decision. "Roger would be sweet and funny one day," she remembered, "and I'd think, *Maybe he's changed.*" Finally in April 1962 she braced herself to announce to Clinton that she wanted a divorce, triggering another explosion. The next day mother and sons packed their bags and left the terrace for the last time.

With the money she had been squirreling away for years, she bought a new home in a development on the southern edge of Hot Springs and defiantly moved her boys into a setting that was fashionably middle class, if not affluent, by local standards. "Earned by my own tears," as Virginia termed it, the house was the latest Gold Medallion all-electric model of the late 1950s. A red-brick ranch-style residence with picture windows and white wrought iron, it boasted a central vacuum system with outlets in each room, a large master bedroom with mirrored vanity and sunken bath, a spacious den, and two added bedrooms. Attached was the obligatory double carport, sheltering Virginia's familiar convertible, a black high-finned Buick coupe Bill drove during high school, and the small aging Henry J that Roger and Virginia had once cavorted in, its top cut off to make another convertible, which Bill took out in the summer.

There were other substantial houses and impressively filled driveways in the subdivision, some with the ubiquitous little cast-iron black groom out front, the small, smiling figure prized here as elsewhere in suburban white America as a touch of genteel history. The neighborhood was an obvious step up from Park Avenue. The Wheatley family, who owned most of the real estate in downtown Hot Springs, lived in the area. Next door was a comfortable Baptist parsonage, whose resident took polite note of Virginia's seasonal appearances, her inimitable yard work in full makeup, halter, tight shorts, and bare midriff. She was amused by the stir she created in a community that included a Baptist minister. Yet the three of them fitted easily enough into the outward respectability of the neighborhood. For two blocks in front of their home was a lush field of rose, pink, and deep purple peonies, harvested by the town each year just in time for Mother's Day. To friends it seemed idyllic. "Amazing!" one of them said of Bill Clinton's sleek new house on Scully Street.

New status did nothing to rescue the family from the old turmoil and relationships. Divorce depositions by both mother and older son that spring revealed only fragments of the violence they lived with. "He has continually tried to do bodily harm to myself and my son Billy whenever he attempts to attack me when he has been drinking," Virginia testified. The accompanying statement of fifteen-year-old Billy supplied details he would later omit—notably Roger Clinton's uncowed and fierce reaction to his defense of his mother, however taller and heavier he had grown. There had been much abuse and violence since that episode in 1960; Bill called the police again as late as April 1962, just before their leaving. "He has threatened my mother on a number of occasions and because of his nagging, arguing with my mother, I can tell that she is unhappy and it is impossible in my opinion for them to continue to live together as man and wife," he swore in language prompted by a lawyer. He added, though, a story with the ring of real life: "The last occasion in which I went to my mother's aid, he threatened to mash my face in if I took her part."

The Garland County chancery court in Hot Springs granted the divorce on May 15, 1962. For a time, Bill even began to escort his irrepressible mother on her rounds of the local nightclubs. "I guess he'd been playing the role since he was four or five," said a close friend, "but with Roger gone, Billy was a daddy and husband for sure now." It was a brief interval. Drawn and gaunt from a sudden loss of weight, Roger Clinton soon appeared on Scully Street, parking his car across the road to wait until Virginia inevitably came out to talk to him.

After weeping and pleading to reconcile, he frequently spent the night on their front porch, she remembered, "like a derelict."

The Clintons told her big Roger was suffering terribly. It was in pity but with affection that she eventually took him back, even though Bill had "conflicted feelings" about the divorce, as she put it in her memoirs. At the time, however, he was utterly opposed to any reconciliation, arguing that his stepfather "would never change," according to a friend. At one point during the period of divorce Bill and big Roger had managed a long talk alone together, in a car parked in another part of town. "A real conversation," as the younger man would call it later, it was in touching contrast to their usual relationship and no doubt part of Roger Clinton's anguished contrition. But not even that had persuaded Bill. "Virginia went back to him in spite of Bill's objections," said another friend. They apparently never discussed the reconciliation again. "Imagine the feeling of loss of control when Clinton could not convince his mother not to remarry Roger Clinton," wrote a psychotherapist discussing the event after it was publicly revealed. But once more Bill had suspended his anger, striving to please his mother. "She felt that Roger [Jr.] needed a father," Bill later explained, omitting, thought one observer, "what seems the obvious and (in this case) the real reason—that Virginia loved Roger."

Virginia often related how Billy went to a Hot Springs judge on his own initiative that summer to change his last name legally from Blythe to Clinton. He did it either for his younger brother, so they would both have the same last names, or as a gesture toward a stepfather he still loved, as she explained it. Asked later by reporters, Bill himself could never remember exactly when or why the step had been taken. In fact, Arkansas court records showed that it was Virginia Cassidy Clinton who petitioned for the change—on June 12, 1962, barely a month after the divorce and well after Roger began to appear so imploringly on Scully Street.

Despite the objections of the new Bill Clinton, Virginia and Roger were remarried on August 6, eighty-three days after their divorce. When big Roger rejoined them, however, he would be sleeping with Virginia in one of the smaller rooms along the hall, supplanted by what they all saw as the "third adult" in the family. As it had from the moment the mother and boys moved in months before, the imposing master bedroom belonged to sixteen-year-old Bill.

Then, as before and after, as always, the boy in the master bedroom energetically concealed his anguished private life behind a cheerful, apparently serene public face. There, as in the old bungalow, Bill gathered friends around him to practice their musical instruments, to take part in activities he organized and led, and often simply to have them there for reasons he could never explain. The Clintons' Baptist neighbor was not quite sure his daughter was entirely safe in a home where the parents drank and gambled with such gusto. But what most of Bill's friends saw was a normal, outgoing, even joyful teenager, especially loving to his half brother. To little Roger, Billy became the hulking and masterful Bubba—in the outside world an indulgent and mentoring big brother, a surrogate parent and secret protector only within the family. Few guessed how demanding both roles were.

Virginia now routinely took little Roger to school before dawn, leaving him with a janitor rather than home alone with his father. Not long after the remarriage, the six-year-old had found Roger Clinton bent over Virginia in the laundry room with scissors at her throat and had run out to find his brother in the next-door parsonage, shouting hysterically, "Bubba! Bubba! Daddy's killing Dado." There was another familiar episode of shrieks and sobbing that ended only when Bill slammed the door in Roger Clinton's face and sent the drunken man careening out of the house.

High school classmates remembered ever-smiling Bubba Clinton driving the little cut-off Henry J through Hot Springs or to out-of-town games, wearing a huge four-foot-brim sombrero that became, like his glibness and ebullience, a personal trademark. Few seemed to notice the underlying melancholy, the periodic anxious telephone calls home to check on his mother and little brother. He was "pretty happy" as a child, Bill Clinton said of himself decades later, though when asked about intimacy with or loving memories of his stepfather he was suddenly at a loss, unable to recall even the warmer moments from Hope. "He took me to St. Louis in a train once," he told a reporter tersely after a prolonged pause. "There just weren't many times. It was sort of sad. . . . I missed it."

"I think it strengthened Bill," his mother said of the tumult and fear. As usual, the older son agreed, at least in public. "She really taught me a lesson that I've always applied to my political life," he once said, "about sucking it up and working through the tough times." Others came to see it in different terms. "He was always taking care of his little brother because big Roger couldn't ever be trusted, always calling when he was out because he was afraid," said a friend who knew them all. "The burden was enormous, and as I look back on

it, Bill Clinton never really had a chance to be a child or a teenager."
Behind the mask, the unrelenting tension between image and reality
was already producing a young man haunted by nervously hidden
bouts of depression, by a sometimes morbid uncertainty, and still more
by the compulsion to win favor—to make peace and make everything
right—at virtually any cost. "One of the biggest problems I had in fully
maturing," he reflected on one occasion, "was learning how to deal
with conflict and express disagreement without being disagreeable,
without thinking the world would come to an end, without feeling I
would kind of lose my footing in life."

Ultimate loss, death itself, seemed to add to the specters and pressures. "I thought about it all the time," he would say about his natural
father's accident. "I always felt, in some sense, that I should be in a
hurry in life, because it gave me a real sense of mortality." One of the
most chilling experiences of his youth, he confided one night years
afterward on the campaign trail, was the enigmatic death of a friend's
older brother, a young man strikingly similar to what Bill Clinton was
striving to be. "He was a perfect kid, handsome . . . smart . . . popular . . . one of those guys who everybody loved," he said in tones his
listeners never forgot. "He went to sleep one night and the next morning they found him dead. No sign of anything. He just died."

Bill Clinton, the boy who had leaped up to answer every question in
the elementary grades, plunged into high school with the same fervor
to please and excel. Never well-coordinated or athletic despite his size,
he made his mark in music and academics. With childhood lessons,
Ozark summer camps, and sheer hard work, he became one of the
most accomplished tenor saxophonists in the state. As band major, he
organized fund-raising on behalf of the high school music program
and had his first peer contacts with African Americans, "the first blacks
Clinton respected," said one account. Eventually he played in his own
talented jazz combo, won state prizes and music scholarships, and in
the process, as one fellow musician recalled, "amassed a large network
of friends throughout Arkansas." But while music remained his fond
avocation, and later even a career asset of sorts, it was never a match
for wider school politics.

"He has an enormous modesty, bordering on inferiority, about his
personal experience. There are a lot of things about him that aren't
self-confident. He needs a lot of assurance and validation that he's
doing good," one of Clinton's closest associates in Little Rock would
later remark. Another observer said, "There's a veil over his voice, a

veil over his face. He has this smile all the time. There is a veil over his whole being."

The principal of Hot Springs High School, Johnnie Mae Mackey, was in a sense his first political patron beyond Uncle Raymond. Widowed in World War II, she worked avidly in the American Legion Auxiliary, held an elaborate Flag Day celebration each year, and in a strong southern voice "boomed her admonitions to patriotism," as one student recalled. When a color guard went by during a rain-soaked football game without receiving what Mackey thought due respect, the large and imposing lady roused the huddled crowd to its feet by crying out, "If there's a red-blooded American in this stadium, stand up!" "Service through elected office was considered a high calling," Clinton's friend Carolyn Staley said, describing the school's robust ethic, "and cynicism was an unfamiliar impulse."

Mackey had no difficulty inspiring the school's gregarious and amicable first-chair tenor sax, whose political aptitude she quickly recognized and proceeded to nurture. But then, Bill Clinton seemed to run for president of every organization he joined and to join every one in reach. With ridicule and rancor as well as good humor, his classmates soon nicknamed him Billy Vote Clinton. Eventually his cheerful grasping moved even the leadership-minded Mackey to put an unprecedented limit on the number of extracurricular groups to which any one student could belong. "Or Bill would have been president of them all," she confessed. As it was, several students believed the high school's political system was "rigged," as one put it, on behalf of nonathletes and other "favored" students like Clinton. "We had a bit of a sit-down strike in the auditorium over it," remembered Peggy Janske, a cheerleader who saw Bill and those like him as "too good to be true," deferring to the administration rather than independently representing students' concerns. "We felt like Mrs. Mackey was catering to Billy," she told a reporter years later.

Close beneath the charm he was fiercely competitive. "I beat Jim McDougal on a math test! I beat Jim McDougal on a math test!" Carolyn Staley remembered Clinton as "just *screaming*" when he bested a local prodigy. Having been president of the sophomore and junior classes, Clinton ran for a senior class office against an old friend and during the balloting told her with grim seriousness, "If you beat me I'll never forgive you." He lost, and they remained friends—though she never forgot the sudden, almost menacing force of the remark or the raw feeling it exposed.

Bill Clinton always enjoyed popularity. There were close friends, many who respected him for his intelligence, others who liked him for his sheer warmth and congeniality. Still, there were mixed reactions among his peers, though few spoke out when the state and national press later came asking about the adolescent who had become a powerful politician. "Several of us looked down on him," a Hot Springs native would say after Clinton was elected president of the United States and the ritual mythology of his difficult but "normal," "outstanding" boyhood was already forming. "In the presence of elders or anyone who could help or hurt him, he was always safely in the background. He'd always hide his true feelings." Another saw the same trait in Clinton's claimed aversion to alcohol and drugs because of allergies or revulsion at his drunken stepfather. "It wasn't because he couldn't or didn't want to get high," said a man who grew up with him. "Bill just didn't have what it takes to risk the disapproval in getting caught, to risk his political future." From early on, the paradoxes of his expedience, opportunism, habitual sincerity, anger, and implacable ambition ignited ambivalence in friends and acquaintances.

"He always had the girls carrying his books home for him after school," Virginia bragged to a friend. Yet, in his early teens at least, a still pudgy Billy was not the attractive or assertive young man he would become with women. "I think there were years growing up that he felt kind of like he was fat and rejected," said one classmate. Clinton himself later seemed to echo some of the same self-consciousness and uncertainty. Encouraging the son of a political friend to overcome his shyness, the then-governor of Arkansas drew the young man aside at a dinner party in Little Rock. "I was a fat boy and the girls hated me," Bill Clinton told him solemnly in an earnest and rare confession. "But look at you. You're skinny, and they'll love you."

In his later high school years, grown taller and slimmer, he seemed eager to make up for earlier doubts. There were proms and parties and long hot summer nights spent cruising Central with girls in the convertibles—though neither Clinton nor most of his circle dated steadily. "Bill's taste ran toward the strikingly attractive, a bent I wholeheartedly agreed with," wrote Virginia, adding, with her unabashed sense of the cosmetic, "I liked what I called beauty queens—girls who wanted to look pretty." The mother later admitted as well that neither she nor her alcoholic husband ever talked with their sons candidly or openly about sex and that they had only a vague sense of the boys' ethical and moral grounding. Bill appeared a "straight arrow" compared to her,

Virginia Clinton reflected, and on matters of values and character "seemed to do all right." Even more than in most families of that time and place, the model of relationships between men and women—matters of sexuality, loyalty, commitment, equity and equality, ultimately intimate friendship and love itself—had been left largely to what Bill and little Roger had seen and felt so sharply at home.

Promoted by Johnnie Mackey, Bill ran for the American Legion's Boys State the summer before his senior year. Wealthy Mack McLarty, his kindergarten friend, was elected "governor" at the state meeting. But as he hoped and maneuvered to do, Clinton won nomination to the national assembly in Washington, DC. There, on July 24, 1963, almost four months to the day before the assassination, John F. Kennedy shook his hand in the White House Rose Garden, producing a memorable photo of the two presidents a generation apart, the self-consciously grinning sixteen-year-old from Arkansas and a handsome young celebrity president almost the same age the boy's father would have been, a politician whose style Bill Blythe's son would emulate in a number of ways.

He went on to lunch in the Senate dining room with the Arkansas senators—his uncle Raymond's friend John McClellan and another idol and a future employer, William Fulbright. He had once considered medicine as a career, "seeing how much his mother looked up to doctors," recalled a friend. But in later legend the Washington trip was said to seal his choice of politics. "I could see it in his eyes when he came back," Virginia told a reporter. "I had decided what I wanted to do well before I met Kennedy," Clinton would confide to a friend. "He always knew what he wanted to be," added the same friend, "a lot more than what he wanted to do with it."

He asked Fulbright's and McClellan's staff, as well as school counselors, about a choice of college. At their suggestion and without much apparent pondering of his own, he applied only to Georgetown's School of the Foreign Service in Washington, drawn by its sheer proximity to government—though he never contemplated a diplomatic career, and his Hot Springs counselor in some confusion thought it one of "the Ivy League schools . . . most difficult for a Southerner to get into." At Hot Springs he would finish fourth in a class of 323, a National Merit Scholarship semifinalist with prizes in Latin and music, feats of memorization in English literature, though surprisingly few other traces of maturing intellectual conviction or originality. In his US history textbook, Perry Miller's conventional *Errand into the Wilder-*

ness, the future president underscored the author's optimistic if nebulous judgment of the American experience on the eve of the 1960s: "This is a chronicle of social self-consciousness."

On Scully Street his sense of ambition was more than ever fortified by his fiercely proud mother. Virginia now framed his band medals on velvet, making a corner of the living room "a kind of Bill Clinton display," as one person remembered. His friends called it "the shrine." Some saw the poignant contrast with the increasingly morose Roger Clinton, who by the mid-1960s seemed to customers and old friends a thoroughly withdrawn and broken man. "Now that I think about it," said one, "Virginia really belittled her husband, went around saying, and sort of winking at, what a weak drunk he was, and made Bill the real object of her pride and affection." She recorded her son's frequent public appearances with a home movie camera, telling relatives and friends that he would surely someday be president. His benediction at commencement she carefully typed out beforehand, sending copies to relatives and others. Ironing his gown, she had wept so much that the tears visibly stained the fabric. "I was so proud of him I nearly died," she wrote her mother about the prayer their boy impressively intoned over the public address system at the high school stadium. "He was truly in all his glory that night."

Georgetown accepted him later in the summer of 1964. The Hot Springs he left behind would change over the ensuing years, its more egregious illegal gambling finally closed down by the reform state administrations of Winthrop Rockefeller in 1967–70. For a time they even boarded up some of the store fronts on Central, prompting hookers and drug dealers to spill out onto the streets more brazenly than ever. Yet the tenor of the place remained. The flow of tourist dollars eventually resumed despite the waning popularity of miracle waters or the absence of back room gambling. Even in the leanest times of its relative legitimacy, the famous Vapors would never gross less than half a million dollars annually, as insiders testified to federal vice officers. Raymond Clinton and other powers of the old Springs found new channels for their wealth and influence. Organized crime adapted and maintained its presence, making Arkansas a pivotal province of its drug empire as it had once made the old spa an open city for its vacationing warlords.

Bill's absence produced what Virginia called a "void" for both her and his brother. For eight-year-old Roger, "there was nobody left whom he knew could protect him *all* the time," she would say. Soon after Bill went to Washington, Virginia invited her mother to come live

HOT SPRINGS • 59

with them. Both soon regretted it.

Of Bill Clinton's friends in the town where he grew up, many would be fellow students, though even more were former teachers and other adult contacts he had made a point of cultivating in his adolescence. They included several people in the town's business community, where he was well known by the Kiwanis, the Elks, and Civitan as a "Junior Businessman of the Year," a Master Counselor of the Masonic Demolay, and other honors he tirelessly accumulated. "He was always a gentleman, showing respect and good manners," said a typical older admirer, "loved by his peers, teachers, and yes, even the civic leaders."

In the end he appreciated them more than most then knew. As he left for Georgetown, Bill Clinton had already meticulously compiled hundreds of Hot Springs names, addresses, phone numbers, and personal notations on small index cards—for future votes, campaign organization, and, of course, fund-raising.

· 4 ·

Georgetown

"They'll Know What I'm Doing Here"

Spread across a hundred acres on the rolling bluffs above the Potomac in northwest Washington, the Georgetown campus was one of the capital's landmarks. Overlooking the river were the Gothic spires of the venerable and picturesque Georgetown College for arts and sciences. The plainer, newer brick building of the School of the Foreign Service was tucked back up Thirty-sixth Street on an old tree-lined cobblestone avenue and, along with the schools of business and languages, formed part of what was called the East Campus. Altogether, the Jesuit-run university bordered the exclusive Georgetown section of Washington, with its fashionable business blocks along Wisconsin Avenue, its undulating colonial brick sidewalks and rows of federal townhouses, and its discreet mansions and even wooded estates.

The curriculum in which Bill Clinton enrolled in the fall of 1964 was prescribed training for prospective diplomats or others in international relations—four years of required courses, mostly in the social sciences and with relatively few electives. Taking a more narrowly vocational approach than most liberal arts colleges, the School of the Foreign Service was "almost a State Department bureaucrat's version of a military academy," said one graduate, "rote without the brass or discipline." With some nine hundred students in the mid-1960s, the school was well known in the country and abroad, largely because of the Jesuits' shrewd promotion. For all that, however, it was never in the first rank of the nation's academic programs in world affairs.

With tuition and expenses comparable to those of the Ivy League,

60

Georgetown drew largely the sons, and still only a handful of young women, of upper-middle-class and well-to-do Catholic America. But there were also conspicuously wealthy international students—"The real money was from overseas," said a graduate—many of them sent from the ruling families of Latin America and the Middle East. "A three-suit school," as one professor called it, the university was affluent and formal compared with less monied parochial campuses like Fordham, Boston College, or Holy Cross. Young gentlemen of the School of the Foreign Service and the other colleges traditionally wore coats and ties to classes. Many shopped in the exclusive men's shop adjacent to the campus and lined the narrow streets around the institution with their sports cars.

In the mid-1960s the university was still clearly marked by a conservative academic orthodoxy as well as by the visible distinctions of wealth. "Intellectual skepticism did not play well with the Jesuits, who ranged like greenskeepers over the Catholic country club that was Georgetown in 1964," wrote Robert Sabbag, one of Clinton's classmates, adding that "money and status at Georgetown—as they have a habit of doing everywhere—traveled hand in hand." "Georgetown was an overwhelmingly conservative institution," said Jo Hamilton, another student at the time, "compared with almost anywhere else, except perhaps the deep South." Clinton and his class enrolled at a historic moment in the larger course of the country. The summer of 1964 had seen the passage of a major civil rights act, the secretly manipulated Tonkin Gulf resolution opening the way to US intervention in Southeast Asia, and the hopeful beginning of Lyndon Johnson's War on Poverty (before Vietnam devoured its budget and before its first challenges to local economic and political power aroused such lethal reaction). Those seminal events would shape much of the national backdrop to Bill Clinton's higher education over the following decade, just as rebellion, war, and reaction shaped the America he would inherit as a politician over the next thirty years.

On the gracious Georgetown campus that autumn, where a future president was intent on the politics of the moment, Virginia Clinton had come to help get him settled, and his provincial Arkansas education had raised eyebrows from the start. "What in the name of the Holy Father is a Southern Baptist who can't speak a foreign language doing in the *mother* of all Jesuit schools?" a priest had asked them smilingly but pointedly when they checked in. "Don't worry," her son had told her. "They'll know what I'm doing here when I've been here awhile." Less than a day later he was campaigning for freshman class president—"had made the decision to run," said his college room-mate Tom Campbell, "before he left Hot Springs."

John Kalell, a freshman, remembered the tall, cheery Southerner coming by the dormitory already leading "a coterie" of students who "had some belief in him," thrusting out his hand to introduce himself, and asking, "How'd you like to sign a petition to have a television placed in the lounge on this floor?" Like so many to come, Kalell thought him "remarkably engaging yet seemingly totally sincere." Campbell and others watched in awe what they called the unabashed freshman's "love of retail politics, talking to everyone, listening to everyone, urging, nudging people a little closer to his position." He seemed to be studying them all and years later would recognize by name the most casual acquaintance, reminiscing with stories about each that no one else remembered. He was forever "practicing his craft," one of them thought. "That phase of his life," said Campbell, "was like that of the gym rat who wants to play basketball so badly that he will spend hours shooting layups and hook shots and dribbling."

Clinton chose another experienced high school student politician, Bob Billingsley, to give his nominating speech for freshman class president and then made Billingsley rehearse with him on the roof of their dormitory. Painstakingly signing each sheet, he passed out hundreds of copies of his proposed platform. "The feasibility of every plank has been carefully considered," it assured voters, promising a newsletter and improved "work on the homecoming float and the Class of '68 dance." He won handily. But in a pattern that would follow him from dormitory to statehouse to White House, he soon felt compelled to explain how his impressive promises might not be realized after all. "The freshman year is not the time for crusading but for building a strong unit for the future," he told a student magazine after his victory, adding a bit archly, if not defensively, "You must know the rules before you can change them." Meanwhile, familiar with at least some of the oldest rules in politics, he named Billingsley and other backers to the most important student committees.

Students soon got to know Bill Clinton as "a junk-food man" who poured salted peanuts into his cola and devoured Moon Pies and peanut-butter-and-banana sandwiches. "Outwardly he bore no signs of homesickness or loneliness," thought a roommate who knew nothing of the grim reality on Scully Street. "He was exactly where he wanted to be." He began as a freshman to date a pretty, willowy blond from New Jersey named Denise Hyland, and they seemed "a steady pair," as a friend put it, over the next three years. Everyone remembered and liked his sheer gregariousness with both men and women—the cease-less politicking and invariable storytelling about Arkansas. Again and again they found small crowds in his dorm room and Bill "just re-galing them with stories."

The impression he gave of himself, quite deliberately, was that of the unaffected country boy, almost the bumpkin. He carried what Rob-ert Sabbag remembered as his "twangy Arkansas accent" and his obvi-ous ambition with an ease that instantly set him apart from his many peers who were trying to affect more sophistication. Most tended toward a weary disdain for the seamy commerce of Washington. It was "a student body almost totally indifferent to politics," said one of them. "In those days, it was not stylish to run for class office . . . even less stylish to openly court every friendly face with a handshake, in search of a vote," recalled classmate Dru Bachman. "But that's exactly what Bill Clinton did with a sunny naïveté." His apparent lack of guile was so original amid the pretensions of the campus that it soon be-came winning, making the most of his natural strengths. "He was some BMOC," said Jo Hamilton. "But . . . he always stopped and chatted. It wasn't as though he was looking down his nose at you. Even though you knew he was political, you at the same time never felt that it wasn't genuine."

Clinton volunteered for the air force ROTC and learned to march and do an about-face, but he turned in his uniform after one term, when the program was cut back and could not assure him a commis-sion. Georgetown's remaining ROTC, an army unit, was already full, and like most other college men in 1964–65, he would take his chances with a selective service that still had meager quotas and routinely granted student deferments. "Life was wonderful that first year at Georgetown," according to Tom Campbell. He and his friends went to basketball games, polo matches, and what one described as Washing-ton's "many women's junior colleges." Campbell, a New Yorker from a Jesuit high school, assumed before coming to the campus that his roommate "with a name like William Jefferson Clinton . . . [was] black." Like so many others afterward, he saw Bill Clinton the white Southerner as "the most unprejudiced person I have ever met." Clin-ton gave the impression that, unlike the southern stereotype, he came from a thoroughly integrated background. He "had grown up with poor black people," others remembered him telling them. "Any mani-festation of bigotry distressed him," Campbell would say. Yet there were no public acts of commitment. Egged on by Cuban exiles, they once picketed the Soviet embassy to protest the Russian presence in

Cuba. But Clinton and his circle did not join similar demonstrations about US politics. Nor was Georgetown entirely passive in 1964–65. "The real activists," one person recalled, "were the upperclassmen who had been down South as freedom riders and teachers."

Typically, Bachman and others saw the affable young man from Hot Springs as determined "to soak up every ounce of information and experience he could find" and doing so "with a hunger and gusto bewildering to those with far less self-assurance." His most lasting academic impression seems to have been a required freshman course, Development of Civilization, a survey of European history taught by Carroll Quigley, one of Georgetown's more colorful professors, who was known to conclude his lectures on classical political theory by flamboyantly tossing Plato's *Republic* or some other masterpiece out the second-story classroom window.

Quigley knowingly explained the connections between money, technology, class, and political power that conventional history often obscured—the role of the stirrup in the rise of the European aristocracy or how a technical impasse in gold mining prompted Roman imperial expansion. Renowned on campus, his final lecture was always on what he called "the key to the success of Western civilization," the "future preference" of both Europe and the United States—"the willingness," as one student remembered it, "to make sacrifices today to secure a better future . . . to prefer the future over the present." Citizens had a "moral responsibility" to build for posterity, the professor admonished them.

Quigley's "future preference" would echo in Bill Clinton's later speeches—"that fundamental truth [which] has guided my political career," he called it. Clinton even mentioned the late professor in accepting the 1992 presidential nomination. But Quigley was also the proponent of a rather less idealistic view of American politics. A consultant to the space program, the Pentagon, and the Smithsonian, he had written a 1,300-page book grandly titled *Tragedy and Hope: A History of the World in Our Time,* in which he extolled the way both the Democrats and the Republicans, while maintaining a democratic illusion for popular consumption, were fundamentally subservient to powerful special interests. Political parties are "simply organizations to be used," and big business has been "the dominant element in both parties since 1900," he wrote. "The argument that the two parties should represent opposed ideals and policies . . . is a foolish idea. Instead, the two parties should be almost identical, so that the American people can throw the rascals out at any election without leading to any profound or extensive shifts in policy. The policies that are vital and necessary for America are no longer subjects of significant disagreement, but are disputable only in detail, procedure, priority, or method."

Quigley was especially impressed by the old foreign affairs establishment, part of a larger Anglo-American financial and corporate elite and what he called a "power structure between London and New York which penetrated deeply into university life, the press, and the practice of foreign policy." He saw the prestigious Council on Foreign Relations as a concerted, if not conspiratorial, international network. Quigley approved heartily of the council's "powerful influence" and "very significant role in the history of the United States"; he "admired its goals and agreed with its methods," concluded a student. He exaggerated the import of the council itself, as apart from the wider sociology of knowledge implicit in its otherwise mincing discussions and publications. But the somewhat awestruck academic did capture much of the intellectual-psychological conformity and co-option of the old establishment, its society of status and orthodoxy so conventional, so linked to corporate and financial power, after all, as to dispense with conspiracy.

Clinton found Quigley "fascinating, electrifying, and brilliant," said a fellow student, Harold Snider. "Dr. Quigley was our mentor and friend. He left an indelible impression on our lives." Quigley had thought one mark of laudable elite dominance in the Washington of the 1960s was "the large number of Oxford-trained men" in the Kennedy and Johnson administrations, and he was alert to make his own students eligible for power. Clinton and others who did well he urged to apply for Rhodes scholarships and similar grants.

By the 1990s, as it happened, the eccentric Georgetown lecturer had acquired a kind of posthumous vindication in the number of likeminded and properly groomed figures crowding the campaigns and appointment lists of both George Bush and Bill Clinton. "If he is to be believed," one former student would say of the late Carroll Quigley during the 1992 election, "it won't matter whom you vote for on November 3."

◆ ◆ ◆

Clinton finished his first year on the dean's list with an impressive 3.57 grade point average, on his way to Phi Beta Kappa. In a letter to a Hot Springs friend, Patty Criner, he described college as "really hard," though he seemed to fellow students to move through most of the courses easily enough. Even with campus government duties, he found time to volunteer part-time in a student-staffed clinic for alcoholics and to spend days earnestly helping Harold Snider, who was blind, find his way around the school and the surrounding neighborhood.

Still, it was politics, both natural and cultivated, that seemed a constant presence. Tom Campbell went home with him that first summer and was impressed by Uncle Raymond's home on Lake Hamilton near Hot Springs, where they water-skied, but even more, as he recalled, by their "long excursions around Arkansas," the numerous friends, and "the dawning awareness that Bill Clinton had been *everywhere* in this state." Another roommate, Tom Caplan, remembered visiting Hot Springs at Easter the next year, driving from the Little Rock airport in a stylish Buick convertible, again courtesy of Uncle Raymond, and then cruising onto Bathhouse Row, top down on a gentle spring evening, crowds of kids on the sidewalk seeing them and crying out, "Hey, Billy Clinton's home! Hey, Billy Clinton's home!" Caplan told a reporter later, "Wherever we went that week it was the same." College friends who saw him in Arkansas, as in Washington, were convinced he was destined for big things politically.

Clinton returned to Georgetown in the fall of 1965 to become sophomore class president as well, making scores of small speeches around the school about "solving parking problems," as one student remembered his platform, "getting off-campus students involved in the class, and getting everyone involved in decision making." That fall he lobbied the Jesuits to lower campus food prices. Eager to meet Robert Kennedy, having met Kennedy's martyred brother, Clinton as class president invited the senator and former attorney general to make a speech at Georgetown and proudly escorted Kennedy around the university. But it was all comparatively tame and respectful by the standards of the time. "Not a word about confrontations with the university administration," Campbell noted, "and no mention of Vietnam," which was rapidly becoming a contentious issue on college campuses and in Washington.

The surges of student unrest and reform in the 1960s had already begun with the free-speech movement at Berkeley, the great civil rights March on Washington in 1963, the founding and spread of the activist Students for a Democratic Society at schools in the Midwest and throughout the country. Now the carnage in Southeast Asia provoked mass protests. Only minutes from the Georgetown campus, twenty-five thousand students had marched against the Vietnam War in April 1965, Clinton's freshman spring, and by the close of that year there would be nearly 200,000 US troops in Southeast Asia. In October 1965, a hundred thousand people had demonstrated against the war simultaneously in ninety cities. A month later, a young pacifist and father of three immolated himself in front of the Pentagon, and within weeks another forty thousand marched again in Washington, DC. "You didn't have to strain your eyes to see the signs of youth upheaval everywhere," wrote one participant. Yet however powerful or obvious, those tides "barely touched Georgetown," as Campbell remembered. By the end of Clinton's sophomore year, there were nearly 400,000 American soldiers in Vietnam. But at that point Bill Clinton would be intent on joining Alpha Phi Omega, the Georgetown fraternity known for its campus political prominence and for running student elections, and then on returning to Arkansas to work in his first statewide campaign, for what even local pols were labeling "the machine candidate" for governor.

He was J. Frank Holt, a former attorney general and state supreme court justice whom an opponent aptly called "a pleasant vegetable." In the 1966 gubernatorial race, Holt eventually lost a Democratic primary runoff to segregationist Jim Johnson despite the backing of the Democrats' old guard and especially of Witt Stephens, the senior brother of Stephens, Inc., the bonding, banking, and holding-company conglomerate in Little Rock that effectively dominated so much of Arkansas's politics as well as its economy. For young Bill Clinton, who conscientiously canvassed for Holt that summer, even from the volunteer fringe of the campaign it was a telling introduction to state politics and power. Like Frank Holt and so many others, he would eventually make his bargain with the Stephens empire.

But the more immediate significance of the campaign was in influence and patronage. Though receiving some scholarship money at Georgetown and a generous allowance from Virginia, Clinton wanted a Washington job to eke out added expenses for his junior and senior years. Now, through a Holt nephew and campaign manager, he arranged an offer from Senator Fulbright's office. There were two part-time positions available, a Fulbright assistant told him. By his own account Clinton answered brightly, "I'll take them both," the office was impressed, and he returned to Washington to start right away. "They gave me that job when I was . . . nobody . . . no political influence—nothing," he said later, omitting the Holt campaign ties—like Uncle Raymond Clinton and others, the beginning of so many discreet Arkansas connections.

From autumn 1966 to the spring of 1968, he was one of the legion of young interns and part-time workers on Capitol Hill, watching and hearing from the echoing corridors and rabbit-warren suites of the Old Senate Office Building the tumultuous years of Vietnam escalation, race riots from Detroit to Watts, draft-card burnings amid antiwar protests everywhere, Democratic Party schism, Lyndon Johnson's presidential abdication, and ultimately the assassinations of Robert Kennedy and Martin Luther King, Jr. It was one of those periods, says sociologist and participant Todd Gitlin, "when history comes off the leash, when reality appears illusory and illusions take on lives of their own." Though mostly in Fulbright's regular Senate office—rather than with the Senate Foreign Relations Committee, which the Arkansan had chaired since the 1950s and where much of the political action was—Clinton had a rare vantage point on the unfolding drama.

Rhodes scholar, law instructor, president of the University of Arkansas at thirty-four, and prominent in Congress by forty, already a four-term Democratic senator, J. William Fulbright was one of the genuine prodigies of Arkansas and national politics. Known for his contemplative intellect and literary bent in a US Senate where both were oddities, he had chaired the Foreign Relations Committee hearings on Vietnam that had begun, in 1965, Washington's own substantive critique of the war. When Bill Clinton went to work for him a year later, Fulbright was directing a further series of inquiries and revelations about US policy in Southeast Asia, in effect leading the opposition against a president of his own party and already despised in the White House and national security bureaucracy. "Senator Halfbright," Johnson called him sneeringly.

Coming up Pennsylvania Avenue every day after classes, Clinton performed the myriad menial chores of a Hill staffer, from filing to clipping to routine home-state services and correspondence—though now with the daily added responsibility of tearing Vietnam casualty lists off a constantly clacking wire-service printer and marking the names of Arkansans, to whose families Fulbright would then send personal letters of condolence. It was a grim, growing task. By the end of 1967 there were nearly half a million US troops in Vietnam and over fifteen thousand killed, some sixty percent of them during Bill Clinton's first full year on the Hill. Aides remembered him dealing quietly and stoically with the casualty lists while otherwise happily rummaging in every other function of the office. He was eager to learn how politicians dealt with disgruntled constituents, locally and nationally, and especially how Fulbright was preparing organizationally and financially for the 1968 reelection campaign in Arkansas.

As Bill Clinton, Uncle Raymond, and others in Arkansas and Washington well knew, there was quite another Bill Fulbright beyond the Rhodes scholar, university president, and war critic. Courtly intellect clothing a protean politician, Fulbright threaded his way uneasily atop an unholy coalition—what he saw as his benighted Arkansas constituency and race-baiting rivals, his wealthy right-wing backers among home-state landowners and financial interests, and his growing liberal, antiwar, and student admirers nationally. Fulbright had signed the infamous Southern Manifesto of congressmen upholding segregation and had voted against every civil rights bill over a quarter of a century; he often vacillated on consumer protection and civil liberties measures and duly perpetuated special-interest concessions like the oil-depletion allowance and other corporate subsidies. His conservative, even reactionary floor votes on root economic and social issues served to keep his native Arkansas caste-ridden and poor, and they were prone to multiply suddenly during election years like 1968.

Among the members of the Democratic eastern foreign policy establishment that Professor Quigley so admired, Fulbright was considered a "dilettante" fond of "calling for bold, brave new ideas," Dean Acheson was said to have quipped, "yet always lacking in bold, brave new ideas." As their private letters and secret documents showed, of course, this description was far truer of Acheson and his shallow establishment colleagues than of Fulbright. But in Washington's venomous and paradoxical jockeying, the twisting record of both statesmanship and squalor ultimately cost Fulbright a historic opportunity—and took an incalculable toll on the nation. While craven on race and other social issues, the Arkansas senator had been extraordinarily evenhanded on the Arab-Israeli rivalry and prescient on Vietnam. When John F. Kennedy thought about naming Fulbright secretary of state in 1961, Harris Wofford (whom President Bill Clinton would face a quarter century later when Wofford was a US senator from Pennsylvania) and other Democrats had mobilized a Jewish, black, and liberal coalition to kill the appointment, opening the job instead to the establishment's anointed Dean Rusk, who would be one of the architects of the Vietnam catastrophe. The same patronage politics, producing much the same sterility and blundering, would haunt President Clinton decades later.

There was substantial irony and wisdom to be gleaned from all this by the late 1960s as Bill Clinton stood by the Senate office ticker with its cascading casualty lists—warnings about political compromise, about intraparty cannibalism, about the lethal puerility of the establishment, and more. But there was no evidence that he came away with the moment's deeper lessons, least of all in his subsequent Arkansas record and presidential appointments. Over almost three decades, Bill Clinton would never reflect publicly on the larger meaning of the extraordinary senator for whom he so gratefully worked. In 1966–68, J. William Fulbright seemed chiefly a marvel of political balancing: scholar as good ole boy when necessary, country campaigner as Capitol Hill statesman. The essential point was the artful playing to every audience. "It wasn't Kennedy, it was Fulbright, the real Fulbright who managed to be so many different things to different folks, that was Bill's model always," said an Arkansan who knew them both well. "He revered Fulbright." Tom Campbell later observed that "in many ways their lives and careers paralleled." Coming from Arkansas, Bill Clinton realized his ambition to be president might not be realistic, "but he certainly thought," one person concluded, "that he could be like Senator Fulbright."

For the first time since starting high school, Clinton decided, during his junior year at Georgetown, to forgo campus office, working even beyond his paid hours on the Hill, learning from Quigley to do with only a few hours of sleep a night and to replenish himself, as he did in a later political career, with twenty-minute catnaps. Friends remembered him in "the more prestigious Copley dormitory" where he now lived, setting his small Baby Ben alarm, lying down to fall instantly asleep, and waking refreshed when others were flagging. He seemed for a moment to be away from his own compulsive politics, absorbed in study and work.

But then in March 1967 he ran for president of the East Campus's student council. Writing in the student *Georgetown Courier* earlier that year, he sounded what seemed a new approach to growing unrest in the country and on other campuses, not unlike some of his presidential campaign rhetoric amid national anguish twenty-five years later. "If elected representative government is to have any meaning at all, it must make a deep commitment to meet [issues] head-on," he wrote. "We cannot adopt a policy of isolation or inaction, or our politics will be without substance. We, as a student body, must urge our representatives to enter . . . where they are most needed, to plant the seeds of improvement, to reap the harvest of beneficial change. The times demand it."

His campuswide campaign was "a sophisticated operation," a roommate recalled, including phone banks to reach off-campus students and hand-colored "Clinton Country" roundels that could be hung on dorm-room doorknobs but cleverly doubled as sportcoat pocket inserts for men and small badges for women. As always, Clinton himself was the most effective campaigner, not least with the opposite sex. "He certainly knew how to speak to girls—and in the way that men talk to women—but it wasn't really flirting," one female student recalled. "He made you feel wonderful when he talked to you." In the end, the candidate's platform proved less than some thought advertised. Clinton stumped tamely for more visibility and funds for the student council, better counseling, and, repeating an earlier theme, better food services—"in the Georgetown political mainstream," Sabbag remembered.

Less organized and much less financed, his opponent and sophomore class vice president under him, Terry Modglin, promptly criticized the campus government for "fiscal and administrative excess," proposed a larger role for students in university policy making, and turned Bill Clinton's easy and familiar campus image against him, calling him the usual "politico," "the establishment candidate," and even a version of "Slick Willie," the epithet that would follow him in later political life. Now as afterward, he seemed outwardly to brush it off, while nursing resentment and anger within. Writing home that year, he had boasted how much other students trusted him. "People—even some of my political enemies—confide in me," he wrote. Only later did the irony seem clear. "It didn't hit me when I first saw it," said a friend familiar with the letter, "and then I asked myself, 'Wait a minute, what's a twenty-year-old kid doing talking about his political enemies?' "

"When I was a student politician I was about as controversial as I have been in my later life," Clinton once said, describing his Georgetown campaigning. In fact, his 1967 run suffered from its very banality, his cautious avoidance of controversy, and a refusal to challenge old authoritarian practices that were already changing nationwide. Not even his personal charm and popularity could defeat the promise of reform. Modglin won by 147 votes out of more than 1,300. In a recurrent pattern, defeat threw Clinton into visible depression. "Bill was down for a while," Campbell said. Also typically, he anxiously studied "the reasons he had lost," as one backer put it, although he never exactly confided the moral he drew. What was clear, as always, was his sheer seriousness and intensity beneath the smiling softness and serene catnaps. "Bill Clinton, a guy who wrote it all down . . . who made all the right moves" was Sabbag's summary. "While the rest of us might have been looking four years ahead, Bill Clinton was looking twenty years into the future."

That spring the air force was flying two thousand sorties a week over Vietnam, and Martin Luther King, Jr., addressed an antiwar rally of more than 300,000 in New York. The 1960s' famous "summer of love" was to follow in San Francisco's Haight-Ashbury and elsewhere. In October 1967, Clinton's senior autumn in Washington, a thousand activists, mostly students, held a chanting "siege" of the Pentagon, while a hundred thousand more kept quiet vigil at the Lincoln Memorial. "None of us took part because we were aiming to be mainstream players and didn't identify with the marchers," said Campbell later, explaining their failure to join the protests. "Bill and Kit [Ashby, a roommate] had their positions on the Hill to protect, and they didn't want to embarrass the men for whom they worked."

For Clinton, at least, there was inexplicable irony in avoiding for the sake of his job a movement Senator Fulbright had done so much to inspire. To be seen among hundreds of thousands in an antiwar demonstration might worry Bill Clinton for his own reasons, his peers thought, but it would hardly worry the chairman of the Foreign Relations Committee, renowned and basking in opposition to Vietnam. Others were more categorical about the motives of the young would-be politician. "Clinton did not take to the antiwar movement until after he left college," wrote Sabbag, "and he did not take to it any more convincingly than he took to dope, apparently, which he discovered at about the same time."

They were "in many ways . . . a generation apart" from their own age group, thought his classmate John Kalell. While some priests and nuns, and even some venerable Catholic schools, were in the forefront of the antiwar and social and cultural reform movements, the affluent university in its exclusive corner of Washington remained largely complacent. "We were the last remnant of a way of life," said another contemporary. Most of the campus was "absolutely unconscious" of the moment, added Walter Bastian, another classmate. "Going into business was judged a good thing, serving in government was deemed useful" was how still another classmate and Clinton friend explained their mentality. "All of the institutions whose reputations were stained during that era were all seen at Georgetown University as honorable places in which to spend one's life."

· ◆ ◆

Through it all there were constant echoes of the old life in Hot Springs. Trying to stem the jealous rages of her husband, Virginia had once given him a sheet signed by hospital coworkers recording her comings and goings for a month. But Roger Clinton had ignored it, and he continued to menace her and little Roger. Knowing their continuing ordeal from frequent calls and correspondence, Bill labored from Georgetown to fill the breach, frequently writing his brother consoling, exhorting letters. "Only remember to treat everyone fairly and honestly. Be as good as you can to everyone," he advised in one. When the child lost a football contest, the older brother was sympathetic but admonishing, citing his own defeat and triumph. "I'm sorry you didn't win the pass, punt and kick. . . . Bubba finished last the first two times I went to tryouts on my horn. But I finished first 10 out of the last 11 times," he told him. "So you see, determination will finally pay off—*if* you want to win badly enough."

In 1965, big Roger had been diagnosed with cancer of the mouth that had metastasized. With the Dude's old vanity, he stubbornly refused the radical facial surgery doctors prescribed, and there followed two years of trips back and forth from Hot Springs to the Duke medical center, where he received experimental laser therapy and other treatment, though to little avail.

Not long after Roger fell ill, Bill wrote him a rare letter of sympathy and encouragement, exceptional documentation of the torturous, otherwise largely mute relationship between stepfather and stepson. It was good that he was now going to church, Bill told him. "I believe, Daddy, that none of us can have any peace unless they face life with God, knowing that good always outweighs bad and even death doesn't end a man's life." In part compassionate, in part bitter, the letter was a reminder, too, of the younger man's relative strength and power, and even of the reconciliation with Virginia that Bill had opposed. "You ought to look everywhere for help, Daddy. You ought to write me more," he admonished big Roger almost as he would the little one. "But the last real conversation we had alone was parked in a car behind an old house on Circle Drive. That was 6 years ago, and you and mother were getting a divorce. I had hoped that things would get better after you got back together, but you just couldn't seem to quit drinking, and since then I have often wondered if you really wanted to."

Next came an especially telling passage, speaking in a few earnest sentences the mixture of confession and denial, guilt and anger that was their shared torment:

> *Of course I know I have never been much help* to you—never had the courage to come and talk about it. The reason I am writing now is because I couldn't stand it if you and Mother were to break up after all these years. I just want to help you help yourself if you can.
>
> I think I ought to close this letter now and wait for your answer but there are a couple of things I ought to say first—1) I don't think you have ever realized how much we all love and need you. 2) I don't think you have ever realized either how we have all been hurt . . . but still really have *not turned against you.*
>
> *Please write me soon Daddy—I want to hear from you. . . . Don't be ashamed to admit your problem. . . .* We all have so much to live for; let's start doing it—together.
>
> *Your son, Bill*

In the spring of 1967 Roger went back to Duke for prolonged treatment. Though preoccupied with the job on the Hill and the coming race for student council president, Bill had gone down to see his weakening stepfather, speeding the 260 miles back and forth to North Carolina in the 1963 Buick convertible Virginia had given him to take to Georgetown. He "would drive down to see him occasionally on weekends," according to Tom Campbell, "and return to school exhausted late Sunday night." Still proud and fastidious, Roger was humiliated that he could no longer always make it to the bathroom. "Bill would bodily pick him up and take him . . . so that he could maintain his dignity," Virginia remembered. He had gone to visit the dying man "just because I loved him," Bill Clinton told reporters long afterward. "There was nothing else to fight over, nothing else to run from." On a last visit Roger had given him his ring. "At least they made their peace," Virginia would say.

The interval produced still more letters back to his mother, "Miss Nightingale," as he called her adoringly. "I hope you will be proud of me in the next few months," he wrote of the campus election. "Win or lose, I'll try to reflect the honor and courage with which I've been raised." Periodically he reported on the visits with big Roger, seizing on fleeting signs of apparent improvement, telling her in detail about an emotional Easter Sunday they had spent together driving among the dogwoods of Chapel Hill—though even then they had characteristically left their feelings unspoken. "There was no 'true confession,' " Virginia would say later.

At that, the dutiful letters to Hot Springs always returned to the special, faceted relationship between son and mother. "Hope you will have some time to yourself other than the races now—probably you will never win that much," he could not resist saying in one, though adding immediately, "What a girl!—I know how hard this has been for you—my goodness, your life has been a succession of crises. . . . Surely I am prouder of you than you ever could be of me."

By the autumn of 1967 Roger Clinton was back in the Springs for the last time, secluded in a back bedroom on Scully Street, now drooling and emaciated at age fifty-seven and still too vain to see even his oldest friends. Before the Thanksgiving break, Virginia summoned Bill home to be with them. As the mother described it herself, eleven-year-old Roger had been praying "for years" that his father would die to end their own suffering. Now he prayed to end it for them all, the sick man's anguished lingering seeming to the survivors "one last act of terrorism," as Virginia Clinton put it. Bill stayed up with the devastated figure through the last nights. Then, weeks later than they expected, as the mother recorded, little Roger's "deepest, darkest prayer was answered."

Scarcely two months afterward, grandmother Edith Cassidy died at sixty-six. Bill had returned to Georgetown but he wrote Virginia instantly. "Never have I been so sorry to be away from you as I was when Mawmaw died.—Surely you will get some years of peace now." As usual, Virginia was rather more candid and blunt about what they had both suffered. In heaven neither Edith nor Roger, she noted in her memoirs, "would ever feel the need to shriek through the night again."

◆ ◆ ◆

That winter, armed with Fulbright's crucial backing and recommendation, and competing in a region that comprised Texas as well as Arkansas, Clinton won his Rhodes scholarship, among thirty-two in the nation and one of the first from Georgetown despite Quigley's establishment recruitment efforts. At an airport on his way to the final interview, Clinton had picked up an issue of *Time* that happened to have an article dealing with questions the panel later asked him. But the award was obviously a tribute to his impressive record, his winning intelligence and personality, as well as luck and formidable patronage.

In addition to its own considerable prestige, it was also a first brush with the power elite of Little Rock who were to be so important in his career and that of his future wife. Among his Rhodes interviewers were senior partners of the famous Rose Law Firm in the Arkansas capital.

Winning the scholarship brought more pride and publicity in Hot Springs, including an interview that April with the hometown Palmer News Bureau. "Students are gathered together in an atmosphere of learning, so they have a great advantage over rank-and-file people in our country," Clinton told the impressed local reporter. "If we learn the facts, we can gain a healthy outlook on domestic and foreign affairs. I think more involvement is necessary." How he truly saw himself vis-à-vis the "rank and file," what his real "outlook" already was would become unintentionally plain over the next two years and would prove more complicated than the ingratiating, slightly unctuous and condescending pose he now struck for the folks back home.

At the same time, his final months of college in 1968 were ones of national turmoil. In January came the shocking Tet offensive in Vietnam, and later in the spring the popularly forced withdrawal of Lyndon Johnson from the presidential race and the murder of Martin Luther King. Like thousands of other students, Clinton would tell his friends he was in favor of the antiwar Democratic challenger that spring, Senator Eugene McCarthy of Minnesota. But like the rest of the Georgetown campus, he remained at a distance from the country's unrest until riots erupted in the Washington ghetto on April 5, the afternoon after King's assassination.

Clinton promptly volunteered for a student relief program in the burning black neighborhoods, had a red cross put on the doors of his white Buick, and drove to a barren corner on the edge of the riot-torn area at Fourteenth and U Streets to distribute food. Visiting him from Hot Springs and riding along, Carolyn Staley remembered him as "numb and shocked at what we were seeing" and somehow annoyed that she wanted to take photographs of the destruction that might "trivialize the moment." Later, back at the dorm, she thought Clinton "very melancholy," muttering passages he had memorized from King's famous "I Have a Dream" speech at the Lincoln Memorial five years before.

At intervals they and other students went to the roof of old Loyola Hall to peer out at the distant billowing smoke as sirens screamed only thirty blocks away. Along with much of white Washington, they were fearful of a breakout, though the riot's rage was, as usual, penned up and turned inward on black homes and businesses. Machine-gun nests had been set up on the White House lawn, troops camped in the Georgetown gymnasium, and someone in pathetic precaution had scrawled "Soul Brother" in soap on the display windows of the University Shop, an expensive "Ivy League" men's store that was, as one student put it, "decidedly not owned by blacks."

Aside from Bill's relief foray, Tom Campbell recalled, they "stayed close to the campus and each other, not certain what was coming next." Later, the disturbances over but block after block of the capital still smoldering, they ventured onto the pacified streets and were shocked anew. Much of northeast Washington was as ruined and skeletal as a war zone, "a part of the city," one Clinton roommate said, "to which we had never before paid much attention."

♦ ♦ ♦

Clinton was to finish Georgetown cum laude, if not at the top of his class or even among its memorable intellectual stars. But the honors were a fitting climax to an energetic undergraduate career. Apart from his ubiquitous campaign politics, he had not been especially social, breaking off the steady relationship with Denise Hyland early in their senior year, though continuing to see her along with other women. He spent most of his leisure time in a circle of male friends, especially the roommates with whom he shared an off-campus house on Potomac Avenue his senior year—Tom Campbell, who deplored the antiwar protesters and would soon enlist as a Marine Corps pilot; Kit Ashby, the son of a well-to-do Texas doctor, who interned for right-wing Democratic Senator Henry Jackson of Washington; Tom Caplan, a Baltimore boy who had interned in the White House and was a gifted writer; and Tom Moore, who was described as "an army brat from Kentucky with an encyclopedic knowledge of the battles of Napoleon."

As in Hot Springs, Bill Clinton would be remembered in college as exceptionally bright, quick, and articulate—very much the apprentice politician. "He was a taster of ideas," one Georgetown friend reflected later, "a kind of grazer, and a skillful user, but not a lover [of ideas] for their own sake." Campbell recalled their frequent dinner discussions on Potomac Avenue about the war, talk that was more immediately political or pragmatic than historical or philosophical. "His objection was not that the United States was immoral but that we were making a big mistake. He wondered how a great nation could admit that and change course. He thought America was wasting lives that it could not spare."

Four days before their June graduation Robert Kennedy was gunned down in Los Angeles on the night of his California primary victory, when the nomination and the presidency seemed within his grasp. Senior-week festivities were abruptly canceled. Commencement was rained out in a thundering downpour. "The entire four-year experience was destined to find its metaphor . . . when the sunlight gave way to darkness suddenly," wrote Robert Sabbag. "The world beyond university walls," he added, "had posted a very dark invitation."

· 5 ·

Oxford

"Every String He Could Think Of"

"It was just a fluke" that he was not drafted, Bill Clinton would earnestly tell the *Los Angeles Times* in 1992. "I certainly had no leverage to get special treatment from the draft board." But two dozen years before, the reality had been quite different.

Though few of his friends knew it at the time, shadows had begun to form for Bill Clinton months before his class left Georgetown. That March of 1968 the Hot Springs draft board, following national policy, had already lifted his 2-S student deferment and reclassified him 1-A, ready for induction. Before his education was completed, before his planned and practiced political career could even begin, he had faced the dreaded Vietnam draft and the prospect of being one more of those names in the Arkansas roll call of the dead that spilled so relentlessly out of the ticker in Fulbright's office. The first thing he had done was to call Uncle Raymond.

◆ ◆ ◆

By the spring and summer of 1968 the Vietnam War had come home to poorer states like Arkansas with special vengeance.

For much of the war, under the post–World War II system of selective service, with its exemptions for higher education, the fighting and dying in Southeast Asia were predominantly a matter of race and class. Secret government documents told the ugly story. According to a typical memo of the time, the selective service was glad to exempt those middle-class or wealthy students who were "busy acquiring approved skills," while it gave exams to ferret out "underachievers." As late as 1966–67, as a historian later revealed, the system "was deliberately using the draft as an instrument of class privilege." Scarcely one college graduate in ten would even go to Vietnam, and only a small fraction of those saw combat. By contrast, young Americans with a high school education or less were more than twice as likely to be called for service, and more than twice as many were sent into battle. The poor, especially African Americans, were gathered into the maw. Black casualties in Vietnam would be twice as high as white.

The results were stark for Arkansas, a state near the bottom of the nation in household income. Of the total US casualties in Vietnam— nearly 60,000 killed and more than 250,000 wounded—week by week, month by month, Arkansas often suffered higher losses proportionately than most other states in the nation. In the small-town and rural high schools of the Mississippi Delta, entire classes of young black men were decimated. Even in more prosperous Hot Springs, Principal Johnnie Mae Mackey's beloved American Legion was continually busy with memorial services and calls on bereaved families. In the Gold Medallion neighborhood of the Clintons, Bill's boyhood friend and classmate Mike Thomas came home from Indochina in a flag-draped coffin.

By the beginning of 1968, with casualties mounting, the wholesale conscription of the poor, uneducated, and nonwhite was no longer enough. The Johnson White House had been forced to lift the old exemptions for graduate study that had kept thousands of middle- and upper-middle-class men free of service. Avoiding Vietnam would now take far more than simply staying in school.

When the question of his 1968 draft status eventually came up in the New Hampshire primary more than two decades later, Clinton himself would never describe the several personal contacts and pleas made on his behalf—though Raymond Clinton and his lawyer regularly told the anxious student and his family what they were doing.

Friends remembered how Bill Clinton, home from Georgetown, especially in his upper-class years, used to taunt his reactionary uncle by deliberately dropping liberal statements in the older man's presence and joke in private about Raymond's notorious racism and shady contacts. "Despite all that Raymond had done for him, I guess Billy had grown a little embarrassed by him and his views," said a member of the family. "I sure didn't agree with old Mr. Clinton. He was a real mossback," one school friend recalled. "But Billy's setup was always kind of cruel." Now that the mocking young nephew was about to be drafted into a bloody and unpopular war, however, the ridicule noticeably stopped. In a sense it was Bill Clinton's first political crisis, and it was his benighted but influential uncle on whom he relied.

He was reclassified 1-A on March 20, 1968, and Raymond Clinton had swung into action. "We started working as soon as [Raymond] got word that Billy was going to be drafted," said Henry Britt, the car dealer's longtime friend and personal attorney. It was a concerted effort "to get Bill what he wanted," Britt would say later, adding, "Of course Billy knew about it."

The circumstances seemed dismal. In February Lyndon Johnson ended by executive order all graduate-study deferments except for medical students. Young men had already crowded National Guard, reserve, and ROTC units to avoid burgeoning draft calls, in which at least one-third of army inductees were now bound for Southeast Asia. But Raymond Clinton appeared undaunted. Late that March he had called an old friend, Commander Trice Ellis, Jr., who was the officer in charge of the local naval reserve unit. The uncle asked the commander "to create a billet, or enlistment slot, especially for Bill Clinton," as one account put it. "Raymond said he had a nephew who was college-educated and the army was about to draft him, and the boy wanted to join the navy," Ellis recalled. Though naval reserve assignments were then filled throughout Arkansas, with lengthy waiting lists, Ellis assured Raymond that he would try to talk the eight naval district authorities in New Orleans into specially arranging another billet. "I was always looking for good people," Ellis recalled. "I said I'd see what I could do."

While the commander lobbied the navy, Raymond went next to another old friend, William S. "Bill" Armstrong, chairman of the Hot Springs draft board and, along with both Raymond Clinton and Commander Trice Ellis, a founding member of the local chapter of the Navy League, a national organization of naval boosters. The uncle now pressed Armstrong hard, citing their shared loyalty to the navy over the other services, as well as Bill Clinton's credentials. "Why don't you give the boy a chance to get into the navy," Britt remembered Clinton importuning the chairman of the draft board. Britt himself would urge Armstrong to "put Bill Clinton's draft notice in a drawer someplace and leave it for a while."

At one point, Raymond and Henry Britt hurriedly drove some distance to buttonhole Senator Fulbright at a dam dedication on the banks of the Arkansas River and get him to ensure that his office, too, would intercede with the Hot Springs draft board. Soon after that ceremony, as board member Robert Corrado remembered it, a Fulbright aide telephoned the Hot Springs office of the selective service to urge that Corrado and his fellow board members "give every consideration" to keeping young Bill Clinton out of the draft so that he could attend Oxford. "Raymond was playing both sides of the fence like a good politician," Britt would explain. "If nothing else worked, he could always get Billy into the navy. He was hedging his bets."

The Hot Springs board members were duly impressed with Bill Clinton's prestigious grant at Oxford. "As old as he was, he would have been at the top of the list to be drafted," said board executive secretary Opal Ellis, "[but] we were proud to have a Hot Springs boy with a Rhodes scholarship." By standards applying to hundreds of others, William Jefferson Clinton was due to be drafted no later than the summer of 1968. But William Armstrong acceded to the manifold political pressures and routinely kept Clinton's draft file back from consideration by the full board. "We've got to give him time to [go] to Oxford," Corrado recalled the chairman announcing at their meetings in a small room in the old federal building, not far from Bathhouse Row.

Meanwhile, Commander Ellis had in fact managed to arrange the special extra naval reserve billet with the New Orleans headquarters and soon called his friend Raymond Clinton to ask, "What happened to that boy?" The car dealer replied cryptically, "Don't worry about it. He won't be coming down. It's all been taken care of."

Eventually Bill Clinton would be scheduled to take his draft physical, though not until February 1969 at a US base in England, nearly a year after it would have been set had he been treated like most inductees. The interval between his reclassification and his examination was "more than twice as long as anyone else" could expect, according to one account, "and more than five times longer than most area men of comparable eligibility" were granted. Of all those classified 1-A by his draft board in Arkansas during the turbulent, bloody year of 1968, Bill Clinton was the only one whose process was so extended.

The behind-the-scenes political intervention of Uncle Raymond and others would enable him to leave the country and complete a first year at Oxford without either a formal deferment or any other promised fulfillment of military obligation. And in the longer sequence of the draft, that interval would be just enough to be decisive in keeping him out of the war. "The board was very lenient with him," Opal Ellis admitted later. "We gave him more than he was entitled to."

◆   ◆   ◆

On the SS *United States* that autumn of 1968, Bill Clinton was a ship-board favorite. Also headed to the United Kingdom were other Americans on study grants, including some Clinton would appoint to his administration twenty-five years later. Soon after leaving the Hudson River docks, he was on deck or in the lounges entertaining clusters of students with his saxophone and the inevitable tales of Arkansas. To the seasick, soon lying in their cramped cabins on the heaving Atlantic, he carried broth like a solicitous relative. Among the queasy was Robert Reich, a future Clinton adviser and labor secretary who remembered opening his compartment door to "a tall, gangly Southerner" holding chicken soup and crackers and saying "with a syrupy drawl," as Reich heard it, "I understand you're not feeling well. I hope this will help."

The only African American in the group and another of those later named to a Clinton regime, Rhodes scholar Tom Williamson was wary at first of the effusive young Arkansan. But he was quickly won over by Clinton's almost ritual denunciation of what they all seemed to associate with his home state—infamous Orval Faubus and the Little Rock school crisis a decade before. Williamson was struck, too, by Clinton's "full command of the lyrics to all the great Motown hits of our time." Several shipmates were impressed with his apparently effortless success with women, a handsome country boy's magnetic lack of pretense, and his use of his music like a kind of pied piper. Bill "insisted that playing the saxophone," Williamson would say, "was a workable substitute for bona fide charm and urbanity in trying to engage a young woman's attention."

The awaiting Oxford was a world-famous symbol of learning. Fifty miles northwest of London, it was the oldest university in England, dating from the twelfth century. In 1968 its ten thousand students were enrolled among thirty-one stately colleges, Clinton's University College one of the three original. Instruction was in the traditional Merton College tutorial system. Unlike American higher education, there were no compulsory courses or lectures, no class quizzes or semester exams, only an assigned tutor who guided the student throughout the undergraduate years, prescribing what should be read and written. The tutorials led eventually to university examinations for either a simple pass or honors bachelor's degree, with a master's available in many fields without further testing.

Yet behind Oxford's dignified image, as American Rhodes scholars and others swiftly discovered, was a rather different, quite relaxed real-ity. "Oxford places the emphasis on fluency and glibness," said one Rhodes scholar. "Serious discussions are not encouraged." With the one-hour tutorial sessions but twice a week, the ungraded essays only to be read out to the instructor, and no examinations at term's end, everything depended on the quality and devotion of the individual tutor. In the late 1960s, as before and after, the discreet little secret of Oxford and its Rhodes scholars was that "intense learning experi-ences" were rare and "hopeless disasters"—or at least a stylish English languor—all too common.

Generations of American students returned from the medieval tur-rets and jade-green fields with stories of feckless, dozing dons, of in-serting outrageous, irrelevant passages in their weekly essays only to drone on unnoticed by the immovably indifferent tutor. An Oxford sojourn had "great snob appeal," was a "ticket to punch" for would-be "American luminaries," one of them acknowledged. And as in all large institutions, there were bound to be exceptions to the predomi-nant false pretense. But in sheer intellectual terms, most Americans were likely to be on their own, largely left to the limits or biases of their undergraduate educations and to their native ability or shallowness, frequently departing two years later intellectually untouched by majes-tic Oxford. "You could do as little or as much as you wanted. It was a kind of a lark," said Dell Martin, a Clinton contemporary in the late 1960s.

Added to the tutorial caprice was the cultivated air of detachment and affected ennui rooted deep in the patrician English prep school system, from which Oxford still drew large numbers of its students. "Hard work is not only unnecessary, it's essentially frowned upon," said David Segal, an American at Balliol College who later wrote of an Oxford "ethic . . . semi-officially codified as 'effortless superiority.' " The experience at this renowned institution might therefore hone the skills of the facile and the articulate, but with few demands on underly-ing substance or sustained intellect.

"Lots of American students, most of whom had been hyperindustri-ous undergraduates, had a hard time adjusting to Oxford's too-clever-to-care chic," Segal recorded. Yet others concluded that US scholar-ship winners accepted the ubiquitous sham and affectation happily, and in any event few were ready to dispel the prestige and reputation they now enjoyed as part of the mythology. Like Bill Clinton himself after two full years, many Rhodes scholars did not bother completing even bachelor's degrees at Oxford. If they were eventually graded in the ultimate examinations, several coasted with gentlemanly "thirds"—the equivalent of "two years," Segal translated, "of straight Ds." "My main impression was just how easy it was," said another Rhodes scholar at Oxford just after Clinton. "There's a sort of a conspiracy of silence not to reveal this."

"Oxford is overrated. And most Americans studying there couldn't care less," one US student concluded. "For them, the main challenge is finding ways to stay amused." Most succeeded. A Clinton contemporary, later a colleague of Hillary Rodham's and eventually a Republican governor of Massachusetts, wealthy William Weld typically remembered his Oxford years as "lager and chocolates, poker games and parties without end, ten sets of tennis every afternoon, played on grass courts so that no one ever got tired."

Neither colleagues nor reporters could later identify an especially influential Oxford "mentor" or a particularly telling intellectual experience for the future president of the United States—or any detail about the reading or writing he did that first year, apart from the mystery novels and other popular literature that everyone remembered his enjoying. "He was better in argument than on paper," his first-year tutor, Zbigniew Pelczynski, told a London paper a bit vaguely in 1992. "His essay technique was not perhaps the best that I have seen, but he was obviously an avid reader." Friends from 1968–69 recalled more clearly his enthusiasm for rugby and how he held forth at his favorite pub, the Turf Tavern, or impressed an English supper circle in University College with Arkansas storytelling or lengthy discussions of Vietnam and other subjects. Clinton was "always given to pontification," said one account. At the same time, as at Georgetown, he could seem uniquely unassuming with more self-important peers, "talking with huge pride about watermelons," as Englishman Martin Walker recalled. Like his undergraduate contemporaries, Americans at Oxford found the naturalness much of his attraction. "Bill was the most comforting figure among the crowd of confident blue bloods," said contemporary Robin Raphael.

Sociable or relaxed academically, he had nonetheless brought to that first year in Britain his own serious preoccupation—the ubiquitous lists and three-by-five cards he had faithfully tended, as one might an impassioned diary, since high school. If Oxford didn't promise Arkansas votes or money, it was a seeding of future contacts and support for a wider ambition. "He meticulously recorded the name of every new person he met," said one writer looking back on their time in England. "Bill would join us at the pubs at night," Brenning McNamara recalled, "but not until he had jotted down the day's names." Some took his ceaseless politicking as provincial wont, others as undisguised opportunism. "It was the eyes that gave it away," Philip Hodson told the London *Sunday Times* in 1992. "They moved on before he had finished talking to you."

When the contacts had been made and the vital names stored away, there was now, more than ever before, an added interest—women. In Oxford at twenty-two and twenty-three, Clinton would display what Garry Wills called "a dangerous talent, part of his gregarious and ingratiating way with all his friends, a puppylike eagerness and drive to please" that young women seemed to find irresistible. "Bill was one of two people I have known who were just amazingly successful with women," said a friend from England. "You would hear him and say to yourself, 'No one is going to believe that line,' but they did." A housemate for a time, the British novelist Sara Maitland, remembered that she had a neurotic fear of hooded hair dryers and that Bill arranged for her to have her hair dried by hand at the beauty parlor. She thought it an example of "the very real way he is sensitive to the people around him."

It was also at Oxford that he began to be drawn to something more than what Virginia called "the beauty-pageant mold," the flossy, stiff-haired surface epitomized by his mother, his parents' nightclubbing friends, and eventually his own dates. On one occasion he even wrote home about his infatuation with a young woman, warning Virginia that the girl was not attractive in the "traditional" way and offending her mightily by adding, "You wouldn't understand, Mother." Still, while pursuing various women in England, he was also sending a stream of love letters back home to Sharon Evans, soon to become a Miss Arkansas. Clinton was involved as well with an English woman, Tamara Eccles-Williams, when Evans visited Oxford in March 1969. His circle marveled at how he juggled his love affairs without apparent collision. "He took this homegrown lovely to an antiwar demonstration one day at Trafalgar Square, then put her on a tour bus and went back to Mara for a while," a friend recalled. A fellow Arkansas scholar remembered being introduced to Evans. "She was a real beauty. He said this was the woman he loved and the future mother of his children. I never saw her again."

He could be publicly delightful as well as seductive in private. Another friend remembered going with him to a lecture by the celebrated Australian feminist Germaine Greer, who admonished the audience that the female orgasm was a factor in gender tyranny and, in any case, vastly overrated. "Bill was sitting there in the hall looking something of the hick," the friend recounted, "in his Hush Puppies, his ginger beard, and his ginger suit." After the lecture, he had thrown up his hand eagerly to be recognized. "About the overrated orgasm," he drawled, "won't you, Ms. Greer, give a southern boy another chance?" He brought down the house and seemed to disarm the imposing feminist herself.

Yet there was another side to the charm and sexuality, a first evidence of utter relentlessness about his conquests. For some, his promiscuity left a nagging question of loyalty and integrity despite the laxity of the moment. "There were big noisy parties, with wine, marijuana and casual sex. It was a time of revolving-door relationships, and Clinton pursued a lot of women . . . including the girlfriends of his friends," wrote Alessandra Stanley. "It seemed for a time there that he was going after and getting every woman who came within reach," another witness remembered. "I don't know that we thought much about what that told about Bill Clinton, or about his women either, for that matter."

By the end of his first year at Oxford, however, everything else would suddenly be shrouded by unexpected events back in the federal building in Hot Springs. Though Richard Nixon had been elected the past November promising to end the war in Vietnam and though the first US troop withdrawals began in May 1969, fighting raged on, with ten thousand more Americans killed. Draft calls were unremitting. New pressure from Washington fell on local authorities. Bill Clinton had passed his physical in February and chairman William Armstrong and his draft board back in Hot Springs now abruptly decided in the spring of 1969 that they could no longer hold back his file, Rhodes scholarship and Raymond Clinton notwithstanding. His induction was set again, this time for April 1969. Only after more intense lobbying by Raymond and others was that date put off once more, to July 28, 1969—"so that he could finish the school term," as one source put it.

They had all been confident that the board would remain fixed from the interventions of the previous spring. Since Raymond had brushed aside the specially created naval reserve billet, Bill was suddenly without even that alternative. Friends at Oxford advised him to manage somehow an ROTC deferment at an American university. But ROTC programs were also notoriously crowded and at best would require him to abandon Oxford. By mid-May 1969, scarcely two months from the newly scheduled induction, Clinton was visibly depressed—"as low as I have ever been," he said. He left Oxford doubting he would ever return, though planning another feverish effort to avoid Vietnam.

One of Clinton's first public displays of temper occurred not long after arriving in Hot Springs when he decided in near despair to go personally to the office of the draft board. There he confronted its executive secretary, Opal Ellis, a twenty-year veteran of the selective service. Ellis remembered Clinton's telling her he was too well educated to go. "He was going to fix my wagon [and] pull every string he could think of." In 1992 Clinton denied he had ever made such claims or threats, suggesting instead that Ellis, a Republican, had "at best a faulty memory." In any event, Clinton left the federal building and began an almost frantic sequence of actions to stave off induction.

He now quickly took an air force officer's candidate examination, only to fail the more demanding physical exam because of a vision defect. He also hurried to take the officer's candidate test for the navy but flunked that physical as well because of a hearing problem— though, like his defective vision, it had not disqualified him on the general draftee physical four months earlier. In mounting despair, as he remembered vividly, he anxiously telephoned and wrote friends about his plight. Then, only eleven days before the scheduled July 28 induction, he suddenly drove up to Fayetteville to the home of Colonel Eugene Holmes, commander of the army ROTC unit at the University of Arkansas. In a two-hour interview on the evening of July 17, as the colonel remembered, Bill Clinton earnestly explained "his desire to join the program."

Among those to whom he had appealed was a fellow Arkansan, Cliff Jackson, a Fulbright fellow at Oxford when Clinton met him in 1968 and a Republican who had worked for the Winthrop Rockefeller campaigns. As Jackson later told the story, Clinton asked him to use his influence with the GOP administration in either Washington or Little Rock to "quash the July draft notice." Ambitious but not yet the bitter rival and enemy he would become years later, Jackson responded by contacting the man he was going to work for that summer, the executive director of the Arkansas Republican Party, Van Rush, who in turn was close to Willard "Lefty" Hawkins, Governor Rockefeller's appointee to head the selective service in Arkansas.

Jackson arranged a meeting with Hawkins for both Clinton and an anxious Virginia, who herself talked with Jackson during the weeks before Bill arrived back in Hot Springs earlier that summer. At the meeting with Hawkins, according to what the colonel later told Jackson, Bill Clinton readily agreed to "serve his country in another capacity later on" if the July 28 draft could be lifted. Hawkins was not sure what was possible. The fall enrollment at Arkansas's army reserve officers program was full, but something might be arranged for the next term. He sent the young man on to his fellow officer Gene Holmes at the university's ROTC unit, and Clinton said he would make the five-hundred-mile round-trip to Fayetteville right away. As Jackson mentioned matter-of-factly in a letter to another student on July 11, his friend Bill was "feverishly trying to find a way to avoid entering the Army as a drafted private."

A much-decorated survivor of the Bataan death march and of more than three years as a prisoner of war of the Japanese, Eugene Holmes was nearing the end of a thirty-two-year military career. Crusty but avuncular, he had lost a brother in World War II and personally ushered both his own sons into Vietnam service; he was "a real believer," according to a colleague. Like others in Arkansas, Holmes was impressed by Bill Clinton's credentials and pleased by the bright student's interest in ROTC. He was proud to be "making it possible," he wrote later, "for a Rhodes scholar to serve in the military as an officer." Holmes methodically explained to Clinton what they both knew—that he would have to enroll at the University of Arkansas simply to be eligible for ROTC there. Clinton said he planned to "attend the Law School," Holmes noted, but naturally needed "some time" at Oxford to put his affairs in order before returning to Fayetteville. "I thought he was going to finish a month or two in England and then come back to the University of Arkansas," Holmes said afterward.

Clinton promised, as he later recalled, to let Holmes "hear from me at least once a month." Holmes said he would immediately begin the processing of Clinton's formal application and would inform the Hot Springs board of his new ROTC deferment. But the delay in England before enrolling at Arkansas, he added, must not be too long. "I couldn't have done it for a year," Holmes said he told Clinton at the time. "That wouldn't have been ethical."

Successful as the July 17 visit to Fayetteville had apparently been, things were not left at that. The "next day," as Holmes would testify in a formal affidavit, there began a concerted campaign of phone calls to him on Bill Clinton's behalf. Hot Springs draft board members themselves were telephoning to say that "it was of interest to Senator Fulbright's office that Bill Clinton, a Rhodes scholar, should be admitted to the ROTC program," Holmes remembered, and "that Senator Fulbright was putting pressure on them and that they needed my help." Whether this was what Opal Ellis described as "fix your wagon" would never be clear. But Colonel Holmes himself felt acutely the political elbowing down the line. "I received several such calls," he swore later. "I then made the necessary arrangements." To the Hot Springs board in late July the ROTC commander sent formal notice of a 1-D deferment for William Jefferson Clinton—"Member of reserve component or student taking military training"—which the board then duly noted and officially entered on August 7. Yet again, this time at the last moment, his ordered induction had been staved off.

On August 7, 1969, Clinton signed the formal letter of intent to join the University of Arkansas ROTC, but he did not legally file it until some days later. In a summer of so much applying and exam taking, he did nothing official to apply to or test for the university's law school. During his 1992 presidential campaign he would claim that the school "informally" accepted him simply on his academic record—though other students with comparable undergraduate records weren't granted any such dispensation. The actual record left no illusions. "He figured this maneuver would get him several more years of deferment, possibly until the end of the war," campaign biographers Charles Allen and Jonathan Portis wrote bluntly of the ROTC exemption.

Clinton began almost instantly to have second thoughts and pangs of guilt. In August he repeatedly called an Oxford friend and another future member of his administration, Strobe Talbott, who gave a version of their conversations in a 1992 *Time* essay supporting Clinton. "He was troubled that while he would be earning an officer's commission and a law degree," Talbott recounted, "some other, less privileged kid would have to go in his place to trade bullets with the Viet Cong."

On September 9, 1969, little more than a month after signing up for ROTC, he wrote a letter to fellow Rhodes scholar Rick Stearns that Talbott characterized as full of "articulate ambivalence . . . confusion, self-doubt, even self-recrimination." He referred sarcastically to his ambition and to the University of Arkansas, mocking his agreement to go to the law school in Fayetteville as "*the* thing for aspiring politicos to do." Indeed, many of his future close associates in Little Rock business and politics were doing likewise at the time. His letter to Stearns described a painful summer in Hot Springs, "where everyone else's children seem to be in the military, most of them in Vietnam."

Clinton wondered aloud if he was "running away from something maybe for the first time in my life." Only a month after his agreement with Holmes, he told Stearns, he was thinking that refuge in the ROTC had been a mistake after all. "I am about resolved to go to England come hell or high water and take my chances . . . nothing could be more destructive of whatever fiber I have left than this mental torment," he told his friend. "And if I cannot rid myself of it, I will just have to go into the service and begin to root out the cause."

Three days after the letter to Stearns, he stayed up through the night at the Scully Street house writing to the chairman of the Hot Springs draft board. As Clinton himself summarized it two months later, he wrote that his signing of the ROTC letter of intent was a "compromise I made with myself . . . more objectionable than the draft would have been." The truth was, he told the board, that he had "no interest in the ROTC in itself" and had only been trying "to protect myself from physical harm." Since he was hereby withdrawing from the ROTC and its deferment, he wished that they would "please draft me as soon as possible." The middle-of-the-night letter ended by earnestly thanking the chairman "for trying to help in a case where he really couldn't."

Clinton never sent his confessional, sacrificial outpouring to the draft board chairman. "I did carry it on me every day until I got on the plane to return to England" is how he told the story afterward. "I didn't mail the letter because I didn't see . . . how my going in the army and maybe going to Vietnam would achieve anything except a feeling that I had punished myself and gotten what I deserved."

On September 20, scarcely a week after his unsent letter to his board, President Nixon announced that there would be no new draft calls for the remainder of 1969 and that graduate students would not be inducted until they completed their current school year. If Congress did not act immediately to reform the draft system, Nixon warned, he would do so by executive order. Headlined throughout the nation, the White House announcement heralded a wholly new conscription system planned to begin December 1, 1969—the draft lottery.

• ◆ ◆

Within days of the agonized September letters and conversations, Clinton was on his way back to Oxford. He stopped in Washington for a time to volunteer at the headquarters of the Vietnam Moratorium Committee, which was planning nationwide rallies against the war for mid-October, to be followed by a procession of nearly a million marchers down Pennsylvania Avenue in Washington on November 15. The antiwar movement had now grown well beyond isolated students and reformers to include much of moderate, older, more affluent America.

Directed at a belligerent, besieged Nixon White House, the moratoriums of 1969 would be increasingly what journalists came to call "mainstream"—"a cascade of local demonstrations, vigils, church services, petition drives," as Todd Gitlin described them, "replete with respectable speechmakers and sympathetic media fanfare." Clinton had earlier met in passing one of the organizers, longtime activist David Mixner—he would call Mixner "a close friend," though they barely knew each other—and now paused briefly in Washington to work with him, making contacts as well for foreign versions of the moratoriums he would join in Britain.

The Washington stopover made him late for the Oxford term, and though he was now banking on the new Nixon draft lottery, he seemed unsure about the months ahead. "Clinton showed up at Oxford that fall," Strobe Talbott remembered, "so uncertain about his future that he didn't even arrange in advance for a place to live." For a time he roomed with Stearns and others, "living the life of an off-campus nomad," a friend said.

But that same autumn, taking advantage of Oxford's ease, he would also make a trip to Oslo, Norway, where he met Richard McSorley, a Jesuit professor at Georgetown and peace activist who was in Scandinavia to visit various antiwar groups. Clinton asked to accompany the priest on his rounds, and they visited the Oslo Peace Institute, as well as talking with American conscientious objectors, Norwegian peace groups, and university students. "This is a great way to see a country," Father McSorley's memoir recorded Clinton as saying when he left Norway. On November 16—the day after McSorley attended the moratorium demonstration of some five hundred Britons and Americans in front of the US embassy in Grosvenor Square in London—he encountered Clinton yet again, this time in another crowd of several hundred at an interdenominational church service for peace in England. "Bill Clinton . . . came up and welcomed me," Father McSorley wrote. "He was one of the organizers."

Ten years afterward, questioned about his "antiwar" activities, Clinton would tell the *Arkansas Gazette* that he had "only observed" protest marches in London and elsewhere. Whatever impressions he gave Father McSorley in 1969 and the Arkansas press subsequently, the reality of his role was always ambiguous. Like others, he had helped stage "teach-ins" at Oxford, once inviting former US diplomat George Kennan, who was critical of the war policy, to speak to the visiting American students. He had helped the moratorium committee organize both the October 15 and November 15 events in England and been one of the speakers at a special rally for American students in London. Yet his was cautiously calibrated opposition. The day before his London speech, British antiwar groups met on the same spot to demand US withdrawal from Indochina. But Bill Clinton had urged others to boycott the event, "deeming it too radical," said one account.

"Theirs was a temperate revolt against the establishment," Alessandra Stanley wrote of the Oxford years. "He was not some extraordinary rabid organizer," said fellow Rhodes scholar Christopher Key, later a supporter. "It was not a Jane Fonda–going-to-Hanoi deal. No one thought of it as being disloyal to our country." Several, in fact, saw Clinton and his circle as self-serving, opposed to the war on their own terms and never carrying their principles far enough to jeopardize their futures in the system. "They all hung out together, and they all played it very safe at the moratoriums, having it both ways," said Dell Martin, an antiwar leader at Oxford in 1968–70 who knew Clinton, Talbott, and their colleagues. "They were conservative, and frankly I had no patience with them. I felt they were careerists—making a place for themselves in a society [that] had caused this war to happen."

During the fall demonstrations Clinton finally found quarters for the year, moving in with Talbott and another American friend from the term before, Frank Aller, a brilliant young Rhodes scholar in Asian studies from the University of Washington. They shared an old row house at 46 Leckford Road, and the setting became a kind of caricature of their moment at Oxford—beards grown, candles burned to the music of the sixties, Clinton's mattress on the floor, shillings fed into a clicking meter for lights and heat against the drab English winter.

It was an interesting household by any measure. The son of a wealthy Ohio investment banker and prominent Republican, Nelson Strobridge Talbott III had himself escaped the draft "thanks to a letter to his draft board from a friendly orthopedist in Cleveland," said one account; he was a young man who "wasted no time on failure, introspection or rebellion." Talbott had been trained as a Russian linguist at Yale and now, at Oxford, was already involved in the coveted job of translating Nikita Khrushchev's CIA-smuggled memoirs for Time-Life, a publishing coup that involved shadowy forces on both sides of the cold war and that would soon lift young Strobe himself to prodigious cachet as a *Time* reporter.

But it was Frank Aller, without wealth or furtive connections to power, who had something deeper, who was "the one you wanted to have dinner with," his friend David Edwards would say, and the one who "paid the price for all of us." He was a talented classical pianist as well as a serious scholar, mastering Mandarin and writing a thesis on the Chinese Communists' Long March. He was immensely likable—gentle, kind, and genuinely modest. A "buttoned-down Kennedy Democrat," as one writer described him, he had been raised in conservative Spokane. "We both grew up on John Wayne movies," Clinton would say, adding that Aller still managed "a very finely developed ethical sensibility." Frank and Bill were close—many thought the closest of friends—talking for hours on end about Vietnam. Even Clinton's seducing one of Aller's girlfriends seemed to have no effect on their own friendship.

But Aller also stood apart from the rest of them. On the day of Nixon's inauguration, January 20, 1969, he had sent a three-page letter to his Spokane draft board, saying plainly, "I cannot in good conscience accept induction into the Armed Forces of the United States. . . . I believe there are times when concerned men can no longer remain obedient." At one point in the letter, he might have been describing Bill Clinton's own, very different approach to their dilemma of career and principle—though it was never clear how much he or any of the others knew of the restless maneuvering and wire-pulling back in Arkansas. Aller deplored "the fact that many of us who have come to disagree with American military involvement in Vietnam have refrained from actions which would imperil our deferred status and have continued to comply with selective service regulations despite moral or political objections to the war." It turned out that Aller had both, with a sophistication amply vindicated by events.

In the end, though, it was courage more than insight that distinguished Aller from the others on Leckford Road. He had no political influence back home, would not apply for conscientious-objector status, because he did not oppose all wars, simply this one. "Finally, he concluded he could not maneuver for an easier way out," said one account. The evening he sent his letter, Clinton and Robert Reich, exempt from service for physical reasons, threw a party for Aller. "It was a raucous gathering," according to one description, "that was partly a mock wake" for someone whose "defiance made him a legend at Oxford." Their most gifted member had become the official resister.

Aller would also be a kind of touchstone for the expedient morality and commitment of his housemates and their circle. "None of them were willing to risk their futures by resisting," writer Alessandra Stanley concluded. "Others were able to live their own need to resist through Frank. Bill had to weigh what it really meant to resist. He understood the consequences more than the others," said a woman who knew them. "Frank was the only guy among the Rhodes scholars who actually did something about the war—who risked himself," colleague David Satter said to a reporter years afterward. "Guess what? He did it and nobody cared," David Edwards would "bitterly" tell the same journalist.

For a while Clinton worried that his opposition to the war—however cautious, whatever the contrasts with Frank Aller, whatever the outcome of his maneuvers with the draft—might still cost him his political career. As an alternative, he told Garry Wills in 1992, he had "seriously considered" becoming a journalist. "I would at least comment on the great events of my time," he said. But that would be unnecessary.

That October—some remembered it was the middle of the month, others the end—Clinton told his family in Hot Springs to inform the draft board that he wished to be returned to 1-A status, making him eligible for the national draft lottery scheduled for December 1, 1969. The board formally reclassified him 1-A on October 30; meanwhile, he had no contact with Colonel Holmes in Fayetteville since leaving the United States. As far as Holmes and the ROTC knew, Bill Clinton the Rhodes scholar was still intending to enroll at Arkansas's law school and join the reserve unit. In the imminent draft reform, his options were by no means closed. Though entering the lottery, he might draw a low number and face induction yet conceivably still make good on his promise to Colonel Holmes and, despite his October switch to 1-A, resecure the ROTC deferment, which remained valid under the new system. If he drew a higher number, setting him clear of induction, he could then make a final decision to discard the ROTC—and inform Holmes as best he could.

That November was a tense countdown. The contorted politics of career and conscience were obviously draining and, for a time, all-absorbing. Talbott—self-conscious about his own dubious deferment, what he called "my gimpy knee . . . enough to keep me out of the Mekong Delta but not off the squash courts and playing fields of Oxford"—remembered how agitated and preoccupied both Clinton and Aller had been on Thanksgiving of 1969. The two friends had stood in the kitchen basting a shriveling turkey for four hours while locked obliviously in an intense conversation about patriotism, service, the war.

Days later, the birth date of William Jefferson Clinton of Hot Springs, Arkansas, formerly if recently 1-A, was drawn number 311 in the selective service lottery—more than a hundred places away from the cutoff for current or even anticipated draft calls. The next morning he jubilantly sent off an application to Yale Law School for the coming academic year and on December 3, after much drafting and redrafting, mailed a telling letter to Colonel Eugene Holmes in Fayetteville. On December 4, Frank Aller was indicted for draft evasion by a Spokane federal grand jury. His housemates remembered that Aller took the news bravely. But there were no parties on Leckford Road.

◆　◆　◆

Friends watched Bill Clinton and men like him send off numerous letters to their draft boards and other authorities. Often addressed to faceless, faraway people who held mortal power, the compositions were among their most serious efforts. "As a rule, those kinds of letters were very carefully crafted and well thought out, as much as or more so than anything else they did at Oxford," said a witness. "If you look closely, what they wrote was amazingly sincere as well as utterly cynical," said another who heard the painstaking epistles read aloud, discussed, and often collectively edited. For those destined for careers in politics or business—areas conventionally assumed to penalize candor or nonconformity—their outpourings on the draft, despite the calculation and ingratiation, were in some ways a fleeting moment of honesty. "At the end of the day," David Edwards would say, "this was our first real struggle over right and wrong." Between the lines, and sometimes explicitly, Clinton's letter to Eugene Holmes was just that—a revealing mark of the man he had grown into, as well as the politician he was becoming.

To the fatherly colonel he began by apologizing for being "so long in writing": "I know I promised to let you hear from me at least once a month, and from now on you will, but I have had to have some time to think about this first letter." He had contemplated the reply "almost daily since my return to England" and wanted to thank Holmes, "not just for saving me from the draft, but for being so kind and decent to me last summer" when he was depressed. "One thing which made the bond we struck in good faith somewhat palatable to me," he told the Bataan veteran, "was my high regard for you personally."

As he had proudly made plain to Holmes in Fayetteville, he had worked for Senator Fulbright in Washington. But there was something about the Senate job Clinton had not admitted in their long interview that summer at the officer's home. "I did it for the experience and the salary, but also for the opportunity, however small, of working every day against a war I opposed and despised with a depth of feeling I had reserved solely for racism in America before Vietnam," he told Holmes, going on to claim, "I did not take the matter lightly but studied it carefully, and there was a time when not many people had more information about Vietnam at hand than I did." Given the genuine expertise on Vietnam in America and Europe as well as Asia, this was a remarkably adolescent boast, made by a man of twenty-three who later left behind no trace of his supposed authority on the subject. If calculated in 1969 to impress someone he thought an uneducated army officer, it also seems a hint of an evolving Clinton bravado, in which a quick mind's glibness might impress a less confident audience yet mask a shallowness or indolence, a provincial conceit and ignorance about what he actually knew and did not know.

He went on to confess that he had "written and spoken and marched against the war." Had Holmes known that when they met, their "admiration might not have been mutual." He had not begun to "consider separately" the draft issue until the spring of 1968, Clinton wrote, alluding to a Georgetown term paper on "selective conscientious objection." He mentioned nothing about the March 1968 induction notice from Hot Springs or the busy local politicking by Raymond Clinton.

"From my work I came to believe that the draft system itself is illegitimate. . . . No government really rooted in limited, parliamentary democracy should have the power to make its citizens fight and kill and die in a war they may oppose, a war which even possibly may be wrong, a war which, in any case, does not involve immediately the peace and freedom of the nation." Accordingly, he thought the World War II draft was justified "because the life of the people collectively was at stake." But "Vietnam is no such case," and neither was the Korean War of 1950–53, "where, in my opinion, certain military action was justified but the draft was not."

Clinton was "in great sympathy," he told the colonel, with those refusing "to fight, kill, and maybe die for their country (i.e. the particular policy of a particular government) right or wrong." Two of his Oxford friends, he said, were conscientious objectors, and he had written for one a letter of recommendation to a Mississippi draft board, "a letter which I am more proud of than anything else I wrote at Oxford last year." He also told Holmes that "one of my roommates is a draft resister . . . possibly under indictment . . . and never able to go home again." Without naming him, he wrote of Frank Aller, "He is one of the bravest, best men I know. That he is considered a criminal is an obscenity."

There followed a remarkably candid description of Clinton's own dilemma about whether or not to be a resister. "I decided to accept the draft in spite of my beliefs for one reason: to maintain my political viability within the system." He went on to describe how he had been preparing for "a political life characterized by both practical political ability and concern for rapid social progress. It is a life I still feel compelled to try to lead." Young Bill Clinton then added an extraordinary and in some ways ironically prophetic passage: "I do not think our system of government is by definition corrupt, however dangerous and inadequate it has been in recent years. (The society may be corrupt, but that is not the same thing, and if that is true we are all finished anyway.)

"When the draft came, I was having a hard time facing the prospect of fighting a war I had been fighting against," he further explained to Holmes, though again without mentioning all the machinations that had gone into that "hard time." His trip to Holmes's house in Fayetteville was crucial. "ROTC was the one way left in which I could possibly, but not positively, avoid both Vietnam and resistance," he wrote. Once more he neglected to add the essential reality—that by changing his classification from 1-A to 1-D and delaying his induction long enough that summer and autumn for the draft lottery, the ROTC had indeed been "positively" a way out of a hated, life-threatening war, as well as out of what he feared might be a career-threatening act of principle and defiance of convention.

Continuing his education at Oxford or elsewhere "played no part" in his joining the ROTC. "I am back here," he wrote vaguely from Oxford that December, "and would have been at Arkansas Law School because there is nothing else I can do." He would have liked to "take a year out" to teach in a small college or "work in a community action project" to decide "whether to attend law school or graduate school and how to begin putting what I have learned to use." Yet all that begged the question of why he had not written Holmes for months, why he had never applied to Arkansas or even prepared to go there as he had promised, why he had returned to England and effectively bided his time and even changed his draft classification directly with the Hot Springs board at the last moment, awaiting the lottery.

After he signed the ROTC letter of intent that August, he "began to wonder" about the compromise, Clinton wrote the colonel. He had "no interest" in the program and only seemed to be saving himself "from physical harm," he admitted. "Also, I began to think I had deceived you," the letter told Holmes, "not by lies because there were none but by failing to tell you all the things I'm writing now. I doubt that I had the mental coherence to articulate them then." These were some but hardly all the misgivings he had expressed at length to Rick Stearns and Strobe Talbott that August and September, when he saw his own "moral fiber" in terms of returning to England to "take my chances," albeit without then telling Holmes and ending the ROTC option prior to the lottery.

"At that time, after we had made our agreement and you had sent my 1-D deferment to my draft board," Clinton now recounted, "the anguish and loss of my self-regard and self-confidence really set in. I hardly slept for weeks and kept going by eating compulsively and reading until exhaustion brought sleep."

It was a recurrent pattern of crisis and personal turmoil he had experienced before and would experience again, though no one among the peace moratorium workers or his Oxford colleagues—except perhaps Stearns and Talbott, who felt his anxieties from a distance by phone or letter—seems to have noted it in Bill Clinton that late summer and early fall of 1969.

He now told Holmes about staying up all night to write, and then carrying around, the unsent confession to the draft board. "I didn't mail the letter because I didn't see, in the end, how my going in the army and maybe going to Vietnam would achieve anything except a feeling that I had punished myself and gotten what I deserved," he wrote. "So I came back to England to try to make something of this second year of my Rhodes scholarship." There was no reference to Nixon's September 20 announcement exempting graduate students for the academic year or to the draft lottery.

He was telling all this to Holmes, he concluded the long December 3 letter, "because you have been good to me and have a right to know what I think and feel." He finished with a plea for the respectability he knew he once enjoyed with the Arkansas officer: "I am writing too in the hope that my telling this one story will help you to understand more clearly how so many fine people have come to find themselves still loving their country but loathing the military, to which you and other good men have devoted years, lifetimes, of the best service you could give. To many of us, it is no longer clear what is service and what is disservice, or if it is clear, the conclusion is likely to be illegal."

Like so many other similar gestures of the time, the words were a poignant reach across generational, intellectual, cultural, and political divides—and like so many others, ultimately in vain. Though he feared exposure at the moment and then, over the coming decades, had rea-

son to believe he had escaped the worst political effects of his maneuvering, Clinton and his very presidency would pay a price for the
unhealed wound visible in the letter to Holmes.

He ended with a surprisingly cloying, almost casual passage, leaving
it merely implicit that he was resigning from the ROTC and never
coming to Arkansas's law school: "Forgive the length of this letter.
There was much to say. There is still a lot to be said, but it can wait.
Please say hello to Col. Jones for me. Merry Christmas. Sincerely, Bill
Clinton."

Holmes angrily canceled Clinton's ROTC enrollment. He sent no
reply to the young Arkansan in England at the time, though his remarks to the press decades later still reflected his reaction. "Bill Clinton was able to manipulate things so that he didn't have to go in," the
retired colonel told a reporter. "Ethically, I think he should have
stayed in ROTC. He'd given his word and was backing out."

In a September 1992 affidavit the ill and elderly Eugene Holmes,
now inevitably a pawn in a presidential campaign in which he obviously
opposed Bill Clinton, made a "final statement" on the episode,
describing their two-hour talk in Fayetteville and the subsequent "pressure" on both the ROTC unit and the Hot Springs board, adding that
Clinton "purposely deceived me, using the possibility of joining the
ROTC as a ploy . . . purposely defrauding the military . . . both in
concealing his antimilitary activities overseas and his counterfeit intentions for later military service." By then the colonel was not the only
one caught up in the partisan controversy and twisting history. "That's
very strange," Virginia would confess when asked about her son's planning to go to law school at the University of Arkansas and join the
ROTC. "I was under the impression when he came home from Oxford
that he was going to go to Yale."

• • •

The specter of Vietnam lifted, Clinton spent the rest of the term and
year at Oxford far more relaxed and carefree. Over the December-
January break he briefly visited Moscow on a student tour, a trip his
floundering Republican presidential opponent would someday try to
exploit. Reading poetry with Rick Stearns one gray day at Oxford,
Clinton set off on a lark to find Dylan Thomas's birthplace and spent
days hitchhiking through Wales in a cold rain. That spring of 1970 he
and Stearns took a bus tour of Spain, reading accounts and touring
battlefields of the Spanish civil war, an experience that left their views
"changed substantially," according to Stearns. "Both of us understood

that it was much more complex than a simple right-versus-wrong," Stearns would say of Franco's fascist overthrow of the elected republic. For Clinton, his companion was to be one of the more important and influential of his Oxford friends, as Rick Stearns's patronage two years later would usher him into valuable local political exposure and authority in the Democratic presidential campaign of George McGovern.

Like the reminiscences of so many others, Clinton's public claims for his Oxford years give only the most nebulous impression of his intellectual pursuits or accomplishments. "I read about three hundred books," he said at one point, invoking the quantity rather than the authors or ideas. Above all, others seemed to understand in England as plainly as they had in Washington that Clinton was without apology a politician in training, "about as transparent as a politician can be" and, in the colliding, polarized opinions of the time, "always . . . what would be called a moderate," his Oxford friend Peter Hayes would say. Watching Bill Clinton talk endlessly at the dining tables of University College's Long Hall, Douglas Eakeley thought him charming and fascinating to the British, "easily the most popular [American] student there." But as always, there were those who saw his congeniality in a different light. It was simply more "networking and glad-handing," a reporter quoted a fellow Arkansas student and later a rival, Cliff Jackson, as saying. "A few of Clinton's contemporaries in England," Jackson and others concluded, had been "crass and self-serving and enough to make you sick."

"It is just almost impossible to re-create the personal agony we felt then," Clinton would later say of the months at Oxford haunted by the draft. He left Oxford the spring of 1970, without a degree, bound for Yale. Still a fugitive, Frank Aller stayed on in Europe, where "loneliness seemed to engulf him," according to one account. "I don't want to become a broken old man nursing a faded ideal which no one else remembers," Aller wrote in a letter in October 1970. Who exactly was that Rhodes scholar who "refused induction?" he asked mockingly in a letter the following month that referred, in contrast, to what they all expected of his more protean housemate. "I'm not sure," came the answer in Aller's imaginary and bitter dialogue. "You mean the guy who was at Oxford when Governor Clinton was?"

Aller eventually returned to the States, ironically flunking his military physical the day that draft-evasion charges against him were dropped. He and Clinton saw each other briefly during a California reunion of the Leckford Road housemates. But the psychological torture of the ordeal had been too much. Back in Spokane in September

1971, less than two years after his ardent talks with Bill Clinton about service and destiny, Frank Aller calmly borrowed the keys to a friend's apartment and there put a bullet through his brain.

◆   ◆   ◆

"Bill Clinton's ties to the intelligence community go back all the way to Oxford and come forward from there," says a former government official who claims to have seen files long since destroyed. The subject of sharply varying accounts, the future president's final months in England were indeed shrouded in some mystery and in inconsistencies never explained—though the very polarity of the suspicions and allegations seem only to obscure what really happened.

Apart from controversy over how he dealt with the draft, the Oxford years were to be a fleeting, paradoxical issue for Clinton in the 1992 campaign. Republican aides rifled passport files in vain for some evidence of Clinton disloyalty while abroad or even of suspect travel by Virginia. Trailing in October, George Bush himself tried almost pathetically to impute something subversively, unpatriotically sinister to Clinton's 1969–70 trip to Moscow or his role in antiwar rallies, demanding on a national talk show that the Democratic nominee tell voters "how many demonstrations he led against his own country from a foreign soil."

It was with similar venom that the Central Intelligence Agency's infamous Operation Chaos of the 1960s had been directed at uncovering some discrediting foreign hand in antiwar activities at home and abroad, to the point of recruiting American student informants and placing provocateurs among the demonstrators. "Get me some commie money and organizers behind this student shit," Lyndon Johnson had ordered during a session of his fateful Tuesday Lunch with national security advisers. The CIA swiftly obliged, using front organizations and foundations that already operated illegally within the United States and sending out a circular cable by its own channel to station chiefs all over Europe—especially in countries where there were large numbers of American students, such as the United Kingdom, or where there were increasingly conspicuous colonies of draft resisters, such as Sweden—to target and penetrate student antiwar movements abroad more aggressively than ever, employing American students themselves as prime sources and de facto agents.

According to at least two former agency station chiefs and two more deputies who received the instructions and directed such covert operations, the inducements for the young informers ranged from cash payments to help with local draft boards and even promised deferments to more general and sweeping proffers of future help and influence with careers. "I could get them some money and accommodations if they needed it and see that selective service stayed off their backs," said one former CIA officer. "And most case officers were telling these young men that their service would be noted and appreciated for future reference. You know, if the agency's in a position to help at some point in their careers, there'd be an institutional memory. The Rhodes and Fulbrights and others were going to be important folks someday, and they knew the advantages of helping out."

The CIA stations were routinely advised not to run afoul of host-country intelligence services in the course of their surveillance of the antiwar movement. But in Britain, where there was a standing agreement between the CIA and their London counterparts not to conduct covert operations on one another's home territory, there was a special problem with Whitehall's MI-5, which adamantly objected to CIA recruitment of US citizens on UK soil, let alone to proscribed spying on activities around British universities. According to several accounts of CIA officers on the scene in 1967–70, Operation Chaos evaded the secret intelligence agreement through an elaborate ruse in which the station at the US embassy in London arranged to contact certain American students at Oxford, Cambridge, and elsewhere and to be "turned down," with word of the attempted recruitment then leaking to the British, who routinely protested the violation but thought the matter ended with the students' reported rejections. "In fact," remembered a ranking CIA case officer, "we went back and got the boys for real. It was kind of blown cover as cover, you might say, and the Brits groused about the dummy approaches but never caught on." In any event, the episode produced even stricter, more furtive security measures around the recruitment of student informers in the United Kingdom than attended most such espionage. "There were very few records kept, frequent purging of the files, and in general a lot of cutouts and other Mickey Mouse," recalled one officer. "Because of the sensitivity of the UK, these kids were treated in some ways like some high-level agents."

It would all befog still more the later allegations of CIA collusion by and around Bill Clinton at Oxford. One former agency official would claim that the future president was a full-fledged "asset," that he was regularly "debriefed," and thus that he informed on his American friends in the peace movement in Britain. Similarly, he was said to have informed on draft resisters in Sweden during his brief trip there with Father McSorley and to have had his room paid for at one of Moscow's most exclusive Intourist hotels, the venerable National just off Red Square, during his holiday trip there at the end of 1969—the same trip George Bush would try to portray as a subversive act. The booking at the National for the usually impecunious student from Hot Springs would raise eyebrows when it became known even back in Arkansas. "Arguably the best accommodation in town," a Little Rock columnist wrote later of the expensive Soviet hotel. Clinton would spend at least part of his time in Moscow with two visiting Americans he had apparently happened upon, Charles Daniels, a contractor from Virginia, and Henry Fors, a farmer who was seeking Soviet help finding a son missing in North Vietnam. But otherwise, ensconced in a hotel usually reserved for more prominent or affluent visitors, he seems to have made an oddly pointless trip, with none of the purpose or application friends saw him bring to other ventures. Clinton "just hung around, always hungry and broke," Arkansas journalist Meredith Oakley quoted another student in Moscow as saying.

One more CIA retiree would recall going through archives of Operation Chaos at the Langley headquarters—part of an agency purge amid the looming congressional investigations of the mid-1970s—and seeing Bill Clinton listed, along with others, as a former informant who had gone on to run for or be elected to a political office of some import, in Clinton's case attorney general of Arkansas. "He was there in the records," the former agent said, "with a special designation." Still another CIA source contended that part of Clinton's arrangement as an informer had been further insurance against the draft. "He knew he was safe, you see, even if he got a lottery number not high enough and even if the ROTC thing fell through for some reason," the source said, "because the Company could get him a deferment if it had to, and it was done all the time."

Several CIA sources would agree nearly a quarter century after the events that there had indeed been several informants among the Americans gathered at British universities at the end of the 1960s, young men who went on to prominence, if not the Oval Office. "Let's just say that some high today in the USG [US government] began their official careers as snitches against the antiwar movement," said one former official who doubted Clinton's own involvement. "Close to Bill Clinton were informants with a more formal relationship than occasional sources," said another ex–case officer. "I can't and won't ever tell you names, but you'd sure recognize them if I did."

• • •

By his return to the United States in 1970, much was clear about who
he was and would be, about the already polished and protected artifice
and artifacts of a career, ultimately a life.

Amid all the spirited or grim discussions of Vietnam, he would be
identified afterward with no ideas or concepts (unlike Frank Aller and
others), no lessons of foreign policy or decision making or larger history. He left behind only the most generic, glossed images—nice, popular, eager to please, bright without being unorthodox, intelligent
without being provocative or memorable, very much a part of his surroundings. No attack by his reactionary opponents later would be
more undeserved than the charge that young Bill Clinton was "radical."

Clinton went through genuine torture over the draft. Many if not
most of his peers among the Rhodes contingent of 1968 had received
some special dispensation, and American students everywhere were
going to some lengths, from political coercion to self-mutilation, to
avoid the war. Some future Republican rivals in Washington, figures
such as Senator Phil Gramm of Texas and House Speaker Newt Gingrich, nimbly skirted the service during the same era, as one journalist
put it later, "without any apparent sign of moral anguish," much less
understanding of the war.

Clinton and most of the rest of his circle were fundamentally questioning the war and their possible sacrifice, not what produced it or
what might come afterward in the America they inherited. "Radicaliza-
tion means building a rational conviction that the social structure must
be altered at its roots, that phenomena such as the Vietnamese war
were symptoms," writes Joseph Conlin, a historian and critic of the
1960s. For thousands of people, including many who served in Southeast Asia, the war left just such a legacy, one far beyond simple nostrums of nonintervention: an understanding of how narrow and
puckered political leaders and policy makers in both great parties had
grown, how venal and resistant were huge private interests, how institu-
tionally and culturally flawed government and policy were becoming.
But Vietnam radicalized neither Bill Clinton nor the small crowd of
equally career-minded young men around him at Oxford and later in
his administration. Nor in basic ways did it prepare them to understand what they would face at the end of the century.

The spring of 1970 brought the invasion of Cambodia and another
surge of antiwar protests that gave the Nixon White House pause. Over

the next year, however, as draft calls waned, American combat deaths plunged from two hundred a week to thirty-five, and with them the urgency and force of much of the antiwar movement. "The slackening of the draft weakened the less committed's incentive for opposing the war," wrote Todd Gitlin. Whatever the cause and effect, the ebbing margin of opposition allowed the Nixon White House to continue the war for another four bloody years, doubling the number of Americans killed and, through massive bombing and the proxy of "Vietnamization," adding nearly a million more Asian casualties.

If the moral and career torments of the moment cut deep wounds, Clinton's scars were all but invisible over those ensuing years of prolonged carnage and after. Having spoken so much in Oxford's Long Hall, on Leckford Road, and even at London rallies, having solemnly discussed the issues and boasted of unique knowledge of the subject in his letter to Colonel Holmes, Bill Clinton the emerging politician of the 1970s and 1980s never again paused to reflect in public on those great questions, never probed in his many Arkansas campaigns or national forums the profound, fateful issues of war, peace, and political obligation that so haunted his youth.

Once his draft crisis was over, it was almost as if none of it had ever quite happened.

·6·

Park Ridge
"She Had to Put Up with Him"

In their own ways, they were casualties of their America and refugees from the depression, much as Virginia Cassidy and Bill Blythe had been.

Dorothy Howell was of Welsh-Scottish descent with French and Native American ancestry as well. She was born in 1919 into the blue-collar tenements of South Chicago, the daughter of a fireman and of a half-Canadian mother who was all but illiterate. Part of the vast migration of the era, the family later moved to southern California, where Dorothy grew up in the sunlit but bittersweet promise of the Los Angeles basin. At high school in Alhambra, she was a member of the scholarship society, an admired athlete, and an energetic organizer of student activities. She left the West Coast almost as soon as she graduated, never looking back "too fondly," as one account put it, on a seemingly painful, unreconciled childhood and adolescence. Intelligent and pretty, with a compelling smile and an abiding sense of independence, eighteen-year-old Dorothy was back in Chicago in 1937, applying for a job as a secretary with the Columbia Lace Company, when she met a witty yet severe and begrudging young curtain salesman named Hugh Rodham.

He was seven years older and had been raised amid English working-class sternness and privation. His own father was brought from the bleak miners' slums of Northumberland to Pennsylvania at the age of three and, while still a child, was put out to work at the Scranton Lace Company, later to marry another English immigrant who had been a

107

winder in a silk-mill sweatshop since her teens. Theirs was an unsparing household, bound by the evangelical Methodism of their origins and the hard-bitten lunch-pail Republicanism of the time. One of three boys and his father's namesake, Hugh managed to attend Penn State on a football scholarship, majoring in physical education. But out of college during the depression, he found himself back in the lace factory himself, a second generation now "lifting boxes for lousy money," as one account put it. He soon fled, laboring for a time in the grim Pennsylvania coal mines, restlessly looking for jobs in New York, then Chicago, where he ended up in the fabric business after all, though in a more respectable, white-collar job as a salesman. He was still engaged to a woman in Scranton, and they had even taken out a marriage license. Then he noticed smiling Dorothy Howell at the office.

Their courtship went on for five years, with "much romantic back and forth," as friends described it. In his late twenties, he already foreshadowed the stinting, harsh husband and father he would become. Dorothy Howell was sadly ahead of her time, enjoying a brief relative independence during the depression and war years and ever after yearning for an equity and opportunity painfully denied in her married life. Proud, quietly ambitious, she had fallen in love with a "Mr. Impossible," as one chronicler of the family wrote. When Pearl Harbor came she was still a working girl, seeing Rodham but with hopes for higher education. She now put off college indefinitely, and they were finally married in 1942.

During the war, Hugh Rodham, with his college degree in physical education, supervised young recruits in the navy's Gene Tunney program, a regimen of conditioning and self-defense named for the former heavyweight boxing champion. In naval stations around the country, instructors like Rodham were expected to be stringently rigorous, austere, and aloof—tight-jawed calisthenics leaders equally free of emotion and flab, withholding praise, unconsoling, mocking of the slightest failure. Believed to harden the erstwhile civilians to a new toughness and resolve, it was all an unsentimental hazing for the warfare waiting outside the gate.

After 1945, the Rodhams were very much a part of the postwar generation of resumed hopes, intent on stability after years of uncertainty. "They wanted secure jobs, secure homes, and secure marriages in a secure country," Elaine Tyler May wrote of anxious millions like them. Just as traveling salesman Bill Blythe dreamed of owning an auto-parts franchise, Hugh Rodham would start his own drapery business. He began to sell custom work to major purchasers like hotels, corporations, and airlines, buying, printing, and sewing the fabric himself, even hanging the curtains. He usually had only one employee—whom he generally treated as a slack navy recruit, with an irascibility those around him struggled vainly to gloss. "Although he badgered his help inordinately," said one account of the business, "there was an undercurrent of good humor in his manner—and nobody took Hugh at face value."

When he came home from the service he and Dorothy lived for a time in a one-bedroom apartment in an area of Chicago only miles from the house Bill Blythe had purchased. In January 1947 she gave birth to a placid 8½-pound girl, "a good-natured, nice little baby," she would say, who was "very mature upon birth." In a small act of unconventionality, she called her Hillary, a family name she saw as "exotic and unusual."

Three years later the family left the city for the new space and status—what many saw as the refuge—of the suburbs, a sedate place comfortably northwest of Chicago on the wooded moraine that gave it its fashionable name, Park Ridge. Taking in a wave of postwar migrants, it was no dusty subdivision of tract houses hammered up on a treeless grid but an established community of shade and character. The locale had been one of the older settlements adjoining Chicago's city limits, the site of a nineteenth-century brickyard that eventually exhausted its clay deposits. With the arrival of the Chicago & Northwestern tracks, the old industrial village gave way to a commuting suburb, suitably changing its name from Brickton to Park Ridge. By the 1950s a neat little town center had thriving small businesses and solid, respectable public buildings. To many this was the prize, the way life in America was supposed to be. "We could have been a Frank Capra set without changing a thing," one resident would say. "Park Ridge was where Dick and Jane lived with their perfect parents and their little dog, Spot," another resident remarked.

When Hillary Rodham grew up there in the 1950s and 1960s, the streets and yards were teeming with the children of the postwar baby boom and suburban exodus, literally hundreds of them in the blocks around her house. Over the decade after her family moved, the population of Chicago proper grew by some 20 percent, but the near suburbs exploded, Park Ridge itself almost tripling to nearly forty thousand residents.

They were hardly a dozen miles from Chicago's Loop, yet Park Ridge was a world apart from the city and even from more diverse suburbs like Skokie, blocks away to the east. Park Ridge was on the rural outskirts of the metropolis. A few miles to the southwest, the area that would become O'Hare Airport, the world's busiest, there was still an apple orchard with cornfields beyond. Nearby were also Chicago's distinct communities of Italians, Poles, Mexican Americans, and Appalachian refugees, even Native American ghettos, and the largest single Jewish population in the metropolitan area. From all that, however, Park Ridge and similar suburbs were cordoned off by discreet but towering barriers of class and ethnicity. Here as elsewhere in the nation, sharply defined, exclusive enclaves of affluent, white Anglo-Saxon Protestants were segregated from unwanted minorities by racist real estate covenants and sub-rosa mortgage discrimination, as well as by income and economic privilege.

For the most part, it was a society of the educated upper middle class, among whom Hugh Rodham, even with a lucrative drapery business and his own new Cadillacs year after year, could seem déclassé. Away from his sewing machine and curtain hanging, he did not socialize with suburbia's "doctors, lawyers, and Indian chiefs," according to his daughter. "I never knew any professionals growing up," she would make a point of telling a reporter a quarter century later. In the social life the family did have, Dorothy Rodham herself would feel sharply the lack in her own background and forfeited education, "so unsure of her knowledge that she would drop out of conversations," wrote Judith Warner, "or simply play supportive audience to her husband's stronger voice." In their prescribed role, the mothers of Park Ridge stayed home to care for their houses and children. "Independent women, admired during the 1930s and the war," wrote one historian, "were now looked upon as neurotic freaks."

"It was a lily-white area," remembered Sherry Heiden, a childhood friend of Hillary Rodham. "I think finally by our senior year there was one black kid in the whole school." They all went diligently to Sunday school and services in lovely brick churches with the requisite steeples and stained glass—and sometimes grew into adults without realizing they were all so numbingly alike. "I was in college before it hit me that everybody and everything was in the same mold," said one. Only in the consolidated high school, enrolling students from neighboring Skokie and elsewhere, did many of them have their first social contacts with Catholics, Jews, or simply children from blue-collar families.

Invariably the politics of Park Ridge followed its social and economic contours, finding expression and lead in the newspaper and broadcast empire of Chicago's legendary reactionary, Colonel Robert

R. McCormack. The area was "white-collar country," as a group of political analysts once described it, "where the Chicago *Tribune* is a staple and where children are brought up to despise and fear the city [Democratic] machine." In a larger suburban district known for conservative sentiment, Park Ridge itself could be uniquely dogmatic and rigid, a contrast even to wealthier but more politically mixed and socially secure suburbs north along the Chicago lakeshore. A fiercely and unctuously dry community while liquor was sold just a township away, Park Ridge elected local, state, and national representatives known almost uniformly as *Tribune* Republicans for their right-wing extremism.

In a familiar pattern of class reaction, many in the town seemed all the more jealous of their exclusivity for having recently emerged themselves from poor or working-class origins. In the 1950s the picturesque community was an early center of the ultrarightist, conspiracy-minded John Birch Society, assailing President Dwight Eisenhower as a "Communist dupe," if not a Soviet agent, and equating Democrats in general with outright treason. So powerful was the reactionary fear taking root in Park Ridge and nearby suburbs that right-wing Republicans won the district's congressional seat in the early 1950s and never let go. Harold Collier, a former match-company personnel manager and a colorless creature of Colonel McCormack's, served nine terms and was succeeded in 1966 by a rotund state assembly politician and affable ideologue, Henry Hyde, who over ten more terms—until his embroilment in a banking scandal in the mid-1990s—would be known as "defender of the suburbs" and the GOP right's "most effective partisan weapon" on Capitol Hill.

In exclusive enclaves around Chicago—as in the Arkansas subdivisions—there were formidable social forces arrayed against honesty and revelation, both within and outside the family. Added to the prevailing cultural images of parents and children and to the postdepression, postwar drive for stability and security were vast corporate powers fastening on the happy new suburban family in its roles as advertising icon and lucrative market. Not least, there were the deeper politics of the moment. In many respects mirroring cold war reaction and conformity on the outside, the conservative male-dominated family regime and ideology of the 1950s and early 1960s abhorred and checked rebellion in the home almost as national policy contained revolt abroad—and often with similar means of reward and punishment. Just as Arkansas folk wisdom taught resignation to the fixity of local power, suburban orthodoxy in Park Ridge posed all the implicit contracts of the new postwar affluence and stability—the approved credentials and paths to success, the cost of dissent or mere nonconformity, the seeming disappearance of the old basic divisions of class and wealth, the manifest superiority of the American system at home and abroad. "Domestic containment," as historian Elaine Tyler May called the ethos of postwar life in the suburbs, "was bolstered by a powerful political culture that rewarded its adherents and marginalized its detractors."

In the same suburbs, it was true, there were warning signs dating from the early 1950s—a growing and affecting literature chronicling discontent and the emptiness of materiality, a six-fold increase in psychiatrists and untold additional patients, and what sociologist Todd Gitlin called "generational cleavage in the making" among the young. There had been all that and more. But behind most closed doors in Park Ridge and its replicas, women and children in particular learned somehow to cope, to go on—perhaps even to feel better about their predicament, to reconcile themselves, though seldom to change the deeper pattern or to question the connections between their own despair or disillusionment and the larger social, economic, and political framework.

America's most powerful First Lady was to come from that crucible and those confines as markedly—and in some ways as painfully—as a future president emerged from his landscapes of Hope and Hot Springs.

◆ ◆ ◆

The Rodhams lived in a graceful two-story stone-brick Georgian house built before the war at the corner of Elm and Wisner. Hillary was soon joined by two younger brothers, Hugh, Jr., and Tony. As the only daughter she had her own bedroom, a cheery yellow with polished oak floors and a sundeck looking out on the pleasant neighborhood. There she grew into an obviously bright, determined, accomplished girl whose experiences were so stamped with the people and cultural setting as to seem now almost apocryphal.

"There's no room in this house for cowards," her mother remembered scolding her about confronting the neighborhood bully. "You're going to have to stand up to her. The next time she hits you, I want you to hit her back." According to the family story, the Rodhams' little girl did just that and won with her own fists a precious male acceptance and a coveted chance to play with the boys in the neighborhood. "Boys responded well to Hillary," Dorothy would say proudly. "She just took charge, and they let her." She also played avid ping-pong, took music and ballet lessons, organized neighborhood "Olympics" and circuses, competed gamely with her athletic brothers, and amused everyone with a biting gift for mimicry that she would carry into her political adulthood. At Eugene Field Grammar School and Ralph Waldo Emerson Junior High, she was "a chronic teacher's pet," by one account. After school, she faithfully went on to the Brownies and Girl Scouts, earning a sash "so loaded with badges and dazzling little pins," thought Martha Sherrill, "that it's amazing she didn't walk with a stoop." On Sundays she was devoutly at the First United Methodist Church. Despite what one recollection called "the burden of that ceaseless public do-gooding," little Hillary Rodham seemed "to love it all." It was what growing up in Park Ridge was supposed to be.

How she reacted to the rest of her childhood was never part of the public myth. In the house at 236 Wisner, Dorothy Rodham was the town's conventional "stay-at-home mother" and child's "chauffeur," as Judith Warner described her. "I spent all my time in the car then," she herself would say. "The mother is the encourager and the helper, and the father brings news from the outside world" is how her daughter later benignly described what she called the family's "classic parenting situation." In that sense, however, the "news" from the world was often harsh, and the solicitous mother could not help her children with what writer Carolyn Susman saw as "a looming presence in all their lives"—the implacably judgmental and exacting Hugh Rodham. "Kind of like the glue that held the family together. But not the way you would think," Hugh, Jr., would say of him after his death. "My father was confrontational, completely and utterly so."

Most of the public memories of the man and his impact were cast after his daughter became famous—and with so much political and personal discretion as to be distorted. Nevertheless, the essence is unmistakable. "The suburban Hugh Rodham was tightfisted, hard to please, and always in command," concluded Norman King. "Though it is not fashionable to be macho today, Hugh fit the pattern perfectly then." There would be ostensibly fond recollections of the father's spending time with his children, devoting himself in a sense—though always with the drillmaster's mania for performance, endurance, proof of worth. One spring, Martha Sherrill noted, the entire family went to a local park and stood watching the man "pitch and pitch and pitch until his daughter Hillary learned to belt a curveball." She became an accomplished shortstop and hitter and applied her categorical intelligence to baseball lore, treating less knowledgeable young fans in the neighborhood with the impatience, if not contempt, her father had shown his children. "She knew everything about the Cubs and every-body else, and really showed it off," said a childhood friend.

In the same way, friends remembered, Hugh Rodham had drilled his daughter on stock prices, requiring her to pore over quotes on the *Tribune*'s stock market page for "good investments" and then praising her sparingly or upbraiding her with his usual rigor, depending on her "success." "You actually got tongue-lashed or sanctioned for losing money in that little game they had, and she learned the ropes fast," one recalled. "Making money like that was always very important to Mr. Rodham, very important," said another, "and it was something he tried to instill in her like everything else. No matter what you did, you weren't worth very much if you couldn't make money."

"Mr. Reality Check," Hillary would call him in the more neutral language of another generation. "I used to go to my father and say: 'Dad, I *really* need a new pair of shoes. My shoes have holes in them,' and he'd say, 'Have you done your chores? Have you done this? Have you done that?' " There were constant reminders of how fortunate—and precarious—their situation was, of what bitter hardships their father had suffered during the depression. He took them to an old coal mine in Pennsylvania to show them the grimy, spectral setting in which he once worked, however briefly. "The youngsters got the point," thought Norman King. "We were probably the only kids in the whole suburb who didn't get an allowance," Tony Rodham recalled vividly. "We'd rake the leaves, cut the grass, pull weeds, shovel snow. All your friends would be going to a movie. After your errands you'd walk in and say, 'Gee, Dad, I could use two or three dollars.' He'd flop another potato on your dinner plate and say, 'That's your reward.' " His approach to avoiding "spoiled" children, according to his wife, was straightforward: " 'They eat and sleep for free! We're not going to pay them for it as well!' "

For misbehavior they were "spanked on occasion or deprived of privileges," as one account put it. Neighbors and friends saw Hugh, Jr., as the family rebel—"a kind of rascal, a roustabout," a local minister would say—but his sister as the obedient, amenable "perfect child." "I was a quick learner," Hillary told Marian Burros. "I didn't run afoul of my parents very often. They were strict about my respecting authority, and not just parental authority. My father's favorite saying was: 'You get in trouble at school, you get in trouble at home.' "

But in Hugh Rodham's family boot camp, the even harsher response was reserved for conformity and success. When his proud little girl came home with straight As, he said to her dismissively, "It must be a very easy school you go to." Later, when she excelled in college prep courses, as Hugh, Jr., remembered, "He would say, 'It must be a pretty small college.'" At his sons' football games, Rodham disdained the bleachers and other parents, carrying a folding lawn chair in order to sit out on the sidelines, nearer the action, alone. After Hugh, Jr., who would go on to play at Penn State, quarterbacked a 42–0 championship victory and completed ten of eleven passes, he came back to Wisner Street to find his father lying on the sofa, ready with the familiar reproach. "I got nothing to say to you," he told the boy, "except you should have completed the other one."

Decades afterward, family and friends tried to interpret the elder Hugh Rodham's motives more gently. "With all of those things, he was not being mean or tactless. . . . He was trying in his own way to show us that we could be better," a son offered. "It's hard out there," Hillary quoted her father, explaining to an interviewer that his "encouragement was tempered by realism." The deeper cost of that tempering, however, no tactful language could conceal. Among both relatives and friends, many thought Hugh Rodham's treatment of his daughter and sons amounted to the kind of psychological abuse and adversity that might have crushed some children—and came close to doing so in Park Ridge. It was not the episodic, detonating, often bloody abuse her future husband suffered in Hope and Hot Springs but a slightly more subtle oppression. The Rodhams were not like the Clintons, with a "crisis every four minutes," Hillary would later tell her future mother-in-law. In a sense, she was right. The quieter, more discreet abuse of Park Ridge had known no intervals. "Her spirit, though, was unbreakable," biographer Judith Warner concluded. Others disagreed. "I don't think there's any question that the real little Hillary was broken," said a longtime observer. "The point is how she got mended, and the person put in her place."

Family and friends adopted Rodham's own pretense—that it was all good for them, however hurtful. Victims themselves, her mother and brothers came to rationalize what had happened to Hillary, arguing that the relationship with the father fortified her and bred her famously fierce determination and endurance. The family story of how she resolved at the age of nine to keep her maiden name when she married was the sort that proved how well she coped and survived and was stronger than most. Yet there was no real hiding the quiet cruelty and pain. The sense of stinted or denied love, a resort to refuge outside the family, the alternating warmth and vitriol, compassion and sarcasm, the tightly controlled yet seething perpetual anger not far beneath the impenetrable shell—all would be visible in the independent but camouflaged woman she became. "She loves talking about ideas. She loves asking questions," Jan Piercy would say of the Hillary Rodham she knew well in the years just after childhood and adolescence. "Ask her about herself and I think you'll find she shuts down. Oh, she may answer your question, but I don't think you'll see much energy behind it." The same verdict would come from the other woman who had watched it all, and felt her own wounds. "Maybe that's why she's such an accepting person," Dorothy Rodham said in a moment of candor about her outwardly strong but long-suffering daughter. "She had to put up with him."

The parents "made no distinction between her and her two brothers," one observer wrote later, but the old shadings were in fact always there. With Hugh Rodham's approval, Hillary might take jobs as a baby-sitter, wading-pool lifeguard, or recreation counselor, but never in the drapery business, where her brothers worked often. At the same time, friends remembered the mother's steady, conscious effort to spur her daughter to succeed in academic and career terms, albeit terms still defined by men. "I've always spoken to Hillary as you would to an adult," Dorothy once recalled, with echoes of Virginia Clinton. The girl growing up in Park Ridge was to be what her mother had never been free to be in Alhambra, Chicago, or the suburbs—above all, a presence, even a power, in the competitive, image-conscious, male-run outside world. That, in some ways, was more important than the trappings of marriage and family, which the mother had without fulfillment. "I was determined that no daughter of mine was going to have to go through the agony of being afraid to say what she had on her mind," Dorothy would say later. "Just because she was a girl didn't mean she should be limited."

One of her fellow students recalled that in the early 1960s their high school was "a big factory but also a really snobby place in its own way. The kids were just like their well-off parents, and everybody seemed headed for college with good jobs for boys, marriage for girls, and big homes and cars just like their folks." Utterly composed, a serious, busy young woman, Hillary Rodham seemed easily a part of that world, those expectations, yet in some ways deliberately separate. Through three years at Maine East, then a final year among some four thousand students attending the huge new Maine South, she continued to excel academically. At the same time, she played field hockey and volleyball, debated, acted in school plays, sang in the variety show. Asked years afterward if she and her friends had ever cut classes or openly challenged school authority, a close friend could only gasp, "Are you *kidding?*"

She dressed conventionally, wearing her society's familiar box-pleated skirts, blouses with Peter Pan collars, kneesocks and loafers, though she remained relatively oblivious to clothes and pointedly spurned cosmetics and hairstyling. "She rejected offers to have her ears pierced . . . didn't smoke in the bathroom, didn't make out with the boys in 'the Pit' at Maine South's library, didn't even wear black turtlenecks," recorded Martha Sherrill. "She was totally unconcerned about how she appeared to people," thought Jennie Snodgrass, a classmate, "and she was loved for that." Dorothy Rodham was less certain. "When she was fifteen or sixteen, and other kids were starting to use makeup and fix their hair, she wasn't interested," the mother recalled. "That used to annoy me a little bit; I used to think, 'Why can't she put on a little makeup?' " There were moments when Hillary might look like the rest, dressed for the 1964 junior prom, for example, in gown and long white gloves, with lipstick and short, specially cut, slightly teased hair. But it was almost as if she were wearing a bizarre, slightly disagreeable costume, and after Maine South she would not return to its like for fifteen years, until the 1980s, when she appeared as the deliberately "made-over" wife of a comeback candidate for governor of Arkansas.

Defiantly unadorned and blithely uninterested in boys, she had little social life beyond her extracurricular activities and almost no dates, taking an old childhood friend to "girl's choice" dances and preferring a college boy from Princeton to her callow peers, though seeing little of him either. Like the makeup and clothes, sexuality was one of the rites of suburban passage for which she had neither time nor enthusiasm. "She wouldn't let some young man dominate meetings if he had nothing to say," said one of her teachers. "She wasn't going to be demure and spend a lot of time looking cute to attract people." To others, however, there was already an air of something more, an edge about her relations with young men. With no patience for her intellectual inferiors, she seemed to seek out intelligent boys, then coolly compete with them, establishing her dominance. It was not a matter of finding equality, some came to think, but a matter of maintaining a respectable superiority. "She was strong and secure and graceful, almost aloof," said Bob Stenson, a classmate who made even better grades. "I always felt a little funny around her. She was a tough competitor and formidable. I was always hoping she'd stumble a little bit."

The high school paper at one point predicted that Hillary Diane Rodham would become a nun, to be known caustically as Sister Frigidaire.

• • •

The politics of the Rodhams were as fixed as their demands on their children. "Hugh always voted Republican," said a friend, "and not just voted, but could be downright righteous and rabid about it." At home they seldom discussed political topics when their daughter and sons were younger. But there were summer gatherings of the larger Rodham clan around lakes in northeastern Pennsylvania, where staunch Republican relatives deplored the Democrats, convinced that John Kennedy had stolen the 1960 presidential election from Richard Nixon by the connivance, among others, of Mayor Daley's notorious Cook County Democratic machine in Chicago.

Meanwhile, there arrived in Park Ridge a gentle, energetic young minister who would change Hillary's life. The Rodhams' red-brick First United Methodist Church was a stronghold of the town's fearful right-wing reaction well into the 1960s. In the wake of the Kennedy murder in Dallas and initial publicity about foreign conspiracies by Fidel Castro or the Soviets, the parish director of Christian education felt compelled to send a calming, cautionary letter to the entire membership of three thousand, "hoping that they wouldn't begin finding Communists under every rock," as one account put it. "There were a lot of John Birchers in that church," one of its pastors said later. The year of the Kennedy-Nixon race, when Hillary Rodham was thirteen, Donald Jones, a new youth minister, was appointed to the church. A thirty-year-old recent graduate of the Drew University Seminary, he brought to the suburb a professorial passion to give his sheltered young Methodists a broader sensibility.

As a seminarian, Jones had been deeply influenced by Paul Tillich, and it was Tillich's robust, socially active, and redemptive Protestantism that now shaped Jones's ministry in Park Ridge. Against the backdrop of the early 1960s—the civil rights movement, the fashion of the Kennedy administration, the first stirrings of a youth rebellion—his Thursday night class for a handful of teenagers became what they called with some awe the University of Life. His group was "not just about personal salvation and pious escapism," Jones would explain, "but about an authentic and deep quest for God and life's meaning in the midst of worldly existence."

He rented a projector to show François Truffaut's classic *Four Hun-*

dred Blows, Rod Serling's *Requiem for a Heavyweight,* and similar films. On his own guitar, he strummed the songs of Bob Dylan and had his pupils analyze the lyrics. There were lively discussions of Picasso prints, readings from Stephen Crane and e. e. cummings, a debate between an atheist and a Christian—all to make real "the feelings of others," as one remembered him telling them, and to enliven the "practical conscience and content" of their faith. "I was used to relating theology to pop culture, theology to art, theology to the world," Jones said later. "By the time I got to Park Ridge, I had read all kinds of things. I got them reading too."

They went on the usual group retreats, swimming and skiing. But Jones's more remarkable outings took them into a different world. He now led them on a startling series of visits to Chicago's inner city, taking them to recreation centers and other churches to meet black and Hispanic youth, even gang leaders. At one point, he carried along a large reproduction of *Guernica,* set it before a ghetto gang and his suburban teenagers, and asked them to relate to their own lives Picasso's portrayal of anguish and suffering in the Spanish civil war. The session, he well remembered, evoked far more candor and feeling among the poorer, supposedly less educated young people of the city than from their more privileged visitors. Eventually they also met the legendary social activist and organizer Saul Alinsky. Proselytizing among affluent church groups like Jones's young people as well as among Chicago's poor, the flamboyant, irreverent, profane, and harddrinking Alinsky was at the height of his now acerbic, now raucous challenges to the domestic power structure. Typically, he had once staged a "fart-in" among protesters at a corporate headquarters and, to wring concessions from the Chicago city council, had threatened a demonstration that would flush all the toilets simultaneously at the new O'Hare Airport. He was another unique encounter for the Park Ridge teenagers. However brief, the meeting would have an interesting sequel. In a college thesis a few years later, Hillary Rodham would reveal much of herself in writing about Alinsky and his strategies, and the crusty organizer himself would offer her a coveted job as a virtual protégé.

Most of the inner-city encounters would be genuine revelations for the Park Ridge group, not least for the earnest, impressionable Hillary Rodham. "I was in junior high and high school and got a sense of what people were up against, and how lucky I had been," she once told an interviewer, still remembering the visits to Chicago with obvious emotion. "I don't think those kids had seen poverty before," Jones recalled, "don't think they had interacted with kids that weren't like themselves." On April 15, 1962, he took the class to Chicago's Orchestra Hall to hear Martin Luther King, Jr., preach a sermon entitled "Remaining Awake through a Revolution." After the address he spirited them down to meet the already famous civil rights leader. Thirty years later, Jones himself and most of the others had forgotten the details of that night, but Hillary Rodham remembered it vividly, recalling that Jones had introduced them one by one and that she had personally shaken hands with King. "To accuse her of taking this message literally would not be going too far," one thought of her response to King's admonitions.

Eventually a Thursday evening discussion of teenage pregnancy filtered back to parents and stirred the inevitable controversy and outrage at United Methodist. Still, Jones mollified his superiors and managed to continue the youth group. By 1962–63 his pupils were busily organizing food drives for the poor and even a baby-sitting pool for the children of migrant farm workers camped amid wretched hovels and open sewage in fields west of the city. Small acts of virtual charity, the efforts touched no real power or politics yet in spirit and sensibility were extraordinary for Park Ridge. The imbued and shared idealism of Jones's young Methodists was plain—if bitterly poignant in terms of so much that followed. "We believed in the incredible social changes that can happen," said Sherry Heiden, "if you change your perspective."

Hillary Rodham began dropping by Jones's church office after school or on summer afternoons, eager to talk more about the new ideas and insights from the class. Responding warmly, he gave her a first taste of modern Protestant theology, in excerpts from Tillich, Søren Kierkegaard, Dietrich Bonhoeffer, Reinhold Niebuhr, and others, and they carried on long, increasingly serious discussions. "She was curious, open to what life had to bring," the young minister would say. "She was just insatiable."

When she was in high school he gave her his copy of J. D. Salinger's *Catcher in the Rye.* "I didn't tell you at the time, but when you had me read *Catcher in the Rye,* I didn't like it, and, moreover, I thought it was a little too advanced for me," she wrote Jones her sophomore year in college. "But now that I've read it a second time, I realize, I think, why you gave it to me. I don't think it was too advanced, as a matter of fact."

The minister introduced her to the larger social-political implications of Tillich's reformism, the quest to subdue with Christian idealism what many theologians saw as the postwar's social alienation and secular loss of values. They talked as well, he remembered, about Kierkegaard's "leap of faith" in the face of rational cynicism, about Bonhoeffer's "religionless Christianity" of public morality and ethics, and especially about Niebuhr's more tragic, unsentimental view of history and human nature and of the necessary force of civil governance. "She realizes absolutely the truth of the human condition. . . . She is very much the sort of Christian who understands that the use of power to achieve social good is legitimate," Jones would say. Yet much of that was in retrospect, when the inquisitive girl of the youth group had become a famously powerful First Lady and when the politics of Hillary Rodham had been shaped by her experience in Arkansas as much as by theology.

At the time, in Jones's small church office, their quiet afternoon talks were less a matter of political tutelage than the tentative discoveries and questions, the first fitful awakenings of critical intellect and sensibility in a spiritually minded young woman. She was at heart, he knew, a cautious, carefully contained, and self-protective girl whose judgments about herself and the world, like her perception of *Catcher in the Rye,* were still forming. "Unlike some people who at a particular age land on a cause and become concerned," Jones said later about what would be a gradual, almost lifelong process, "with Hillary I think of a continuous textured development."

Jones was to leave students like Hillary with the habit of carrying small Methodist devotionals with them for comfort. The warm and ultimately loving personal relationship with him, unique in Hillary Rodham's life, was obviously crucial at the time. Jones was not only intellectually exciting and nurturing but fondly approving and accepting. A "world beyond . . . growling Hugh Rodham," Martha Sherrill called it. "Boys liked her," Reverend Jones once said, defending his favorite student to a reporter questioning her lack of social life in high school. "And not because she was flirtatious. She was not—she wasn't a raving beauty, but she was pretty enough. What attracted guys around her was her personality, her willingness to talk to them, at parity with them." It was a memory, some thought, that mirrored more accurately the maturity and affection of the thirty-year-old minister than the common attitude of suburban teenage males in the 1960s.

To Don Jones, as to no one else, she would continue to bring her questions and reflections. "I wonder if it's possible to be a mental conservative and a heart liberal?" she wrote at one point, charting the inner division that began in her adolescence. Before she finished high school the minister was gone, assigned to another church after little more than four years in Park Ridge. (He would eventually go back to Drew for a PhD and a teaching career free of rancorous congregations like First United Methodist.) She was elected vice president of her junior class at Maine East but in the spring of 1964 ran for senior class president at Maine South and lost, producing a rambling, "philosophical" letter to Jones about reconciling herself to defeat. "Hillary," the pastor remembered clearly, "hated to lose." The letter was only the beginning of her correspondence, usually single-spaced and crowded onto both sides of the page, sent faithfully to him over the next three decades from Park Ridge, college, law school, Washington, Arkansas, and finally the White House.

Not long after he left Chicago in 1964, she wrote about the disapproval she felt from the new minister who had taken his job. "He thinks I'm a radical," she told her confidant and mentor with some exasperation. It was, after all, an irony they both understood.

◆　◆　◆

In the autumn of 1964 Park Ridge backed with unusual enthusiasm the conservative Republican candidate for president, Senator Barry Goldwater of Arizona. "AuH$_2$O '64" bumper stickers seemed to fill the driveways, and Hillary Rodham, to the delight of her parents, joined the campaign as an official Goldwater Girl, wearing her straw boater and sash to rallies, briskly canvassing the already solidly Republican neighborhoods, and "[speaking] out for the right wing," according to Judith Warner, "with all the passion of a teenager." Elected to the student council as a senior the same fall, she organized around the national election an elaborate mock political convention in the new Maine South gym, showing her appreciation of the rituals of politics and even planning political demonstrations in the aisles. In November Lyndon Johnson crushed Goldwater by some sixteen million votes, though Park Ridge was unreconciled, its bumper stickers unremoved, fading irreconcilably in the midwestern sun over the years to come. That December Hillary Rodham wrote one of the ritual senior self-portraits in the Maine South paper. She chose to recount her high school experience in terms of a prosecuting attorney pursuing a case that has gone on "literally for years." To the routine question about her ambitions she answered pertly and, to some, a bit unexpectedly, "To marry a senator and settle down in Georgetown."

She graduated fifteenth out of a thousand in the class of 1965. Most of her affluent friends were bound for college, although many young men from lower-income suburbs were soon destined for Vietnam.

Some saw their class as a last charmed moment before the upheaval of the rest of the 1960s. Hillary Rodham was voted the girl most likely to succeed. The boy named for the same honor killed himself with a drug overdose before the end of the decade.

She had been a National Merit Scholarship finalist and National Honor Society and student council leader, known almost uniformly for her toughness, competitiveness, and strong convictions. Fellow students said she spoke out for things that she believed in, took unpopular stances, reconciled conflicting positions, and never exhibited a rebellious nature.

Like her future husband's, Hillary Rodham's high school poise and achievements shrouded a deeper loneliness and hurt—and decisive influence—few saw at the time. If Bill Clinton's models had been Roger Clinton and Virginia, hers were no less the long-suffering Dorothy Rodham and her stringent husband. But unlike Bill, she also had a genuine intellectual mentor and an exposure to ideas and to the diversity of American life otherwise as uncommon to Park Ridge as to Hot Springs. The essential contrast in their experiences was in many ways the difference between Uncle Raymond Clinton and the Reverend Don Jones.

Yet she seemed to take away nothing so much as the mark of her childhood place and time. "What people don't seem to realize is that Hillary's so conventional, so traditional, so midwestern, so middle class," her friend Sara Ehrman once said with unintended irony. "Her taste in art is middle class. Her taste in music is middle class. Her clothes. . . . She's very simple, brilliant, a nice person, and a product of her upbringing."

At the urging of two young Maine South teachers, she considered some of the most prestigious women's colleges in the East, including Radcliffe and Smith. "She was set on going to an all-girls' school," her mother said later. She had chosen Wellesley, as she told the story, the moment she saw pictures of its bucolic Gothic campus outside Boston—"the lake in the middle, the quaint Victorian classrooms, the tiny surrounding town."

Her parents drove her to Massachusetts in the fall of 1965 in Hugh Rodham's Cadillac. Saying good-bye, the mother, at least, realized how insular, how much within the sustaining, punishing family her daughter's life had been. "Aside from a few trips away with girlfriends, Hillary hadn't really been away from home," Dorothy remembered. "After we dropped her off, I just crawled in the back seat and cried for eight hundred miles."

· 7 ·

Wellesley

"Tomorrow, When You Are the Establishment"

Of America's most exclusive women's colleges, Wellesley was the wealthiest, its endowment one of the twenty largest in the nation among private schools overall. In the academic world, the college had been known since opening in 1875 primarily for lavish art and library collections and, after the war, for well-funded science laboratories. Even by the mid-1960s, however, Wellesley remained largely what it had been for decades, a staid, prestigious, conservative institution performing a traditional role for daughters of the upper classes. It was part liberal arts college, part finishing school, the intellectual reputation of its faculty and students never matching in rank—or expected to match—its financial assets.

To take classes among the picturesque Oxford-inspired buildings and green lawns, Wellesley students generally paid higher tuition and fees than even Princeton or Harvard men did. Their campus sat beside rustic Lake Waban and the neat, expensive colonial villages of Wellesley and Wellesley Hills, a still comfortable fifteen miles from Boston Common. First-year students could not have cars, be out after nine on most nights, or leave for weekends without parental permission. "Women in those places in those years weren't really encouraged to *go* to a school but to *be* educated and *be* well-bred," said one of them. "You have to remember that, for all its money and name, Wellesley was still mainly just a 'girls' school' in that sense."

Hillary Rodham found it "all very rich and fancy, and very intimidating to my way of thinking," she said later. She had "stayed apprehensive for about three months," she told Arkansas reporter Mara Leveritt. At the same time, others saw her as an eager, proper fresh- man who "at once signed on with the campus Republicans," accord- ing to one account, "and sat down to tea." "I was worried about her," her mother told a friend, "but Hillary adjusted to Wellesley without a problem. She joined clubs and was active immediately."

Fleeing their cloistered setting—"The biggest social life on campus was tea . . . one lump or two," said her classmate Kris Rogers— Wellesley women in numbers traditionally took the Boston transit trains on Fridays and Saturdays into Harvard Square, and Hillary joined the migration from the beginning. Not long into her first se- mester she began to date Jeff Shields, a quiet, diligent Harvard junior destined for law school. They saw each other more or less steadily over the next four years, in an essentially platonic relationship he remem- bered as "based on a lot of discourse."

There were dances, football games, parties at Shields's Winthrop House, strolls along the Charles in Cambridge and around Lake Waban back at Wellesley. At the beginning she was quiet, "tended to listen more than talk," Shields recalled. Her reticence soon disap- peared. "The things that I remember most were the conversations," he told a writer. "She would rather sit around and talk about current events or politics or ideas than go bicycle riding or to a football game." The young Harvard man "fell in love with her earnestness," professed author Gail Sheehy, though while they were dating she also saw other boys from time to time, all of them, like Shields, "poli-sci, earnest- idealist, policy-activist, good-government types, not wild-eyed radicals," according to Rogers.

Her freshman speeches took the Republican side of current issues, including Southeast Asia and Lyndon Johnson's War on Poverty. But the winter and spring of 1966 were also spent in her own methodical, characteristic sampling of college preoccupations, as if she were trying them on for style as well as substance. In the beginning she had been the grind, then the partier. "After six weeks of little human communi- cation or companionship, my diet gave me indigestion," she wrote Don Jones about her regimen of reading and composition. "The last two weeks of February here were an orgy of decadent indulgence—as decadent as any upright Methodist can become." Having played "so- cial reformer" for the month of March, involved in assorted campus improvements, as she told Jones, she turned in April to become a thirty-day hippie, painting a flower on her arm. By May it was gone and she had returned to a more familiar role.

Jones thought her then and ever afterward in searching, often sharp rebellion against what they both called "sentimental liberalism"; a "sense of human frailty" pointed up for her, he told writer Donnie Radcliffe, the "difficulties of achieving justice and even the necessities of using power." The imperfection and irrationality of the mass seemed both to excuse the oppression of institutions and to render futile a more direct confrontation with power. In either case she came out of her freshman identity tasting with more scorn than ever for radical student movements. Earlier she had taken a black student with her to the Wellesley Methodist Church. "I was testing me as much as I was testing the church," she confided to Jones about her symbolic act. But when riots erupted in Chicago ghettos the following summer, giving new prominence to Martin Luther King, Jr., and Stokely Carmichael's Student Nonviolent Coordinating Committee, she was caustic about the more insistent young activists. "Just because a person cannot approve of SNCC's attitude toward civil disobedience," she wrote Jones, "does not mean that one wishes to maintain the racial status quo."

◆ ◆ ◆

During her sophomore year of 1966–67, a new militancy on Vietnam and civil rights was already marking other college campuses. With a handful of other students, including some of the African American women beginning to trickle into the college (ten attended that year), she began to urge greater black enrollment. Civil rights leaders were invited to speak to a sea of white female faces about the moral imperative of racial integration. "We were all still afraid to talk about it," Jan Piercy remembered.

Later, as a member of the student senate, Hillary would become one of the leaders of the exclusive school's version of the 1960s rebellion— protesting Victorian curfews, asking for a reduction of mandatory courses, advocating a pass-fail grading system, even proposing to lift the century-old ban on men in Wellesley dormitories. Conducted with no reproach to administration or alumnae, it was tame and polite reform, hardly comparable to the chanting, fists-in-the-air student upheavals at other colleges throughout the nation. Like Don Jones's taking his youth group to the forbidden interior of Chicago, her Wellesley acts would seem daring if only because of the stolid setting. The wider ferment of the 1960s merely opened the way for relatively modest reformers like the young woman from Park Ridge. Her reforms addressed outmoded or embarrassing conditions while posing no threat to the basic arrangements of power.

Her college protests would be "a Hillary-style rebellion," wrote Martha Sherrill, "methodical, rational, fair." She was intent on being individually successful in her causes—though success, as always in such easy pragmatism, increasingly defined the cause itself. "I wouldn't say she was angry," Jan Piercy said, comparing her to other student activists. "Intense anger is sometimes the result of frustration, from not being effective. And Hillary has always been effective."

By her junior year she was a recognized student leader, seen as serious but not too bookish and known as a natural go-between in increasing controversies pitting students against the administration. She had earlier chaired and held in check a volatile campuswide meeting on racial discrimination in admissions, what black students had attacked as Wellesley's "secret quota policy," and she would later act as a mediator between an African American women's group and college officials. "She had a talent for serving as a bridge between different groups of students . . . tried to keep everybody talking," Kris Rogers remembered. For the moment she had found a role and obviously relished it. "Hillary couldn't say no to a meeting," thought Martha Sherrill. "Get out the Robert's Rules of Order and she would come flying through the door."

Some still wondered about her own eventual political purposes. An admiring, affectionate Jeff Shields saw her as "someone who wanted to be involved and have an impact but didn't exactly know how." Apart from her good offices in campus issues, friends observed a change in Hillary over her last two years at college, a growing involvement, as one put it, in social issues away from Wellesley and a steady shift from Republican to Democratic politics. Despite a busy schedule, she would volunteer to teach reading to poor black children in Boston's ravaged Roxbury ghetto and later help out at one of the new alternative newspapers springing up in the city. As a Young Republican she had favored the right's old nemesis, GOP moderate Nelson Rockefeller, or Representative John Lindsay of New York against more conservative rivals Richard Nixon and Ronald Reagan. Now, by the winter of 1967–68, with opposition to the Vietnam War reaching a crescendo, she joined the student supporters of Senator Eugene McCarthy of Minnesota in his challenge of Lyndon Johnson.

Her Wellesley roommate, Johanna Branson, remembered Hillary's returning to their dorm the night of April 4, 1968, after hearing the news of the assassination of Martin Luther King, Jr., in Memphis. "She came in, the door flew back, and her book bag went crashing against the wall," Branson said. "She was completely distraught about the horror of it." While young blacks rioted in eighty cities and students prepared campus uprisings at Columbia and other universities, Hillary and a small group of Wellesley women put on black armbands to join a somber memorial march in Boston. She and others planned to march in Wellesley itself, only to have local veterans' groups threaten, as a young local minister remembered, "that we'd have our heads beaten in if we did."

In the wake of the King murder, the mood on campus was tense. She was among those asking students to boycott classes and attend a teach-in on civil rights issues, and when a professor scolded them for not giving up "weekends, something we enjoy," her reply in the college paper was instant, the first of many sharp responses to public criticism. "I'll give up my date Saturday night . . . but I don't think that's the point," she wrote. "Individual consciences are fine. But individual consciences have to be made manifest." Her own was soon plain. Within weeks she was running a carefully organized campaign for president of the student government. Like her two opponents, she advocated more student control over Wellesley's social regulations and even a role for class leaders in the institution's decision making. But like them as well, she was "vague as to exactly how they would implement the change in the power structure," as the *Wellesley News* put it in refusing to endorse Hillary Rodham or the others. When she won the race, she was astonished at her popularity and acceptance, despite her organization and the reputation she had cultivated for three years. "I can't believe it. I can't believe it," she told a faculty friend incredulously.

Her election was only the beginning of a remarkable series of events over the months between her junior and senior years. In early June 1968—the bleak moment of Bill Clinton's graduation from Georgetown—she was in riot-scarred Washington on the Wellesley Internship Program. One of thirty chosen from among three hundred applicants to aid Republican congressmen in assignments directed by Wisconsin representative (and Nixon's future secretary of defense) Melvin Laird, she spent the next eight weeks working routinely in the office of reactionary Harold Collier from Park Ridge's district. But the internship also gave her a chance to research and write for Laird and others on issues of revenue sharing and to meet several ambitious young rightwing aides who would later be prominent in the Reagan years.

In this first exposure to Washington, she left, as always, the impression of an assertive intelligence and effectiveness, whatever the substance. "She was for it," Laird would say of the Republican plan to "share revenues," shifting control of federal money and programs to states and localities. On the surface it seemed a benign scheme to dilute distant federal dictation and return decisions to communities where tax money was spent. But as is so commonly true on Capitol Hill and in state legislatures and courthouses, bland principle masked brutal politics. The vaunted "sharing," as many well knew, would simply turn over the money in state after state to more parochial, conservative, often corrupt local regimes, who could be counted on, in turn, to blunt whatever change or impact the original policies and appropriations might have intended. "Hell, can't anybody see it," a frustrated, courthouse-tutored Lyndon Johnson would say to his aides. "They want to share revenues with the boys that got all the real revenues to begin with."

From the Washington internship she went briefly to the Republican Convention in Miami, where she worked in the already failed campaign of Nelson Rockefeller to head off the presidential nomination of Richard Nixon. Like her passing involvement with Gene McCarthy's insurgency in the Democratic primaries earlier that winter and spring, her commitment to Rockefeller was spurred by his apparent promise to end the Vietnam War and address social and urban problems anew. There was, of course, a naive inconsistency between her work in Washington and that in Miami: the men she had served and impressed on Capitol Hill, the issues to which she devoted herself as an avid GOP intern, belonged to Richard Nixon and to a Republicanism that deplored Rockefeller and his policies as much as it did the Democrats. About Hillary Rodham's whole heady summer of national politics in 1968 there would be the air of the freshman sampler, trying on Congress one month, the convention the next, a matter more of scouting than of conviction.

Back in Park Ridge later that summer, she spent what was left of her vacation in languid poolside talks with old friends, punctuated by heated political arguments with her father at home. If she remained the moderate and the mediator at Wellesley, her political evolution felt far sharper in Park Ridge. "When fights flared between them," Judith Warner recounted, "the bottom line always was politics." In late August she and a neighbor, Betsy Johnson, took the train to Chicago to see for themselves the stormy demonstrations surrounding the riven Democratic Convention.

Inside the Chicago Amphitheater, the Old Guard, in the form of

Mayor Daley's machine and presidential nominee Hubert Humphrey, suppressed the last remnants of Vietnam dissent in the wake of the primary defeat of McCarthy and the murder of Robert Kennedy. Blocks away, near the Conrad Hilton Hotel, a symbolic spectacle took place. There had been bloody clashes earlier in the week, with student demonstrators chanting their familiar "Fascist pig" and "Hell no, we won't go" and Chicago police shouting back, "Kill the Commies" and "Let's get the bastards." On a sultry Wednesday night a disorganized crowd, already teargassed, milled about near the hotel, "most of them pacifically inclined middle-class kids," a reporter scribbled in his notes. Then suddenly, without warning, cohorts of billy club–swinging police charged. What a later inquiry termed a "police riot" was seen in part by shocked television viewers, including young Bill Clinton in Hot Springs, and the initial revulsion in the national press was widespread. "The truth was," Tom Wicker wrote afterward in the *New York Times,* "these were our children in the streets, and the Chicago police beat them up."

"We saw kids our age getting their heads beaten in. And the police were doing the beating," Betsy Johnson remembered. "Hillary and I just looked at each other. We had a wonderful childhood in Park Ridge, but we obviously hadn't gotten the whole story."

In the longer aftermath of the fury, there was a systematic backlash against the victims, Mayor Daley calling the student demonstrators "a lawless violent group of terrorists [threatening] to menace the lives of millions of people." "I think we ought to quit pretending that Mayor Daley did anything wrong," presidential candidate Hubert Humphrey would say of the repression at the convention as well as in the streets. "He didn't." Within only weeks, polls showed much of the public agreeing with Daley and Humphrey. Protests continued to rage on campuses, but the nation watched with a growing unease and resentment, despising the dissenters for being wrong, hating them for being right. Having broadcast the bloody images from Chicago and deplored the brutality, most of the press soon shed its initial editorial indignation and fell in behind the recoiling public mood.

Symbolic of the divide within a generation, Hillary Rodham watched the brutality at a political as well as a physical distance—shocked, as Betsy Johnson remembered, yet detached and apart in many ways. Elected president of the student government association, she would return to Wellesley to help organize teach-ins on the war, after similar meetings at other universities. Later that autumn, while many students boycotted the election, Hillary seemed far removed from the screams outside the Hilton or the disillusion in their wake, leaving Wellesley again and again to drive through New Hampshire and western Massachusetts, avidly distributing literature and working on phone banks for the long-compromised Hubert Humphrey, with his "politics of joy" a cheerleader still for Washington's war policy.

♦ ♦ ♦

Hillary Rodham's last year at Wellesley was a combination of public accomplishment and personal disquiet. As student government president she continued to be the campus conciliator, with a genuine "empathy" for both sides, as Kris Rogers and others saw her. She was in favor of change, they remembered, but never too committed to it, thought the status quo oppressive or wasteful but was never too outraged by it. "She was really very mainstream . . . not a counterculture person . . . going to drop out or become radical, even in her thinking," Jeff Shields would say. "Because even when she became definitely liberal, it was always within a fairly conventional scope."

She presided over her own small salon in the common area and dining room of her dormitory. "Not a frivolous person in the least," remembered Eleanor Acheson, the granddaughter of Secretary of State Dean Acheson and a coworker in the Humphrey campaign. Acheson also thought her friend free of the usual family pressures. So many students were "tortured by insecurity, have parents driving them," Acheson told a writer decades later. "Hillary never had any of that." Her relationship with Jeff Shields ended early in her senior year. "Read between the lines," said a classmate, "that she just wasn't getting in bed with him." But despite her successes, the years at Wellesley were often more difficult than she acknowledged. Looking back on a presidential race fraught with personal attacks, her mother would insist to Judith Warner that "the trials Hillary faced as an adolescent . . . made the troubles of the 1992 campaign look like a cakewalk." At that, her undergraduate years seemed still worse. "The most difficult time of her life," Dorothy Rodham would say, "[was] when she was at Wellesley."

There had been no one for her at the college quite like Don Jones. Among the faculty, Patsy Sampson thought her very "intense," giving her A-pluses in child psychology courses, which Hillary obviously relished. Alan Schechter, a young political science professor who taught constitutional law with a devotion to civil rights and liberal politics, saw her as "the best student I had taught in [my] first seven years . . . at

Wellesley." It was with Schechter that she wrote her senior thesis on the community-action programs of Lyndon Johnson's War on Poverty.

No subject could have been more prophetic of the politics she and her future husband would inherit. Born in the euphoria of Johnson's early power in the mid-1960s, the larger antipoverty program was rooted in the faith of liberal economists that US postwar growth would be constant and that no meaningful redistribution of wealth or power was necessary for the realization of American democracy. "Poverty could be abolished without anyone's pocket suffering," as one historian described their presumption. The Democrats could "achieve the millennium without changing the system."

Yet there had been a fatal flaw from the beginning. A new cigarette tax in 1964 might have provided crucial billions for a direct, less politically vulnerable jobs program for the thirty to fifty million poor. Under powerful pressure from the tobacco lobby, however, Johnson and the Democratic congressional leadership had abandoned the tax. They chose instead to concentrate on regular Capitol Hill appropriations for "community action," designed to encourage economic power and popular participation at the grass roots in both urban slums and rural depressed areas. Barely two years later, by mid-1966, the efforts were doomed—not only starved of money and attention in the vast sinking of resources into the maw of war in Southeast Asia but also under attack by Democratic officeholders all over the country, threatened by the new political and economic assertiveness of the dispossessed. Governors and mayors, congressmen and legislators had lobbied Vice President Humphrey, and Humphrey in turn warned Johnson, who with escalation of the war could afford no major defections in the ranks.

"The poor were being organized against the establishments," wrote historian Robert A. Levine, "and, not surprisingly, the establishments didn't like it a bit." Politicians of both parties were soon joined by a resentful middle class—its own status threatened by the fiscal and social catastrophe that was Vietnam—finding it easier, then as later, to blame those below and nonwhite than to understand political economy.

This vivid story of reform and reaction Hillary Rodham now viewed in her Wellesley thesis. Like the author of a literate but blanched bureaucratic report, she meticulously described various programs and assessed their clinical impact. In the spring of 1969 she judged that the already moribund community-action programs had been "constructive" and that the poor would now require something "broader" and more "sustained," as one of her thesis readers recalled her conclusion.

But she stopped well short of analyzing the actual political murder of the programs or of discussing what the episode revealed in a larger sense about power and politics in America.

In the thesis she dealt in passing with Saul Alinsky. Since meeting him in Jones's youth group, she had heard him speak in Boston and had even gone to see him in Chicago before coming back to Wellesley for her senior year. His own reformer's approach to poverty—"an embarrassment to the American soul," he called it—had evolved to an elegant simplicity. The poor were poor because they lacked power and must be locally, practically organized to acquire it. Hillary Rodham judged Alinsky and his methods only marginal at best. "Organizing the poor for community actions to improve their own lives may have, in certain circumstances, short-term benefits for the poor but would never solve their major problems" is what Professor Schechter remembered as her thesis conclusion. "You need much more than that. You need leadership, programs, constitutional doctrines." Though she never defined precisely what the "much more" entailed, hers would in some respects be a sound verdict on the era that followed, when Alinsky and his disciples around the nation won hundreds of meaningful small battles for the poor and disenfranchised only to see poverty and disenfranchisement grow as never before. Packing a city council or embarrassing a corporate board here and there would be no real remedy to the massive corruption of federal power and the lethal redistribution of national wealth and resources in the 1980s. Yet to focus on Alinsky's localism and organizing tactics was to miss just that, the other dimension of his larger critique, the apportionment of power itself. Like her appraisal of the community-action programs, her self-confident dismissal of the old Chicago hero and nemesis did not come to terms with the underlying point of it all—politics.

Schechter and three other graders gave her As on the thesis. Her adviser thought her, like himself, a "pragmatic liberal" in the spirit of the early 1960s, someone who shared what he called his "instrumental liberalism: using government to meet the unmet needs of the society to help those people who are not fully included within it." He had "high hopes for Hillary and her future," he wrote in a recommendation to Yale Law School. "She has the intellectual ability, personality, and character to make a remarkable contribution to American society." Her Wellesley thesis, however, would not be part of that contribution. Not long after graduation, enmeshed, like her husband, in politics, she instructed the college to seal her senior thesis from the public, even the tactical criticism of Alinsky and nebulous call for "leadership" having become possible career liabilities. "Hillary can't afford the negative image of the sixties," an admirer would explain a quarter century later.

Friends remembered her as in search of a "calling" those last months. The overwhelming majority of her class were still anticipating no more than marriage and family, but "feminists visiting Wellesley . . . turned Hillary toward a legal career," according to Martin Kasindorf. She had decided on Yale Law after an encounter with an arrogant and sexist Harvard Law professor. "She's trying to decide whether to come here next year or attend our closest competitor," a Harvard friend said, introducing her to the faculty member. "Well, first of all, we don't have any close competitors," the man had replied. "Second, we don't need any more women."

The choice led to one last encounter with Saul Alinsky. She had once contemplated following Alinsky's example and "doing something in the area of organizing," Hillary would tell the *Chicago Daily News* in a special graduation interview. She thought his view of change through social agitation "a good point," like his political concern for the sensibilities of the middle class, "the kind of people I grew up with in Park Ridge." But when Alinsky himself offered her a job that spring as an organizer, she turned him down, telling him she was going to Yale. "Well, that's no way to change anything," he had said. "Well, I see a different way than you," she replied. "And I think there is a real opportunity."

Afterward there were repeated testimonials to her more idealistic purposes at the time, repeated surprise at the life she eventually led. "She didn't go to law school because she was interested in being a lawyer," thought Jeff Shields. "Not for the purpose of making money or becoming a corporate lawyer, but . . . to influence the course of society," Schechter would add. "I'm not interested in corporate law," she herself would declare. "My life is too short to spend it making money for some big anonymous firm." Shields believed her undecided about a career but, in any case, fiercely independent. "She didn't have any fixed ambitions in terms of knowing that she wanted to be elected to some office," Shields remembered. "She certainly didn't give any indication that she was looking to attach herself to a politician—and I'm sure probably would have been offended by that concept if someone had raised it at the time."

With Schechter's sponsorship and a concerted last-minute campaign within the class, she became Wellesley's first student commencement speaker. An apprehensive college administration stipulated that the speech reflect a "consensus" of the class of 1969 while also being "appropriate." A drafting committee was formed, and student ideas poured in, urging her to speak candidly about the war, the assassinations of King and Kennedy, the Chicago riot, campus protests, and more from their turbulent last years. In the end the committee proudly refused to submit the speech for final review by the college president.

Though her mother stayed in Park Ridge with her brothers, Hugh Rodham drove to Boston to hear his daughter speak. The ceremonies began with Senator Edward Brooke, a Massachusetts Republican and the only African American in the Senate, making a perfunctory speech not even alluding to the war or popular unrest. Hillary Rodham followed with an unrehearsed response, "chewing out" the United States senator, as one account described it, "for being out of touch." To audible gasps from the crowd she scolded Brooke for his fey performance, "gave it to him, no ifs, ands, or buts about it," Schechter recalled. "I find myself in a familiar position, that of reacting," she said, "something that our generation has been doing for quite a while now." "Hillary just sort of launched off on her own," Eleanor Acheson said. "Some people, largely mothers, thought it was just rude."

She began her prepared text with words from a classmate and poet. "The challenge now is to practice politics as the art of making what appears to be impossible possible. We are not interested in social reconstruction, it's human reconstruction. . . . You and I must be free, not to save the world in a glorious crusade, but to practice with all the skill of our being the art of making possible.

"The issues of sharing power and responsibility, and of assuming power and responsibility, have been general concerns on campuses throughout the world," she said of the unrest of 1968–69. At stake were "integrity and trust and respect." Students were struggling to "come to grips with some of the inarticulate, maybe even inarticulable, things that we're feeling," she told them. "We are, all of us, exploring a world that none of us understands and attempting to create within that uncertainty." Only minutes into the address she seemed already to be losing some of the audience. "A murmur of whispered commentary buzzed under her words," said one account. "But there are some things we feel," she went on. "We feel that our prevailing, acquisitive, and competitive corporate life, including, tragically, the universities, is not the way of life for us. We're searching for more immediate, ecstatic, and penetrating modes of living. And so our questions, our questions about our institutions, about our colleges, about our churches, about our government, continue." In more elaborate language it was the plaint of so many in the paradox of postwar prosperity: "Is this all there is, all we have to look forward to?" But her speech brushed the larger political reality only to retreat to abstraction, without asking or venturing more.

"Every protest, every dissent, is unabashedly an attempt to forge an identity," she said. "That attempt at forging . . . has meant coming to terms with our own humanness." At one point she seemed utterly lost in ambivalence: "Within the context of a society that we perceive—now we can talk about reality, and I would like to talk about reality sometime, authentic reality, inauthentic reality, and what we have to accept of what we see—but your perception of it is that it hovers often between the possibility of disaster and the potentiality for imaginatively responding to men's needs." By now there was a small background din of people shifting noisily in their chairs, whispering, even beginning to move restlessly in and out of the long rows.

Closing, she tried earnestly to reconcile dissent with the old order. "There's a very strange conservative strain that goes through a lot of New Left collegiate protests that I find very intriguing because it harks back to a lot of the old virtues, to the fulfillment of original ideas." But that idea, too, she left dangling and ended abruptly on a banal, almost nationalist note: "And it's also a very unique American experience. It's such a great adventure. If the experiment in human living doesn't work in this country, in this age, it's not going to work anywhere."

Her class, a few of the more recent alumnae, and some parents gave her a standing ovation, though the distraction during the address had been telling. Twenty-four years later she would look back on the speech as "full of uncompromising language." Puckered Wellesley thought so at the time. Uttered as it was only in passing in her reproach to Senator Brooke, the word *Vietnam* did not appear in the officially printed version of her address, and the college's first student commencement speaker appeared nowhere in a 1975 official chronicle of the institution. Yet what stood out then and later was the uncertainty and equivocation of what she had actually said, when so many others of her generation were coming to grips more simply with realities of "power and responsibility." Had she spoken at Harvard, a reporter wrote years later, the speech would have "invited a mass walkout." As it was, a few miles away at Brandeis University, more typical of the class of 1969 and sadly more prophetic, a student commencement speaker was talking about the rule of "an economic elite in our society . . . which has a vested interest in preserving the social order on which their holdings depend." Valedictorian Justin Simon put it plainly: "If you support the war in Vietnam, pay for it. Don't have tax lawyers out making sure you don't pay too much."

Excerpts of her address were published by *Life* in a collection of student commencement speeches, accompanied by her first national photograph, showing a round-faced austere young woman with long straight hair, peering out through thick rimless glasses, the fingers of her outstretched hands joined pensively in front of her. In the same feature was a future White House aide and her own later collaborator on health-insurance reform, Ira Magaziner of Brown, who admonished his classmates, "The way things should be has got to be the way things are. . . . We should lose sleep because we are doing things that are wrong and we're allowing things that are wrong to go on in our society and we're accepting them." Beside the students was a premonitory passage from Vice President Spiro T. Agnew, who denounced the "sniveling, hand-wringing power structure" tolerating the era's "violent rebellion." He seemed at one point to be speaking to the Rodhams and Magaziners in particular. They should accept the "rational" status quo and reject "immature" dissent, Agnew advised them scarcely four years before he left office in a bribery scandal. "Ask yourselves which kind of society you want for tomorrow—tomorrow, when you are the establishment."

Hillary Rodham graduated from Wellesley already a paradoxical, guarded, concealed woman. Combing the same ground decades later, even the most sympathetic reporters would be troubled by how one-dimensional she then seemed, how "rational, cerebral," as one account described her, with "pain . . . fears . . . dreams" all seemingly missing. "She rarely, if ever," concluded Frank Marafiote, "is described by friends or family members as creative, innovative, emotional, empathetic, intuitive, introspective, sensual." Ultimately, he thought, she seems "unknowable, certainly to others, and perhaps more ominously, to herself."

After the commencement speech she left the crowd, including her father, for Lake Waban, indulging a last act of ritual revolt by stripping to a bathing suit she had worn under her graduation robe and dress and plunging into waters where student swimming was strictly prohibited. While she was out in the lake, a school security guard happened by and spitefully took her things, including her thick-lensed glasses.

She finally told the story at a 1992 Wellesley commencement. "Blind as a bat," she remembered, "I had to feel my way back to my room at Davis." The audience laughed. No one seemed to notice the more poignant meaning of the incident: literally and symbolically, she had spent the triumphal moment of her college career much as the years before and after—ultimately, defiantly alone.

· 8 ·

Yale I

"She Saw Right Past the Charm"

It was the same summer of 1969 that Bill Clinton spent so anxiously in Hot Springs trying to escape the draft, and Hillary Rodham started her life after graduation with another act of restless independence. Shunning a contentious summer at home in sultry Park Ridge, she struck out for Alaska—to the consternation of both family and friends, even hitchhiking part of the way. There she took a job in a cannery, soon to be fired when she earnestly told the manager that the fish they were packing for US grocery stores seemed tainted. "They really were dark and half spoiled," she told a friend, "but I guess nobody wanted to know that." She had come back from the Northwest with a new air of self-sufficiency, if not cynicism, her friends thought, and that autumn, as Clinton returned to Oxford with his ROTC deferment to await the lottery, she confidently enrolled as one of the few women at Yale Law.

People remembered her flannel shirts, thick glasses, and sheer plainness, austerity worn as a notice—or warning—the overall impression "somewhat intimidating," in Gail Sheehy's later description. She immediately joined the moratorium protests against the war and led her own campaign to have tampon dispensers placed in the women's rooms at the law school. There would be softening recollections of her Tammy Wynette records and of whispering and giggling with girlfriends. But above all, her Yale classmates marked her as "studious and solemn," and often solitary. The ever-disciplined daughter of Hugh Rodham trooped regularly to the Yale undergraduate gymnasium to follow her own regimen of calisthenics.

From the beginning, there seemed no question about the strength and even passion of her scholarship. For an interval she worked on the founding editorial board of the short-lived *Yale Review of Law and Social Action,* a consciously progressive competitor to the school's traditional review. Given to indignant but duly cited articles on government repression of groups like the Black Panthers and on other political issues, the new journal represented a lively challenge to the law school's orthodoxy. "There was a great amount of ferment and confusion about what was and wasn't the proper role of law school education," she remembered. "We would have great arguments about whether we were selling out because we were getting a law degree."

She dated little in her first year, and some thought her lonely despite her outward, sometimes flaunted indifference to sex and convention. "Hillary was deliberately dowdy and colorless as a young law student but a radical and feminist only of sorts," said a close friend. "As I look back on it, regardless of her pose, I think she always wanted male attention as much as anything else." Whatever her deeper sense of self or of men, there were soon social frictions. "I think that those years were those of her greatest challenge," her mother would say. "She was a young woman and was the equal of men. At that time that wasn't yet accepted." But it was not only a matter of sexism. At twenty-two she was already unable or unwilling to mask a blunt, impatient, often acid distinction between those who interested her, seemed worthy of her attention and courtesy, and those who did not. "She was direct, she could be sharp, but she could also be very warm to people she liked and trusted," recalled Alan Bersin, a friend. "In other words," added another male friend, "Hillary could be extremely nice, or else she could be a real bitch. Not a lot in between."

Still, she continued to impress both peers and elders. As she had done at Wellesley, she volunteered to chair stormy campus meetings on protests against the school regarding community controversies, including, in 1969–70, a New Haven trial of Black Panthers, for which she organized shifts of students to monitor the courtroom under the direction of Yale constitutional scholar Thomas Emerson. As always, she seemed at once engaged and strangely disengaged. Ever neutral, coolly summarizing the less artful or more agitated speeches of other, more committed students, the young woman with the heavy glasses and severe demeanor was soon accepted here, too, as crisp campus moderator and the available mediator between student dissidents and a nervous, groping administration—though she made sure, some thought, that she took no stand that jeopardized her own position. "She was so ambitious . . . already knew the value of networking, of starting a Rolodex even back then," a classmate told journalist Connie Bruck. "She cultivated relationships with teachers and administrators even more than with students."

Unlike at Wellesley, however, her role cast her in a different light for more discerning students and faculty. "In the years since, she has dissembled about her own ambition, but at Yale Law School she did not dissemble about her desire to be an important political figure," another related to Bruck for a 1994 profile. "Here were all these great struggles over rights and foreign policy and all the rest, and she always seemed to join the fray yet hold back any conviction," said one peer who watched her. "I think her great struggles may have been over gender and professional opportunity, but most of all it seemed to be over her own viability. Her real cause was Hillary." A veteran of Washington politics in the Kennedy era, Yale law professor Burke Marshall thought her highly intelligent, hard-working, magnetic, but in the end unexceptional, even pedestrian, in her approach to politics. "A run-of-the-mill Democrat," he would call her afterward.

After *Life* published the excerpt of her Wellesley commencement address, she was invited to a League of Women Voters conference of "young leaders of the future," one of a series of anxious efforts by the two parties, as well as by conventional nonpartisan groups like the league, to deliver sixties student leaders from the sins of radical protest. It became Hillary Rodham's introduction to a discreet nexus of Washington contacts—"candidate members of the establishment," as one observer called the younger political figures assembled to mingle with students at such gatherings. There she first met various congressional staff and other capital figures later instrumental in the political rise of her future husband. Typical among them was an ambitious young black voter-registration attorney named Vernon Jordan, who twenty-three years later, having evolved into a wealthy corporate lobbyist, would preside over Bill Clinton's presidential transition.

More immediately, however, the gathering prompted an invitation to speak at the league's fiftieth anniversary observance, and in the spring of 1970, in the wake of the Cambodian invasion and the atrocities at Kent State and Jackson State, she delivered what some would look back on as the most telling speech of her career from Park Ridge to the White House. Her address was suffused with much of the sense of epiphany, and frustration, of the moment, as the character of the

Nixon regime became painfully evident and the shadows of war seemed to lengthen without visible end. "Here we are on the other side of a decade that had begun with a plea for nobility and ended with the enshrinement of mediocrity," she told the audience at the league's national convention, appealing to them "to help stop the chain of broken promises" that marked her coming-of-age. "Our social indictment has broadened," she went on. "Where once we advocated civil rights, now we advocate a realignment of political and economic power. Where once we exposed the quality of life in the world of the South and of the ghettos, now we condemn the quality of work in factories and corporations. Where once we assaulted the exploitation of man, now we decry the destruction of nature as well." They were not powerless, she admonished the largely white, upper-middle-class women, if only they asked and answered the right questions: "What kind of stock one owns? What do you do with your proxies? How much longer can we let corporations run us? Isn't it about time that they, as all the rest of our institutions, are held accountable to the people?"

In terms of what followed, the passages proved stunningly, sadly ironic. It would be as if the Hillary Rodham of 1970 were mocking the Hillary Clinton of two decades later—the Arkansas First Lady who condemned neither the exploited labor nor the environment of her adopted state, who had held her own highly lucrative stocks in a corrupt commodities market and in companies profiting from racist South Africa. She would sit on the boards of, and serve as counsel to, several corporations and would long since have ceased to advocate a "realignment of political and economic power." The evolution of one into the other was foreshadowed by much that was already shaped in her life, and it could be explained further by the most elemental forces of love and ambition yet to play out. But the league speech, soon forgotten, revealed with rare clarity the character of her passage from what she might have been to what she became. Hillary Rodham Clinton had, after all, once known the difference.

Contacts at the league gathering smoothed a next step in her career. One of those she met was a former aide to Robert Kennedy, Peter Edelman. When his wife, children's rights lawyer Marian Wright Edelman, later spoke at Yale, Hillary was instantly impressed and asked her for a summer job with her Washington Research Project. Supported by a Yale grant, she worked briefly at the project and then, on the recommendation of both Edelmans, went on to a coveted staff job with Senator Walter Mondale's Subcommittee on Migratory Labor, studying firsthand the plight of children and their families in wretched, disease-ridden migrant camps in Florida and elsewhere.

Mondale staff aides remembered her that summer, only two years after she worked on the other side of the aisle for the right-wing Harold Collier, as a quiet, dour assistant—"an apparent liberal," one called her—intensely involved in the subcommittee's inspection and documentation of one of the crueler by-products of American politics and economics. Through Don Jones's Methodist youth group she had known some migrant families passingly, but nothing prepared her for what she now found. The experience, she told friends and fellow workers, was "shocking." Late in July 1970 the subcommittee held hearings on the gruesome conditions in the camps, including those run by Coca-Cola through its newly acquired Minute Maid subsidiary. When Coca-Cola president J. Paul Austin arrived at the Senate hearing room to testify on July 24, he was accosted in the corridor by what onlookers, including other members of Mondale's staff, saw as a furious young Hillary Rodham, uncharacteristically emotional and "losing her usual cool," as one said. "She was really something, this young activist breathing fire," a company lawyer said later. "We're going to nail your ass," more than one of them remembered her angrily blurting out at the astonished executive. "Nail your ass."

Austin blandly promised the subcommittee to improve treatment of migrant workers, and the hearings eventually trailed off with no essential change in the conditions. In Washington's enveloping culture of money, exposure and reform had a way of dissipating in discreet irony. When Mondale ran as the Democratic candidate for president in 1984, it was with Coca-Cola's onetime corporate counsel as a ranking adviser and with large contributions from many of the same agribusiness giants who profited from the migrant agony revealed in the 1970 hearings.

Coca-Cola and Austin were hardly the only names implicated in the scandal. Hillary Rodham and a gasping hearing room heard witnesses describe what one called "some of the most squalid, inhuman conditions in the world" in migrant camps in Texas, where the laborers and their families toiled for, among others, a former congressman and millionaire landowner named Lloyd Bentsen. In 1970 Bentsen was a successful candidate himself for the US Senate on the strength of a fortune made in banking and insurance as well as migrant labor—and later, in 1992, would be chosen as secretary of the Treasury in the Clinton administration.

Rodham returned to Yale soon after the hearings concluded. Proud of her work for the subcommittee, she would be visibly angry about the migrant labor scandal for months afterward. Yet that ardor, too, faded. Only seven years later, in an extensive public résumé that listed every other remotely notable accomplishment and affiliation all the way back to her undergraduate record at Wellesley, Hillary Rodham omitted her senatorial staff work on the migrant camps, not to mention her fervent Washington confrontation with Austin and her prophetic speech to the League of Women Voters.

That autumn of 1970 the members of a new law school class were already much in evidence in New Haven, prominent among them a charming, garrulous young man from Arkansas with "Elvis sideburns" who talked proudly about the miraculous watermelons of a place called Hope.

Repeated often in the 1992 presidential race, the story of the first meeting of Hillary Rodham and Bill Clinton at the law school library became a kind of political celebrity folk tale. As another student tries in vain to persuade him to join the stodgy law review, he is staring down the long reading room at Hillary. Eventually she gets up, walks all the way to where they are standing, and says drily, "Look, if you're going to keep staring at me and I'm going to keep staring back, I think we should at least know each other. I'm Hillary Rodham. What's your name?" It is a line, Martha Sherrill writes later, "worthy of Lauren Bacall." In Clinton's own version, it leaves him uncharacteristically speechless, grappling for his own name.

In terms of both the private turmoil and public gravity of the relationship that followed, the charm of the story was less revealing than the roles of the two people at the moment. The young woman of studied plainness, always proving her seriousness, is in effect picking up the tall, handsome, story-spinning Southerner she has unavoidably noticed around campus. He, who has been tirelessly selling himself like Hope watermelons to everyone for years, suddenly finds himself the customer. As the two of them described it later with obvious candor, both fell in love with the unexpected—or at least the novelty in their own felt experiences. "He wasn't afraid of me," she would explain. "I could just look at her and tell she was interesting and deep," he told one writer.

Before the introduction in the library, he had tried to approach her but had held back as perhaps never before; for a time he even sheepishly "stalked her," as Gail Sheehy described it. "I had just broken up with another girl," Clinton told a biographer, and there was no question that Hillary Rodham was only the latest in a long line of encounters for him. "Before Bill Clinton, Hillary had dated a number of men at Yale," her own biographer wrote later. Others remembered men "in and out" of her life, as Donnie Radcliffe related. But one man who did see her socially before Clinton insisted that she had been with no one often—or in an intimate relationship, as she was with Clinton from the beginning. "She certainly wasn't his first, but he may well have been hers," he said, "and that's as significant as anything else in what followed."

◆   ◆   ◆

Entering the law school that autumn, William Coleman III was the son of a well-to-do Nixon cabinet secretary and one of ten African American students in a class of 125. He remembered in particular the "friendly fellow with a southern accent and a cherubic face . . . plopping himself down at the 'black table,' " around which Coleman and his fellow African Americans promptly segregated themselves in the law cafeteria. But Bill Clinton soon drew them in, as he had so many others, with his cheerful openness and infectious conversation. "He had the gift of a true storyteller," Coleman would say. "He could take the simplest event and, in retelling it, turn it into a saga complete with a plot and a moral."

Along with the personableness was an ease about, almost a condescension toward, the law school courses most others took far more seriously. Yale friends remembered Clinton's joining a "countercourse" during the first semester, a student-organized study group trying to reach beyond interpretations or opinions in the prescribed curriculum, and his carefully writing and rewriting occasional papers. None of his peers doubted how bright, quick, or articulate he could be behind that soft drawl. But here as elsewhere, he was more practice and persona—jaunty, warm, magnetic, ever sincere—than substance or conviction. Over their three years in New Haven, Coleman and several others thought him "somewhat casual about his formal studies," attending few classes, paying little attention to significant precedent cases or legal and constitutional theory, avidly reading murder mysteries or novels but rarely the law itself. "He did not spend lots of time trying to master *Marbury v. Madison*," a classmate said bitingly. What they did recall was his inveterate last-minute cramming. Three weeks before the end of the term Bill Clinton would borrow several sets of notes from his more conscientious friends, hide himself away, and emerge to do "quite well," as one of them put it, on the final examination.

There was never any coyness at Yale about his patent ambition to run for political office at the earliest opportunity. Nor was there disapproval or discouragement from peers or faculty. "He was a very good student, he's very, very smart. But I'd never have thought Bill Clinton was law-firm material," Burke Marshall told a writer. "He was obviously going to be a candidate." Clinton was unashamedly someone, said a Yale roommate, "who at the age of twenty-four was prepared to define himself as a politician." As at Georgetown, his boyish gregariousness and seeming lack of artifice dispelled any suspicion or distaste. "After all, nobody in law school was cheerfully announcing, 'I'm going to be an ambulance chaser,' but what he did was a little like that," remarked one classmate. "In Bill Clinton there just didn't look to be any real cunning, though that, I guess, was the point." The backwardness of his home state could even justify to some the skimming and skating through law school. William Coleman thought "his ambition . . . so reasonable," the plan to put "a political apprenticeship ahead of scholastic pedigrees" quite practical, because Clinton would have a realistic chance of being elected in "the congenial environment of a small state" like Arkansas. "To Clinton," as Gail Sheehy summed up how most of them saw him, "law school was just a credential."

Lost in the prodigal image, of course, was something deeper, and less flattering to them all—the implicit assumption that politics and high public office might require credentials or prestige but not serious substance or knowledge, that a would-be state governor, say, *needed* to be glib and facile, *needed* to cram, do well on the final, and move on. "Whatever it tells you about Bill Clinton," one professor said of the future president's approach to Yale courses, "it tells volumes about this law school." Clinton discovered early that the heralded "paper chase" was not often the television image of dedicated, grinding, overworked law students extending the frontiers of justice. "Let's face it. I taught a kind of vo-tech for Wall Street mechanics and other shysters," one disillusioned professor said later. "There were the few serious and the many hacks, and the curriculum was such that they all did well." "In many ways it was a sausage factory," said another who studied, taught, and then administered at Yale Law, "an impressive trade school, but a trade school nonetheless."

Only weeks into the 1970 fall term Clinton moved to a four-bedroom beachfront house on Long Island Sound about twenty-five miles south of New Haven, sharing it with Coleman, fellow Rhodes scholar Doug Eakeley, and Don Pogue, a midwesterner from a working-class family. The breezy house soon became a popular social venue where Clinton's classmates remembered his relish and conquest of young women and, in seeming equal measure, his gluttony—his frying everything in sizzling, spattering grease and then customarily devouring it "in one continuous motion from frying pan to plate and into the mouth," as one housemate recalled with amazement.

One of the few sixties student radicals in their circle, Pogue thought his new friend from Hot Springs had "a reserve of decency towards everybody he met that just kept him going." While Clinton talked long and agreeably with other students—with Coleman and other African Americans, deploring Arkansas's racist politicians like Orval Faubus; with Eakeley, pressing the virtues of southern literature—he argued long and loudly with Pogue about foreign policy and, most often, about the advantages and pitfalls of "working within the system," as Coleman recalled. He left behind no enemies from these arguments, they agreed, but also no doubt about "his commitment to politics"— that he would embrace the system as he found it, as he had already embraced it, smilingly confident he could handle any compromises a Don Pogue might warn against.

Clinton was as frequently absent from the beachhouse as from Yale classes, absorbed in a series of political campaigns and other part-time work. Though he had been given a Yale scholarship and continued to receive ample subsidies from Virginia's seemingly inexhaustible resources back in Hot Springs, he took various jobs to eke out expenses, teaching in a community college, working for a local city councilman, and investigating civil cases for a New Haven lawyer, a job that afforded him a fleeting glimpse of the teeming backstairs of urban America. "I wound up going into tenements where people were shooting up heroin, doing stuff like that," he once recalled. "I mean, I had some interesting jobs." (The next time he was near such casual drug use would be in very different surroundings and circumstances, at the posh cocaine parties of Little Rock speculators and his own political funders more than a decade later.) His errands into the inner city as a law student were the future president's only authentic exposure to this portion of the nation's underside. He would never work again at the street or neighborhood level of that world of chronic poverty and deprivation, never live in or around it, never genuinely touch its urban or even worse rural reality in Arkansas—never even tour its wreckage except in the crafted, sheathed role of candidate or officeholder.

Clinton's principal jobs continued to be political. At Yale he would work in the campaigns of a Connecticut state senator and a local mayoral candidate. But the more significant experience and connections came at the federal level. Back from Oxford, he had used his Rhodes contacts, notably Rick Stearns, to get a job for the summer of 1970 with Project Pursestrings, a Washington lobby backing the Hatfield-McGovern amendment to cut off appropriations for the Vietnam War. There he met Carl Wagner, a future Democratic political consultant and backer, and Anthony Podesta, who in turn steered Clinton that autumn to the US Senate campaign in Connecticut of the Reverend Joseph P. Duffey. An antiwar insurgent and former Gene McCarthy supporter, Duffey had won a primary against the old Democratic machine and was running in a tortuous three-way race in the general election. On one side Duffey faced the scandal-ridden incumbent Democrat Thomas Dodd, who had dropped out of and then reentered the race as an independent, and on the other a lavishly financed Republican congressman, Lowell Weicker, heir to the Squibb drug fortune.

As his classmates were buying law books and taking notes at their first lectures, Bill Clinton was busy organizing for Duffey the precincts of Connecticut's Third Congressional District, a heavily industrialized, largely Italian area gerrymandered out of New Haven and surrounding towns. The mainly ethnic, evenly divided blue- and white-collar constituency was resentful of Yale and fearful of the small but exceptionally vocal African American community around the university, which amounted to a mere 2 percent of the district population. Nominally Democratic, the district was represented in Congress by what amounted to a right-wing Democrat who voted consistently with the Nixon White House on root issues of class.

Building on past third-party congressional antiwar candidacies in the district, using the most advanced methods of telephone banks, data files, and student volunteer canvassing door-to-door, Clinton would mobilize the Third District for Duffey, everywhere emphasizing the minister's reasoned argument against the war but avoiding more volatile, if basic, economic and social issues. Despite Clinton's efforts, Duffey was to split the usual Democratic machine vote with Dodd and lose decisively to Weicker statewide. The gain for the law student from Arkansas was in further contacts: Duffey himself was a chairman of the Americans for Democratic Action and would be a future official in the Clinton administration, while Duffey's campaign manager and eventual wife, Ann Wexler, became a prominent Washington political consultant, corporate lobbyist, and Clinton backer.

What was to be called in 1992 a New Democrat would derive in large part from Bill Clinton's experience in Arkansas in the 1980s and from a thinly refurbished version of the old mercantile southern Democrat of the earlier postwar years. But in some measure, it would trace to Connecticut's third district in 1970, where a beset middle class might deplore "radicals" or resent assertive minorities, might be prey to reactionary manipulation, and still be efficiently organized to vote Democratic without confronting their fears or ignorance.

◆   ◆   ◆

Once asked if she had ever experienced one of those "ecstatic . . . modes of living" she had hoped for in her Wellesley commencement address, Hillary Rodham answered without pause, "Falling in love with Bill Clinton." One friend said, "She saw right past the charm and saw the complex person underneath. I think he found that irresistible." In temperament, thought, style, they seemed the ideal complement in a fitful new era of relationships between men and women, her own conventionally "masculine" force, rigor, endurance matching the best of his "feminine" warmth, feeling, responsiveness. "Rationality meeting intuition," her biographer Judith Warner wrote. Not least, it was the convergence of ambitions. "She not only understood how nakedly he wanted to be president but that he really could be," said someone who knew them through the years. "She got that right away." Many sensed her further calculation as well. "And she's always seen she could have political power with him—just not elected," another intimate told Connie Bruck.

"They have been looking at each other," Gail Sheehy wrote more than two decades later about their famous library meeting, "with mixed feelings of fascination and apprehension ever since."

Early in 1971 Hillary Rodham became a regular visitor and guest at the beachhouse, where the texture of their love affair and alliance became more apparent. Increasingly they seemed a partnership as well as a pair, Rodham helping him occasionally with courses in his otherwise relaxed approach, the two joining as what seemed an unbeatable team in the moot-court competition of Yale's Barristers Union. Under her discipline, they prepared meticulously. She organized the substance of the case, as friends remembered, and they all coached the rambling Clinton to focus on breaking the hostile witnesses. Yet in the end they lost the prize trial. "I just had a bad day," Clinton told a reporter twenty years later, still feeling their shared failure.

He was unrelenting in his own habits, then regretful, reluctant to face her judgment above all—while she could be just as unsparing as he feared, yet abiding. There was, everyone saw, genuine passion and affection, though with blunt edges from the start, and then a marriage of political convenience with pain and bitterness—though never one-dimensional. Clearly one of the most significant love affairs in twentieth-century politics, it is a drama being played out between two people that has immeasurable effect on the governance of a nation. "I can still hear Hillary's humorous and fond admonition of Bill when he would wax a little too eloquent on some idealistic vision," a friend is quoted in a 1992 campaign biography as saying demurely of their beachhouse exchanges. "Oh, for Chrissake," another witness more candidly describes Hillary as exclaiming in the same setting. "Come off it, Bill. We've all heard it before."

In 1971–72, her senior year at law school, they lived together in a small colonial house near the campus, attracting as a couple much of the social life Clinton and the others had drawn to the beachfront, including later advisers and appointees like Robert Reich. To the outside world, Clinton was still the pungent storyteller, although in the fall of 1971 somewhat subdued about his own usually ardent ambition. "The best story I know on them," he wrote in a November 17 note to an Arkansas friend asking about White House fellowships, "is that virtually the only non-conservative who ever got one was a quasi-radical woman who wound up in the White House sleeping with LBJ, who made her wear a peace symbol around her waist whenever they made love." But then he struck a more serious note in remarking on the friend's own political ambitions. "If you can still aspire, go on; I am having a lot of trouble getting my hunger back up, and someday I may be [so] spent and bitter that I let the world pass me by." He concluded the typewritten letter on Yale Law School stationery, "So do what you have to do, but be careful."

To what Dorothy Rodham herself admitted was a "chilly" reception, Bill Clinton visited Park Ridge during Christmas vacation. "To be honest, I sort of wanted him to go away," the mother said about opening her door to the first young man remotely serious about twenty-five-year-old Hillary. "I knew he had come to take my daughter away." He stayed with them "a whole week," as she remembered. The Rodhams were at pains to ensure that Bill slept in one of the brothers' rooms and that "he stayed in there." Typically, Dorothy was soon charmed by Bill Clinton's encouraging her to go to college and his readiness to discuss her academic interests with her, signs of respect she had quietly longed for and never been given in her comfortable suburban house.

They talked politics incessantly. "It was always the same subjects," she recalled. "Okay, you'll go back to Arkansas to realize your ideas, but what about my daughter?" Dorothy Rodham asked the tall, handsome young suitor at one point. It was the question of a woman who had sublimated herself and hoped for more for her daughter. Clinton had already announced his intentions to his own family. "He told them long before that he would never marry a beauty queen. He was going to get the smartest girl in the class," said a longtime Arkansas friend. "You have to remember," said another, "that Billy grew up where women who dressed flossy and used a lot of cosmetics were 'available,' and he wasn't ever going to *marry* that kind." Leaving from the Little Rock airport after a brief visit in 1971, Bill had turned to Virginia suddenly and blurted out, "Mother, I want you to pray for me that it's Hillary, because if it isn't Hillary, it's nobody."

Virginia met her in passing during a trip to New Haven. But it was not until Bill brought her to Hot Springs in 1972—the young woman looking particularly plain and "scraggly," as the mother remembered—that the first of many clashes took place. Bill had been coming home lately with "so many girls from all over," Virginia would reminisce, "all beauties" he took around to his favorite haunts and then out to the lake for a speedboat ride. Now there was this girl "with no apparent style." Virginia and sixteen-year-old Roger were disapproving and distant to the point of rudeness. When Hillary left the room to unpack, Bill took them both aside for an angry rebuke, his eyes boring through them, Virginia wrote, "like my mother's used to do." He told them then, according to the family story, "I've had it up to *here* with beauty queens. I have to have somebody I can talk with."

His scolding suppressed the mother's hostility for the moment. It was only the beginning, Virginia admitted later, of "a long, long road ahead of us." At the same meeting she thought Hillary "quiet, cool, unresponsive . . . offended." She was right. "The tension and contempt for the mother was there from the first time she set foot in that house," said a Rodham family friend. "She didn't particularly care for Arkansas, and she sure as hell didn't care for her future mother-in-law and nasty little brother-in-law."

Afterward they all explained the instant and enduring mutual dislike by what Bill Clinton himself called "a kind of cultural tension" between the distinctive Arkansas mother and the Chicago suburban daughter-in-law, by Virginia's later confessed envy of Hillary's intelligence, and even by some underlying similarity between these two strong, strikingly different women. "Well, the only thing I know," Virginia remembered Bill's telling her, "if you and Hillary don't like each other, then you don't like yourself."

· 9 ·

Yale II

"She Never Drew Her Identity from Him"

In the autumn of 1971, the Duffey forces in Connecticut had called on their former organizers to join the presidential campaign of Senator Edmund Muskie of Maine, Humphrey's running mate in 1968 and now the putative front-runner for 1972. "We got everyone in the room except Bill," Ann Wexler recalled. "He said quietly and firmly that he was for McGovern."

Against a cautious, grinding Muskie, already a captive of the party's Washington establishment and its major individual and corporate contributors, George McGovern embodied both an authentic commitment to end the war and, seemingly, a more open, representative governance. The earnest South Dakota senator would attract at the grass roots hundreds of potential insurgents against the Democrats' constricting core of Washington lobbyists and hangers-on, who gravitated to Muskie or even the spent Humphrey. Though many McGovern operatives were eventually absorbed into Washington's mercenary culture, two decades later the old distinction from 1972 still marked the Clinton administration. Onetime McGovernites became lesser officials in the White House and various departments, while many in the cabinet and among Clinton's senior advisers in economic policy and foreign affairs were former Muskie or Humphrey backers. "It's a little too clear who won in the end," one of them would say.

Weeks before the Duffey meeting, Clinton's earlier contacts around Project Pursestrings—Carl Wagner, Anthony Podesta, and Rick Stearns (who was among the first hired by the McGovern campaign)—had led

153

to an offer to play a meaningful role in the challenger's race. "We gave Bill Clinton in his twenties a chance to direct whole states in a presidential campaign, and to be a player in Arkansas as well," said one former McGovern adviser. "Hell, he couldn't turn it down even though a lot of us knew that deep down he probably preferred Muskie and those people."

A year later, in October 1972, McGovern having won the nomination to run against Nixon, one of the senator's aides, Sarah Ehrmann, drove out early to the airport in San Antonio, Texas, to meet the candidate as he arrived for a rally at the Alamo. She was surprised to find someone already there on the tarmac, eager to greet the campaign plane, "a tall young fellow dressed in a white linen suit," as she remembered him, "standing at the foot of the stairway." That's Bill Clinton, another aide said. He was one of the campaign's state coordinators in Texas and would be briefing McGovern personally on the events and politics at hand. Talking later to the figure in the ice-cream suit, Ehrmann was duly impressed. "That kid is really going somewhere," she remembered saying to herself.

The scene in San Antonio came at the climax of a pivotal period for Clinton. Both he and Hillary, who volunteered to do voter-registration work for the Democrats, spent much time in 1972 away from Yale, particularly in Texas, at one point sharing a small apartment in Austin with Taylor Branch, also a McGovern volunteer and a future biographer of Martin Luther King, Jr.

Canvassing as a registrar in the dusty sun-bleached barrios of San Antonio, Hillary Rodham thought her rounds "a big eye-opener," as she later told the *Arkansas Times*. She had always believed that "politics is the process of change—you get involved and you can affect the outcome." But in Texas she found "stunning" indifference, apathy, and fear. These were "American citizens," she remembered in evident astonishment, "who *wouldn't* register to vote."

Clinton's own experience, as a McGovern envoy within the protocols and rites of the state Democratic organization, was as different from hers as the world of party politics was from that of ordinary people. Texas liberals were behind McGovern. But they had to be kept happy as the campaign reached out to appease Bentsen and other conservatives as well. Here, as in so many other states, the process was played out less in substantive issues than in acts of petty tribute—seating arrangements at a rally, private moments with the candidate or his people, due deference to minor satrapies. Branch found himself appalled at the contrast of "the gravity of the issues at stake with the silliness of the decisions we had to make on a daily basis.''

Bill Clinton "loved the game," Branch remembered. He moved from faction to faction, audience to audience, with an instinctive and utter fluency, paying every obeisance, telling each just what they wished to hear. "He seemed fully at home in a roomful of county chairmen or a roomful of radicals," according to Branch. "Look, we've got to expand our base to appeal to people who don't see the world the way we do," Hillary remembered his "always saying" in 1972. But in sprawling oligarchic Texas he made expedient campaign allies rather than converts to McGovern.

Working out of Austin, Clinton met an ambitious local operative, Onie Elizabeth Wright of Alpine, Texas. Shrewd and acerbic, she was a chain-smoking organizer who had been an activist at the University of Texas in the 1960s and the youngest president ever elected by the state's Young Democrats. Later known in Little Rock as the "enforcer," the proud, fiercely devoted, crisis-managing Betsey Wright was to be one of Clinton's closest advisers and a tireless gubernatorial chief of staff for nearly a decade. By the 1992 campaign she was entrusted to guard his most personal and redolent Arkansas files as well as to compile dossiers to discredit knowledgeable local critics. Still later, though a lobbyist pointedly outside the administration, Wright was once again the de facto damage-control officer coping with revelations of prepresidential philandering and other Arkansas scandals. But in 1972 she was simply a Texas country girl in awe of the extraordinary young couple living with Branch. "I'd never been exposed to people like that before," she remembered. "I mean, they spent the whole semester in Texas, never attended a class—then went back to Yale and aced their finals. They were breathtaking.''

That fall of 1972, as Betsey Wright and others apparently did not know, Hillary Rodham had already graduated from Yale Law School and was doing independent research for the university that allowed for political diversion, while Bill Clinton, in his senior year, was sloughing off his classes and showing up to cram for finals much as usual. Wright, an ardent feminist herself, thought the serious young lawyer from Park Ridge might possess the drive and ability to lead a new generation of women politicians and once told a friend she was more impressed with Rodham's potential than with Clinton's. Rodham hardly seemed ready to determine her next step, much less to commit herself to a life in politics. Branch remembered that, "whereas his purpose was so fixed, she was so undecided about what to do.''

Before Texas Clinton had worked for McGovern in Connecticut, where he extracted from the national campaign the authority to make his first real political foray into Arkansas. In early June 1972, with McGovern already assured of the nomination, Clinton went to Little Rock to mend political fences at the Democratic state convention prior to the national convention and, most of all, to establish his own presence. Whenever home from Yale, he ritually made rounds at the state capitol, enlisting Raymond Clinton's old Hot Springs contacts like Arkansas House Speaker Ray Smith to introduce him to legislators and other local politicians. Now, only weeks short of his twenty-sixth birthday, he came as one of the presidential candidate's men, suddenly dealing with Arkansas's ranking Democrats as a peer and—equally important—with the local media as the prodigal he would represent to them for long to come. Cultivating McGovern support without offending Arkansas's powerful congressman Wilbur Mills in his vain favorite-son candidacy, he was "treading softly in Arkansas political circles," the Arkansas Gazette prominently reported. "I was asked to come to Arkansas essentially to make as many friends as I could," he said of his deferential contacts with Mills, Governor Dale Bumpers, and others.

In an interview that emphasized his impressive credentials at Georgetown, Oxford, and Yale, Clinton pointed out that his formative experience in politics, unlike that of most other young people of his generation, was not with a Gene McCarthy or a Bobby Kennedy but in the ranks of familiar, respectable homegrown Arkansas politicians like Frank Holt and Senator Fulbright. Despite doubts about McGovern in the South, native son Bill Clinton would work with anyone, regardless of their views.

In the aisles of the state convention, Clinton would be far more aggressive. Claiming to have inside information on the various races, he tried to pressure delegates into withdrawing in favor of McGovern supporters who would vote for his man on a second national-convention ballot after the pro forma Mills delegates were released. Stephen Smith, then the youngest state representative, whom Bill had met at the capitol in Little Rock the year before, resisted his blandishments, won a delegate race, and nonetheless became a fast friend of Clinton's, going on to become one of his aides.

The sequence was a small foreshadowing of the public and private Clinton, a congenial image and rather more conniving reality. Campaigning for McGovern against Nixon in Arkansas in the summer of 1972, Clinton carefully avoided the great issues of the day: Nixon's racist appeal throughout the South, the GOP attack on poverty programs vital in Arkansas, a major escalation of the war that May as the US carpet bombed Hanoi and mined the port of Haiphong, even the Watergate break-in of only weeks before, which was already linked to the White House. He was "light stepping" in a "ticklish situation," the *Gazette* observed sympathetically of the young man it called "a good politician."

Meanwhile, coming with him to Arkansas for the first time, Hillary Rodham seemed typically less concerned with appearances. While he made the rounds to see his old circle in Hot Springs, including former girlfriends, she stayed home reading. Several people noticed. "There were hardly any other women who had been in Bill's Clinton's life who didn't try to spend all their time with him," said a former date. "She had her own interests and never drew her identity from him."

◆ ◆ ◆

"The wonderful thing about going into a McGovern headquarters is to find that there is no ego-tripping," Clinton told an Arkansas reporter on the eve of the convention that July in Miami. "Most of us on the staff—however good we are—realize that we are only mediaries [*sic*]," he said, diminishing his behind-the-scenes performance at Miami. Through Stearns and others high in the campaign, Clinton had positioned himself to be the nominee's sole coordinator for the Arkansas delegation. His small desk and direct phone to the floor were jammed in among other state coordinators' in the "boiler room," the candidate's mobile trailer drawn up next to the arena—where the operation would be generally known for its freedom from the usual petty jockeying, jealousy, and hierarchy. As many remembered vividly, however, Bill Clinton and his state were the glaring exceptions.

"He was going to *be* somebody in Arkansas, which was not the case with others on the staff, and so he *did* Arkansas. You couldn't touch Arkansas, no contact by anyone other than Clinton, like barbed wire around the state," said one McGovern aide. "You'll always have to work through Bill on Arkansas," a caucus worker remembered being told. If anyone encroached on the authority Clinton reserved to himself they faced not the usual sunny smile but a florid, yelling rage. "Hell, he really blew up at the slightest cross on that," said a coworker. But Clinton had the ranking Rick Stearns "running cover," playing the "enforcer or protector" for him. "I'm working the phones inches away from him," one campaign coordinator in the boiler room remembered, "and I resented that I couldn't talk to [Arkansas delegate] Brownie Ledbetter or anybody else on resolutions or other things I was working on. A lot of us resented it." "You didn't horse around," said yet another McGovern aide, whose desk was only a few feet away from him. "Bill Clinton was going to be governor of Arkansas or something, and everyone came to see it was a lifetime ambition, that he was obsessed."

On the convention floor, meanwhile, there was the desired effect. Hot Springs's own Bill Clinton was the voice on the headquarters-to-floor phone, from the inner chamber of power. Arkansas delegates, many decisive in Clinton's career, saw and heard him once more as a prodigy, already influential at the national level. "I was thoroughly impressed at how well this twenty-five-year-old Yale student moved among the famous and powerful in the party," said Stephen Smith, who like others was unaware of the "barbed wire" around Arkansas in the boiler room. Among Clinton's Miami delegation conquests, too, was a thirty-seven-year-old Springdale, Arkansas, lawyer and former Fulbright aide, James B. Blair, whose inseparable connections and advice were to be not only vital in Clinton's political rise but also instrumental in the personal enrichment of Hillary Rodham.

◆　◆　◆

In November, barely six months before the first testimony to Watergate prosecutors and Senate investigators, Richard Nixon won reelection with a landslide of nearly eighteen million votes, the largest numerical margin in American history. As Clinton and Rodham watched their efforts overwhelmed in usually close-run Texas, Nixon crushed McGovern by more than a million votes, or over thirty percentage points. Only days after the election, at a private dinner in Washington, one of McGovern's exhausted campaign managers, Frank Mankiewicz, fascinated the room with what seemed a frustrated loser's fantasy. "In a little while we'll rediscover the Watergate scandal the press buried for the election," he told them. "We'll find we've elected a crook after all, and it'll all be so ugly that nobody will ever want to know what really happened in 1972."

As if to bear out the prophecy, two great myths promptly fastened in the aftermath of the debacle, despite Nixon's fall. The first was that McGovern's campaign represented an aberrant radicalism in American politics. The second, equally fixed, was that voters had turned in some vast, consciously reactionary tide toward historical reversal of the New Deal, to what Theodore H. White called "slowing the pace of power" in public control and balance of private wealth and corporate influence.

Missing in the simplistic imagery was how diverse and even conservative the McGovern ranks had been, from their mild South Dakota leader on down, how much their common opposition to the war hid deeper differences among them about root issues of equity and power. "The glue holding it together was the war, and people in the campaign really didn't talk about other issues. It was Humphrey and the Democratic hacks attacking McGovern in the primaries, and then later Nixon, too, that sold the radical label. Take the war out of the McGovern camp and it doesn't exist," said one ranking aide. "None of the men running the campaign, like Gary Hart or Rick Stearns, were exactly sixties protesters or real reformers. They were yuppies, politicians-in-training wanting to take power themselves, which some did eventually—not redistribute it or clean it up," another veteran of the campaign reflected years later.

Lost as well in continuing demagoguery around the myth of national reaction was the extent to which American government and politics were being marshaled to intervene on behalf of vested economic power, while the public was supposedly deploring the "intervention" visible in programs for minorities or the powerless. The 1972 election itself would be a watershed in the gushing of big money into congressional as well as presidential races, the corruption growing apace despite the later so-called Watergate reforms in political finance. Not surprisingly, it was the Nixon-Ford regime and accompanying Congresses of 1973–76 that laid the foundation for the bloated Pentagon budgets of the 1980s and other unprecedented corporate plundering of the federal Treasury. "Nobody will ever want to know," as Frank Mankiewicz had presciently told his fellow diners.

As the Democrats moved fashionably and lucratively rightward, demonizing their spurned 1972 candidate, Bill Clinton went with them. "What was so disturbing to the average American voter was not that [McGovern] seemed so liberal on the war but that the entire movement seemed unstable, irrational," Clinton told columnist David Broder in a solemn postmortem on his first foray into presidential politics. "This campaign and this man did not have a core, a center, that was common to the great majority of the country."

Running for office, Clinton would never again mention his once-impressive McGovern ties in Arkansas, and his own politics reflected the post-1972 contrition among certain Democrats, who began to see themselves through the eyes of Richard Nixon, as it were. Though several former McGovern aides arrived at the same accommodation— Mankiewicz himself became a highly paid Washington lobbyist—others stood apart. "Those who were willing to make compromises with the system that took over after '72 were successful, and Clinton was a classic case in point," said one who had been beside him in the boiler room in Miami. "Bill cared enough about the morality of the war," remembered another. "But he was not a liberal who later sold out, [or] a progressive who grew up. He was one of those who was just a lot less liberal to begin with, a Muskie-ite at heart, I guess."

"Clinton may actually have started out that campaign much more liberal than he's let on over the years since," said someone close to him in 1972. "In Arkansas he'd learn how to hide, to be a closet liberal, and having done it for so long, you have to wonder where the 'there' is. What did Bill Clinton take from the McGovern experience? That's pretty clear—at the human level you can have good values, but in this political system, after *that* election, everything was negotiable."

◆ ◆ ◆

They came back to New Haven, still living together, he to finish his law degree before returning to Arkansas for a first political run, she to complete the research she had arranged in order for them to stay together at Yale his last year.

However compelling Hillary's love for Bill Clinton, her postgraduate work in 1972–73 was more than just a convenience. Under a special program of Yale's law and medical schools and its Child Study Center, she was assigned to review the legal rights of children in terms of public policy as well as legal doctrine and judicial practice. Her interest in the subject dated from her study of child psychology at Wellesley and had been furthered by her shocking exposure to migrant children with the Mondale subcommittee and in her study of family law at Yale. The postgraduate project would result in three articles published between 1973 and 1979 in the *Harvard Educational Review,* the *Yale Law Journal,* and an academic anthology entitled *Children's Rights: Contemporary Perspectives.* It was the beginning of a long career of speaking out on children's issues.

Unlike later speeches or lectures, her writing at Yale was unaffected by Bill Clinton's electoral career, and thus they stand alone as rare documents, glimpses of what Hillary Rodham then believed about the society she and Clinton were one day to lead.

Her studies were prompted and funded amid a wave of discussion of children's rights arising out of the political and intellectual ferment of the late 1960s. For a time she worked as a research assistant to Yale law professor Joseph Goldstein, whose edited collection with Anna Freud and Albert Solnit, *Beyond the Best Interests of the Child,* was one of the prominent volumes of the moment, along with social psychologist Kenneth Keniston's *All Our Children,* which she also helped research.

Hillary Rodham's articles from the 1970s, written as the skeletal legal briefs they were, would seem to many relatively ordinary. She stopped short of advocating the emancipation sanctioned by some at the time and appeared to suggest only that the courts stop automatically regarding minors as legally incompetent until eighteen or twenty-one and that instead judges or other arbiters decide on a case-by-case basis if younger children might be competent to make certain specific, defined decisions about their parents, at least on the gravest matters. "I prefer that intervention into an ongoing family," she wrote, "be limited to decisions that could have long-term and possibly irreparable effects if they were not resolved." Her views likely would have been destined only for footnotes in the field had the words not been written by a future First Lady.

Behind the pages were flesh-and-blood choices and family drama— issues such as abortion, surgery, selection of residence or schools, often the well-being and emotional or physical survival of a child. She had already witnessed agonies of abuse and deprivation firsthand while working during 1971–72 in the local federal Legal Services program for the poor and for the New Haven Legal Assistance Association, an organization then litigating with Connecticut over the state's gruesome bureaucratic neglect of foster children. The work left her critical of figures like her former employer and ostensible children's advocate, Senator Walter Mondale, for often casting such human agonies in fiscal terms. Mondale "upset her at times," remembered a New Haven colleague.

Like her experience with the subcommittee on migrant labor and in voter registration in the Texas barrios, this was exposure to another America. Yet later critics would find a disturbing absence of human reality in what Hillary Rodham recommended as legal practice and public policy. "There is something overly abstract and unsatisfying about these articles," wrote one; in them, this critic said, "functioning families are not organisms built around affection, restraint and sacrifice. They seem to be arbitrary collections of isolated rights-bearers chafing to be set free. And there is no indication in her writing that what children want and what they need are often quite different." Some, like Margaret O'Brien Steinfels, writing in *Commonweal,* judged the most important of her writing "historically and sociologically naive." Though Steinfels and others do not, of course, suggest as much, it is not hard to see the shadows of Park Ridge and Hillary Rodham's oppressive father behind the young woman lawyer of the 1970s who is sometimes angrily "opposed to the principle of parental authority in *any* form," seeing advocacy of children's rights as "another stage in the long struggle against patriarchy."

Her proposal for children's legal competence "amounts to a defense of bureaucracy disguised as a defense of individual autonomy," concluded the eminent historian Christopher Lasch, who thought her an unoriginal echo of earnest reformers of the early twentieth century. "Only trying to help," as Lasch described their unctuous credo, the "child savers" of the Progressive era left behind a structure of arbitrary state power as prone to its own abuses of children as any torturing family was.

But what may have been most revealing about Rodham's Yale writing was not so much psychological or historical as political. Behind her explicit indictment of "incompetent" families was a looming reality no juvenile court or earnest social program could touch. If families were disintegrating, if there were cruel deficits in neighborhoods, schools, and institutions, the havoc could be traced to the very heart of the nation's society and culture—and to a political system that served the special-interest arrangements that made the country what it was.

America's children were the most naked results of those values, that array of power and priorities. Theirs was the highest toll under the rule and example of the political fixers' market, in which corporate giants gorged while schools and other public institutions starved, in which vast official subsidies and exemptions to wealth were only good business while public day care and health insurance and free higher education were insidious dependence and state interference. It was children who suffered most the destructive, stunting bondage to rampant commercialism and material consumption. Most of all, there was the immutable lesson that American children sooner or later learned so graphically, that in the "real world" money and power—and their inevitable companion, hypocrisy—are what prevail and endure, nowhere more plainly or cynically than in politics and government.

"Unless we have a family policy in this country," Rodham wrote in the mid-1970s, "then whatever we do on behalf of children in relation to their families will continue to be band-aid medicine, lacking clear objectives and subject to great abuse." At no point in her deeply felt advocacy of children, then or later, did she come to grips with the larger system responsible for their plight—the national ideology of private gain and the political culture of collusion and complicity in

Washington and in state capitals. No more now than in her Wellesley study of poverty did she seem to see politically beyond the obvious symptoms of that deeper problem. As it was, the system she ignored continued to make her own advice "band-aid medicine."

◆　◆　◆

Their last weeks together in New Haven in the spring of 1973 were fraught with the tensions of Dorothy Rodham's unanswered question, "What about my daughter?" Several people remembered Clinton's genial possessiveness toward the fiercely self-possessed woman with whom he lived. To everyone he bragged about what a "star" Hillary was, "a little like he owned her," said a friend. For her part, she was completing one struggle for independence only to face a new dilemma of love and ambition. It was not easy to follow Bill Clinton back to Arkansas. "He was from somewhere. . . . He knew what he wanted to do there," she once told a reporter. Her own place and purpose, if she went to Arkansas with him, were far less clear. He obviously wanted her to like and adopt the place. Picking Hillary up at the Little Rock airport on her first visit, Clinton had taken eight hours to drive the fifty miles to Hot Springs, boyishly squiring her to every scenic overlook in the soft green hills, every favorite haunt and drive-in.

"She's a feminist and she's just wonderful," he told his Democratic Party friend Brownie Ledbetter, a Little Rock activist involved, like her, in family issues. She would need a local job that was "not just some make-work thing," maybe something in her field of children's rights. In Arkansas, though, there was little choice in work of that sort—or in suitable work for a woman connected to an ambitious politician.

In the early 1970s, in fact, Arkansas was just awakening to the possibilities of public-interest law. There were only the first grass-roots consumer movements and community action, the first steps toward holding local governments accountable, the first broader civil rights, labor, and gender challenges to the oligarchy that ruled the state. Lawyers and activists who did that work stood to be low-paid, operating out of dingy offices and run-down houses, often unappreciated by their own constituencies, dismissed or grinningly despised by the regime and social elite. They were a lonely remnant facing long odds against the money, lawyers, and politicians of the Little Rock power structure.

"It was a job to help people and maybe make a difference, but not in any conventional sense, somewhere to help yourself or make your husband governor," remembered one public-interest lawyer who knew both. "The name on *those* letters and briefs," another said about public-interest challenges to Arkansas power, "was *never* going to be Hillary Rodham Clinton."

How much the couple recoiled from local public-interest law as a sacrifice to Clinton's ambitions, how much was her personal choice, was never clear, though friends believed the implicit decision as much hers as his. They had agreed on her career independence and the political imperative as well. "There certainly was a period of time when they were working out how they might do this. And I don't think there was any problem in terms of their personal relationship about her independence—he was perfectly open to that—but perhaps her feeling was that she might somewhat harm his political career, which was so clearly what he was aiming to do," Brownie Ledbetter told a writer later. "That relationship was a lot more complex than a lot of people say."

They left Yale in May without undergoing the ritual graduate interviews with prestigious law firms. As he had always promised he would, Bill Clinton simply headed home. He stopped along the way to call almost casually for a job teaching at the University of Arkansas Law School at Fayetteville, where he had once told Colonel Holmes he would be a student, impressing them now with his Oxford and Yale credentials, charming the dean with his apparent guilelessness. "You might want me to come teach up there a year because I'll teach anything, and I don't mind working," Clinton told him, "and I don't believe in tenure, so you can get rid of me anytime you want."

Using earlier Washington contacts as well as her research project patrons, Rodham went back to work with Marian Wright Edelman, now as an attorney for Edelman's fledgling Children's Defense Fund, a foundation- and corporate-financed Washington group that lobbied and litigated at national and state levels on behalf of poor, minority, and handicapped children. It seemed to her friends a natural, defining choice, though in the summer of 1973 she also took the bar exam in Little Rock.

"What in the world are you doing here?" asked Ellen Brantley, an astonished Wellesley acquaintance whom she ran into at the test. She explained that in her Washington job she was required to pass a state bar, could take it anywhere, and had simply "chosen Arkansas," as Brantley remembered.

She had been with the Children's Defense Fund less than six months when she was recruited by John Doar, the new chief counsel to the House Judiciary Committee for its historic 1974 inquiry and hearings on articles of impeachment against Richard Milhous Nixon. A Wisconsin Republican who joined the Justice Department during the Eisenhower era, Doar stayed on under Kennedy and Johnson, conducting dramatic civil rights prosecutions before leaving to head Robert Kennedy's Bedford-Stuyvesant Restoration Corporation in New York. He was a vanishing breed, an old-fashioned GOP moderate, incorruptible, someone reflexively associated with integrity and intellectually respected on all sides. To assemble a staff he had called his old Justice Department colleague, Burke Marshall at Yale, who gave him the names of both Bill Clinton and Hillary Rodham—the latter, Marshall thought, "very smart, very articulate . . . an organized mind." Already absorbed in his congressional campaign, Clinton turned down the chance but quickly recommended his girlfriend. "I'd have called her anyway," Doar said drily.

In mid-January 1974 Hillary Rodham started work with the new impeachment inquiry staff. She was at the lowest rank among forty-four lawyers, who were joined by some sixty investigators, clerks, and secretaries. Most of the attorneys, both junior and senior, came from corporate practices in Doar's circle in New York and Washington. "We were considered the radicals," said Fred Altshuler, a westerner whose legal background was not corporate and who soon befriended the young woman from the Children's Defense Fund. "I think we were both somewhat affirmative-action choices." More typical among her other young associates was the well-connected William Weld, a future Republican governor of Massachusetts. "This was a very conservative, gold plate–law firm kind of group," said a member of Doar's staff, "mostly an establishment posse out to hunt down the heavy-handed Mr. Nixon."

The inquiry staff moved into the slightly seedy old Congressional Hotel, across the street from the Rayburn House Office Building. The job also meant implicit, if not overt, gender discrimination. "Capitol Hill in general was incredibly sexist," Altshuler recalled. Rodham would be one of only three women on the professional staff. Subjected to the usual slights and remarks, she often bristled but was careful here as elsewhere not to appear the zealot. "She was sensitive to the issue, and without being shrill at all," an older male colleague would say afterward in his own telling terms.

In this, her first taste of government, Hillary Rodham was literally surrounded by dirty little secrets, immaculately kept. Doar turned the staff's floor of the hotel into a grated, guarded, wired fortress, sealing off the mounting evidence of the inquiry. He insisted on an air of scrupulous nonpartisanship among his staff and on mute confidentiality with respect to the media and the public. "We're so damned secretive," complained one Missouri congressman on the Judiciary Committee, "that we're going to impeach Nixon in secret and he'll never know it."

She told stories later of being assigned to hear some of the infamous Nixon tapes, saying she listened to one they termed the "tape of tapes" as the haunted president was recorded reviewing his own Oval Office conversations, muttering exculpatory interpolations of what he really meant at the time. But young staff attorneys rarely if ever had such privileges or responsibility. The traditionalist Doar relied principally on documentary evidence and testimony from other hearings, distrusting computers or other electronic "gimmicks," as he called them, painstakingly compiling material on some 500,000 index cards in "a cross-filing system," noted one observer, "with a level of precision that approached life." Nor in the strict staff hierarchy did junior lawyers have any appreciable contact with the politicians or politics of the Judiciary Committee, a grave role reserved to the chief counsel and his most senior men.

Instead, she was assigned under other male attorneys down the line to tend the process of the inquiry, dealing with subpoenas, submission of evidence, the role of White House defense counsel, and similar questions of form. Procedural work, it held her largely on the fringes and was never the sort of exposure that some others received to Watergate's seething evidence of political abuse. Even under Doar's imposed secrecy, however, the staff constantly talked about the scandal among themselves, and, whatever her duties, Rodham had an exceptional vantage point.

Into that spring and summer they worked grueling hours, their lives consumed. Like most of the others, she lived a spartan existence in a single room at a friend's place not far from the Capitol. Doar himself slept in the shabby basement apartment of an old rowhouse a block from the Congressional Hotel. She and Bill were "in constant touch by telephone," wrote Donnie Radcliffe. At one point Clinton scheduled a trip to Washington, and Hillary told a more senior staff attorney, Bernard Nussbaum, who was already in politics, that she wanted him to meet her "boyfriend," as Nussbaum remembered it. "He's really good," she pronounced with casual certainty one night driving home. "He's going to be president of the United States." At that Nussbaum "went a little crazy," as he put it. "We're under a lot of pressure on the impeachment, and here was somebody telling me her boyfriend is going to be president." They apologized to each other the next day and Nussbaum went on to stay in touch with Hillary Rodham over the years, passing legal business her way and, eventually, for a brief and ill-fated tenure, becoming White House counsel.

By midsummer 1974 Doar's methodical work from his index cards reached a climax. The committee pored over more than forty loose-leaf notebooks with their innocuously named "Statements of Information" detailing the generic beast of Watergate. It was John Doar's inquiry, resented and ridiculed by the regular House Judiciary Committee staff, publicly overshadowed by special prosecutors Archibald Cox and Leon Jaworski, that in the end constitutionally dealt with Richard Nixon. Its work brought the formal House vote of articles of impeachment, forcing the president's resignation before a convicting Senate trial.

Despite Doar's precise accounting, the larger and more ominous dimensions of the abuses were publicly understood only after Nixon's resignation and subsequent pardon by Gerald Ford. The political process that disposed of a corrupt president by moving toward veritable impeachment also, in a sense, closed in around the corruption rather than cleansing it. The tainted political money exposed by Watergate, and even some of the more thuggish political methods, would survive the era's superficial reforms in new forms and new places into the 1990s.

For the young woman who handled Doar's procedural issues there were special ironies. Two decades later, as First Lady, Hillary Clinton would witness Richard Nixon's triumphal return to Washington as an honored elder statesman welcomed by the Republican leadership on Capitol Hill and admired even by the Democrats. When Nixon died in the spring of 1994 her husband would lead a national chorus of eulogy and homage. At the lavish funeral in Yorba Linda, California, they would hear Watergate's unindicted coconspirator canonized as a hero and statesman. It was as if the inquiry staff's grim "Statements of Information" had never been published.

◆ ◆ ◆

Following Nixon's resignation in early August 1974, Hillary Rodham made the decision to join Bill Clinton in Arkansas. "It was not on her radar screen," Fred Altshuler said of her going. "It was not the sort of thing she had set out to do." Some thought she would return to work for the Children's Defense Fund, some that she might strike off on her own political career.

A few saw career advantages for her in Arkansas, but "there was some fear on her part that she would simply be an adjunct to him," Carolyn Ellis recalled. "My response at that time," Ellis told Judith Warner, "was that she had no political base of her own, and that she could do an awful lot down in Arkansas with her talent."

For a first job Clinton smoothed the way by promoting her with the University of Arkansas Law School much as he had sold himself. Already introduced by him to the dean the summer before, she called the school in August and received an offer to teach "right away," as they told the story. Nonetheless, she interviewed at the same time with the prominent Washington lobbying and political firm of Williams and Connolly, where partner Steven Umin was ready to hire her. Umin remembered Hillary Rodham as "already the Washington type at the faded end of summer 1974. She knew how things worked here, and she knew her way around the Hill."

Her inquiry staff colleague Fred Altshuler and others saw in the end her hesitation about teaching in Arkansas. "It was not what she had worked for," he said afterward. "She had anticipated something more, and I think she had a hard time with it." He described to Donnie Radcliffe a "poignant" last dinner of Doar staffers at which they all seemed to be going on to "exciting jobs," Altshuler himself to a public-interest practice in San Francisco, while Hillary's future was what they all saw as the backwater of Fayetteville. "I think the ultimate trade-off was the White House, not to mention the ultimate revenge," said another, reflecting on that moment, "and she worked hard to get both."

Their friend Sara Ehrmann drove her from Washington to Arkansas, trying to dissuade her all the way. "Why are you throwing your life away for this guy?" Ehrmann asked when they stopped only miles outside Washington. "We haven't gone that far. You can still change your mind." They were standing at Monticello, where little more than eighteen years later Hillary Rodham and her husband would begin their triumphal inaugural entry into Washington.

They drove into Fayetteville on a warm Saturday, the day of the Arkansas-Texas football game and went first to Clinton's campaign headquarters, a run-down bungalow owned by Uncle Raymond close to the school. A lone volunteer was thumbing through the worn index cards and small wrinkled notes that Clinton, typically, had spilled out onto a desk, expecting someone else to order them all. Hillary Rodham was "stunned," one person recorded, "at the absolute anarchic lack of discipline at Clinton's headquarters." It would not be the last time. From the nearby stadium the two women fresh from Washington could hear the screams, "Sooooieee, sooieeee, pig, pig, pig," the ritual Arkansas Razorbacks' chant of "calling the hogs."

"For God's sake, Hillary, are you crazy?" Ehrmann finally asked her. "How are you going to survive here?"

"I love him," she answered.

The next day Ehrmann watched her determined friend take over the campaign office with her usual command and efficiency. Then Ehrmann heard Bill give a campaign speech, and suddenly Hillary Rodham's sacrifice seemed somehow justifiable, politically as well as emotionally. "I knew that he was going to be president of the United States," the former McGovern aide remembered, "and I didn't question her judgment anymore."

· 10 ·

Fayetteville

"An Aura of Inevitability"

Bill Clinton began to run the moment he returned to Arkansas, days out of Yale. It was the start of a career, a life's purpose, spent solely in the winning and holding of political office.

With long, shaggy hair and an easy style, he was an engaging, if somewhat feckless, young law school lecturer. Students remembered his enthusiasm and "incredible sense of fairness," as one described it, though also that he "was not always well prepared and seemed preoccupied." They learned to endure annoying delays in Clinton's marking of final exams, which came back months late. At a golf tournament on Labor Day, 1974, one of his students stopped play to yell excitedly across the course to another that Bill Clinton "just posted his grades for the spring semester." Still, he attracted future political supporters and appointees among his students, a few of whom came and went in disillusion, others of whom remained loyal. His associations with some would haunt him later in the White House.

As soon as he began the law school job he asked Fulbright to help pave the way politically. The senator called state representative Rudy Moore, Jr., and others in Fayetteville to say his former intern was coming. Clinton immediately made the rounds, pouring out his plans with each new friend and speaking "lovingly" of Hillary Rodham, as one person recalled. Moore remembered the couple's almost magical, instant prominence in the Ozark community—first his, then theirs together—because of "the buildup that preceded them." After only a few days in town Clinton began talking openly about running for something important, and his sheer ability, charm, and enthusiasm seemed to cancel any questions. "It was only a matter of finding the right office," Moore would say, though Clinton saw no need for apprenticeship in lesser positions and never "gave any thought to running for a local office or for the legislature."

In 1973–74 Arkansas had a number of attractive young Democratic politicians, all formidable, all on the move. Governor Dale Bumpers, at age forty-eight, was finishing the second term of what Moore called "an enormously popular reform administration." Preparing to challenge Fulbright himself for the Senate in 1974, the attractive and thoughtful Bumpers was already mentioned as a potential presidential or vice presidential candidate. Ready to fill the governorship was thirty-nine-year-old David Pryor, who had served three terms in Congress, where he had become known nationally for a bold investigation of nursing home abuses, and in 1972 had lost only narrowly a Senate challenge to the entrenched John McClellan. Finally, there was Jim Guy Tucker, widely called a wunderkind of Arkansas politics, at twenty-seven a Little Rock prosecutor, and in 1972, two years later, elected state attorney general. In the summer of 1973 they all seemed to stand in the way of Bill Clinton for years to come. Their eventual dispersion and relative eclipse over the next decade would be one of the crucial elements in his rise to the presidency.

"It didn't take long for him to settle," Moore said later. Barred from high state office by popular Democrats, determined to run for something, he quickly chose the only plausible race in sight, challenging four-term Republican congressman John Paul Hammerschmidt in Arkansas's Third District. Comprising the western and northwestern portion of the state, including Fort Smith, Arkansas's second-largest city, and Fayetteville and Hot Springs, the largely white, rural, blue-collar district was what one observer called "the closest thing to a swing district in Arkansas," the only congressional seat where there had been any genuine bipartisan contest over the past decade. The so-called mountain Republicanism of its northern Ozark counties, dating to the Civil War, was the only GOP remnant in otherwise one-party Democratic Arkansas. But the race was still a long shot for Clinton.

Hammerschmidt, a wealthy lumber company owner with no visible interest in ideas, had upset the district's longtime Democratic congressman in the anti-Johnson surge of 1966 and had since erected his own incumbent's machine. Known amiably around the district as John Paul, he was a common type in Congress, the painstaking tribune who attends to every individual request, claims credit for every act of federal dispensation in his district or state, and, in a routine of power few notice, votes mercilessly against the interests of the majority of his constituents. His House record was relentlessly reactionary. He was against clean-water legislation, publicly funded health care for local miners suffering black-lung disease, economic and social rights for migrant farm workers, lowering the voting age to eighteen, and ending the Vietnam War. He found his passions in support of logging in public parks, "no-knock" entry by police into private homes, and the ravaging of the community-action programs Hillary Rodham and others already deemed pathetically inadequate. On Capitol Hill he became a close friend of another 1966 Republican freshman, Houston oil millionaire George Bush. In the late 1960s the two were often together aboard Bush's speedboat racing down the Potomac, raising a wake and joking casually about young George's becoming president someday.

Hammerschmidt also readily accommodated the great timber, poultry, mercantile, and utility interests in northwest Arkansas and throughout the state. The congressman "ingratiated himself with Democrats and Republicans alike," as one witness put it, and thus was always well financed. "Even by 1974," wrote one political observer, "John Paul . . . had become an institution."

Against such fortified local power Clinton confidently counted on the onrushing scandal and public disillusionment of Watergate; he "became convinced," said one observer, "that Nixon would take Hammerschmidt down with him." Organizationally, the Clinton campaign began modestly. Rudy Moore escorted him around the Third District to meet key Democrats. Rural leaders in the north had made their bargains with Hammerschmidt and were cool to the newcomer, and in the towns "a few of the city fathers," as Moore recalled, "didn't like Bill because they thought he was too young and too liberal." But there were also old ties. On a Sunday he showed up unannounced at the home of a childhood friend in Hot Springs and asked her to coordinate at least two counties, spilling out on the kitchen table the worn pile of four-by-six index cards on which he had carefully recorded contacts since high school. "Bill always kept those cards," said the friend, "and now there they were."

He soon found he needed more rank-and-file names and promptly got them a few weeks later when he befriended Carl Whillock, a University of Arkansas administrator who had been an aide to the Democratic incumbent whom Hammerschmidt had unseated. One night that autumn of 1973, sitting on the floor in front of Whillock's fireplace in Fayetteville, Clinton said he was running despite the odds, and the older man climbed upstairs and brought down his former congressman's dusty card file. Bill reacted to the favor with obvious emotion. "No one but his mother, until then, had encouraged him," Whillock remembered his saying.

"The only reason I ran for Congress is they couldn't get anybody else to do it," Clinton was fond of telling reporters, even though at nomination time there were three other Democratic candidates. In his political debut Bill Clinton was hardly a reluctant candidate. "He showed up at the Pope County picnic . . . our traditional political kickoff," remembered one Democrat, "opened his mouth, and everyone just knew."

Moore and other Clinton volunteers believed their young candidate lacked "political heavy hitters," as one said, "who could raise a few thousand dollars for him here and there." Behind the scenes was a different reality. He did not command at the beginning the traditional party money raisers in the Third District, the older legislators, and local officials and their longtime patrons who would contribute to his later races. Nonetheless, he came to politics in 1973–74 with his own heavy hitters. From the start, Clinton received money from a newer, younger breed of Arkansas bankers and lawyers and from unexpected quarters like the stepdaughter of former Republican governor Winthrop Rockefeller. There were also substantial contributions from outside Arkansas, including $1,000 from New York banker E. David Edwards, money from friends at Oxford, Yale, and the McGovern organization like Texas housemate Taylor Branch, and $400 from one Hillary D. Rodham, listed as "the attorney for the Children's Defense Fund."

But the decisive early sum came in a $10,000 personal loan to Bill Clinton in January 1974 from the First National Bank of Hot Springs—an amount equal to the yearly earnings of many families in impoverished Arkansas. The loan required special help. Making his appearance as he did so often at critical moments, Uncle Raymond Clinton had walked "in and out of that bank in a matter of minutes," said a relative. "Raymond promoted him when he really needed it, you bet he did," said another member of the family. "Billy'd never've got that loan without him."

It had all been arranged at a meeting hosted by Virginia at the Scully Street house soon after her son told her he was running. Cosigners on the otherwise unsecured note were Raymond himself, later identified discreetly on campaign reporting forms as R. G. Clinton, a "retired investor," and G. Crawford, "druggist" of Hot Springs, ever-present Gabe, the backroom bookie operator who had been Roger Clinton's abusive, pugnacious drinking partner. At the same meeting Raymond said he would provide some old houses he owned to serve as rent-free campaign headquarters, and Crawford offered his own private plane as well. "They had all been involved in his raising," the mother wrote later about those men who brought so much tortuous family history and shady ties to Bill's political start. "And now they were helping him become the man he wanted to be."

By late March 1974, two months before the primary, the Hot Springs bank money gave Bill Clinton an overwhelming seven-to-one advantage in campaign funds over his nearest Democratic competitor. It was the first of so many local loans, so many discreet arrangements for crucial support from the very beginning to the presidency itself. His backing didn't stop, however, with banks or the old Hot Springs connections. Clinton had gone as well to his old friend Vincent Foster. Educated at Davidson and Vanderbilt, graduated with high honors from the University of Arkansas Law School just two years before, Foster was already on his way to becoming a partner in Little Rock's powerful Rose Law Firm. The relationship between Foster and Clinton grew convoluted over the years, ending in tragedy after a fateful White House phone conversation between them one night twenty years later. But in 1973, he welcomed back his boyhood playmate with unalloyed warmth. Foster was surprised at Clinton's run against Hammerschmidt. "I . . . questioned that decision," he told a reporter. "But it indicated a real can-do attitude." As always, he was prepared to help. Soon afterward, with the approval of the Rose senior partners who knew the young candidate from the Rhodes scholarship interview years earlier, Bill Clinton enjoyed his first lucrative, anointing political fundraiser among the Little Rock business and financial elite—in the dignified offices of the Rose firm itself. "They did their part and then some," recalled a former Rose attorney who was there.

By mid-May, two weeks before the primary, he had collected more than $36,000, dwarfing not only the funds of his Democratic opponents but the war chest of a complacent, slow-starting Hammerschmidt as well. His primary contributions would eventually total nearly $50,000. It was a small sum compared to that collected in many districts and later campaigns elsewhere, including Clinton's own statewide runs. The money was decisively huge for the time and place. In the dark green hills and mountains of Arkansas's Third District in 1974, the strength and presence it purchased gave him a crucial advantage. In the May 28 primary election, Clinton led with 44 percent of the vote, against three relatively better-known opponents, including a state senator and mayor. He went on to win a runoff with nearly 70 percent. He was a stunningly good candidate.

Clinton had been equally effective and comfortable in raising the money, seemingly without effort much of the time. He had a natural affinity with his funders, aides recalled, his manner as easy in the suites and affluent living rooms of Little Rock as in small-town offices or on the telephone. National organized labor—the United Steel Workers, the machinists, and others—made generous contributions. Yet most of his money came from business, banking, and insurance executives as well as from lawyers who served the same interests—from the constituencies of vested advantage and power more than from any other. "Money from the money folks made the difference then and from there on," said one Democrat. "It was the difference between the white knight who went up against Hammerschmidt and went on to big things and just a smart, nice young fella who once ran in a primary in the Ozarks."

Clinton set an impressive pace, often working eighteen hours in a day. First in a dusty 1970 Gremlin, then in a small Chevrolet pickup with Astroturf lining the bed, he traveled the curving highways across the wooded ridgelines and hollows of the northern counties. He amazed campaign workers with his energy, especially his nocturnal restlessness. At first he used Gabe Crawford's plane only occasionally, preferring to drive and stop at will, but in the last two months of the race he flew often, frantically trying to cover ground. He would land at midnight on remote airstrips lit by the headlights of volunteers' cars, only to emerge eager to shake more hands. "Oh, we've got to talk to these people. We've got to go to that store that's still open," Patty Criner remembered his insisting.

His beard was shaved and his thick hair trimmed, but he was still "bushy-headed and sideburned," as Carl Whillock remembered, and thus faced what colleagues saw as "not only mistrust but also dislike" in the wary, isolated countryside. To win the locals over he invariably reverted to what he was underneath his impressive education: a home-grown boy from Miss Mary's kindergarten, ready to talk through differences, to make it right regardless of what they thought of him or the issues. Whillock, Moore, and others saw it again and again in drugstores, on street corners, at barbecues and potluck suppers. "I was convinced that Bill could persuade two of every three voters to support him," Whillock would say, "if he could have one-on-one conversations with them."

Unlike many politicians who relied on glad-handing, however, he also spoke sweepingly, if vaguely, about programs. The district was poor and correspondingly contemptuous of Washington's "handouts" yet always ready for its own congressional pork. Clinton spoke about the need for more federal aid to education "within a structure of local control," national health insurance that would "help everybody," and political reforms to prevent scandals like Watergate. He was in favor, he told people, of taking aggressive anti-inflation measures, improving teachers' skills and retraining workers, imposing an excess-profits tax and tighter regulation of oil companies in the wake of the Arab oil embargo, when spiraling gas prices aroused fresh anger.

"I was astonished to hear this twenty-eight-year-old law school teacher addressing conservative Rotary Clubs on the dangers of corporate abuse of power," wrote a reporter who covered the race. "Beware of the multinational corporations, he said. The Rotarians applauded." Yet the rhetoric, like the applause, was never alien to Arkansas, whose voters, including small businessmen like the Rotarians, were traditionally given impersonal foreign or Wall Street villains on whom to vent their frustration rather than face abuses—and politicians—closer to home.

Clinton's appeal and reception among such audiences mirrored, too, the larger moment of national disquiet in 1974, when the American economic decline from postwar preeminence was already beginning abroad and at home. Amid Nixon's forced resignation, it was an interlude when a kind of populism—or what sounded like it—was the bipartisan fashion. "Our nation's capital has become the seat of a buddy system that functions for its own benefit, increasingly insensitive to the needs of the American worker who supports it with his taxes," said one contemporary critic of the era, voicing many of Clinton's themes. "Today it is difficult to find leaders who are independent of the forces that have brought us our problems—the Congress, the bureaucracy, the lobbyists, big business and big labor." The speaker was Ronald Reagan.

To many in northwestern Arkansas, the young Democratic congressional candidate seemed to feel acutely their as yet undefined sense of public impotence. "He is most committed to making Congress a body of strength, a body that will check concentrations of power working against the people's welfare, whether it originates from other branches of government or from the private sector," said the *Baxter Bulletin* in an endorsement. "The good government we love has too often been made use of for private and selfish purposes," he told a party meeting that fall. "Those who have abused it have forgotten the people." As for Congress, the challenger would reform it by choosing committee chairs in party caucus and by reducing committees overall, along with the number of committees on which any one representative could serve.

But the political realities that lay behind those "concentrations of power" and "private and selfish purposes" were not a part of his dialogue or agenda of reform—the tyranny of money in congressional and gubernatorial as well as presidential politics, burgeoning lobbies, the narrowing, careerist party establishment he witnessed firsthand in the McGovern campaign. Like Hillary Rodham anguishing over the plight of American children, he began his quest for "good government" with sensitivity and indignation but then approached the essence of the failure, the larger menace, only to walk past it, seemingly unseeing.

Later that summer and fall, under mounting attack from Hammerschmidt for being "immature" and having "a radical left-wing philosophy," he voiced more and more, albeit in coded language, the old prejudices of the district—a simplistic nativism on foreign policy, resentment of government bureaucracy, and on matters of crime and punishment an atavistic sense of vengeance. "We want America's needs to be met first. Charity begins at home," he told the Democratic state convention in September, going on to attack Washington's "wasteful spending and bloated bureaucracies. These middlemen of government meddle with our lives without increasing the common good." At another point he seemed to be talking both about bringing Richard Nixon to account and dealing harshly with common criminals as well.

The rhetoric of that first campaign was, like the money, a portent. It was an often brilliant blending of tone and tenor, of a populism and progressive impulse with an expedient demagoguery and pandering to reaction, that would be Bill Clinton's unique mark as a modern politician. A politics for all customers and all sales, it was "a powerful message," one writer recalled, "which he has not abandoned to this day."

◆　◆　◆

Meanwhile, family crises roiled this first campaign. Before he returned from Yale, knowing Hillary was not coming with him, Clinton had turned on his mother in a series of bitter recriminations. "I hadn't displayed the warmth toward her that was my nature . . . wasn't treating her with the respect she deserved," Virginia remembered his telling her. Her chill reception in 1972 had no doubt only added to Hillary's reservations, though it was never clear how much. "If Hillary had second thoughts to begin with about Arkansas," said one local acquaintance, "she must have had third, fourth, and fifth after meeting Virginia and Roger and seeing where he came from." In any case, what had been only rare in his high school and college years now became more common—shouting fights with his mother that reminded her closest friends of nothing so much as the raging of his stepfather. He would treat her, witnesses thought, as he came to treat other intimates, as he treated his wife, with affection punctuated by tantrumlike explosions, followed by sullen contrition and then the sweetest of gestures and amends.

On the usually redoubtable Virginia the effect of his anger was shattering. Stubborn and proud, basically unreconciled to the distant young woman whom her son had settled on and whose contempt for her and her Arkansas was barely concealed, yet fearing the loss of her son, she took the once-in-a-lifetime measure of apologizing, in effect, for who and what she was. Driving home one day from a trip to Hope, as she related the story, she decided to write Hillary an abject apology. In her mind, she said, she "made peace with her." The younger woman did not reply, and over two decades they never talked about the letter, though Virginia at least felt a sense of relief. "I began to live again," she remembered.

She had married her hairdresser, Jeff Dwire, in 1969, to the initial dismay of her oldest son. Dwire had recently served time for investment fraud, and Bill was at first "apprehensive about our relationship," as Virginia put it. But the impeccably dressed, fun-loving hairdresser was also a bright, warm, engaging man—indulgent toward teenage Roger, tender toward Virginia—and Bill had been reconciled. "Whatever, mother," he told her casually in a call from Oxford when she announced that she would marry only months after Roger Clinton's death. By 1974 Bill had drawn Jeff into the campaign, and Dwire, sensing the tension between his wife and her son's lover, was even given to calling Hillary at headquarters for friendly, conciliatory, implicitly commiserating chats.

Then, in August 1974, Dwire died suddenly of complications of diabetes, and at fifty-one Virginia had lost her third husband. Clinton paused in the race to deliver a moving eulogy, seeing in the dead man a decency and selflessness he had never known in his stepfather yet unconsciously speaking, too, of a legacy that could have applied to both men and in a sense to his own destiny—"the bad with the good, the torment of his past, the frustrations, the unfulfilled hopes." After-ward Hillary sent Virginia a copy of the address with a warm note that was, in its way, a kind of belated response to the mother's mea culpa and plea for forgiveness. "I have never known a more generous and stronger woman than you. You're an inspiration to me and so many others," she wrote. "A letter that meant the world to me," Virginia would call it.

As it was, the mother was characteristically persevering. Enlisting Rose Crane and other neighbors and friends, she threw herself into the campaign, phoning incessantly to gather contributions and volun-teers, covering her big brown Buick with "Clinton for Congress" post-ers and bunting and herself with the buttons, sashes, and hats she would put on for her son each time in eight more races over the next eighteen years. Behind the scenes she had brought together Raymond Clinton, Gabe Crawford, and others for crucial backing and continued to do everything from eliciting old backroom money from the Springs, to buying her son a proper seersucker suit, to staffing his offices. The morning after Jeff Dwire's funeral, after she had spread his ashes over his favorite lake, she was back at Clinton headquarters, "my makeup as impeccable as it had ever been," she said. For the rest of her life she would keep the black size 13 shoes Bill Clinton wore out in his first political campaign.

◆ ◆ ◆

In most followers he inspired a dedicated, sometimes even selfless loy-alty. The campaign's Hot Springs office was in what a visitor called "an undistinguished suite" at the old Arlington Hotel, busy with devoted staff volunteers who unabashedly importuned reporters come for an interview. "We hope it's a good article. Your paper can bring us a lot of votes," one journalist remembered being told "repeatedly" by young retainers who exuded their own "hardihood and charm." It was an early manifestation of the zeal—the constant, often naive promotion and assumptions of shared sympathy—that the press encountered in his presidential campaign eighteen years later. Clinton staffers would commonly project a bitter animus toward political opponents or even partial critics and recoil angrily, almost as if betrayed, when a journalist covering their champion did not soon enter in.

The volunteers were largely women, drawn by the issues and by the candidate's sheer personal appeal. "Former campus politicians, join-ers, and gadflies," as one account called them, they had an idealism Clinton readily tapped into. "These are the kind of people," Michael

Glaspeny wrote for Fayetteville's alternative paper, the *Grapevine*, "who stand in the rain at high school football games to distribute campaign leaflets." But after spending time with the staff as well as the candidate, Glaspeny also saw something less innocent in the slavishness that a Clinton candidacy seemed to produce, if not require. "The workers are influenced by the Dexedrine-like effects of campaigning white-line fever," he wrote in September, 1974, "an inversion that naturally seizes the members of a cult. The volunteers are extremely reluctant to talk about themselves. They constantly mutter the aspirant's name in hushed tones: 'Bill thinks . . . ,' 'Bill feels . . . ,' 'Bill does. . . .' I feel as if I am either in a confession box or am party to the recitation of a first-grade primer: There is a monotonous circularity to all the conversation."

Hillary Rodham soon took over the headquarters in the peeling bungalow in Fayetteville, reorganizing the effort and managing the staff much as she would in later races. In a display of support for both of them, as well as to see their daughter's apparent chosen ground for themselves, her entire family came from Park Ridge to join the campaign for a time, Republican Hugh Rodham manning the telephones, her brothers excitedly hanging posters around the district.

In this first race there were several premonitory signs of problems that would grow. "His mind and operations are mainly instinctual, and somewhat manic, making it difficult for him to focus on only one process at a time," one observer complained. But the liberal National Committee for an Effective Congress, having briefly watched the articulate candidate and his dedicated aides wage their battle, would pronounce Bill Clinton's "the most impressive grassroots effort in the country today." The committee's praise was widely publicized national recognition, the first of much to come. To help out the promising amateurs the committee promptly sent to the Ozarks a professional political consultant, though he had little impact for much the same reason the committee had been so impressed to begin with. "The principal strategist and tactician in that campaign was Bill Clinton," said David Mathews, a future Arkansas legislator who was one of his drivers in 1974.

By the last weeks the race had come down to a plain contest— Clinton's own tempered reformism against the incumbent's personal hold on his constituency in spite of Watergate and the Nixon resignation. The "John Paul factor" seemed to frustrate Clinton's most energetic efforts. "I get sick and tired of hearing how nice Hammerschmidt is!" Clinton screamed at an assistant in the closing days. Like his outburst at the Hot Springs office of the selective service five years earlier, however, such displays of temper remained largely hidden. Hammerschmidt's own deliberate mildness had the effect of shielding his political vulnerabilities. After a handful of initial attacks on Clinton's "radical" views, he said remarkably little about his young challenger.

The cruder smears spread in the Republican campaign had the unintended effect of obscuring Clinton's background for years to come. In 1969 a Vietnam veteran had lifted a mattress into a willow tree across from the University of Arkansas's student union and had camped there to protest the war until his arrest a few days later. Now there were Republican-fed rumors that the famous tree-climbing radical had been Bill Clinton, a myth that would persist in Arkansas politics for the next several years. Then, too, there were whispers about Bill Clinton's being unmarried, a good-looking boy in his late twenties, already beyond the age for settling into a "normal" family life as it was assumed in the hills and towns of northwestern Arkansas. "They were even trying to say behind the door that he was a little queer," said a local editor who heard the gossip.

Clumsy fictions were as near as the Republicans, the Arkansas press, or anyone else seemed to come to the real story of Clinton's machinations to skirt the draft, his antiwar involvement, or even his involvement in the McGovern campaign—any of which could have been liabilities in much of the district. For his part, Clinton said as little as possible about either the war or his role in the 1972 campaign. Behind the scenes, however, he was visibly agitated about how his escape from the draft might be exploited by the Republicans. He was "red-faced scared," said an aide who heard him discussing it with another campaign volunteer, and the result would be the first of many vain efforts to suppress or obscure the record.

In June or July of 1974 Clinton had confided in a supporter, Paul Fray, about the 1969 letter to Colonel Holmes, and Fray, according to his own account nearly two decades afterward, told the young candidate that "he could get into a pickle" if Hammerschmidt somehow obtained the letter. Fray urged Clinton to "try to get the original back." By then the colonel himself had retired. But Clinton again, as five years before, brought manifold pressures on the aging officer, including calls from Fulbright's people, a forceful intervention by Uncle Raymond and his friends, and now also earnest pleadings from Holmes's former associates in the University of Arkansas administration whom Clinton had ardently cultivated in Fayetteville. "They laid down another barrage on the old guy to make that letter go away," said a friend of Raymond Clinton's. Late that summer Holmes would telephone a noncommissioned army instructor named Ed Howard at the university ROTC office and tell him, as Howard put it later, that "he wanted the Clinton letter out of the files." Too junior to act on the request, Howard called his commander, Colonel Guy Tutwiler, then on maneuvers in Kansas at Fort Riley, and Tutwiler ordered him to give Holmes a copy of the Clinton letter but to retain the original. Someone from Holmes's family came promptly to the campus ROTC headquarters to get the letter, Howard remembered. According to still other sources, the letter was soon passed on to Clinton through a university intermediary. Apparently no one noticed or worried that it was a copy rather than the original so laboriously drafted and typed on Leckford Road, and everyone, including the nervous candidate, assumed that "the situation was done with," as Fray put it, and that, in the words of a university cohort in the purge, "this ghost of wars past had been put to rest."

The same day as Howard called him, Tutwiler called back to instruct Howard to take the original of the Clinton letter, as well as any other similar documents pertaining to Vietnam War dissidents, and send them to him at Fort Riley by certified mail. Tutwiler subsequently told Howard that he had "burned the file," since the army no longer kept files on dissidents, at least officially, and that he did not want the correspondence "used against [Clinton] for political reasons." Neither the two army men nor the beset Colonel Holmes—and least of all Bill Clinton—knew then that still another copy of the letter had been made earlier, by Holmes's deputy commandant, Colonel Clinton Jones, who like Eugene Holmes had been appalled by the 1969 episode but who was overlooked by the anxious Clinton camp.

◆ ◆ ◆

On election night they waited anxiously at Uncle Raymond's place in Fayetteville. There were cheers and hugs as Clinton carried some of the old Hammerschmidt strongholds in the Ozarks and other rural areas on his way to winning thirteen of the district's twenty-one counties. But as the night wore on, Hillary irritably began to call the remaining areas where returns were strangely slow. Numbers from Sebastian County and Hammerschmidt-dominated precincts in and around Fort Smith were delayed for hours. When the returns finally came in, it was with notably larger GOP proportions than anywhere else in the district, even where Hammerschmidt was running well. It seemed almost as if those ballots had been in response to Clinton's early pluralities. Clinton would lose his first election by a razor-thin margin, Hammerschmidt slipping back into office with 51.5 percent, the narrowest victory in his three decades in Congress.

"Those votes were just 'lost' for hours, and I have no doubt the election was stolen," one Clinton county coordinator said afterward. "I *know* it was," insisted another in 1993. Hammerschmidt's strong showing in Fort Smith had been combined as well with suspect returns even in Clinton's home Garland County, where voting machines were being used for the first time. "There were nineteen machines in Garland that weren't right," acknowledged one poll watcher years later. "I don't know that Hammerschmidt himself was involved personally or exactly who did it," judged another prominent Arkansas political figure, "but that election was sure as hell stolen fair and square." Determining as it did that Bill Clinton would now go on to Little Rock, to the singular crucible of Arkansas state politics rather than to the somewhat more visible arena of Washington, the obscure and petty local fraud of 1974 would shape the future of the presidency.

Rudy Moore remembered Clinton that night in Fayetteville. "I think he was genuinely shocked that he lost. Most of us were surprised that he had come so close." Though reports and rumors of the fraud echoed for weeks and even years, there would be no challenge of the results. Clinton himself seemed gracious, even self-deprecating in defeat. Before the Arkansas Press Association a few weeks after the election, he deplored the incumbent congressman's advantages of franking privileges and a paid staff but said nothing about the suspect votes. He would now "try to be of whatever service he could to the Democratic Party," said the *Arkansas Democrat,* reporting his modesty and deference.

Everyone seemed to take for granted the victory in his defeat. "Clinton did something during that campaign that I don't know how to explain. He achieved an aura of inevitability. It became a foregone conclusion that he would hold a state office soon," said Bill Simmons of the Arkansas Associated Press. "He was anointed by political elites as a soon-to-be governor or US senator," thought Art English, a University of Arkansas scholar already watching Clinton's career.

Afterward there were fashionable myths about Clinton's underdog fight in 1974—how, spurning a tainted last-minute contribution that might have made a difference, he finished $45,000 in debt, how he had struggled to be "almost as well funded" as his GOP opponent, as *Newsweek* wrote in 1994. The less romantic truth—and, among politicians and their funders, far the most important lesson of the race—was that young Bill Clinton had overwhelmed everyone in campaign finance.

When it was over—not counting all the in-kind and under-the-table gifts of Gabe Crawford's airplane, Uncle Raymond's property, and the rest—Clinton reported amassing nearly $181,000, then the largest amount collected for a House race in Arkansas history and clearly besting Hammerschmidt's $97,000. As a challenger he outraised and outspent in 1974 even the Democratic congressional *winners* around Arkansas by more than two to one and marshaled as much as Dale Bumpers or others in the party had ever brought to gubernatorial races statewide. He had done it by drawing on many of the same sources that would later make him governor and ultimately president.

❖   ❖   ❖

Bill and Hillary lived together in Fayetteville that fall and winter, renting separate apartments for the sake of appearances. Her friends elsewhere were "bewildered," she would say, that she was still in Arkansas. But there were many in Clinton's circle as well, including old girlfriends and women from the campaign, who still wondered about his attraction to her. "It was fascinating to his friends," said one account, "that Bill, with his reputation as a ladies' man, chose . . . the brainy and frumpy-looking Hillary."

After the election she stood back for a moment, not fully joining the law faculty until January 1975. But as soon as the race was over, Clinton turned to their courtship as a campaign of its own, arranging for the wives of political friends to invite her to their homes, surrounding her with the warm hospitality of the culture, drawing her in. "Bill beseeched us to make her feel good about coming to Fayetteville," Carl Whillock remembered. "He was afraid she would feel out of place."

With Clinton himself talking up her impressive background with John Doar, she came to the lecture rooms of the provincial law school as something of a "celebrity," one student remembered. In her "hippie clothes and northern accent," as Judith Warner described her, she "benevolently terrorized her students."

She plunged into her new work outside the classroom as well, becoming director of the University of Arkansas Legal Aid Clinic and setting up new inmates' rights programs at the notorious penitentiaries at Texarkana and Cummins, programs that might have been common in other states but were exceptional and obviously needed in Arkansas. In her first forays into the state's court system she fought blatant discrimination against what Arkansas judges still called "lady lawyers." At the university she pressed trustees to include women in the search for a new chancellor and enthusiastically helped brief a newfound faculty friend and political science instructor for a debate with Phyllis Schlafly on the Equal Rights Amendment before the Arkansas legislature.

At every turn there were reminders that it was "*his* state and *his* political future," a colleague remembered. As part of the prison project Rodham had soon joined in the writing of an empassioned brief opposing capital punishment that resulted in a successful appeal for a convict on death row. Later, when her husband was governor and a presidential contender, she would ardently support the death penalty, even helping stiffen his resolve in carrying out executions at critical points in their political climb. Then, too, though her legal aid clinic saw in a year some three hundred otherwise unrepresented clients, she also spent "a lot of time placating the bar association," as a student recalled, soon agreeing under pressure to place the clinic's criminal cases with the usual local lawyers, whom many poor clients ended up paying anyway, "as if the clinic was just a lawyer referral for the ole boys," said one disillusioned participant. Meanwhile the friend she coached for the Schlafly debate, Diane Divers Kincaid, was soon to become the second wife of Jim Blair, the corporate lawyer whom Clinton had impressed with his "boiler room" mastery of the Arkansas delegation at the 1972 convention. Blair already represented the Tyson Foods chicken empire and other local and regional giants, and the four of them socialized together and became the closest of friends. A prominent Democrat, Blair was in the process of becoming Bill Clinton's most influential adviser and patron. Beyond issues of women's rights or civil liberties, there was always present the larger shape of vast concentrated power in Arkansas, the forces that would determine the Clintons' future.

Early in 1975 Hillary Rodham stopped by a Marine recruiting office in Arkansas to ask about joining "either the active forces or the reserves," as she revealed later. For those who knew her childhood, it was not strange that the daughter of Hugh Rodham would consider the military. Nor was the ethos of the Marine Corps at odds with her deeper political or social convictions. But mainly what she was looking for was an escape from the decision closing in around her that spring. It ended in what became a joke. "You're too old, you can't see, and you're a woman," a female recruiter told the twenty-seven-year-old law instructor. "Maybe the dogs [army] would take you."

◆ ◆ ◆

In the summer of 1975 she set off around the country, visiting friends in Chicago and the Midwest before going on to Washington, Boston, and New York—hoping to discover, as she told Gail Sheehy, "anything out there that I thought was more exciting or challenging than what I had in front of me." Afterward some believed that she was still genuinely looking for alternatives, others that the journey was only a ritual in a decision already made.

Talking with one couple who had been particularly close to her over the past few years, she confessed with painful intimacy what some already knew well in Arkansas, that Bill Clinton was often involved with other women even as he ardently courted her. In the midst of the 1974 congressional campaign, even as she worked eighteen hours a day on his race and slept with him whenever they were together, Clinton was flaunting other conquests on the road. "I met a young woman, the daughter of a prominent Arkansas politician, who told me she was Bill Clinton's fiancée," remembered one witness. "Of course Clinton had lied to her. He was then living with Hillary." Despite all that, Hillary told her friends she loved him and believed in him and would take her chances in the relationship. She would fortify herself for love and marriage as she did everything else, with reserves of resignation as well as grit. "I know he's ready to go after anything that walks by," they remembered her saying. "I know what he's doing, but I'm going to go as far as I can."

"It was two people who needed and fit each other. It was love. It was also a kind of bargain," reflected one of the friends later. "But even at her most cynical or calculating I don't think she could have bargained for what she got." "It was just ironic," thought another, "that she chose so consciously to live out her life through a man when she, of all people, could have led her own." Still others came to believe that there had been a crucial imbalance all along. "There was always this something special about Bill, an identity, a place and a purpose, even if it was Arkansas," said someone who knew them both from law school. "Deep down there was this ordinariness about Hillary. She needed to belong somewhere." Yet most friends would later agree that she made her choice for no single reason but out of some swirling combination of motives—"Hillary's usual mix," one called it. The wounded, derogated little girl from Park Ridge who found resources within herself early, the formidable young woman of potential, now made, they concluded, a Faustian bargain with her own heart—out of love, ambition, disappointment, hope, and perhaps even a guarded cynicism.

After some weeks she headed back to Fayetteville. "I just knew I wanted to be part of changing the world," she told a writer in 1992 but then added what seemed a remarkable confession of the sacrifice she felt: "Bill's desire to be in public life was much more specific than my desire to do good." In her absence Clinton had purchased a painted brick and stone cottage behind a rock wall on California Street in Fayetteville, a small house she had once admired. Now he surprised her with it as he drove her home from the airport. As usual, Dorothy Rodham was more frank than most in her memories. "It was just a little, tiny house, only worth a handful of money. I think there were only two rooms," she told *Paris-Match*.

Her mother flew to Fayetteville not long before the early-autumn date quickly set for their wedding. They were still painting and putting together the small cottage. At the last moment Dorothy took her daughter to buy a traditional white wedding gown at Dillard's department store. Hillary had "not thought that much about it," said a friend; she "was in kind of a haze once it was all set . . . not like her, really."

Virginia had driven up from the Springs and was having breakfast with friends at the Holiday Inn the morning of the wedding when Bill came by and told her he needed to talk with her about something. The table fell suddenly quiet. "Hillary's keeping her own name," he said. He began to explain his own lack of concern or his approval but never finished. His mother burst into tears while the women with her fought to keep from doing the same. "Pure shock," Virginia remembered her reaction, "I had never even conceived of such a thing. This had to be some new import from Chicago." Nineteen-year-old Roger Clinton's reaction was equally vehement, adding to his own distance from his new sister-in-law.

A simple ceremony was performed by a Methodist minister on October 11 in the hastily refurbished cottage, and attendance was limited to the immediate family. Dorothy Rodham's mixed feelings were audible later: "To see these two brilliant students loaded with diplomas, which could have brought them all the luxury and money in the world, there, in Arkansas, in that modest house because they had dreams of realizing their ideals. It was so moving."

The reception followed at the spacious old Fayetteville home of

Morris Henry, a state Democratic chairman. "Hundreds of guests . . . from all over the Third District," as Ann Henry remembered, milled about the house and yard on a balmy Saturday evening. The party turned into one of the biggest political affairs not only in the district but in the state itself. Having shed her glasses and curled her hair for the occasion, a radiant Hillary Rodham seemed unrecognizable to many. Everyone appeared to understand that it was part wedding reception, part rally—that Bill Clinton was running again. At one moment she had made a point of being photographed standing on a step, a head taller than her groom, smiling knowingly at the man whose fortunes were now her own.

Among the guests was Arkansas attorney general Jim Guy Tucker, who was already planning a 1976 run for the House seat of the disgraced Wilbur Mills, a move that would open his current office to Bill Clinton. Here again was a chance to climb the Democratic ladder. The two men had discussed it earlier that summer while Hillary traveled. "Just an absolutely terrific job to have," Tucker remembered telling him. Clinton had seen the possibilities right away, had been "capable," Tucker told a reporter, "of understanding what you can and cannot do with the law."

Clinton had argued that with the coming campaign he could not afford the time for a honeymoon. Dorothy Rodham, however, had presented the newlyweds with inexpensive tickets to Acapulco and had bought them for all the Rodhams as well (pointedly excluding Virginia and Roger in what was called a "family" excursion). "We had a marvelous time," the father said in a rare public comment about his daughter's famous marriage. The couple returned from Mexico that autumn to begin planning the race for attorney general in the May Democratic primary.

Hillary Rodham told friends she would certainly keep her maiden name, as she had resolved long ago as a little girl. She would be "a person in my own right," she assured Ann Henry and others, not the usual "sacrificial" political spouse. When Governor David Pryor's wife, Barbara, was ridiculed in Arkansas that autumn for an exotic hairdo and when the Pryors separated at the end of 1975, Hillary was incensed, showing up at a dinner of Clinton backers with her own hair frizzed in "support" of Barbara Pryor. "I thought that was a real principled thing to do," one of them told Donnie Radcliffe. They had all praised her at the time, and she was clearly pleased. The woman who had once lectured the League of Women

Voters national convention on corporate responsibility and realignment of power would increasingly express her protest and principles in such symbolic gestures.

"Hillary made her trade-offs early on," Jan Piercy said of her Wellesley roommate, "and I think she steeled herself not to look back."

BOOK II

◆

· 11 ·

Regnat Populus
"The People Rule"

From every part of the state they came to listen, parking their old trucks and cars and wagons in the dusty town squares, standing for hours in a burning sun. There were workers with no jobs, owners of small businesses struggling to survive, debt-crippled sharecroppers white and black, anxious young people whose prospects were grim, elderly couples whose savings were exhausted—and everywhere, from the Ozarks to Little Rock to the Delta, the gaunt, unsmiling children standing beside weary parents. Again and again the politician made the same speech. Again and again they nodded and cheered.

"We have more food in this country than we could eat . . . and yet people are hungry. . . . We have more houses than ever and yet people are homeless." They all knew why, he told them. Corrupted by wealth and power, their government was like a restaurant with only one dish. "They've got a set of Republican waiters on one side and a set of Democratic waiters on the other side," he would say, "but no matter which set of waiters brings you the dish, the legislative grub is all prepared in the same Wall Street kitchen."

It was August 1932, and the legendary Huey Long of Louisiana was barnstorming Arkansas on behalf of Hattie Caraway. Widow of a US senator who died in office, she had been sent to fill the remaining year of her husband's term while squabbling Democratic bosses back in Arkansas settled on a successor. But then the petite Mrs. Caraway proved rather too independent, even deciding to seek election herself, and the Little Rock machine set out to crush this upstart woman in the

193

primary. Long had sat next to her on the Senate floor, fondly called her "the little lady" as she joined his votes against monied power in both parties. Sharing her enemies, savoring his own grand ambition, he decided to help her in her underdog race, and now he swept the state in a campaign never equaled, covering 2,100 miles, making thirty-nine speeches to a quarter of a million people in just a week. His purpose, wrote his biographer T. Harry Williams, was "to arouse into a full fury . . . into a genuine class protest" the restiveness of what many saw as the most oppressed state in the union. He would do just that. Hattie Caraway won an upset victory and returned to the Senate. For a few fleeting summer days, telling crowds in the dusty squares what they already knew, Huey Long had "set Arkansas ablaze." In the politics of the place, it was a moment like no other—before or after.

H. L. Mencken referred to "the miasmatic jungles of Arkansas" and called it "the worst American state." Its nineteenth-century founders, a local writer observed with casual certainty, "were a band of thieves." Others described the state more clinically, but the essence was, and remained, the same. In his classic study of southern politics between the 1930s and the 1960s, Harvard scholar V. O. Key thought Arkansas second only to Tennessee for "the most consistent and widespread habit of fraud." As if describing some benighted and distant foreign despotism, Key concluded that the unfortunate state still lacked "the essential mechanisms of democratic government."

Distrust of politics ran deep among the state's settlers, who were fleeing the class-dominated societies of the old Confederacy. As savagely and blindly as anywhere in the South, Reconstruction left still more aversion to government. Built for inaction, the modern state constitution hedged the power of both the executive branch and the legislature. Most tax legislation required a formidable three-fourths vote. A simple majority overturned the governor's veto. Yet the deliberately enfeebled structure proved easy prey for the state's omnipresent special interests. The regime in Little Rock subjected its wary citizens to a new, singularly Arkansan form of corrupt republic. Institutional rigidity thought to protect and curb became the protection of privilege and the curbing of reform. Supposedly passive government was relentlessly active in its insider concessions and favoritism. "Free enterprise in Arkansas," said a beneficiary, "was everything you were free to get out of your friends in the capital." The debauchery of the ruling Democrats was unrelieved, and even the few Republicans relished their own spoils. "About five old men who sat on a porch until there was a

Republican president and then held out their hands for some patronage," one observer said of the state's GOP in the 1960s.

Beneath the political shell lay the implacable reality of Arkansas's economic and social power: the absolute, essentially colonial supremacy of a small financial elite and handful of corporate giants. First had come the planters, bankers, speculators, and owners of tenant farms, then the great extractive industries in timber, oil, and minerals, the big utilities, the huge mercantile and poultry operations. Open to raw profiteers as well as to courtly gentlemen, the Arkansas oligarchy propagated through money and influence far more than through birth or breeding. Its paternalism was now cruel and crude, now mincing and discreet, though above all constant. By the 1970s there had grown a new ganglion of banks, bond houses, holding companies, and, inevitably, law firms. Epitomized by the colossal Stephens, Inc., the nation's most formidable investment banking empire outside of Wall Street, all were bound up by retainer and return, mutual interests and mores, by an incestuous society and political sociology that made up Arkansas's singular culture of venality and power.

The system might seem on the surface almost banal, merely another example of legendary local vice in American politics. "We're no different, just more," one of its practitioners would say. But then, Arkansas's "more" was itself the difference. The state's farmers, found one study, were "the nearest approach to medieval serfdom ever achieved on the North American continent." Examining skeletal remains from the early twentieth century uncovered in an African American cemetery near Hope, anthropologists were shocked to find a people more ravaged by chronic starvation and disease than any other group in comparable findings from either prehistory or the modern era. Observers were invariably struck by the enormity of what a local paper nimbly called "great wealth in a poor state," the spectacle of one of the richest areas in the United States home to such widespread want, such a narrow, exclusive concentration of wealth and power. Inequity of income was vast, with only a relatively small middle class wedged precariously between the exceptionally wealthy and a mass of the working poor or destitute. "Nowhere in America is the range so great as in Arkansas," wrote the *Arkansas Times* in 1992, "from the multibillionaire status of the Wal-Mart Waltons to the abject poverty of the Delta region." A local minister put it simply in 1993: "Oh, there's plenty of riches to go around in old Arkansas. The problem's that only a few folks got most all of it, and it ain't goin' around."

Self-proclaimed populists and reformers came and went more visibly than in much of the South, in a dreary pattern of promise and default. "Transient demagogues," as one writer called them, they were habitually absorbed by the enduring order, leaving ever-hopeful voters only "with memories." Nearly a half century after Huey Long campaigned for Hattie Caraway, the state remained "a wrenching mixture of beauty and squalor," according to a local writer. "It had about one country club—full of rich people and landowners—and two million peasants, sharecroppers, and struggling shopkeepers." Over them all unfurled Arkansas's mocking motto, *Regnat Populus,* "The People Rule."

As elsewhere, racism was a tool of demagoguery and division, masking the root economic exploitation of white as well as black. There had been an exodus of African Americans after the cotton collapse of the 1920s, leaving them scarcely 16 percent of the population, concentrated in a pale of veritable Third World poverty in the Mississippi Delta. The black vote was to be a crucial bloc for Bill Clinton in the 1980s, though civil rights politics on the whole were always less relevant than they were in more progressive states. Grateful to be rid of an overt racism so recent and so ugly, Arkansas's African American community would seem to many largely numbed and complacent—if not politically suborned—in a system that gladly conceded them the forms of democracy without its economic substance.

The state's newspapers and broadcast stations were in the hands of ruling interests, their editors and reporters cowed or bought off. The rare independent journalist was soon made an example. Trying to expose ballot-box stuffing and other corruption through the 1960s and 1970s, publisher Gene Wirges survived nearly a dozen attempts on his life, was indicted seven times on trumped-up charges ranging from slander to conspiracy, and was once sentenced to three years at hard labor, only to be saved when the main prosecution witness was proven to have lied. Arkansas was just like Mexico, Wirges would tell friends, a tawdry one-party dictatorship in democratic guise in which the police and justice system—including the Democratic Party–dominated courts—were used to coerce and suppress dissent. With the equally venal, if less numerous, Republicans cooperating, third-party movements and other organized dissent would be ruthlessly eliminated by both legal means and crude coercion. Naturally enough, many of Wirges's professional colleagues, like the co-opted press of Mexico City, learned early to skate the surface of Arkansas's deeper political reality, tweaking its figurehead politicians but never going too far, never straying into a darker world they knew only through gossip or glimpses in the occasional court case.

By the closing decades of the twentieth century, however, the essence of the regime had become a matter not so much of blatant manipulation as of something more subtle, something unique to a state regarded as a painful hillbilly joke in the rest of the nation. Of the many legacies of repression, none was so ingrained, from the Ozarks to the Delta, as the popular sense of inferiority and resignation, overlaid with fierce sensitivity, a victim's pride and prickliness. It produced still more irony among Arkansas voters: not only a weary acceptance of their lot but a ready, grateful credulity toward politicians earnestly promising to change it. As in the old Communist tyrannies of the Soviet Union and Eastern Europe, there was often only resentment toward outsiders pointing out the enduring disgrace, a native refusal to face reality that further fortified the system. In "modern" Arkansas, gone from tenant serfdom to chicken processing and corporate law with no real break in its caste-ridden regime, morale was a last resort. "We just had to *feel* better about ourselves," one community leader said in 1993, "whatever the realities of politics."

◆ ◆ ◆

"He warn't getting nowheres," poet John Gould Fletcher said of the common man who worked in factories, farms, and small stores. "Them politician fellers in Little Rock had never done a danged thing for him or his kind." The politicians' neglect was not, he might have added, accidental or temporary. Meeting biennially, its lawmakers plied with what a witness called "boodle and booze," the legislature was a haven for incumbents, a bastion of one-party domination. Arkansas's regime seemed to many a perpetual caricature, even by the most notorious southern standards, "a sort of unholy meshing of public and private interests," historian Harry Ashmore had written in the late 1950s, "without any effective restraint from an electorate bemused by other, perhaps more important matters."

So complete was the incest and co-option that lawyers and lobbyists "swarmed on the chamber floors . . . and frequently joined in the voting," according to one observer, while legislators brazenly drew from corporate payrolls. By the late 1960s seventeen of thirty-five state senators still received regular salaries or other retainers from the Arkansas-Louisiana Gas Company. "ARKLA didn't have to worry too much about regulations or rate controls," chuckled one longtime lobbyist. A representative shrugged off the pandemic corruption still flourishing a decade later: "Hell, we wouldn't have a government if there were no interest groups."

Across the domed capitol in Little Rock—aptly enough a replica of the building in Washington—the governor was strong only by default, collusion, or dint of extraordinary effort. Limited to two-year terms until 1986, executive power came "bastardized," as an aide put it— fragmented by tangled jurisdictions and legislative feudalism. Still, the lack of genuine parties or issues lent the office what historians called a potent "personalism." Arkansas governors drew power from their personalities or appeal rather than from sustained principles or programs, and a politics of expedience and manipulation, fealty and personal accommodation became the habit of the office.

In that mold were four somewhat paradoxical figures of the late 1950s on. Son of an ardent back-country socialist, Orval Faubus was both the national villain of the 1957 Little Rock school crisis and a relative progressive for Arkansas, funding education and services, exposing the nightmarish state asylum where Edith Cassidy was committed, and eventually even reaching out to blacks and other opponents after his notorious confrontation. Winthrop Rockefeller, the era's first Republican governor, proved a feckless administrator and fitful reformer, a political moderate but a hopeless alcoholic whom one writer called "the failed hope of Arkansas liberalism." Yet he nonetheless tugged the state forward, courageously leading a chorus of "We Shall Overcome" on the capitol steps after the murder of Martin Luther King, Jr.

Defeating him in 1970 was Dale Bumpers, a small-town lawyer who ran on little money, even returning a check from the imperial Stephens, Inc. Bumpers went on to provide some relief from regressive taxes, create a governor's cabinet, and affect other changes. "They hated him, but they had to work with him," one admirer said, remembering his public distance from the old bosses. "He didn't seem to know you couldn't do those things," an editor commented. Following Bumpers came David Pryor, who, despite his ever-ingratiating pose as "ol' David," was the first to appoint blacks and women to ranking state offices in 1975–78, signaling a break with the traditional whites-only, good ole boy patronage.

All four men modernized the governor's office. All four puttered at the ragged edges of the system. Outwardly polished and progressive while sufficiently "down-home," Bumpers and Pryor both epitomized what a local writer called Arkansas's "more presentable politicians," a refinement demanded by the times and by the comparatively sophisticated patrons of the state's newer financial elite. In their more presentable train, they drew women, minorities, and young idealists formerly excluded from politics. Yet in Arkansas it all happened at the margins of genuine power. None of the four confronted the abiding rules or rulers of a state they governed in name only.

While Faubus lingered as a political relic, Rockefeller dissolved in alcoholism, and Bumpers and Pryor vaulted to the Senate, Arkansas power remained what and where it always was. The speculative bloat of the Reagan-Bush era added to the lineage of old planters and plungers new practitioners of monied control and political patronage. They worked in the discreet confines of executive suites and bank boardrooms, law offices and country clubs, and they lived in the gracious columned houses of Little Rock's White Heights and in sprawling pseudoplantations nestled among the Ozark hills and valleys.

It was in this setting that Bill Clinton entered state politics in 1975. When he left in 1993 he had been governor for twelve years, as long as Rockefeller, Bumpers, and Pryor together. He presided over the prospering political-corporate nexus in Little Rock as no other politician in the state's history ever had. What he did in and for Arkansas, he claimed, qualified him to govern the nation. And in a sense, ironically, his record there shaped and explained his presidency as much as any events in Washington did.

◆ ◆ ◆

"I been shakin' hands all day, and on the phone raisin' money all night," Clinton laughingly told a relative during his 1976 race for attorney general. Behind the banter was a smooth, well-financed campaign in which, as an aide put it, "he was almost handed the key to the office." He "breezed into" it, wrote a reporter. "Willing to hew wood and draw water," according to someone who watched him at meeting after meeting, he prepared through avid work in party organization. Then, against two older, lackluster primary opponents, he far outorganized and outspent both together.

There were many of the same volunteers and in-kind gifts as in 1974, Uncle Raymond's real estate and other offerings, and crucial early contributions of over $30,000, the money flowing principally from banking, insurance, and real estate interests, including funds channeled from the Stephens financial empire in Little Rock. But his campaign funding also listed $15,000 of his own money, a surprising amount, given his meager law school salary. It was cash that came again through the quiet auspices of Raymond Clinton and old family ties.

With a Stephens executive as his deputy, Clinton coordinated Jimmy Carter's 1976 campaign in Arkansas even as he ran his own race, adding national contacts and eventual federal patronage to his strength. He was obviously confident of his victory yet cautious and calculating to the point of turning against original allies. "Believing it hindered his candidacy as much as it helped," the *Arkansas Democrat* noted, Clinton now spurned the union support he had courted and depended on in his congressional race just two years earlier, pointedly refusing to oppose the state's "right to work" law and beginning a long, bitter feud with local labor.

He was constantly advised by his new wife, who was doing freelance legal work that spring in addition to teaching. "She called him all the time, every day several times a day, it seemed like," said a senior attorney who worked beside her. "And I'll tell you, she was a cold-blooded heifer, telling him exactly what he had to do with this group and that, who to dump and who to charm to win that election, no matter who'd backed them before." Another saw her as "a great pusher and mover," making sure that there were enough little American flags at his rallies, that supporters were dispersed through the crowd to give the impression of wide support. "By the time he arrived," said Clarence Cash, one of his primary opponents, "she had set things up for him perfectly."

When the candidate's own professional experience as a lawyer was questioned he quickly claimed he had represented clients from fifteen counties in cases from divorce to felonies to disability compensation, though in reality he lacked any such practice and had rarely been inside a courtroom in his three years as a law school lecturer and perpetual candidate. The misrepresentation was soon forgotten as his campaign showered the press and public with what he called "a set of comprehensive position papers"—including plans to toughen criminal penalties—released each day in the last weeks before the election. In the May 1976 primary he won 60 percent of the vote. Standing unopposed in the general election, he was, as one local editor anointed him, "obviously heir apparent to the Bumpers-Pryor moderate-progressive legacy."

With the office won, he went on to plan his attorney general's staff while directing the Carter presidential run in Arkansas, and in August Hillary made her own move into the Carter camp, joining the campaign as deputy director in Indiana and staying through the fall as she took a leave from both the law school and Arkansas politics.

◆ ◆ ◆

The job came from Betsey Wright's lobbying of Carter operatives, though Hillary and her husband were already recognized in the party. The work provided political seasoning as well as capital with a likely president. Yet campaigning for Carter, whom the Clintons had met briefly during his visit to the university and whose candidacy they backed during the early presidential primaries, also involved for both of them a choice about competing forces and futures in the Democratic Party.

Running against the Georgia governor in 1976 were two of the party's last independent leaders, Congressman Morris Udall of Arizona and Senator Fred Harris of Oklahoma. Once they had been defeated there would be no escape from the party's growing bondage to big political money and Washington's oppressive lobbies and bureaucracies—from the bipartisan corruption of Congress itself, in which Democrats would become virtual mirror images of their Republican cohorts. The triumph of money was implicit in Jimmy Carter's coded mercantile politics of the "New South." It was inherent, too, in the Clinton's choice of Carter in 1976 and would be reflected vividly in their rule of Arkansas over the next decade and, even more, in their own White House politics and policies seventeen years later.

Indiana was expendable in Carter's calculations, conceded from the start to incumbent Gerald Ford in a strategy that counted on a southern base and a split in the old Democratic strongholds of the Northeast. But the new deputy director from Arkansas seemed to give away nothing herself. Colleagues remembered Hillary Rodham's campaign management in Indianapolis for its old-fashioned professionalism, its characteristic astringency, and the Carter-party distaste for what was now seen as the unrealistic principles of the past. The new politics, according to the *Washington Post*'s Donnie Radcliffe, were "an antidote to the party's idealistic binge of the 1960s," by which he seemed to mean the democracy of Kennedy, Johnson, Humphrey, and the Vietnam War Congresses.

Like Bill Clinton in Texas four years before, Hillary Rodham was now coolly attentive to all the details of ego, protocol, and deference, as much at ease with old rural or town bosses from the state's decrepit party as with corporate lawyers and student volunteers. When a county chairman became embroiled in a delegate selection battle, she labeled him "radioactive," as he recalled, and kept him largely out of the campaign. With grim determination she set up a phone bank in a former bail bondsman's office across from the jail and hired inmates out on bond because the rent and labor were both cheap. She rallied her staff as Carter stumbled toward the finish line with a series of tactical campaign blunders, portents of an administration she privately regarded with dismay and disgust. Most of all, staff members remembered, she disciplined those who made mistakes in her own ranks. "Hillary took no prisoners," one writer recorded. When the networks came on with their coverage early on election night, they instantly awarded Indiana to Ford. It had been no real contest from the beginning. Still, she stayed on at the dispirited headquarters, looking far beyond Indiana in 1976. Carter finally won the close national race in the predawn of the next day.

She would return to Fayetteville with both local and national contacts for Bill Clinton's eventual presidential run and with her own hard-won reward. At the close of his first year in the White House, Jimmy Carter recognized his Indiana deputy by appointing her to the national board of the Legal Services Corporation, the congressionally funded public corporation charged with providing legal services to the poor. On the corporation's board she was to work with Mickey Kantor, another campaign appointee, a former Democratic Senate aide and lawyer-lobbyist who would be the titular manager of the Clinton campaign in 1992. Back in Arkansas Clinton would join Senator Bumpers and the powerful Jackson Stephens of Stephens, Inc., a Carter intimate and major contributor, to dispense a dozen choice presidential appointments in the state, including appointments to the federal bench. There was one major disappointment. For chairman of the Federal Home Loan Bank Board, with its vital role in the nation's savings and loan industry, neither Attorney General Clinton nor his politically talented wife were able to seat their candidate—their Springdale friend, Tyson lawyer Jim Blair.

◆　◆　◆

The attorney general's office in Little Rock was a time-honored rostrum for the state's ersatz reform, a place to denounce special interests while leaving their power intact. "It was a populism as natural and unabashed in Arkansas as hogs in a pen," wrote University of Arkansas political scientist Art English, "and Clinton fit right in." He promptly announced plans to intervene aggressively on behalf of consumers in cases dealing with utility rates, pledged to "clean up and rationalize" property taxes he termed "a raving mess," and filed suit against alleged milk price-fixing, telling one applauding group that "some" big dairy companies "stole from you, just as if they'd broken into your house and taken it." To similar applause he strongly supported the death penalty as "a deterrent to crime," a conclusion for which he had "no statistics," the thirty-year-old Clinton told audiences, but "a gut feeling based on my observations over many years." At one point the new attorney general even ventured into foreign policy and international economics, deploring the "terrible shape" of the entire country as a result of Mideast oil prices and sinister Arab investments in America.

Everywhere he turned, it seemed, the new attorney general was lauded for what he was and would certainly become. Typical of the acclaim was his being named one of the state's "Outstanding Young Men of the Year" by the Arkansas Junior Chamber of Commerce after only two months in office. Yet even such seemingly unqualified honors held unseen irony. The young politician who carried the state's black precincts with overwhelming margins now received his award at the whites-only Little Rock Country Club. The admiring judges who selected him were Bill Bowen, a wealthy local banker and future aide, Clinton's old intimate Thomas J. "Mack" McLarty, and a third political friend whom Clinton would appoint to the bench and who would go on to administer a federal loan program and ultimately testify in a 1995 grand jury against the president of the United States—an enthusiastic Democratic lawyer named David Hale.

Despite her late-summer and fall absence in Indiana, Hillary Rodham was, from the outset, an unusual presence in her husband's tenure as attorney general. Not only standing beside him at the ritual rallies and receptions, she now appeared alone and spoke out herself on various issues, from the handling of evidence in rape cases to the media's deplorable preoccupation with "investigations" rather than with "presenting the news," as she put it to a sympathetic audience. "One of our problems is trying to control a press that is far out of line because of Watergate," she told a Little Rock Rotary Club in 1977. By then she no longer taught or ran legal clinics for the unrepresented, was no longer simply the attorney general's wife, but belonged to one of Arkansas's oldest, most formidable, most fundamentally conservative institutions, the Rose Law Firm.

The ultimate determining decision in her own career was made almost casually, as an extension of her husband's politics and—typically—with discreet inside arrangements. Preparing to move to Little Rock after the 1976 primary, Clinton had called Rose partner Herbert Rule III, a former legislator who had raised money in his 1974 race. "I got the word from Bill Clinton that she was coming and I tracked her down," Rule said later. At the time the firm had few women or even Ivy League law credentials, and Rose rarely recruited from law school faculties or legal aid clinics. "Hillary was just a law professor, that's all," remarked one partner. But the firm saw her obvious value, offering the twenty-nine-year-old attorney a salary just under $25,000—far higher than the pay in Arkansas for teaching or public-interest law and well more than Clinton himself would make as attorney general. Friends could not remember her even pausing to consider an alternative. "The decision had been made when she decided to marry, to go with his career as the engine for her own ambitions and power," said someone who knew them since Yale. "By the time Rose came across with the offer, she was going to do whatever was best for Bill, whatever would get them to the top—and I mean all the way to the top—as fast as possible." At the same time there was a sense, some believed, in which Hillary Rodham's joining Rose was not so much entering into Arkansas as rejecting it, relishing the caste distinction between Little Rock's most sophisticated and nationally prestigious law firm and the rest of the state and much of the political world her husband frequented. She was finding her own place, a refuge.

Both sides recognized the mutual compact in Rose's employing the wife of an attorney general and politician on the rise. "She had an interest and talents that would indicate that she would make contributions beyond the mustiness of law," Rule added coyly. "Sure, she was bright, but she brought us no special litigation skills or expertise otherwise," recalled a senior partner. "Hillary was this huge political asset, pure and simple."

For the firm she was the most natural hireling. Formed before statehood and named for a founder of the American Bar Association, Rose had numbered among its partners judges and state supreme court justices, mayors, legislators, a US Senator, and, above all, the intimates of those in power, figures who exerted their force more discreetly, without potentially awkward public visibility, without accountability. It was a matter of appearance and reality in an Arkansas when the two were frequently not the same. For a century and a half Rose represented and wielded the influence of the most powerful forces in the state—in land, timber, retailing, insurance, investment banking, agriculture, financial services—and, with governments at all levels, virtually the entire enveloping grid of political privilege and consequent private profit from the Ozarks to the Delta. What Arkansas was the Rose Law Firm had been well paid to make it—and to protect and maintain the result. The discreet firm's own fortunes were inseparable from the economic and social system it served. Beyond any considerations of gender, résumé, or name, Hillary Rodham's presence on the letterhead was in a long tradition.

◆ ◆ ◆

They had been in Little Rock only months when a tectonic shift took place in Arkansas politics with the passing of one of Raymond Clinton's most powerful political friends, eighty-two-year-old Senator John McClellan. The death set off a scramble for the seat by two rivals, Governor Pryor and Congressman Tucker, and so opened the governorship to Bill Clinton, with the added bonus that at least one of his party rivals might be eliminated by the Pryor-Tucker fight. He began the campaign virtually at McClellan's funeral.

With money raised partly and discreetly, as always, through the Rose firm, he published in January 1978 a sleek "Attorney General's Report," celebrating his year's record in what one reader called "rapturous terms." Only later were the discrepancies clear. Clinton claimed to have recovered hundreds of thousands of dollars for buyers in a General Motors recall, though the rebates came out of a class action by other attorneys general. He boasted of aggressive policing of utilities, though his much-publicized appearances and statements at regulatory hearings added no meaningful consumer rights, and an unchallenged coal contract actually threatened higher rates. "I had to press over and over again for him to be aggressive at all," said a deputy who worked on regulatory problems, "but in the end he was mostly just talk."

Clinton had also given general "help for the elderly," said the report, though he had refused to confront a cruelly regressive sales tax on necessities. The attorney general had provided "official oversight" in the transport of hazardous materials, he assured voters, though what he had actually done, as in almost every other promise of his 1976 race, turned out to be far more rhetoric than legislation, executive action, or litigation. With some justification a later opponent would accuse Clinton of mostly "chasing headlines" as attorney general, and one reporter thought the vaunted report a typical "hype." Yet the extravagant claims, expensively packaged, had the effect of obscuring the authentic record. "We did push truth in advertising for optometrists and embalmers," a Clinton aide said later with a smile, "and two handbooks on the Freedom of Information Act."

In March 1978, after only fourteen months as attorney general and less than five years after leaving Yale Law School, Bill Clinton did what many had long assumed but few expected quite so quickly: he declared his candidacy for governor of Arkansas. Flanked by his wife, his beaming mother, and his brother, he told reporters and backers that the statehouse was the job he "really wanted because a governor could do more for more people than any other office." "Any office," he added with what one person saw as a "self-conscious" grin, "except the president."

With fifteen paid workers, a mobile phone, a rented plane, and Jimmy Carter's own advertising firm for television spots, plus more than a dozen offices with hundreds of volunteers, the 1978 Clinton campaign was the most modern and opulent Arkansas had yet seen, "a well-disciplined and well-equipped 'army,'" wrote one reporter, "spread into every city and hamlet." Working from predawn shifts to late-night receptions, eager assistants attended the candidate. "Clinton will snap his fingers and the aide will come running to record the voter's name or perhaps some information about a complaint," journalist Carol Griffee wrote, describing the ritual that made each voter feel duly noted. It was a campaign built "with painstaking care over four years, without question the best organization ever put together in Arkansas without machine support," said columnist John Robert Starr, who compared it to the old Faubus coalition of Little Rock money and rural bosses.

With obvious differences of style and content, Starr might have noted, Clinton's was already a machine of its own. Against four minor opponents—a rural judge, a lawyer, a legislator, and a turkey farmer— he raised nearly $600,000, twice what his two closest rivals raised together and three times as much as any primary run had yet garnered. "Clinton's hoard," one account called it. Beginning with the quiet blessing of Stephens, Inc., his backing included, in fact, most of the old powers behind Faubus and others, as well as newer forces in the financial elite, "many of them from big business interests," one reporter noted ironically, "that he had challenged as attorney general."

His first gubernatorial campaign money came from presidents of most of the major banks in the state; from investors, planters, and corporate farmers, realtors, oilmen, brokers, attorneys, developers, timbermen; and in substantial amounts from the growing political action committees of banks, utilities, and the health industry. The donors included "R. G. Clinton of Hot Springs, retired"—the ever-present Uncle Raymond giving the maximum individual contribution of a thousand dollars—and other members of the Clinton family and Raymond's old Hot Springs circle. Dotting the list were names later prominent, some notorious—the Tysons of the poultry empire, kindergarten playmate McLarty, who was again Clinton's campaign finance chairman, an expansive Little Rock bond dealer named Dan Lasater, and another old friend, now an ambitious developer and would-be financial magnate, James McDougal.

The politics of money could be crass or muted. Typically doubling as "consultant" for the state's Associated General Contractors, a state senator abruptly switched his patrons' support to Clinton when the candidate they first endorsed was rash enough to suggest more competitive bidding for highways. After a private meeting with the legislator-cum-lobbyist, Clinton himself "took no position" on the bidding issue, as he told the press, signaling to road builders a perpetuation of millions in the old sweetheart contracting. He vigorously opposed a constitutional amendment exempting groceries and prescriptions from sales tax, warning solemnly against "lost revenues." Promising "new ideas" and "constructive reform," he carefully avoided any discussion of how such tax relief for the poor or elderly might be made up by reform of the state's regressive corporate, income, and property taxes, all of which spared his own major contributors.

Part of the campaign money would go for the first in a succession of expensive political advisers from outside Arkansas, notably a thirty-year-old professional campaign consultant from the Upper West Side of Manhattan named Richard Morris, or Dickie as he would be known by grateful clients, grudging admirers, and embittered enemies. He had been organizing elections and managing candidates since his childhood at PS 9 and New York's Stuyvesant High, shocking his own candidates with his constant obsession with the next election, beginning the day after the last one. Bill Clinton had met him in 1977 and the two had immediately struck up what Morris called afterward a "close intimate relationship" as "political tactical soulmates," though the virulent, often fiercely combative adviser was even more a favorite of Hillary's. Eventually there would be serious questions about the integrity of Morris's polling methods as well as his temperament. Within a few years he would become too obviously one of the caricature mercenaries in the nation's emerging politics of money and manipulation, hiring out to huckster the election of well-heeled right-wing Republicans in the Reagan eighties as zealously as he contracted with Democrats, all with his trademark abrasiveness. His "style," said one account, "could irritate even those closest to him . . . a tendency to treat every conversation like a negotiation, the way he would weave back and forth between flattery and veiled threat, and the seemingly emotionless way he could launch attacks." The protean Dickie Morris's hold on the Clintons now and later was to be a kind of blood tie, sometimes strained but never broken. "Dickie's dictum," as some called it, was the epitome of the new characterless politics of self: the politician existed to be reelected. There was no "separating means from ends; governing and campaigning were one and the same," as *Washington Post* reporter David Mariness wrote. "This Eastern sharpie . . . one of the smartest little sons of bitches," a Clinton aide would call the New Yorker. "Mean. But God was he good."

In 1978 Morris would evidently demonstrate both characteristics, not so much in the lopsided gubernatorial race as in plotting with Clinton Governor David Pryor's Senate primary victory over Congressman Jim Guy Tucker, whom a reporter called "Clinton's main competition for the title of Democratic golden boy." Though Morris was distrusted and even despised by some around Pryor, including his wife, Barbara, Clinton eventually prevailed on the governor to take Morris's advice and air the savagely negative ads against Tucker that Clinton and Morris had devised together in long hours in the attorney general's office. It seemed to many an unusually naked case of intraparty fratricide. Several who watched the two men working and then the broadsides against Tucker thought Bill Clinton had never been more passionate than he was in the destruction of this young rival in his own party. "They killed Jim Guy with more sheer zest than they ever brought to Republicans," remembered a lawyer who knew them all. "But then Tucker was the only real long-run threat to Billy, and they all knew it."

"Virtually flawless," an aide called Clinton's 1978 run. No special attacks from the Dickie Morris arsenal were necessary, although the race had its premonitory moments. When rivals called him "liberal," Clinton assured crowds there was "no validity" to the unfair "charge" and "name-calling." Besides, he added at one point, Arkansas voters "have almost never responded to a negative campaign." As for those unfair taxes, those cost-of-living raises for state employees, and those needed public works, all required "further study," he told voters. "He is running the classic front-runner's campaign," noted a writer traveling with him, "taking few firm stands on controversial issues."

There was a fleeting shadow out of the past as a retired air force lieutenant colonel and Republican partisan named Billy Geren accused Clinton of being a "draft dodger" by reneging on the 1969 ROTC commitment that conferred its crucial deferment before the lottery placed him beyond call. But the candidate quickly insisted that the ROTC agreement was canceled "shortly after it was made" and that he "never received the deferment"—the 1-D Colonel Holmes had in fact secured for him nine years earlier. He had decided to "take advantage" of the ROTC option, Clinton told the *Gazette* on October 27, 1978. But after returning to Oxford in the fall of 1969, he went on solemnly, he had written to Colonel Eugene Holmes at the ROTC unit to say he would not accept an ROTC deferment and wanted to "get it over with" by entering the draft. He had told Holmes, he added, that he would enter the ROTC program if the commander wanted him to, but he preferred to take his chances with the draft.

It was, of course, a total and brazen lie, an invention of Eugene Holmes's actions as well as Clinton's. Believing that he had pressured Holmes in 1974 to remove the embarrassing letter from the files, and thus that there could be no documentation for the charges, Clinton now reckoned still further on the elderly colonel's coerced silence or agreement. Aides remembered a frenzy of activity in the hours after Geren leveled his charges, Clinton closeting himself and making a series of agitated phone calls, at one point yelling so excitedly that he could be heard through a closed door. "I don't know what they said to that old man then, but there was a lot of heavyweight leaning from the university people and others," said a campaign assistant watching the crisis. In the event, when he was inevitably called at his Fayetteville home by Little Rock reporters, Holmes said simply that he could not "recall" Clinton's particular case, that there had been "thousands" of students since then—though his memory of the episode would still be vivid fourteen years later.

To Clinton's seemingly detailed and confident denial, Geren could only respond that he had once seen documentation of his allegation, which indeed he had, and he only knew "what was in the file." If he was now wrong, if Clinton had not received a deferment, he would apologize. "It's obvious to me," Clinton responded dismissively, "that he didn't know the facts and that he didn't want to know them." With the record still buried in a lone surviving copy of the letter outside Clinton's control, with the press stopping at Holmes's demur, with Bill Clinton's exasperated categorical insistence—not unlike the stand he would strike more than fifteen years later as a president besieged by Arkansas scandals—the issue died once again. A future governor and president had lied with an impunity in part secured by his own pressuring of a witness, in part by the abdication of the media and others. As a Clinton aide acknowledged years afterward, understatedly, "It was not a pretty sight." For the moment, he had once more put the draft issue aside.

Though somewhat more discreetly in the background than she was in the 1976 primary, Hillary Rodham was his principal strategist and adviser, along with Dickie Morris. Even with Morris's repugnant bellicosity, it would be she who provided the campaign's harder, more cynical, warlike edge. While Clinton moved sunnily down the row, eager to like and be liked, his wife, campaign director Rudy Moore told Connie Bruck, saw the "darker side": "He's not expecting to be jumped, but she always is." One of the primary opponents referred caustically to her use of her maiden name, but when aides brought up the issue, she was adamant as usual and no one thought the race close enough for the name to matter.

Questions of conflict of interest were also raised in 1978—and skirted in much the same way as they would be fifteen years later. Barely a year after she joined Rose, Hillary Rodham was suddenly retained by the Little Rock Airport Commission, displacing their former counsel; one of the commissioners was a prominent Little Rock figure named Seth Ward, whose son-in-law was Webster Hubbell, one of Hillary's colleagues at Rose and already a close Clinton friend. She had also already represented in court a Stephens subsidiary and other interests doing major business with the state her husband served as chief law enforcement officer and now aspired to run. Meanwhile, the attorney general himself had failed to intervene as promised in a $45.5 million rate increase by Arkansas-Louisiana Gas Company, whose board members, including Mack McLarty, were among his backers. What might happen, wondered attorney John Harmon, one of his primary opponents, "if Ms. Rodham were the First Lady of Arkansas" while she and her Rose firm advanced and profited from such questionable clients or if Bill Clinton as governor discreetly shielded his patrons. "Don't you feel the propriety of this arrangement deserves your closest examination?" Harmon asked a party caucus about the airport commission.

In 1978 the indignant reply was much the same as when similar questions were posed in the presidential campaign and in the White House itself. They committed no wrongdoing, Clinton insisted without offering details, and Hillary was the victim of vicious personal attacks. "I don't care what any of these fellows say about me," he said, "but

. . . they ought to be careful when they talk about my family. . . . I wouldn't attack theirs." He'd been on a plane over Hot Springs in turbulent weather, he told one group: "I started praying, and I even forgave my opponents for all those terrible things they've been saying about me." The audience loved it. Like the denials on the draft, his very resilience, earnestness, and good humor seemed to banish the issue.

Clinton denied advocating gun control, though he had seemed sympathetic to it before audiences known to favor it. To sheriffs and prosecutors he stressed his fervent belief in capital punishment; to critics of the death penalty he insisted he would approve no executions until the Supreme Court ruled on Arkansas's law and even then would be inclined to commute sentences or forestall execution. The attorney general announced his office had "no evidence" of manipulated loans during his tenure, though realtors, bankers, private lawyers, and those in government knew that racist redlining and similar practices were commonplace, discrimination that would later be documented among his contributors' institutions in Little Rock and around the state. Radio ads boasted that he had intervened for consumers in "every" gas rate case; when a reporter pointed out the falsity, Clinton argued in a "clarification" that the ad should have said, "every case that had major impact on residential customers and in which [the] staff had recommended intervention."

Nonetheless, in a field otherwise marked by folksiness and fundamentalism—"Till the last dog is hung," one of his opponents was given to repeating every few phrases in his speeches and conversation—Clinton won near-unanimous black support and the endorsements of teachers, community reform groups, and even some of the labor movement he had turned against so abruptly two years before. As in 1974 and 1976, the agile young candidate and his coolly intelligent young wife radiated idealism and commitment as well as a smooth, seemingly effortless political professionalism. "He showed good," primary opponent John Harmon would concede. Attracting loyalty and devotion from supporters of widely varying sophistication, the couple had the ability to make questions and doubts melt away, seem relatively insignificant, especially in the light of what the two of them, with their evident talents, could do for a stricken Arkansas. To many, the end of having them in office would justify their means—though the full means were known to only a handful of the closest backers; few of their warmest supporters knew the details of campaign finances or other crucial relationships. "He was *always* better than the other guys," said

Ernie Dumas, a friend and *Gazette* editor who watched him from the beginning, "or so it seemed."

In the May election, carrying all but four counties and the black community en masse, he swept the nomination with nearly 60 percent of the vote, "an unheard-of margin in a race for an open office," wrote John Robert Starr. Meanwhile, on the strength of the Clinton–Dickie Morris negative ads, Pryor soundly defeated Tucker in a runoff for the Senate, leaving young Bill Clinton, barely five years after entering politics, Arkansas's preeminent politician at the state level. With a victory in the Democratic gubernatorial primary tantamount to election, he hardly campaigned in the general race, though he continued to receive generous financial support from wealthy interests, including a $10,000 line of credit from a friendly bank. He would win the governorship in November by over 60 percent.

On the night of his triumph the *Gazette* found the thirty-two-year-old Clinton, about to be the second-youngest governor in state history, "choked with emotion" as he stood before a wildly cheering Little Rock throng with an adoring Virginia and a visibly wide-eyed Hillary. "I am very proud of the campaign we have run," he told the crowd, characteristically biting his lower lip. "We have held the high road."

◆ ◆ ◆

In August of 1978, sure of election, they paused to enter a potentially lucrative private real estate development deal. It began one night at the Black-Eyed Pea restaurant in Little Rock, where Bill's old friend, Jim McDougal, made a familiar Arkansas proposition.

McDougal, then thirty-eight, was already something of a legend in the state's nexus of business and politics. "A classic of the type," one person called him; "a country-boy charmer with a sharp mind," said another. From a town of eight hundred in north-central Arkansas, he had been even more of a prodigy than Bill Clinton. At nineteen he ran John Kennedy's 1960 winning campaign in the state and went on to Washington, where he worked first for John McClellan and then for the powerful secretary of the Senate, dated one of Jacqueline Kennedy's social aides, and sipped bourbon over shaved ice in a hideaway Capitol office with family friend Wilbur Mills and other prominent politicians. "It was a helluva deal," McDougal would say later, but adding, too, "It was the end of the fun in life." When his father died, he had come back to run the family feed store and continued to build his political reputation by taking over the Young Democrats in a 1965 intraparty feud. By then he was also a legendary drinker of extravagant tastes and erratic behavior, and he suddenly disappeared for a time in what a colleague called "a sea of whiskey."

McDougal had soon come back to manage Fulbright's reelection run in 1968, though only after convincing Fulbright's people that he was a committed member of Alcoholics Anonymous. In that campaign he first met Clinton, charming the younger man with his marvelous imitations of Franklin Roosevelt and becoming a kind of mentor; his own alcoholism gave him a sense of kinship with Bill's tales of his stepfather. Clinton had "an inordinate desire for acceptance," McDougal would say. "Let's just call it the teacher's pet syndrome." Six years older, he was "protective about Bill" from the start. "I always felt like he was still just a kid and I was supposed to be looking after him," he remembered. He gave money and advice to both Clinton's 1974 and 1976 races and meantime went to teach at Ouachita Baptist College, where his wife-to-be, Susan, studied and where he resolved to use his unique background and talents to become what he called a "populist banker." By the time he walked into the Black-Eyed Pea in 1978 he had a hand in various schemes neither his friends nor his associates fully understood. He was "sort of a political businessman," he explained. "Everybody I know is in politics. That's my circle."

What he now proposed to the future governor was one of those deals for which the "circle" was well known. A group of "good ole boy businessmen," as one observer called them—including Kearnie Carleton, Clinton's campaign coordinator in the area—had recently purchased in a bankruptcy sale some thirty-six hundred acres on the popular White River, not far north of Little Rock. They were now looking to sell 230 riverfront acres, choice land where Crooked Creek joined the White. A part of Bill Blythe's old Ozarks sales territory near the Missouri border, it was alluring country for retirement or vacation homes, and the land could be subdivided, the lots sold at a substantial profit amid the growing migration to the South and a predicted boom in real estate. The McDougals and Clintons, Jim explained, would form a development partnership and "make a lot of money together," as a friend remembered.

The financing of the deal was even better than the setting itself. Although the land cost more than $200,000, they could buy it in effect with no down payment. Part of the price would come from a friendly bank supporting Clinton's election, and some $183,000 would be financed by yet another helpful local institution, Citizens Bank and Trust of Flippin, conveniently run by James N. Patterson, one of the men from whom they were buying the tract to begin with. Moreover,

Susan and Jim McDougal would manage the business and bear most of the risk and liability, personally guaranteeing nearly $200,000 of the total loans, while Bill and Hillary, at the statehouse and at Rose, would still enjoy a full 50 percent ownership. The Clintons could even deduct interest paid on the loans—$10,000 for 1978 and $12,000 for 1979—an immediate, profitable tax break on the ripening prospect.

Altogether it was a remarkable enterprise for a young couple who less than two years before were modestly paid law school instructors. In 1977 their combined taxable income in Little Rock had been only $41,000. Ordinarily they would never have qualified for such lavish financing or investment opportunities without conventional collateral or capital. At the same time, the deal was typical of Arkansas, much like arrangements that Uncle Raymond had made and that the Clintons' new, well-connected friends in Little Rock now had, a scheme of the kind the Rose firm itself crafted and burnished at vastly higher sums but with the same discreet advantages and accommodations. Late that August the purchase was concluded. Bill and Hillary now talked themselves of building an impressive house on a beautifully wooded bluff over a bend in the river. "They had big plans for that whole thing," said a Rose lawyer. "Nobody said a word about what it might cost, in any terms," another remembered. The venture was named Whitewater.

But real estate development was not their only good fortune. Less than two months after launching Whitewater, Hillary Rodham began extremely profitable trading in the volatile cattle futures market on the Chicago Mercantile Exchange. She would act on the advice of another intimate and well-connected friend, Jim Blair, the Springdale attorney for Arkansas's Tyson Foods and other agribusiness giants. Blair was even closer to Clinton than Jim McDougal, their failed candidate for chairman of Carter's Federal Home Loan Bank Board, who was himself heavily and profitably invested in the commodities market, "winning millions," he would say himself.

As in Whitewater, there were to be discreet special arrangements for this as well. The future First Lady of Arkansas was allowed to open her account with Blair's Fayetteville broker that October with only a $1,000 deposit, rather than the $12,000 that Mercantile Exchange rules required for ordinary investors. In the first few days she realized a $5,300 profit on her initial trading, and she would make some $27,000 before the end of the year, on the way to what would amount to nearly $100,000 in cattle futures profits over the ensuing months.

The Clintons might have lost thousands if the trades had gone otherwise, far more than their earnings or estate. It seemed they were uncharacteristically gambling everything they had worked for. Yet Hillary Rodham had never appeared worried. "She was attentive," said a colleague who saw her deal with the broker from time to time. "But she just seemed to know that it would go her way."

On the eve of Bill Clinton's inauguration as governor of Arkansas, the couple had quietly become land speculators despite a lack of capital, and beneficiaries of risky market windfalls without advancing the requisite cash—all with the help of well-placed friends. "That's my circle," as Jim McDougal would say.

◆　◆　◆

"A little bit like running for class president" is how Clinton later described his first race for governor. Still, he was taken seriously. As he won the governorship the *New York Times* called him "the 31-year-old whiz kid of Arkansas politics," quoting him as saying that his victory went beyond "traditional ideological terms" and was of historic importance in symbolizing what he called the "new compromise progressive candidates" in the Democratic Party. Personal attacks against him and his wife had failed, Bill Clinton told the *Times* in his first national interview, because the voters "no longer fear change."

· 12 ·

Little Rock I

"A Guy Who Supposedly Has
an IQ of a Zillion"

There seemed no doubt about the advent of youthful new style and glamour at the statehouse. The theme for the inaugural celebration was "Diamonds and Denim," emblems of Arkansas and of the Clintons' own cosmopolitan unpretentiousness. The young governor, announced the *Arkansas Gazette*, was assuming office with "brilliant auguries for success." Even an editor of the more conservative *Arkansas Democrat* thought it the beginning of Little Rock's own "Camelot at the Capitol."

In his inaugural address Clinton spoke dramatically of the need to ease the burdens of the less fortunate: "We live in a world in which limited resources, limited knowledge, limited wisdom must grapple with problems of staggering complexity and confront strong sources of power, wealth, conflict and even destruction, over which we have no control and little influence." Even so, he would lead as no one had ever before, moving the people and the state into "a new era of achievement and excellence." He promised long-suffering Arkansas "a life that will be the envy of the nation." Huddled together on the capitol steps, shoulders hunched, shivering in an unusually bitter and raw January cold, the crowd cheered, and some wept at his words.

Earlier an old legislator had pulled Clinton aside to deliver a private, less rhetorical promise. "Son, I've been in politics since you were born and I'll probably be here when you die. I'll sure enough be here when you're governor," he drawled, "and then you'll *wish* you were dead!" The governor-elect laughingly told the story at a party before the inauguration, and his backers and appointees thought it a nice joke about the notorious and crusty political order they were encountering. "Nobody took it as a *prediction,* for God's sake" said one, "which is about what it turned out to be."

◆   ◆   ◆

Clinton appeared uniquely serious and well-prepared for the task of governing. From an unprecedented $100,000 surplus of campaign money he spent a sizable portion to hire Price Waterhouse to consult on the management of the state's budget. Prior to his election he had asked for advice from the National Governors' Association and Washington think tanks; before taking office he made highly publicized trips to the White House, meeting with President Carter, and to the Democrats' 1978 special midterm convention in neighboring Memphis, where he chaired a hearing on the urgent matter of national health-insurance reform, and coyly appeared with Senator Edward Kennedy amid speculation that, despite being a year younger than the constitutional requirement, he might even be Kennedy's 1980 running mate in a brewing challenge to Carter.

Meanwhile his prospects looked equally promising back home, where fresh command and initiative, it was now said, might still overcome the stagnant, interest-dominated regime, whatever the warnings of old pols. "While the legislature was potentially a strong stumbling block if aroused, it had no internal forces to start and drive itself and was very receptive to leadership," one political analyst said. "The intimacy of politics in Arkansas lent itself to the personal energy of a legislative leader like Clinton."

Then, with almost baffling suddenness, it all began to come apart. Preparations had not been as careful as they seemed; the devoted and showy young governor was not as skillful as he appeared. "He was so brilliant, or thought he was so brilliant," said a close aide, "that he assumed he could really coast, and that was fatal." Within weeks, observers remembered, Bill Clinton was squandering the momentum of the inauguration.

Though he had watched his predecessor, David Pryor, avidly, there was now little of Pryor's deliberateness or maturity. "Bill was like a kid with a new toy that first term," a friend would say. A legislature and a public that seemed receptive in December were by spring bristling at the governor's affable, boyish hypocrisies as much as at his policy initiatives. One version described him as "so prone to conciliation that he chooses congenial duplicity over honest confrontation." "He'd pat you on the back while pissing down your leg," a labor leader said. Under scattered leadership, his senior staff of three was soon rife with its own politics, the proposed reforms lost in political scapegoating. "Supermen, deputy governors, and whiz kids," one lawmaker called Clinton's staff members contemptuously. "The three stooges," another said simply.

For the next two years there were many promised changes and little true change, new budgets that ended with old priorities, heralded policy innovations never quite sustained, seemingly ambitious legislation yet no authentic challenge of the established regime, record numbers of women and minorities appointed to offices, boards, and commissions but much the same resulting governance. There were alliances abandoned or betrayed, enemies accommodated. There were seemingly constant Clinton appearances and consultations with national organizations yet scant impact on the life of ordinary people in the state. There were repeated and articulate explanations by the governor at town meetings and county picnics while the realities of power in Little Rock remained largely unspoken and unchallenged.

Afterward the actual record of the first term was shrouded not only in the usual political claims and attacks but in a widely accepted mythology of Bill Clinton's ideological evolution from callow young liberal and progressive to a more centrist, pragmatic leader. "He was a punk kid with long hair, he had all those longhaired people working for him, and he was a liberal," a reactionary legislator would repeat to the press years later. In fact, the underlying reality was more prosaic, far less a matter of haircuts or labels than characteristics of both the man and the political culture of the state.

In Little Rock as in Washington, government's influence began and ended with money—how the state raised and spent its revenues, the priorities and arrangements it sanctioned for both public policy and private interest. It was that system which held hostage genuine initiative or change, starved new programs and fattened old interests; and in 1979, by both statute and custom, the principal budget and fiscal priorities of Arkansas were long fixed by the traditional legislative powers and lobbies, "carving up the carcass," as one of them would describe it. While he moved to centralize and modernize the bureaucratic budgeting process itself, Clinton from the outset did nothing to challenge either the means or the larger ends of the old system. "It relieved him of the real tough decisions," said an attorney and friend, "but it also reduced him, like everybody else before, essentially to dealing on the edges of power."

At those margins the new governor struggled gamely, and often in vain, with his own visibly conflicting impulses—to improve his state's often shameful conditions yet not to confront the cause or entrenched powers too openly or disturb his support among those powers. His initial education budget thus carried the largest increase for elementary and secondary schools in the state's history. Facing serious opposition in the legislature, however, he quickly withdrew a school district consolidation and reorganization bill that might have made the added money meaningful, and he stood by in relative silence while the interest-dominated Public Service Commission slashed the big utilities' already underassessed property taxes by several million, dooming his second-year education budget increase. Similarly, in the wake of the 1970s energy crisis he introduced a new state department of energy, to be endowed with broad powers of conservation, development, inspection, and even intervention in the old commission, with its corrupt oversight and rate setting. But there, too, he watched almost timorously as the authority of the new office was crippled by the utility lobby and as the giant Arkansas Power & Light, some of whose major shareholders and partners were among his wealthiest backers, publicly postured, then reneged on financing consumer conservation measures.

When his own aides later uncovered a scheme by AP&L to evade even the pliant Public Service Commission and gouge Arkansas ratepayers for the dubious Grand Gulf nuclear power plant in Mississippi, Clinton was incensed, putting his name to a staff-written exposé to be published in the *Gazette* in the summer of 1980. Then, at the last minute, the governor backed out—"took his name off the byline after he felt the AP&L heat," said one witness—though the article had already been edited and set at the *Gazette* and it was too embarrassing in that quarter to stop publication altogether. In classic Arkansas fashion the Grand Gulf controversy and its attendant publicity slowly petered out. The Clinton administration eventually entered a series of empty agreements with the utility, and local ratepayers ended up a decade later paying the largest share of the original toll. Clinton's image as a utility watchdog would still endure. "I understand he's always taken on the utilities," a writer would say years afterward to a onetime energy department aide. "Are you kidding? Not 'taken on,' stroked," the former official replied, explaining the obscured record. "Bill Clinton did like being seen fighting the utilities," said a journalist familiar with the Grand Gulf episode. "He just liked the good ole boys of AP&L and their contributions a lot better."

Some episodes were stark premonitions of issues in his presidency. Facing a crisis in medical services—Arkansas had the highest rate of teen pregnancy in the nation and other problems—Clinton promptly commissioned new officials and studies with some fanfare, even appointing Hillary Rodham to chair a task force on reform of rural health care. But then the ensuing proposals for rural clinics run with practitioners and other nonphysicians quickly aroused the fear and fury of the state's formidable medical establishment, "a very tight, exclusive union," as one writer called them, echoing Virginia Clinton. The opposition to the country clinics even included close relatives of such Clinton friends as Congressman Beryl Anthony and the Rose firm's Vince Foster. As the reform was soon demolished by medical money and lobbies, however, the governor appeared puzzled, then numbed, then simply intent on salvaging anything for political appearances. A supporter had told Hillary Rodham what was happening to health initiatives in the legislature and elsewhere, and she had urged him to tell Clinton as well. When he did, the governor only turned away. "She saw it, but he didn't want to know," the man remembered. "He just wanted one of those clinics open in time for reelection, and that was it. I told him people were being screwed and he just glazed over and walked off."

The killing of health reform was hardly his only reminder of vested power. Though rapacious clear-cutting of Arkansas forests had ravaged much of the state by the 1970s and though Dale Bumpers had confronted the problem years before, hearings by a Clinton timber management task force drew predictable anger from powerful timber companies, represented by Rose lawyers, among others. At first the governor had seemed gleeful. "He loved the idea of sticking it to 'em, though it was just rhetoric and both sides got into the hearings," said one observer. A task force aide, Steve Smith, recalled that he used the term *corporate criminals* but later had to apologize under orders from Clinton, though subsequent studies on environmental abuses found the description all too accurate. Under mounting attack, however, Clinton eventually repudiated Smith, and the forest issue, like others, faded away. It was much the same story for aides on economic development, who found Clinton's initial emphasis on new small businesses opposed by large interest-dominated chambers of commerce and thus soon dropped in favor of the old low-tax, low-wage industrial concessions and bond promotion for brokerage houses and developers.

Having campaigned on promises to repair the state's crumbling roads, Clinton planned the necessary $45 million in higher fuel taxes and other levies and proportional increases in registration fees for heavy trucks and luxury cars. His original proposal actually reduced license costs for the older, lower-priced cars owned by most Arkansans. But then the state's huge trucking industry and its allies like Tyson forced Clinton and the legislature to reverse the formula, shifting "a disproportionate share of the tax," according to one study, to "those least able to afford it." When the lobbies were through in 1979 there would not be enough money to make a difference in most country roads and instead there would be what a Clinton aide called the "political catastrophe" of "outraged" citizens standing in line at state motor vehicle offices, the handsome young governor's photograph smiling down on them as they waited to pay higher fees for their tags and transfers.

It was never quite clear to most witnesses whether Bill Clinton had "caved in," as one assistant put it, or merely fashioned a "pragmatic compromise" in the face of insurmountable forces. "He was weak more than venal, always," said one first-term aide. "But there was one thing he never did," added still another. "He could have said to the folks, 'Look here, the big truckers and rich boys are costing you your bad roads and want you to pay the freight.' He could have said that, but you'll never catch Bill Clinton tellin' this much truth." There was no statehouse mobilizing of conservationists to rival the timber companies, no front of the medically needy to balance the medical lobby; no overcharged ratepayers were summoned to match AP&L. To genuine grassroots efforts by others Clinton responded only hesitantly, expediently. After a 100,000-signature petition drive and volunteer citizen lobbying he reluctantly agreed in 1979 to lift the regressive sales tax on prescription medicines, though not on groceries.

"Generally it took a huge effort to get Governor Clinton to commit himself on an issue," said Little Rock poverty activist Zach Polett, summing up more than a decade of experience. Like many others, Polett thought in that first term that "he didn't reach out to the constituency groups . . . nor did he bring representatives from their ranks into his administration. In short, he pissed off a lot of people."

Through the 1980s Bill Clinton worked tirelessly to marshall large business interests. He persuaded them to support school reform or economic development measures that were not always a matter of their immediate profit or advantage. He personally borrowed, then paid back with wealthy backers' contributions, hundreds of thousands of dollars for initiatives that bolstered his record and career but that were not necessarily on their agenda. He spent lavishly on television, radio, and newspaper ads, direct mail, consultants, travel, polling. But that was something else. Beyond boardrooms and law offices and discreet calls, this remarkably empathetic, people-touching young politician rarely if ever sought seriously to raise the people themselves in any cause save his next election. It was almost as if he, like many of his powerful patrons, were uncertain—or afraid—of the force itself.

Aides typically saw him, in the words of Rudy Moore, Jr., as a "vibrant . . . exasperating" executive, what local historian Phyllis Johnston called "a combination of the moralist, manager and popular persona." He was given to open-ended discussions or ruminations with staff or other politicians and often to long, aimless conversations with visitors or even passersby, usually regardless of schedule, though he constantly fumed about having no free time, was "out-and-out cranky," said Moore, and "threw his regular fits," as a former secretary recalled. Allies and enemies alike came to view the governor's office as a site of vigorous activity and few conclusive results, decisions emerging, especially on politically troublesome issues, only wrenchingly, ever subject to amendment or reversal.

He installed his own loyalists throughout state offices as few governors had before him, "extended the reach," wrote Johnston in her study of the administration, "deep into the bureaucracy." Yet he did nothing to disturb the old lines of legislative and lobbyist influence, nor did he keep oversight of his regime.

After little more than a year the senior staff triumvirate around Clinton was in disarray. Moore, the former state senator and campaign manager, was promoted to chief of staff, only to face worse trials. John Danner, an outsider, a lawyer and management analyst from San Francisco who was originally a friend of Hillary's, left early in 1980 in obvious frustration. Smith, the other former legislator and a longtime supporter from Fayetteville whose son was the Clintons' godchild, was exiled with his timber report and other initiatives to a windowless basement office. Men in their early thirties (Moore and Smith quintessential "local boys"), they were scarcely the radicals demonized by primitive legislators playing on fears of youth, long hair, and proposals that were merely standard for the rest of the country, even if they were threatening in Arkansas.

Like many of their successors, these three men were drawn by Bill Clinton's compelling intelligence and, though dismayed by his retreats, betrayals, and fey practices, remained doggedly loyal, despite their humiliation and abandonment, to what he perennially seemed to promise. "It was pure cannibalism," said one witness in the governor's office in the capitol, "but you could never tell who was eating whom." None survived to later, less controversial terms or to the White House—though they constituted ominous history. Clinton's original failure as a young governor to discipline himself or manage his most important subordinates, to defend them effectively against petty ideological smears, to confront his own faults rather than offer up underlings made for the larger failure of his first term and haunted those that followed. At stake was far more than office rivalries or administrative efficiency. In Little Rock, as in Washington, people and method determined policy and result. It was the oldest lesson in politics: the somber difference between running for office and running a government.

No bureaucratic bloodletting saved the administration from its legislative and lobbyist predators or from an unremitting series of exposés and attacks by a resurgent *Arkansas Democrat*. In 1979–80 the paper was challenging the dominant *Gazette* and was newly edited by a vain, crusty, political reactionary, John Robert Starr, a former local AP reporter. Not long after the auspicious inauguration stories began to appear that were virtual parodies of what Starr happily called "misfeasance, malfeasance, and nonfeasance" under the new young governor. There were reports of a building services director's doing public business with his own hardware company, of vastly inflated land appraisals on purchases for a state park, of discrepancies in the granting and policing of liquor licenses, of a cabinet member's spending $450 a month for potted plants in his office, of Clinton's driving to a rally at more than eighty miles an hour after ordering a crackdown on violators of the new fifty-five-mile-an-hour speed limit, of the usual state police infighting and excesses, of Rudy Moore's being caught in a violent incident with a girlfriend, of an expensive departmental retreat at a local lake, of souvenir wine and corkscrews at another official conference where dining and entertainment cost thousands, of dubious grants to an Ozark institute for rural development, of more wasted money in an energy-conservation woodcutting program and by a Clinton appointee in the state purchasing office.

As the governor railed against the *Democrat* in angry phone calls to the publisher and even personal tongue-lashings in his office, then tried ingratiatingly to "explain" the incidents, Starr amplified the stories in his own caustic column and instituted a "Sweet William" award for readers who selected the worst government waste of the month and a "Slick Willie" award for "profligate" officials. It was showy but legitimate, sometimes even penetrating journalism, and it struck a deep chord in the state.

Paradoxically, Starr and his newsroom devoted no comparable probing or indignation to the vast knot of private and political power before them, the brokered, lobbied, lawyered arrangements of bipartisan plunder around Clinton and every other Arkansas politician, arrangements that were and would be the far greater abuse. The *Democrat*'s stinging little awards never named the major thieves. Justifiable as such journalism always was in the cause of good government, in Arkansas the depth of the problem gave it all grim irony. The exposures only fed the public's reflexive misapprehension that its pain came mainly from venal, heedless bureaucrats in ways and sums they could readily grasp, rather than from a more subtle world of statute, finance, contracts, and collusion seldom seen or understood. "It was like nailing people with unpaid parking tickets while the Mafia ran the treasury," said one local journalist.

Starr's self-satisfying coverage of the administration's peccadilloes even missed much of the target in the governor himself—the already sizable, often seedy reality of the Clintons' financial dealings and other indiscretions. In that the *Democrat* was hardly alone. Ironically, part of what annoyed and drove Starr was the governor's discreet, cozy, sometimes co-opting relationship with the other major newspaper in the capital and state.

Long a lone voice of progressive values, taking a brave stand, for example, during the desegregation crises of the 1950s, the rival *Arkansas Gazette* was gleeful at the coming of the educated and compatible governor, who socialized with friendly editors and reporters and struck up warm friendships with senior journalists and managers living, like many of his backers, in the shaded white heights of Little Rock. Many believed the relations went beyond congeniality. "Some of those boys became a kind of kitchen cabinet for Bill," one official remembered. While its articles and editorials were commonly more thorough and measured than the *Democrat*'s, more meticulous about the public record, and more conventionally liberal, the widely respected *Gazette* also mostly kept its own distance from Arkansas's deeper realities of power during the Clinton years, at the end of which the paper finally collapsed and was absorbed by the *Democrat*. "The truth is, for all their good work, they went in and out of the tank on the big stuff," a former reporter there in the 1980s said sadly, "and the result was pretty much the same as with those other clowns."

◆ ◆ ◆

"MS. RODHAM?" the *Democrat* headlined in February 1979, in one of its more benign features on the new governorship. "JUST AN OLD-FASHIONED GIRL." She was conspicuous from the first weeks of his administration. "We realized that being a governor's wife could be a full-time job," she told a women's page reporter while conducting a tour of the mansion's kitchen and living quarters, a ritual she would repeat often over her ensuing dozen years in the house. "But I need to maintain my interests and my commitments. I need my own identity, too."

Beyond her work at Rose, Hillary Rodham was also available for numerous speaking engagements. She invariably spoke on generational values, deploring the "unsettlement" of the 1960s, the "excessive narcissism" of the 1970s, and "selfish politics" in general. She kept her maiden name, she made a point of telling young women, because not only was it "a smart professional move" but it also made her feel more like "a real person."

As her husband took office she remained involved with the Children's Defense Fund in Washington and drew national attention as the first woman chair of the Legal Services Corporation. But she was plainly restless for more. "These organizations . . . satisfied only pieces of her ambition," wrote Nina Martin in a study of her earlier career, "perhaps because they were essentially bureaucracies whose paths had largely been determined by other people." She readily found her part as a major force behind the scenes in her husband's governorship, advising him on "everything political," said one aide, as well as shaping major policies. The role was neither one of equal partner nor one of ordinary political wife, neither public figure in her own right nor mere consort; she didn't "have to go to ladies' lunches or travel with him," a close friend observed, but she had to "be next to him and not speak."

When she did speak in private and political sessions, it was with an authority, impatience, and bite few had heard before. "Let's just say his staff didn't like her much," said one of the journalists in the putative kitchen cabinet. "She was hard, always pressing," said another. Tommy Robinson, a former small-town police chief who became Clinton's controversial director of public safety in the first term and later a congressman and acrid political rival, "had to put up with her tirades," he later told the *Gazette* in 1990, calling her "the *real* Governor for 10 years." "She is one very professional tough bitch," Robinson added still later for *The New Yorker*. "I have a great deal of respect for her. . . . She did not want screw-ups of any kind. She was *all business.*"

By some accounts, she now matched that sort of sexism and resentment with her own slashing temper and profanity, countering what aides saw as Bill Clinton's habitual pandering or slovenliness with antidotes of cynicism and ruthlessness. "I'd never heard *anybody,* male or female, talk like that," one staff man recalled.

The language made what Robinson called her "tirades," and her sometimes puzzling, self-exempting politics, all the more memorable. "There at the end of the 1970s and into 1980 she'd be ranting about how bad Reagan and the Republicans would be for the country, how much everything would be run by the rich and corporations if they won," remembered a departmental aide, "and I wondered, here she was a lawyer for some of the same kind of people and corporations at the Rose firm." Her ultimate interest and loyalty always sounded clear enough. During the intramural crisis in the summer of 1980 over whether Clinton himself would sign the exposé of AP&L's Grand Gulf fraud, Hillary had telephoned from the Democratic Convention to discipline aides working anxiously at the mansion to get the information out. "Here's Bill up here working his ass off to save the party and you little bastards are only makin' trouble for him," one aide remembered her saying. "No one appreciates what we do."

If white-collar aides felt the Rodham disdain, the First Family's state police escorts were treated still more contemptuously. Officers Larry Gentry and Roger Perry would remember the temper tantrums both Clintons threw, sometimes in the back seat of the official limousine, throwing any object at hand at each other or their bodyguards. A "bitchy" Hillary was openly hostile, given to calling them "pigs." She "loathed" them, the officers recalled, and it was part of "their condescending attitude toward employees in general and Arkansans in general." "Deep down," said another officer, "that woman really hated this state, the people in it, and almost everything else except being top dog."

Friends saw them both in these early years as relatively tentative and insecure. Bill himself didn't have a bit of background. "He didn't really care much about money per se, but he was always yearning to be a part of society," said a member of one of Little Rock's most renowned families, who knew them well. "Bill just didn't have it [background], and the truth was that Hillary didn't either."

Others thought it was the class acceptance Clinton so coveted that his transplanted wife now found she missed most in their larger prestige and plans. It was not enough for Hillary Rodham, after all, to be the wife of a prodigiously successful young politician, however integral she was to his career, whatever the reflected status and derived power. "They both had a very strong sense of needing to belong, to arrive," said one. At any rate, it was Hillary who now began to tend avidly to one of the marks of the status they both sought—their personal wealth.

◆ ◆ ◆

Less than a year into the Clinton governorship, Hillary Rodham had made $100,000 in the commodities market under circumstances that were part of a growing pall over their Arkansas associations and involvements—and over their own integrity.

As in the case of Jim McDougal and Whitewater, it was their friend Jim Blair who had come to them with the prospect of making some ready money after Clinton won the 1978 primary and was certain to be governor. Blair was then a forty-three-year-old attorney, a divorced father of three children, with a thick black watch cap of hair framing a pleasant face, heavy dark-rimmed glasses, and the modish wide ties and collars of the era. Born in tiny 400-soul Elkins, southeast of Fayetteville, he was a 1957 honors graduate of the University of Arkansas Law School, a rising figure among the younger nonofficeholders in the state Democratic Party, who had succeeded McDougal in helping manage Fulbright's losing race against Bumpers in 1974. After two decades in practice, a senior partner in a nine-man firm in Springdale, he worked only a few miles from his birthplace.

Jim Blair was a principal outside counsel for Springdale's mammoth multibillion-dollar Tyson Foods, "whose operations," one person observed, speaking both literally and figuratively, "gave the small Ozark town a pungent, penetrating odor." His firm's other clients numbered comparable giants of the state, region, and nation, including Ralston Purina, Welch Foods, Safeway Stores, Wilson and Company, Arkansas-Louisiana Gas, and International Paper, along with several large food industries and Arkansas trucking lines, all of them linked in the intricate web of agribusiness marketing, packing, and shipping.

By 1978 Blair was also making "several million dollars trading commodities," as he later boasted to the New York Times. "I was on a streak, on a streak that I thought was very successful," the small-town lawyer would say, "and I wanted to share this with my close friends, as I did." His clients, as it happened, were not only large, market-linked corporations, but also a freewheeling, poker-playing pal, a commodity broker in Springdale named Robert L. Bone, known to his clients as Red.

Bone had worked for Tyson for more than a dozen years before founding the Springdale office of Refco, Inc., a rapidly growing Chicago trading firm with a reputation for aggressive, highly profitable trading in a notoriously risky market. No ordinary brokerage, the Ozarks branch of Refco was there principally to cater to giant Tyson's own enormous stake in the market, as well as to the investments of a handful of wealthy Arkansas speculators. Red Bone was certainly no ordinary trader. In the early 1970s, while still at Tyson Foods, he had been handed an eleven-month suspension by the government's Commodity Futures Trading Commission, and had "settled charges," as the *New York Times,* the *Village Voice,* and others reported, in what regulators found to be an intricate and vastly lucrative scheme by magnate Don Tyson, him, and others "to manipulate the eggshell futures market," as one account described it. Bone ultimately settled with the commission without admitting or denying guilt. Only a month before Hillary Rodham opened her account with him, he had completed a one-year partial suspension for serious exchange rules infractions and would subsequently receive another, more stringent suspension for still other professional violations.

Market authorities also disciplined Bone for "serious and repeated violations of record-keeping functions, order-entry procedures, margin requirements, and hedge procedures," according to a Mercantile Exchange complaint. In the commodities trade, these were major offenses that might allow unscrupulous brokers and their collusive customers to evade the initial required margin deposits or even ongoing "calls" for further margin money to be put into the customer's account in the course of the high-risk speculation. Far more serious, such violations might also enable the broker to "allocate" trades, to assign winning contracts to some selected clients and losing contracts to the rest, in effect changing the bet after the game to reward favored investors with either unearned gains or, equally common, false losses to be used as tax write-offs. The stakes were gigantic. Winners, whether legitimate or fraudulently "allocated" by their broker, stood to make or save fortunes large and small.

There were far more losers than winners, especially among novices in the cutthroat commodities market, and entire nest eggs could be wiped out in a few trades. This form of arcane speculation had enormous impact on food prices and even on international trade and humanitarian aid to starving millions around the world.

Commodities futures were a dangerous gamble as well for those who knew the game. Jim Blair had obviously come to think of himself one of those few. He had been Bone's lawyer in the controversial broker's disciplinary proceedings and other legal disputes and was now, in 1978–79, one of Red's extraordinarily successful customers in the Springdale brokerage. "There were days of exaltation and days of terror," Diane Divers Kincaid, Blair's girlfriend at the time and later his wife, recalled. "Jim was tense. It was always apparent whether it was a good day or a bad day."

In the midst of all this, Blair had also advised the Clintons on their Whitewater venture; despite the colossal risk and liability in the commodities market, he had set Hillary to trading her limited funds with his friend Red Bone. On October 11, 1978, her first transaction—netting within days a $5,300 gain on a $1,000 investment, a return many later thought "mathematically impossible if exchange rules were strictly followed"—took place even before her check was cashed by the brokerage. "Like the Whitewater thing," said an associate who knew of both schemes, "it was going to take care of Bill and Hillary, fix 'em up for the future." Within hardly a week, the wife of the next governor of Arkansas had won another $7,800, and $7,200 more only days after that.

Following Blair's advice, she got out of the cattle futures market in July 1979, having parlayed an initial investment of $1,000 into nearly $100,000, never having to add to her original cash despite at least one market "margin call" for a larger deposit to cover her speculative purchases. Her spectacular 10,000 percent return on her investment was more than five times the rate of profit made even by such investors as had bought when she did and sold at the peak of the market during the same period. Commodity windfalls added more than $26,000 to their income in 1978, over $72,000 in 1979. At the end of Clinton's first term they were showing nearly $160,000 annual income in an Arkansas governorship that paid $35,000 a year.

Years later, when the remarkable trades were eventually revealed by *New York Times* investigative journalist Jeff Gerth, the episode was shrouded in questions. At a moment when the Clinton rise was being launched so auspiciously, had the usually careful, personally conservative Hillary Rodham been singularly daring, foolhardy, or somehow just lucky? Had the little girl Hugh Rodham drilled over the *Chicago Tribune*'s stock pages become a trader of exceptional skill, "buying ice skates one day," as Mark Powers, editor of the respected *Journal of Futures Markets*, put it, "and entering the Olympics a day later"? Had the Clintons, who ran for and won the presidency righteously damning the speculative greed and grasping of the 1980s, been profiteers, inside traders, and thus hypocrites themselves? Was it true, as one critic wrote, that "the way a president has been willing to make money speaks volumes"? The answers lay in details and fragments of the story not always seen together.

First, there was the overwhelming evidence that the Rodham trades took place amid pervasive fraud in her brokerage and within a wider market manipulation to which it was linked. During the entire nine-month period she had been their client, Red Bone and Refco were under investigation by the Chicago Mercantile Exchange for systematic violations of market rules. Official investigators believed that in October 1978—the very month Jim Blair had taken the future First Lady of Arkansas into the supposedly unpredictable market—Bone and others at Refco had virtually cornered that market in what brokers called a classic squeeze. They found, too, that the brokerage had routinely allowed favored clients to trade heavily and profitably without ever putting up enough money to cover the speculation. A broker at the Refco office in Springdale would admit under oath that they had been trading in "blocks" of contracts and "allocating them to customers after the market closed." In a technique that later was rendered virtually impossible on Wall Street, there had been blatant falsification and manipulation of records, often involving brokers' setting back the time-stamp clock to cover the fraud.

Moreover, the trade press reported that in April 1979 Bone and other brokers improperly controlled nearly 70 percent of one side of the cattle futures contracts on the Chicago exchange, holding almost fifteen thousand more contracts than regulations allowed. In December 1979, climaxing its investigation and settlement of what it called "serious and repeated record-keeping and procedural violations of Chicago Mercantile Exchange rules," the market fined Refco $250,000, then the largest penalty in the exchange's history, and suspended Red Bone in Springdale for three years, one of its most severe sanctions short of criminal prosecution.

At the same juncture there were added charges from market sources and even Congress, where Democratic representative Benjamin Rosenthal of New York contended that a conspiracy of food-processing executives and brokers, including Refco, had managed an insider-trading scheme to manipulate prices and make millions in "turnaround profits" in the summer of 1979. Alerted by other traders and market officials appalled at the piracy, the House Small Business Committee staff, including a former trader on the market, determined that "the entire commodities exchange was awash in scandal," as one account put it, from January 1978 to April 1979. House staff investigators became convinced that more than thirty insiders had colluded in some fifteen "secret signals" that allowed them to manipulate futures contracts for themselves and others, "an interlocking group," as one account described them, making over $110 million in illicit gains—some 70 percent of the total profit on the entire exchange over that period.

Under Blair's tutelage, the Arkansas governor's wife had been in the market when nine such secret signals were given, according to congressional records, five of them sent by the market manipulators during the weeks and months when she was receiving the bulk of her own $100,000 profit, though only one of her trades coincided with the precise dates identified in the House staff investigation. Still, her last weeks of trading exhibited an inexplicable recklessness and abandon. Suddenly losing more than $26,000 in June 1979, she came back in July to do her boldest betting, "going both short and long," as one account described it, "on separate block of fifty cattle contracts, her largest position yet." In one humid week that July the governor's wife grossed more than $54,000, her largest winnings to date, and she then abruptly quit the commodities market after only nine months, never to return. Looking at the record fifteen years later, exchange professionals and other traders would be baffled. "They almost never see behavior," one reporter recorded, "like Hillary's last-minute killing and sudden exit."

As the proof of larger market manipulation became more compelling, it would be the surviving evidence of Hillary Rodham's personal account that established beyond any plausible doubt what happened. To begin with, as Dow Jones analyst Caroline Baum and commodities trader Victor Niederhof documented in a later study, she had again and again defied the trend in the biggest bull market in the history of cattle in North America, a phenomenon simply too unlikely to be either dumb luck or skill. In her first two trades, her final two, and her most profitable in the interim, she had invested from the short side, banking on a decline in cattle prices that flew in the face of all market logic as well as the herd-reduction theory Blair himself was supposed to be following. The confirmations for her two most lucrative trades would later be found missing, while the known details of her transactions defied belief. Her purchases and sales were consistently made at virtually the most favorable prices of the day; if legitimate, the odds against such prescience and mastery would have been "about the same as those of finding the Dead Sea Scrolls on the steps of the State House in Little Rock," as Baum and Niederhof put it.

More telling still was the lethal, unbelievably reckless risk she and Blair ran with such apparent abandon, and with only the vaguest and most general memory afterward. According to market records, in November and December 1978 and again in the flurry of July 1979, literally the beginning of Bill Clinton's gubernatorial career, Hillary Rodham's liability stood at more than $1 million for days on end, and on two occasions for as much as three weeks. Between November 1978 and July 1979, as the Baum-Niederhof study shows clearly enough, a minuscule fluctuation in the market in any one day would have resulted in a loss equal to at least five times the Clintons' annual income and five times their net worth. On July 17, 1979, alone, the liability on her newly opened positions plus her deficit from the day before would have obliterated the family's salaries and assets *without* any adverse move in the market. She had to win—and evidently knew she would—to avoid financial catastrophe only six months into the governorship.

The vastly privileged treatment of the new First Lady by her brokerage also told a story of fix and favor. In the autumn of 1978 and again the following summer, her account was undermargined by $50,000 to $130,000 for periods of days. While customers on the exchange were usually required to maintain an equity of five times the margin requirement, the governor's wife was allowed to average an equity of less than one-fifth the required margin, and far less at crucial moments. Again it seemed obvious that Blair, still wheeling and dealing with Bone in the millions, was covering for his trading protégé and his old friend the governor, though no discretionary forms were ever filed as legally required for the thirty out of thirty-two Rodham trades he had placed for her. Numerous other records of her transactions were missing or contained unaccountable discrepancies, and her first two monthly statements would show identical typing misalignments and faulty strokes.

"After each big win, she withdrew the spoils," recorded the Baum study. She would go on to the end trading with the bravado of a person with limitless resources, on three different occasions dealing with contracts that would have required a million dollars in equity, once controlling 62 contracts with a market value of nearly $2 million, in her last winning gambit trading 115 contracts with a value of $3.2 million, though the equity in her account was a negative $18,000. At one point she doubled up, in effect bet everything, when her required margin was $115,000 and she properly owed $135,000 to her broker. "Mrs. Clinton was allowed to trade like a millionaire, in the process violating numerous rules and procedures that industry professionals have developed to prevent financial catastrophe to customer and brokerage house alike,'' Baum and Niederhof concluded. "Only if she had held a confirmed round-trip ticket would someone in Mrs. Clinton's position have been willing to risk the farm in such a high-stakes game.''

The windfall had "all the trappings of prearranged trades,'' said a former career attorney with the chief counsel of the IRS. In 1995 economists at Auburn and North Florida Universities ran a sophisticated computer statistical model of the First Lady's trades for publication in the *Journal of Economics and Statistics,* using all the available records as well as market data from the *Wall Street Journal.* The probability of Hillary Rodham's having made her trades legitimately, they calculated, was less than one in 250,000,000.

Over the same period in 1979 Congressman Rosenthal and others would charge that the manipulations accounted for an "unexpected and unexplainable'' sudden 12 percent rise in the price of meat in mid-August 1979, worsening the nation's already rampant inflation and further jeopardizing Jimmy Carter's prospects for reelection in the following year's race against Ronald Reagan.

After soaring nearly 60 percent over the previous two years, cattle futures took a dive in the late summer and autumn of 1979, wiping out those who had lingered too long. Blair himself reportedly suffered a $15 million trading loss, and on October 15, 1979, he filed a lawsuit charging his old poker friend Red Bone and Refco with repeatedly bilking customers. Charges included joint manipulation of the cattle futures market in which Refco was accused of secretly giving false assurances to customers like Blair and then "squeezing,'' or trading against, them. Such maneuvers cost Blair and his "trading group,'' his complaint alleged, even more than the $15 million he had recorded in his bankruptcy filing. The suit seemed to implicate Blair, if not a relatively small-fry Hillary Rodham, in the company's purported schemes to manipulate the markets. "If this was such a rogue outfit,'' the *Wall Street Journal* mused after the trades were exposed fourteen years later, "how could a Yale-Watergate staff lawyer believe that by doing business there she was playing by the rules?''

Refco went on to be sued successfully for questionable practices by several other customers and associates, including former brokers in the Springdale office. Cocounsel on one of the lawsuits against Refco after the cattle crash would be Rose's own Hillary Rodham. Soon to become a major power in global financial markets, however, Refco was later implicated with the notoriously corrupt and scandalous Bank of Credit and Commerce International (BCCI), "the central bank," wrote one authority on its history over the 1970s and 1980s, "for terrorists, spies, arms dealers and drug lords."

Yet when presented with congressional evidence of rigged trading, including some names of the insiders who allegedly sent the "secret signals," the Chicago Mercantile Exchange prevaricated, then simply interred the larger scandal in inquiries never completed, findings never announced. "There were too many big interests, too many big names involved," said one trader familiar with the cover-up, which he saw as business as usual for the troubled market. In the light of such abuses, Thomas Eagleton, the former US senator from Missouri and Democratic vice presidential nominee, himself a governor of the Chicago Mercantile Exchange, called in vain for more public oversight of commodities speculation, deploring the supposed regulation of futures trading as a "Chicago mirage . . . something of a myth" and the exchange's enforcement mechanism as a "sleeping pygmy." But such pleas were no match for the political power exerted by the market. The exchange would command some of the most extensive lobbies of insiders in Washington and some of the richest political action committees and most lavish contributions in American politics—all ensuring that futures trading would continue largely under its own dubious self-regulation.

By October 1979 Hillary Rodham was free and clear and opened a $5,000 account with a Stephens broker in Little Rock with whom she had dealt in small transactions since 1976. Stephens, the past and future major Clinton supporter, would have crucial business ties with both Refco and the criminal BCCI, including an instrumental role in introducing BCCI into the American banking system. With the Stephens brokerage she now invested again in more conventional stocks, including the DeBeers and Engelhard corporations of South Africa, both notorious for their role in the apartheid regime there. At one juncture her account showed a $26,894 profit, and she even made three trades, bringing in $10,000, the week of her daughter's birth. But without Red Bone or Jim Blair her more magical market prowess deserted her, and she closed out the relatively modest, cautious trading in the spring of 1980 with a net profit of only $6,500 (wrongly reported as a $1,009 loss on the couple's tax return).

The Clintons made a down payment on another house and purchased further property beyond Whitewater, in addition to making added securities purchases, including tax-exempt municipal bonds to begin what they called a "nest egg" for the child they had conceived during their windfall. As for her most lucrative and high-risk venture in 1978–79, Hillary Rodham would always claim to have known nothing of Red Bone's wrongdoing and exceptional penalties or of the pandemic corruption on the Chicago Mercantile Exchange, well publicized at the time in the trade press and among avid market watchers and investors. For his part, questioned fifteen years later about the 1978–79 trades, Red Bone could not even remember her as a client. "In Arkansas you remember everyone," a local politician would say, "by remembering no one."

Soon after the elaborately manipulated commodities boom, which enriched large corporate investors as well as individuals, both Jim Blair and Red Bone went to work for Tyson Foods full time, the lawyer as well-paid corporate counsel, the infraction-prone trader as official company broker. Tyson, like Stephens, would continue during the Clinton years in Little Rock to be one of the most powerful forces in Arkansas, and together the two companies would be the beneficiaries of tens of millions in state-promoted business and literally billions in ongoing income derived under a regime of regulatory, tax, and other political advantages.

◆ ◆ ◆

Jim and Diane Blair were married by the governor in September 1979 in the same room where he and Hillary had their own reception. Clinton donned white tie and top hat, his wife acted as the Blairs' "best person" with her glasses off and a flower in her hair. Over the coming years the two couples continued to be the closest of friends, regularly vacationing at the Blairs' Ozarks lake retreat. Jim Blair came to be widely known as the governor's most intimate adviser on matters both governmental and personal. "He'd never make an important move without him," one associate said. Later the Clintons would encourage Diane Divers Blair to write a history of the 1992 presidential campaign, in which she participated as an aide. She had previously written a text on Arkansas government and a book based on Hattie Caraway's journals. Of all the old Arkansas friends, the Blairs were among those most frequently in the White House in 1993–94.

For those who watched such relationships and then later learned of the commodity windfall there was little doubt about the essential financial and political commerce at Red Bone's brokerage from the autumn of 1978 through the torrid trading of 1979. Jim Blair had obviously had the money to cover for his friends. The commodity trades were only the beginning of the money and favors the Clintons would enjoy— money and favors that would leave them consorting not only with unsavory characters and practices but with a covert, manipulative world outside the law. "The cattle deal was just a form of money laundering, that's all," said a prominent lawyer who had been a US attorney during the era. "It was a way to fix up Bill and Hillary a little without being too direct about it."

Hillary Rodham had taken what one peer called the "sweet deal" without apparent hesitation, had taken advantage, had taken the profits and left under egregiously suspicious circumstances. Not long afterward, she would evince the same ethical and legal myopia when the couple's Whitewater debt was suddenly being paid from suspect sources, by a partner whose piratical banking practices she knew intimately. "You have to understand," said an old friend from Yale, "she took what she thought they were entitled to in making such a sacrifice in this steamy, raw, backward place." She had perforce given up her own Washington potential and, with it, much of the idealism of her past, the lessons from the Reverend Don Jones, her outrage at the migrant labor camps, and more. Tallied on buy and sell slips from Refco, the crucial missing statements, and the revealing shards that survived was not merely another market scam but a gifted young woman's bargain with destiny as well.

Historians and political analysts came to believe that the Carter presidency never quite recovered from the inflationary forces and widespread sense of economic uncertainty fed in part by the sudden summer jump in meat prices in 1979. With such "relentlessly bad news," Jack Germond and Jules Witcover concluded their study of the 1980 election, "political diversion was impossible." That summer, sorely perplexed amid Washington's frustrations and his own failures and isolation, Jimmy Carter had purged his cabinet and made his famous "malaise" speech, warning that "special interests" were running amok while the nation suffered "paralysis, stagnation, and drift." Carter's decline only deepened as Ronald Reagan, once feared for his own right-wing devotion to the same special interests, gained acceptance by default. "It's a bitter pill," a Carter White House aide said, looking back. "Things like that cattle market deal really got the president and helped elect Reagan, and people like the Clintons were in it themselves, and nobody thought twice."

◆ ◆ ◆

The corrupt commodity trades were but one watershed event in their paradoxical relationship of uneasily merged careers and tangled feelings. With a husband already well known for his financial insouciance Hillary Rodham was now clearly the rainmaker and money manager of the marriage. Observers watched as she evolved from the unmercenary young woman into the sharp-eyed overseer of their political and material fortunes.

She announced her pregnancy at the end of September 1979, saying that the governor was "ecstatic" and that she did not know how soon she would return to Rose after the delivery. "Oh, it'll be Clinton," she said when asked by local reporters about the child's destined surname. At Chelsea Clinton's birth in February 1980 both parents were "overcome" with joy, as a friend remembered.

By then Hillary Rodham had been promoted to full partner at Rose, and her professional attachments were growing. At the firm she was close to partners Webster Hubbell and Bill's childhood friend, the courtly young Vince Foster, who "worshiped" her, according to a mutual friend. By 1980 she was also thoroughly enmeshed in Rose's own considerable intramural politics and their nexus of power in the statehouse and throughout Arkansas. Despite the expected restraints of motherhood, she seemed to many to be more than ever "her own woman" and a strong figure of tangible independence beside her husband.

Amid the quiet investments and market windfalls, the public pregnancy and celebrated birth, a fitful ebb and flow of tension and quarreling was ongoing in the personal quarters of the mansion. From Clinton's first years as attorney general, Little Rock had been awash in gossip about his blatant womanizing, often unhidden from staff aides and escorts and seeming to accelerate after 1980 with the birth of his first child.

What Rudy Moore and others called the first couple's "marital troubles" became well known to an ever-widening circle in the city's incestuous society. The excesses or problems of those in power, including members of the legislature and other political figures, were a staple in the living rooms or country clubs of Little Rock. Among others, Winthrop Rockefeller had indulged his legendary drinking, Faubus his country boy's pleasures; even the relentlessly serious Dale Bumpers was rumored to have an eye for the ladies, and most recently the relatively more modern and urbane Pryors had gone through a painful marital split. But with the Clintons, many believed, there was from the beginning a quantitative and qualitative difference: there were too many women and too many stories to be a matter of a temporary lapse or of smears by opponents, too many bitter and violent fights at the mansion to be dismissed.

Still, the code of social and political silence held fast, as it long would, for the usual reasons—discretion, fear, indecision, shame, indifference, pride, ambition. "Hillary was said to be devastated and humiliated by his behavior during this period," Connie Bruck wrote later, "but to have determined that she would not leave the marriage, in which she had invested so deeply." Even the state troopers whom Hillary treated with scorn were struck by her stoicism. A young woman lawyer in Little Rock claimed that she was accosted by Clinton while he was attorney general and that when she recoiled he forced himself on her, biting and bruising her. Deeply affected by the assault, the woman decided to keep it all quiet for the sake of her own hard-won career and that of her husband. When the husband later saw Clinton at the 1980 Democratic Convention, he delivered a warning. "If you ever approach her," he told the governor, "I'll kill you." Not even seeing fit to deny the incident, Bill Clinton sheepishly apologized and duly promised never to bother her again.

The indolence of the Arkansas press toward their prowling governor might be difficult for those outside the culture to fathom. There seemed to be a tacit acceptance of the governor's escapades, even though much of the womanizing occurred on state time with the troopers standing guard. It was as though the inherent abuse of his wife and of at least some of the women were not a matter of character in the state's highest-ranking elected official. Reporters were unwilling or unable to document the ubiquitous allegations, much less ponder the individual or social pathology of what they might find.

For Hillary Rodham, despite her carefully cultivated roles and prominence, the agenda remained his, and it was to his culture and system, his career, his indulgence, fickle discipline, political survival, and self-defined success to which her choice had bound her. For all the trappings of independence, some thought, she was already, at thirty-two or thirty-three, in many ways as subordinated to her own "modern" young husband in Little Rock as her mother had been to Hugh Rodham in Park Ridge. "She'd rather be run over by a car than admit it, but Hillary really was a fifties wife with nice eighties accessories," said a friend. "I think the truth is that by this time in that first term she was the last thing she or Mrs. Rodham planned for her to be—another woman victim" and one frustrated by faithlessness as well.

Bill's womanizing seemed to repay sacrifice with emotional savagery and to drive humiliation still deeper. "You always have to remember," said someone who watched them through the years, "this is a woman who could have been a big-time lawyer and made a hundred thousand whenever she wanted without playing anybody's market, somebody who could've gone into politics herself, been a damned good governor or senator, ended up running herself in 1992 and, I'd bet you, beating Bill Clinton—among other things, on the character issue. Funny, isn't it?"

◆   ◆   ◆

At the Democrats' 1978 midterm convention Clinton had already sided with the party's emerging ultraconservative wing against the Mc-Govern remnants, what his Arkansas supporters contemptuously called "the wildies of former days." Forerunners of his own ostensible New Democrats of the 1990s, these were a shifting coalition of elected officials from the South and West, politicians funded and programmed by the same powers that lay behind their increasingly indistinguishable GOP peers, along with the ever more powerful Washington faction of lawyers and lobbyists, who were ultimately paid by the same elements. Clinton's avid maneuvering to know, and be known in, these circles continued during most of the first term despite periodic local warnings about the perils of unsightly overreaching. "He insisted on flirting with national office," thought editor Starr, "when his state office was in danger."

But Carter's waning strength soon became an issue that overshadowed the Democratic Party's inner shift of power. Clinton was one of many who chafed at the administration's disarray, a product of Carter's own stale establishment appointees and aborted promises. In the summer of 1979 Clinton was summoned, along with his fellow governors, to Camp David, where he warned that President Carter was now even weaker in Arkansas than he had been in 1976, before he ran as a relative unknown.

Clinton's self-promotion and his jabs at Carter were undisguised at the 1980 Democratic Convention in New York's Madison Square Garden. Behind the scenes he was involved for a time in the ultimately abortive efforts to reconcile Carter and Senator Edward Kennedy, at least for the sake of appearances. In the mediation with other prominent Democrats, Clinton carefully threaded his way between the two factions, "always thinking about his own future," said one witness. His convention speech, carried only briefly by one network but proudly reprinted in Arkansas, had been carefully edited by Hillary and gave evidence of what was to come in 1992—both his empathy for the nation's problems and the intrinsic limits of his vision of politics and governance.

Pointedly acknowledging "the faults of our party . . . and this president," he seemed to recognize the longer-term "breaking down" of the postwar economy, the rising force of "special-interest politics," and the demagogic attraction of Ronald Reagan, whose reactionary voice was "clear, consistent, and committed." The Democrats should now "speak to the millions of Americans who are not here—who do not even watch us . . . or listen to us. Who do not care. Who will not bother to vote or, if they do, will probably not vote for us." Yet there was no need to dwell on what he brushed aside as "the past" of Franklin Roosevelt and the Democrats' attempted healing of old wrongs: "We have proved that our party is more sensitive than the Republicans to equality and justice, to the poor and the dispossessed." Now, instead, the tasks were not political in the classic sense of the distribution of wealth and power but instrumental, technical. The Democrats needed to offer "creative and realistic solutions to our economic and energy and environment problems."

Between the lines was much of the ideological paradox he would perpetuate as a presidential candidate and eventually as a president. There was the leery turning away from issues of equity at a moment when the GOP right was exploiting a vast blue-collar and middle-class unrest rooted in the failure to resolve those very issues. Growing economic precariousness, social tensions and decay, crime, misshapen fiscal and tax policies—all that and more were the legacy of the 1970s and a prologue to the illusionary, painful decade to come. But his speech took for granted the post-McGovern myth that Democrats must be more mercantile than their far more practiced Republican rivals, more "fungible," said one observer, "like oil or gas, able to flow across normal political boundaries and assume new shapes."

Clinton's call to transcend special interests, coming as it did from a governor whose home state was, and would remain, a singular haven for vested power and political money, was most ironic. "Defending the status quo and calling it new," one writer saw as the current among ambitious young Democratic politicians like Clinton, belonging to "a party that can no longer state coherently what it believes (and whom it represents).'' But ''the ideological bankruptcy of the Democrats as a governing party'' was not a topic the politicians, least of all Clinton, wished to debate that humid week in Manhattan. His scolding speech to the convention almost a respite, he flew back to Little Rock to face his own troubled race for reelection.

At home he seemed besieged by a series of crises, all set against the backdrop of a sagging economy. In the spring of 1979 and again a year later, tornadoes had plunged down to wreak havoc across the state; a murderous heat wave followed in July and August 1980. The Ku Klux Klan held a tense, embarrassing national rally in Little Rock. ''Good evening, white people,'' crowed David Duke as he began the proceedings. *Soldier of Fortune* magazine was billing Arkansas as a haven for mercenaries, Klansmen, and other paramilitary movements. In May 1980 AP&L's Nuclear One power plant sprang a radioactive leak. That September a Titan II missile was accidentally launched from a silo barely forty miles north of Little Rock, crashing into woods nearby and nearly detonating a nuclear warhead seven hundred times as powerful as the Hiroshima bomb. In each crisis Clinton had been an attentive governor, rushing to the site of the accident or natural disaster, relaying reassuring information from local or federal officials. But the events, like the general state of the Arkansas economy, were anything but political assets.

The most damaging episode came in May 1980, when the White House decided to resettle Cuban refugees at Fort Chaffee, near Fort Smith. Within weeks they numbered nearly twenty thousand, making the camp one of the largest population centers in the state. When disturbances broke out in the teeming, squalid compound, nearby residents were ''arming themselves to the teeth,'' a sheriff told a reporter. While Clinton squabbled with the White House and Pentagon about controls and conditions, a thousand refugees broke free on the night of June 1 and stormed down the highway. They were stopped only by a thin line of Arkansas state troopers, National Guardsmen, and deputies at the entrance to a small town bristling with guns.

It was a scorching encounter with the notorious incompetence of Carter's staff, as well as with the military's inertia and recalcitrance, and it dragged on for weeks as the governor was first praised for patient statesmanship ''in the grandest of American traditions,'' as the *Gazette* exulted, then accused of ''Mississippi madness'' or ''Faubus tactics'' by the *Pine Bluff Commercial* and others who thought his interference with federal authorities political grandstanding. In the welter of meetings and lengthy, often antagonistic phone calls, Clinton's demeanor alternated between cool deliberation and audible panic.

While Senator Bumpers and other ranking politicians scurried to distance themselves from the debacle, Clinton seemed trapped. By autumn Bumpers, tutored by Reagan campaign operatives, began his campaign as Republican candidate for governor of Arkansas with grim television ads featuring the worst of the rioting, showing only black refugees, and intoning that it happened here because Bill Clinton "did not stand up to Jimmy Carter." A righteous Clinton lashed back at his opponent for trying to "redneck" on the issue, a fact everyone understood all too clearly. But the ads played on to considerable effect.

In a Little Rock television station, as Clinton walked in for an interview, an old Democrat muttered to a reporter, "What kind of man lets a woman keep her own name?" In small towns elsewhere in the state there were snide remarks about the "unmanliness" of the fleshy young Clinton, who could "not even control his wife," as one person remembered the talk. Months before the election there were signs that Hillary's manifest independence was openly resented in what one native aptly called "the exquisite pecking order" of Arkansas. She had only added to the ire with her shapelessly "unfeminine" clothes and what many saw as a manner of downright insolence. The governor's wife even had the effrontery to read a book while seated next to her husband at an Arkansas Razorbacks football game.

In the face of gathering discontent the Clinton reelection campaign was now strangely heedless and impotent. Everywhere he went, it seemed, the governor found the same complaints and questions: about the Cubans at Fort Chaffee, about his wife's name, about government scandals and out-of-state aides, about his presidential ambitions—and always, about the higher cost of car tags. "Rudy, they're killing me out there," he told Moore after a swing through the dirt-poor rural southern counties, where they were paying as much to license a ten-year-old Chevrolet as the Little Rock bankers paid on a new Cadillac. "They tell me I kicked them in the teeth." He talked about calling a special session of the legislature to change the tax law, but he talked about it only briefly, according to Moore. The trucking lobby, Tyson, and the rest were far too powerful, and it would only mean a major fight with some of Clinton's own backers. "Nothing was done," Moore recorded.

They had been complacent to begin with, putting the campaign in the hands of too many Clinton camp followers with no experience in a statewide race. The May primary was a warning. Monroe Schwarzlose, a seventy-seven-year-old retired turkey farmer who finished last in the 1978 primary with less than 6,000 votes, now picked up nearly 140,000, or 31 percent. Still, the Clinton camp remained mired in bickering and inertia. "He wouldn't make the decisions that would bring the campaign out of its lassitude," Moore wrote later. At an early point Steve Smith brought him a stinging populist ad attacking the telephone company for higher charges on toll calls. "The man in this building wants to raise the amount you pay," it said against the backdrop of Southwestern Bell's corporate headquarters in Little Rock, then shifted to Clinton's office at the capitol, "and the man in *this* building is going to keep him from doing it." But Clinton perfunctorily rejected the ad as "demagogical and unnecessary," one staff member of them remembered.

As usual, Hillary Rodham supplied her blunt corrective. "Bill, don't be such a Pollyanna," she would say in staff meetings. "Some of these people you think are your friends aren't." Yet he appeared oblivious, and even she "did not seem to be fully engaged," as Moore saw it. As the campaign foundered, the governor's office was further shaken by its chronic rivalries and his own evasions. An angry group of staffers had gone to Moore about finally pushing out the already marginalized John Danner, along with his wife, Nancy Pietrafasa, both of whom were personal friends of the Clintons. Presented with a virtual ultimatum from his underlings, Clinton quickly agreed but insisted Moore fire their friends, "a terrible way to handle" the problem, the chief of staff remembered, "but . . . he simply couldn't do it."

Bill Clinton would go on, as one aide put it, "in search of a magic consensus," telling everyone what they wanted to hear, then simply failing to fulfill his commitments. It was not out of "any duplicity . . . from cunning, or in the pursuit of power or money or even in the pursuit of his own self-interest," Rudy Moore and others maintained, but rather simply "from his nature, which was to trust everyone and to want everyone to like him and to see the worth of what he was trying to do." At the same time there was now another dimension beyond the old habits. "Bill Clinton was not the same person psychologically in 1980," Moore would say, alluding to "something personal, perhaps in his relationship with Hillary." Others thought the disarray in the candidate and campaign only a continuation of his personal style and administration. "He never thought he was going to lose, but the distraction was nothing new," one supporter told a local reporter. But there was no question about the toll of the bitter quarrels in the mansion and Clinton's own agonized response, which would evolve over time. The personal turmoil and indiscretion might be their own business, "a private matter," as they both would say defensively. From the beginning, however, there was no real separating the private from the public, personality and character from performance and governance. In their tangled relationship—who they were together, the impressive strengths and the poignant weaknesses—shaped much of what he was and would become, as president of the United States.

◆　◆　◆

His opponent was Frank White, whom a *New York Times* reporter called "an affable, unimaginative Republican with a blustering style and an aversion to syntax." A forty-seven-year-old former Democrat from Texarkana who had served in the Pryor administration but broken with it over a patronage squabble, White was an Annapolis graduate, a cheerful, open-faced broker and banker whose main distinction was a booming voice that required no public address system and that "he rarely lower[ed]," according to one listener, "even in conversation." He formally defected to the GOP only at the beginning of 1980 and was encouraged to run by state party leaders. At first his campaign had been "hesitant," as the *Gazette* recorded. He had even asked the advice of old Democrat Orval Faubus, who told him in inimitable Arkansas style, "Organize and raise money. Issues mean nothing."

Then the primary exposed Clinton's vulnerability, and White appealed for help from the Republican National Committee and Governors' Association, which finally "allowed" him, as he remembered, to attend a school for Republican congressional candidates in Arlington, Virginia. "I was the only gubernatorial candidate there," he told a reporter. "I knew nobody in the Republican Party. I was just the man who came from Arkansas. It was kind of a joke."

What followed struck no one as funny. White returned from his school with much of his campaign staff and substantial resources now provided by the national party. His platform style grew polished and his advertising far more professional, slick, and negative, epitomized by the implicitly racist footage of black Cubans breaking out of Fort Chaffee. Widely shown, too, was a photograph of Frank White with a smiling Ronald Reagan, then leading presidential polls in Arkansas. Most of all, there was a felt change in the tenor of what Republicans and the Clinton opponents they enlisted were now saying, a new assault not only or even mainly on the governor's record but on his wife, her maiden name, who and what she was as a woman. A decision had been made in Arlington to go after Hillary Rodham. "They were saying that there was this smart-ass bitch out there in Arkansas, and she could be used just like the Cubans or anything else," said someone familiar with what happened. "That kind of thing. Tough politics."

Sequels proved ironic. The concerted personal attacks would be more than a matter of "tough" campaigning. The election of 1980 was to be a crucial event in the Clintons' lives, affecting both their future governance, their personal relationship, and ultimately their presidency. The issue of her status as a woman and wife and her eventual change of both name and personal style became in themselves substantive. In any case, the affably venomous Frank White's misogynist campaign drew continuing and ardent support from the national GOP, with Republican handlers from Washington to Little Rock shaping and inciting the wider anti-Clinton, "bitch" strategy. Among those watching the spectacle from high in the Republican camp was David Gergen, the former Nixon loyalist from the Watergate White House who became a tactician for Ronald Reagan. It was Gergen who scripted Reagan's famous jab at Carter in the 1980 presidential debates, cueing the former B-movie actor to ask a television audience, "Are you better off than you were four years ago?" Little more than a dozen years after that bitter campaign, with hopes he might perform similar services for the new employers his old ones had once attacked so malevolently, David Gergen would be named a ranking official in the Clinton White House.

♦　♦　♦

Once again Mack McLarty was Clinton's campaign treasurer, and once again Clinton drew contributions from many of the state's corporate giants, major banks, and other forces, including the ever-present Stephens, Inc.—all of them familiar with the transaction implicit in donation and influence. "The road construction companies poured money into Clinton's campaign," Associated Press analyst Bill Simmons wrote two days after the election, pointing to the irony of the higher license fees' losing votes while gaining money. "His revenue laws meant business for them through the state Highway Department." Clinton would spend over $477,000, with a deficit of more than $63,000, only a little less than he paid to win handily in 1978. But now it was Frank White who set records. In the richest GOP campaign in Arkansas since Winthrop Rockefeller's largely self-financed runs in the 1960s, the challenger listed more than $442,000, including $50,000 of his own money, and heavy support from vested power the Clinton administration seemed to threaten if not actually affect—utilities such as AP&L, timber combines like Georgia Pacific, physicians and others still angry about his rural clinics. The interests, though by no means all of them, had put money behind an Arkansas Republican as never before, and some hedged their bets by contributing to both candidates.

Desperate as the race wore down, Hillary Rodham placed what one account called "an emergency phone call" to their old adviser Dickie Morris. Only months after the 1978 victory, Clinton had deliberately cast aside the controversial consultant, and eventually he dropped their contract. "Whether he didn't think he needed him ever again, or just thought Dickie was too nasty for Arkansas, or what, I don't know," said a friend. "I suspect it was as much good old arrogance as anything." Morris himself had seen their rift as Clinton's fatal distinction between governing and running, as if leadership should be somehow above politics. "There was a feeling that I got that I was something dirty, that they didn't want to touch me with gloves," Morris remembered. "Sort of like, 'This was my sordid past when I was running for office, but now I'm governor.' " Now, in October 1980, Hillary finally located Morris in Florida, where, with characteristic flexibility, he was managing a reactionary Republican who was running for the Senate, his third GOP client of the season. There were differing versions of how Morris responded to her plea for help. "I got the impression he told them to go screw themselves," one aide recalled. "He took one look," remembered another, "and knew it was gone." In any case, Hillary Rodham's frantic summons to what other advisers called "the hit man" did nothing to change the character or the outcome of the campaign.

"I have never felt more comfortable and at ease before an election in my life," Clinton told the press in mid-October, denouncing in particular "that Republican campaign school." With audience after audience he spoke of his governorship as "the most humbling two years of my life" and confidently outlined the next term. Local polls showed him in the lead by as much as twenty points with a week to go. Yet callers to radio shows and questioners at meetings continued to ask about his "high-paid" staff from out of state, the petty scandals, his national ambitions, Cubans, car tags, his wife's name.

On election night first returns came from Miller County, in the far southwestern corner of the state, where Bill Blythe had once courted Virginia, and Clinton knew that his margin there was not enough, that the race was lost. The Republican of less than a year's standing was only the second of his party to win the statehouse in the twentieth century, Bill Clinton the first incumbent to lose reelection since Faubus won in an upset in 1954. At 77 percent the turnout would be the highest in Arkansas in decades. White won by 32,000 votes out of more than 800,000.

Beneath the surface, as the numbers were understood at the mansion and in Little Rock's suites, it was a rout. The *Gazette* thought the outcome "could almost be termed a landslide." Clinton carried only twenty-five of the state's seventy-five counties, compared to at least fifty in each of his previous statewide elections. White won the Third Congressional District with 60 percent of the vote, carrying some old Clinton counties two to one. In the presidential election Ronald Reagan won Arkansas, the state with the greatest single shift of voters from the Carter victory four years earlier. Yet there was no GOP sweep. Though the Cuban refugees affected everyone's margin, Dale Bumpers was reelected to the Senate with 59 percent of the vote, and other Democrats won handily. In Arkansas's fiercely local politics White was the only GOP exception, outpolling even Reagan. However they voted in other races, the voters had repudiated Bill Clinton.

Though he comprehended the returns at one level, as the night wore on there was deepening shock in the war room Rudy Moore had set up at campaign headquarters in Little Rock. Clinton stayed in seclusion at the mansion for hours, refusing to meet reporters or even a rally of supporters at the capitol. He emerged at midnight to make a choked five-minute statement of concession to the stilled, weeping Clinton camp at the Camelot Inn, then hurried out a back door, flanked by his state police bodyguards.

◆　◆　◆

The next morning, his wife at his side holding eight-month-old Chelsea, Virginia and Roger behind them, he met a crowd of supporters his staff had hastily gathered in the backyard of the mansion. "Hillary and I have shed a few tears for our loss," he began, in what would be an emotional little speech about his boyhood "in an ordinary working family in this state," his caring for the people even "when the right course may not be popular," his leadership in "crisis after crisis when . . . people could have been harmed and our reputation irrevocably damaged." "I want you to be generous with me in defeat," he told them, his voice cracking. "I want you to be determined with me to go on fighting for our future." Roger Clinton, in "full rock-and-roll regalia," as a reporter described his dress, walked about the grounds punching the air with his fist and chanting, "We'll be back! We'll be back!"

Afterward they went to lunch with the Blairs, the governor "half-laughing, half-crying," Diane Blair remembered, "their sorrow and shock and self-reproach almost impenetrable. . . . It was all going to be over, and defeat was burned into his political soul."

For more than two weeks he continued to avoid the press he had so avidly courted. Starr was scathing about the backyard farewell that had barred reporters' questions. "And there he was on the patio of the mansion, blaming everybody except himself for his defeat, telling the people of Arkansas, in effect, I knew what you wanted, but I also knew what was best for you, and that is what I tried to give you." If mute in public, Clinton had been privately calling legislators and politicians all over the state, talking about "a need to enhance his public image and to stabilize his political future," as one of them told a reporter.

Finally, in late November, Clinton consented to a handful of screened interviews. "A guy who supposedly has an IQ of a zillion did something stupid," he told the Associated Press, talking about the unexpected "voter hostility" to the license fees but saying nothing about how it had all happened, his original road tax proposals, the fatal surrender to the truckers, Tyson, and the rest. His defeat was the result of the fees, the Cubans, the "mood of the times," and his own image as "too young, ambitious, arrogant, and insensitive," he told a friendly John Brummett of the *Gazette*. He had been perceived, wrongly, "as being a liberal rather than as an activist governor." Now he was simply going to lead a private life and look into a law practice.

Both publicly and privately he blamed a large cast of villains and enemies, including several within his own ranks. Many of his "publicized problems as governor were inherited," he told reporters in unveiled criticism of David Pryor. As for his own Democratic Party, Clinton thought it "spoiled," "asleep at the switch," and in "pretty bad shape," as he put it during an early December radio interview. He would not blame his wife or her maiden name for his defeat, he told the *Democrat* at the end of the year, but his opponents were "loose with the truth" and the "biggest hypocrites." The "press and . . . campaign workers had not taken White seriously enough." People misperceived his ambition when his "only desire had been to be governor for six or eight years."

When one loyal aide came to his office that December to report on a governmental issue, Clinton brushed the topic aside and was grimly furious. "He looked me right in the eye, and said, 'You were the major

cause of my defeat,' " the official remembered. "I was astounded because my issues never even came up in the campaign. . . . But he
railed at me. It was all my fault." State trooper and bodyguard Gentry
overheard the couple in the mansion rancorously deploring their benighted electorate. "They always held themselves to be quite a bit
above the average Arkansan," Gentry told Meredith Oakley in 1993.
"They went on and on, talking about how stupid the people of Arkansas were for electing Frank White. God, they were mad."

The final weeks in office were filled with such postmortems. Voters
judged him too big for his britches, thought he'd come too far too fast,
he would say; they had decided to "send a message," though they
"didn't really expect or want" him to lose. Meanwhile, there were
offers of consolation and of the ritual sinecures, some tendered out of
mixed motives. Governor John Y. Brown of Kentucky, a social and
political friend whose own unsavory associations would intersect with
Clinton's more than once in the years to come, telephoned "several
times," as McLarty remembered, trying to persuade Clinton to take
the presidency of the University of Louisville, a position that, whatever
its other virtues, would almost certainly have removed the young Arkansas politician from a then-implicit national rivalry with Brown. "Bill
saw that one for what it was," said a statehouse aide. For days in December he toyed with running for the open chairmanship of the national Democratic Party he had just denounced as "spoiled." Now a
national committeeman, Jim Blair lobbied for him feverishly in Washington. But at the last moment Governor Jerry Brown of California
held back a crucial endorsement and the national post was gone. En-
mity toward him would be long and deep, extending into both the
public forums and the back alleys of the 1992 campaign.

Democrat columnist and Clinton nemesis Meredith Oakley saw the
episode over the chairmanship as another example of his childlike
"coy" ambitions and predicted that one more rejection "might wound
even his massive ego beyond recovery." However partisan, her observation was more accurate than most knew. Clinton was plunged into
what one account called "bitter depression," issuing in a burst of womanizing, a seemingly desperate search for conquest that shocked even
his most indulgent and cynical intimates. "What am I supposed to do,"
he asked one of them, "when all these women are there and want
me?"

But above all he plotted his return. "I felt sort of sick," he later
confided. "But the next day [after the election] I resolved that I was
going to run for governor again. I knew at some deep-down emotional

level that I would have to run again in 1982 in order to live with myself the rest of my life." As he left office he had begun to attack White in the wings. It was as if he were again the fresh young challenger and outsider, with no burden of a record. Arkansas would be "back to dead last in everything," he told an audience in Hot Springs, if White's regime could not "renew faith in government." At a Razorbacks game that fall he felt an odd mixture of elation and immobilizing depression. "I'll be governor again," he announced to a surprised Woody Bassett, who had just heard from all their friends how "shattered" Clinton was.

Imagery was now everything, perception the key to both his history and his future. He fixed on his opponent's "misconception" of his liberalism, that he was too active, too bold, too assertive, when the reality was tragically different. At a quiet dinner of backers that Christmas one pulled him aside gently with the unwanted but historically accurate verdict. He had failed not because he had confronted the old system too hard, said the friend, but because he had done so too little. He had compromised and given way again and again. "If I believed that," Clinton replied dismissively, "I'd stick my head in a goddamned oven."

· 13 ·

Washington I
"A Slow-Motion Coup d'État"

As the defeated Clintons left the governor's mansion at the end of 1980, the Washington they would meet a decade later as president and First Lady was already taking shape. In the growing convergence of the Republican and Democratic Parties there was a slow-motion coup d'état in American politics and governance. Its origins went back to the early postwar days, the time when Bill Blythe was killed outside Sikeston and the Rodhams moved to Park Ridge.

Both parties had become far less than the sum of their electoral parts. The Republicans were in thrall to a newly minted ultraconservative ideology. An unmourned extinction of moderates compressed the Grand Old Party into an ever-narrower constituency of reaction and prejudice in the service of privilege. Democrats meanwhile became all the more expedient and deliberately undefined. Shunning old principles as a political or bureaucratic liability, they were intent on congressional feudalism and establishment jockeying, their own wanton politics of self further and further from the wider electorate they once claimed.

Despite alternating victories and ideological facades, the two old parties were becoming less representative. As Lord Bryce observed of the factions of another era in *The American Commonwealth,* they were like bottles, each with its own label, both empty. Despite seeming differences they were closer than ever in their common, unprecedented captivity to the base elements of money and power. "Indispensable enemies," political writer Walter Karp called them even before the

Carter or Reagan presidencies. Just how revealing and poignant his description was would not be evident for years.

Behind all the later rhetoric about "gridlock" and "breakdown" was in fact an elaborate, refined system that hummed with its own energy and equilibrium. It was this Washington that Bill and Hillary Clinton would meet in the 1990s.

♦ ♦ ♦

The presidency of Ronald Wilson Reagan officially began on January 20, 1981, with its own symbols. Even jaded Washington was taken aback. In limousines, private planes, furs, and jewels, the claimants of the new regime enveloped the city, flaunting wealth such as had not been seen since the notorious Gilded Age a century before. As if to mark the restoration, one group of GOP contributors rolled into the capital in the plush Pullman once ridden by legendary spoilsman J. P. Morgan, the Wall Street banker who had owned, it was said, not only the train but the tracks to Washington and the government at the end of the line.

Reagan's 1981 inauguration—the most expensive yet (and much of the spending illegal)—cost five times more than Carter's in 1977. In events both official and private there was a ready heedlessness about money and privilege. Georgetown parties were grander, more exclusive. Once-public ceremonies could be attended by invitation only. Even at $10,000 each, boxes for white-tie balls were in brisk demand. Outside the old Union Station on Capitol Hill, the neighborhood's homeless people caught the aroma of gourmet food at a reception inside and managed to crash the gate by squeezing among the stream of official guests. Politicians and lobbyists in formal dress recoiled from the smell and filth of the derelict intruders.

While Reagan took the oath of office, household staff rearranged the White House for new masters. To a place of honor in the Cabinet Room they brought from storage the portrait of Calvin Coolidge, the expressionless Vermont Republican whose administration supposedly epitomized the economic and social values Reagan was to employ. His White House would evoke nostalgia for some imagined schoolbook past. "He wrests from us something warmer than mere popularity, a kind of complicity," Garry Wills wrote of Reagan's soothing appeal. In 1984 the president's reelection theme was to be a soft, tinted commercial with the comforting announcement, "It's morning again in America."

Reagan and his regime were also the less comforting agents of "the most reactionary administration of the century," as a chronicler would epitomize them later. They had come seeking vengeance for the many reforms enacted since Calvin Coolidge—and they had come on the strength of a popular dismay at changes in postwar America. "The most original thing about Reagan," said a journalist, "was his uncompromising unoriginality." What followed the inauguration was without precedent in American politics. In weeks the administration had its plans moving through Congress and the bureaucracy. An assault on both the Democratic and Republican past, on a wide range of policy in effect over the past half century, the proposals called for a radical new tax structure favoring wealth. There was to be wholesale deregulation of business and finance. New budgets made a vast reallocation from domestic social programs to weaponry. While mocking government, the new conservative administration would actively use the enormous force of Washington as no government had before, bending it from public purpose to private gain.

For a moment it seemed the new legislation might atrophy in the usual congressional inaction. Then came the attempted assassination of the president outside the Washington Hilton on March 30. Reagan's recovery was far feebler than carefully staged public appearances suggested. But his very survival boosted his popularity and conferred fresh power. No filibusters now blocked his actions. No formidable Washington lobbies or inspired public mobilization stopped the promised change. Within the first 160 days Congress passed the new taxes and weapons buildup. By August the White House broke the air traffic controllers' strike with utter impunity. The Roaring Eighties had begun.

Then and later, many thought Reagan a mere figurehead. But at least part of the force of the administration traced to the character of the seemingly simple yet enigmatic man himself. "Reagan enunciated a set of ideological convictions quite at odds with the status quo he inherited. And he never, ever drew back from them, never apologized for them, never even acknowledged their defeat even when he was badly beaten," recalled an unsympathetic journalist, William Greider. "We remember him as a strong leader, though Reagan lost on many major issues. . . . Yet he still seemed like a winner."

When the Republicans left office a dozen years later there were the usual political arguments about achievement. They claimed credit for the fall of the USSR and the end of the cold war. Yet the collapse of the corrupt Soviet regime was purely internal as few in history were—and might have happened sooner but for the diversion posed by a new US bellicosity in the 1980s. The Republicans claimed to have cleansed and simplified government. Yet their Washington was befouled by scandal, a capital where some bureaucracies burgeoned while others decayed in place. Most of all, they claimed to have altered the course of the nation. "We are the change," Reagan boasted in a farewell address. "What a change it's been." And about that, at least, there was no question.

Over the 1980s and early 1990s there would take place what one study called "the largest transfer of wealth in the nation's history." The money neither appeared nor disappeared by magic. It was wrested by political means from the vast majority of Americans and given to the already affluent and powerful. "The nation traveled from the New Patriotism to the New Greed all within a mere decade," journalist Haynes Johnson would write. Inseparable from that passage, there was also a manifest change in America's consciousness of itself—a deepening sense of insecurity and uncertainty for the first time in half a century, since people like Bill Blythe and Virginia Cassidy, Dorothy Howell and Hugh Rodham went through the depression and World War II. "I don't really know what happened," said a typical worker in 1992, "but things now only get worse and not better, like they were supposed to."

In the bleak morning after, as the toll was counted, there were many who blamed Ronald Reagan and George Bush. Yet it was never that simple. What had happened to the nation was not—could not have been—at the hand of Republicans alone. Whatever its pretenses or the charges of its rivals, the rightist regime that took power amid such extravagance in January 1981 marked not a revolution so much as an evolution of forces long at work. The Reagan-Bush era would emanate from the converging histories of *both* parties, and in the Washington of the 1990s the larger political ethos was nothing if not bipartisan.

◆　◆　◆

Within the GOP Reagan's victory settled old scores. His election marked the triumph at last of the party's ultraconservative wing, which had long been denied power, not merely by Democrats but by a train of moderate Republican leaders. From the nominations of Wendell Willkie and Tom Dewey in the 1940s through the postwar presidencies of Dwight Eisenhower, Richard Nixon, and Gerald Ford, the reactionary right remained largely on the fringe—brooding and planning.

Republicans of both factions prospered in the great red-baiting of Democrats in the late 1940s, the kind of hysteria that enveloped Hillary Rodham's Park Ridge hometown, with its John Birch Society and its fearful suspicion or hatred of outsiders. But the repression by government and culture at large—the acceptance of domestic dirty tricks and covert actions, a more than forty-year cold war against dissent at home—worked to poison the grassroots citizen base of moderates themselves, stifling creative political thought and initiative among Republicans no less than among Democrats. J. Edgar Hoover's ranting against "pinks, punks, and pansies" would be a prelude to the bigotry of the fundamentalist Christian right of the 1990s, preparing the way for a zealots' seizure of the Grand Old Party once thought unimaginable. The Republican moderates' own irresistible chauvinism, concluded a historian, ultimately contained "the seeds of destruction."

The politics of the cold war could not resolve the philosophical rivalry within the Republican Party. The two wings remained divided about the role of government, about economic and social policy, and ultimately about class, wealth, and power. In the moderates' acceptance of government regulation and efforts at social welfare, conservatives saw craven betrayal of principle. And behind the right's orthodoxy of unrestrained markets and limited government, moderates sensed a greed and inequity the nation could no longer endure.

It was a schism marked by rancorous personal rivalries. Urged to unite behind a young Richard Nixon for the vice presidency in 1952 after a brutal internecine fight, Nixon's fellow California senator, conservative William Knowland, asked bitterly, "I have to nominate that dirty son of a bitch?" The same gritty hatred stoked the thunderous boos cascading down from the galleries on moderate Nelson Rockefeller at the 1964 Republican Convention, which nominated conservative Barry Goldwater—the convention that Hillary Rodham, a Goldwater Girl, imitated with such colorful detail and enthusiasm in her presentation at Maine South the following autumn, albeit without the venom of the original. There was the old animus, too, in the defeat of Reagan himself in bids for the nomination in 1968 and again in 1976. The extreme right deplored "Democrat" liberals, as everyone knew, but GOP moderates they truly despised. For more than three decades following World War II, including sixteen years of Republican presidents in the White House, the factions fought savagely behind the scenes, maintaining in public an uneasy, if enduring, balance. Their stalemate sustained a bipartisan consensus on federal policies evolved since the 1930s.

Reagan's triumph was now part of the end of that consensus. To the inveterate Old Guard he married his California base and the throbbing new corporate and personal fortunes of the South and the Sun

Belt West. Not least, he ensconced in Washington a fresh generation of right-wing ideologues seized with the linear passions, and career opportunities, of Coolidge economics. J. P. Morgan would have recognized in their newfangled supply-side economics the old fetish of laissez-faire. Lower taxes on wealth, reduced regulation of corporate and financial practices, enormous new military spending and reactionary concessions to large interests, a draconian attack on "waste" in welfare and social programs, the legions of displaced and undereducated—it all meant more money and power in the hands of the monied and powerful. The reactionary ideologues moved—suspiciously like their Democratic peers—into well-paid government offices or corporate-funded Washington think tanks, lobbying suites, and other sinecures. Settled within the legendary Beltway, they would soon become one more self-styled elite of hangers-on in the capital, still more political floorwalkers touting their wares. In everyone's best interest, the theory and practice of the new administration was to be what its inauguration proclaimed—a government of, by, and for unrestrained wealth, propelled by unbridled corporate greed.

The significance of Reagan's victory was hardly a matter of ideology. It also gave powerful precedent and impetus to a politics of manipulation that blurred principle and took its practitioners—in both parties—farther from the nation they governed. The trend was plain for decades as the mass advertising culture of the postwar engulfed the older, more personal politics of the first half of the century. Republicans in particular cultivated the new methods to win the White House even while remaining a minority. There would be careful insulation and "handling" of the candidate, highly skilled "management" of media images, obsessive organization and targeting of constituencies around parochial privilege or prejudice. Ronald Reagan, the Great Communicator, became the champion of a leisure class in an "age of illusions."

There were many symbols of the shifting power in the Republican Party, but none more graphic than the moment at the Detroit convention in 1980 when Reagan reached out to select, and politically absorb, his running mate. After a quixotic attempt by aides to accommodate a supposed "dream ticket" with former president Gerald Ford, the nominee called one of the men he defeated for the nomination, George Herbert Walker Bush.

He was the son of the legendary Prescott Bush, a handsome, patrician, lion-maned Connecticut Yankee who went from Wall Street to the Senate in the old GOP eastern establishment and soon became a pillar of the moderate wing. Golfing partner of Eisenhower and champion of Ike's consciously middle way in defiance of profiteers and bureaucrats in both parties, the senator earned distinction as one of the few politicians in the nation who stood up against Joseph McCarthy's red-baiting in the 1952 presidential campaign. The elder Bush went on to an equally historic role behind the scenes in the Republicans' orchestrated purge of their Wisconsin demagogue. The legacy left his son and successor the natural heir to GOP moderation—and made his cupidity and complaisance all the starker.

The younger Bush compiled a restless résumé, shuttling from place to place without sustained accomplishment anywhere—popular at Andover, Skull and Bones at Yale, eager navy pilot, West Texas oil wildcatter seeking his own fortune, Houston congressman, defeated Senate candidate, UN envoy, Republican Party chairman during Watergate, director of the Central Intelligence Agency, ambassador to China, failed presidential contender. Some came to believe that he was never so moderate or liberal as some of his supporters liked to think. With George Bush, his prospecting in Texas but his patrician family home in Maine, it was always perhaps more style than substance. But along the way he offered up one surrender after another to the growing reaction in his party—small, self-defining retreats on civil rights, abortion, gun control, foreign policy, and finally on right-wing fiscal and tax policies he had once called "voodoo economics." No single career charted the eclipse of the moderates, but Bush epitomized their decline. In the end the man who had once bravely stood up to racism in the Houston suburbs would run blatantly racist campaign ads to win the presidency. The politician who deplored supply-side voodoo would as president yield to the incessant pleas to lower the taxes on his friends' capital gains.

When the call from the victor came that summer of 1980 Bush was sitting in his Detroit hotel suite in moody, disconsolate silence. Facing the wall as he took the phone, thinking he was to be told of the Reagan-Ford ticket, he listened for a moment in disbelief, then suddenly broke into his crooked grin and turned back to give an exultant thumbs-up to his wife and his aide James Baker across the room. He agreed to be Reagan's running mate, to the nominee's right-wing positions, without hesitation. "Why yes, sir. I think you can say I support the platform—wholeheartedly!" he blurted out, ending in seconds, in the glee of ambition, a historic struggle for the Republican soul.

In a sense George Bush would be the first and last of the twentieth-century GOP moderates so momentously co-opted by the right. Even in his dearly purchased one-term presidency, his own embarrassingly vacuous vice president, Dan Quayle, was a sop to reactionaries. His own administration was crowded with Reagan loyalists who privately distrusted, if not despised, him. His reelection effort would be sapped by an angry revolt on the right led by former Nixon ghostwriter Pat Buchanan and, not least, by a national convention that frightened the nation with its unadorned fanaticism in prime time.

Still, there would always be some doubt whether George Bush ever fully understood the significance of the thumbs-up he gave to that call from Ronald Reagan. Back when Hillary Rodham heard her father's family talk about the controversial Kennedy-Nixon race of 1960, their GOP was still overwhelmingly a party of middle-class, moderate mainline Protestants. By 1994 the party grass roots were increasingly in the grip of a self-possessed evangelical minority driven to impose its religious and reactionary tenets on an increasingly diverse and changing nation. It would be these extremists who provided most of the decisive troops and organization for the GOP primaries, and who held hostage at last the GOP's presidential candidacy.

The sun-faded "AuH_2O" bumper stickers of the mid-1960s had now been replaced by a social and political mania that repelled Goldwater himself. The right attacked abortion, homosexuals, art, literature, public programs for the poor, and with thinly veiled racism, the new ethnic diversity of American life—all these social vexations and more, it seemed, but not the predatory economic ethic and power that so largely shaped the America they found abhorrent. "Conservatism means letting people live their lives as they see fit," an aging Goldwater would try to remind them. In return they would agitate to erase his name from public buildings in his native Arizona. "We've gone from Bob Taft to Reverend Jerry Falwell," said one longtime Republican, "without passing through civilization."

Meanwhile the Democrats were taking another, equally telling path to the Reagan inauguration and to the Washington of the 1990s beyond.

In the late 1940s the ruling Democrats—including their feisty little machine-politician president, Harry Truman—had been ready and unquestioning recruits to the new rivalry with the Soviet Union. The Democrats' own Washington lawyers, lobbyists, and bureaucrats were the original architects of vast national security budgets and bureaucracies, from which many of them would incidentally benefit. Yet not even their authentic or expedient chauvinism could save them from losing office, from being driven out of the White House and the executive departments they had held for twenty years, as the red scare raged in the 1940s and 1950s. In the face of Republican jingoism and cold war demagoguery, most of the party would be simply craven. Clinging to the fixed, safe center of political dialogue, they promptly became part of the crust of conformity that closed over the nation.

By the late 1950s they had begun to run at Dwight Eisenhower and even Richard Nixon from the *right* on international issues. They charged the White House with a missile gap that they knew never existed. They beat the drums for an invasion of Castro's Cuba though they knew the ill-fated venture was already being planned. They joined disgruntled officers in crying for larger Pentagon budgets. They proposed more aggressive counterinsurgency in places like Vietnam. "God help us," Eisenhower the old general would say to an aide in the Oval Office in the late 1950s, "when there's someone here who doesn't know the military like I do."

For most of the postwar, the Democrats were still a party of colorful, sometimes grim diversity, liberal and conservative, North and South, urban and rural, city machine and county boss, Bible Belt and cathedral, the old patchwork democracy of racist Uncle Raymond Clinton and protean Bill Fulbright in Arkansas, the Kennedys in Boston, Adlai Stevenson in Illinois, and the prairie druggist's son and civil rights champion, Hubert Humphrey, in Minnesota. But across all their apparent differences, from southern reaction to northern liberalism, Democrats of the era had one conviction in common—the anathema of a democratic left. It was what made the Republican smears and red-baiting so ironic, often so grotesque, throughout the country. Orval Faubus's father, a pioneer socialist in the Ozarks, had seen workers' meetings savagely broken up by Democratic sheriffs, and farm organizers, like troublesome blacks, burned out by hooded men who were minions of the governing party. But for once, benighted Arkansas was hardly unique. There was also prosperous Minnesota's merged Democratic-Farmer-Labor Party, of which liberal Hubert Humphrey and his protégé Walter Mondale were leaders. In 1947 their faction had taken over by wantonly smearing opponents as "Reds" and bloodily clubbing Farmer-Labor dissidents in what one witness called "an unmerciful beating" in the corridors of St. Paul hotels. "The caucuses were frauds, and they were won more by baseball bats and labor goon squads than by votes," former Minnesota governor Elmer Benson observed years later.

In Minnesota as elsewhere, the postwar brought a renewed and bitter clash between Democrats and their few but vocal critics on the left.

The battle was defined not only by debates over cold war foreign policy but by very different visions of the future at home. "Farmer-Laborism attacked concentrated wealth, monopoly . . . the power of the few over the many," concluded a scholar of the Minnesota struggle; the Democrats of Humphrey and Mondale, like those of Raymond Clinton and Fulbright, were meanwhile drawing money from large business interests.

While Republicans like McCarthy or Nixon railed about "pinks" and "Communists" among the Democrats, there was never any question about the suppression—and fateful silencing—of the party's grassroots and intellectual left. Unlike in the GOP, with its reaction old and new, there would be no larger, systematic critique among Democrats of the special-interest "liberal" system both parties fashioned together in the decades after World War II. Alone among the free nations it led, postwar America would have no major party with a democratic left to match the enduring right—no balance, as one historian wrote, to "the powerful emotions and interests that always work for conservative policies."

When Bill Clinton excitedly shook hands with John Kennedy in the Rose Garden that summer of 1963, much of the reckoning had already taken place. Like Republicans in the White House later, the Democrats were suffering the gap between the glamour of a media-age president—this first one of the television era a virtual icon and idol—and his ability to govern. Kennedy's aides writhed under his disorganization and indecisiveness, later cataloged chillingly in the documentary record opened by Richard Reeves and other scholars. In the Bay of Pigs disaster, in the beginning of the entanglement in Vietnam, in halting enforcement of civil rights in a violent South, the stylish young president was again and again stymied by the sheer narrowness of his conventional party politics, his party view of the nation and the world. Nothing so testified to the gathering failure as the poignant claims of his staff and admirers after his murder—that everything would have been so different in his second term.

There was a brief interlude—a momentary revival of the old coalition of urban and rural, northern working people and southern poor—with Kennedy's martyrdom and the succession of Lyndon Johnson's manipulative genius and home-preserved populism. It was the now towering, now shrunken Johnson, the endlessly paradoxical politician of what biographer Robert Caro called "threads bright and dark," who dominated the Democrats during the mid-1960s as Hillary Rodham and Bill Clinton came of age. It was his administration of fitful promise and exhausting, disillusioning disappointment that shaped politics as they first encountered them. He had been, after all, not a winning new media president of the emerging era but a successor, an inheritor by political murder, and a relic, still essentially a creature of the old politics. But he was also a product of the same constricting Democratic mentality, and he would only hasten the larger party evolution and decay.

Symbolized by the stillborn poverty programs Hillary Rodham assessed so ambivalently and incompletely at Wellesley, Johnson's interval of equity and reform quickly ended in the opposition of Democratic barons and bosses and in the blood and folly of the Vietnam War, a result of the Democrats' self-conscious chauvinism and agitated sense of historical analogy. But Vietnam was also very much the work—as history often ignored—of the perennially bloody-shirted Republicans, who in Congress and as candidates for president cheered the war on, blocking every attempt by a small minority of Democrats like Fulbright and a few GOP moderates to stem the disaster or even to expose endemic official lying and criminal acts on the pretext of national security, abuses that were becoming the governing habit of both parties.

The red scare had not only frightened and silenced Democrats but stolen their judgment. The most prominent casualty, Johnson himself, described the gnawing, indiscriminate dread of retribution by the reactionaries for any seeming weakness in foreign policy. He had watched, he once confided to a friend, as postwar Communist advances in China and elsewhere fed McCarthyism and destroyed even the most powerful Democrats. "And I knew that all these problems taken together were chickenshit compared to what might happen if we lost Vietnam." His monument—and that of the majority of Republicans and Democrats who joined him in the calamity—would be a polished black granite wall, five hundred feet long, fifty-eight thousand American names chiseled into it.

While Republicans thrashed in factional strife the Democrats tore apart under the pounding tides of the 1960s. The wave of reaction was not only opposition to the war, a phenomenon largely outside the party and power, after all. A youth rebellion against the hypocrisies and conformity of the 1950s—against the worlds of Hot Springs and Park Ridge—was already stirring an angry generational reaction among the older Americans whose era it was. The civil rights movement was already hastening defection of whites to the GOP in the South and elsewhere. And those intertwining tensions of war, values, and race widened still further the sullen rifts of class and culture already opening between the party's old blue-collar constituency and younger, more affluent professionals.

It all climaxed in the convulsive year of 1968 that Hillary and Bill watched so closely as ambitious young would-be politicians. Like a series of sharp explosions in the night, there would be Gene McCarthy's insurgency, Johnson's abdication, the murder of Martin Luther King, the belated run and then assassination of Robert Kennedy, a riot-shattered convention and party, the narrow defeat of Humphrey by Nixon in a three-way race with Uncle Raymond's idol, George Wallace.

As any bloodied young demonstrator from Chicago could have testified, the Democratic Party in 1968 remained more than ever in the possession of its established powers and their backing money. They were epitomized in 1968 by grinning Hubert Humphrey, financed by his longtime friend Dwayne Andreas, a multimillionaire agribusiness magnate and commodity market player later to be involved in price-fixing on a global scale. Andreas's habit was to contribute hundreds of thousands of dollars to both presidential candidates—including, eventually, Bill Clinton. But right-wing Democrats like Lloyd Bentsen in Texas and others, to say nothing of the Republicans, set out to vilify their intraparty rivals with the frightening images of "radical" students, and the ostensible smear, like the red-baiting before it, stuck in many cases. By the end of the decade the Democrats would be politically branded, partly by Democrats, with unsettling causes and changes they enlivened or tolerated only in part—causes and changes that their own misrule had in some measure provoked and that they had bitterly, violently resisted, had tried to extinguish no less than their Republican counterparts had.

In the grip of its own reaction, squirming under its ironic labels, this was the party in which Hillary Rodham and Bill Clinton formed their own politics and sense of forces in Wellesley, New Haven, Texas, and Arkansas. During eight years of opposition and divided government under Nixon and Ford, as the war raged on and a Republican White House crumbled in corruption, the Democrats struggled only hesitantly to recover the old presidential coalition that elected Kennedy and supported the early, reforming Johnson. From surviving centers of power on Capitol Hill—and especially among the ever-growing Washington and New York establishment of officials from past administrations—they drifted ever rightward in domestic policy. In those precincts it was hardly surprising that they were coming to represent vested interests. The Democratic Congress was ever more dependent on big money contributions from those quarters for its incumbency. The establishment were mostly hirelings of the same interests.

As their books and speeches graphically show, they were also increasingly in thrall to the money-raising and media success of their opponents and eagerly mistook the GOP's manipulation of popular fear and prejudice for the expression of popular interests. It was a strange echo of the "me-tooism" the old GOP conservatives of the 1940s and 1950s used to accuse Republican supporters of the New Deal of exhibiting. In the harsh light of Nixon's 1968 victory, went a common argument by the Democrats' right wing, the party should tailor its appeal to the "real majority," a mass of middle America whose conservative values and flag-waving nationalism were supposedly betrayed by the party's affinity for antiwar protesters and unsettling minorities. Once more ironies were sharp. The party was never to be one of minorities or protesters. And the same middle America—always more blue-collar and marginal than inflated official definitions of "middle class" admitted—would indeed turn away from the party, would not even bother to vote, because its interests, jobs, welfare were increasingly ignored or betrayed by Democrats aspiring to look, and to be handsomely financed, just like Republicans.

Born out of the strife of 1968, rule changes in 1972 were supposed to open party processes. But then the Washington-anointed front-runner, Senator Edmund Muskie, lost the nomination to George McGovern, heading a renewed wave of activists. While reluctant party leaders appeared to accept McGovern in an uncoerced convention, maintaining the facade of reform, they quietly and methodically moved to control the insurgents, absorbing them, forcing them either to join or to leave the unreformed system. Withholding contributions, endorsements, and votes, the Democratic leadership in 1972 went on to abandon McGovern to crushing defeat by a Nixon already shrouded in corruption. "I threw open the doors of the Democratic Party," McGovern himself would say later, "and they all walked out." The unwanted Democratic candidate was "gonna lose," one party leader told a television interviewer with rare candor late in the race, "because we're gonna make sure he's gonna lose."

Several veterans of the McGovern run left Washington and politics, never to return. Comanager Gary Hart went on to the Senate and a seemingly inexorable presidential candidacy himself, only to be destroyed in a sex scandal that private investigators and others believed was facilitated by both right-wing Republicans and a CIA nervous about Hart's potential reforms in national security. Others from 1972 stayed in or around Washington, growing adept at the game, and twenty years later joined a Clinton administration that had become what they saw as their last chance at government. The so-called McGovernites—of whom Hillary Rodham and Bill Clinton would be the most famous and, in many ways, the most typical—left no visible resistance to the increasingly distorted distribution of governmental and thus economic power in the 1980s. In most cases they were merely part of it, takers of the spoils.

When the Watergate scandal made a Democratic victory likely in the 1976 presidential campaign, the party establishment and its special-interest money turned to the corporate-sanctioned right, to a relatively unknown but mercantile-minded Georgia governor named Jimmy Carter. Soon familiar for his smile and easy drawl (his temper, willfulness, and brooding vacillation yet to be discovered), he was a politician of the more presentable New South, a prototype of the later Clinton New Democrat, who would appreciate the local natural dominance and political dispensations of banks, insurance companies, and low-wage industries and the other freebooting that marked the southern arrival at modern economics.

What was happening to the old democracy could be counted in one small way that year in the party's ostensibly more open system for nominating its presidential candidates. In the still machine-dominated party of 1960 John Kennedy entered seven primaries. In 1976 Carter ran in thirty. But then the propagation of primaries, and later the "front-loading" of voting dates early in the year, several on the same day, only fixed the race even more for the heavily financed, front-running establishment candidate. There would be no more "McGovern accidents," as one Washington lobbyist put it. Like other Democratic reforms, the primaries ultimately shifted power to the regulars and insiders, to the money. "The result," said one veteran Democrat, "was to create the appearance of more choice while actually allowing less."

Even against a Gerald Ford weighed down by his pardon of unindicted coconspirator Richard Nixon, Carter won the White House in 1976 with the narrowest electoral college victory since 1916 and the poorest voter turnout in three decades. Having campaigned on a popular pledge to "turn the government of this country inside out," he promptly installed a regime vividly reflecting the decaying leadership of his party. Wealthier by far than its Republican predecessors under Eisenhower, Nixon, or Ford, the Carter cabinet would number several Democratic establishment millionaires and retainers.

Fleeing to a secluded Minnesota lake to ponder his plight, Vice President Walter Mondale, the party careerist from the bloody 1940s, nearly resigned in despair at the Carter administration's disarray. "These sons of bitches don't know how to govern anything," he told an aide. Through 1979 and 1980, as Bill Clinton and others tried to warn Carter of the impending disaster, he only drifted while Senator Edward Kennedy jockeyed to seize the nomination despite Chappaquiddick, numerous indiscretions, and a lethal shallowness in early national appearances. It was a nasty, bitter fight—much like the bloodletting between the GOP's right and its moderates—with Carter refusing to speak to Kennedy for years to come. As it was, the battered president managed to muster what was left of the old party machinery, the new corporate money already enveloping the Democrats, and his institutional White House patronage to stave off the challenge. But then in the race against Reagan there were the ever-flickering television images of American hostages in Iran, blindfolded silhouettes of impotence abroad as at home—and in the background, a tremulous, inflation-weakened economy that exacted its worst toll from the majority of workers and owners of small businesses already abandoned by both parties.

Weeks after his 1976 election Carter had spurned a congressional reauthorization of wage-price controls even Richard Nixon had used a few years before, and by 1979, with wages stagnant and the consumer price index climbing at as much as 14 percent annually, he had no means to stop the spiral. The surrender to the orthodoxy of vested interests would be called with fine irony "neoliberalism." In the political economy of the Democrats and their wealthy sponsors, the well-heeled Carter administration had done little, if anything, to stem a slow decline for millions of Americans. In fact, the Georgian who had once drawlingly called the US tax system "a disgrace to the human race" had begun another process altogether, practicing his own Coolidge laissez-faire. In 1978 he and his men had joined to bring about a major reduction in the capital gains tax and a lowering of corporate tax rates that one writer called "the most regressive measure since the 1920s."

In the fall of 1980, as Bill Clinton complacently faced his own reelection, the frustrated national electorate voted its seething discontent. Like the black Cubans charging down the Fort Chaffee highway in Frank White's ad, menace and uncertainty seemed to loom before the voters—with neither party able or willing to tell them what was happening to them. Reagan won in what was typically described as a landslide, by more than eight million votes, sweeping forty-three states besides Arkansas. Victory brought GOP control of the Senate, the first since 1952 and only the third in a half century. Thirty-three new GOP seats in the House reduced the Democrats to an uncertain fifty-one-vote majority. "It's sort of an expression of joy," one Republican lawyer said afterward, "like a flower coming up in the spring." Others were not so sure of a clear result for party or doctrine. Many voters now called themselves conservative, yet millions more were added to the ranks of deliberate nonvoters. Only a little more than one in three eligible Americans had bothered to go to the polls in any election since 1974, and thus there was a vast new party of the politically dispossessed, outnumbering Democrats and Republicans together. "This is not the conservatism of people genuinely wed to the status quo and to the protection of their privileges," one writer predicted well before the 1980 results were in. "It is the pseudo-conservatism of people with blighted hopes."

What followed was indeed part of the longer, larger slow-motion coup, a culmination of the betrayal and lingering death of democracy in both parties, a series of decisive, bipartisan political acts led by Democratic Congresses as well as the Republican White House.

It had begun in 1978 under Carter with the cuts in capital gains and corporate taxes and the deliberate disavowal of government as the balancing force of public interest against private power.

In 1981 came the initial Reagan tax legislation, drastically reducing rates for the rich and devising still more subsidies and windfalls for corporations and wealthy individuals. The spectacle appalled Reagan's own budget director, David Stockman, one of the administration's staunchest ideologues. "The hogs were really feeding," he confessed to a journalist afterward.

By 1982 sweeping financial deregulation set loose a speculative frenzy in the financial markets resulting in a plague of business seizures at a cost of hundreds of thousands of jobs and billions in productivity, public revenues, and rifled pension funds.

In 1983 a new $200 billion social security tax fell overwhelmingly on the working poor and middle class, amounting to what one Senate witness would call "embezzlement," another "robbery."

By 1985 the regressive redistribution of wealth in federal budget mandates was enshrined in the Gramm-Rudman balanced budget act.

In 1986 heralded tax reform did little for the majority of Americans but quietly gave another $20 billion in windfalls and subsidies to upper incomes, making "spectacular beneficiaries," as one account put it, of those making $200,000 or more.

In 1990 a deficit-reduction bill scheduled $140 billion in future tax increases, but with scarcely 11 percent to come from corporations. Most of the rest was taken from those with incomes beneath $50,000.

All the while, the states themselves followed Washington's example. Their own local taxes became increasingly regressive. The ten wealthiest states grew 36 percent richer during the 1980s, surpassing the other, poorer forty in an inequity "getting dangerously worse," as the *Economist* warned by 1992.

When it was over, Americans of average means were paying proportionately far more in taxes, and the wealthy were getting off easy. Most people were comparatively poorer and less in command of their own lives than at any moment since the Great Depression and World War II. The few at the top were richer and more influential than ever. The most powerful US corporations escaped an estimated $92 billion a year in taxes (compared to their early postwar contribution), their share of federal revenues cut by four-fifths since the 1970s, down to 8 percent. Foreign corporations were taxed at a fraction of what most American families paid. Even government largesse in the name of national security—a $250–300 billion military budget and over $36 billion in yearly arms sales—profited only the few. To close the circle, the redistribution of wealth and taxes, along with gigantic weapons spending, fed a fulminating national debt, and interest on it, too, flowed to the wealthy at home and abroad who held its notes.

◆ ◆ ◆

As the toll and the governance that exacted it became more stark, it would be clear that the Reagan reaction beginning in 1981 had not truly transformed Washington. It had merely merged with it. There was less a Reagan-Bush revolution than a continuing corrupt evolution of both parties, particularly of those institutions that made up the real government of America—the money-dominated Congress and executive, the lobbies and the media, the interests, methods, loyalties, rewards, consequences they all shared. It was a culture that had grown naturally, organically out of the past yet had now taken on historic proportions. If it seemed different in kind, it was because its abuses had become so enormous, so common, so accepted.

· 14 ·

Little Rock II

"You'll See They Love You Again"

Not long after losing the 1980 election, Bill Clinton met with three
Pentecostal preachers who ministered to his defeat as if it were some
ghastly disgrace or disfigurement, "holding hands with him and praying together," Donnie Radcliffe recounted, "as they reassured him
that even if he had lost they loved him." Revivalist themes of guilt and
absolution—of being "loved" and elected again—were typical of
much that followed, though the scenes were not always so sanctified.

As it had before, the thwarting of his ambition amounted to an
emotional crisis for the man and the politician. It produced in the
thirty-five-year-old Clinton distinctive reactions—in public a desperate,
obsessive contrition, in private a despondent, often bitter recklessness.
Defeat—and then the feverish comeback—also exacted a toll on Hillary Rodham. The period 1981–82 became a crucial juncture in their
marriage and in their rise to the presidency.

Over a first bleak winter after the election, well-placed patrons eased
their exit from power. Still disconsolate after a brooding vacation in
Puerto Vallarta, Clinton retreated from the statehouse to a sinecure
with Wright, Lindsey and Jennings, a growing Little Rock law firm
serving some of the nation's largest corporations, including Ford,
AT&T, General Electric, and Westinghouse; an array of national insurance giants, among them Hartford, Kemper, Nationwide, Northwestern National, Allstate, and Travelers; and several of Arkansas's big
timber, food, utility, financial, and trucking concerns. Formally of
counsel rather than a partner, Clinton was to be paid $55,000 a year, a

respectable Little Rock retainer at the time and more than the $49,290 his wife was receiving as a junior partner at Rose.

Some in the firm hoped the former governor's name recognition might attract clients, though no one aware of the arrangement expected him to practice law. His brief was his own political resurrection and the rewards it promised on all sides. "The son of a bitch cost this firm a lot of money just to park him here between terms," one senior partner complained. But the bargain was implicit. "We gave him a salary and an office for a reelection campaign for governor, pure and simple," said another of the firm's attorneys, "and everybody around here understood more or less what was going on." Under Clinton statehouse administrations to come over the next decade, Wright, Lindsey would enjoy influence and fees far beyond what many in the local business community thought it could have expected otherwise, surpassing in lucrative state-bond work even Rose and other, more venerable firms. "A helluva return on the investment," one of its partners remarked afterward. "You might conclude," said a rival, "that they were wired."

Clinton owed his comeback haven to senior partner Bruce Lindsey, a thirty-three-year-old Arkansan educated at Southwestern in Memphis and at Georgetown Law School. The slight, taciturn, diffident Lindsey was a lawyer of ordinary abilities who worked doggedly to cultivate his already lucrative practice. He was always in the shadow, many thought, of his more impressive father, who worried that the son would never be more than a political hanger-on. "The boy was not his old man," said a close friend of the father's, "and I can tell you that Bruce's daddy wondered if he wasn't just a gofer at heart." The younger Lindsey had moved from minor job to minor job for Fulbright, Bumpers, and Pryor before returning to Little Rock to join the firm. There he found his niche, personally as politically, with Bill Clinton, soon becoming a slavishly loyal acolyte to the quicker, more outwardly imposing politician. A "preternatural, supernatural loyalty," one observer called it.

Lindsey would be an intimate in the rise of a future president of the United States. Adviser during the 1980s in the Clintons' thickening web of financial and political connections, he became an impervious man Friday, traveling at the candidate's side in 1992, serving as sounding board, orderly, and warder. It would be Lindsey who saw to it that the campaign plane's pretty flight attendants were nowhere near Clinton when cameras were readied and that they and other young women politely declined the governor's insistent invitations to "work out" with him at a local gym. "Bruce was like the guy who comes along behind," another aide would say, "shoveling up after the parade." Later, among the small Arkansas inner circle in the White House, he would be one of the very few at the core of the Clinton presidency who knew its deeper provenance in Little Rock.

Barely a month after joining Lindsey's firm Clinton also became one of three directors of a seven-month-old Arkansas corporation called Intermark, described in a press release as "an international trade-and-management company," said to be engaged in "promotion of foreign markets" for Arkansas products as well as in "importing and in forming joint ventures involving Arkansas and foreign interests." In what the *Gazette* called "Clinton's first job with a private company," his fellow directors were Intermark president John W. Priest and J. Stephen Stoltz, former and current chief executives, respectively, of Polyvend International, a Conway, Arkansas, sheet-metal corporation that was becoming one of the country's leading manufacturers of vending machines and would hold, under the second Clinton administration, the lucrative state contract to make Arkansas's "Land of Opportunity" license plates. A subsidiary of Polyvend, Intermark was "expected to have sales in the millions during its first year," Clinton himself boasted to the *Gazette* in February 1981. The former governor, Priest added, would be "a strong asset," playing "an active role in company affairs." With that, however, Intermark and Clinton's involvement with it promptly disappeared from public view.

What sort of company was Polyvend, and what was its relationship to state government? Exactly what did the new Intermark do for its predicted large profits, and how much did it actually earn? What "active role" did Bill Clinton play as the only outsider on its three-man board, and was he paid or otherwise compensated as a director of a reputedly multimillion-dollar concern? Even in 1981 there were intriguing elements of the association for a young Democratic politician. Polyvend had a major branch in South Africa. The home company in Arkansas was noted for its reactionary antilabor posture. Holder of the Polyvend founding fortune through a controversial inheritance, Steve Stoltz was a decided conservative and a staunch supporter of Republican candidates yet now was also a free-spending social friend of Democrat Bill Clinton; they were "partying buddies," one person remembered. "I guess they were an odd couple," said a member of Stoltz's family, "unless you really knew Arkansas."

But like the relationship with Jim McDougal in Whitewater after 1978 or with Jim Blair in the commodities market in 1979–80 and as an intimate adviser ever after, like the bargain struck with Bruce Lindsey's firm in 1981, like the various links with wealthy backers and enormously powerful local figures like chicken king Don Tyson, like Hillary Rodham's connection with her Rose partners and their practice, like, for that matter, the Clintons' notoriously tortured marriage, the Intermark arrangement went largely unremarked. In Little Rock's tacit code of ruling-class discretion it was merely one more piece of business amid a banal intermingling of public office, private profit, and personal excess.

On the strength of both the new retainer at Wright, Lindsey and Hillary's brokerage windfalls the year before, the Clintons now moved to a gracious home on Midland Avenue in the capital's fashionable Pulaski Heights. Purchased for $112,000, with a down payment of $60,000 from the commodities profits, it was an airy old Victorian residence of tasteful soft yellow trimmed in white, with a sweeping porch, four large bedrooms, and an impressive library to display Bill's much-noted accumulation of books. "I always remember all those books," said a former aide. "It showed how smart he was." Their home was literally around the corner from many of Little Rock's most imposing houses and estates, the friendly precincts of the business and professional caste where Clinton won majorities of over 60 percent, even against Frank White. "That was the kind of place that made them part of the 'right neighborhood' and 'right people' in Little Rock, or at least as 'right' as you could be in Arkansas," said a neighbor at the time, "and that was really important to both of them, especially Hillary."

Yet neither the law firm sanctuary nor the respectable address seemed to assuage his anguish over his defeat. Restlessly he prowled offices and restaurants, even grocery stores and shops in and around his prestigious new neighborhood, seeking out familiar faces or, as often as not, strangers to accost with what journalist and friend Max Brantley called "this Hamlet soliloquy—'All is lost, what can I do?' " Many observers thought it a kind of emotional panhandling. "It was pathetic," one told Connie Bruck. "It seemed as if you might find him, almost any hour of the day or night, at this supermarket out on Markham—he'd catch you at the end of the aisle, or he'd be waiting at the register, and he'd say, 'You know, I used to be governor, and . . .' "

Later, advisers would urge him to make a campaign theme of apology and humility, to "admit" what older Arkansas political figures and wealthy backers saw as the "radical" liberalism and rash reforms of his first governorship. Yet in the weeks after he left office the personal abjectness and mortification were far more impulsive and disturbing—

not yet crafted political tactic but a stark sign of his deeper inner frailty, of how completely political acclaim and advance already defined his life. "It was supine, really a craven kind of crawl from one place to another, begging to be taken back," said one who watched. "It was an extraordinarily appropriate reaction," Edith Efron observed, "for a man whose sense of reality is dependent on the perception of others." At the time, his sternest critics were as dismayed and embarrassed as his staunch friends were. "He apologized so often and with such remorse," John Robert Starr recorded, "that even I begged him to stop."

In 1992 campaign interviews the Clintons both recalled how much the 1980 election and its aftershock had evoked memories of Bill Blythe's premature death and thus the son's own sense of precarious mortality. "I would seize everything," Clinton told Gail Sheehy in an interview for *Vanity Fair.* "Not just in his political career," Hillary explained to Sheehy. "It was reading everything he could read, talking to everybody he could talk to, staying up all night, because life was passing him by."

In the same months friends and former aides heard him speak contemptuously about the "rednecks and peckerwoods" who deserted him, "stupid people who didn't deserve what he had to offer," as one recalled. There were also stories of the former governor's carousing as never before at parties where cocaine was as common as liquor. Clinton would be seen with a young woman or even two women at a time, a red-eyed, puffy figure delivering himself of a profane running commentary about the treachery of voters.

There had been persistent rumors of cocaine use in the wider Clinton social circle during his first term and more open charges of pot smoking. "I can remember going into the governor's conference room once," state representative Jack McCoy said years later, "and it reeked of marijuana." A convicted drug dealer and onetime bartender at Le Bistro nightclub, reportedly where Roger Clinton's band played and Bill went often in 1979, later told stories of selling cocaine to Roger, who "immediately gave some to his elder brother," according to one account. The frequent nights out in 1981 only added to such increasingly common lore. Some of Little Rock whispered about wild "toga parties" at the Coachman's Inn outside the city, half sophomoric fraternity bacchanalia, half more serious spectacle. It was the beginning, some believed, of a still sharper divide between the politician's public face and private reality. Bill Clinton came to seem all the more calculating on the outside, all the more wanton behind the screen, his personal excesses taken in compensation or even revenge for his buttoned-up public persona. "He was deeply hurt and deeply angry," said an aide, "and along with the oh-so-sorry Bill there was also a screw-'em-all Bill."

◆ ◆ ◆

Only ten days after the election he reached out to Hillary and his Texas friend and organizer from the McGovern campaign, Betsey Wright, persuading her to hurry to Little Rock to begin managing his comeback before he even left office. "She came when he begged her," said a mutual friend, "and when no one else would work for him." Since the 1960s Wright had been what a colleague called a "loaded gun for hire," serving Democratic candidates of various stripes, including Humphrey, Carter, and Clinton, in his 1974 congressional run. In 1980 she was working for a women's political action group in Washington. Like Lindsey and others, she now cast her lot with the unseated Arkansas governor, seeing him, despite his loss, as one of the young comers in the shaken party at a moment when Republicans had won both the White House and the Senate. "Only a couple of years," a friend remembered her saying in 1980 about her stay with Clinton. She ended up spending more than a decade. The essence of her career would be in the shadow of what she found—and joined—in Little Rock.

Smoking five packs of cigarettes a day, given to baggy sweatshirts, slacks, and a manner that instantly set her apart from conventional Arkansas political women, Wright was ensconced with suitable funds in an office conveniently near the Lindsey firm. There she immediately began to plot Clinton's reelection. "I found his entire political life on index cards in shoe boxes," she said of the records that dated back to high school in Hot Springs and that by now contained scribbled notations of each Clinton contact or encounter, a meeting here, news of a family death or success there, literally hundreds of tireless entries in a politician's exhaustive scripting of spontaneity, memory, intimacy. With the help of a Clinton supporter Wright now cross-referenced names, addresses, and telephone numbers by county, zip code, and level of support, creating sophisticated computerized files of past and future backers, current and potential enemies. Over the next twelve years she was to be what one associate called "the keeper of the keys and of the skeletons behind the locked door." Like most handlers and votaries of her kind in modern American politics, she also buried her own convictions, whatever substantive views she may have once held, as an ardent feminist serving a politician with a superficially enlightened, deeply paradoxical, often crudely depreciative attitude toward women.

From the beginning Wright pushed and disciplined Clinton as no other aide had. "Betsey was the only one who could and would challenge him, who'd scream and yell," said a man who watched the relationship for years. She was also characteristically, singularly candid—often tart—about what she discovered the moment she became his manager. "He got crazy in the incessant quest for understanding what he did wrong," Wright would say of the period following the 1980 loss. "Bill was always very careless," she once related, hurrying to explain, "out of an unbelievable naïveté. He has a defective shit detector about personal relationships sometimes. He just thinks everyone is wonderful. He is also careless about appearances."

To Gail Sheehy in 1992 Wright confided her own "frustrations . . . watching the groupie girls hanging around and the fawning all over [him]. But I always laughed at them on the inside because I knew no dumb bimbo was ever going to be able to provide to him all of the dimensions that Hillary does."

With that other equally strong and acerbic woman on the scene, Wright soon formed an implicit bond of perseverance and discretion. "Hillary got on with her because she wanted someone to say no besides her," said a longtime friend of both, "as well as somebody else to keep the secrets, to keep quiet where they had to." Still, Wright's frankness and fierce pride broke the silence. Around the campaign office and later the statehouse, she was defiant of the primitive sexism of the Arkansas political world, confronting any sign of discrimination or exploitation, while watching Clinton's personal antics and his marriage with sometimes irrepressible dismay. "Her tolerance for some of his behavior just amazes me," she would say of the governor's wife, the woman confronted with so many of what they both chose to call "dumb bimbos."

In the winter of 1980–81 friends saw Hillary Rodham successively hurt and enraged by her husband's woeful reaction to defeat, then eventually resigned and grimly determined to salvage her choice. "In some ways, I guess, this was the first time she'd actually seen that side of the real Bill," said one witness. More than one friend urged her simply to give up and leave. "She was only thirty-three, with great earning power and plenty of reason to be her own person, for God's sake—a lot more going for her than many mistreated women have," said a Yale classmate who remained her confidante.

But Hillary Rodham resolved to stay and recover their original quest. She would force a certain necessary compliance in the relationship for electoral purposes, even if she couldn't meaningfully curb the private appetites and habits of her ever-promising, ever-charming, politically gifted husband. "It absolutely was not an alternative that she gave him," Betsey Wright remembered. Clinton's friends described him as "terrified" of losing his wife, with "a deep sense," as one put it, "of having failed Hillary by losing the election." The recurrent fear and guilt, they agreed, always brought only expedient adjustment and a grudging, fitful accommodation, never self-searching, authentic change or meaningful sacrifice.

With earnestness and effect Clinton began appearing every Sunday at Little Rock's massive Immanuel Baptist Church, which he had never attended so regularly before. He was now seen prominently in the choir, just beyond the pulpit, as carefully arranged television cameras carried the service—and with it the former governor's grinning, nodding, hymn-singing presence—to thousands of viewers throughout the state. He would also attend a publicized church camp in the Redfield community, where he was broadcast harmonizing with a quartet of pastors.

Inside Immanuel Baptist, monumental and prosperous in an otherwise struggling quarter of the city, the setting was a classic of its kind. Light blue carpet and Wedgwood decor framed the great forty-two-pipe organ and red-velvet baptismal chamber recessed into the wall above the altar. Beneath the domed ceiling, bathed in television lights, sat the well-coiffed minister and choir, a front-pew phalanx of deacons, and an overwhelmingly white, middle-class congregation of a thousand or more, all stiffened by seemingly uniform hair spray and by a robust theology intoning the "attitude of gratitude" and the "subtlety of the serpent." "Perfect place for a soft reentry in ole Arkansas," a fellow politician said later of the Sunday-morning televised scenes.

Away from the choir Clinton struck what the couple's friend Diane Blair called "a new note of religiosity" in his still frequent public declarations, pointedly reminding listeners of the power of redemption for wayward governors who had tried to do too much, as for other lost souls. "We have always sort of specialized in forgiveness of sinners," he said of his "home" church. "If in his first dazzling rise to the governorship Clinton had most nearly resembled a child prodigy," Blair said, "in his reincarnation he had become the prodigal son."

The invariable apology was for radical rule, for not "listening." It was in many ways a Clinton version of the wider Democratic reaction to the Republican victories around the country, a new postmortem orthodoxy that the party should accept the characterization of its reactionary opponents and turn to the right after 1980, much as after the Nixon victory in 1972. Others saw it in simpler Arkansas terms. "He'd just learned that the big boys run the state," said one adviser. "That's all."

But even more impressive and lasting than the contrite message was the distinct manner of the slightly pudgy, still boyish young politician of unique earnestness. He would respond to the charge of heedlessness by listening as never before. More intense, more purposeful than even the highly personalized style of the early Clinton, his new approach would first appear now, in the almost desperate recovery of early 1981, and evolve over the years as what Alexis Moore described as "The Look": "The Look makes the moment his. As the citizen says his or her name, Clinton's eyes widen in an intense, focused gaze that says, 'Yes, yes, you, you are the one I've been waiting for; yours, yes, yours is the single voice to which I listen; you, yes, you are the One Who Matters.' When The Look appears, he leans forward or down to see eye to eye. This stream of light permits no escape. When The Look hits, the citizen, whether hostile, disbelieving, or supportive, can't help but respond. Hunched shoulders relax, anxious faces smooth, fast talkers slow, shy folks emerge garrulous."

Not long after his defeat, Clinton went unexpectedly as well to visit one of Diane Blair's political science classes at the University in Fayetteville, as eager to talk to students as to any other group that would listen. Leaders were a combination "of darkness . . . and of light," Blair remembered his saying in his discussion of various figures from Lincoln to Hitler to Lyndon Johnson. "Great politicians don't give a rip about public opinion," he told the students. Clinton said nothing about his own predicament. Asked why he pursued politics, he paused, shrugged, and answered almost offhandedly with his reflexive grin, "It's the only track I ever wanted to run on."

Many came to believe that it was in the early months of 1981 that Bill Clinton made fundamental choices about himself and about power. "It didn't matter what he had been or hadn't really been in his first term, how progressive or idealistic or not. This was the moment when Bill lost his guts," said a colleague from earlier campaigns. "From there on, he'd do whatever necessary to get elected and stay elected. He made his deal with the devil."

•   ◆   •

He was not alone in facing a choice. Some thought Hillary Rodham had taken the loss as hard as her husband had, though her manner of dealing with defeat was as different from his as her taut Methodism was from the display at Immanuel Baptist.

Nominated by the outgoing Carter for another term on the Legal Services Board, she went unconfirmed by the new Republican-controlled Senate in 1981. Personal rejection seemed to propel her back toward her own role in Clinton's fate and thus toward confronting both the meaning of the 1980 defeat and the essence of their relationship. "The experience of watching Bill screw up made Hillary realize she should jump into the breach," an adviser told Connie Bruck. "She had to—he was so shaken, and was not a particularly good strategist anyway. There was no way he was going to win again unless she came in." What followed, however, was always far more than taking charge of a reelection campaign.

No single act came to symbolize so vividly her role and sacrifice as the surrender of her maiden name. Friends and advisers were alternately grave and flippant in urging her to give up the most visible vestige of independence. "Early one morning she was cooking me and Bill grits, and I told her she had to start using her husband's name," Washington lobbyist Vernon Jordan remembered of a visit to the mansion just after the 1980 debacle, adding fatuously, "She understood." For his part, Jim Blair was mocking about the local mores they were appeasing. "Have a ceremony on the steps of the capitol where Bill puts his booted foot firmly on her throat, yanks her up by the hair and says, 'Woman, you're going to go by my last name and that's that,' " he told them. "Then wave the flag, sing a few hymns, and be done with it." They all laughed, as Diane Blair related the scene.

Blair's caustic acknowledgment of the political liability was also, of course, another expression of the profound inner contempt of the homegrown elite for their "beloved" Arkansas, the "hillbillies and white trash," as one of Hillary's fellow lawyers put it—the same society the devout ex-governor smiled out on from Immanuel Baptist, people whom many of Blair's clients and Clinton's contributors were profitably exploiting through low wages, regressive taxes, and the larger special-interest tyranny of state government.

The name change was only part of a larger transformation, calculation, capitulation for the former First Lady. Treating her overall appearance as a political expedient, she shed her glasses for contact lenses though she found them difficult to wear, styled and lightened her hair, began using cosmetics, and hired a fashion consultant to help her buy a wardrobe. "She conformed, eyes batting. She hated it, for a while resented it no end, but she became what Arkansas wanted her to be," one of the Clintons' closest aides would say. "I saw them a little while after they left office and looked at this woman and thought, 'Jesus, he's dumped his wife after all,' " said a legislator and lobbyist, "and then I realized . . . it was Hillary."

Equally important, her makeover included a more demure and ingratiating public manner. The coolly intelligent and crisply decided, often abrasive young woman was less aggressive and outspoken, careful, if not wholly concealed. Her exterior change was never so abrupt as some thought afterward; it was more nearly an evolution and unfolding, each alteration tried on and absorbed in turn.

Clinton himself would be given a shorter haircut, and his wide-lapelled 1970s wardrobe would be replaced with more subdued, conservative clothes. Swiftly Hillary purged from campaign circles "the squirrels," those young "long-haired radicals" of a supposedly brazen, bumptious administration. In this and more, Clinton himself was diffident, quietly acquiescent in watching old backers swept aside, some from the first days of his congressional run.

As part of a wider new expedience and opportunism in both their social and their political contacts, she established her own subtle and not-so-subtle distinctions as to who could be useful—who, in effect, would be their society—not only on the way back to the governorship but on their path to the ultimate prize of the White House. "Why are you hanging out with these *losers?* They're not successful, not rich," a Clinton friend said, describing to Connie Bruck Hillary's attitude toward many of their associations. "I think she has assigned a usefulness quotient to everyone in her life: Whom do I need to accomplish this? Everyone is part of a team to get from this point to the finished product. . . . Are you wealthy? Are you powerful? Have you written a book I like? Are you a star?"

Longtime Clinton friends who were her rivals for influence and intimacy were eliminated, as were aides like Steve Smith, Rudy Moore, and others who recognized the irony in the cliché that the first term had been fatally radical. "These folks cut out were sure as hell not *her* buddies from Rose or the corporations," said someone who watched the retribution, "and it was easy to blame a lot of good folks for losing that election."

The resulting Arkansas claque was deemed more useful—corporate executives, wealthy figureheads and lawyers, or simply politicos with stakes in the status quo, men like former highway commissioner W. Maurice Smith, a small-town banker and fund-raiser; former auditor and adjutant general Jimmie "Red" Jones; Bill Clark, former head of the notorious Highway Commission; onetime Detroit Tigers star and highway commissioner George Kell; and Mack McLarty. "When you understand that the highway slots are the nearest thing to royalty in Arkansas," one legislator said of the good ole boy commissioners, "they were the princes of the system." Maurice Smith, campaign finance chair in 1982 and for each subsequent gubernatorial run, would be especially important, with what one source called "all his rich friends, and all their rich folks' point of view." Elevated by what some saw as Hillary's "great purge," the new circle around Clinton only furthered his "repentance" and disavowal of a mythical first-term progressivism.

Hillary soon called back their talisman from the first statehouse victory, Dickie Morris. Between clients, many of them now right-wing Republicans in the vogue of the 1980s, Morris made his reappearance in Little Rock in 1981. By several accounts, he spent long hours at the law office and at the Midland Avenue house charting the campaign just as he and Clinton, at an easier time three years before, had plotted not only winning the governorship but Pryor's elimination of Tucker as well. Now Clinton was likely to face the jobless and still ambitious Tucker himself in the gubernatorial primary, and Morris and he discussed how to build on the attacks and negative images they had confected so effectively for Pryor.

But the consultant's advice, according to some who heard it as well as read internal memos, now went well beyond the primary or the general election. Morris was facing not the confident, trade-fluent politician who had unctuously dismissed him but a deeply shaken, unappeasably remorseful loser. With a sense of vindication and personal dominance he now pressed on a ready audience the most self-serving nostrums of the career politician. Clinton must make his use of every popular cause, even Republican initiatives, in order to shield himself from attacks and, if possible, find his own enemy to demonize, so as to deflect controversy to others and define himself in a safe middle. In the 1981–82 campaign some would call it "getting one's shots," inoculating oneself against any dangerous image or label—in Clinton's case, acquiring immunity by admitting past mistakes and adopting some version of the conservative criticism of his record. Most crucial, Morris instructed him, he must do nothing in governing that he would not say or do in the midst of a political race, make no dispensation for policy or leadership in a term that was simply another phase of the endless campaign. "You're always running. That's all you do," one remembered as the kernel of the indoctrination. Heaped on top of Clinton's already frightful sense of vulnerability, the ultimately apolitical, antidemocratic cynicism of his acrid Manhattan handler further fixed the mode of a comeback and subsequent career.

Meanwhile, inside the camp and despite the relative anathema Dickie Morris represented to most of Clinton's close retainers, the new, softer, flossier Hillary continually "played 'bad cop,' " as Judith Warner put it, "to complement his often too-accepting manner." Again and again, many remembered, she struck out at what she saw as staff laxity and her husband's own gullibility or slackness. Friends found themselves making some casual observation in their presence, only to have Hillary suddenly seize on it to drive home her side of a private argument. Carolyn Staley recalled a time on Midland Avenue when Hillary burst out at hearing Staley take for granted a report about Clinton's record in the press. "She just screamed, 'See Bill! People do believe what they read in the paper!' " Clinton invariably responded sheepishly. "By now she ate him for breakfast," quipped a friend who grew up with him in Hot Springs. Some thought it another mark, too, of deeper differences of character between the two. "But facing opponents, standing on principle, defending himself on views that were possibly unpopular, wasn't Bill's strong point," Warner concluded. "It was hers."

If Bill Clinton tended to be politically craven and vacillating, too prone to expediency or unprincipled compromise, those traits were only reinforced by the tactics and people he and Hillary adopted together for the comeback—as much at her insistence as out of his desperation. "Hillary . . . was somewhat disturbed by Clinton's excessive self-flagellation, but apart from a few offhand comments she kept her peace," Warner reported. "It was her respect for what he chooses to do," Betsey Wright offered.

Temperamentally repugnant as Hillary might find some of his public remorse, whatever her "respect" for his choices, the essence of their crafted comeback was to be accommodation and concession—like her own new eye shadow, hair tints, and tightly managed public persona. It was also, after all, the convention of their local advisers and of the national Democrats recoiling from the Reagan victory, the resort of the Blairs and the Vernon Jordans alike. "Hillary was always very, very comfortable as the Democrats went right," an old friend would say. "She had sold out corporate and yuppie as fast as any Washington lawyer." Who was to say where "principle" lay for a shattered young politician equating office with life and a far more composed wife, the Rose partner, untroubled in the cause of the firm's clients, of the old power and privilege she served in Arkansas? Their differences always a matter of style more than of character or root values, their mutual strong point would remain a single-minded dedication to their own inextricable advance.

Her discipline would have unintended, ironic consequences in the long run. To curb the philandering as well as make the early public comeback more efficient and discreet, she now hedged about his time and schedule as much as possible. When a driver was caught indulging Clinton's "campaign stops" at bars and clubs for the inevitable female "constituents," Hillary promptly fired the young man, adamant that Clinton be escorted by "professionals." Later, back in the mansion, she would insist for similar reasons that he have Arkansas state troopers as bodyguards and drivers, men whom she first trusted, then soon came to despise for what she saw as their dutiful good ole boy collusion in the governor's extramarital indulgences. Later still, as the Clintons were finishing their first year in the White House, a few of the same troopers would reveal glimpses of the couple's tortured private life in Little Rock, an exposé that indirectly led to the media and legal inquiries into Whitewater.

Clinton himself seemed, as always, to shrug at the short-lived, ultimately ineffectual efforts to rein in his sexual habits. Aides remembered how much he welcomed his wife's much larger role in the campaign, comfortable now with Hillary as a media filter and political strategist, even more active and publicly prominent than in their earlier races. "Make no mistake about it," said one, "she ran things in those two years of his recovery at a level beyond Clinton or Betsey Wright." At the apparent nadir of their fortunes she found, too, a fresh authority and warmth with Clinton, speaking to his rawest vulnerabilities and feelings. Judith Warner recorded Hillary's coaxing and encouraging him, as one might a frightened and sullen child, to attend Little Rock's annual lampoon show for press and politicians in April 1981. "Make them laugh, and you'll see they love you again."

After the performances and applause for both of them, however, there was no doubt about the depth of her own submission. For their ambition, their comeback, she was "willing to knuckle under," as their Arkansas friend Brownie Ledbetter said with characteristic bluntness.

"This new personality or person that I was developing," Hillary would say vaguely of the change begun in 1981–82. "She was a bit uncertain how to describe it," said another of her new exterior, "because whatever it was, it wasn't her real self."

On February 28, 1982, she stood next to Clinton holding Chelsea, now two, as he formally announced his reelection bid. "I don't have to change my name; I've been Mrs. Bill Clinton since the day we were married," she responded archly to press questions, admitting she would be "strictly 'Mrs. Bill Clinton' for a while," though still signing her legal briefs Hillary Rodham. Barely a month later, weeks before the primary, wearing her studied new wardrobe and hairdo, she pointedly changed her voter registration to Hillary Rodham Clinton.

◆ ◆ ◆

On a chill Monday night in February 1982 Clinton performed for the entire state what he had been doing before smaller audiences almost constantly for more than a year. In a thirty-second television ad repeated throughout the week, viewers saw a sad-eyed Clinton biting his lip and staring intently into the camera. The focus was at such close range that the top of his newly styled hair and even the tip of his drawn-up chin were off the screen, his face looming with sudden intimacy in living rooms all over Arkansas.

Deeply apologetic for what he had been and done as governor, he asked their forgiveness, especially for those license fees. He had learned from defeat and from all the people he had talked to since leaving office, and he wanted and deserved a second chance. "You can't lead without listening," he summed up the bitter lesson. Crafted in part by Dickie Morris, by a Little Rock ad agency, and by other out-of-state political consultants and approved by old backers like Carl Whillock as well as by Hillary, Wright, and other advisers, it was still largely Clinton's own much-rehearsed script and emotion. "A humble pie advertising campaign," Starr called the matching spots on television and radio. "The airwaves," he noted, "were saturated with them."

Beyond public view his campaign was less contrite, often fierce and cynical. By the summer of 1981, only seven months after moving out of the mansion, Clinton was locked in battle for the 1982 gubernatorial nomination against the other defeated prodigy, thirty-eight-year-old Jim Guy Tucker. The *Democrat* reported that both candidates were "burning up Arkansas highways seeking support in the hinterlands." That autumn Wright ordered a poll showing enough Clinton popularity to raise major early money, financing the ubiquitous "humble pie" ads the next spring. Meant to reassure and solicit, however, the survey did not match him against rivals like Tucker and foreshadowed none of the slashing among the two young politicians in the primary, much of it echoing Republican rhetoric. When Tucker promised teachers a pay raise, Clinton attacked him for pandering to "special interests." For his part, Tucker deplored Clinton's "palace guard" of radicals in the governor's office and the way he coddled criminals, commuting so many sentences "I find it hard to imagine." Typically, Clinton reacted with television commercials apologizing for commuting sentences or for being "out of touch," implying he was misled by alien staff. Privately, he lashed out at the Arkansas Education Association for endorsing Tucker. "You are trying to end my political career," he told AEA leaders early in 1982, "and I will beat your brains out." Like his rupture with the labor unions in 1976, the episode began, despite public amenity from time to time, a bitter behind-the-scenes feud. Just as antilabor animus shaped his later governance, the rancor with teachers in the desperate 1982 comeback was a furtive influence for years to come in Clinton's educational policy and politics, including his much-advertised Arkansas school reforms.

Beyond Tucker and Clinton the primary field of five included Joe Purcell, a former lieutenant governor and attorney general who had run a losing race for governor in 1970; an obscure state senator; and the perennial gadfly turkey farmer Monroe Schwarzlose. Though Betsey Wright's vaunted organization was now "sputtering," as a reporter saw it that winter and spring, Clinton overwhelmed them all with money. By February, with Maurice Smith tapping heavily into contacts around the state and region, Clinton raised some $200,000 on top of the intensive, costly ad campaign already bought and begun. Altogether he took in nearly $800,000, then a record for Arkansas primaries and, at that, only part of the backing. As always, the money had come from wealthy individual backers, bond brokers and stockbrokers, oil and land fortunes, the state trucking, merchandising, and agribusiness giants, insurance companies, the medical industry, banks, corporations, and various other large interests as well as from the proliferating Arkansas lawyers, consultants, and agents who represented them.

To all of them he would repeat his ritual contrition, accepting the interests' characterization of his callow and misguided regime, implying a far more "mature" conservative rule to come. It had all been a matter of personal style and attention, something he could outgrow. "I made a young man's mistakes. I had an agenda a mile long," he said on the eve of the primary. "I was so busy doing what I wanted to do I didn't have time to correct mistakes." But whatever the public smears and apologies, it was in the suites and by checkbook that Clinton quietly eliminated Jim Guy Tucker, the only formidable obstacle to the comeback. Tucker ran without substance or program, his empty theme "the Arkansas way" and his comparatively few ads focused on images of him playing the guitar and hunting. In the end the former congressman had simply gone broke while Bill Clinton, as usual, cornered the market in political dollars. Starr found a dispirited Tucker at his headquarters days before the primary, "out of money, members of his staff . . . at each other's throats."

Clinton won his first political resurrection with only 41.7 percent of the Democratic vote and was forced into a runoff against Purcell, who extolled "clean" politics, called every opponent "my friend," and refused to criticize a rival. "How about the devil, Joe?" someone asked. "The devil is my friend," Purcell replied earnestly. His forbearance was little help in what followed.

Clinton's "organizational machine," as one account put it, "went into overdrive for the runoff." In the coda to the most expensive primary in Arkansas history, the barrage of Clinton ads and apologies ran constantly. Public attacks on a benign Purcell likely to appear unseemly, there was now a concerted whispering campaign about the fifty-eight-year-old candidate's health, false rumors so virulent that at one point reporters were sent scurrying to local hospitals after anonymous calls about "old Joe" collapsing on the campaign trail.

Even though Purcell had bravely stood up to a racist and red-baiting opponent in the 1960s and held a creditable civil rights record for an Arkansas politician, slurs about his racial views were bruited about in the black community and substantial money was dispensed to leaders and organizers in Little Rock and the Delta. "There was *beaucoup* cash crossing the brothers' palms in that election. You better believe it," said an African American lawyer who witnessed the get-out-the-vote payments to ministers, funeral parlor owners, and other traditional "drops" for the money. Once more the cynical supposition and silence of the local press was numbing. "It was simply taken for granted that in some communities, particularly in the Delta, black votes were for sale and had been bought," Meredith Oakley of the *Democrat* wrote, explaining with embarrassingly unveiled racism the lack of reporting by her colleagues on the ubiquitous allegations of bribery and kickbacks in 1982. On runoff day, black voters appeared for Clinton in record numbers; Purcell was actually shut out in one large ghetto precinct.

The onslaught of smears and corruption broke even the loser's legendary equanimity. Despite a formal "do right" pledge among Democrats, despite a lifetime of party loyalty, in a farewell press conference an embittered Joe Purcell refused to endorse Clinton in the general election, many of his aides furiously offering to work for Frank White.

When it was over, Bill Clinton had the nomination by a margin of thirty-two thousand votes out of nearly half a million cast—the slim, harshly won margin of a comeback, a career, and ultimately a presidency.

◆ ◆ ◆

At a candidates' forum in North Little Rock in May 1982 Hillary Rodham appeared in her husband's place just after the governor delivered his familiar criticism of Clinton's first-term record. "Frank White, I hope you're still out there to hear this," she said, "lighting into" the florid Republican, according to a reporter, as he tried in vain to ignore her and mingle with the crowd. Afterward someone asked about the force and obvious emotion of her counterattack. "Well," she said matter-of-factly, "politics is conflict."

It was not a sentiment much associated with Bill Clinton then or later. Even some inside the campaign thought Hillary chiefly responsible for the aggressiveness in the primary and in the still harsher race against White in the general. Her sternness and discipline were unrelenting. On a campaign flight back from a tiring string of appearances by both of them in western Arkansas, Clinton had cheerily agreed to aides' suggestion that they all go out for an impromptu party that night at a favorite capital bar—despite the fact that White, a teetotaler, had made a minor issue of drinking by the Clinton staff. Listening to the exchange, Hillary was livid. "I can't *believe* you'd say all right," aides heard her screaming at him above the roar of the small aircraft's engines. "She yelled at him all the way to Little Rock," one remembered.

Such scenes in front of staff or friends—Clinton typically absorbing her sharp reproaches in embarrassed silence—tended to obscure how much he passively resisted, evaded, and himself aggressed in other settings and times, often on more serious matters. "He rebelled against the pressure in his own way," said a friend. Her withering temper also eclipsed his own anxious anger and venom in the comeback, always there beneath the happy or ingratiating politician's manner.

Out of office, struggling to come back, Clinton remained the darling of the *Gazette,* most of whose reporters and editors showed unconcealed enthusiasm for his reelection. Apart from occasional, usually tame editorial criticism, neither the respected Little Rock daily nor any other media in the state reported in depth on either of the Clintons, least of all on the Rose firm and the ganglion of political-business connections of which Hillary was an active part. Throughout the 1980s the Clintons would enjoy relative impunity from the scrutiny of investigative journalism, making the later uncovering of their provincial world by outsiders all the more unexpected. In 1982, though, there was still the right-wing and potentially troublesome *Democrat,* embodied in a vain, raspy John Robert Starr and his record of superficial but barbed "exposés" of Clinton and his first-term cabinet.

Their remedy was simple. Having met, carefully courted, and visibly impressed Starr at a political dinner early in 1982, Hillary pointedly began to have lunch with him, pressing on him the more conservative, more "responsible" bent of her husband's politics. "They knew that . . . Starr had a tremendous ego, that he was weak, that they could pander to him," said rival *Gazette* reporter and editor Ernest Dumas. "We found it nauseating." Frequent lunches with Hillary only began a routine of lavish attention to their onetime nemesis, including regular tips and calls from campaign press secretary Joan Roberts and others and "standing orders," as another remembered, "to check with Starr every morning, see what he wanted, and give it to him."

"It worked like a charm," a fellow editor said. Almost immediately, Starr was praising Clinton. "He is no longer a radical," Starr wrote on the eve of the runoff against Purcell. "He is still a bit of an idealist, but his idealism has been tempered by realism that one can learn only from rejection and defeat." They had "made a deal," the editor said later, that Starr would not remind voters of Clinton's old blunders if his comeback remained a "clean campaign." "Clinton is liberal, but he is not as liberal as he was and is more liberal than he plans to be," Starr wrote approvingly that October.

Whether liberal or conservative, Little Rock reporters almost never ventured into the uncharted wilderness of serious power and systemic corruption in Arkansas politics and economics. As it was, the fawning and feeding begun with Hillary's tête-à-tête at lunch in 1982 assured Starr's discretion in covering Clinton for the next ten years. "Nauseating" as the *Gazette* found the toadying to Starr, its own compromise and neglect were too much akin to the *Democrat*'s, and together the two papers left it to others to unearth, only well after the 1992 election, the unseemly origins of the presidency—in many ways too late for Arkansas, the Democratic Party, and the nation.

◆   ◆   ◆

To the alternating delight and disgust of the press and the public, Clinton waged in the 1982 general election his own portion of what became one of the most acrimonious campaigns in state politics. "Bill Clinton was *the* dirty campaigner," Starr told a colleague years later, though he had tactfully withheld that conclusion at the time. "I hope you don't want me to try to out–Frank White Frank White . . . to get down on that level," Clinton announced to a radio audience, describing vividly how the governor had set out to "poison the people's minds against me last time by being constantly critical." White, he maintained, was only a tool of special interests, a governor in the habit of "shaking down" those who did business with the state. "I'm not kidding," he told a crowd in Magnolia. "He's got half a million dollars because the people who wanted decisions from the governor's office paid for them."

It was all "an outrageous abuse of public trust," Clinton repeated in speech after speech. He reminded audiences that White had watched the doubling of the price of prescription medicine for Medicaid recipients while giving an added $12 million tax exemption to big businesses. As a recession deepened nationwide and unemployment soared in poor Arkansas, utility rate hikes had cost consumers $130 million and boosted utility profits 50 percent, in some measure because Frank White had dismantled Clinton's energy office, removed its watchdogs, and packed regulatory bodies with industry flacks. At one point Clinton signed with a flourish a petition to vote on a constitutional amendment to make the state public service commission an elected rather than an appointed body, a proposal that unnerved many of his own powerful supporters before it was eventually struck from the ballot in an industry-backed legal challenge for "faulty" language. "He toyed with it, but he knew that one would disappear into the Bermuda triangle," said a journalist with a wink.

White proclaimed his 1980 election a "victory of the Lord" and sponsored a "creation science" act (promptly struck down as unconstitutional). Prone to accepting rides on corporate jets and asking business friends publicly "how to do the job," he soon became known by capitol reporters as "Governor Goofy" and was guilty of most of what Clinton charged. Like some in Arkansas politics, he had ties to the interests that were at once too naked and too artlessly explained. White tried to argue that Clinton's own close friends, contributors, and campaign officials—most prominently, Mack McLarty of ARKLA and Richard Herget of AP&L—were members of utility boards with the same connections Clinton now deplored. The governor of Arkansas would go on television with a live leopard to remind people that apologetic Bill Clinton wouldn't change his spots. His commercials featured twanging Texan actors impersonating Arkansans who declared that they were voting for good ole Frank.

Yet neither then nor later could the jowly, voluble Republican quite tar Bill Clinton with the same brush—the corporate tax breaks, compromised regulation, favors to contributors, cozy rides on company jets, and more. "No matter how hard Frank hammered, he and other right-wingers couldn't have it both ways," said a state government attorney who worked for both men. "They couldn't say Bill was a radical and also a sellout to the big boys at the same time, and besides that there wasn't anything wrong with the big boys when Republicans ran with 'em too." It all amounted to an impenetrable hypocrisy, institutionalized in the state's unique politics of pride, submission, denial.

Through the autumn the two camps flailed at each other in what one observer characterized as "an unending series of negative spots threatening wholesale prisoner releases, massive utility rate increases, devastating harm to the elderly, and even mass gun confiscations should the other be elected." Against White the "interest-dominated plutocrat," as Diane Blair saw it, "Clinton was just a caring and concerned down-home Baptist family man who wanted nothing more than another chance to fight the fat cats in behalf of the little guy." The *Gazette* called his commercials "cute, sophisticated, and nearly always negative." Yet the sheer wealth and demagoguery of the campaign were reinforcing. Nervously, some thought even frantically, Clinton poured much of his gushing campaign money into five major polls and several lesser surveys in September and October alone—and each seemed to indicate that he did better with the electorate, even raised more money, if he matched White blow by blow, charge by charge. "They were watching it like a prize fight," said a Clinton supporter, "and they loved to see blood."

Clinton would tell friends later, "If you have twelve good people who really believe in you, you can still carry a rural county." By the climax of the 1982 run Betsey Wright and the richly financed campaign had in fact mobilized thousands around the state with what she called "a passionate mission." They organized telephone blitzes that in some counties reached every listed number, regardless of registration. With military precision they mobilized the African American vote. "You and I know there's no such thing as a real Democrat for White," Clinton reportedly told black audiences. "You and I both know what they ought to be called: 'White Democrats for White.' " One civil rights lawyer observed, "They waved everything in front of 'em but white sheets with eyeholes, and knowing Arkansas, it was enough to scare hell out of everybody anyway."

Still, no strategy was more decisive than the candidate's "new" wife. She would take a full year off from Rose to manage the race and in effect run herself, making almost as many stops as her husband did, taking their daughter with her when it was opportune but often leaving the little girl with Dorothy Rodham or sitters. The Little Rock press and others welcomed what they called her "major shift in attitude": "Eight years in Arkansas have almost totally eradicated most of those Yankee tendencies, leaving behind a first lady who embraces her adopted state with the characteristic fervor of a convert . . . accepted by a remarkable number of Arkansans." Starr had it on reliable authority that "some of those who still don't think Clinton is a real person are now convinced that Hillary is." They "know her now as Mrs. Bill Clinton," a *Gazette* writer recorded approvingly, and "are already calling her by yet a different name—Chelsea's Mommy."

In the final weeks of the race Bill Clinton took nothing for granted. "He shook every hand at every stop," a worker said of Clinton. "He worked like a demon." Woody Bassett remembered him standing in the freezing rain in the middle of the night as the shift changed at the Campbell Soup plant in Fayetteville and moving on to another plant at six in the morning, then to a dawn breakfast and reception as the campaign day was just beginning. Privately, he alternately cajoled and strong-armed Democratic county chairmen and trade associations as never before. Betsey Wright had talked about the "up-beat feeling" after a lengthy meeting with party officials. "More like beat-up," one remembered long afterward.

Three weeks before the election Bill Clinton, carelessly answering a questionnaire from the National Rifle Association, said he would favor the reporting of firearm sales to a central computer system for law

enforcement, prompting White and the NRA to denounce his suggestion as dreaded gun control. Within hours Clinton had taped and was
broadcasting a radio commercial denouncing gun control in principle;
he "saturated the airwaves with it, up to and including election day,"
reported John Brummett.

In addition to the ads, he immediately circulated thousands of pam-
phlets repeating his dedication to the NRA position and, in the process, even managed to attack White's handling of sportsmen's license
fees. The blanketing commercials and flyers were luxuries afforded by
his swollen campaign chest. "It was a marvel of backtracking and recovery," said one aide who was involved. On a crowded, crucial Saturday of appearances, Clinton suddenly changed his schedule and went
back home to Hempstead County for a Frontier Day Festival, to be
seen and photographed, as a reporter noted, "admiring and fondling
the antique guns that would be on display there."

On election eve he amazed aides by recalling his exact vote totals,
county by county, in the 1980 race and by methodically, accurately
predicting his likely numbers now. The next day he crushed White
with nearly 55 percent of the vote, winning thirty-two counties lost two
years before and becoming the first governor in Arkansas history to
come back from defeat for another term.

There were several measures of the triumph. As in the primary and
runoff, the decisiveness of his black support was graphic. In a race won
by seventy-eight thousand votes statewide, the ninety thousand African
American votes he took in Little Rock and the Delta were clearly the
margin of victory.

So, too, was the more than $1.6 million he assembled for the richest
campaign ever waged for the statehouse. Only later was the abiding
reality of Arkansas power evident in a careful reading of the campaign
finance lists: almost a fourth of Maurice Smith's big contributors to Bill
Clinton represented major lobbies in the state, and they had given to
Frank White as well.

For now, however, none of that seemed to matter among the
once and future governor's jubilant volunteers, many of them still,
as in that first race for Congress in 1974, hopeful idealists seeing
their articulate, attractive champion as an exception to the state's
gangrenous old politics. For scores of workers and supporters it was
once more a triumph of youthful progressivism over the special-interest misrule of a buffoon Republican; it was a fresh challenge as
well to the venal, torpid Democratic legislature. "AN OBSESSED CLIN-

TON," the gratified *Gazette* headlined afterward, "LED THE DEVOTED IN NEAR-PERFECT RETURN TO POLITICAL GLORY."

In contrast to his morose seclusion and fugitive appearance two years before, Clinton came early to his headquarters on West Capitol as the initial returns heralded victory. When he entered, as the accommodating Starr recorded for posterity, the gathering "exploded in exultation."

· 15 ·

Washington II

"A Little Too Much Like
What It Really Is"

As the Clintons were making their comeback in Little Rock the tyranny of political money was transforming the nation with historic consequences.

Dominance of wealth was the congenital disease and disgrace American democracy was supposed to avoid. In national myth, George Washington might be the symbolic father of his country, his own political accommodations to money suitably muted, but Alexander Hamilton and his mercantile patrons in the Northeast and the planter oligarchs of the tidewater were its political-economic godfathers, practicing what Jefferson called "the general prey of the rich on the poor." Now furtive, now garish—a subject most histories discreetly overlooked and politicians duly ignored—money was the arbiter of most Congresses and presidencies after the Civil War. Power came to be embodied not only in wealthy individuals but in the vast corporations spawned by industrial concentration and conformity.

Yet as late as the 1970s it was still possible to run for the US House and Senate for sums that did not necessarily pawn the candidate—less than $100,000 in some states, far less in others. Even presidential money and its legendary abuses could still seem slight in retrospect. In 1960 John Kennedy drew laughter from the press, and no awkward questions, when he disarmingly referred to stories that his wealthy father had corrupted the crucial West Virginia primary—as indeed he did with last-minute payoffs of thousands of dollars, not to mention what FBI wiretaps later showed to be large Mafia donations on behalf of the future president. Old Joe Kennedy, his own fortune made in smuggling and stock market manipulations typically condoned by local and national governments, had sent his son's campaign a stern telegram. "Don't buy one vote more than necessary," JFK mockingly quoted it as saying. "I won't pay for a landslide."

By the next decade contributors were doing just that, and no one was laughing. All proportion vanished with the cost of the new manipulative weapons of media campaigning. Consultants, polls, and the inevitable television ads devoured millions. After 1976 the cost of running for the Senate rose sixfold, the House fivefold, the presidency more than sevenfold. A typical 1980s senator spent $3.6 million for a seat, soliciting an equivalent of more than $12,000 every week of a six-year term. House races averaged a half million, demanding $5,000 raised week in, week out over the two years in office. In both chambers 60 to 80 percent of contributions now commonly came from outside the home state or district, from interests far removed from constituents. In Capitol Hill's version of the quick and the dead, there were now only two kinds of politicians—those "never free of the money-raising fixation," as one put it, and those retiring or dying in office.

As costs soared, corrupt money poured in. It reached a climax in the Nixon campaigns of 1968 and 1972, awash in bribes from rogue corporations and even foreign juntas. Watergate brought sensational if only partial exposure. In the open for a moment, abuses long known in Washington prompted the obligatory shock and reform. Under hasty new laws, individual contributions were limited to $1,000 per candidate in each primary and general, $25,000 a year for all federal races. Political action committees might hand $5,000 to each federal candidate with no limit on their total. For the presidency, both individual and PAC donations were eventually confined to primaries, with $40–50 million publicly funded for the general election. But Watergate laws only channeled the cash into new currents, creating a surface of legality while corruption swirled beneath.

For would-be presidents money would be more powerful than ever in an electoral system deliberately designed to put a premium on winning the first primaries. Money anointed the front-runners for both Democrats and Republicans, rewarding the early winners and turning a summary thumbs-down on the losers, effectively sealing the nominations of the two kindred parties before most of the nation ever voted. In the general election cash—"soft money"—flooded into the system through a cavernous loophole. Given to parties free of restrictions on candidates, it bought the White House outright in spite of the partial public financing of campaigns.

In sums of $100,000 to $200,000 or more, fat cats supposedly tamed by reform were by the late 1980s passing out a total of more than $30 million to each presidential ticket. Hedging their bets, several individuals and interests showered cash on both sides. Insurance, tobacco, liquor, oil, and entertainment companies, banks and brokers, arms merchants, developers, the most prominent manufacturers and the more discreet sweatshops, a flourishing medical industry, the vast military-industrial-energy combines of the cold war—all these interests and many more swelled the coffers of the men competing for the White House. They became the faceless makers and breakers of the American presidency.

On Capitol Hill, as at the White House, rich individual donors outspent all others. But it was the political action committees that most vividly embodied the corporate seizure of power in Washington. The money coup d'état of the 1970s and 1980s coincided with a major resurgence of big business in the manipulation of politics and government, an intervention more massive and concerted than any in the annals of oligarchic politics. By the early 1970s—with the continuing growth of federal regulation, with huge budget or tax largesse for those who could control legislation, and with new sophistication about means and ends, about the sheer corruptibility of politicians—corporate America moved from shareholder to full-fledged proprietor.

The stakes were enormous—multiple tax exemptions and credits, preferential interest rates, subsidies to entire industries, tariffs, banking and bankruptcy laws, licenses, contracts, and myriad other concessions worth hundreds of billions. In the early 1970s corporations had sent only a handful of agents to Washington. By the end of the decade more than four hundred of the Fortune 500 corporations had encamped in "public affairs" offices. Hundreds of other large interests hovered with hireling lawyers, consultants, trade groups. Most of all, there were their PACs. Multiplying from five hundred in 1974 to more than four thousand by the 1990s, they passed out tens of millions a year. What had once been the old game of the rich or of big business winning government favors now became a continental shift of power.

The wealthy ruled. For the 249 members of "Team 100" who gave George Bush $25 million in 1988, there were returned favors to make nineteenth-century spoilsmen blush. A grateful White House killed a two-year-old criminal investigation of a team member's company. It approved a questionable airport project with windfalls for another team investor. It revised the Clean Air Act to benefit a product and a corporation after a Team 100 stalwart intervened with the president himself. It reversed a twenty-six-year-old government practice and standing presidential policy of imposing tariffs on foreign cement. It made suitable arrangements as the savings and loan bailout became what one witness called "a bottomless welfare program for the politically well-connected," and members of Team 100 were some of the biggest purchasers of forfeited real estate from the Resolution Trust Corporation. On and on went the deals, tax shelters, environmental exceptions, regulatory interventions, friendly appointments. According to a detailed accounting by the Washington watchdog agency Common Cause, the 249 members of Team 100 who contributed $25 million received in return—in subsidies and concessions, issues evaded or ignored—federal favors worth well over $100 billion.

"When these political action committees give money," Bob Dole, Republican leader of the Senate, would say in his dour sarcasm, "they expect something in return other than good government." Taking millions himself, a major violator of even tepid campaign finance laws, the former prosecutor from Russell, Kansas, was in a position to know. Every law and most lawmakers were reliably assumed to have a price. Two hundred medical PACs gave $60 million to both parties in congressional races between 1982 and 1992, ensuring that any "reform" would be written by the industry itself.

Arrangements were mutual. On top of the usual campaign funds, senators and representatives took generous gifts to their own personal "back pocket" or "leadership" PACs, dummy foundations or other fronts from which, in turn, they dispensed donations to fellow members in their own monied patronage. Until the practice was ended by public outrage in the early 1990s, they might also pocket unlimited amounts of unused campaign moneys at retirement or take large honoraria for speeches to interest groups that already funded them and commonly drafted the speeches themselves. But even after the retirement and honoraria scandals, the politicians merely devised inventive new schemes for personal payoffs and enrichment, from payment for their "academic" lectures and political training courses to backing of "issues" groups and committees. "I guess we have our own united ways," laughed a young congressman.

Author and journalist Philip Stern documented a typical case in which AT&T's PACs put out $1.4 million in the mid-1980s and received special tax exemptions of over $12 billion, a net return of 867,145 percent on the investment. By the same measure, General Electric realized a 673,759 percent return on its political money, Sears, Roebuck 510,581 percent, and so it went. The real killing of the 1980s was never on Wall Street, political donors knew, but more discreetly in the marbled corridors and paneled committee rooms of the US Capitol. While politicians extolled risk taking and free markets, enough money in the right places made Washington in the 1980s and 1990s as close to a sure thing as any venture on the planet.

By 1992 less than 1 percent of the gross national product would be spent on human welfare, and most of that was taken by Social Security. Altogether states would spend less than $23 billion (some $262 per family) on welfare; meanwhile, the nation spent $87 billion (or $1,000 per family) to bail out the executives of failed savings and loans. Washington would grudgingly appropriate $25 billion for food stamps, nearly $30 billion for subsidies to agribusiness, and another $100 million each year for international market promotion for more than a dozen Fortune 500 companies. It was, after all, what the political money had paid for. *Harper's* editor Lewis Lapham described in his 1993 book, *The Wish for Kings*, a reality Washington knew only too well:

> The politicians dress up the deals in the language of law or policy, but they are in the business of brokering the tax revenue, . . . redistributing the national income in a way that rewards their clients, patrons, friends, and campaign contributors. They trade in every known commodity—school lunches, tax exemptions, water and mineral rights, aluminum siding, dairy subsidies, pension benefits, highway contracts, prison uniforms—and they work the levers of government like gamblers pulling at slot machines. As with the subsidizing of the farms and the defense industry, so also with the paying off of the bad debt acquired by savings and loan associations. Except for the taxpayers (who, as always, didn't know what was being promised in their name), none of the ladies and gentlemen privy to the workings of the swindle took the slightest risk.

By the late 1980s Washington's most prominent figures were its parodies—Senate Democratic majority leader George Mitchell, Republican minority leader Dole, and assistant leader Alan Simpson; in the House, Democratic Speaker Thomas Foley, majority leader Richard Gephardt of Missouri, GOP minority leader Robert Michel of Illinois, and minority whip Newt Gingrich. They would average more than

$250,000 a leader among the millions passed out by the health industry over 1982 to 1992. From insurance companies, drug makers, hospitals, and others, the reform-stifling money was again only a small portion of the millions the same men garnered altogether, election after election, from other interests for other issues. Much of their slush funds came from PACs—70 percent of House Speaker Foley's war chest in 1990, for example. Each session they might also take hundreds of thousands in blatant "conflict of interest" cash from those for or against legislation that they effectively controlled from introduction to passage.

No tribune of the money tyranny would be more mercenary—or more casually hypocritical—than the fiercely ambitious future Speaker of the House, Newt Gingrich. While savaging Democratic Speaker Jim Wright in 1987 for ethics violations in accepting special-interest favors, Gingrich was quietly—sometimes secretly—building an empire of political finance large enough to dwarf Wright's typical graft. By the early 1990s, as he got ready to make a first nationwide bid to be Speaker, his GOPAC had accumulated over $7 million, the Friends of Newt Gingrich campaign committee over $6 million, a front foundation another $2.3 million, all in the cause of the pudgy, driven politician who would be ruler of the House. Though a loophole in the reporting laws would allow many of the donors to remain hidden, they were, for the most part, what the *New York Times* eventually described as "a predictable array of bankers, health-care executives and other benefactors whose contributions could raise conflict-of-interest questions when Republicans act on proposals governing business." They would be known as Newt, Inc.

A restless young academic described by the press as "an environmentalist critical of the business establishment" when he first ran for Congress in the mid-1970s, the protean Gingrich swiftly evolved into a self-styled "conservative revolutionary," decrying handouts to the poor and brazenly promoting any policies or legislative schemes that could enrich his sponsors in insurance, finance, pharmaceuticals, telecommunications, or other interests. While he denounced socialism for the inner cities, his affluent suburban Cobb County, Georgia, would be the third-largest recipient of federal funds of any suburb in the nation, its take 55 percent higher than the national average, its gated, guarded white subdivisions bolstered in part by weapons contractor Lockheed, in whose Pentagon contracts Gingrich found no small incentive.

With his artfully cultivated fortune Gingrich would erect a sophisticated 1990s political machine of indoctrination and recruitment, fealty and favor—all with a cocky confidence and insouciance and with a contempt for his Democratic rivals so richly deserved that critics were largely disarmed. "The first duty of our generation is to reestablish integrity and a bond of honesty in the political process," he told the conservative Heritage Foundation in a 1990 speech. Even Dole had called him and his ranks "the young hypocrites," but the bold disingenuousness was in many ways the essence of the money tyranny. The *Atlanta Journal and Constitution* would later more aptly quote one of his GOPAC donors, a real estate developer who had given nearly $200,000. "My dad used to say," Fred Sacher recounted unabashedly, " 'What we've got to do is just get those corrupt, dirty Democratic crooks out and put in some nice clean Republican crooks.' "

In the boom that began in the 1970s—in the politicians' greed and the interests' unprecedented aggressiveness to match—the parasites multiplied as never before, a caste of lawyers, fixers, and advisers without substantive portfolio, men and a handful of women who raised the money, implicitly peddled the influence, and frequently ended up, as part of their reward, in government themselves, in cabinet offices or in other prominent positions.

Alongside them grew the thriving industry of campaign consultants and those who concocted political ads, technicians and soothsayers who, like the money pushers, were thought to command special gifts, and high fees in any case. From the White House to the back rows of Congress, they were widely consulted on all matters affecting money and elections, which was to say, sooner or later, everything in American politics.

Some thought the result "an aristocracy of money," others a seedy oligarchy worthy of some minor satrapy. By any name, it produced a largely permanent Congress. Incumbency alone gave senators a more than six-to-one advantage in PAC funds, representatives ninety-seven cents of each PAC dollar in the House, and both groups three to four times more money overall than challengers. Through much of the 1980s there was a numbing 97 percent reelection rate in the House regardless of party. From 1988 to 1992 thirty-three of thirty-nine Republican incumbent senators won reelection, forty-two of forty-five Democrats. They outspent challengers by $200 million. Seats open owing to retirement or death were the only chance for renewal. But those races, too, were quickly dominated by special-interest money that captured the winners, most of whom soon became money-obsessed, entrenched incumbents themselves.

In 1990 a self-motivated Democratic challenger named David Worley was making inroads against a corrupted and brazenly hypocritical incumbent by attacking him on congressional pay raises and other issues. Yet Worley found his own Democratic Party refusing to support him because he had violated a backroom bipartisan deal on Capitol Hill not to fund challengers who raised the pay-hike issue against either party. Outspent by $1.5 million to $333,000 in a race he might well have won with comparable support, Worley narrowly lost by 974 votes out of 151,000. The winner was Newt Gingrich.

By the 1980s the oppression of money made the US Congress less competitive, with less turnover, as Ronald Reagan once observed, than the old Soviet Politburo.

◆　◆　◆

For Republicans, lost was the heart of the old faith, a genuine restraint and skepticism about intrusive government. Behind the worn ideological facade of limiting the state, ever-hungry and pragmatic business donors to the GOP now required just the opposite—proper management and manipulation of the government appropriations on which they had developed, said one observer, "an abject dependence."

Glib opportunists like Gingrich made careers of railing against the "liberal welfare state," urging cuts in services for the poor and minorities while pushing deregulation and privatized services. By 1992 the GOP had occupied the White House for a dozen years, controlled the Senate for six years during the 1980s, held the balance of power in the House for more than a decade, and for years had dominated the federal courts. Yet over the same period the demonized federal government grew larger, more expensive, more bureaucratically ponderous. While taxes were reduced for the wealthy and corporations fattened at the public trough, Republicans had stoutly refused to address vast middle-class "welfare," including education, highway, and farm budgets. The fastest growing federal spending during the Reagan-Bush era was on GOP constituencies, the agribusinesses, for example, that received an extra $20 billion in 1986, "nearly three times," as one account noted, "the entire federal contribution to Aid to Families with Dependent Children that year." Meanwhile Ronald Reagan "piled up more debt, in inflation-adjusted dollars, than Roosevelt and Truman had incurred to win World War II," David Frum wrote in the *Wall Street Journal*. "In just four years, George Bush accumulated three times more debt . . . than Woodrow Wilson had taken on to fight World War I."

Hypocrisy this grand called for the oldest of political tricks: acting out of self-delusion, calculation, or a combination of both, the Republicans simply lied. They would blame taxes on the indolence and demands of the poor, regulations on the antibusiness venom of a phantom liberal elite. Debt they ascribed altogether to Democrats. Amid the social ravages of their political economy, they would spend hundreds of millions to change the national subject from politics and economics to the cultural fears and social resentment their oligarchy had so aggravated by unprecedented inequity. The middle-income sectors were to be convinced that their problem, their enemy, was the poor—and not simply people down on their luck, as Americans had defined the victims of the depression in the 1930s, but rather a class apart, separate and ultimately menacing.

A single mother with three children was expected to practice rugged individualism on $400 a month while corporations and their inflated upper payrolls were doled out billions. "The problem is that corporate welfare has created a culture of dependency that has encouraged certain industries to live off the taxpayers," an independent research group found in the early 1990s, charting over $51 billion in direct subsidies to large businesses and, in a single session of Congress, another $53.3 billion in special tax breaks. More than ever before, America's corporations depended on government's suborned taxes, budgets, regulations, and other benevolence. It was always done discreetly, in congressional committee markups, secret budget negotiations, and deals few saw in crucial detail. Serving such furtive politics, Republicans became the quintessential party of centralized power and state intervention. Descendants of Calvin Coolidge and Barry Goldwater evolved into special pleaders for tax breaks and government dispensations—capitalists by blustery political day, socialists for their engorged patrons by still legislative night.

Politics was not somehow apart from the system; it *was* the system. The capital's silence was captured in the epigram of an elderly western senator. "Be careful what you say, boys," he once warned his colleagues. "It looks a little too much like what it really is."

Among the Democrats the ironies seemed still sharper. "What was once the party of the common man," wrote Ronnie Dugger, "is now the second party of the corporate mannequin." Whether the Democrats had ever been quite so democratic, there was no doubt about what had happened by the 1990s. "The whole tragic decline of the Democratic party," one of its many disillusioned voters would write, "can be traced to the soft, manicured hand from which it is accustomed to feeding." Three hundred pairs of hands would be there for the 1992 election. A Democratic version of Team 100, donors were accorded the accurately proprietary title of "trustee" for their gifts of $100,000, "managing trustee" for $200,000. As with the GOP, money set the bounds for Democratic policies, which in wan mimicry of Republican practices produced everything from bloated Pentagon budgets to regressive taxes. Even the remnant of Washington's Democratic think tanks and promotional groups were now commonly founded and effectively run by lobbyists for the interests and financed—"de facto owned," admitted one of their directors—by corporate money.

The epitome of the courtesan organization, the Democratic Leadership Council, in which Governor Clinton himself was prominent, again and again took tens of thousands in corporate underwriting in the 1980s to discover the virtues of more corporate-oriented Democratic policies. Accordingly, the council and its satellites churned out policy papers and "reform" proposals, advising that Democrats should practice fiscal responsibility by cutting social programs and avoiding awkward revisions of the tax code. They could win back the great resentful middle of the electorate, the council told its members, by indulging popular resentment of the poor in sterner welfare measures, zeal on crime, and other issues that did not intrude on more basic questions of money and power. Naturally enough, DLC financial patrons included several who were also generous in their support of President Reagan and President Bush and some of the most reactionary GOP senators and congressmen. Meanwhile, beyond Washington, the skylines and back streets of American cities, so long the political preserve of Democrats, reflected the same venality. To believe the party was redeemable, critic Norman Solomon wrote, "you'd have to forget the . . . miserable urban Democrats who run our big cities, hacks utterly in the grip of local real estate and banking interests who promote downtown development above all else."

Like its state clones, the national Democratic Party was bereft by the late 1980s not only of meaningful financial support from and contact with ordinary voters but of independent ideas and alternative policies. Typical citizen contributors were now in their seventies, a dwindling vestige of New Deal loyalty. Local parties had degenerated into voter-turnout operations that sent volunteers home after the job had been done, with no further help needed. While Republicans aggressively recruited younger grassroots contributors to their corporate-approved and corporate-enriching "populism," Democrats could find no genuine popular cause not at odds with the aims of their own backers among the same interests. And it was the chief intellectual distinction between the two parties in the 1990s that Democrats, unlike the zealots of the GOP, could not even conceal their betrayal beneath a demagogic fig leaf. The real cost of the Democrats' co-option was that their space on the national stage was silent. Corruption rendered them mute and intellectually sterile, leaving the theater to Republican mythology, with its social divisions and political diversions. Worse than the loss of their integrity, the Democrats had surrendered the very terms of the political dialogue.

Reduced to a countinghouse, the party saw its millions in "soft money" controlled by congressional leaders or a presidential candidate—and at the state level by governors and legislators indebted to the interests. "If the Democratic party began to act like a real political party, the money would be cut off," wrote a longtime Washington journalist on the eve of the 1992 election.

But then Washington also understood that the tyranny of money would loom over any new president, especially a Democrat. If he did not confront it immediately and unequivocally, regardless of the culpability of his own party and past, his every other promise would be betrayed.

◆   ◆   ◆

Only slowly over the 1980s and 1990s did the toll of the corruption become clear. In the richest agricultural economy in history, farmers despaired as their homesteads were auctioned off. In the cities of the world's last superpower, families boarded up their windows against the anarchy of gang violence. There were waiting lists at the most fashionable restaurants and long lines of the hungry at shelters and soup kitchens. In the guise of national security, government planes took off secretly from remote airfields in the South to fly illegal arms to Central America and elsewhere, returning with drugs to be sold by a criminal empire on the streets of Little Rock and Knoxville, Los Angeles and New York. Capitalism triumphed in the cold war, and in the United States the largest single private employer was an agency for temporary help.

The historical adjustment to world economic challenges would have been difficult enough, the transition to a new postindustrial economy a national trial. But coinciding with the money tyranny in Washington, the impact was in many ways lethal.

Jobs vanished at a rate and with a finality worse than in the Great Depression. Nearly two million disappeared in manufacturing alone, and hundreds of thousands more than official figures ever acknowledged. There were layoffs, plant closures, the flight of corporations and export of jobs abroad. In the place of once-decent pay millions found only minimum wages, instead of full-time employment only part-time work stripped of benefits and rights. The average earnings in 1994 were some 15 percent less than two decades earlier. Even as American workers' efficiency and productivity rose, their wages stagnated or fell—breaking what the *New York Times* called "one of the most enduring patterns in American economic history." Meanwhile farm values plunged along with collapsing commodity prices. Their unions broken or impotent, their land sold at auction, American workers and farmers returned to a vulnerability and powerlessness not seen since the nineteenth century.

They were only part of a larger decay of the economy. Never before had the country been so challenged by competition from abroad. Its aging infrastructure and industrial base were already straining in the 1970s. The fabled American commerce of the midcentury faced retooling and renewal at best. Yet by 1992 even that ominous condition seemed some distant, nostalgic past. Arresting the decay meant confronting corporate America and the whole elaborate structure of power by which business folly and abuse were protected, sometimes rewarded. It was the very task a money- and corporate-dominated government could never do.

When it was needed most, investment in plants and equipment had fallen drastically. A vast accumulation of wealth at the top had once again failed to "trickle down." Instead, there was plunder of healthy corporations and institutions. Speculators made fortunes seizing and destroying businesses through stock manipulation. Executives once answerable to shareholders, if not to the moral restraint of public leadership, sacked company holdings for salaries and other perquisites nearly 150 times the wages of their employees. Savings and loan institutions sank in an orgy of shady loans at the cost of hundreds of billions in depositors' ruin and taxpayers' liability.

America went from the world's greatest creditor to its deepest debtor, the annual budget deficit approaching $400 billion and the national debt climbing toward an unimaginable $4 trillion. As a conservative convert in the early 1960s Ronald Reagan liked to draw gasps from his audiences by evoking the Democrats' scandalous national debt as dollar bills stacked "eighteen miles high." By the time he and George Bush left Washington, as one writer reckoned, the same figurative pile reached over 250 miles.

The binge of spending and debt came alongside a deliberate impoverishment of public services. Washington slashed domestic social programs by more than a third between 1981 and 1989, aid to cities by 63 percent, housing by 82 percent, jobs programs and other services by more than half. As support for schools fell over the decade by more than 35 percent, America invested less in education than did any other industrialized nation and trailed most in literacy as well as science. Once proud of its quality of life, America came to rank behind even Third World countries in the health of its babies.

Of the fifty to sixty million Americans—one-fourth of the nation—living in poverty in the early 1990s, at least three million were homeless and seven million more at risk. In 1993, 26 percent of American children under the age of six were officially poor. Despite working full time, nearly ten million American workers—and eight million spouses and children—remained poor. Moreover, they represented more than twice the number of adults on welfare. By 1994 nearly one in five full-time workers were counted among the poor even by woefully unrealistic government measures of poverty. Their curse was neither welfare dependency, lack of education, nor poor skills but the oldest economic disadvantage of all—low wages. More than thirteen million full-time jobs—one in every six and nearly half again more than in 1979—now paid less than it took to raise a family of three out of poverty. In 1970 the minimum wage had been more than 50 percent of the average worker's salary; by the early 1990s it was 30 percent and still declining in relative terms.

As part of the same trends there was a relentless growth in the old impoverished black ghettos. By 1992 nearly six million blacks lived in urban slums, 36 percent more than in 1980. Half of all African American children were born and raised in poverty. There was no question about the social disintegration in such neglect—abuse, illness, suicide, drug addiction, a pandemic of crime, the costly cycle of imprisonment and still more crime.

The collapse of public services, the economic exclusion, and the profound cynicism and alienation were inseparable. The nation now led the world in the percentage of children living in poverty, teen pregnancy, murders of young males, and murders by handguns for all ages. Five million of its children under twelve went hungry every month. It imprisoned more of its citizens than the former totalitarian Soviet Union had. In social and class terms, the nation's penitentiaries were de facto prisoner-of-war camps, though without benefit of the Geneva Conventions. In many urban communities of color, police were a veritable occupying force, their implicit role to contain as well as control. Though politicians and the media found it too frightening to call by its right name, there raged in many US cities in the 1990s a virtual race and class war.

Nationwide, race was only the knife edge of a larger crisis, whose essence was class. The poor of 1992 numbered twice as many whites as nonwhite, especially in the so-called New South, where blacks, though they could at last hold office in the local courthouse, were still, as one book portrayed it vividly, "surrounded by white merchants who own and run everything else." Single-parent families, the uneducated, unemployed, and unemployable, the poor and near poor, always a paycheck or two from disaster, were in every locale, including the more than five hundred suburban communities newly classified as poor by 1989 and the hundreds soon to follow. An official study in the mid-1980s found that more than half of all Americans over twenty-four died in relative poverty, their assets "at the low end," as the report discreetly put it. A 1993 report revealed that five million of the elderly, despite incomes above the official poverty line, were suffering what was delicately defined as "food insecurity."

The wreckage included the once-thriving middle class, though more than 50 percent of the adult working population now received hourly wages, which were what traditionally defined the working class. Median family income, mired at $35,000 in 1990, no longer purchased the status of a generation earlier. Suddenly the children of Middle America were half as wealthy as their parents had been, and with less chance for college, career, property, or secure retirement. Home ownership, once the proud badge of the middle class, became a privilege of the relatively wealthy. Hundreds of thousands of Americans refinanced their homes because their wages were stagnant or they lost their jobs. Equity fell by a record $300 billion over the 1980s. The median cost of a new home rose fivefold in twenty years. Combined with falling real wages, the spiraling costs cut in half, to a little over 30 percent, the percentage of families able to buy their own homes. It all struck at the heart of what Georgetown professor Carroll Quigley had taught the young Bill Clinton about America's unique "future preference," the nation's stoic readiness to sacrifice and postpone so long as there was the prospect of "a better future."

No condition was more telling than the crisis in health insurance at the beginning of the 1990s. Neither destitute enough for Medicaid nor old enough for Medicare, the working poor and middle class accounted for most of the thirty-seven million Americans without health insurance and the sixty million more with inadequate coverage, all facing ruin in a major illness. As premiums shot up nearly 200 percent and medical costs tripled, the employer-paid insurance common in the postwar covered less than a third of the nation's families. The ravenous $800 billion yearly cost of the medical industry—14 percent of the gross national product and nearly twice that of other advanced countries—undermined even larger businesses. But its massive burden, like much else, had been shifted to fall most heavily on the least affluent, the least powerful. By the early 1990s experts estimated that a hundred thousand deaths took place each year simply because the uninsured victims could not afford basic health care; lack of health insurance, something uncommon in other civilized nations, caused three times more fatalities in the United States than AIDs.

◆ ◆ ◆

In the sum of suffering and shattered dreams, there had been a historic change in the political economy of the United States. By 1989, before most Americans realized the first shot had been fired, the class war was effectively over. While the ranks of the poor were teeming and the middle class was shrinking by the millions, those reporting incomes of a half million dollars or more grew from 17,000 in 1980 to nearly 200,000 by the end of the decade. Those earning between a quarter million and a million dollars a year rose by some 700 percent, and multimillionaires by unprecedented numbers. These inequities in wealth were far greater and more swiftly inflicted than any since the inception of the nation.

Few causes and effects were so direct as the dominance of money in politics and the emergence of an economic and political overclass. Altogether, there was the largest gap of money and power separating the rich from other income earners anywhere in the developed world. "The once-egalitarian United States," said an analysis of the 1990 census, was becoming "more stratified and polarized than Europe." As economist Timothy Smeeding would document for the Congress in the early 1990s, the nation tolerated "a level of disadvantage unknown to any other major country on earth." This would be the America that Bill Clinton wanted to govern. How much he truly understood of the national forces at work would never be altogether clear in the campaign, though his apparent empathy for the suffering and complaints of ordinary people became a compelling part of his candidacy.

The Washington he ran against was a deeply ingrained culture with its own tribal habits and mores, a culture of complicity the new president, if his promises were to have a chance, would have to understand and confront as directly as he faced the other challenges. To both Washington and the nation, in any case, he came from his own peculiar history in the Arkansas of the 1980s, a place with its own money tyranny, human toll, ugly secrets. And that, too, would eventually have to be seen for what it really was.

· 16 ·

Little Rock III

"Best of the New Generation"

To the bond dealers it was Slam City, and *Forbes* named it America's "scam hot spot." Even in a decade of legendary excess, rampant speculation, and corporate intrigue, of celebrated greed and flamboyant wealth, there was a stark contrast in Little Rock between its outward appearance and its inner reality. "A wide open town in a wide open state where a lot of money got made fast with no questions asked," one federal agent remembered. "I didn't know what life in the fast lane really was," said a Wall Street broker, "until I got to little old Little Rock."

Below the white heights and a trendy new west side of shopping malls and residential sprawl, the city of 175,000 might still appear languid and provincial, its venerable black ghetto cordoned off by a freeway, the poorer bottomland of North Little Rock often veiled in a haze of pollution beyond the gray-brown moat of the Arkansas River. A sparse, stubby new skyline rose over the worn downtown, its somewhat incongruous high-rises the monuments of homegrown fortunes like Stephens and Worthen Bank. Beneath them the heart of the city remained implacably shabby and forsaken, too many blank storefronts, too many parking lots paved over the empty sockets of failed enterprise. "On a business day," thought one visitor, "the place seems as sleepy as some others on a peaceful Sunday."

The taller buildings stood in contrast as well to the grinding want of the rest of Arkansas—some two million people who remained among the poorest in the nation, their average yearly income less than the

$20,000 annual fees at the Little Rock Country Club. The old colony was always there, not far from the capital's modern glass towers, in communities riven by railroad tracks, race, and caste; in the polluted company towns of the Ozarks; in the migrant workers' shanties sprawled on the southwestern flats; and most of all in the Mississippi Delta, with its Third World privation, its houses with dirt floors, bleak counties where infant mortality was worse than in much of Africa or Central America and where the only viable industry was likely to be the local crack house. "The economy of plantations and sharecropping gave way to no economy at all," Memphis journalist Guy Reel wrote of the Delta in the early 1980s. "The dirt was all anyone knew."

More than ever, the affluent and powerful of Little Rock lived comfortably apart. More than ever, from corporate suites, law firms, and banks, from the corridors of the legislature, from discreet political fund-raisers emulating the political money parties in Washington, they controlled it, held it at bay—in part, as always, by laughing contemptuously at what surrounded them. "How do you measure the wealth of the average Arkansas household?" went a familiar joke. "By the number of dogs killed when the front porch collapses."

Behind the tinted windows of Little Rock's skyscrapers, in offices grafted onto the now-fashionable old Quapaw quarter, there was an air of showy new money and brash prominence. To many it seemed symbolized by savings and loan magnate Jim McDougal, gliding through town in an unmistakable blue Bentley or in one of his twin green Jaguars. His voluptuous wife, Susan, starred in a familiar local television commercial, wearing a skintight outfit and spurring her white stallion over the countryside to promote land development schemes with names like Gold Mine Springs, Maple Creek Farms, or Whitewater Estates. Diamond Jim and Hot Pants, as the couple was known, were intimate social friends, political backers, and business partners of Governor Clinton and the First Lady. Diamond Jim was in succession a statehouse aide, legislative liaison, and principal fund-raiser for the governor. Hillary, in turn, was not only intimately involved in their joint real estate venture but also worked as a lawyer on special retainer for the McDougals' Madison Guaranty, the savings and loan that soon became notorious for the profligate spending, borrowing, and shuffling of depositors' money and government loans that fed a lavish lifestyle and an intricate if gossamer web of interwoven companies, including the cash-hungry Whitewater half owned by the Clintons.

In the Little Rock of the 1980s few questioned such ties to publicly insured and regulated institutions or even a sitting governor's close, collusive partnership in the manipulation of other people's money. So natural a part of the political and economic landscape went unexamined by the capital's media, still widely thought to be among the most vigilant in the New South. "There was a certain selectivity in what they chose to cover," *Democrat* columnist Meredith Oakley wrote afterward. About the Clintons' flashy friends and other backers in Little Rock there was acceptance of their simply being on the make, whatever the stakes or methods, however dubious or seedy the atmosphere. It was "the milieu of a David Mamet play," the *Wall Street Journal* said, "in which glib five-and-dimers swim along the edges of the real economy, living on fancy talk, cutting corners, and hoping that one of the big boys will offer them a piece of the $100 sure thing."

The "big boys" and some of the "real economy" were there, amid Arkansas's enduring poverty, with a magnitude and force unique in the nation. Even the high-living McDougals, with their statehouse intimacy and bountiful flow of cash, could seem almost modest beside the larger boom. In the shade of a state government known for its agreeable regulation and its friends in high places, there was a torrent of money, a wheeling and dealing unlike anything in the history of the region. In the early 1980s billions poured through Little Rock bond houses. Around what they called "the pit" in firms like Lasater and Company, eager bond daddies worked the phones in a frenzy. Accounts might appear overnight with huge earnings and just as swiftly and mysteriously vanish. "Bo knows bonds," one of them would say later with a grin about the proverbial fast-talking southern salesman.

Among the issues they hawked were a publicly insured state agency called the Arkansas Development Finance Authority. ADFA was to be a model of Governor Clinton's economic development policy, a program to ease financing for low-income housing and small businesses, which were too rarely supported by conventional capital. Instead the bond agency would become what one person called a "piggy bank" for the politically connected, discreetly shunting its privileged finance to crony companies, its expensive legal work to favored law firms, its lucrative underwriting to select Wall Street houses and local bond brokers—almost all of them backing Bill Clinton. Under a scheme quietly contrived by the Rose firm, ADFA at one point planned to channel nearly a hundred million dollars in taxpayer-guaranteed bonds to capitalize a vast profiteering in nursing homes partly owned by Stephens. With similar license the authority husbanded other deals of suspect character, including investment of state money in surreptitious off-shore companies, commonly with records that later proved lost or not quite complete.

Immense amounts of money, often shady, seemed everywhere, from local fly-by-night ventures to exotic foreign transactions, from the levies of the Arkansas River to the shores of the Persian Gulf. Begun by a peddler pushing Bibles, belt buckles, and the proverbial southern bonds, the mammoth Stephens, Inc. now dealt in billions worldwide. The financial house took public burgeoning local companies like Wal-Mart and Tyson and made them all still vaster fortunes. By the 1980s Stephens not only stood atop the local economy with control of banking, utilities, and other holdings but counted numerous politicians among its income-producing properties. From its Little Rock headquarters the combine now reached out as well to international clients and partners in the Middle East and Asia. Stephens had brokered the first penetration of legitimate American business by the infamous BCCI. Through a company called Systematics it provided sophisticated computer services for banks, services that came to afford intimate and privileged access to financial systems throughout the world—and that some saw as lending itself to alleged links with the shadowy new computerized world of post–cold war espionage, to money laundering and front companies, to intelligence agencies' surveillance of private bank accounts and manipulation of funds. As if to trumpet its ultimate power, the Stephens empire would go on, at a fateful juncture in the 1992 election, to put up a few of its millions to rescue—if not ransom—a future president of the United States.

But then, the speculators and bankers, however immense their reach, were hardly alone in netting the profits washing over Little Rock. So flush was the moment that Internal Revenue Service monitors noted warily a "major increase" in the number of large cash transactions in Arkansas, despite the state's chronically stricken economy. The IRS began to alert other law enforcement bodies to what its agents called the region's "enticing climate" for drug trafficking and money laundering. As it was, the worst official suspicions rarely matched the grainy picture emerging in law enforcement files and other documents.

At raucous parties on sprawling estates and aboard private jets, cocaine lay piled in ashtrays, was passed about on silver platters or in small vials, was even bagged in festive pouches hanging as ornaments from Christmas trees. Regular party guests—powerful businessmen and politicians from Arkansas and beyond—had "all the coke they could snort," as one witness told the police—and were supplied, too, with pretty teenage girls from Little Rock high schools as well as with the most fashionable black prostitutes from the capital or Memphis or New Orleans, women who later told stories of suffering cigarette burns and other abuse in the houses and suites of some of the city's most wealthy and prominent citizens. "They were animals," said a West Memphis sheriff's deputy who listened to some of the accounts.

It was all done with seedy abandon and, for most involved, utter impunity. Drug dealers corrupted local police for protection, hiring off-duty officers as bodyguards, and in any case kept up a steady stream of contributions to local officeholders and charities. At one point gruesome testimony moved prosecutors to bring a few cases. But inquiries never went too far, and the token convicts were soon forgotten, the most famous among them pardoned by Governor Clinton. "I guess there was an accountability of sorts," one official would comment bitterly. For their own purposes at least, according to government informers, representatives of organized crime made videotapes of the politicians cavorting at the parties.

Meanwhile, in the remote pine-forested Ouachita Mountains, some 160 miles to the west on the Arkansas-Oklahoma line, in country once the refuge of border bandits and anarchists, local officers happened onto suspect air traffic, stores and truckloads of weapons, and even Spanish-speaking strangers carrying out military exercises in camouflage uniforms. Nearby a local IRS agent and state police investigator glimpsed the silhouette of a multibillion dollar gunrunning, drug-smuggling, and money-laundering operation, an enormous criminal traffic carried on for at least five years with what the US government's own documents secretly recorded as the collusion of organized crime, the Central Intelligence Agency, and other Washington institutions. By their sworn statements, couriers for the operation carried duffel bags stuffed with cash into local Arkansas banks, then watched as obliging bank officers apportioned the money among the tellers for cashier's checks, each transaction just under $10,000 to evade the IRS reporting requirement.

A tentacle of the Iran-Contra scandal, and only part of a larger, still darker underworld of national security policy run amok, the vast crimes were effectively sanctioned by Ronald Reagan's White House and later covered up by George Bush's. Yet what went on in the Ouachitas in the 1980s was essentially condoned as well by a third and future president then sitting in the Little Rock statehouse, where the drugs and intrigue were topics of avid interest and frequent discussion among the governor and his state police escort. The episode was destined to be known for the obscure town where the principal smuggler and government operative based his aircraft, a tiny Arkansas county seat named Mena.

Over it all, linked directly and indirectly to the people and even the more bizarre events, was Arkansas's gregarious young leader, who by the mid-1980s seemed to have taken up permanent residence in the governor's imitation Georgian mansion. There was no longer any doubt about Clinton's accommodation to the state's largest interests old and new, or about their stake in him. "Put sessions" were what the gatherings were called at which the local movers and shakers came together to "just put up or shut up," as business editor Kane Webb described the ritual. In his 1982 comeback and afterward, Clinton would raise some $10 million from them, an average of over a million dollars a year. When he made his long-expected run for the presidency in 1991–92, they would be there with millions more.

Yet there was something now beyond the usual statehouse favors and the ceaseless ambition. The palpable ethic of Little Rock, of the 1980s as an era, became that of the Clintons as well. Albeit in different ways perhaps, he and his impressive wife were personally very much a part of the city's racy new style, drawn like Mamet characters into the ethos and habit of its grasping.

As she had done earlier in the commodities market, the First Lady of Arkansas took advantage of the easy money. She swiftly joined the McDougals in their fast shuffling of loans and land and assumed an active role in exploiting with punitive real estate contracts the specially targeted, often gullible low-income elderly buyers of Whitewater lots. Typically, too, she used her political status to garner lucrative retainers or seats on corporate boards and was one of a handful of Little Rock insiders in a high-yield franchise investment scheme spun by a figure who, like Red Bone, would be discovered afterward to be shrouded in allegations of fraud and manipulation.

Meanwhile, commonly said to care little about making money, an impression he casually cultivated, the governor was privately avid in his own financial pursuits. He unabashedly solicited friends like Jim McDougal for not only campaign funds but even legal retainers for his wife. "McDollars," Clinton would laughingly call the money that always seemed available through the owner of Madison Guaranty. From other friendly banks he borrowed, without collateral, hundreds of thousands of dollars that went into his personal campaigns and toward other uses for which there was no comprehensive accounting. Beyond the ten million dollars in recorded campaign contributions, he extracted more from the large interests to wage elaborate propaganda in the service of his legislative agenda and his national reputation, again evading a complete reporting of the funds.

In the vivid recollection of aides who handled the wads of bills, the governor was provided thousands of dollars each year in "pocket money," cash that went for everything from petty kickbacks in friendly precincts to payments made by state troopers for gifts for his mistresses—all this, too, evidently unreported on tax returns or in other accounting by a Bill Clinton who meticulously ticked off dollars and cents in tax deductions on discarded underpants and socks. Not least, there were the incessant favors, the gifts, the flights on corporate planes and on the private jets known for their ashtrays filled with cocaine, the complimentary suites and boxes, the parties with the teenage girls and tortured prostitutes.

According to numerous witnesses who slowly emerged from the shadows, drug orgies were hardly the governor's only sensual pleasures. According to their sworn testimony and the consistent accounts of several of the women themselves, his state trooper bodyguards served as veritable procurers of sexual partners, both the consenting and the simply vulnerable, as Bill Clinton swept through public appearances from conventions to county fairs or made his habitual forays into nightclubs in Arkansas and elsewhere while traveling on official business. For hours of their official shifts, troopers stood lookout, the state limousine furtively tucked away up a driveway or around the corner. The governor's sexual compulsions on and off public time were common knowledge in some Arkansas circles, even among the "selective" Little Rock press, and, like his business associations and financial practices, were unexamined, condoned, accommodated.

To those who had access to official files and insider knowledge, the abuse of Hillary Clinton and the exploitation of young women, even the misuse of public office in the conduct and coverup of the acts, could seem comparatively trivial. One of the governor's closest friends and principal backers, the beneficiary of commissions on hundreds of millions of dollars in state bond transactions, was a drug dealer of some magnitude, one of Little Rock's cocaine party hosts who was also under suspicion for narcotics smuggling elsewhere in the nation.

Other influential Clinton friends and contributors, too, had thick investigative dossiers, several with the special code numbers reserved for suspects appearing with some frequency in the records of the federal Narcotics and Dangerous Drugs Information System. Police files brimmed with allegations of drug running, ties to organized crime, and even murder alleging the involvement of a well-known Arkansas businessman and some of the governor's closest supporters.

In many ways Bill Clinton knew the underworld reality as well as he knew the relatively open issues of state governance he described so impressively to visitors. He was known for expounding on almost anything of import in his small, self-conscious state. Yet about the darker provinces in Arkansas, about much that made the place far more than its hillbilly caricature—from the debauchery of the powerful to the immense wealth and influence to the international intrigue and crime—the voluble politician was uncharacteristically reticent. On some subjects, it seemed, even Bill Clinton would say as little as possible.

♦ ♦ ♦

In his 1983 inauguration speech Clinton movingly evoked his roots in Hope, telling the old story of how Eldridge Cassidy had wept because he was too poor to buy his little girl Virginia an Easter frock. "It was very humble and watery," recalled an aide. Meanwhile Hillary Clinton moved back into the mansion with a relish and design that struck even casual observers. To the comparatively modest inaugural ball—"no Camelot now," a reporter noted—the reinvented First Lady wore a decidedly traditional gown, what the editor of the *Democrat*'s society page thought "a pleasing set of feminine contradictions" and a less reverent observer called "something you'd find at the Eastern Star dance in Pine Bluff." Their friends from out of state were "shocked," as one recalled, that the carefully coiffed and made-up Hillary now also spoke with an audible southern drawl. "I had to think twice," said a Yale Law School classmate.

In place of what Starr had deplored as the young "squirrels," there was now banker and money raiser Maurice Smith, "grizzled, gravel-voiced . . . unprepossessing . . . one of a series of father figures in Clinton's life," as Oakley saw him, a good ole boy who "knew where the skeletons were buried but . . . had no interest in disinterring them." Just below Smith was the acerbic Betsey Wright, serving again as guardian of Clinton's public image and political flanks.

His staff had shrunk to fourteen members from the seventy-eight it had been four years before, and only one member was from outside Arkansas, compared to twenty-six in the past. Clinton for now closed the Arkansas office in Washington, renouncing out-of-state travel or national forums as ardently as he had once sought them. "Gone native," the staff of the National Governors' Association would say sarcastically of the thirty-seven-year-old politician they watched move with such expedience from local to national poses.

There was an anxiously displayed new accommodation in legislative policy as well, what an intimate witness called "the care and feeding of the interests." Even the conservative Starr thought Clinton's second-term agenda a "pale shadow" of his first administration's. Utility reform now went unmentioned, the Grand Gulf swindle he had played against White all but forgotten. Even before Tyson and the shipping combines lobbied for it themselves, Clinton on his own initiative would press for the truck weight concessions they had wanted two years earlier. To the mounting distress of the small public-interest community in Arkansas that still supported him, he acquiesced from the outset in corporate environmental abuses and continued company dominance of state regulatory commissions.

The young governor might still occasionally rail against a faceless "they" who financed his opponents in the legislature as lavishly as they bankrolled him, though it was now public indignation with a broad Clinton wink. "He knew it was popular to attack them, but he was on the phone with them before and after, telling them it was just good politics, keeping and making peace," recalled a legislative aide. "He became a student of the political process, not truly governor but ultimately a master of what elects and what doesn't," said a supporter at the time. "Any real policy would have gotten in the way. He wouldn't offend the money."

At meetings early in the second administration the governor might still ask aides who was most affected by the action they were discussing. Were there people not present who really cared? "But that happened less and less," said a participant, "and there were fewer and fewer voices in the room other than the status quo." As in the first term, as in his campaigns, Clinton would continue to promise and renege, appeasing each audience as it came, infuriating even his most consistent clients among the interests with an incorrigible vacillation and evasiveness. "The son of a bitch couldn't ever really be trusted. Ever!" one of them would say years later.

Yet not even his habitual caprice could balance the constant calculus to satisfy the patrons. "He never challenged them again," a prominent Arkansas Democrat said of the corporate giants. The craven wont of the comeback now became his fixed political method and governmental custom. The "care and feeding" evident in the first weeks of the second term would shape power and politics in Arkansas for the rest of the decade and beyond.

The widely publicized "reform" of Arkansas education in 1983—an episode the Clintons were to advertise as a major achievement in running for the White House—embodied what many saw as both the best and the worst of the administration and, in any case, was a fateful prototype of the ill-fated national health reform to come.

By every measure, the state's schools had long been a disgrace, among the poorest in the nation in terms of course offerings, dropout rates, teachers' salaries, number of accredited districts, or any other standard. "They do worse," a member of the state Board of Education said of Arkansas students in 1980, "the longer they stay with us." At once symbol, cause, and effect, the deep-seated mediocrity in education went to the core of Arkansas's tormented, defensive self-image of backwardness, and Bill Clinton was to play effectively, sometimes brilliantly, on that paradoxical mixture of pride and prejudice.

Policy that the Clintons later presented as a bold, original initiative actually derived far more from the political moment and the work of others. Even in Arkansas, educational reform had been a recurrent if ultimately vain theme for governors dating back to the postwar Mc-Math administration. By 1983 state supreme court decisions made necessary at least some overhaul of the system, and education had also become a fashionable issue among the newer generation of modernizing, mercantile-minded southern governors in states from Mississippi to South Carolina, from whose already evolved reforms the Clintons would borrow "liberally," as one reporter put it. In that setting what now unfolded would make education a kind of emblem of Clinton governance: a pressing problem both simple and subtle, addressed with seemingly dramatic solutions, soon immersed in expedient, often contradictory politics, and ending with a substantive result far less meaningful than the eventual claim.

As late as the transition—there had been no real commitment to such a major initiative during the 1982 campaign—the Clintons settled on the priority and potential of the issue and moved quickly to seize the political moment. "Slick Willie . . . dominated the regular, do-nothing session of the legislature," one skeptical editor noted of the weeks after his second inauguration. But with the newly reelected governor lobbying energetically, the 1983 legislature did create an Educational Standards Commission to hold public hearings and recommend reforms, though some believed—aptly, it turned out—that most measures had already been decided by the governor's office. Kindergartens, mandatory attendance, smaller teacher-student ratios, a small raise in teachers' salaries, new course requirements, a longer academic year, limits on teachers without appropriate credentials, and more—the proposals were a roll call of what was starkly absent in the old system. "Only in a state like Arkansas," one writer concluded, "would such a minor package . . . be labeled 'reform.' "

Yet the most startling innovation for many—bringing a "statewide gasp," said one account—was the governor's appointment of his wife to chair the commission, thrusting her into the political process more openly than ever before, to act now as advocate and lightning rod for an issue on which they were both banking heavily. The selection was more than political calculation. Reelection hardly stanched the draining emotional wounds of the defeat and comeback. "The period preceding her appointment had been one of the most turbulent of their marriage," Nina Martin wrote of those months in 1982–83. Now, in a pattern to be repeated often, the formal, overt sharing of power, whatever the intimate balance between them, proved to be both personal appeasement and adept politics. Hillary Clinton plunged into the effort with obvious ardor. "She did it with more delight than in anything I'd ever seen her do in Arkansas," said a friend. "She was really ready."

The job seemed both to compensate for the accumulating pain and betrayal in the marriage and to vest her all the more in the fate—and myriad compromises—of her husband's persona and politics. By then some of her oldest friends thought that her lot was long since cast, others that the educational reform was still a watershed, a point from which she might yet have somehow turned back or aside. "After she got out front on the education thing," said one of them, "there was no doubt about where she'd end up, or how consciously she chose it."

Together in the promotion of a public policy, the Clintons were unlike anything the state had ever seen and in many ways more concerted and collaborative than they would be again until the 1992 presidential run. While the governor worked what aides called "the inside," restlessly lobbying legislators, school superintendents, and others, the First Lady crisply held the often tedious pro forma public hearings in each of the state's seventy-five counties, ate her discreet lunches with Starr, and courted, impressed, and ultimately won over the broad public they had targeted. The audience was ready, albeit in an Arkansas still prone to use deplorable education as an excuse for much else and always opposed to the taxes involved in paying for a better system. Most important, they encountered no real opposition among the dominant interests. "The good suits," as they were known, would at least be neutral, if not supportive. In fact, Clinton would raise more than $130,000 from wealthy contributors and major companies for television ads and other promotions selling better schools as a tool for economic development, a source of jobs, and a spur to state pride. He merchandised the proposed legislation as if it were a consumer product, pitching educational standards to the public, said one account, "as a way of giving them something for their money."

Even with powerful backing and broad consensus, however, the Clintons were never to confront the basic problem of school district consolidation, the one essential reform that could have given meaning to the rest. Splintered into its local enclaves and preserves, most of Arkansas would never have the resources or renewed talent to make the new standards truly count in terms of a more educated populace. Though longer years of mandatory attendance, more course offerings, and higher salaries for teachers would be legislated, these changes would occur within the old and overweening system. "Real change meant going to the grungy heart of education as pork and bureaucracy," said someone who worked on the reforms in the statehouse— "the difference between policy as playing politics and policy as real problem solving and reform whatever the difficulty." In the end even the Clintons' limited improvements, modest by national standards, would be mortgaged by that failure.

After the statewide hearings and just before legislative action, they responded to the urging of Starr and others (and ignored the despair of many of their supporters) by adding to the package a one-time qualifying test for teachers. Questions of competence were all too real, but the test, the governor's office understood, was a case of class cannibalism in a state where teachers, whose pay was at the bottom of the scale nationally, still made as much as 50 percent more than Arkansas's average wage. As expected, the test aroused angry opposition from the Arkansas Education Association as well as from civil rights groups rightly fearful of the toll on black teachers. Their cries provoked the calculable backlash. At a stroke the Clintons could now cast the essential issue of reform as teacher accountability, and teachers as a whole and blacks in particular as ready scapegoats before the poor white electorate.

As the corporate-financed ads and other statehouse pressures intensified through late 1983, polls soon showed a two-to-one margin in favor of the teacher testing. It was with that condition that the rest of the new school standards eventually passed the legislature at the end of the year. Later leaked to the press, the test was a cruel mockery. While rates of failure were predictably higher in the most impoverished black districts for all the usual cultural and political reasons, and some 3.5 percent of teachers flunked despite repeated attempts, several of those who took it in Little Rock's White Heights "came out laughing," as one journalist recounted. Anyone with an eighth-grade education, even in Arkansas schools, might have passed, Meredith Oakley noted cautiously, proof only that most teachers "were at least as competent to stand at the front of the classroom as the average Arkansan."

The same "average Arkansan" was to suffer the new tax levy that was the other precondition of the package. Having promised a 1 percent increase in the state's notoriously low corporate and severance taxes and having proposed the teacher test "as a bone to businesses . . . to give them accountability in return for a tax hike," as one version described it, both Clintons would now stand by in studied silence while the interests—many of the same giants who had given to their propaganda fund—quietly turned their lobbyists full force on legislators to block any rise in corporate or severance rates. "The big boys were for better schools so long as the rednecks paid," a ranking woman in the Clinton administration recalled. "Spectacle to behold, spectacle to behold," drawled a lawyer who saw it at the capitol. "Lots of winkin' and noddin' Arkansas-style." In the process and with the same ethic, Clinton would earnestly promise antipoverty and senior-citizen groups a rebate on any tax affecting the poor, then casually abandon them by refusing to press the relief against the opposition of legislative barons and corporate lobbyists.

When it was over after a six-week special session of the legislature in the autumn of 1983, the entire cost of the stillborn reform typically fell on those least able to afford it—in a regressive one-cent rise in the sales tax—"the largest general tax increase in the state's history," one journalist recorded. "Business and utility interests emerged unscathed," Oakley noted. Country club fees were specifically exempt from the sales tax. With Jim Blair lobbying, a third of the new funds would be siphoned off, without even the pretense of higher standards, for state colleges and universities as mediocre as the lower schools, leaving elementary and secondary institutions far less of the regressive tax money than ever planned, for reforms already more guise than substance.

Outwardly Clinton scored a public-relations triumph. Conservative local critic Paul Greenberg deemed it Clinton's "finest hour" and proclaimed that the governor "came of age as a political leader" and that "Slick Willie [was] almost invisible at the special session." The change, due largely to Hillary, "wouldn't be the first time that the key to a man's growing up would prove to be a woman." It was a verdict about both of them widely shared in local journalism and lore.

Only later was there deeper public scrutiny of the actual effects of the legislation, let alone the raw politics that enveloped it. Like the rest of the Clinton legacy, the sum of his education policy, including the new standards, could not be fairly drawn until the 1990s, though year after year from 1983 on, even with the added funds, the state remained consistently among the worst two or three in the nation in spending per capita on public schools, while most of the other dismal indicators there at the beginning remained largely unchanged. Few understood the implications of the $130,000 given to the governor by the interests to sell the package, the subsequent cynical lobbying against progressive taxes to which both Clintons acceded, and then the almost perfunctory statehouse treachery on the rebate for the poor.

If teachers came away feeling exploited and deceived by Hillary's expedient resort to the testing issue and then her sudden disappearance from the process after her public accolades—and just when the corporate lobbying and sordid inner politics began—they were not alone. Scarcely a year into Clinton's second term, there was a gathering sense of his emerging pathology as a political leader. "I think he's a habitual liar. He's done it all his life, and it's just the way, business as usual," former close aide and fund-raiser Bert Dickey would say later, echoing a judgment that began to form for many in the 1983 maneuvering. "I don't think he's got a conscience. He can be true-blue one minute and then the next minute you're out of there." At the same time, aides and others found an imperious double standard. A legislative assistant thought Clinton "very casual about the truth himself yet very scrupulous about what somebody else told him." One of his liaison lobbyists observed that, "beginning with that second term and particularly in education, which meant so much to his reputation and national ambition, Bill himself was tougher and more ruthless than anyone in getting what he wanted. He was abusive and full of violent language at any hint of betrayal by anybody he thought was an underling."

A decade later some saw the education-reform episode reflected in the extravagantly promoted but ill-fated effort at national health-insurance reform. Once again, the First Lady was thrust out to hold hearings and impress the audience, and once again, supposedly open reforms were secretly sabotaged beforehand. Once again, there were promises and betrayals, an elaborate outer image and hidden inner politics. In Washington, however, the opposition would be far more formidable than Arkansas' scapegoated teachers or civil rights groups. The insurance combines, the medical industry, and more would be arrayed against change with overwhelming force, and there would be a crushing defeat. Once again, too, the First Lady would leave the field just as the real politics began, unable to confront either her husband's habitually refracted politics or the deeper power of the system she professed to understand and challenge. "If you knew what truly happened in the education deal," one of their statehouse aides would say, "you didn't need a crystal ball for what was going to happen to health reform in Washington. You just knew."

At the end of 1983 in Little Rock, however, the Clintons basked in victory, and much of the state in the impression, if not the reality, of change, the all-important "feeling better about themselves" that the governor and his wife would repeatedly bring to an abject constituency. Through her skillful public rounds Hillary especially had "engag[ed] the people of Arkansas for the first time in a real conversation about education," former Clinton education aide Don Ernst said afterward. For many it was enough. That new standards, persuasively presented as reform, had passed the notorious legislature seemed proof of statesmanship, especially since the governor and his wife had "faced down a long line of special interests," by which Greenberg and others meant the teachers and the blacks. Demagoguery on the test, collusion with the interests, failure to confront consolidation—all seemed subtle and obscure by comparison. So, too, was a larger precedent: an avowedly populist governor artfully turning on people ostensibly of his own constituency, isolating or stigmatizing them on class or racial grounds to appease what he saw as broader support. It was a foreshadow of what would be called "the Bubba factor," a consummate cynicism taken into the presidential race of 1992 and later into the White House.

After only a year of his second term Bill Clinton stood at the zenith of his popularity in Arkansas. He was still unrivaled in his own party and faced no credible Republican opposition on the way to a historic third term in 1984. The first such extended tenure for a governor since Orval Faubus, reelection would bring sweeping patronage in commissions and other bodies that would make him the most powerful chief executive in state history. Then, just as that historic victory and power appeared certain, there was a fleeting intrusion of that other, darker Arkansas, stirring private turmoil behind the public facade and frightening Bill Clinton into a needless last-minute debt that would haunt his presidency.

◆ ◆ ◆

Roger Clinton's locally famous name began to appear in the narcotics files of local and federal law enforcement agencies in the first weeks of 1984, and some officers believed there had been even earlier reports that were subsequently purged. It was in the late spring of that year, as Virginia remembered, that she first learned that twenty-seven-year-old Roger was in trouble for drug dealing, though "Bill had known for weeks that this moment was coming." What her sons had actually known and done, however, and for how long, not even Virginia was prepared to face.

Roger's dissolution had posed a potential embarrassment since Clinton's first term in the mansion, though each time the episode was fixed or covered up. After Roger was arrested in 1981 for ignoring repeated speeding tickets, the governor quietly arranged for his release to the custody of a relative who chaired the state's Crime Commission. Clinton had already appointed his half brother to, of all things, the Crime Commission's Juvenile Advisory Board, though Roger would soon be removed for nonattendance. There was another troublesome arrest, this time for drunk driving and possession of narcotics, in March 1982, on the eve of Bill's carefully orchestrated announcement for reelection. Containment required intense intervention behind the scenes, and after a year of maneuvered postponements the charges were discreetly dropped. "The sheriff's office and the prosecutor succumbed to political pressure," one journalist wrote after the fact. "They leaned till they cracked," said a lawyer who knew the case. Knowing what lay in store for them if they brought charges, local authorities generally continued to look the other way through 1983 as Roger repeated his father's pattern of public drunkenness and brawls.

According to later testimony, including police stakeout video film, informers' hidden tape recordings, and his own statements to investigators, Roger Clinton had begun using cocaine in the late 1970s and was soon addicted. Eventually he was slave to a four-gram-a-day habit, snorting the drug some sixteen times during his waking hours and "getting close to a lethal dose," as a therapist told the court. He supported the addiction and a rakish lifestyle by dealing drugs himself, with contacts in New York winding all the way to the Medellin drug cartel in Colombia; he had, on occasion, walked smugly through Little

Rock's small airport with what he described as "thousands of dollars" in cocaine hidden on his person. "I can get you a quarter pound," the half brother of the governor would be heard saying to a wired police informer in negotiations for $10,000 in cocaine during the early 1980s. "I can get you what you want if you come up with the cash." Yet it was clear from the evidence, too, that Roger Clinton was hardly one more petty drug dealer and addict. As his own trial and related ones revealed, the drug trade flourishing around him involved some of the most noted figures in Little Rock and around the state.

New York and Medellin suppliers began extending credit to Roger Clinton on learning "who his brother was," Maurice Rodriguez, one of the middlemen, testified. Roger's frequent drug-buying trips to Manhattan reached a peak in the fall and winter of 1983 after Bill's reelection and as his popularity and power in Arkansas soared. On trial, the younger Clinton would deny or evade any implications that he was blackmailed or otherwise exploited by his drug connections to exert influence on the governor. "Both sides were 'Jack be nimble, Jack be quick' about that subject," said a government attorney who monitored the case. "They were all Arkansas lawyers and it was enough they had Roger. They didn't want the other cans opened." The potential for corruption was obvious. One state police tape recorded Roger being propositioned to persuade Bill Clinton to help remove a ban on new buildings in Hot Springs in return for a kickback from the profits on the sanctioned construction, but Roger denied ever having done anything improper.

Yet according to the local narcotics officers who made the tapes, video surveillance footage showed Roger discussing various payoffs of $30,000 to arrange government approval of sewer lines for a large development that was an interest of a close Clinton friend and major contributor, multimillionaire bond broker and later convicted drug dealer Dan Lasater. "I need $10,000 for my brother to take care of EPA regs and other environmental oversight problems," the officer quoted Roger as saying on the tapes, which were turned over to the state police, never to be presented at trial. City police officers who shot the tapes were told the portions dealing with imputed involvement of the governor had been forwarded to the Public Integrity office of the Justice Department in Washington early in 1984, but then they heard no more. "I guess they just got lost," one officer said bitterly a decade later.

At the least, Roger Clinton put on an impressive show of his intimacy with the state's chief executive. Had he ever taken women for sex "over to your brother's place," a wired informer once asked him. "Yeah. There was the mansion and the guest house," Roger answered. "Oh, they love it." Even sketchy state trooper entry and exit logs at the governor's mansion would bear him out, showing him coming and going at the family quarters or the guest house, often accompanied by "females," "girl," or "a friend," at least thirty-six times after February 7, 1983, the height of his drug trafficking. The guards recorded visits within days of his July 1984 indictment and as late as January 13, 1985, only two weeks before his sentencing, when the registry showed "Roger in with two females to change for party." Commonly the logs might note "Roger and girl" going to the mansion for two hours or more during the night, then Roger moving to the guest house alone and leaving from there late the next morning, though with no further record of the whereabouts or eventual departure of "girl." "They used the home of the governor as a whore hotel," said one narcotics investigator.

On one of the 1983–84 videotapes filmed by local narcotics officers, Roger Clinton was said to tell a supplier jauntily, "Got to get some for my brother. He's got a nose like a vacuum cleaner." Years later, after the suspicious murder of her husband, Jane Parks, the resident manager of an expensive Little Rock apartment complex, would tell Ambrose Evans-Pritchard of the London *Sunday Telegraph* that during the summer of 1984 Roger Clinton had been a nonpaying guest there for two months. The governor was "a frequent visitor," the *Telegraph* reported. "There was drug use at these gatherings . . . and she [Parks] could clearly distinguish Bill's voice as he chatted with his brother about the quality of the marijuana they were smoking. She said she could also hear them talking about the cocaine as they passed it back and forth." As at the mansion, there were said to be numerous women, often strikingly young. Tenants complained of the noise made by the partying Clinton brothers in B107.

There would be still others to substantiate similar accounts. A teacher and social worker named Sally Perdue would describe similar occasions in her late-1983 affair with Bill Clinton when he would smoke marijuana and use cocaine regularly, pulling joints out of a cigarette case and shaking cocaine out from a small bag onto a table in her living room. "He had all the equipment laid out, like a real pro," Perdue told a reporter. Still another witness, a convicted drug dealer and informant named Sharlene Wilson, who was a bartender at Le Bistro nightclub in Little Rock, testified to a 1990 federal grand jury in Arkansas that she had sold cocaine to Roger Clinton as early as 1979 and had watched, at both Le Bistro and at the infamous toga parties at the Coachman's Inn on the outskirts of the state capital, as Roger passed the drug to Bill, who "would often snort cocaine."

Roger Clinton's world had begun to unravel in the winter of 1983–84. Beyond the savage addiction that left him so dissipated physically—he had "eyes and nose like an announcement," a friend said later—someone had stolen $8,000 of cocaine from his car, slashing the top of a new convertible Virginia had given him. Aghast at the vandalism, Virginia had started to call the police. But when Roger nervously insisted they could not report the incident, as she told the story later, she suspected and did nothing. Her other son apparently had no illusions. Roger Clinton would later admit that his drug creditors had threatened his mother and even Bill, though there is no record that the two half brothers ever discussed the problem. Instead of advising Roger to go to the proper authorities with his predicament or reporting the convertible slashing himself, the governor of Arkansas simply moved to get his drug-dealing relative out of town. According to an FBI report, Bill Clinton had swiftly gone to his friend and backer Dan Lasater, imploring him to find a place for Roger at his thousand-acre thoroughbred farm outside Ocala, Florida. "Clinton asked him [Lasater] to give his ne'er-do-well half brother Roger a job," said one summary of the FBI document. Lasater did just that. "Mr. Lasater remarked at that point that he owed the governor a lot of favors," John Fernung, the farm's manager, said afterward.

Roger not only took the job but asked Lasater to loan him the $8,000 he owed his drug connections, money the millionaire handed over as quickly as he had the job Bill Clinton requested. Cocaine dealers were "putting the heat on him and something might happen to his brother and mother," Lasater told the FBI Roger had said. If Ocala was intended to be more than a hideout, however, it was hardly the place for an addict's recovery. Those who worked there described the same sorts of wild drug parties for which Lasater was known in Little Rock. It was suspected that the racehorse trading business was being used as a mechanism for the laundering of drug money. On one holiday, according to a trainer and veterinarian, small pouches of cocaine were hung as favors on a huge Christmas tree, and an eager guest nearly set the house ablaze when he lunged for a packet and toppled the densely lit tree. "You could tell Roger Clinton was really strung out the whole while he was at the farm. I just remember he was always using, always saying he had been on the phone talking to his brother the governor, not worth a damn as hired help," recalled a senior employee. "I was told we were stashing him for some politician Mr. Lasater was working." At that, the favors from the contributor may also have gone beyond refuge and the $8,000. When Roger returned to Arkansas, eventually to face narcotics charges in Hot Springs, his team of defense lawyers would feature the same prominent attorney, William R. Wilson, Jr., who then represented Lasater and Company in Little Rock and who in 1993 would be appointed a federal judge by President Clinton. Assisting Wilson would be his partner, Stephen Engstrom, who would be called to aid Betsey Wright in countering state troopers' testimony about the president's alleged cover-up of his personal excesses in Arkansas.

The videotape and wire recording case developed against Roger Clinton by both local police and state investigators might well have been quietly quashed if not for dissident state police who schemed to get at least some of the evidence out. "Some troopers put it out on the street where it couldn't be ignored," said an investigator. "They took a real risk." One former federal prosecutor remembered clearly, "Roger Clinton was about to be swept under the rug by both the US attorney and the local boys, no question about it." In any case, in the spring of 1984 the younger Clinton was back from Lasater's Florida haven and was now the target of a federal grand jury investigation. By the time state police commandant Tommy Goodwin formally told the governor in June of the imminent indictment of his half brother—"Goodwin knew of that investigation real early and had alerted Bill Clinton directly," said one officer—the case was "already handled" by federal prosecutors, as Goodwin told a reporter later, insisting that the governor could not have interfered. "Just go ahead and handle it like you would any other case," Goodwin recalled the politician's stoic response.

But dissidents in Goodwin's own ranks were convinced that Clinton would intervene and they managed to get details of the case to Hillary Rodham Clinton as well, counting on her to force the governor to keep his hands off as a political precaution. By the dissidents' account, the First Lady reacted exactly as they hoped, rushing to Clinton with her own report on Roger and ordering that he do nothing to warn his half brother or stave off the arrest, actions that might be exposed and used against them in the 1984 reelection campaign or later. "I don't think she ever knew how much coke Bill had snorted with Roger or how many girls they'd done together," said one state policeman, "but we knew she'd tell him to feed ole Roger to the feds for the sake of his career, and that's what he ended up doing." On August 2, 1984, as he later recounted to the press, Goodwin came to the capital to tell the governor that the indictment of Roger Cassidy Clinton on six counts of drug dealing and conspiracy was about to be announced. Clinton called a press conference for a brief statement with no questions, reading his remarks red-faced and "visibly shaken," as a reporter noted. "My brother has apparently become involved with drugs," he said with irony and hypocrisy only a few insiders could appreciate, "a curse which has reached epidemic proportions and has plagued the lives of millions of families in our nation, including many in our state."

Damage control began immediately. Local narcotics officers who had developed much of the original and most compelling evidence against Roger—and the most damning for the governor—were deliberately excluded from the arrest and systematically cut out of the subsequent investigation and evolution of the prosecution's case. "We had a lot more than just Roger, like Lasater and who owned who in places like Springdale, and buys that included the state police," said one local officer close to the case. "But Roger cops out, our narcs get taken out, and the case stops there." On August 14, represented by Lasater lawyer Wilson and his partner Engstrom, Roger Clinton was arraigned before Oren Harris, a former Democratic congressman and one of the more infirm judges on the federal bench, who was known locally for his relative deafness, his dim eyesight, and "a propensity," as Meredith Oakley noted, "for nodding off during prolonged testimony." Roger pled not guilty to every count. After less than ten minutes before the doddering Harris, he was released on $5,000 bail, with trial scheduled for November 9, days after the general election. Governor Clinton, spokesmen assured the public, "had no idea he had even tried drugs," as a reporter summed up the claims, "let alone that he had become addicted to cocaine."

Roger continued to come and go at the mansion with some abandon. Virtually from the hour of the arraignment there had been negotiations to arrange a plea bargain, so long as the formal admission of guilt came only after the election. In return for testifying against certain accomplices, the younger Clinton would avoid his own potentially revealing trial, face fewer counts, and receive a lighter sentence. In partial preparation for the plea bargain and sentencing, Roger and his immediate family attended token sessions of counseling on drug addiction and codependency. Even these cursory sessions, which both Virginia and Bill described later in general terms, opened the "rawest wounds," as one account put it. Though neither Virginia nor Bill mentioned it, it was Hillary who, according to Judith Warner, her biographer, "took a leading role in the discussions and was quite astute at pointing out patterns and weaknesses to the assembled family." Warner adds pointedly that, "though he was grateful, her participation didn't always endear her at the time to her husband." According to friends who heard contemporaneous accounts from Virginia, her daughter-in-law raised unexamined questions of denial and irresponsibility and other topics that sent the mother away in tearful fury and the thirty-eight-year-old governor into yet another round of distraction and debauchery.

On November 9, 1984, three days after his half brother's resounding victory at the polls, Roger Clinton was back in court to change his plea to guilty of conspiracy and a single count of drug distribution. He was "one tentacle of cocaine distribution in Arkansas," said Republican US attorney Asa Hutchinson, though most of the other arms of the figurative monster would never be pulled in. In a subsequent trial Roger testified for the government to convict a boyhood friend, Sam Anderson, Jr., a Hot Springs lawyer and the son of Virginia's old attorney. But there the inquiry stopped for the moment. "I guess I'm going to do Roger's time for him," Anderson would say bitterly the following March. In his last days at large the younger Clinton took women in and out of the governor's mansion for parties and went on with his cocaine habit despite the certainty of discovery before sentencing. On January 28, 1985, when Roger again appeared before Judge Harris, now "exceptionally alert," as Oakley saw him, there was no denying that he had used drugs consistently even after his arrest and during his months on bail. A dour, publicity-conscious Harris suspended the three years on the distribution charge but for the count of conspiracy imposed two years in the federal prison at Fort Worth. Both the governor and Hillary stood there with a lip-biting Virginia as Roger Clinton—"a fourteen-year-old in a twenty-eight-year-old's body," as his mother now came to see him—was summarily handcuffed and driven off by marshals. At no point in the five months of bargaining, suppression, and calculated betrayal of cohorts had there been an inkling of the videotaped footage implicating the governor or even of the graphic physical evidence of Roger's addiction, which would have belied the governor's bland protestations of ignorance. "I feel more deeply committed than ever before to do everything I can to fight illegal drugs in our state," Bill Clinton said in a rehearsed statement outside the courtroom as his half brother was taken away.

In the little more than a year Roger served in prison, as Virginia told the story later, he would "grow up some." Out on probation in the spring of 1986, he worked with a construction crew building bridges "on the winding old Benton highway," Virginia recorded, "the one Bill and I had taken years before on those horrible Sundays when we had gone to visit my mother in the state mental hospital."

◆ ◆ ◆

As that small drama of the darker Arkansas played out, largely in the shadows, honors poured in on the attractive young couple in the governor's mansion—one world oblivious, as usual, of the other. Bill and Hillary Clinton were named Public Citizens of the Year by the National Association of Social Workers. *Esquire* magazine celebrated them as among the "best of the new generation," young leaders of "courage, originality, initiative, vision and selfless service," who had received "a torch . . . passing between generations . . . approaching the full bloom of adulthood." With the endorsement of an admiring Starr, even the once-critical *Arkansas Democrat* proclaimed Hillary Rodham Clinton "Woman of the Year."

Clinton would run for reelection with a nervous zeal. For a time he had put out rumors that he might run for the US Senate against Pryor or take just one more term as governor before challenging Bumpers in 1986. "I think he was always toying with one idea or the other," said an aide. "Pryor was kind of a friend, though that wouldn't have stopped Bill if he thought he could beat him, and he downright hated Bumpers"—the latter a feeling that a *Gazette* editor called "entirely mutual." Clinton's "original script," as Starr and others saw it, would have had him running for the Pryor seat in 1984. But the 1980 defeat had obviously altered timetables, and the extraordinary power of a third term and beyond in the statehouse still seemed to promise the ultimate prize of the presidency. The local spoils were historic. A third term— with control of even more autonomous commissions and boards, bodies most crucial to the big interests—would be the guarantor of Little Rock's most powerful political machine of the century, allowing the governor "to literally walk off with the state of Arkansas," as one old pol told a reporter years later, "dome and all." Looking beyond even that, Clinton quietly raised more than $100,000 to push a state constitutional amendment on the 1984 ballot establishing a four-year term for the governor beginning with the 1986 election, a provision that would allow him to run for the White House in 1988 and still hold on to the governorship and its base for yet another attempt at the presidency in 1992.

The political landscape of their base was still vintage Arkansas. To

Congress the Second District would elect that year former Clinton director of public safety and sheriff Tommy Robinson, who called a black appointee to the federal bench a "token judge" and had promised he would not "coddle" convicts, which some of his audience understood to mean black prisoners, with "fried chicken and watermelon" but would have them "out on the road gang cleaning the ditches where there are copperheads and water moccasins." Opposing court-ordered consolidation and at least partial desegregation of the Pulaski County schools in and around Little Rock, Robinson's celebrated political ad of 1984 showed "a little white girl waiting for a school bus on an ominously dark and empty country road," as Diane Blair described it in her scholarly book on state politics. "Arkansas ain't part of the Midwest yet," Paul Greenberg wrote of the Robinson ad.

With typical irony, both national and local Republicans continued to portray the state Democratic combine as "a plaything of the left." Apart from ritual differences in platform that disappeared in practice, the GOP demagoguery could be reduced to what one aide laughingly called "contributor envy." By 1984 the governor had assembled the most impressive list of corporate and individual donors ever recorded in the state, and one of the more notable in the nation for a nonfederal politician. Investors in neither "playthings" nor "the left," his backers included Union Pacific, Pepsi-Cola, Weyerhauser, Reynolds Metals, Wendy's, Paine Webber, Salomon Brothers and other investment houses, Washington patron Pamela Harriman and several others of her ilk, even Hillary's onetime anathema Coca-Cola—in addition to the Rose Law Firm, the Lasaters, the usual anonymous donors, local banks, utilities, and other giants. Other contributors beyond ideology reportedly also appeared in force. "That was the election when the mob really came into Arkansas politics, the dog-track and racetrack boys, the payoff people who saw a good thing," said a former US attorney who watched the FBI's tracking of organized crime figures and their interests. "It wasn't just Bill Clinton and it went beyond our old Dixie Mafia, which was penny-ante by comparison. This was eastern and West Coast crime money that noticed the possibilities just like the legitimate corporations did."

Local money passed under the table as never before. "If you wanted to sit on the Highway Commission or the Fish and Game Commission or another commission, well, it would cost, and that's how they laundered money," former state party official and Clinton fund-raiser Bert Dickey admitted later. Locally prominent, a man with a doctorate in education, Dickey, like many others, was approached early by the campaign to do some crude money laundering. Asked to give $3,000 to Clinton, he demurred. Would he and his wife then give a hundred each? "Well, yeah," Dickey recalled his answer. "So they gave me twenty-eight hundred-dollar bills and said, 'Put this in your farm account and write two checks [to the Clinton campaign] for fifteen hundred dollars.' " What if the IRS checked on him? Dickey asked. "We'll just tell them you sold a piece of used farm equipment to somebody and they paid you cash." During the 1984 campaign, according to several accounts, the unrecorded or soon-to-be-laundered cash flowed in such a gush that it was carried around by the bagful, often in stacks of "banded money" brought fresh from some bank by special aides designated to tote the sacks just as they held on to the governor's briefcase and billfold.

As usual, special betrayal was reserved for Arkansas's black community, whose pivotal vote was always a crucial Clinton advantage. "It's impossible to overestimate the importance of Clinton's lock on the blacks," one politician said, echoing a widespread view among those who knew the state's electoral realities. Yet at any sign of restiveness in the vital, ordinarily quiescent bloc, the governor could enlist reactionary allies to put it down. "He called me once and said the blacks were on his ass," the *Democrat* editor Starr remembered. "I told him, 'Don't worry. I'll go after the blacks—I'll get them so mad at me they'll forget about you.' I called them 'pip-squeak preachers.' " Meanwhile the black share of plentiful campaign funds was duly dispensed as "walking-around money." An aide who claimed to have guarded and carried the bags of money later told the *American Spectator* that it was variously handled in 1984 not only by Betsey Wright but also by black aide Robert Nash and Delta boss Rodney Slater, and by Democratic National Committee agent Carroll Willis. Wright or Nash, by this account, often handed "paper bags of cash over . . . for safekeeping in the governor's mansion or the official car," from there to be given back to Nash, Slater, or Willis for doling out. "We'll just have to spread a little money around," the aide recalled Betsey Wright's typically saying, adding himself, "That's the real world. That's how things happen." Supposedly limited to individual amounts of fifty dollars "to stay within the realm of the law," as Willis claimed later in denying any wrongdoing, the black payments in fact, as several witnesses remembered, came and went in rolls and stacks, with local bosses expected to "spread it out." Those in the ranks who didn't get their cut were not above calling the governor directly to complain about inequities.

"That motherfucker hasn't spent that money! He hasn't spread it around," the aide in charge of the bags remembered Clinton's yelling at a diffident Bobby Nash in a characteristic outburst. In 1984 Arkansas's black votes again went overwhelmingly for Clinton, some precincts by more than 90 percent. "Stunning numbers," said an analyst looking at the figures a decade later, "what the mathematicians call 'unnatural anomalies.' "

Interviewing Clinton in 1984 about his education initiatives, southern author Marshall Frady found the ultimate desire scarcely hidden in the still young and prodigal governor. If the school reform was an "authentic passion" for Clinton, there was something more. "Within his eager earnestness," Frady wrote, "one also sensed an instinct for close pragmatic computations, and a ferocious ambition already larger than his native state could contain."

In the general election, with Roger yet to change his plea and with no politically damaging evidence in the case yet bruited, Clinton crushed his hapless and relatively unfunded Republican opponent, a Jonesboro contractor named Woody Freeman, by more than 200,000 votes and twenty-seven percentage points. Yet at the eleventh hour, leading by more than twenty-five points in the polls, the governor "panicked," as one campaign aide put it. "He came up with this sudden obsession about some last-minute turnaround," said another who traveled with him, "as if something was going to blow open, which is what it would have taken since people hardly knew anybody named Freeman was running." Insisting on a flurry of thirty-second television commercials to blanket the state during the last week, Clinton found that even the hundreds of thousands in laundered and other tainted money had been committed. He turned to aide and mentor Maurice Smith, asking that the small Bank of Cherry Valley, which Smith owned, grant him a personal loan of $50,000. Made to both Hillary and Bill and secured without collateral, the loan produced the cash that Clinton contributed to his own campaign on October 29, 1984, for the final ads.

Maurice Smith had long coveted the next ten-year seat on the Arkansas Highway Commission, and Clinton promised it to him even though he had long beforehand pledged the same appointment to the candidate of his own First Congressional District backers. This patronage conflict produced the first crisis of his new term in January 1985, "during which," Oakley noted, "Clinton reportedly bit his nails until his fingers bled." In the end the weight of the district machine forced him to renege on his promise to Smith, who would be compensated with a prompt appointment as a University of Arkansas trustee. Three years later Smith was made executive director of the Highway and Transportation Department. "The catch was," said an aide, "Bill still felt after the commission screwup that he ought to get that loan paid back faster than he might have otherwise." To erase the debt, Clinton decided, he would turn to a source that during 1984 had provided "a constant flow," as one account described it, his old friend Jim McDougal.

As his third term began, however, none of this was publicly visible. Unlike their modesty of 1983, the Clintons planned an extravagant inaugural. A regal First Lady was photographed on the mansion staircase wearing a three-piece ensemble of gold lamé, her makeup by Chanel, her faille shoes by Yves Saint Laurent, her hair by Little Rock's own Hair Care, Inc. Under huge American and Arkansas flags in the Governor's Hall at the Convention Center, there would be a thousand-pound ice sculpture of the old Confederate statehouse and screens displaying a continuing show of Arkansas scenes. It was, the *Gazette* declared, "the party of the year."

· 17 ·

Washington III
"A Culture of Complicity"

Not long after the Clintons entered the White House, when it was clear they came heavily burdened by their past, it was fashionable in Washington to look back disdainfully at poor provincial Arkansas, at the seamy associations and inveterate practices that mortgaged a new administration. Only a few people were willing to recognize how much the settings were alike—how much the Little Rock that was the crucible of the Clinton presidency was only a smaller version of the culture on the Potomac.

Like Little Rock, Washington had its own ruling interests and oligarchs, its native caste of panderers and plungers, a quaint, corrupted legislature, a compromised executive, an incorrigible bureaucracy, insatiable lobbies, and, not least, its own media whose shallowness and self-absorption amounted to collusive mediocrity. Not yet facing up to the futility and fraud of promised change by a changeless regime, never quite appreciating what they were up against, the rest of America was not so different from the Ozarks or Delta after all. If Washington regarded the Clintons' Arkansas with condescension and contempt, it was in many ways seeing only itself.

As early as 1980, historian James David Barber recorded the disappearance of the old Washington, the familiar "village of ambition." Taking shape, he saw, was quite another reality: "something more fundamental than the circulation of elites or the shuffling of structures. Something more powerful. Something visceral. Something at the heart of the enterprise . . . a set of inherited modes of belief and expectation that gripped the city's practitioners at least as powerfully as did the organization charts . . . a set of mores—values thought natural—increasingly divergent from the country's common sense. . . . Inside the capital city, isolated from the criteria of performance the rest of us took for granted, a peculiar tribal ethic had developed, subject to anthropological analysis."

By the early 1990s political Washington had evolved into the republic of fix and favor that was the reality behind the facade of the Clinton administration, and which would rule with a force and permanence beyond any single presidency or Congress, law or institution. For most of those who made careers and fortunes in and around the system, differences of race or class, ideology or policy, personality or party were superficial, almost ephemeral. What mattered most—the daily reality of governance—was their own part of that "peculiar tribal ethic."

◆　◆　◆

Congress lived by its own institutionalized connivance, the "backslapping, backpedaling, backstabbing ways of Washington," as one observer called it. The evolution on Capitol Hill was graphic. "The difference between Congress now and fifteen years ago is the difference between chicken salad and chickenshit," longtime Democratic pol Robert Strauss confided to a Canadian ambassador in the early 1980s. "If you don't understand that, you'll understand nothing about Washington."

Money contorted careers from the outset, determining who would run, who survived the cockfight for the rare open seat. Wealthy individuals and corporate interests were there to welcome the new congressman or senator, generously paying off campaign debts, a favor never forgotten. The money pushers also shaped the clawing for committee assignments in a Capitol where "PAC heavens"—committees dealing with energy, finance, weapons, and other founts of federal subsidy—were vital to the inevitable next election. Part of the congressional leaders' fearsome power was to reward pliant freshmen with seats on those committees and to punish would-be reformers to the hell of lesser ones.

New members naturally thought themselves free agents. "You don't lie awake those early nights thinking of your corruptibility," one remembered. But few resisted the old rotten bargain. By the 1980s the money tyranny commanded the largest majority ever to sit in the United States Congress. Only four of 100 senators and twelve of 435 representatives were independent, well-financed enough to refuse PAC dollars or similar blandishments. The vast majority fell swiftly into the weekly routine of personally soliciting PACs and donors whose interests coincided with their committees, however distant from their own agendas or constituents' interests. The richer the war chests grew, the more hostage the "successful" candidate became. The system pulled freshmen and second-term lawmakers ever further from whatever grassroots loyalty or sensibility they brought to begin with.

Their preoccupation as lawmakers was not domestic or foreign policy but fear of losing. To hold it at bay, they commonly used their staff payrolls to hire campaign organizers and media flacks or provide patronage for contributors and lobbyists. They became obsessed with image, practicing sound-bite government to satisfy the folks back home as well as the interests, ceaselessly mongering "the taxpayers' largesse and Congress's free media," as one veteran put it, "into a steady stream of favorable publicity that no lurking opponent could hope to match." The Hill's quickest death, aides only half joked, was to walk between a sentient member and a television camera.

Unwritten rules were unanimously understood and observed in both the House and the Senate. Senators and representatives routinely schemed to exploit any subject, including natural calamities, for political advantage and predictably evaded any that could not be. "Ask not what your member can do for the issue," went a congressional staff credo of the 1990s, "but rather, what the issue can do for your member." Legislators might vote one way for the sake of appearances, then work discreetly before and after the tally to nullify the effect. At the same time, alongside the anxiety and calculation, the 535 little career dramas, there was knowing contempt for the audience, for the performance. "Let's face it," one Republican told an aide in 1992, "you have to be a bozo to lose this job."

Hard beneath Capitol Hill's oily deference and camaraderie was remorseless cannibalism. "He does exactly what his constituents want him to do—namely, steal from the voters of other districts," one reporter wrote, describing a typical congressman, "a man," he went on, "with the ethics and moral courage of a hookworm." "All anyone ever wants is a special advantage over the next fellow," Jamie Whitten of Mississippi, chairman of the House Appropriations Committee, said. "Understand that, and you've understood the intent of every law ever passed."

Above all, there were what everyone suitably capitalized as The Numbers—approval and trail-heat polling back home. "The Numbers run everything," a former House aide explained in a 1992 memoir. PACs and other donors studied them to protect their stake and avoid long shots. Would-be opponents were emboldened or broken by them, bankrolled or written off. When The Numbers were good, a member would "shop around the results . . . to prove he [was] still a blue-chip investment," one staffer recalled. When The Numbers were bad or worrisome, they had to be obscured, discounted, reversed.

Unrelieved politics of self-preservation produced flagrant neglect as well as corruption. Members moved warily from issue to issue, sound bite to sound bite, while substantive authority gravitated more than ever to the committee barons, chairmen, and ranking minority figures. Regardless of party, nearly all were mouthpieces for the interests and often the bureaucracies they were supposed to monitor. Intent on lim-iting its own liability, Congress had shifted responsibility to the states and surrendered prerogatives wholesale to federal agencies. For a mo-ment in the early 1970s, in reaction to executive abuses and grandios-ity, the "imperial presidency" of Johnson and Nixon, Congress seemed on the threshold of broad new responsibility, exacting ac-countability from the executive branch for how laws were carried out and appropriations spent. But the money tyranny soon cut off that progress.

Born to public fanfare and innocent hope, legislation went forth as an administrative orphan, soon to be raped and prostituted. Washing-ton knew the bloody battle of passage was only a prelude to law, that the essence was not in the letter but in the execution, that lobbies and bureaucrats were always out there, ready to capture and twist the law in their own interests. Without sustained oversight, the most explicit and forceful bill was "naked and defenseless."

With less than 10 percent of Congressional testimony under oath, both houses gave up their constitutional duty to draw out the reality of governance in public hearings. Witnesses trooped to the Hill, it was true. Testimony before multiple committees devoured the time of ranking officials and lent an appearance of scrutiny. But most sessions were understood to be ritual performances for the cameras on both sides, and as any watcher of C-Span could tell, questions and answers were politely oblique, rarely if ever touching on the realities of power. "White lies, big lies, lies in all colors and sizes," a House subcommittee chairman described the routine exchange, "and the thing is, the peo-ple facing each other know it's one kind of lie or another and almost never the straight truth." Even the Senate had largely defaulted on its confirmation powers, staging a few major hearings for cabinet or Supreme Court appointments, while waving through hundreds of key executive officials without serious attention. Nominees "can be crummy, mediocre, not qualified, even in industry's pocket," an aide told a reporter early in the 1990s, "and if they haven't done anything criminal, they're approved."

A parody of the practice burst into view in the 1991 Judiciary Committee hearings on Bush Supreme Court nominee Clarence Thomas and the testimony against him by Anita Hill. A classic of Washington gender politics, the Thomas-Hill affair had it all. Several women and men would have substantiated Hill's account of sexual harassment. They were never called by a craven committee chairman, Democrat Joseph Biden. Yet under the lash of Thomas's ardent backers, Republicans pursued a patently partisan vendetta against Hill. Just as typically, Democrats cringed at GOP attacks and Thomas's staged outrage at his "lynching." When it was over, a precept of Congress was reiterated. "Possession of the truth can amount to nothing," the *New Yorker*'s David Remnick wrote, "in the face of an overwhelming ambition to win."

◆ ◆ ◆

Certainly there was no rescue in the Hill's own bureaucracy. Committees multiplied from 38 in 1947 to 283 in 1992, aides from some 600 to nearly 2,000 in the last two decades, employees overall to more than 24,000. The staff as shadow legislative branch were often assumed to be better and brighter than their notorious employers, an assumption frequently shared by the aides themselves. A 1992 account described a typical chief of staff as "a petty humorless despot who regarded himself as far smarter than his boss and therefore the real congressman—a totally common phenom[enon], apparently." Just as familiar was the staff's own corrosive cynicism and mediocrity, the same resignation and conventionality that overtook the bosses. "A mil? One lousy mil?" an aide asked sneeringly on hearing about million-dollar poker hands among Wall Street brokers of the 1980s. "I can do *ten* mil with report language and not even have to ask the chairman."

They called themselves "Hill rats," as a 1992 memoir of the same title by John Jackley announced. "Lord Acton was only half right. Power might corrupt, but absolute power is a blast," the book quoted one of the species as saying. "Hill rats learn self-importance at a very callow age, usually right out of college," a reporter said of the aides thronging the Capitol. If more now came with advanced degrees, most were without intellectual distinction or relevant experience, making them lethally dependent on lobbies, the executive, or private "experts" for substantive knowledge. In droves they whisked through the Hill's revolving door with the same lobbies, bureaucracies, corporate-kept think tanks, businesses, and law firms, often at double or triple their ample congressional salaries. Many arrived the other way—recycled bureaucrats, retired military officers come to inform and stiffen the amateur civilians on the armed services, intelligence oversight, or foreign relations committees—all with the same certification and approval of the interests. "He's a brilliant fellow," an "energy lobbyist" said gratefully of one staff director. "He has an intuitive sense of politics." These were people who could be relied on to draft to order, to observe the implicit limits of discussion, to honor the culture that was their ethic as well as their livelihood.

Moving from member to member, even party to party, those who stayed on the Hill levitated to senior committee jobs or the personal staffs of entrenched legislators. Nearly four hundred of them made $108,000 a year or more by the 1990s, living comfortable lives in fashionable Washington enclaves or upscale suburbs of Virginia and Maryland, suitably removed from the America whose laws they wrote. They were, above all, bureaucrats themselves, reflecting and magnifying the mores of the corporate world they paralleled. Even if their patrons or parties were defeated, they were likely to find sinecures with lobbies, captive organizations, or think tanks, perhaps even slip into the bureaucracy.

Discrimination legally denied other public institutions or contractors Congress discreetly reserved to itself. Racism was still subtly the office rule in the 1990s, minorities occupying a small fraction of key staff jobs. Sexism was equally implicit and thus rampant in a workplace where women still occupied preponderantly clerical jobs. Of more than 140 "principal" leadership and committee staff members listed in 1992 in *The Hill People,* only 26 were women and none were in ranking jobs dealing with the manly preserves of the military, foreign affairs, energy, or intelligence. The overwhelmingly white, affluent, careerist male clerkdom of Congress possessed a unique vantage point from which to measure the toll of the 1980s. They had seen in the ornate committee rooms the intent of the tax windfalls and vast subsidies, had noted in the stream of statistics and wounded witnesses the wreckage of abandoned public services and gross economic inequity, experienced again and again in offices and hallways all over Washington the immutable, banal realities of misgovernment by both parties. "We knew," one senior figure said of the savings and loan scandal.

"Hell, yes, we all knew." Yet no line of whistle-blowers emerged from behind the marble columns to explain the abuses. In one of the most scandalous periods in American lawmaking, there were no resignations of note among House or Senate staff members. Congress might encourage executive whistle-blowers, pass statutes to reward or protect them, but its own whistles were mute. Revolving-door careers were obviously more important, collusion rationalized too easily. Faceless Hill bureaucrats were not simply spectators to the tyranny, after all, but an integral part of it.

A bleak generational irony marked the Congress of the 1990s. Members elected in the wake of Watergate reform two decades before had seemed brighter, better educated than any single class to come to the Capitol. Yet they were also more affluent, less connected as a matter of class and sensibility to middle-income and poorer families, more technocratic and more prone, in their glibness and affluence, to the corrupting professionalization of politics. On the surface they might have been legislators straight out of a civics textbook. Yet they became what one reporter called "our elected . . . ruttish whores to big money." For all their promise, their monument was now the singular disgust felt by those who knew their world best. "The House of Representatives," another journalist wrote in language typical of that contempt, "is now widely regarded as a holding pen for unindicted felons."

Exceptions might still arrive, men and a handful of women who spurned the forced conviviality, the worst compromise. But Congress was a place newcomers always found harrowing, ultimately defeating. Sooner or later most succumbed to what one poignant account of a valiant Nebraska freshman called "the encirclement." Even if they escaped the blanketing venality and hypocrisy, they were left no real room for sensibility or imagination, for authentic change that threatened so much, so many. Where expedience and self-interest were the predictable norms, conviction became aberration, principle an abhorred deviance. Those who acted on beliefs could not be trusted and were treated accordingly. "You never know what the bastards will do," a chairman warned a young congressman.

So systemic was the corruption by 1993 that integrity itself seemed part of the contrivance. Of certain Democrats' votes against the status quo, political author Michael Ventura observed, "It's not only tolerated, it's encouraged. Those 'good' Democrats make everything *look* like a political process—and most of them know it. If they had any real integrity they'd quit the party." As it was, few found voice for the melancholy, the isolation, the bitter resentment many felt after leaving office. "The most chickenshit institution I've ever been a part of," James Aboureszk of South Dakota said on leaving the Senate in 1978 after one term each in both chambers. Scores shared the sentiment, yet candor was rare. Co-opted by sinecures or traditional pretense, most veterans could be no more honest about the institution after leaving it than while inside.

Publicly derided as never before, Congress responded with neither confession nor authentic reform. Instead it resorted to what columnist Robert Kuttner called "cohabitation," the continuing collusion of officeholders and system regardless of views or personalities. In the larger sweep, partisan politics mattered little. In the postwar era Democrats had nominally controlled the House for nearly four decades, the Senate for more than thirty, inflicting petty oppressions of procedure and prerogative on the Republican minority. But the GOP held the White House for twenty-six of those years, and all the while a de facto coalition of Republicans and conservative Democrats ransomed the actual substance of Congress, with no law or debate beyond their grip. Despite bickering over parking places, patronage, and prestige, the real majority belonged to the money. Nothing was more natural than a bipartisan coalition against genuine reform of the laws and rules regulating campaign finance or the role of lobbyists. Beyond partisan hypocrisy or petty ambition, the "ruttish whores" had far more in common with one another than with the nation. They would stick together to the end.

◆ ◆ ◆

The presidency was by the 1980s more than ever about money. Its deeper, subtler corruption was thus its people, the White House staff, cabinet officers, and other ranking appointees drawn from or into Washington's pervasive mercenary culture. Most simply shifted from Congress, state capitals, the ubiquitous campaign industry, or directly from special interests and their fronts. They were overwhelmingly of the system, hangers-on who made the White House merely another Washington precinct. If the presidency at the close of the century seemed increasingly without character regardless of occupant, it was largely because of its characterless retainers and their numbing conformity.

Not surprisingly, their preoccupation was image. Staged events in the Rose Garden or the East Room, briefings open and secret, discreet fund-raising and influence peddling—all reflected on a grander scale the merchandising that 535 legislators undertook at the Capitol. Incessant touting of the president, indistinguishable from campaign to Oval Office and back again, had long since become routine. Well executed, it was a spectacle of manipulation. Washington expected fraud; it only deplored it if done ineptly. Flackery had reached new depths with the culturally appealing presence of Ronald Reagan. By surprisingly simple means, presidential image "handlers" fed and flattered the Washington media until "communications" were synonymous with co-option. Reagan aides like Michael Deaver, later charged with influence peddling and convicted of perjury, or David Gergen, one of the oilier survivors of the Watergate White House, provided cover for what was actually happening—and thus for a good deal of the reactionary "success" of the Reagan-Bush era. As much as anyone, thought a historian of the Reagan era, touts such as Gergen and Deaver made the 1980s "a time when the national political debate was dominated by a bundle of ideas that almost without exception were contradicted by objective facts, common sense or both."

Touts were part of an ironic pathos inherent in the presidency. There was a growing isolation at this pinnacle of government as Washington politics cut the White House off not only from the rival Congress and the permanent bureaucracy but even from its own appointees in the departments. As the money tyranny divided government, captured parties and politicians, and fortified feudalism on the Hill and elsewhere, the White House was all the more alone and all the less powerful, left to play to its shifting audience without true allegiances. In a barren landscape of selfish ambition, where loyalty was an expedient, the most famous office in the world could be a theater of the abject. The postmodern presidency was always dying a little from within.

By the time of Bill Clinton's election in 1992, any real differences between administrations, like differences between the two old parties, had withered. Even the most public-spirited bills drifted down from the abdicating Congress without oversight, precision, clear enforcement language, or organized public constituencies. Defenseless, left to lobbyists and kindred clerks, unwanted laws were "anesthetized," as one account described it; the public interest, those awkward rules of equity and social responsibility, was simply put out of its misery.

On the White House itself, with its incurable courtier politics and absence of institutional memory, the fixers fastened their hold with special vengeance. Beyond the ken of tourists or most reporters, the effect was to turn the American presidency into an arena of unrelieved special pleading. But then again, intervention and unction were everywhere in Washington, from the supposedly sacred Federal Reserve to the obscure Home Loan Bank Board, which regulated the savings and loan industry, from the Food and Drug Administration to the Nuclear Regulatory Commission, from the Treasury Department to Transportation, from the Pentagon to Commerce, and on to the least-known offices.

To those who looked closely—as few did—there was now crippling compromise before, during, and after any meaningful legislation. "A lawless swamp," one writer called Washington on the eve of Clinton's election.

◆　◆　◆

Tamper-prone regulators represented only a fraction of the vast career clerkdom that was the executive. In Washington and its colonies around the country, some three million souls belonged to a federal service whose insular culture reinforced the capital's tyranny at almost every turn. For a time it was fashionable to explain that the bureaucracy was victimized by successive waves of postwar abuse—by demagogic Republicans and cowardly Democrats in the red scare and, later, by the much-publicized hostility toward government work and workers among the Reagan reactionaries. "The federal government . . . is increasingly unable to attract, retain, and motivate the kinds of people it will need to do the essential work of the Republic," warned one of the periodic studies done in the late 1980s. At hand, a blue-ribbon panel concluded, was "the worst of all possible worlds—mediocre civil servants and mediocre subordinate political appointees as well." Yet politics accounted for only part of what the bureaucracy had become. Most of the disaster they managed by their own devices.

Their rules were implicit and immutable. From Washington to the farthest outpost, the successful bureaucrat existed to secure or enlarge the budget, to maintain the seniority that protected jobs and power, to build on the prevailing buddy system that had long since twisted civil service recruitment into a self-preserving nepotism. Like most of Washington—and unlike more and more of the rest of America—the bureaucrats enjoyed vastly inflated titles and pay. While middle-class families worked two jobs or more and real wages plunged for most Americans, federal paychecks rose and perquisites increased. Median family income nationally hovered at $30,000, and nearly forty million people were officially below even the anachronistically low poverty line. But federal officials with "responsibilities comparable to those of a manager of a Safeway store," as one study put it, made between

$83,000 and $115,000, with full health and life insurance and generous pensions. Beyond Congress and the White House, over ten thousand bureaucrats got more than $100,000 yearly. Above all, there was job security, entrenchment as existed nowhere else, save in Congress itself. Regardless of pay or rank, a 1991 study found, the bureaucrat's chance of being fired was exactly one in forty-three hundred.

Over the dozen years of Reagan-Bush, so-called conservative Republicans entered the career bureaucracy to an extent surpassing even the Democratic influx of the New Deal. After 1988 they were organizing regular Washington seminars to instruct their own refugees from America's harsh rigged economy how to burrow into and then rise in the civil service. Conservatives had learned to love the highly paid faceless bureaucrats of their old demonology—especially when the bureaucrats were they themselves. As a result, agencies from the Forest Service to the Foreign Service experienced unprecedented "ideological cleansing," as one account described it, with GOP appointees penetrating all the way down to desk positions. "They're trying to find openings—or force openings—for political appointees that they want to bury as what we call 'moles' in the department," one Justice Department official explained to *Barron's* at the end of the 1980s. "They bury these moles at the Department of Justice so that even the next administration can't find them." Right-wing infiltrators would be there waiting for a new president. "The Clinton entourage will decamp in the District of Columbia, pick up their government phones, and find at the other end . . . the late nineteenth century," a writer said of the seizure.

More than ever before, government departments represented, or covered for, those interests they had long since ceased to police or balance. Agriculture colluded with agribusiness, Treasury with the brokerage and financial world, Commerce and Labor with corporate interests, the Pentagon with its military suppliers, Energy with the power and fuel giants, Housing with its own client real estate and construction industries, Interior with old land and resource concessionaires, Justice with some of the very executive-suite outlaws it was supposed to pursue, and so on through the *Federal Register*.

More than ever before, career officials slid back and forth through the door marked private money. Even those in once more seemly diplomatic positions degenerated into a new species of stock-option bureaucrat. Keen to assist Chinese clients, General Alexander Haig, former secretary of state, was to remark in 1992 that human rights violations in China should not be allowed to interfere with American investment there. He and another former secretary of state, James Baker, developed as well an avid interest in oil and gas deals in Turkmenistan, enjoying lucrative consultancies for a US firm, Enron, interested in concessions to build natural-gas pipelines in the region. Trading on previous public careers as if they had been shrewd investments in pork bellies, others such as Brent Scowcroft, Nixon's and Bush's national security adviser, and Lawrence Eagleburger, a former Foreign Service officer and Bush's proxy secretary of state, parlayed their bureaucratic ranks into million-dollar-a-year consultancies, advising corporations and foreign powers eager to manipulate Washington; their firm was that of their old boss, former presidential adviser and secretary of state Henry Kissinger, whose Kissinger and Associates was seen by many as the epitome of public service prostituted to private profit.

Nowhere were the stakes and costs greater than in the national security bureaucracy, often considered the higher caste of clerkdom. Masked by congressional and media diffidence as well as by official secrecy, it easily survived the cold war as a state within a state, harboring zealots and racketeers in the guise of defense or intelligence and a stagnant guild of timeservers in the name of expertise. Bloated national security budgets held public investment and much of the economy hostage, literally at gunpoint. From US complicity in genocide and torture to collusion in gunrunning, drug smuggling, and arms trade, from obscure blunders to the enormities of war and famine, the overt and covert record in national security policy was a bipartisan calamity never fully appreciated outside the capital. Foreign press accounts, scholarly writing, occasional investigative journalism, even minimal congressional hearings all brimmed with case histories. But the capital had far fewer public-interest groups in foreign affairs than in domestic, most of its think tanks sinecures for bureaucrats and establishment figures shuffling to and from office, exchanging jobs on the narrow, arguable margins of policy. Absent front-page scandal or demonstrators blocking traffic, statecraft was left to the "experts." Washington treated amassing evidence of their abuses with cynical resignation, if not blithe acceptance.

In the Departments of State and Defense, on an overgrown National Security Council, in a warped Central Intelligence Agency, and elsewhere in what was called the community, bureaucrats looked down on pedestrian colleagues in Agriculture or Interior while living the same code of avoidance. Many were content to be fey protocol officers to Washington's mercenary regime. Others actually had a hand in policy.

All came to know what ethic they served. Getting along to go along, they accumulated trackless policy disasters. Someone else's suffering they accepted in a convention of professional indifference well beyond moral abdication. Lobbies and special pleaders, they knew, perverted foreign affairs no less than they did domestic. Distinguished gentlemen of the establishment frequently turned out, on closer scrutiny, to be fools or knaves. Governance in foreign policy was often shockingly ignorant of the world and hypocritical and contemptuous of the public. But as in Congress, whistles rarely blew and few people resigned out of conscience. Washington was a capital many national security veterans found as distasteful as the seediest foreign posting—its culture the subject of ceaseless clubby complaints, head-shaking gossip, and bitter jokes. Yet nothing so marked that self-styled elite as keeping the lurid misrule to themselves. "The Great Silence," one called it.

Everywhere, in bureaus domestic and foreign, the result was more nervous preservation of the status quo, more stifling of change. "The present system is designed to protect those within it," Charles Peters wrote on the eve of Clinton's inauguration, "not to serve those outside." Yet "outside," as Clinton's Arkansas itself would show, there was still another quasi-governmental world that led to an even deeper and more sinister corruption. If the bureaucracy and its figurehead superiors could not cleanse banal office politics, what were they to do about the national security state within the state? About CIA renegades or contractors with their criminal empire along a southern arc? About massive scandals deep within the DEA, the FBI, the Customs Service? About the gruesome mercantilism of a government whose operatives and associates freebooted with official permission, if not collusion, in narcotics, guns, infants' body parts? On that dark side of the American system, too grim for press or public, critiques of right and left met in a single verdict: a bureaucracy so self-corrupted it was unfit for democracy.

◆　◆　◆

Watching with interest were Washington's other notable one hundred thousand, that occupying army of the capital politely known as lobbyists. While executive-branch lobbying was conveniently exempt from the most basic accounting and while many corporate interests failed to list their agents, even registered lobbies now numbered more than eleven thousand organizations, swelling by 20 percent in the early 1990s. If special-interest money overwhelmed Washington, these were the people who embodied and dispensed it.

Their mix of old-fashioned boodle and modern tax-subsidized fees and expense accounts transfigured the largely middle-class city of the 1970s into a preserve of luxury hotels, exclusive shops and restaurants, opulent office buildings, and enormously inflated real estate. As the capital's sullen slums festered, as median family income languished at $30–35,000 in the rest of America, metropolitan Washington's household income rose by 1986 to more than $75,000, making its bureaucrat-lobbyist-lawyer–crowded bedroom counties in Maryland and Virginia the richest in the country. "The capital of democracy is seated in a city where citizens of average means cannot afford to live," wrote one journalist. When Congress voted its controversial pay raise from $89,500 to $125,000 in 1989, much of the capital thought the increase negligible. "Only in official Washington, where even young lobbyists and lawyers routinely made more than $100,000 a year," wrote a *Wall Street Journal* reporter, "did $89,500 seem like a pittance."

Inside the real and symbolic boundary of the Beltway, lobbyists were variously known as the "enforcers," the "pimps." They were "the last of the rogue institutions," as one account put it in 1993, "another link in the great chain of favors" that was the government of the United States. By any name, they were everywhere, practicing, as *Wall Street Journal* writer Jeffrey Birnbaum described it, "the brazen manipulation of both lawmakers and the public." Attorneys, public-relations flacks, specialists of varying education, they earned their handsome retainers and offices by a number of more or less discreet functions. Some became the valued "experts" in the intellectual wasteland of congressional staff and civil service. Unabashed "guns for hire," as Birnbaum called them, they constituted the unpaid staff on whom self-absorbed or indolent officials came to depend. They thus became the best-informed in the city on many intricate issues, albeit issues made intricate by the web of special-interest concessions they themselves had woven.

There was no question of the lobbyists' reach and importance. Many of them literally promoted politicians and staff, offering lucrative non-government work for the interests. In Washington's ingrown society, former aides and their employers, colleagues and rivals, husbands and wives, fathers and sons might all end up lobbying one another sooner or later. Where substance was deliberately wrung out and fresh independent ideas perceived as threatening, the labyrinth of personal relationships was all that was left and, in many cases, all anyone knew how to manage.

For all their apparent authority, lobbyists represented what Birnbaum and others called a highly paid "underclass," disdained as the prostitutes they were. In the White House, on Capitol Hill, especially in newsrooms, they were ridiculed and looked down on, albeit by many who had been or would soon became much the same. The emptiness and fraud of their work were widely known—"lots of locomotion masquerading as cerebration," as one of them admitted, and their parasitic personal economy produced little of value beyond the next fix. Forced into coalitions with other hirelings, lobbyists might be defeated in a given battle, yet they always survived to lunch and insinuate again. Win or lose, they continued to overwhelm the remnant public-interest lobbies ten to one in numbers and millions to one in financial resources.

Flacks and former officials crowded payrolls of foreign interests arrayed against both American business and labor. Congressional and executive aides-turned-lobbyists wrote ventriloquist speeches for senators and congressmen masking the criminal and drug empire of the notorious BCCI and other outrages. The infamous "iron triangle" of Pentagon weapons contracting—lobbies, Congress, and the Defense Department bureaucracy—regularly funneled nearly $200 billion in government money to a handful of favored contractors and locales. "Public" lobbies like the American Association of Retired Persons extracted millions in dues, stoutly resisted any change in subsidies to the affluent, then wallowed in offshoot businesses, bloated staff salaries, highly paid consultants, and luxurious offices while their largely unknowing members back home held bake sales. By the 1990s even once-avid public-interest groups like Common Cause and others had, as Washington editor and author Sam Smith noted, "become capital institutions, part of the ritualized, status-conscious, and very safe trench warfare of the city."

Through it all, Washington's omnipresent lawyers manipulated at $300 to $400 an hour on behalf of interests foreign and domestic, with a venality as casual as it was epic. Private legal "services" became the prime growth industry in the capital. The profession's prevailing ethic was legend. "The highest compliment inside Patton, Boggs that one attorney can pay to another," said one lawyer of the firm prominent in Democratic politics, "is that he or she will do anything for money."

By the time the Clintons came to the White House, lobbyists had long since replaced both the Congress and the executive as what one account called "the primary actors" of Washington, just as their provincial counterparts dominated Little Rock. It was *their* government that was now permanent, beyond the facade of elections and inaugurals. At the beginning of 1993 that regime was stronger, richer, better-prepared than ever for a struggle whose rules and weaponry, facts and fictions, they already controlled. If issues of change in a Clinton presidency were to be fought on the old grounds—were even to be addressed before the suborned system itself was fundamentally challenged and changed—the battle was over before it began.

◆ ◆ ◆

To such pervasive misrule in America there was to be one ultimate constitutional remedy, one final line of defense—a free, conscientious, insightful journalism. Even the most widespread abuses of power could not withstand honest reporting of what a government did and was. That, at least, was the democratic ideal.

The relationship of journalism to power in the Washington of the 1980s and 1990s was very different. Despite an apparently free and influential press, the money tyranny flourished. American journalism managed little substantive understanding of or concern for governance and posed no genuine check to the real regime's billowing power.

"It is in the things not mentioned that the untruth lies," John Steinbeck had learned from his experience as a correspondent in World War II. The "things not mentioned" and thus the essential lies of the Washington media were many and decisive, numbering not only all the consciously and unconsciously buried stories but what the profession knew of its own corruption. Like a battlefield of brutal waste and wreckage, the political landscape was littered with the corpses of failed journalism—reports killed, left to die, never pursued. A few hundred insiders—among them officials, politicians, government agents, lawyers, private investigators, criminals, political contributors, the handful of writers who deserved to be called investigative journalists—knew that quite another world existed in America. But it was almost never visible in mainstream media, much less in public discourse or education.

Why was so much missed, at such cost, by so many seemingly talented, ambitious journalists? For one thing, the media themselves had, by the 1980s, become the chattel of concentrated power. Most reporters worked out of some cubicle of a monopoly and took their subsistence and pensions by its favor. Twenty-three corporations controlled most of the nation's twenty-five thousand sizable outlets. Twenty-nine media conglomerates were among the Fortune 500. Thus General

Electric owned NBC; a billionaire, CBS; another conglomerate, ABC; and behind them was a web of shareholding and interlocking owner- ship in which shadowy giants like Wells Fargo International Trust, Fi- delity Management and Research, Bankers Trust, and Capital Research and Management were among the controlling interests in all the net- work parent corporations. Like the pollsters and political consultants, they would be wed to the tyranny not only by shared values but by millions in profits from political advertising.

Subsumed in an "information cartel," as one writer termed it, jour- nalism was now far less a profession or an art than a subsidiary of an immense profit-worshiping clerkdom, carrying its innate curse of lad- der-climbing bureaucrats, company conformity, implicit and explicit gags on integrity. In the most fundamental economic and institutional terms, the press and broadcasters were no longer an independent con- stitutional element, conscience, or antagonist of the system; they *were* the system. And in political coverage the first casualty would be report- ing about the inner realities and outrages of that world, not to men- tion the political arrangements that allowed them. "A built-in, chronic tilt," wrote the eminent journalist Morton Mintz, "chills mainstream press coverage of grave, persisting, and pervasive abuses of corporate power."

In commercial television, journalists' reporting was shrunk to sound bites and reality to a hackneyed rendition read off by vacant "talent." Though some began to venture out, capital reporters still languished, too, in hoary "beat" journalism that kept them "on the reservation," as their handlers called it. In Washington they were beset by 750 press secretaries on the Hill and hundreds more in the presidency, by bu- reaucracies, lobbies, think tanks, embassies, and satellite organizations, most devoted to getting their attention, some to avoiding too much, all to manipulating for boss, business, career.

As in Congress, rivalry was relentless if selective—competition, like literacy, a virtue never carried too far. Scores stood in line for report- ers' and editors' jobs in Washington. Many coveted the exclusive big piece. By the 1990s editors were anxiously measuring the worth of revelation by calling up on their computers what "mainstream" peers had written. In their fear and inertia, the media resembled nothing so much as Washington's bureaucrats they scorned. "They remain trapped in a purgatory," editor Sam Smith said of his colleagues, "be- tween the disdain of the public and ineffectualness within their own bureaucracy."

Yet none of this larger corruption and careerist inanity was necessarily decisive. With exertions not many people saw, good reporters could and did find their way around. If journalism missed the real Washington, if it seemed more aggressive and unctuous while less revealing or relevant, it was not alone a corporate curse. The answer was also in the who, what, where, when, and why of journalists themselves, in their informed adult consent to the corrupted system. As elsewhere in the culture, a few journalists stood apart. But the essence of American political journalism was how common failure and folly had become. And like government, it was a matter of substance.

On the surface the men and the token handful of women reporting Washington seemed better-educated and more discriminating than their relatively unschooled, poorly paid predecessors of the 1930s and 1940s—men who swallowed their leaks, like their liquor, unmeasured and who left the archives of political journalism in many respects a dingy embarrassment of indolence and co-option. Now some reporters were thought quotable themselves, celebrities if not quite authorities. Performing on their own television shows, they were famous in their own right, attended and courted. "Some of the country's best mouths, not its best minds," said one of them. They came "experienced"—the Washington assignment a stamp of superiority—but then, too, practiced in the crippling conventions, career politics, superficiality, smugness of the culture. No less than in other corporate settings, compromise and mediocrity were often implicit in promotion. "Experience," as the *New York Times* book critic John Leonard wrote earlier, "often as not means upward failure."

Covering and explaining the tyranny beyond personalities and surface politics simply demanded more than many had. A tabloid intimacy with personal scandal now passed for investigative reporting, even political understanding. Nothing so epitomized the end-of-century shallowness as the treatment of politicians' philandering: there was little reflection on the underlying issues of abused wives, misuse of office in the inevitable cover-up, implicit questions of psychology and integrity, or the misogynistic victimization of numbers of women. Meanwhile, few grasped the dense, fugitive, often squalid pageant of government; and of those who did, many grew cynically indifferent or indolent, reconciled to what they did not report. Few pondered the demands on integrity and intellect posed by a capital culture that was devoted to a finely layered deception and that defined success as conformity. Those monitoring compromise were co-opted themselves. More lucrative and stylish, more sassy than ever, their full-color, cappuccino journalism of the 1990s was closer to the yellowing rewrites of their cigar-champing predecessors than most could admit.

What stunted coverage was not always so simple or crude as plain censorship. "The process is more sophisticated. . . . Self-censorship is the primary shaper," one editor observed. "The problem has three names," another said bitterly, "substance, substance, and substance." Underlying ignorance and uncertainty made most reporters, no less than politicians, crucially dependent on the culture's so-called experts. Thus the corporate wards of the interests' think tanks and lobbies appeared again and again in newsprint and on television screens, paraded as "fellows" of an "institute" or "center" whose background or whose underwriting by business or even foreign governments went unexamined. Prominent "discussion" programs like ABC's *Nightline* and public television's *MacNeil/Lehrer NewsHour* or Charlie Rose descended into journalism-by-Rolodex, confining dialogue to the safe, stagnant right of center and their guests to the same predictable officials, former officials, club members, and flacks of much-rehearsed banality.

Pressures to conform to accepted opinion were everywhere, from lunches and dinner parties with sources and colleagues to editorial meetings and the ceaseless hail of manipulative press releases and calls. Enterprising reporters were ostracized and their careers shattered throughout the 1980s, notably at the *New York Times,* with editor Abe Rosenthal's rancid national security orthodoxy and establishment-censored coverage of Central America. But the effect was much the same at the major news services and magazines. In the publicly unmourned and all but unnoticed ruin of their peers' careers, journalists repeatedly saw the dangers of departing the comfortable prison of the right quotation marks. "It is not smart to come up with information that conflicts with White House briefings, State Department 'white papers,' or cocktail party assurances from senior administration officials," wrote one veteran of the purge.

In other quarters there might be no reluctance to embarrass the government, to get a story that showed malfeasance or worse, but even that relative readiness was usually crippled by the reporters' or editors' underlying ignorance of how government truly worked beyond. The dark side was not a world most reporters knew or understood or even wanted to ponder. To acknowledge its revelation as authentic journalism—rather than as "sensation" or "conspiracy theory" unbefitting "serious" reporting—was to question the shared political myth of the system. To expose it was to pose unwanted questions of what had happened to democracy and what must be done. In that, reporters submitted not only to the government's concealment or authority but to a professionwide superficiality and ultimate cowardice.

By the mid-1990s the long list of vital censored stories of the past fifteen years would belong to history. The journalists who had turned them up continued to reside on the fringes. Dissent and dissenters were digested, domesticated, and allowed an occasional outlet if convenient, marginalized and, in effect, repressed if not. The de facto censorship left only the money tyranny's party line, "Washington's approved version of reality," as one observer called it.

It was not only an agreed-on set of facts and considerations but more essentially a habit of mind, a way of seeing and thinking about politics and people, about what journalism was expected to tell—and, most crucially, what it might naturally, necessarily neglect and hide. It was to this bondage—however conscious or hypocritical the individual surrender—that most Washington journalists lent themselves. Like the social and psychological captives in Congress, many privately chafed and railed at the manifest corruptions and frustrations of their world. Yet shockingly few declared aloud their loss of confidence in the system. "At any given moment there is a sort of all-prevailing orthodoxy," George Orwell wrote, "a general tacit agreement not to discuss some large and uncomfortable fact."

Most of the industry found its coveted "center" well to the right of the old postwar political spectrum on basic questions of wealth and power, issues fundamental to all others. In the timorous senior ranks of news organizations, there were not many who could now describe themselves, as Dwight Eisenhower once had unabashedly, as a "militant liberal." News executives and reporters might deplore the primitive social prejudices of groups like the Christian Coalition or pay homage to token feminism, gay rights, artistic freedom, or civil liberties, but they could not confront the inequity of income and power that was the crux of their own status and against which even the conservative crowds flailed, though for the moment conveniently diverted by social issues.

As in the federal bureaucracy, ideological reactionaries penetrated journalistic ranks during the 1980s in unprecedented numbers. More telling than any infiltration by zealots or change of heart in formerly "liberal" institutions, however, the shift overall reflected the intellectual sterility of Washington's governing culture. The stunted media agenda, after all, was no more or less than the range of issues and depth of inquiry defined by the interest-dominated Congress, presidency, bureaucracy, and lobbies—the permissible confines of "serious" public discussion within the money tyranny. Once more, it was in "the things not mentioned" that practical censorship lay.

Reporters thus learned early to stay within the shallows of the corporate and political worlds. Within tamely accepted limits, the mythic obligation of media "objectivity" became its own Orwellian newspeak, sanctioning journalists to assemble the readily available prepaid and predigested data, the safe pedestrian quotes, but almost never to call political cause or effect by plain, unequivocal "unprofessional" names like hypocrisy, injustice, inequity, bigotry, demagoguery, crime, corruption, lie. In a distribution of power and sterilized public dialogue neither balanced nor fair, ideals of journalism turned into a mockery—"balance" became subterfuge or contrivance, "fairness" a guarantee that any criticism of vested advantage would always be rebutted.

Coverage dwelt long and self-indulgently on personalities, rivalries, designated symbolic events, and the city's endless narrative gossip, rarely on the classic questions of politics—who gets what, why, and how, at what cost to others. Knowingly, cynically, journalists might report the regime's worst infractions, the occasional politician, like the occasional major mobster, exposed, perhaps even tried and convicted. Otherwise, whatever they knew or said in private, they dealt professionally with institutions, policies, and politics very much at face value, as if nothing truly fundamental had happened since the 1970s, as if democracy itself had not been transformed and virtually extinguished. Their industry was witness to the coup and the ensuing decay. Like workers in an emergency room who watch a patient bleeding to death, they had chatted, taken notes, whispered to themselves, perhaps turned away now and then in boredom or distaste. But almost no one had sought the cause of the hemorrhaging, moved to stanch the flow or ease the agony or even testify later as to the actual cause of death. "Educated journalists, it turns out," wrote William Greider, one of the few exceptions, "are strong on the facts and weak on the truth."

With intellectual shallowness came, too, the sheer class pandering, cronyism, and shrunken sensibility of reporters, producers, and editors. They not only reflected, relied on, and parroted the opinions of the regime but were eager social peers as well. At the top—where bylines and television stand-ups mattered most, after all—they cohabited with the powerful and the interests' hirelings in numerous ways. They lived in the same neighborhoods, bought their children into the same exclusive private schools, entertained one another at intimate dinner parties, shared implicitly the inside-the-Beltway bond of Washington's sophisticated society. "When you add corporate caution to social climbing and the inoffensive product favored by much of the media," wrote one student of the industry, "a huge news hole develops in Washington." Like the comparatively wealthy and isolated government, like the six-figure lobbyists of K Street, they were far away from foreclosed farms, layoffs, lapsed health insurance. The ferocity of their own stricken Washington ghetto seeped only occasionally into their preserves. Driving through its Beirut-like slums to get to Capitol Hill, they locked doors, avoided eye contact, and worried about the potential consequences of a flat tire or an overheated engine.

To expose the regime was in many ways to expose themselves. Each revelation was a kind of acknowledgment of their own past compromise. Rumors might abound that news organizations and the prominent were corrupted by corporate power, even by the CIA or organized crime, "mobbed up," as the term had it. But conspiracies were rarely necessary. Wherever control lay—as in most closed systems holding out money and status—sociology and psychology took care of most potential dissent.

In the guise of "news" and "public affairs," corporate-sponsored television shows presented what one irreverent political writer, Eric Alterman, called the capital's "punditocracy," parading as journalism the views of a narrow group of the city's columnists and courtesans. Yet many reporters watched the debasement of their field in discreet silence, aspiring to be celebrities themselves. Rarely did they examine how many of their fellow Washington journalists now worked directly or indirectly for foreign interests. In the end, it was their own special treason, for if the media constituted the new intelligentsia of modern American politics, their blithe ignorance and conformity amounted to betrayal of duty. Journalists, after all, were still the self-proclaimed guardians against the very excess they had joined.

By the inauguration of Bill Clinton, there was no counting what might have been done or avoided over the past several years of plunder had the media not abdicated so completely. Corrupt money might still have overwhelmed—and a reeling public largely ignored—even vigilant, fearless, sophisticated, and truth-telling journalism. But exposure might also have stayed some of the worst abuses of the era and hastened the disaffection of the public. The nation would never know. As it was, reporters and their superiors would be there in 1993 and after, contemplating not their own crisis in integrity and responsibility, not what to do in fulfillment of Thomas Jefferson's democratic "first object," but rather what they would now *think* of the new First Couple.

"The real war will never get in the books," Walt Whitman wrote after seeing firsthand the corruption of Civil War Washington. More than a century later, his prediction remained sadly true for American politics. History and biography might discover a rogue or knave in a politician safely gone from office but tended to treat money as a slightly distasteful footnote rather than the essence of governance. Twentieth-century presidents went from disdain to favor and back again on waves of ideological fashion or literary-academic vogue, with little accounting of who owned whom and what in national power. The two old parties and many of their candidates might be well financed by shady, even criminal money, the Democrats especially benefiting from the largesse of the drug trade in the 1980s, according to law enforcement sources. But such outrage was discreetly confined to FBI wiretaps or safe-house bugs, known only by a few insiders hoarding their knowledge like doctors finding and concealing a malignancy.

Still, by the time the Clintons came to the White House in 1993, what had happened to American democracy, how long and how deeply the decay had been at work, was scarcely a state secret. Never before in American history, in fact, did the titles of an era chorus such debacle and alarm—books with names like *America: What Went Wrong?*, *The Best Congress Money Can Buy*, *Who Will Tell the People: The Betrayal of American Democracy*, *The Politics of Rich and Poor*, *Fooling America*, *Mink Coats Don't Trickle Down*, *S & L Hell*, *Beyond Hypocrisy*, *Sleepwalking through History*, *Honest Graft*, *Money Talks*, *Golden Rule*, *Dirty Politics*, *Boiling Point*, *Declining Fortunes*, *The Worst Years of Our Lives*.

It would take others beyond power to acknowledge how embedded the culture of complicity and denial had become, how utterly bipartisan, how irreparable. "Who will tell the people?" William Greider asked of the "well-kept secrets" of misrule so widely known in Washington. "No one in authority if they can see no clear advantage to themselves." A larger society made the regime what it was, enabled it to run on a daily basis: ten thousand of them worked around the Congress, a hundred thousand in the executive, another hundred thousand as lobbyists, and thousands more in the media and nongovernmental centers and satellite organizations. Beyond Washington was a wider privileged caste of three to four million "ambitious and well-connected individuals," as Lewis Lapham described the dominant 5 percent of the population, "united in their devotion to the systems in place and the wisdom in office."

In the cruder oppressions of Eastern Europe, such people had been among those who eventually turned on the hypocrisy of the regime, finally declared openly at the risk of their lives as well as their fortunes that the fraud and exclusion were no longer endurable—if not for them then for others. If one element of the US regime were to defect—a president, a segment of Congress, whistle-blowing bureaucrats or lobbyists, a genuinely independent voice in the "mainstream" media—many others would be there to cover, isolate, subvert, ultimately to nullify. The deeper mark of the institutions was that none dominated; all were hostage to the others.

The Washington Bill Clinton glimpsed along the way to the presidency—as a high school delegate shaking John Kennedy's hand or lunching with Uncle Raymond's friend John McClellan that distant summer of 1963, as a Georgetown student and Fulbright intern in the turbulent late 1960s, as a young attorney general visiting the Carter White House in the 1970s—no longer existed in 1993. Awaiting him was not even a Washington as it might have looked from Little Rock in the 1980s, during his ritual encounters with Congress and the White House or in "policy seminars" with some of the capital's corporate-paid courtiers as he plotted a presidential run. It was not even the caricature he ran against as an "outsider" in 1992. The Washington he entered with such ceremony and hope in January 1993 was fundamentally different.

Many thought later that Clinton had not understood what he faced during his first years in the White House. Despite the similarity between Little Rock and Washington, despite the cliché that Bill Clinton was master of his home state politics, there persisted a sense that he was somehow unprepared for the sheer force of Washington's insidious culture. Clinton himself would speak the language of an innocent's frustration and newfound cynicism. "All the old rules are still the ones that count," he said in angry self-justification at the end of 1993, as if both marking a rueful discovery and reiterating the obvious. Yet all that was belied by the president's own clouded past—by a Bill Clinton who was neither neophyte nor defector in America's money tyranny but one of its more wanton and prodigal offspring.

· 18 ·

Little Rock IV
"A Feller Could Live Off the Land"

Bill Clinton's plentiful "McDollars" of 1984, and of the years before and after, poured out of a relationship that was a classic of its kind in American politics from courthouse to White House—a glib, buccaneering businessman cultivating the special favor and protection of government and an ambitious, eagerly patronized officeholder garnering in return his own advantage from their two-way traffic in power and money.

For a time, the benefits were nicely mutual, the personal relations warm and intimate. The businessman flaunted his considerable influence, escaping for years and through tens of millions of dollars the public accountability or even simple notoriety a less friendly government might have exacted. He could intimidate questioning officials with the threat of political retaliation by their superiors. He was known to command the ear of the governor himself when money or concessions were needed from third parties. He would even hire the governor's wife on special retainer as his company lawyer, putting the state's First Couple on the payroll, as it were, and further fending off regulatory problems in the bargain. But then, the politician got his share as well. He profited from their joint land venture. He marveled at his patron's dependable and generous campaign contributions of suitably discreet origin and handling. He and his wife realized several thousand dollars in personal income from the legal retainer they both plaintively solicited. Not least, year after year they watched the quiet repayment by others of their own recurrent and sizable debts—money, like the campaign cash, flowing through the friendly businessman, either from him directly or from other sources they did not question.

Eventually, as such stories often go, the bonds of money and influence frayed and, with them, affection and loyalty. By the time the businessman was finally called to account and became a public embarrassment, the politician had turned away and moved on. He soon became president of the United States, living in the White House while his onetime intimate and patron, now bankrupt, lived in a trailer back in Arkansas. And though the relationship later came to haunt the president, to symbolize a larger, more generic corruption, at the time it flourished in the 1980s the politician, the businessman, their wives, and those around them took it all very much for granted. "The moral of that story was never, 'Don't do it,' " said a lawyer who knew their dealings. "It was, 'Do all you can and don't get caught.' "

◆ ◆ ◆

Jim McDougal had drifted from venture to venture before entering the Whitewater partnership with the Clintons. He speculated in raw land with his old boss Senator Fulbright and for a while in the 1960s styled himself an "export broker," farming crabs and black mussels in order to sell their crushed shells to Japanese "pearl manufacturers." From the mid to late 1970s he ran what his résumé called the Great Southern Land Company, as well as "various other small family-owned companies which dealt in land investment." None conjured the quick wealth, social status, and commensurate political power he wanted so keenly. He was still an obscure, small-time speculator and salesman when he began Whitewater in the late summer of 1978, just before his young partner's election as governor.

With Bill Clinton in the statehouse, however, Jim McDougal's fortunes began to improve markedly. Not long into the first term he joined the Clinton personal staff as the official gubernatorial liaison with the Departments of Highway and Transportation and Economic Development and with the state Securities and Bank Commissions; he also directed the Governor's Task Force on Investments and Capital Expenditures. Although he was drinking heavily, McDougal was clearly in a position of influence and prestige with powerful interests throughout Arkansas. "It was understood Jim spoke for the governor," said one official who dealt with him, "and that Bill was behind him in whatever he did in the state government or in business, that they were real, real close."

At the same moment, their joint land venture was off to an impressive start. During 1979–80 alone, the valuation of Whitewater had risen from $203,000 to $250,000. Over the first two years of the partnership—and again under favored terms similar to those of the original loan for purchase—the Clintons and McDougals borrowed another $47,000 for gravel roads and surveys and spent $40,000 of it carving the land into forty-four homesites. What was more, the worth of the development promised to spiral even higher than the margin of improvements or natural appreciation, thanks to a time-honored Arkansas gambit involving public money and private gain. Early in 1979 state records noted that the Game and Fish Commission had received a quiet donation of a riverfront lot near Whitewater Estates for a boat ramp. As developers and other insiders well knew, acceptance of such a "gift" meant that the commission would promptly build at public expense—spending federal marine fuel tax money channeled through the state Highway and Transportation Department—an asphalt access road to the ramp from the nearest major highway, at once saving the owners major expense in opening the development and adding substantially to the overall value and marketability of homesites. With Whitewater's joint owners now both wielding power at the statehouse, their development quickly became one more beneficiary of the thinly disguised subsidy. In his first term Bill Clinton soon "appointed two old-line commissioners who promptly fired the independent director of Game and Fish," as one account described it. By the fall of 1979 the donation of the riverfront parcel near Whitewater was officially "accepted" by Game and Fish, with the lucrative, tax-paid two-mile access road from Highway 101 to follow.

During the bitter 1980 campaign against Frank White there was brief publicity about Jim McDougal's continuing management of Whitewater while on the governor's staff. McDougal resigned not long afterward. Yet the story was hardly a revelation of collusion. At the time there was no exposé of the fishing ramp–road building racket or even a hint of any impropriety by McDougal's profiting co-owner, the governor himself. State records would show later, in fact, that Clinton planned to promote his friend and business partner to be Arkansas representative on the crucial Ozarks Regional Commission, whose role in planning and finance offered further potential benefits for Whitewater or other development schemes. It had not been political embarrassment but rather McDougal's own business fortunes that prompted his leaving the Clinton statehouse, and the prospect seemed even more lucrative than the Ozarks Commission or other capitol favors. By the autumn of 1980, little more than two years after beginning Whitewater and only months after joining Bill Clinton's staff as liaison to powerful commissions, the once-struggling fly-by-night operator and alcoholic was about to become a banker.

Financed by a $390,000 loan from the same friendly Union National of Little Rock whose board included one of Clinton's main fund-raisers—and whose $20,000 unsecured loan to Hillary had helped pro-vide the Clintons' Whitewater down payment—McDougal took over the small Bank of Kingston in a corner of Clinton's old Third Congres-sional District in northwest Arkansas. He began as one of seven inves-tors, including spurned Clinton aide Steve Smith and former congressman Jim Guy Tucker. It would be McDougal, however, who ran the bank in what soon became his notorious style, effectively con-trolling and dispensing for his own purposes millions in depositors' publicly insured funds, "lending money right and left," as Smith put it later, supposedly on the theory that it was tight credit that held back poor Arkansas. "Populist banking," McDougal called it. Maybe so, but one of the small institution's first loans after its takeover was to the McDougals' and Clintons' own popular cause. The nearly 20 percent interest rates that haunted Carter and helped elect Reagan were dis-couraging lot purchases at Whitewater Estates, and in the wake of Clin-ton's 1980 defeat, the partners moved to spur sales. On December 16, McDougal's Bank of Kingston loaned Hillary Rodham personally $30,000 to erect a model home on Whitewater's Lot 13.

The loan marked the beginning of the tangled skein of deals, trans-fers, and co-mingling of individuals and corporations that later investi-gators found riddled with legal and ethical discrepancies. At the time, even a dubious public record provoked no questions. Land and tax documents showed Whitewater Estates taking in almost $300,000 be-tween 1979 and 1983, well more than the outstanding mortgage and other indebtedness, yet with no recorded profits as income to the own-ers or corporation. As only one example, the twenty-eight acres over-looking the scenic bend of the White River, the parcel the Clintons had wanted themselves, turned out to be one of the first pieces they sold in 1980, for more than $1,000 an acre. Yet tax stamps listed the price of the property as only $2,000, some $30,000 less than the actual sale recorded elsewhere and later confirmed by the buyer.

Obscure, furtive, missing money seemed part of the Whitewater landscape from the beginning, and nowhere more typically than in the twisting history of Lot 13, where Hillary had borrowed to put up the model home. As investigative writer Martin Gross, Congressman Jim Leach of Iowa, and others later tracked the transactions, there were serious questions of legality or propriety at every turn. To begin with, it had been Hillary who took out the loan, because McDougal was now managing shareholder in the Kingston bank as well as in Whitewater, and to give himself the money would have been a blatant violation of banking law. On receiving the loan, however, the governor's wife had promptly deposited the $30,000 in the Whitewater account, the corporation then buying a modular home and proceeding to make payments on the principle and interest of the loan, with Hillary personally deeded both the house and land. If she was thus acting as the corporation's agent, as she obviously was, the same state banking laws made a loan to her as improper as a loan to McDougal himself. Moreover, the friendly bank in Flippin holding Whitewater's mortgage had released Lot 13 from indebtedness, and the corporation simply transferred it to Hillary personally, at no cost or consideration of any kind. But those acts, too, had been a clear violation both of proper banking practices and, ultra vires, of the corporation's legal authority under its charter.

In 1982, during the Clintons' comeback campaign, Hillary proceeded to "sell" the model home she never legally owned to a Hillman Logan for some $27,000, though again with no record of who received Logan's $3,000 down payment. The $24,000 balance was to be paid to Whitewater on an "installment contract," with Hillary retaining the deed. When Logan soon went bankrupt and died, however, she personally bought the house back from a bankruptcy court for only $8,000 and then resold it, again as a personal transaction, for $28,000, making a profit of $20,000 though later declaring only $1,640 in capital gains to the IRS.

She was not alone in tending Bill and her stake or in finding favorable financing. While over $7,000 of her debt at Kingston was eventually repaid by Whitewater, Inc.—largely, it turned out, with unaccountable funds from a subsidiary of McDougal's newly acquired savings and loan—it was during the period of the sale to Logan and her resale that the development corporation ceased to meet payments on the loan. To retire the remaining balance, Bill Clinton personally and without collateral borrowed $20,000 from the Security Bank of Paragould, owned by Marlin Jackson, one of the bankers involved in the initial financing of Whitewater and soon to be appointed by Clinton as state banking commissioner. Whitewater, Inc. eventually paid back much of this Clinton personal loan as well, again mainly on the strength of unexplained deposits in its corporate account from McDougal's savings and loan. All the while—through loan, sale, resale, and loan to cover loan—Whitewater carried Lot 13 on its books as a wholly owned asset, despite Hillary's personal ownership and profit recorded elsewhere. So it went in a thickening mix of shuffle and evasion as the Clintons regained the governorship and resumed their climb to the presidency, ceaselessly jockeying for their own share of profit and percentage in the investment that was supposed to make them hundreds of thousands of dollars.

◆ ◆ ◆

It might have remained one more petty, slightly unsavory flier among so many in the grasping 1980s, but for the flamboyance of Jim McDougal.

His own political ambitions ever aflame, he ran in vain for Hammerschmidt's congressional seat in 1982, winning the Democratic primary but overwhelmed by the entrenched incumbent in the general. That winter, with Bill Clinton reelected, McDougal was back again briefly in the statehouse as one of the governor's liaisons with the 1983 legislature. Within weeks of the session, however, he had returned to business, dickering with Worthen Bank and other backers to buy a struggling little savings and loan in sleepy Augusta, across the White River from his own native Bradford in north-central Arkansas. By the end of 1983 the deal was done and McDougal was opening a branch in his hometown with some fanfare, talking up land deals with local investors and making extravagant plans for his new savings and loan.

McDougal lured local depositors small and large by advertising high interest rates and attracted money from Wall Street and from brokers around the country by offering "Jumbo CDs," up to the $100,000 maximum now backed by federal deposit insurance in the sweeping 1980 deregulation of savings and loans. Under the same drastically revised laws that allowed federally insured thrifts to speculate widely, McDougal would then invest depositors' money as never before in real estate and other ventures in Arkansas and elsewhere, most of them spun off in a web of Madison subsidiaries run by him or his wife, Susan. It was a dream come true for the frustrated politician and speculator, in effect his own private bank to finance his irrepressible deals.

"He wanted to see how much he could make to prove who he was," said Steve Cuffman, who later succeeded him as chairman of the savings and loan. "All that money for high-stakes speculation and spreading around was sure as hell going to make him a player," said a federal prosecutor. Soon after taking over in Augusta, McDougal planned his decisive move to the marketing and financial center of the state in Little Rock, finding an old block-long laundry plant to renovate in gentrified Quapaw. He needed only the approval of state regulators to open in the capital and begin his spree. To inspire public confidence and respectability, the new thrift was to be called Madison Guaranty.

What followed was a parody of the Arkansas system and typical of the larger savings and loan scandal. Jim McDougal's big break came in September 1983—six months after he left the governor's staff for a second time—when the Clinton administration gave him permission to move Madison Guaranty to Little Rock. In the midst of the governor's mounting campaign on education as well as his rising popularity, the event drew little attention. The new branch bank, the *Gazette* noted in a brief booster announcement, would have the "limited purpose" of providing mortgages for what the paper called "a booming Madison Guaranty real estate venture—Maple Creek Farms." Like Whitewater, 1,300-acre Maple Creek was one of McDougal's raw ventures, and "neither . . . was booming," as Meredith Oakley caustically noted afterward. In the offing instead was an explosion of a different kind. Carrying off with characteristic flair exactly what he planned, McDougal would drive up deposits at the stylish new Little Rock branch from an initial $6 million in 1983 to over $123 million scarcely three years later—or so Madison's books seemed to show. What had opened in Quapaw was not the *Gazette*'s solid supplier of home mortgages but a fount of speculation, self-dealing, and insider abuse remarkable even for the time and place. And from the beginning there were several unmistakable warnings.

That same autumn Clinton's own new banking commissioner and Whitewater creditor, Marlin Jackson, prepared to order McDougal's Bank of Kingston—now itself renamed Madison Bank and Trust—to cease what Jackson called "imprudent loans." In little more than two years at the tiny institution, McDougal had already become notorious for "too many risky loans and too many loans to friends," as one report put it starkly. Among other infractions, the state Banking Commission cited the $30,000 model-home loan to Hillary Rodham, though only because Whitewater was outside the statutory lending area of the bank. The multiple other questionable steps in that loan, apparent infractions involving Whitewater and the Clintons directly as well as the bank, went unremarked.

By the fall of 1983 McDougal had also aroused the suspicion of examiners from the Federal Deposit Insurance Corporation, who were growing concerned that the small rogue bank in Kingston was now concealing unsound practices and a consequent weakened condition by shifting troubled loans to Madison Guaranty. That autumn, in fact, state officials already doubted Madison Guaranty's own solvency, Charles Handley, a ranking aide in the Arkansas Securities Department, would admit years later.

The following spring the Federal Home Loan Bank Board found that Madison's investments through one of its real estate subsidiaries were worse, as one summary worded it, than "double the level allowed by Arkansas law." At the same moment, in March 1984, FDIC examiners filed a formal memorandum deploring Jim McDougal's recklessness, alerting the supervisory Federal Home Loan Bank authorities in Dallas, and setting in motion a "special limited examination" of the thrift. Issued in June 1984, that first partial inquiry, while not a formal audit, was "based on an analysis of information obtained from the institution's records and from other authoritative sources," as the report indicated. It found "unsafe and unsound lending practices" and concluded plainly that "the viability of the institution is jeopardized."

McDougal had not used "prudent investment practices," the report went on, and "substantial profits . . . on the sale of real estate owned have been improperly recognized." From only a preliminary review, federal examiners determined that accounting at the institution was highly suspect, and legal bookkeeping would show Madison Guaranty "in an insolvent position" even by the lenient standards of the time, a conclusion widely shared in the regulatory community. "The federal government had done an examination . . . and I agreed with it," remembered state securities official Handley, "which showed that Madison had a net worth of only 1 percent of total assets [when] the benchmark was 3 percent, which wasn't very high itself." Altogether, as Lee Thalheimer, the director of the Arkansas Securities Department, advised his federal counterparts in a letter that spring of 1984, McDougal's violations were "very serious."

Dire as their 1982–84 warnings may have been, state and federal officials had only glimpsed what was going on at Madison Guaranty. Behind McDougal's bravado and brash plans, the thrift was hemorrhaging money from the beginning. Behind what were later revealed to be false appraisals, cleaned-up books, and constant check kiting of dizzying circularity between Madison and its kindred companies—including Whitewater—government examiners and prosecutors would eventually find that huge sums of depositors' money had been manipulated and diverted to the gain of a few insiders. By one official estimate, Madison lent some $17 million solely to its own directors, officers, and executives. Like an elaborate shell game played with other people's savings, and ultimately at taxpayers' expense, money darted from account to account, subsidiary to subsidiary, covering this overdraft with that loan, this loss with that gain or new loan, though with a ceaseless flow of "commissions," fees, salaries, and other perquisites for those inside. "It was not particularly unique in the looting of financial institutions," a federal investigator said afterward, "but real bad stuff."

The resulting extravagance was anything but secret. The ubiquitous television commercials for Madison Guaranty developments became famous in themselves, with "Hot Pants" Susan McDougal riding her white stallion over picturesque territory. "She was kind of a local sex celebrity," said one lawyer. On billboards and in newspapers, Madison speculations like Castle Grande, near Little Rock, would be a familiar part of the advertising and commercial landscape of the small capital. The McDougals themselves were "always good gossip," as one local described them, "and always seemed rich and successful in those days." Susan was known to live mostly alone in their lavish house, while her deal-making husband often stayed in an apartment to be near his aged mother, though the devotion took nothing away from his reputation for extravagance. Now called Diamond Jim, McDougal basked in the apparent wealth and prominence, of which the Jaguars and Bentley were vivid symbols.

Still, for all their flashiness, the McDougals might have been one more pair of high rollers in boom-time Little Rock, save for their extraordinary connection with the state's First Couple. "In their heyday in Little Rock it seemed the Clintons and McDougals couldn't get enough of each other," the *Washington Post* noted a decade later. "An unbelievable relationship," Susan McDougal would call it.

Afterward, there could be no doubt how much and how currently the Clintons knew the business habits of their intimates, knew the essence of what was happening at Madison Guaranty Savings and Loan. Even apart from the social affinity and active partnership in Whitewater, Banking Commissioner Jackson had officially advised the governor of the 1983 findings of lending violations at McDougal's Kingston bank. To underscore the wanton acts at Madison Guaranty, lawyers and investigators in the state Securities Department sent the governor's office a copy of the blunt conclusions of the federal "special limited examination" of 1984—though its receipt was never acknowledged. "We knew it got to Betsey Wright and other folks, and finally to Bill Clinton," said one official, "but they just kept quiet and waited for it to go away."

To Jackson's formal notice of McDougal's infractions, Clinton's reaction was circumspect. "The governor's response to this," according to one account, "was to urge him to ignore politics and treat all banks alike." Jackson obviously was aware of McDougal's special ties, and both understood what "politics" meant in this case, as Jackson himself would recount. The Banking Commission's discipline of the bank at Kingston would eventually result in Hillary Clinton's own $30,000 Whitewater note being called, a sequel later claimed to show the governor's scrupulousness in dealing with Jim McDougal. But by then, of course, Bill Clinton had already covered the Kingston loan with yet another unsecured loan, from the Paragould bank owned by the same Marlin Jackson. While state banking officials curbed a few of McDougal's worse loans at Kingston, his other excesses with Madison Guaranty in Little Rock, Whitewater, and similar ventures went forward unquestioned—and known by the governor and his wife in some detail.

For much of the period, in fact, it was literally a matter of both Clintons being unable to go to work, whether at the statehouse or law firm, without sooner or later confronting at least some unmistakable and relevant knowledge of Jim McDougal's practices. As early as the fall and winter of 1981, the Rose firm had represented his Madison Bank and Trust at Kingston in litigation with another bank. Two years later, as McDougal was taking over Madison Guaranty, he was still a Rose client, and the partners at the time, including the state's First Lady, were heatedly discussing McDougal's business troubles, an unpaid legal bill McDougal contested, and their continuing representation. "Pursuant to your discussions with Hillary Rodham Clinton," began an October 13, 1983, letter to McDougal on the disputed billing of Madison, which Hillary had persuaded her partners to reduce. "She knew McDougal was a renegade just a step ahead of the regulators, and she was still arguing for some give on the billable hours," one Rose lawyer remembered. "Hillary was the point person on everything to do with McDougal and his banks and deals from the beginning," recalled another former partner. "Most of us were aware, I guess, that she and Bill were into Whitewater with him, and she knew the McDougals and that S & L mess inside and out."

Associates and would-be adversaries soon discovered Jim McDougal had powerful friends. As he bought the savings and loan that would become Madison Guaranty in 1983, he had also started another local real estate development, named Gold Mine Springs, in partnership with Freddy Whitener, a retired Bradford construction worker. Whitener remembered vividly that, when a state geologist officially warned them that the term "Gold Mine" was false advertising and that he would complain to the Arkansas attorney general, McDougal said dismissively, "When he's sitting in the attorney general's office, I'll be sitting in the governor's office." That night the geologist was calling Whitener to "apologize," as the partner told the story, asking him to make sure he told McDougal about the concession and adding bitterly, "I've been told that if I don't apologize to you by midnight, I'll lose my job."

With the same apparent ease with which he disposed of the false-advertising complaint, McDougal would go on to secure a $1,300-a-month government lease for a state revenue office in one of Madison's buildings, the kind of small yet stinging favor that rankled commercial competitors as the blatant political influence angered officials, though both felt themselves powerless. "You may have thought McDougal was way out of bounds," said a Little Rock businessman who dealt with him more than once, "but you also knew you had no recourse to the authorities while Clinton was governor."

It would never be clear how much McDougal's political muscle was brought to bear in what followed with federal regulators, in the wake of the stark findings of Madison's "insolvency." As it was, local pressure was seldom necessary to rescue outlaw savings and loans at the time; the larger system was enough. After summoning Madison Guaranty's directors to Dallas on June 26, 1984, and despite the alarm of state as well as federal officials, Federal Home Loan Bank authorities neither closed down the bank nor seriously disciplined McDougal. Instead they entered a perfunctory "supervisory agreement," what one account called "a relatively mild form of probation" that prescribed new accounting and debt procedures but little more, allowing McDougal to go on essentially unchecked for another twenty-six months. By September 1984 the examiner who had found Madison Guaranty insolvent months before had been hired away by McDougal to be one of Madison's senior officers, and the Home Loan Board approved a "debt restructuring" that erased, on paper at least, more than half a million dollars in "improperly recognized profits."

If Jim McDougal began his wild ride as one more gambler with public money loosed by savings and loan deregulation, he now became a beneficiary as well of the partly feckless, partly deliberate federal regulatory failure that only fed the savings and loan crisis once it erupted. "They doubled the deposit insurance and took the regulatory cop off the beat," one observer would say of Washington's bipartisan collusion. As an industry hurtled toward a half-trillion-dollar toll on taxpayers, as federal regulators closed down fewer than thirty thrifts among the troubled dozens in 1984–86, as federal deposit insurance ran out while the looting spread, Madison Guaranty was hardly unique.

◆　◆　◆

Throughout 1984 ties between the rogue banker and the future president grew ever closer, and ever more lucrative for Bill Clinton. A federal investigation later found evidence of at least $60,500 siphoned from Madison Guaranty to Clinton's 1984 reelection campaign, and the governor's official campaign committee would be named in Justice Department criminal investigative documents as an alleged coconspirator in the diversion of depositors' funds. Even then, the suspected siphoning appeared to be only a fraction of the McDollars that campaign aides saw cascading into the 1984 race.

Late in 1984, after his reelection to the unprecedented power of a third term, Clinton interrupted his morning jog to appear unannounced at McDougal's Quapaw office. Clinton was perspiring and breathless as he came in and, much to McDougal's dismay, sprawled heedlessly on an expensive new leather chair. As his host watched nervously, the governor then launched into a familiar and forlorn complaint about his personal income and expenses, that his statehouse salary and Hillary's law partnership were not enough. "I asked him how much he needed, and Clinton said, 'about $2,000 a month,' " McDougal later told the *New York Times*. In response the banker promptly put Hillary on a $2,000-a-month retainer, with the unusual arrangement that it be paid to her personally rather than to or through the firm. "I hired Hillary because Bill came in whimpering they needed help," he remembered.

As it was, Clinton's sweaty lament was not the only plea for personal income. During the same period the First Lady had also paid a visit. "Hillary came in one day and was telling us about the problem. The problem was finances, her finances," Susan McDougal recalled. "She came to Jim's office. I remember Jim laughing and saying afterward, 'Well, one lawyer's as good as another, we might as well hire Hillary.' " To the McDougals and others at the savings and loan, the mercenary pleas of the governor and his wife, both already enmeshed with the McDougals and Madison, became an office joke. "She was on retainer," Susan went on. "I remember everyone sitting around laughing and saying, 'We need to hire Hillary Clinton.' "

Yet being on the Madison payroll was no mere whimsy for the First Couple. The governor was there at the Quapaw office on his morning jog regularly each month to pick up the check, and on occasion Hillary herself came for the money. "It was really at her behest, the McDougal retainer," said a Rose colleague. "She felt they needed it, and after they won in 1984 she felt it was only right they get some more money. That was her attitude about their quote sacrifice unquote," recalled another lawyer. When the tale of the governor's jog and resulting retainer inevitably made its way into White Heights gossip, there were accounts of other soliciting as well. "I realized when folks talked about this," said an older lawyer and former official, "how much Bill was constantly making calls for her on one thing or another, that here was the governor of the state, with all that implied, out drumming up business for Hillary and Rose." Most who knew about it took the grasping for granted. "All of the risks, including Whitewater," Martin Gross observed, "were part of that overriding need to become rich." "No one thought of this as something to be covered up or worried about," said an aide. "This was money they were supposed to get, as everybody saw it."

As the Clintons prepared the lavish third-term inauguration and as Jim McDougal began his more than two-year grace period from accountability, with the governor's wife on legal call, relations between the partners settled into an easy rhythm of mutual favor. That December McDougal arranged for a renewal of their old Whitewater note at Citizens Bank and Trust of Flippin, despite the absence of the Clintons' signatures on legal documents. In mid-January 1985 the newly inaugurated governor replaced the outgoing state Securities Department director and McDougal critic, Lee Thalheimer, with Beverly Bassett, an attorney with a Little Rock firm that had done work for Madison. Bassett was McDougal's preferred candidate and he had urged her appointment on Clinton. "It would be to our advantage," he said later. Then, as if on cue, within days of the Securities Department patronage, Clinton came back for his own favor. As McDougal remembered, the governor telephoned in late January and asked him to "knock out the deficit" of the 1984 campaign, meaning the $50,000 Clinton had borrowed personally from Maurice Smith's Bank of Cherry Valley for a final barrage of television ads. "Bill's in trouble, and we're going to have to get together and help him out," Madison employees remembered McDougal's telling them after Clinton's call. Some were "promised," by one account, that they would be "reimbursed" for donations, though from what source was not clear.

So it was that on a balmy Little Rock evening in April 1985 Diamond Jim McDougal hosted a select but lucrative fund-raiser for his friend

Governor Bill Clinton at the Art Deco headquarters of Madison Guaranty. Between fifty and a hundred people sipped wine and made out checks in the fashionable lobby, including Madison executives and employees there on command. Of the $35,000 McDougal now raised to retire Clinton's loan, federal auditors found some $12,000 in certified checks drawn on Madison Guaranty yet attributed to "phantom contributors" who made no donations. Investigators suspected thousands more in such "orphaned" contributions. Provoked by the bogus checks, an examination of Madison books would show similarly suspicious movements of cash—inflated closing costs, commissions, and transfers—coinciding with the final, free-spending weeks of the Clintons' 1984 run.

Shady money would continue to flow unremarked and unpoliced. But the April 1985 party in Quapaw became a touchstone, first for the groundbreaking journalism of Jeff Gerth in the *New York Times* in 1992–1993, then for the Whitewater special prosecutor. Just as the specter of Roger Clinton and drug scandal had prompted the eleventh-hour loan from Maurice Smith in the 1984 race, the imbroglio over Smith's promised spoils on the Highway Commission had led in turn to Clinton's anxiety to clear the debt and to his quick resort to one more favor-for-favor with McDougal. It all came together at the Madison Guaranty fund-raiser that spring night—the money, the politics, the fretful yet flippant air that was now so often the Clinton style. "I guess you could say in a way that Jim McDougal paid for Roger and the coke. Kind of poetic, isn't it?" said a Clinton aide. "Whatever else it was," a legislator observed, "that little get-together at the savings place was one too many."

◆　◆　◆

The sequel for the Clintons and McDougals, for Madison Guaranty and the public seemed to some a caricature.

The Clintons' choice for state Securities Department director, the ostensible public guardian against abuses like McDougal's, had numerous personal bonds to the wider system. A bright, pretty thirty-two-year-old, Beverly Bassett was the sister of Clinton's former student and aide Woody Bassett and would become the wife of Archie Schaffer, a Tyson executive and a nephew of Senator Bumpers. She had worked for Clinton in the 1974 House race and then in the attorney general's office. As a lawyer in one of Little Rock's more political firms, which included Jim Guy Tucker among its partners, she did some work on a land scheme that involved one of the Madison subsidiaries and even wrote an internal memo in 1984 noting the company's "willful" failure to comply with federal disclosure laws. Afterward, however, Bassett would claim that she had never even met the same Jim McDougal who urged her appointment "to our advantage" that winter of 1984–85, had never heard Bill Clinton speak his name. She was not aware of Whitewater or of the Clintons' conspicuous close ties to the McDougals, much less of the sub-rosa McDollars coursing into the governor's campaigns, she insisted. Bassett and other local apologists later contended that her office had neither the money nor the authority to do more than it eventually did to deal with the Madison scandal. As the pivotal official between the governor and his rogue patron, they argued, she did nothing unusual. In Arkansas terms at least, it was true. On the available record, she apparently showed Diamond Jim no exceptional favor. It was enough that the new securities director governed—and McDougal responded—much like the rest of the system.

Six days after taking office in January 1985, Bassett signed without qualification formal department orders, drafted the previous fall under her predecessor, approving various Madison land speculations, including the real estate deal she had dealt with in private practice months before. All were projects ostensibly devised to restore the bank's squandered solvency. McDougal was to use the twenty-six-month hiatus gained in the 1984 Federal Home Loan Bank Board "supervisory agreement"—and given state sanction—to float several such promotions. His prevarications only deepened and prolonged the plunder of the bank, at crucial points with the influential assistance of the Rose Law Firm and Hillary Rodham Clinton, as well as the diffident acquiescence of her husband's administration.

One episode was emblematic. That spring of 1985, just as the governor was asking McDougal to "knock out" the latest campaign debt, the speculator proposed to state regulators that Madison Guaranty be allowed to issue nonvoting preferred stock. It was an expedient suggested by federal officials and already adopted by some straining Arkansas S & Ls but also a device that would allow Diamond Jim to raise still more capital for his maneuvers without sacrificing either his control over the institution or the federal insurance coverage that made the public ultimately liable for his ruinous practices. Given McDougal's history, the stock scheme aroused immediate concern among rank-and-file regulators in the state Securities Department, who urged that Bassett refer the proposal to be reviewed formally by department lawyers.

But then came two letters to Bassett from the Rose firm, pointedly referring to Hillary Clinton as the senior lawyer on the matter and pressing for swift approval of the stock plan. Citing a favorable internal audit of Madison, Rose told the securities director categorically that McDougal "anticipates . . . no deficiency . . . in the near future" for the bank, and even "improvement of its financial conditions and services"—though neither assurance was valid at the time, much less supported by the troubling record. The second Rose letter arrived across town at the Securities Department scarcely three weeks after the April 4 Clinton fund-raiser. Both letters showed clearly that Hillary and her Rose associates were aware that Madison had not met federally mandated requirements for cash reserves. Still, the assurances of imminent solvency and diligence gave Clinton's new securities director the condition she needed. Promptly, on May 14, in a return letter just as pointedly addressed "Dear Hillary," Beverly Bassett ruled to approve McDougal's issue of the stock, despite continuing vocal opposition among her staff professionals, many of them expressing what one account called "strong reservations."

She had no choice but to approve McDougal's proposal, Bassett would claim long afterward, on grounds that the scheme was technically legal in Arkansas and that the Rose firm's urgings were backed up by Madison's own audit, conducted by the accounting firm of Frost and Company. Frost's chief auditor in the McDougal-commissioned examination turned out, however, to have two outstanding loans himself at Madison, and not surprisingly, the audit was eventually found to be tainted. Moreover, Bassett's pro forma approval of the preferred-stock scheme also blithely ignored the severe criticism and warnings by both state and federal officials over the preceding year. For all that, though, no conspiracy or heavy-handed gubernatorial intervention was needed for McDougal to continue to do business in Arkansas. All it took was a homegrown official willing to take highly suspect matters at face value.

As it happened—through no fault of accommodating government regulators—McDougal never carried out the preferred-stock plan, which might have required disclosure Madison could hardly afford and, in any case, would have only added to the mounting disaster. Yet the swift unqualified approval by the governor's securities director was part of a pattern of official tolerance, if not indulgence, during 1985–86, when the looting of the savings and loan steadily worsened, including more than $700,000 in "commissions" paid to Susan McDougal and two of her brothers. All the while, Jim McDougal continued to entice depositors and investors, drawing in another $60 million, "fattening the load . . . picked up by taxpayers when the bank finally went bust," as Peter Boyle wrote in the *New Yorker*.

The Rose firm enjoyed its own characteristic sequel in the stock episode. When the FDIC itself eventually sued Frost and Company in 1989 over the compromised audit used to mask McDougal's excesses, Rose actively sought and won the retainer to represent the US government against Frost, discreetly neglecting to mention its previous representation of Madison, not to mention Hillary Clinton's myriad ties to the bank and its head. As if to compound the exploitation, the firm settled the $60 million suit on behalf of taxpayers for a token $1 million, far below the accounting company's insurance coverage, much less what the public interest deserved, with Rose taking a $400,000 fee in taxpayers' money. Once more the pattern was repeated: the ignoring of McDougal's ominous record, the shrouded Frost audit, the relentless pillage of Madison while the state regulator stood by in fastidious silence, Rose's deplorable practices in the later federal suit— all with the knowledge and often direct participation of Jim McDougal's lawyer, Hillary Rodham Clinton, and all at the cost of the public. What one relationship between the Clintons and McDougals did not cover, the others seemed to provide. "I need to know everything you have pending before the Securities Commission [*sic*]," McDougal typically wrote an assistant in July 1985, "as I intend to get with Hillary Clinton within the next few days."

♦ ♦ ♦

As McDougal continued to wheel and deal with impunity in 1985, the siphoning of money from Madison Guaranty not only underwrote his incessant land bubbles but also benefited Whitewater Estates and its prominent owners. A preliminary federal investigation of the surviving records in 1992 revealed more than $100,000 drained into the McDougals' and Clintons' enterprise in the mid-1980s, some $70,000 in one six-month period alone. To federal examiners and eventually to House Banking Committee investigators, what might have begun as a legitimate business initiative had obviously become by 1985 a form of white-collar bank robbery.

The pace of McDougal's maneuvering with Whitewater quickened with his twenty-six-month grace period from federal regulators and with the effective free pass from Bassett and the Clinton administration at the state level. Whitewater, Inc.—and thus the Clintons as co-owners—not only had the development's mortgage and other sustaining costs paid by funds manipulated at Madison but made the land venture another vessel in McDougal's dizzying financial shell game. By the mid-1980s, "tens of thousands of dollars were passing through Whitewater's account at Madison," as the *Washington Post* described it afterward, the flow seeming "to bear no direct connection to Whitewater's lot sales or home development activity." So egregious was the shifting and co-mingling that federal auditors would find that Whitewater had become inseparable from the larger abuse at Madison Guaranty and its subsidiaries. "Any attempt to extract Whitewater as one entity from the rest of the McDougal-controlled entities involved in the alleged check kite," a Resolution Trust senior criminal investigator would tell her superiors in 1992 after an initial inquiry, "will distort the entire picture." Investigators came to believe that by 1985 Madison Guaranty Savings and Loan amounted to a veritable slush fund for the Clintons' land business as well as an alleged kitty and countinghouse for their reelection campaigns. In some respects, federal auditors would conclude, the First Couple themselves had become parties to the sacking of the small thrift.

Yet for some, the shuttling of money from one account to another in Quapaw was no more shocking than what was happening on the banks of the White River. While a slow market prevented Whitewater Estates from becoming the boon its owners had hoped for, the development nonetheless had a sometimes brisk trade during the latter half of the 1980s. And it was in those transactions with ordinary people, as much as any intricate insider self-dealing at Madison or furtive political-legal favors in Little Rock, that the character of the operation seemed laid bare.

Advertising in publications like *Mother Earth News* and targeting low-income retirees and senior citizens looking for pleasant rural property to live out their years, the Clintons and McDougals always made a point of offering what seemed at first glance the most attractive terms. "Poor man's real estate financing," as a local lawyer called it, the deals appeared to be the Whitewater application of Diamond Jim's "populist banking" or Bill Clinton's own perennial claim to be a champion of consumers. Elderly couples on fixed incomes might buy lots for low or token down payments, with no credit checks or appraisals and only modest monthly installments at low interest. Many did just that. They were generally retired blue-collar workers from Texas, Missouri, or Oklahoma, as well as Arkansas, husbands and wives planning to build a small fishing cottage or a place where grandchildren could come. Commonly they used the bulk of their savings for money down and barely scraped together monthly payments. It was they who provided much of the $300,000 that Whitewater collected in lot sales between 1979 and the summer of 1990. But what began as a modest dream often ended in painful nightmare.

Behind the Whitewater advertising lure was the fine print of a harshly punitive real estate contract. If the elderly buyers defaulted on their monthly installments for more than thirty days they found that all their previous payments were classified merely as "rent" and that they had no equity in the land at all, regardless of how much they had put down or paid in. The results could be devastating. Clyde Soapes, a grain-elevator operator from Texas, put $3,000 down and faithfully made thirty-five monthly payments of $244.69 to the Clintons and McDougals, altogether just short of the $14,000 price of the lot. When he fell desperately ill in 1987, however, he could no longer make his payments and quickly lost the land and all his previous investment.

Soapes was a typical case. More than half those who bought Whitewater lots from the future president, his wife, and their extravagant partners would lose their land and all their equity payments. Partial records showed at least sixteen different buyers paying in more than $50,000 and never receiving property deeds. Meanwhile Whitewater carried on a flourishing traffic in repossessions and resales, selling some lots over and over when aged buyers faltered or when someone else simply came along and unilaterally bought out the purchasers and took the land by completing the payments. Typically, Clyde Soapes's planned fishing retreat was resold to a couple from Nevada for $16,500, then taken back again after only a few payments, and resold to yet other buyers—all for the same middling but pitiless profit wrung from the struggling and the old. "That is clearly not a very consumer-oriented method of selling at all," an American Bar Association real estate expert would say. Others were less delicate. "They screwed people left and right," said a local businessman who watched the sales. "Taking advantage of a bunch of poor old folks on a land deal. . . . The future President and First Lady. That ought to be the *real* Whitewater scandal."

It was all technically legal and not that uncommon in the Clintons' Arkansas and in similar settings, especially in the South, though many states around the nation had long since moved to protect consumers in such ensnaring escrow or contract sales, making repossession and loss of equity at least more difficult as the buyer's investment grew. Jim McDougal had used the same lure with the same summary penalty in other land schemes. He was a known quantity. The speculator would defend the practice as either affording lots to people who could not ordinarily qualify for bank loans or else as providing a safeguard against the "impulse buying" common at resort properties.

It was a rationalization that could embarrass even his profit-eager partners in the governor's mansion. Hillary Clinton evidently had second thoughts in her own shuffling of lucrative Lot 13. The first owner, Hillman Logan, had defaulted before he went into bankruptcy and died, and Whitewater could have automatically repossessed the lot with all his payments. On behalf of Hillary, a Rose lawyer initially wrote to the executor of Logan's will arguing that the estate should "consider abandoning" the dead man's $8,000 equity. But then the future First Lady suddenly recanted in 1988 and paid the estate the $8,000 for the land—still going on to make a sizable profit in the resale, albeit less than she would have realized by merely seizing the model home like all the others. When the case became known after the Clintons had come to the presidency, the White House would explain simply that Mrs. Clinton paid the unnecessary $8,000 "to safeguard her interests in the property." As always, there were other versions. "Logan was from Mississippi and had a lawyer involved in his affairs, which most Whitewater owners never came close to," said an attorney familiar with the case. "This one could have gotten out of hand and been a little embarrassment, so she just paid that money to put it to sleep."

The frequent repossessions and rolling profits continued through the decade and almost to the eve of the Clintons' 1992 presidential campaign, well after Madison Guaranty had finally collapsed and ceased sluicing funds to Whitewater and other entities, well after the Clintons had taken over the records of the development and begun to shun a bankrupt and mentally ill Jim McDougal. For years, however, it had been routine—the sales bait for the elderly buyers, the repossessions and expropriated equities, the petty profit taking, the sick men or the widows who could no longer make the payments, the broken dreams. Like McDougal's use of the savings and loan, Whitewater embodied business practices, morality, and ethics that the future president and his wife never questioned or even acknowledged openly, much less repudiated. At the end of a road so helpfully paved by taxpayers' money, the scenic lots on the White River took their place in the long chain of advantages and subsidies the First Couple came to enjoy in Little Rock. In the end, there was a sense in which no one more than Bill Clinton himself symbolized the larger irony and mockery of Whitewater's brochure assuring buyers of their private paradise. "A feller," it promised, "could live off the land."

• • •

There were final, similarly revealing sequels to be played out in the Whitewater sequence as McDougal and Madison Guaranty careened toward ruin in 1985–86.

David Hale was a familiar and ingratiating figure in Little Rock's Democratic establishment, a soft-voiced, open-faced lawyer of ordinary ability who had been drawn to politicians since his adolescence. Eager to please, he relished both his access to the powerful and his own patronage sinecure. He had been a president of the national Junior Chamber of Commerce, and in 1979 was appointed by Governor Clinton to be the first judge of Arkansas's new municipal small-claims court in Pulaski County. By 1985, in his early forties, Hale was still proudly presiding over what had become the state's largest court, where he was known for occasional displays of temper at the common citizens before him, in contrast to his fawning behavior toward the politically prominent. Meanwhile he made investments of his own and also ran Capital Management Services, Inc., a six-year-old family-owned small business investment company (SBIC), licensed and funded by the federal Small Business Administration to channel commercial loans to women and minorities in Arkansas obviously "disadvantaged" in the conventional credit and banking system. Hale's own entrepreneurial ventures—a theme park based on Bible stories was a typical example—were hardly successful. But the SBIC was a "gold mine," as one account called it, allowing him to control millions in federal funds with relatively little oversight. He yearned to be remembered as a good judge, David Hale told friends. Yet it was in his other, more mercenary role, dispensing government loan money, that he was destined to make history.

According to Hale's own sworn and repeated accounts, it began in the autumn of 1985 when he was asked to meet Jim Guy Tucker, who was both his lawyer and a client debtor who had borrowed heavily from Capital Management for a local cable company. From Tucker's office they drove to Castle Grande, one of Madison's developments. Waiting for them was Jim McDougal, whom Hale had met only casually years ago as a student in the Young Democrats but who now questioned Hale intently about how much the small business investment company could lend him. Soon after, the two of them met again and McDougal told him engagingly, "We're going to need your help," adding in words David Hale later readily recalled, "We need to clean up some members of the political family. How much money have you got in your SBIC?"

True to his reputation, Hale was eager to accommodate the more prepossessing and powerfully connected McDougal. He duly began to prepare a series of loans. One was for a Madison venture on rocky, fog-shrouded Campobello Island, off the coast of Maine, the site of Franklin Roosevelt's summer home, which reverential Democrat McDougal thought a natural draw; he himself had already sunk nearly $4 million into bleak, tide-stranded home lots that would prove unmarketable. Another loan was to go to former Clinton gubernatorial aide Stephen Smith, reportedly to pay back Smith's own loan from Madison that had earlier drawn the attention of federal regulators. The paperwork on the loans was to absorb Hale through the holidays and into 1986. But only days before Christmas he got impressive new evidence of the rank and importance of the "political family." Waiting for a ride at the state capitol, Hale was surprised to be approached by Bill Clinton himself, whom he knew only slightly. "Are you going to be able to help Jim and me out?" the governor asked him matter-of-factly. "We're working on it," Hale answered agreeably, and Clinton smiled broadly and moved on without saying more.

Within weeks—by Hale's account, sometime in late February 1986—he was to meet Clinton again for a far more intimate and revealing exchange on the money. "Jim McDougal asked if I could meet with the governor at Castle Grande after work," the judge remembered. Hale found McDougal's trademark green Jaguar parked in front of the development's real estate office and, inside, a casually dressed Clinton and McDougal engrossed in a conversation about Frank White's running again in 1986. Eventually turning to Hale, McDougal asked him directly for a $150,000 SBIC loan—"for Clinton's benefit," according to one account of the meeting—to be channeled through one of the Madison subsidiaries run by Susan McDougal. "Jim said, 'We'll put it in Susan's advertising company,' " Hale recalled. "My name can't show up anywhere," Clinton had interjected. "We've already taken care of that," McDougal shot back, though he gave no more explanation and the governor did not ask. "What he meant I don't know," Hale said afterward.

When Hale asked what security should be listed on the routine federal loan documents Clinton offered that he and the McDougals owned property in Marion County, meaning Whitewater. But even the tractable Hale balked at the development as too remote and problematic to list as collateral. "That's not the end of the world, but you can see it from there," he later said of the isolated lots. At any rate, with or without creditable security, the loan would go forward. After scarcely twenty minutes Hale left, agreeing to provide the federal money. As he walked out, the two partners and old friends went back to talking avidly about money and politics, as if Hale and his promised funds had been only a brief diversion.

Once more, within only days McDougal called Hale about the requested loan for Clinton, now suddenly asking him to double the amount to $300,000. Hale agreed yet again. On April 3, 1986, ostensibly on the basis that the federal funds were going to a "disadvantaged" businesswoman and at a moment when the McDougals had a net worth of over $2 million, David Hale made out Capital Management check number 458 for $300,000, payable to "Susan H. McDougal, d/b/a [doing business as] Master Marketing." Promptly deposited without endorsement, the check would be stamped, "Guaranteed by Madison Guaranty Savings and Loan Little Rock."

What happened to the money next would be disputed. Of one fact at least there was no doubt: the government loan was never repaid. Part of nearly $800,000 overall that Hale's federally financed company would give a tottering Madison Guaranty and its related companies, the check to Susan McDougal turned out to be typical of the bustling manipulation of public money in provincial Little Rock. A later General Accounting Office study found that Hale had passed out federal funds to more than a dozen businesses that he secretly controlled. Still other records from 1985–86 showed Hale himself receiving some $825,000 in loans from the same Madison Guaranty his SBIC was propping up. They had enabled the savings and loan and the investment company to "clean up" their books, Hale later told federal investigators. Even when the parties were confronted with criminal indictments, there was a familiar Arkansas artlessness about what they had done, about what had been utterly natural and expected. "I've been involved in politics with these people since I was eighteen years old," David Hale once explained, as if it were self-evident. "They needed help and I helped them."

By the time Hale wrote his $300,000 check for the "political family," Jim McDougal's string at Madison was finally running out, and there were already predictable strains between the beleaguered speculator and his partner the governor. In the first week of March, days after the meeting at Castle Grande and hardly a month before the loan, Clinton intervened personally with the state Health Department when McDougal complained about a departmental ruling routinely requiring him to install a sewage system before building his Maple Creek housing development south of Little Rock. McDougal had planned to put cheaper septic tanks on hundreds of lots at Maple Creek. But officials refused to waive the common standards of public safety, and at the beginning of March a furious McDougal called Clinton, who immediately set up and agreed to attend himself a face-to-face meeting on March 5 between his patron and the director and deputy director of the department.

The session began with the governor gently urging the exemptions and the two summoned officials feeling unmistakable political pressure. "They went expecting to be called on the carpet Clinton-style, a nice slick shaft to do the deal," said one of their aides. "At the outset of the meeting," a summary of an official report noted, "Clinton talked as if he wanted to grant McDougal's wish." Then, as the Health Department director and his deputy repeated their misgivings, McDougal lost his temper in a wild outburst, with what one account termed "abusive behavior" toward the officials. It was the kind of cowing that had succeeded before in the Gold Mine Springs case and others, albeit more indirectly or discreetly. Now the same manner was an obvious embarrassment to Clinton, who "turned red in the face," as the summary of the official report described him, and "explod[ed] in anger" himself. The meeting broke up without a resolution, and after a still agitated McDougal had left, Clinton "apologized" to the officials, as one of them told federal investigators, "for the way his friend had talked to them." Eventually the state approved only twenty Maple Creek lots for septic tanks, McDougal never receiving the favor he had seemed about to get so routinely from Bill Clinton in the first moments of the March 5 meeting. It was the beginning of a swift series of defeats for him, though the partnership with Bill Clinton endured.

That same March—barely nine months after Hillary Clinton and Rose assured Beverly Bassett that Madison was free of its old problems and safe for new investors and depositors—Federal Home Loan Bank Board auditors issued a seventy-eight-page confidential audit that exposed the starkly different reality. It was a catalog of unrelieved abuse, accounting discrepancies, and missing records. "Management blatantly disregarded numerous regulations," the examiners concluded. "The problems discussed in this report (conflicts of interest, high-risk land developments, poor asset quality, rapid growth, inadequate income and net worth, low liquidity, securities speculation, excessive compensation and poor records and controls) constitute a significant threat to the continued existence of the Institution." Nowhere did this first legitimate audit of Madison specifically mention Whitewater or the Clintons, though the development and their relationship with the McDougals were typical of the way the bank had been used. If Whitewater records at Madison were among those now missing—as many of Whitewater's own records would be later—the recklessness and collapse charted in the federal audit was still clear enough. The point of both Madison Guaranty and Whitewater, Arkansas old-timers would say, was always in plain sight. What the Clintons and McDougals had done was not somehow secreted within the system—it *was* the system.

Events now moved rapidly. In the spring of 1986, confronted with the devastating federal audit, Beverly Bassett began talks with federal officials about the need to remove McDougal from control of Madison. That June, Federal Home Loan Bank Board examiners paid a visit to the Quapaw headquarters and, according to one report, were incensed to see the McDougals' Jaguars pulled up in executive spaces in the employee parking lot. "Let's close the place down," one auditor muttered to a colleague.

Regulators from both the FHLBB and an already struggling Federal Savings and Loan Insurance Corporation soon decided to do just that. On July 11, 1986, Bassett and members of her staff flew to Dallas to see their federal counterparts for an intercession with Madison's board minus McDougal. In what Bassett herself remembered as a "long and confrontational meeting," the thrift's board and lawyers—pointedly not including Hillary Clinton at this stage of reckoning—"appeared stunned" at the charges of exploitation but did not oppose the cease and desist order now backed by both Arkansas and federal authorities, removing McDougal and leaving the debauched savings and loan effectively in state custody until federal tax money could be found to pay its betrayed depositors. Even with a governor he had done so much to reelect and enrich and a securities director whose appointment he helped secure, Jim McDougal was now too public a liability. In the end, like so many political patrons who become an embarrassment, he was alone.

For all that, however, there were signs that Bill Clinton shared McDougal's rage over at least some of the events of that summer, just as he shared their still entangling financial interests. At the same moment in July 1986 as officials were at last moving against Diamond Jim, David Hale was shopping at the University Plaza Mall on the booming west side of Little Rock when the governor of the state literally came running up to him. Bill Clinton's mood was obvious. "You could tell he was perturbed or upset," the judge remembered. "Have you heard what that fucking whore Susan has done?" Clinton blurted out. But before Hale could reply the agitated governor hurried away as abruptly as he came. The implication in approaching Hale with such unconcealed disgust was clearly that the matter was somehow related to the $300,000 loan funneled through Susan McDougal. But exactly what she had done—whether crossing Clinton and McDougal on the money or some other betrayal or blunder—was never clear to Hale.

On October 10, 1986, scarcely three months after McDougal's forced removal from Madison Guaranty, the Clintons joined him in yet another land speculation. Under the aegis of the Whitewater Development Corporation, it was known as Lorrance Heights, some 810 acres owned by International Paper a dozen miles south of Little Rock, land largely covered by a raw softwood forest that had proven uneconomical for the timber giant to cut. With a flourish, the Whitewater partners now bought the parcel from International Paper for more than half a million dollars, paying $80,000 down with another $30,000 due in sixty days and a mortgage of $440,000 held by the corporation over a six-year term.

Afterward there would be charges that the $110,000 came from Hale's $300,000 loan to the "political family" through Susan McDougal. While Susan was now still a legal partner in the Lorrance Heights venture, the mangled records of Whitewater and Madison would not make clear how the major new purchase related to Clinton's fury at the shopping mall only weeks before. There were unanswered questions as well about the coincidence of the purchase and a special $22 million tax concession to International Paper that Governor Clinton had recently steered through the legislature, though there seemed no obvious favor in the deal, the Clintons and McDougals paying "well over the market price," as an International Paper executive later told a reporter. In any case, at the moment of the International Paper purchase the partners were said to have much the same ambitious plans they had once held out for the land on the White River, intending to develop and market lots for both year-round homes and vacation houses.

Only sixty days later, in still more fast shuffling, McDougal suddenly transferred Lorrance Heights to his old speculative entity, the Great Southern Land Company. With this shift, apparently made without the legal signatures of the Whitewater partners in the mansion, the Clintons seem to have lost their ownership of the new property at a stroke—and along with it their own presumed $55,000 share of the down payment as well as their $220,000 liability on one-half of the mortgage note held by the timber corporation. Yet there was no question that the Clintons knew about the transaction and benefited from it. On their tax returns for 1986, as investigative reporter Martin Gross reported, the governor and his wife duly deducted $10,131 for interest paid to the Great Southern Land Company.

McDougal and Great Southern did not fare so well. This time it was the speculator who could not make the mortgage payments, and two years later, in the fall of 1988, International Paper moved to foreclose. The corporation secured a $514,000 court judgment against McDougal and later resold the Lorrance Heights property to another developer at an overall profit. "Taste of their own medicine for manhandling all those old folks in Whitewater," a Little Rock lawyer and former Clinton aide would say afterward, "except by that time Bill and Hillary were off of old Jim and on to their next best friends."

◆ ◆ ◆

In November 1988 Hillary Clinton wrote a formal letter to the close friends she had once seen so often, asking them for Whitewater records and for power of attorney so as to sell off remaining property and "get all that behind us by the end of the year." According to Susan McDougal's later account, she sent to the governor's mansion "every sheet of paper . . . every file I had, all the purchase agreements, copies of the deeds, all monthly payments by customers, all checks written by the corporation, all correspondence."

By 1989, facing a federal indictment in one of his land schemes, McDougal himself was nearly destitute and begging the governor for help. But Clinton gave his old friend no help and McDougal continued to face his ordeal without his longtime ally. At his trial in the summer of 1990 on eight counts of bank fraud and conspiracy, prosecutors concentrated on two tangled land sales by a Madison subsidiary. With McDougal's attorney invoking his frail mental state as part of the defense and contending mismanagement rather than conspiracy, the speculator was acquitted of all charges when the jury deadlocked, though one of his associates was convicted of a related crime and served a short term in prison. For the moment, it was to be the only legal or public reckoning. "His involvement with many of the state's most prominent politicians was but a footnote in the resulting stories," Meredith Oakley noted long afterward.

With his old partner running for president and with the appearance of the first national reports on Whitewater, by the *New York Times*'s Jeff Gerth, McDougal reappeared briefly during the campaign for a tape-recorded conversation with Clinton's old Republican rival Sheffield Nelson, making dark allusions to some Clinton tax fraud and generally speaking as a man who knew far more than he had ever divulged, even in his own trial defense. In a transcript later made public by the GOP, he would tell Nelson that the Clintons never paid him interest for the Whitewater mortgage though the First Couple had deducted several thousands of dollars in such payments from their taxes. One loan repayment in particular McDougal claimed was made by the corporation and thus was "overreflected on their income taxes." At another stage in the transcript McDougal asked pointedly about the "statute of limitations for tax fraud" and insisted to Nelson that "every bit" of money the Clintons put into Whitewater was "income they didn't report." With that, however, the speculator disappeared again from public ken, going off to live in a trailer in Arkadelphia as his former partners went to the White House.

He returned in the first months of 1994, as Whitewater suddenly became the object of renewed attention. His head shaven, Diamond Jim was again a local celebrity of sorts, running once more for Congress, selling old Whitewater deeds as souvenirs to raise money, variously contradicting or muddling previous statements about his now-famous partners and their land deal, and leaving "some with the impression," observed *USA Today,* "that [he'd] gone slightly around the bend." At least the fresh notoriety seemed to improve his social standing in Arkansas. "I'm treated," McDougal told the press, "with a deference and delicacy reserved for wounded Confederate officers."

If somewhat more dignified, the Clintons' own subsequent accounting of Whitewater could seem equally bedeviled. Stories multiplied about the First Couple's "losses" in the development, from the $69,000 claimed in a "report" commissioned by the presidential campaign to as much as $88,000 and as little as $46,636 in later figures. But several of the checks they counted as "losses" turned out, as McDougal had suggested to Nelson, to have been repayments of loans from Whitewater, Inc. to begin with, and the initial attempts at accounting sank into the mire of discrepancies that came of Whitewater's chaotic bookkeeping, delinquent tax returns, and convoluted, overdrawn, inexplicably revived accounts at Madison Guaranty. When House Banking Committee investigators did their own calculations of the Clintons' balance sheet on the investment—their real-dollar gains from interest deductions, their capital gain on the model house on Lot 13 and other proceeds, their share of the known injections of capital into Whitewater from Madison, the corporate repayments of their personal loans, the McDougal retainer for Hillary and Rose, their half of the alleged diversion of the Hale loan for the Lorrance Heights purchase—the total profit was over $150,000, and more than $100,000, even subtracting the latest White House "loss" figures. In contrast, judging only from the surviving and uncontested records, the McDougals seemed to have paid out personally some $268,000, most of it after they took over Madison Guaranty, and ended up officially "losing" nearly $100,000 in the supposedly equal partnership.

"People knew," onetime *Arkansas Gazette* editor Max Brantley would say about the Clintons' involvement in Whitewater. Yet only a handful had been knowledgeable about even part of the details, and no one— least of all, it seemed, the Little Rock press—had seen or cared to discover the larger character of what was happening at Madison and related companies like Whitewater Estates. In Arkansas and Washington after 1993, it was possible to minimize and dismiss, if not simply justify, the history. The affair was said to be less serious because Madison Guaranty was so small an institution, as if $70 million were now minor or as if the abuses might somehow have been different or have never happened at all if the available money and the ultimate public toll had been larger. The Clintons were said to have continued in their relationship with the McDougals only because it would have been a political embarrassment to leave and face the resulting questions, as if the meaning of their staying, and the implicit assumption that Whitewater would remain unexplored and thus unembarrassing as they rose higher in public trust and responsibility, were not far more telling. Whitewater was said by one editorial writer to be "not a crippling scandal" in itself, as if in its sheer banality it had not been representative of an ethic that haunted a state and a nation.

"When the ripoff artists looted our S & Ls, the president was silent," Bill Clinton would say accurately enough of George Bush in his 1991 announcement of his presidential candidacy. Few saw the bitter bipartisan irony at the moment. Beyond the standard political hypocrisy, it was more of what the *New York Times* came by 1994 to call "the Arkansas Defense."

"Shoulda, coulda, woulda," Hillary was to say at a 1994 White House press conference in answer to a question about why the otherwise studious Clintons had never been curious about the money paying off their Whitewater mortgage or about other unaccountable infusions of capital into their development. "If you know that your mortgages are being paid, but you aren't putting money into the venture, and you also know the venture isn't cash flowing, wouldn't you question the source of the funds being used to your benefit? Would you just assume that your partner was making those multithousand-dollar payments out of the goodness of his heart?" a federal banking investigator later bluntly asked her superiors in an internal RTC memorandum. "Wouldn't you wonder even more if you knew that your business partner's main source of income, an S & L, was in serious financial difficulty, which by 1985 was fairly common knowledge?" To those questions and more the only White House reply would be the First Lady's coy joke.

Diamond Jim and Hot Pants McDougal might have seemed caricatures of the Clinton-era boom in Little Rock. But their collapse and ostracism were hardly typical among the monied interests backing Bill Clinton. And the hundreds of thousands of dollars swirling around them in depositors' money and federal funds could seem petty compared to the flourishing traffic, legal and illegal, in other quarters of the capital and state over the same period. For all the maneuvering, Whitewater, McDougal, and Madison did not amount to much in the Clintons' overall fortunes either. The couple's effective gain from other sources, from private dealings, public perquisites, and political loans and contributions—from a world that included the grander, more enduring patrons as well as the McDougals—was well over a million dollars by the end of the decade.

Not even McDougal's buccaneering practices, which continued to intrigue a series of investigators and prosecutors, could approach a multibillion-dollar gunrunning and drug smuggling operation based only a few hours' drive from Madison Guaranty or the multimillions cascading out of the bond business and out of corporate expansions and exemptions crafted only blocks away in Little Rock. However belated and costly, there had been some accountability for Jim McDougal in the end, at least a creaking framework of regulations that eventually curbed his run. In those other, far more lucrative and formidable quarters, the still larger collusions seemed to go on without limits, without rules. Whitewater and its kindred abuses would be relatively minor after all.

· 19 ·

Little Rock and Mena
"A World Nearly Devoid of Rules"

In the spring of 1982 a lone small plane began its approach to an obscure airport in the secluded mountains of western Arkansas. At the controls was Adler Berriman "Barry" Seal, old Thunder Thighs, as close friends knew him, a renegade pilot and freelance intelligence agent who had become a major drug smuggler and gunrunner in the netherworld where government and crime were joined.

The scene below him was picturesque, with its own vivid history. Circled about the airport, as if standing guard against the outside world, was the dark emerald ridgeline of the Ouachita range. To the northwest rose Rich Mountain, one of Arkansas's highest peaks, often wreathed in lowering clouds and a thick gray fog. The densely forested slopes and valleys had long been a haven for renegades, a rendezvous for Civil War guerrillas and border bandits in the nineteenth century and, more recently, for dealers in moonshine and red-dirt marijuana.

Nestled against the low mountains was the small county seat of Mena, named for Queen Wilhelmina by the Dutch investors who financed the local railroad. About 160 miles west of Little Rock and 80 miles south of Fort Smith, the only sizable settlement in the remote area near the Arkansas-Oklahoma line, Mena had its political lore as well, including speeches at the old city hall by William Jennings Bryan, Carry Nation, and Huey Long in his 1932 campaign for Hattie Caraway. The region was known for its inhabitants' stony individualism. Nearby was the site of the former Commonwealth College, where adherents of the American Co-operative Movement had tried to teach

389

more benign, collaborative methods of business and agriculture, only to be charged under Arkansas statutes with fostering "anarchy" and to see the school seized and sold by the Mena justice of the peace. By the 1980s that blighted history seemed long past. Like most of the rest of small-town Arkansas, the community of five thousand appeared settled into slightly shabby obscurity, its chief distinction the local high school team. "Home of the Bearcats," Mena announced itself on the main highway.

A few miles out the same road, however, was a very different point of interest. With its lengthy runway and cavernous hangars designed for large, continental-range aircraft, Intermountain Regional Airport was obviously no ordinary rural landing field. The facility was a state-of-the-art installation known in select circles for rapid aircraft rehabilitation and maintenance, for providing a stopover point for discreet official flights between military bases or other obscure airports, and, not least, for its cryptic government and private customers, who quietly housed and serviced their planes there and of whom Barry Seal was now the latest.

The smuggler would prove by far the most successful of the Ouachita outlaws. His well-connected and officially protected smuggling operation based at Mena accounted for billions in drugs and arms from 1982 until his murder four years later. Yet Seal belonged to the political history of the place as well. The very name of the small town would become synonymous not only with a vast criminal traffic but also with a larger dark side of American politics, with links far beyond western Arkansas to Little Rock, the nation, the world—and with collusion and cover-up implicating three US presidents, including Bill Clinton.

Almost from the beginning of the Clinton presidency stories circulated about what had happened around Mena a decade before. Popularized on a videotape produced and widely distributed by anti-Clinton elements, the sometimes wild, unsupported charges joined an underground right-wing litany of alleged evil in the Democratic president's past, despite the fact that events at Mena also incriminated Republican presidents. At the same time, the larger media—with the notable exceptions of the *Wall Street Journal* and a lone report on CBS News— ignored or even ridiculed the subject, as if partisan exaggeration, or simply the intimidating implications of the story, absolved journalists of what could and should be known. Yet the truth behind the extremes of hyperbole and negligence was that many of the imputed crimes of Mena were all too real, documented in state police files and in federal law enforcement records from the IRS, the FBI, and other agencies, in

investigative reporting by alternative and local journalists, substantiated eyewitness testimony, and not least by some two thousand personal papers of Seal himself—from the smuggler's tax returns, sworn
testimony, and tape-recorded conversations to his letters, codes, dia-
ries, and scrawled notes. Even that mass of evidence was only the start
of uncovering a hidden history. But by standards of scholarship as well
as of journalism, much of what had gone on around Mena, Arkansas,
in the 1980s was beyond doubt.

◆ ◆ ◆

Barry Seal flew into western Arkansas in 1982 with a storied past. "Full
of fun, full of folly," as his hometown Baton Rouge high school captioned him, he was a man of talents beneath a beguiling surface—an
astute businessman and intriguer of defiant, almost playful cunning,
with a passion for beautiful women and for aircraft of any description.
"He didn't fly an airplane," said one account, "he wore it like a suit of
clothes." At twenty-six Seal had been one of the youngest command
pilots in the history of Trans World Airlines. Seven years later, in 1972,
he lost his TWA job when he was caught by US Customs trying to
smuggle seven tons of plastic explosives to anti-Castro Cubans in Mexico. The case was quietly dropped on the pretext of "national security." Before TWA, he had been involved in the 1960s with the US
Army Special Forces and had already established contacts with the
Central Intelligence Agency, some of whose underworld hirelings were
embroiled in the Cuban explosives plot.

Within four years after being fired from TWA, Seal was a successful
aircraft "broker," the mask for a flourishing traffic in guns, marijuana,
cocaine, and heroin. By the late 1970s he had his own cadre of pilots
and mechanics, a web of criminal and corrupt official contacts from
the United States to South America, and ongoing ties to the CIA and
others in the intelligence bureaucracy. His personal records showed
him a contract CIA operative both before and during his years of drug
running in Mena in the 1980s.

It was a role he played with flair, brazenly attending the trials of
fellow smugglers to take notes on technique, talking casually to relatives about covertly working for one arm of government while defying
others. At home he could be the devoted family man, taking snapshots
of his children frolicking in piles of cash and lavishing attention on his
beautiful and devoted wife, Debbie, while on the road he was a swag-
gering rogue running a multibillion-dollar international business with
a pager and rolls of quarters, speaking in code from random pay

phones. "One must find the perfect balance between his career and personal life in order to be perfectly happy and keep his loved ones content," he noted in a diary as if he were one more harried professional. Forty-three when he shifted his base from Louisiana to Arkansas in 1982, Seal was already a legend in the cocaine trade, a figure of more than 250 pounds known to Latin cohorts as El Gordo, the Fat Man with muttonchop sideburns who devoured candy bars but did not smoke, drink, or take drugs and who moved easily between governments and the drug lords they claimed to hunt.

Much of the work Seal performed for the CIA—and also for the Pentagon's Defense Intelligence Agency, where coded records reportedly showed him on the payroll beginning in 1982—would be buried in Washington secrecy. What he did while based at Mena, however, was plain from his papers and other sources, including his own videotapes. His drug runs followed an almost invariable routine. After being flown in from Latin America, duffel bags packed with cocaine were methodically lashed together—loads averaging three hundred pounds of cocaine and worth at least tens of millions of dollars—and parachuted with practiced precision onto specially cleared remote sites in Arkansas and elsewhere in the South, there to be picked up by helicopter or other means and carried on within a distribution system that included large trucks and railways. Seal was "only the transport" into the United States, the smuggler would remind his government handlers, pointing to the extensive network of distribution run and tended by a southern-based crime family, Latin suppliers, corrupted officials, and others in the chain who took over in Arkansas and elsewhere after his emptied planes headed home to Mena.

Though he flew duffel bags of cocaine into Intermountain Regional only occasionally, Seal spent thousands at the airport to house, maintain, and specially equip his aircraft with features like added fuel bladders and modified cargo doors for drug drops. When not there himself he was in constant contact with his Arkansas base. In one brazen act Seal brought drug cartel kingpin Jorge Ochoa to Arkansas to show off his operation. In the years that Seal's traffic was based in Mena it brought tons of cocaine and heroin to American cities, affecting an incalculable number of lives. A partial estimate, Louisiana's attorney general informed Attorney General Edwin Meese in 1986, suggested that Seal had "smuggled [drugs worth] between $3 billion and $5 billion into the US."

Only relatively small change from the traffic spilled into western Arkansas, though with resounding impact. Secretaries at Intermountain Regional later told an IRS agent that, after some Seal flights, "there would be stacks of cash to be taken to the bank and laundered." Couriers were told to buy cashier's checks, each just under $10,000 to avoid federal reporting. "The bank officer went down the teller lines," is how one witness described what happened when an airport employee brought a bag of money into a nearby bank, "handing out the stacks of $1,000 bills and got the cashier's checks."

For years Mena buzzed with stories of shoeboxes and suitcases stuffed with cash. In 1982–83, according to IRS and state police calculations, hundreds of thousands washed through local banks, a minor fraction of the profits taken from Seal's Mena runs (most of the money was laundered elsewhere). Law enforcement officials believed it was at least a portion of the Mena-related cash that showed up in later IRS monitoring of financial institutions in Arkansas, marking the otherwise impoverished state as what agents called a "magnet" for drug-money laundering, with telltale rates of savings and cash transactions far higher than levels supported by the legitimate economy. The obscure town in the Ouachitas, it turned out, was far more than the home of the Bearcats. By the sheer magnitude of the drugs and money its flights generated, tiny Mena, Arkansas, became in the 1980s one of the world centers of the narcotics trade and the base of what many believed was the single-largest cocaine-smuggling operation in US history.

But drugs were only one commodity in a bustling commerce. Especially after the spring of 1983, Seal's flights to Latin America to pick up cocaine commonly carried arms for the Contra rebels fighting to overthrow the Sandinista regime in Nicaragua. Part of what was later exposed as the Iran-Contra affair, they were one channel of the CIA and the Reagan White House's efforts to evade congressional restrictions, including the Boland amendment, that went into full effect in the autumn of 1984. Though major, the Arkansas precincts of Iran-Contra remained unexplored in the circumscribed investigations by both Congress and the independent counsel.

Along with arms pouring into the Mena airport from US arsenals and the private market, nationally and internationally, weapons bound for the Contras also came from local Arkansas sources, including a Fayetteville gunsmith named William Holmes, who had been crafting weapons for the CIA since the mid-1950s and now produced for the agency a special order of 250 automatic pistols with silencers. Under oath he later told a federal court that he was taken to Mena twice to meet Barry Seal, who paid for some special orders in cash. Though

Holmes dealt with other CIA agents, too, he regarded Seal as "the ramrod of the Mena gun deal." Not long after Seal's operation began, the terrain around Mena, similar to the landscapes in Nicaragua, became a CIA training ground for Contra guerrillas and pilots. Like the money laundering, the flow of weapons and the covert maneuvers supplied Mena with still more whispered stories, of crates of arms unloaded from unmarked black trucks, of Spanish-speaking pilots who flew practice runs in and out of the airport, of state game wardens in the backwoods who came upon contingents of foreigners in camouflage and armed with automatic weapons; of caches of weapons secreted in highway culverts and mysterious nighttime road and air traffic around neighboring Nella.

Though the CIA and other intelligence agencies routinely denied responsibility for Seal and Mena, security for the operation was generally careless; cover-up from Arkansas to Washington seemed taken for granted. There was a paper trail of federal aircraft registrations and outfittings. Some of Seal's fleet, which included a Lear jet, helicopters, and former US military transports, had been previously owned by Air America, Inc., widely reported to be a CIA proprietary company. Another firm linked to Air America outfitted Seal's planes with avionics. Between March and December 1982, according to law enforcement records, Seal fitted nine of his aircraft with the latest electronic equipment, paying the $750,000 bill in cash. Senior law enforcement officials happening onto his tracks in Arkansas were quickly waved off. "Joe [name deleted] works for Seal and cannot be touched because Seal works for the CIA," a customs official noted during an investigation into Arkansas drug trafficking in the early 1980s. "Look, we're told not to touch anything that has Barry Seal's name on it," another ranking federal agent told a colleague, "just to let it go."

At the same time, customs officers and others watched the Mena contraband expand far beyond the Contras to include the export of munitions to Bolivia, Argentina, Peru, and Brazil—a hugely lucrative black market in arms variously called the Southern Tier or Southern Arc. By any name, intelligence sources described it as a CIA operation, often under cover of bogus front companies, though occasionally with the knowledge of executives and workers in "legitimate" corporations providing spare parts. The smuggling was known to have made millions in criminal profits for CIA rogue operations, mainly from what one former air force intelligence officer called the "clockwork" transshipment of weapons and other contraband from "meticulously maintained" rural airports in Arkansas, Mississippi, Kentucky, Alabama,

Louisiana, Florida, and Arizona. According to several official sources, Mena was not only the base for Seal's traffic in guns and drugs but also a hub in this clandestine network of government crime.

Like the Seal runs, Southern Tier flights came and went with utter immunity, protected or "fixed," as one law enforcement agent called them, by the collusion of US intelligence and other agencies under the guise of "national security." The most telling evidence in Seal's own thick files would be what was so starkly missing. In hundreds of documents revealing fastidious planning—Seal's videotapes even recorded him rehearsing every step in the pinpoint drop of loads of cocaine, down to the seconds required to roll the loads to the door of the plane—there was no evidence of concern for cross-border security or how the narcotics were brought into the country. Engaged in one of the major crimes of the century, neither he nor his accomplices showed the slightest worry about being caught. The shadow of official complicity and cover-up was unmistakable in Seal's papers. In 1996, a former Seal associate would testify to congressional investigators how the operation had been provided CIA "security" for flights in and out of the US, including a highly classified encoding device to evade air defense and surveillance measures.

Those who met Seal in Mena in the fall of 1983 found him at the zenith of his influence. He was already a businessman of note in Arkansas, with an address book listing some of the state's well-known names, and contacts in Little Rock's banks and brokerage houses, and what a fellow CIA operative called a "night depository" for bags of cash dropped from "green flights" onto the ranch of a politically and financially prominent Arkansas family. An associate, a pilot who came with Seal from Louisiana in 1982, would later testify about their first weeks in Arkansas, when they were introduced to pivotal figures in state government and business. "Barry Seal knew them all, and they knew him, the Clinton machine," he remembered. "There was no limit on cooperation by the good ole boys," a federal agent would say of Seal's Arkansas friends.

At the height of his Mena operation, Seal made daily deposits of $50,000 or more, using a Caribbean bank as well as financial institutions in Arkansas and Florida. He casually admitted to federal agents that he took in $75 million in the early 1980s, and under court questioning said he made at least $25 million in 1981 alone. A posthumous tax assessment by the IRS—which officially noted his "C.I.A.-D.E.A. employment" and duly exempted him from taxes on some of his government "income" for the years 1984–85—would show Seal's estate owing $86 million in back taxes on his earnings in Mena in 1982 and 1983. Far from entertaining thoughts of paying taxes, Seal detailed in his private papers his own plans for the money, including setting up a Caribbean bank and dozens of companies, all using the name Royale—from a television network, casino, and pharmaceuticals firm to a Royale Arabian horse farm.

By 1984, the Seal operation began to unravel. While the Mena traffic flourished, he was charged by elements of the Drug Enforcement Agency and federal prosecutors—a group of agents and government lawyers not compromised in the Arkansas operation—for trafficking in Quaaludes. Suddenly facing a prosecution and prison sentence his intelligence patrons either could not or would not suppress, he scrambled to make his own deal. With typical aplomb ("Barry was always smarter than most government folks he dealt with," said an associate), he flew to Washington at one point to dicker with the staff of Vice President George Bush. By the spring of 1984, Seal was DEA informant number SGI-84-0028, working as an $800,000-a-year double agent in an elaborate sting operation against the Medellin cartel in Colombia and individuals in the Nicaraguan regime who had been dipping into the drug trade themselves.

The same elements of the US government involved in Mena were now eager, for political advantage, to expose the Sandinistas in drug dealing. That summer of 1984, CIA cameras hidden in his plane, Seal made the incriminating flights to Medellin and then Managua, only to have the case against the drug lords and his own life jeopardized when the Reagan administration gleefully leaked the evidence of Sandinista involvement, including the smuggler's own film, to the *Washington Times*. In a scribbled note, Barry Seal recorded with knowing cynicism the malignant juncture of politics and crime: "Government misconduct," he wrote, and then of himself, "Operate in a world nearly devoid of rules and record keeping."

In February 1985 Emile Camp, later identified as a member of a Louisiana organized crime family, one of Seal's expert pilots and the only witness to many of his more significant transactions with both drug lords and US intelligence agents, was killed—some thought murdered—when his elaborately equipped Mena-bound Seneca unaccountably ran out of gas on a routine approach and slammed into the Ouachita Mountains. The flight was carrying the original logs of one of Seal's other planes, a Vietnam-era C-123K Seal had christened the *Fat Lady;* these were missing when the wreckage was discovered. Meanwhile Seal himself was becoming a star witness for the US government against his old Colombian associates. Though still cocky, he was now becoming increasingly anxious about his own safety. As if personal publicity could offer a shield, he confessed a few crimes to local Arkansas investigators in a recorded interview and even agreed to an in-law's request that he cooperate in a documentary on his operations for a Louisiana television station. Nevertheless, he withheld the secrets of wider and higher official complicity in Arkansas. The Mena traffic remained relentless. "Every time Berri [*sic*] Seal flies a load of dope for the U.S. Govt.," one local law enforcement officer noted in a log on August 27, 1985, "he flies two for himself." The bargain seemed plain: "Seal was flying weapons to central and south America," an agent noted, recording what "was believed" within the DEA. "In return he is allowed to smuggle what he wants back into the United States."

By the summer of 1985 Seal's usefulness to the government had expired, and a scapegoat for the illegal operation in Mena was imperative. That same year the CIA abandoned him, refusing even to acknowledge in camera to a federal judge his role in the Sandinista sting, much less his long and seamy clandestine service. In a tangled plea bargain on the old Quaalude charges, a bitterly defiant Seal, still holding onto his Mena secrets and still contemplating a profitable return to Arkansas, found himself on a court-ordered six months' sentence to a Salvation Army halfway house in Baton Rouge. It was there that assassins found him alone in his trademark white Cadillac on a wet February night in 1986. With remarkable dispatch and no further inquiry a group of Colombians, said to be working for Medellin, were arrested and sentenced to life. That same winter President Reagan went on nationwide television to denounce the Sandinistas as drug runners, using Seal's covert film to demonstrate his outrage. The Seal family buried Barry in Baton Rouge with a Snickers bar, his telephone pager, and a roll of quarters, under the ironic epitaph he had dictated for himself—"A rebel adventurer the likes of whom in previous days made America great."

◆ ◆ ◆

Only hours before his gangland-style assassination, Seal had been making his habitual calls to Mena. After the killing, activities in the Ouachitas continued unabated, proving the operation went far beyond a lone smuggler. In October 1986 the *Fat Lady* was shot down over Nicaragua with a load of arms for the Contras. In the wreckage was the body of copilot Wallace "Buzz" Sawyer, a native of western Arkansas; detailed records on board linked *Fat Lady* to Seal and Area 51, a secret nuclear weapons facility and CIA base in Nevada. It would be the head-line-making confession of the *Fat Lady*'s lone survivor, Eugene Hasenfus, that would hasten a partial public airing of the Iran-Contra affair. Though the Mena operation remained largely concealed in the ensuing exposé, records showed that there had been several calls around the time of the *Fat Lady*'s ill-fated mission from one of the CIA conspirators in Iran-Contra to Vice President Bush's office in Washington and to operatives in western Arkansas.

"After the Hasenfus plane was shot down, you couldn't find a soul around Mena," remembered William Holmes, who now found that the CIA refused to pay him, reneging also on one of the last gun orders. The hiatus at Intermountain Regional was brief. By early 1987 an Arkansas state police investigator noted "new activity at the [Mena] airport," the appearance of "an Australian business [a company that would be linked with the CIA] and C-130s." At the same moment two FBI agents warned the trooper, as he later testified under oath, that the CIA "had something going on at the Mena airport involving Southern Air Transport [another concern linked to the CIA] . . . and they didn't want us to screw it up."

Since the CIA is expressly prohibited by law from conducting any such operations within the US, the documented actions constituted not only criminal activity by the intelligence agency, but also suborned collusion in it by the FBI. In August 1987, eighteen months after Barry Seal's assassination, an FBI telex advised the Arkansas State Police that "a CIA or DEA operation is taking place at the Mena airport."

In the late 1980s, as intelligence sources eventually confirmed to the *Wall Street Journal,* a secret missile system was tested, CIA planes were repainted, and furtive military exercises were carried out in the Ouachitas. As late as the fall of 1991 an IRS investigative memorandum would record that "the CIA still has ongoing operations out of the Mena, AR airport . . . and that one of the operations at the airport is laundering money." When the story of those more recent activities leaked in 1995, the rival agencies behaved in time-honored Washington manner with the media, the CIA furtively explaining Mena as "a rogue DEA operation," the DEA and FBI offering "no comment."

Months before Seal's murder, two law enforcement officials based in western Arkansas—IRS agent Bill Duncan and state police detective Russell Welch—had begun to compile what a local county prosecutor called a "mammoth investigative file" on the Mena operation. Welch's material became part of an eventual thirty-five-volume, 3,000-page Arkansas State Police archive dealing with the crimes. Working with a US attorney from outside Arkansas, a specialist in the laundering or "churning" of drug proceeds, who prepared a meticulous presentation of the Mena case for a grand jury, including detailed witness lists, bookkeeping records from inside the operation, numerous other documents, and an impressive chain of evidence, Duncan drafted some thirty federal indictments on money laundering and other charges. "Those indictments were a real slam dunk if there ever was one," said someone who saw the extensive evidence.

Then, in a pattern federal and state law enforcement officers saw repeated around the nation under the all-purpose fraudulent claim of "national security," the cases were effectively suppressed. For all their evidence and firsthand investigation, Duncan and Welch were not even called to testify before appropriate grand juries, state or federal. At one point a juror from Mena had happened to see hometown boy Russell Welch, a former teacher, at the courthouse and "told the others that if they wanted to know something about the Mena airport," as one account described it, "they ought to ask that guy out there in the hall." But "to know something about the Mena airport" was not what Washington or Little Rock would want. Though the Reagan-appointed US attorneys for the region at the time, Asa Hutchinson and J. Michael Fitzhugh, repeatedly denied, as Fitzhugh put it, "any pressure in any investigation," Duncan and Welch watched the Mena inquiry systematically quashed and their own careers destroyed as the IRS and state police effectively disavowed their investigations and turned on them. "Somebody outside ordered it shut down," one would say, "and the walls went up." Welch recorded his fear and disillusion in his diary on November 17, 1987: "Should a cop cross over the line and dare to investigate the rich and powerful, he might well prepare himself to become the victim of his own government. . . . The cops are all afraid to tell what they know for fear that they will lose their jobs."

◆ ◆ ◆

After 1987, some nine investigations met similar obstruction. Typical of the quashing at the Washington level, a 1988 General Accounting Office inquiry scarcely started before it was suppressed by the Reagan White House and the National Security Council. A US Senate subcommittee report in December 1988 noted that the Mena cases had been dropped, despite evidence "sufficient for an indictment on money laundering charges," because "the prosecution might have revealed national security information, even though all the crimes which were the focus of the investigation occurred before Seal became a federal informant [in 1984]."

For its part, Arkansas looked back on the crimes it housed with a characteristic mixture of weary resignation and evasion. Mena towns-people knowingly referred to Intermountain Regional as Barry Seal Memorial Airport but nervously scoffed at the story when approached by outsiders and reporters, who seldom went beyond their denials. The airfield was also a major employer in struggling Polk County, and as so often in Arkansas, government contracts of any kind were welcome. "MENA TIRES OF RUMORS," read a 1988 *Gazette* headline over a story dis-missing the worst allegations. Reportedly "ordered" off a Seal investi-gation himself, the local sheriff, A. L. Hadaway, would be typical of many who wanted to forget. "The community where it occurred did not and does not give a damn about what occurred," he wrote causti-cally a few years after Seal's murder. Still, the sheriff himself had taken revealing testimony about the crimes, was said to have resigned in 1986 partly over the drug running, and could also tell a reporter bitterly, "I can arrest an old hillbilly out here with a pound of marijuana and a local judge and jury would send him to the penitentiary. But a guy like Seal flies in and out with hundreds of pounds of cocaine and he stays free."

Columnist Jack Anderson; Rodney Bowers, an independent journal-ist in the *Gazette*'s Fort Smith bureau; and a team at Channel 5 in Fort Smith kept the story alive for a time in 1987. Mena was in John Hammerschmidt's congressional district, but when a local deputy and eyewitness who also worked at Intermountain Regional sent Ham-merschmidt a moving appeal for an investigation of the crimes, the Contra supporter and close friend of George Bush never answered. Meanwhile, vivid if obscure testimony seeped out of the Iran-Contra scandal confirming much of the Mena connection and the Southern Tier, including what fellow smuggler Michael Tolliver and others called Barry Seal's "federal umbrella." Yet neither the national nor the Arkansas press pursued the evidence, and political barriers re-mained impervious in both Washington and Little Rock.

By 1988 Charles Black, a deputy prosecuting attorney for Polk County, viewed the continued federal inaction with mounting dismay. In some desperation he had gone to Governor Bill Clinton to ask for "any available state-level financial aid" to probe "the rather wide array of illegal activities by Barry Seal and accomplices, in Polk County." Clinton, who was also being lobbied by Bill Alexander, a Democratic congressman, to press an investigation, had assured him, Black re-

called, "that he would have someone . . . check on the availability of
financial aid and get word to me." But the prosecutor heard nothing
more from the governor or anyone else in the administration. Years
later there were reports of $25,000 in federal funds earmarked for
Mena—a sum Black thought "tantamount to trying to extinguish a
raging forest fire by spitting on it." Yet even that token money was
somehow mired in the state bureaucracy, and still another chance for
inquiry stifled.

The Alexander and Black approaches to Clinton seemed to set off a
further sequence of cover-ups. As *New York Post* columnist John
Crudele later revealed, it was at that same moment in 1988 that "superiors" in the Arkansas State Police began the destruction of papers in
the Mena file. In sworn testimony, a former staff member of the Arkansas State Police Intelligence Unit would describe a "shredding party"
in which she was ordered to purge the state's Mena files of nearly a
thousand documents, including those referring specifically to Iran-
Contra conspirator Oliver North and Seal associate Terry Reed.

Later, in reaction to a subpoena for the Mena documents by Reed's
lawyer in a federal court case in Kansas, state police officials were said
to have further "dismantled" the already purged archive. From a special locked cabinet at state police headquarters in Little Rock, various
reports about Mena were sent back to the originating federal, state,
county, and local offices—to all appearances a routine action, as if the
case were closed, but one that effectively defied the federal subpoena.
Eventually, from the testimony of those who saw both the shredding
and the dispersal and of others familiar with the documents, the nature of the Arkansas State Police investigation into Mena would be
clear. Never the product of a serious, coherent inquiry beyond Welch's
individual work, the ostensible "file" was a vacuuming up of all the
sightings, suspicions, and related evidence—from state game wardens'
reports to citizens' complaints to FBI telexes—a mass of material held
like hushed witnesses, unquestioned, largely unknown to the public or
any one of the sources.

The issue briefly came to public attention in Arkansas in 1991, almost a decade after Seal flew into Mena. Attorney General Winston
Bryant had made Mena something of a campaign issue against his
Republican opponent, Asa Hutchinson. In May 1990 Bryant forwarded
to Iran-Contra independent counsel Lawrence Walsh a petition signed
by more than a thousand Arkansans imploring Walsh to investigate
Mena and specifically "why no one was prosecuted in Arkansas despite
a mountain of evidence." A month later, spurred by a group at the

University of Arkansas urging further inquiry, Bryant and Congressman Alexander jointly took sworn depositions from agents Duncan, Welch, and others and found anew what Bryant told the press was "credible evidence" of the crimes, with a cover-up to match. "I have never seen a whitewash job like what has been executed in this case . . . a conspiracy of the grandest magnitude," Alexander said gravely to one reporter. He and Bryant then arranged to see Walsh's staff in Washington in September to turn over "two boxes of information," including some of the Duncan-Welch evidence.

Their meeting produced a flurry of publicity in Little Rock and the local media's first general attention to Mena, prompting a September 11, 1991, press conference at the capitol by the state's chief executive. At a moment when the IRS was documenting CIA flights and money laundering still "ongoing" at Mena, and barely a month before he declared his candidacy for president, it would be Bill Clinton's only public statement as governor about the crimes of Mena.

He was "pleased" the issue had been raised "again," Clinton began. The state "did all it could do," he said, to investigate the "allegations" about the Mena airport's being used to run drugs and guns. "I've always felt we never got the whole story there, and obviously if the story was that the DEA was using Barry Seal as a drug informant . . . then they ought to come out and say that because he's dead," he went on without waiting for questions. In any case, the state police had conducted a "very vigorous" investigation several years ago, and the inquiry raised questions "that involved linkages to the federal government."

As governor he had authorized the state police to assure local officials that the state would help pay for a special grand jury, which he expected to be unusually costly because of the need to bring witnesses from out of state. "Nothing ever came of that," he said vaguely of the grand jury, adding that he did not know "whether federal officials pressured the local prosecutor in any way." When county attorneys took no action, the state police turned over their "file" to the US attorney, who convened a grand jury that returned no indictments. There was a state police investigator in the case, Clinton added, apparently referring to Welch, but he had been called to testify "rather late in the proceedings." Moreover, he was asked "a rather limited range of questions," Clinton said, implying that it was not the state's fault that there had been no indictments. After the grand jury failed to act, the "state" gave its "investigative file" to a subcommittee of the House Judiciary Committee.

Asked about Barry Seal's murder, Clinton told the press that he thought the smuggler received "inadequate security," and then added gratuitously that the Seal case "raised all kinds of questions about whether he had any links to the CIA and if he was involved with the Contras . . . and if that backed into the Iran-Contra deal." One observer remembered the assembled television and print reporters scribbling hurriedly, as usual, to take down the governor's flowing and seemingly informed comments. But then, after the remark about the Iran-Contra deal, there was a rustling silence, "as if no one knew what to ask next," the witness remembered. With that, the press conference was over. "CLINTON: STATE DID ALL IT COULD IN MENA CASE," the *Gazette* announced the next day.

No national journalists knowledgeable about Seal, Mena, Iran-Contra, or the drug trade were present, and even the local media had not assigned the press conference to their most informed reporters. At any rate, almost nothing Clinton offered them about Mena was quite true. Only a handful of insiders could appreciate how disingenuous the governor had been. Not only was there never a "vigorous" state police investigation, as Welch and others well knew, but evidence had been effectively suppressed and never adequately presented to a grand jury, and much of it had been shredded or burned. There had been no real help for a state grand jury, and when a congressman and a local prosecutor did ask for help, their request had triggered a further obstruction of justice in Little Rock. And as investigators in both Arkansas and Washington were aware, the state police had never given an "investigative file," in any serious sense of that term, to either prosecutors or a House committee. No such file ever existed, and hundreds of documents had been destroyed or scattered when there seemed the risk of outside scrutiny.

What did a crime so enormous imply about the state's law enforcement, the governor's administration? If there were federal "linkages," political "pressure" on prosecutors, or misconduct in a grand jury, as Clinton seemed to imply, why hadn't he spoken out or acted? Why hadn't the state's chief law enforcement officer shown the same alarm as had his fellow Democrats Bryant and Alexander, whose current charges of crime and cover-up "of the grandest magnitude" he pointedly did not join in raising? And why hadn't Bill Clinton the presidential candidate seized on the issue by attacking the Republicans, including George Bush, for conducting a lawless gunrunning operation that flew tons of cocaine into Arkansas?

Clinton had casually and successfully avoided dates, details, and any discussion of his own role. He would leave the impression that he was knowledgeable about the Mena charges yet knew nothing with authority. Even by the most cynical political standards, it was an extraordinary deception by a future president.

◆ ◆ ◆

Early in 1984, a twenty-nine-year-old Arkansas trooper named Larry Douglass Brown was eagerly applying for work with the Central Intelligence Agency.

Brown was no ordinary state policeman or routine CIA applicant. Known at the mansion and the capitol—and by CIA recruiters—as Bill Clinton's "fair-haired boy," he was the governor's conspicuous favorite among the troopers assigned as his personal bodyguards. Ten years Brown's senior, Clinton treated the avid but less polished young man from Pine Bluff with an avuncular, patronizing warmth, urging on him books from his own collection and engaging in more substantive conversation than the small talk and ingratiating vulgarity he usually reserved for his state police escorts. Yet L.D., as his friends and colleagues knew him, was far more than a protégé. His wife-to-be was Chelsea Clinton's nanny, his future mother-in-law the mansion's administrator. Guard and driver for many of the governor's trips out of state as well as around Arkansas, he was one of several troopers and other aides serving as procurer or cover in Clinton's ceaseless quest for extramarital sex—and claiming what he called "residuals" among the women the governor wasn't interested in. He was also among those who saw evidence firsthand of the far more serious and sustained affair, dating from the mid-1980s, between Hillary Clinton and Rose partner Vince Foster.

As he told his story with impressive substantiation from other accounts a decade afterward, Brown had been privy to some of the Clintons' most personal liaisons, their biting relationship with each other, their behind-the-door bigotry toward "redneck" Arkansas, and other intimacies; he and a stoic Hillary had even talked earnestly about problems in their respective marriages. At one point in the early 1980s, Brown had come in contact with Vice President Bush during an official gathering. The "rather conservative" young officer, as one friend described him, had been impressed by Bush. Afterward Clinton had twitted him about his Republican "hero," though the two remained close. Regarded as among the better state police officers, Brown received some of the most sophisticated training that national law enforcement agencies offer regional police officers, including advanced courses provided by the DEA and Customs in intelligence gathering, drug importation, and conspiracy cases. Because of Brown's extensive training, Clinton handpicked him to serve on a state committee studying the drug epidemic to help develop educational programs in Arkansas, and Brown wrote several of the panel's position papers later cited as evidence of the state government's fight against narcotics.

Brown and the Clintons eventually had a falling-out when the governor reneged on a state job offer in 1985 and later on his half of a political bargain to raise the pay of the state police, whose association Brown headed. Brown gradually went from favorite to outcast, menaced with a prejudicial "investigation" of his work and smeared as a liar and incompetent by aides who not long before had been jealous of how much Clinton trusted and respected him. Yet the deeper break had begun in the autumn of 1984, when Brown had witnessed matters far more serious than the Clintons' personal excesses.

By Brown's repeated accounts, including hundreds of pages of testimony under oath and supporting documentation, the sum of the story was stark: The governor had clearly been aware of the crimes of Mena as early as 1984. He knew the Central Intelligence Agency was responsible, knew that there was major arms and drug running out of western Arkansas, believed the smuggling involved not only Barry Seal but also a cocaine dealer who was one of Clinton's most prominent backers, and seemed to know that approval of the Mena flights reached as high as Vice President Bush. Brown remembered how Bill Clinton had encouraged him to join in the operation—"Clinton got me into this, the governor did," he would testify—and how Clinton had then dismissed his repugnance at the evidence that Seal was trafficking cocaine under CIA auspices. The state policeman watched in "despair," his brother recalled, while the governor did nothing about the drug smuggling. Brown would still think a decade later that Bill Clinton "was surprised only in that I had found out about it."

Clinton had urged him to answer a newspaper ad for CIA employment that ran in the *New York Times* on April Fool's Day, 1984. "L.D., I've always told you you'd make a good spy," Clinton remarked to him when Brown showed him the paper and asked "if this is for real?" "Well, you know that's not his name," Clinton said of a personnel officer listed in the ad, "but you need to write him a letter." Brown did just that two days later. "Governor Clinton has been an inspiration for me to further my career in government service," he wrote, "and in particular to explore the possibilities of employment with your agency."

Clinton proceeded to show an avid interest in Brown's application. He urged Brown to study Russian for an intelligence career, and Brown characteristically took the advice to heart, practicing the foreign script in a copybook and artlessly, proudly informing the CIA of his "understanding of the Cyrillic alphabet." He and Clinton talked, too, of the role of an operations officer, with Clinton explaining the CIA's diplomatic cover abroad and the recruitment of informers. "It was strange, you know. He was into the fiction aspect of it and intrigue," Brown remembered.

At one point Clinton told him he would personally call the CIA on his behalf. "He, obviously, from all our conversations, knew somebody," Brown recounted in a sworn deposition. "I don't know who he called, but he said he would. He said he did. I made a note one day that he made a phone call for me." But in a private conversation Brown would go even further with the story of the call. Clinton, he said, had not bothered to go through any officeholder's liaison or other formal CIA channel in Washington but had simply telephoned someone directly at the agency, someone whom he knew on a first-name basis and with whom he talked for some time. As usual, Brown was impressed with his boss's knowledge and contacts. Early in the process the governor had begun to greet him whenever they met with a grinning question they both understood to refer to Brown's relationship with the CIA. "You having any fun yet?" Clinton would ask.

As part of his CIA application Brown was to submit a writing sample, and together he and Clinton chose as a topic the current foreign policy controversy over the wars in Nicaragua and El Salvador. "We decided that I would write a paper on Marxism in Central America. Governor Clinton and I." Typing in the troopers' guardhouse at the mansion because he had no typewriter at home, Brown wrote what he thought "a pretty decent essay," which he gave to Clinton to read. Some eight hundred words, it was a rough, largely unpunctuated, and simplistic rendition of the Reagan administration's own views, warning of the "growing threat of spreading Marxism south of this country's borders." Clinton made some word changes and suggested what he should "expound on," but the final essay remained, with Clinton's approval, very much "about defeating Marxism in Central America and aiding the Contras in the United States and the domino theory and all that," as Brown testified later.

At odds with more informed views of his own party in Congress and even in the Democratic foreign policy establishment, Clinton's response to Brown's essay is one of the few surviving marks of his opinions on the subject. To the extent that he agreed with what he left unaltered, it was obviously a reactionary, rightist approach to the raging controversy over Central America, accepting the myth that the leftist but fiercely independent Sandinistas were tools of Soviet expansion in the Western Hemisphere, implicitly viewing social revolution in the Americas as a sinister threat to US security. Whether conviction or calculation, the tone seemed well suited for CIA recruiters. Brown himself was never sure his essay reflected the governor's thinking, whatever Clinton's urgings to "expound." They had played the bureaucratic game. "To be quite frank, I think we both thought it was something they wanted to hear more or less," Brown testified in 1995.

By the end of the summer of 1984—four months after taking and passing a CIA entrance examination—Brown had met with a CIA recruiter in Dallas, someone named Magruder, an "Ivy League–looking guy" who spoke "admiringly of Clinton," and whom Brown would later recognize in photographs and identify to congressional investigators in 1996 as a onetime member of Vice President Bush's staff. This was the man who asked him if he would be interested in "paramilitary" or "narcotics" work as well as "security." Brown said he wanted to be considered for such assignments and, in the course of the interview, duly signed a secrecy agreement. Somebody, he was told, would be giving him a call.

On September 5 he received formal notification of his nomination for employment. Scarcely a month later the expected CIA call came to his unlisted number at home. As Brown testified, the caller "talked to me about everything I had been through in the meeting in Dallas, . . . made me very aware that he knew everything there was to know." He asked Brown to meet him at Cajun's Wharf in Little Rock, a popular restaurant and bar off Cantrell Road in the Arkansas River bottoms just below the white heights. His name, he said, was Barry Seal.

At their meeting, the corpulent Seal was memorable for the athletic young state trooper. "Big guy. He had on one of those shirts that comes down . . . outside your pants, big-guy kind of thing." Seal was cryptic but again seemed clearly to know details Brown had provided on his CIA application. "He knew about the essay and everything I had done, so absolutely there was no question in my mind," Brown testified. Seal also spoke vaguely about working for the CIA: "He'd been flying for the agency, that's all I knew." In conversations over the next few weeks, Seal referred casually to Clinton as "the guv" and "acted like he knew the governor," Brown recalled. He invited Brown to join him in an "operation" planned to begin at Mena's Intermountain Regional before sunrise on Tuesday, October 23, 1984.

Impressed with the gravity of it all, Brown told no one about the talk with Seal, except the governor, who seemed "excited" as usual at Brown's progress with the agency. Seal was nothing like the CIA Ivy Leaguer he had met in Dallas, Brown told Clinton. "El Gordo" Barry Seal "was kind of devil-may-care." Again Clinton seemed knowing, encouragingly nonchalant. "Don't sweat it, you can handle it," he told his bodyguard. "You'll have fun."

Arranging his shifts at the mansion to make time for the flight, Brown met Seal at the Mena airport in the predawn darkness and was surprised to find them boarding not a small private craft but a "huge military plane" painted a dark charcoal with only minimum tail markings, its engines roaring with a "thunderous noise," he remembered. "Scared the shit out of me just taking off."

Seal ordered him matter-of-factly to leave behind all personal identification, including his billfold, keys, and jewelry. Along with Seal at the controls sat a copilot whose name Brown never learned, and in the back of the aircraft sat two men, "beaners" or "kickers" the trooper called them. Though he did not know it, Brown was aboard the *Fat Lady,* and his later account marked the flight as one of Mena's routine gun-and-drug runs.

After a refueling stop in New Orleans and the flight to Central America, the C-123K dived below radar, then climbed and dipped again for the "kickers" to roll out on casters large tarp-covered palettes, which were swiftly parachuted over what Brown could see out the open cargo door was a tropical, mountainous terrain. Later Seal told Brown the loads were M-16s for the Contras. On the return they landed in Honduras, where Seal and the "kickers" picked up four dark green canvas duffel bags with shoulder straps, which Brown did not see again.

Back at Mena Seal handed Brown a manila envelope with $2,500 in small bills, presumably as payment for his time—"used money just like you went out and spent," Brown recalled—and said he would call him again about another "operation." As the ambitious young trooper testified later, he was diffident about this apparent audition with his CIA employers, reluctant to ask questions, even about the cash. "This guy [Seal] obviously knew what he was doing and had the blessing and was working for the agency and knew everything about me, so I wasn't going to be too inquisitive."

At the mansion on Brown's next shift following the run to Central America, Clinton greeted him with the usual "You having any fun yet?" though now with a pat on the back. With a "big smile" Brown answered, "Yeah, but this is scary stuff," describing "a big airplane" which he thought "kind of crazy." But Bill Clinton seemed unsurprised and unquestioning, casual as always about what Brown told him about the CIA, Seal, and Mena. "Oh, you can handle it," he said again. "Don't sweat it."

Brown was startled at the governor's obvious prior knowledge of the flight. "He knew before I said anything. He knew," Brown testified. Asked later under oath if he believed the Seal flight had been sanctioned by the governor, Brown would be unequivocal. "Well, he knew what I was doing. He was the one that furthered me along and shepherded me through this thing." Did he have any doubt that Clinton approved of the flight from Mena to Central America? "No," he testified. Did he believe the Seal run "a sanctioned and approved mission on behalf of the United States?" "Absolutely. I mean, there is no doubt."

Not long afterward, in the later fall of 1984, Seal called the trooper as promised, again inquiring about Clinton: "He always asked me first thing, how is the guv?" They talked about the first flight and Seal, ruminating on his service for the CIA, confirmed that they had dropped a load of contraband M-16s for the Contras. "That's all he talked about was flying and [the] CIA and how much work he had done for them, and that's all he did. That's all we would talk about," Brown recalled. They met again, this time at a Chinese restaurant near the Capitol, and arranged for Brown to go on another trip in late December.

On Christmas Eve, 1984, once more with the governor's encouragement, Brown again flew with Seal to Central America on what he still understood to be some kind of orientation mission for his CIA employment. Seal picked up two duffel bags on the return through Hondurus, and just as before, back at Mena he offered Brown $2,500 in small bills. Yet this time Seal also brought one of the duffels to Brown's Datsun hatchback in the Intermountain Regional parking lot and proceeded to take out of it what the former narcotics investigator instantly recognized as a kilo of cocaine, a "waxene-wrapped package," as he called it, "a brick."

Alarmed and incensed, Brown quickly told Seal he "wanted no part of what was happening" and left, speeding back to Little Rock in mounting agitation, not least over the role of the state's chief executive. "I'm just going nuts in my mind with all the possibilities," he would say. "I'm thinking, well, this is, this is an official operation. Clinton got me into this, the governor did. It can't be as sinister as I think it is. . . . He knew about the airplane flights. He knew about it and initiated the conversation about it the first time I came back."

Returning to the guardhouse, Brown first called his "best friend," his brother Dwayne in Pine Bluff, who remembered his being "terribly upset" and later went to the mansion to see him when the Clintons were away. According to the two men, Brown told his brother part of what he had encountered, though without mentioning the CIA involvement. "Who's pushing this. Who is behind it?" his brother asked at one point. In reply, as each recalled clearly, Brown "nodded over towards the governor's mansion."

Brown decided to approach Clinton directly about what he had seen. When they were together soon after the second flight, a smiling Clinton seemed about to ask the usual question. But Brown was angry. He asked Clinton if he knew Barry Seal was smuggling narcotics. "Do you know what they're bringing back on that airplane?" he said to Clinton in fury. "Wait, whoa, whoa, what's going on?" the governor responded, and Brown answered, "Well, essentially they're bringing back coke." More than a decade later, Brown would testify to his dismay at Clinton's response: "And it wasn't like it was a surprise to him. It wasn't like—he didn't try to say, what? . . . He was surprised that I was mad because he thought we were going to have a cordial conversation, but he didn't try to deny it. He didn't try to deny that it wasn't coming back, that I wasn't telling the truth or that he didn't know anything about it."

In waving off Brown's questions about Mena, Clinton had made another remark as well, added as what seemed both justification and warning. "And your hero Bush knows about it," he told Brown. "And your buddy Bush knows about it."

Brown was chilled. "I'm not going to have anything else to do with it . . . I'm out of it," he told Clinton. "Stick a fork in me, I'm done," he added, an adolescent phrase from their shared Arkansas boyhood. The governor had tried to calm him: "Settle down. That's no problem." But Brown turned away, hurried to his car, and drove off, leaving behind his once-promising career. "I got out of there, and from then it was, you know, not good."

The trooper immediately called the CIA to withdraw his application, albeit discreetly. "Just changed my mind," he recalled telling them. But he saw no recourse, no appeal to some higher level of government in a crime in which both the governor of the state and Washington were knowledgeable and thus complicit. "I mean if the governor knows about it . . . and I work for the governor," he remembered thinking, "exactly who would I have gone to and told? I mean, the federal government knows that this guy is doing this . . . I don't know what authority I would have gone to." More than a year later, as they were having drinks in Jonesboro, Brown would tell the commandant of the state police, Colonel Tommy Goodwin, but even then he acted out of a desire to confess his unwitting involvement rather than out of any expectation that Arkansas would move on the crimes. All the while, he was bothered by the role of his onetime hero at the mansion. "Number one," he would testify later of Bill Clinton, "he didn't deny it. I wanted him to tell me, *oh, good gosh, that's terrible. We've got to report this.* And I wanted him to deny knowing anything about it or to explain it away to me . . . *they've got a big sting planned, and they're trying, you know, to make a case on such and such,* but no. It was no surprise to him. He was surprised, I think—this is what I think—that Seal showed it to me. That's what I think to this day."

At the time, the bodyguard had been inconsolable. From the moment of the second flight on Christmas Eve, 1984, until L.D. left the governor's security detail in June 1985, his brother thought him at "a high level of despair." What the eager and patriotic young trooper had discovered about government, Dwayne Brown worried, had left him almost suicidal.

But perhaps what had most disturbed L. D. Brown was a direct reference by Clinton to a member of the governor's own inner circle. Clinton "throws up his hands" when Brown mentions the cocaine, as if a crucial, somehow rationalizing distinction should be made between the gunrunning and the drug trafficking.

"Oh, no," Clinton said, denying that the cocaine was related to the CIA Brown was hoping to join. "That's Lasater's deal."

◆   ◆   ◆

The name Clinton threw out so effortlessly was no stranger to L. D. Brown or any of the other troopers assigned to security at the mansion. The governor was talking about millionaire bond broker Dan Lasater. The Arkansas public may have only known the name Lasater—if they knew it at all—from the Little Rock social pages as a donor of toys to poor or sick children and a supporter of Clinton campaigns. They might also have known him to be an occasional social friend of the governor and First Lady, to whom he generously loaned his private plane for Hillary's trips on behalf of charity.

But Brown and other insiders knew another Dan Lasater as the big contributor who was as intimate as any of Bill Clinton's associates or aides, coming and going at the mansion like family, "through Miss Liza's kitchen," seeing Clinton for closed-door meetings at his brokerage office several times a month whenever the governor was "in the neighborhood," hosting him at his notorious parties with silver platters of cocaine, flying the Clintons to the Kentucky Derby at a time he was handing $300,000 to another ambitious governor by way of a major drug dealer. Still largely unknown was that US attorneys in Arkansas and Nevada as well as the Kentucky State Police suspected Lasater had ties to organized crime; that he dealt cocaine in Arkansas and would be probed by federal undercover agents for major drug trafficking in New Mexico; that his bond brokerage had been disciplined repeatedly for shady dealings with subsequent suspicions of money laundering and was nonetheless the beneficiary of millions in state commissions under the Clinton regime.

In the winter of 1984–1985, however, not even the troopers at the mansion, who waved him through the back gate so often, yet knew that the FBI, the DEA, and others would have a thick criminal investigative file on "Lasater," if not his "deal" at Mena.

"Oh, absolutely. Dan Lasater," Brown would testify years later. "I had met him a lot, you know, through the governor."

Yet if Clinton's incriminating remark about Lasater was not entirely surprising, the invoking of George Bush is less readily explained. "Why would Clinton, when given evidence of criminal activities in his own state, have sought at once to make a bipartisan matter of it?" wondered one who heard Brown's story. Why would an ambitious Democrat, who was already contemplating a presidential run for 1988, have silently condoned the unlawful actions of a Republican administration? It was at a juncture where the corruptions of national security met the comparatively petty yet sometimes kindred corruptions of Arkansas, where in a sense "your hero Bush" and "Lasater's deal" were joined, and where the embroilments for Bill Clinton, because of his very ambition and own abuses of power, became largely inseparable.

To begin with, as Clinton's encouragement of the Brown CIA essay and other evidence would show, there had been no little sympathy and much accommodation in the governor's mansion in Little Rock for the primitive anti-Communism and interventionism that were Washington's ideological rationale for the Contra weapons flown out of Mena.

For some, the pretext embraced even the return traffic in cocaine, ostensibly intended to provide money for still more illegal arms.

When other Democratic governors protested the use of their state reserve units for "training" in Central America in the mid-1980s— missions that might be used to evade congressional restraints on backing the Contras—Bill Clinton allowed the Arkansas National Guard to be sent to Honduras for annual maneuvers. The Reagan White House later pointed to Clinton's "patriotic" cooperation as it attacked other Democrats, including Governor Michael Dukakis of Massachusetts, the 1988 presidential nominee, for their "shameful refusal." As it happened, sources later revealed, some of the opponents' worst suspicions were justified: in a Pentagon subterfuge, the Arkansas Guard's arms were declared "excess," and—with Clinton's knowledge and tacit approval—units in Honduras were reportedly instructed to leave behind on the ground weapons to be passed illicitly to the Contras.

As if to underscore those events, in 1988, well after the Iran-Contra scandal had broken, Governor Clinton pointedly issued "Arkansas Traveler" honorifics to Adolpho and Mario Calero and to General John Singlaub, "three of the most notorious figures," as one journalist described them, "in the *contra* nexus." That, too, was no coincidence. "Are you kidding?" exclaimed a former statehouse aide. "Traveler certificates may be cheap handouts, but they were always checked to avoid any political embarrassment to Clinton, like crooks or kooks, and those Contra ones got reviewed like any other and got express approval, like an order."

Clinton's readiness to support the Contras and a covert criminal operation in that guise was consistent with his acceptance of other controversial policies cloaked in "national security." He would welcome and even encourage in Arkansas—notably at Pine Bluff and Pea Ridge—military arsenals and storage of dangerous materials that other governors of both parties spurned. "These were dumping grounds nobody else wanted," said a former military officer, "and Bill Clinton could be counted on to take 'em." With the same alacrity he would welcome to the state companies like the Wackenhut Corporation—well known for its links to right-wing elements from the 1950s and to the CIA—to provide security guards for local industries, who would eventually be involved in violent clashes with striking workers in the mid-1980s.

Clinton supporters, some themselves perplexed by the ties, would explain them as a combination of conviction, boosterism, and politics. But some thought his undifferentiated zeal for many of the same forces he had apparently deplored in the Vietnam War was a compensation, a kind of political atonement, for his antiwar stance. "I think he was always trying to be the tough guy to live down any doubts about the draft or being a McGovernite, both in himself and the gallery he was always playing to," said an old friend.

Yet a few saw still darker compulsions as well. There was always the shadow of Leckford Road at Oxford, and Clinton's own alleged early ties to the CIA, and the history of friends like Strobe Talbott. How much had that connection—young Bill Clinton the cooperative patriot to some, the treacherous informer to others—been continued, either willingly or as subtle coercion?

What Clinton's national security patrons came to know about his personal excesses and abuses of power long before he became president would be interred in official secrecy. In any case, there were knowledgeable observers in both Little Rock and Washington who believed him substantially compromised by the mid-1980s, whatever his views on Marxism in Central America. "Let's just say this," said one intelligence officer. "Clinton was in no position to say no or blow the whistle on any op[eration] in his backyard."

In a civil trial in the mid-1990s growing out of the Mena cover-up, investigators found eyewitnesses who swore they recalled ranking CIA and other national security figures discreetly visiting Governor Clinton at the mansion during the height of the Mena operation. By the same account, in September 1991, on the eve of Clinton's announcement of his presidential candidacy, Hillary was said to have ordered that entry logs no longer be kept at the mansion. Then there was a similar action—the origin of this order was not as clear—to remove archival state logs recording visitors to the mansion by name and times of entry and exit during the Clintons' first term, 1979–80, and since their return to power in 1983, altogether more than a decade of state records. Troopers and others familiar with them believed the logs contained evidence bearing on a number of indiscretions, and the motive for spiriting them away might have been avoidance of personal scandal. "I think she was worried about the girls mainly," said one who believed Hillary was behind the removal—though there were also reports indicating that the logs would have shown frequent visits to the mansion by Hillary's own intimate, Vince Foster, during the governor's absences. In any event, against the larger backdrop of Mena and "national security," seizure of the logs would have the effect of ridding the candidate of potential questions far beyond adultery.

Hillary Rodham Clinton had also, as always, brought her own views and history to the concerns of Mena. Some remembered her as what one called "a closet Contra supporter" in the early to mid-1980s. She generally muted her opinions for the sake of their relations with congressional Democrats and others who opposed the interventions in Central America and who would be important financially or politically to their eventual presidential bid. "It wouldn't have been smart for him to take a high profile on that issue at sixes and sevens with most of his own party, and certainly not for her," said one woman familiar with the often bitter foreign policy politics of the time. Nonetheless, the First Lady quietly let what was described as her "self-conscious tough-mindedness" be known in Little Rock, where her allegiance discreetly aided Contra fund-raising and where, as elsewhere in the state, there was an ardent clutch of Contra backers.

Outside the state, on national boards and in other capacities, Hillary was circumspect as well, though noted in those settings, too, for quiet lobbying against people or programs in Central America or Washington inimical to the Contras or to the Reagan-CIA policies in general. As late as 1987–88, amid some of the worst of the Iran-Contra revelations, colleagues heard her still opposing church groups and others devoted to social reform in Nicaragua and El Salvador but labeled leftist by the Republican White House. Like her husband's, of course, her more reactionary foreign policy views did not necessarily imply support for the covert and illegal CIA weapons shipments, much less for the drug trafficking or wider black market of the Southern Tier. But their furtive bias or expedient—hers typically stronger than his— obviously made it easier to accept the figment of "national security" used to dress the crimes.

There were business linkages as well that would prove questionable if later scrutinized by outsiders. At Rose, Hillary would join partner Webb Hubbell in representing a company called POM, Inc., Park On Meter, of which Hubbell's in-laws, the Wards, were owners. In the relentless incest of Little Rock, Hubbell's father-in-law, Seth Ward, was tied as well to Jim McDougal, Madison Guaranty, and the Castle Grande development, later found by federal investigators to be a "sham" in which Ward was a "straw buyer"—and for which Hillary Clinton billed some sixty-eight hours of legal work, including more than a dozen telephone conversations with Seth Ward. Hubbell's own lawyering for his wife's family was thought later to have been part of a massive billing embezzlement he perpetrated on Rose as well as on the government—a fraction of which Hubbell would plead guilty to in 1994. Yet Seth Ward was not simply a controversial client implicated in an alleged banking fraud; nor was POM merely a parking meter manufacturer linked to the Clintons and their associates.

Located in Russellville, not far from Mena, the corporation was the recipient of some of the most select classified Pentagon contracts, including, reportedly, for reentry nose cones for nuclear warheads and parts for rocket engines. A prosperous beneficiary of the military budget, POM was also one of the first local businesses to receive a loan from the Arkansas Development Finance Authority, the Clinton-initiated program of state-guaranteed bond capital ostensibly designed for struggling fledgling enterprises. At the close of 1985 the authority loaned the flourishing Ward company $2.75 million, with the documents signed by Hubbell as corporate counsel. Later published accounts would cite two separate sources inside the Seal-CIA network who would implicate POM in the Mena operation as a supplier or at least an eager would-be provider of equipment and Contra weaponry. The Wards would indignantly deny the allegations. In a memoir entitled *Compromised*, written with investigative reporter John Cummings, former Seal associate Terry Reed would further allege that he had understood from Seal that a Ward farm and ranch was one of the drop sites for cash from the Mena "green flights." Still later, sworn testimony in a Reed civil suit growing out of the scandal would link Seth Ward to men alleged to be involved in a cover-up of Mena and the collusion of Arkansas officials.

How much the future First Lady knew about her client and friend Seth Ward, how much she knew of the company she and Hubbell represented, what she heard or discussed with her husband or others regarding Mena would never be clear.

For three years of their presidency, none of the official inquiries enveloping the Clintons would seem to look seriously at the far more ominous scandal in western Arkansas. Yet the surviving evidence of their links to the CIA drug smuggling was much the same as the evidence linking them to Whitewater and Madison. There was no single incident, remark, or tie but many, no startling circumstance or coincidence but a numbing accumulation. The Clintons' lines of direct or indirect knowledge and association had laced unmistakably through and around the crimes of Mena.

♦ ♦ ♦

Danny Ray Lasater would signify their most telling relationship of all—the man Bill Clinton mentioned on impulse when he assured his security guard, "That's Lasater's deal."

Three years older than Clinton, Lasater was born in remote White County, Arkansas, not far from Jim McDougal's hometown and only miles from Whitewater. As a boy he had moved to Kokomo, Indiana, and after high school worked as assistant manager and manager of a local McDonald's. He was not yet twenty, he later told the FBI, when he became partners with his father-in-law, a former sheriff, and with a Kokomo car dealer in a fast-food restaurant. In a meteoric rise that others would later find remarkable, he and his partners would open their own chain of Ponderosa steakhouses, branching out into various states with a succession of investors. With someone else's ample capital, he would at twenty-three become part owner of a chain, and at twenty-nine a multimillionaire. Neither Lasater nor Ponderosa was ever charged with wrongdoing. But his quick fortune—made in a largely cash industry that federal and state law enforcement saw increasingly exploited by organized crime and characterized by what one US attorney called the "skim and scam" of the cash profits by managers—attracted the attention of investigators in several states.

Early in the 1970s Lasater took his company public, sold his shares, and invested his millions in thoroughbreds—another industry rife with allegations of penetration by organized crime, drug-money laundering, and other corruption. With farms in Kentucky and Florida, Lasater would attract the top breeders, and his horses would be among the leading money winners. Along the way he developed a close relationship with Kentucky's Democratic governor, John Y. Brown, and other related figures, including Brown's old friend and partner Jimmy Lambert, whose links to the mob and conviction on drug charges in the mid-1980s would shake Kentucky and help shatter Brown's own presidential plans. The Lambert ties placed Lasater himself under investigation by the Kentucky State Police for his own relationship to organized crime. It was also "Jimmy," as Lasater told the FBI after Lambert's indictment, who gave him his "first" cocaine around 1978 at Lambert's Cincinnati and Lexington nightclubs. But by then Dan Lasater had moved back to Arkansas, first trying a new restaurant, then a more profitable Little Rock bond brokerage—and, not least, acquiring a close relationship with another ambitious governor.

In Little Rock he became part of the drug scene, sniffing cocaine with the Clintons' friend Barrett Hamilton, Jr., and others in the white heights and holding raucous parties at his impressive home or his Quapaw Towers apartment, which happened to be ten floors above that of a local television reporter named Gennifer Flowers. In partnership with a state legislator, Lasater's "bond daddy" brokerage made a million dollars in profits by 1982 but was already infamous in local investment circles for its flow of cocaine as well as its shady financial practices. Lasater himself commonly snorted the drug at the office. "Cocaine was so pervasive in the investment banking community," a Lasater broker was reported to have confessed to a local judge, "that he feared it would be hard to stay away from the drug if he remained."

Like Red Bone's commodity brokerage in Springdale, Lasater's company received professional censure after censure—in 1982 from the National Association of Securities Dealers for excessive markups and unlicensed sales, in 1983 for buying and selling bonds for a savings and loan without authority of the thrift's board, in 1984 for making more unauthorized trades, and over a period of time for violating multiple securities rules and regulations. The state securities commissioner under Frank White's governorship sanctioned the firm for "cheating customers" in 1982.

By 1983 Lasater had personally given thousands and had held fund-raisers producing tens of thousands more for Clinton's gubernatorial campaigns, most crucially the 1982 comeback. As those most familiar with the governor's routine well knew, however, Danny Ray Lasater was never merely another big donor to be paid special deference but rather an extraordinary intimate whom Clinton visited regularly at his brokerage and who came to the mansion whenever he pleased, entering by the back gate and walking through the kitchen.

Entering through the domain of the mansion's commanding black cook, Elizabeth Ashley, was a privilege reserved only for family and the most senior staff. In the mid-1980s Lasater enjoyed it as no one else outside that circle. It was no wonder, as Clinton's closest aides knew, that the governor had turned to Lasater to give Roger Clinton a job or that the millionaire had loaned the governor's addicted half brother money to pay off a drug debt during Roger's 1983–84 crisis.

Lasater was given to "drop-ins," as trooper bodyguard Barry Spivey put it, "just kind of off-the-cuff. Day and night, weekends, all day, he just came when he wanted to." Spivey, who served at the mansion from 1979 to 1984, remembered that throughout his tour, "Dan never was shown in through the front door." Another trooper recalled that, "there is [sic] not many people that just drive through the back gate and their driver pulls them up and they go in the back door. . . . He was a fixture." Among the many ironies of the troopers' waving him through the back gate was that Lasater's chauffeur was not simply a "driver" but a convicted murderer who carried a gun and was widely known to deal drugs on the side.

The governor and the bond dealer saw each other frequently, and with the same familiarity, at Lasater's brokerage, where Clinton would stop for unscheduled visits, telling his state trooper escort to take him to Lasater's office if they happened to be in the vicinity. "A lot of times he would just be in the area and he would say run by Dan's or run by Lassiter's [sic] for a minute," Spivey testified. "We very seldom were in the area when he had any time on his hands that he didn't run in." Clinton's state police drivers would circle the block or simply sit and let the limousine idle while the governor and Lasater "would be upstairs and behind closed doors or something," as one remembered.

When Bill Clinton told L. D. Brown that the Seal cocaine smuggling was "Lasater's deal," he was not talking about someone he met from time to time or knew only in a limited context but rather about the most intimate of friends and associates.

Beyond frequent private meetings at the mansion and Lasater and Company, there were extensive social contacts as well. Other troopers remembered accompanying Clinton to Lasater's large homes or his downtown apartment, to his private box at Hot Springs's Oaklawn track, where Lasater courted the governor's mother as well, or aboard his Lear jet. Some escorts, like Brown, were concerned about the cocaine spread so lavishly at Lasater's parties, extraordinary even amid what Brown called Little Rock's "real robust party atmosphere." At Lasater's apartment, one witness told the FBI in a handwritten statement, cocaine was given to high school girls in a special "graduation party," and on another occasion Lasater threw a party for a woman friend and impressed everyone with his extravagance by writing "Happy Birthday" in cocaine on the glass coffee table. At one typical gathering Brown tried to usher the governor out to avoid a scandal, though it was clear that Clinton knew about the rampant drugs. "There was a silver platter of what I thought was cocaine and I got the governor out of there. I said we need to go. Let's get out of here," the state trooper remembered. "He had to have seen it. There were a lot of people there, a lot of girls there. He had to have seen it. I mean, it was obvious. . . . He said something to Lasater and I got him out of there."

The millionaire would lend his plane to Clinton for campaign trips and, in 1985, for flying celebrities to a charity function organized by Hillary. In May 1983, less than five months after Clinton's triumphal return to the statehouse, trooper Barry Spivey would accompany Lasater and the Clintons on a flight to attend the Kentucky Derby, where they met the host governor, John Y. Brown, who was a friend of

Clinton as well as Lasater but whose longtime positioning for the presidency was already beginning to be clouded by questionable associations. With Roger Clinton "running bets for Dan and Bill," as Spivey recalled, all of them made money on the winner, Sunny's Halo. But behind the gathering of smiling political notables was another reality as well.

Law enforcement agents would remember that 1983 Derby as one of the most heavily surveilled sporting events in history. State and federal plainclothes agents rubbed elbows with the celebrities and the crowd at Churchill Downs as part of a still incipient but widening probe of organized crime, money laundering, and other corruption in Kentucky and surrounding states. Lasater was among those being watched, though the FBI and other agents would not learn until later that Lasater had given a paper bag containing $300,000 in cash to Governor Brown by way of Jimmy Lambert. The Kentucky governor had asked Lasater for a million dollars, a Lasater partner told the FBI, but the broker had decided to give "only" $300,000. "I just took care of John Y's money problems," an associate recalled Lasater's telling him afterward.

Questioned years later under oath about the cash, trooper Spivey could not remember any "money in a paper bag" aboard Lasater's jet as they flew the Clintons to the Derby. But FBI documents would show that the passing of the cash had happened very near the time of that flight, if not on the trip itself. In any case, it was not long afterward, Arkansas troopers remembered, that Hillary began to hector her husband about his contact with Lasater. The First Lady habitually called the state police security unit to keep tabs on her chronically wayward husband, and troopers soon learned to put her off not only when the governor was occupied with a woman but when he was with Danny Ray Lasater as well.

But whatever her concern with appearances, Lasater enjoyed an impressive and ever-growing share of state business. Listed to underwrite state housing bonds in 1983, soon after Clinton was sworn in and only a year after the brokerage was formally established, Lasater and Company began to rake in management fees and still more in sales commissions. Despite being "the new boy," as a US attorney called him, Lasater suddenly ranked fifth in the established and competitive field of state housing bond underwriters, ahead of major concerns and longtime Clinton supporters such as Goldman, Sachs and Merrill Lynch. When, at Clinton's initiative, the Arkansas Development Finance Authority took over most of the lucrative state bond offerings in

1985—under legislation drafted in part by Webb Hubbell and with the governor and his political appointees to the ADFA board personally approving each issue—Lasater and Company would continue to be a major beneficiary of the ubiquitous fees and commissions spread among Little Rock investment and law firms. In the brief period prior to the fall of 1986, ADFA would award it fourteen issues worth more than $600 million, and brokerage fees to Dan Lasater of $1.6 million.

At the same time, almost every Lasater public appearance in the mid-1980s would have its dark shadow. In Little Rock society the broker was a showy philanthropist for children's causes, but in private he was a relentless purveyor of cocaine. In 1984 he purchased the fashionable Angel Fire ski resort in northern New Mexico for nearly $20 million and was given free rein to use Bill Clinton's name commercially to help promote the isolated development in the mountains east of Taos. Undercover law enforcement agents later found the resort a center for drug running, what a US Customs investigative report called "a large controlled-substance smuggling operation and large-scale money-laundering activity." While Lasater held "Arkansas Week" at the resort with Governor Clinton's endorsement and entertained politicians from Santa Fe as well as Little Rock, local New Mexico sheriffs and district attorneys were hearing reports from Angel Fire reminiscent of Mena—strange nighttime traffic, sightings of parachute drops, even hikers' accounts of a "big black military-type cargo plane" seeming to come out of nowhere and swooping low and almost silently over a deserted mountain meadow near the remote ski area.

Over the same period, witnesses told investigators, Lasater was bragging about fixing horse races, "putting one in the boot," as he described it to an employee. He was also said to pay frequent visits to Las Vegas, where he allegedly laundered cash in the time-honored manner of the old mob-dominated casinos, losing money, according to an associate, and then winning it back, plus some.

In Little Rock his political influence seemed stronger than ever. By the mid-1980s Lasater and Company had its own ties to Madison Guaranty, what one account called "significant dealings." A decade later the Whitewater special prosecutor would reportedly be moved by the record of these dealings to investigate whether Lasater used the thrift to funnel money to the Clinton campaigns in 1984 and 1986. Whatever happened with the swirling accounts at Madison, Lasater continued to be a fund-raiser for the governor as well as a major public contributor. Like the employees of Madison Guaranty, brokers at Lasater and Company were urged to contribute to Clinton, with the boss offering higher commission to compensate for the donations—thus "bundling" the Lasater donations to exceed the individual or family limits. But the relationship between Lasater and Clinton now also went beyond the discreet but constant contacts at the brokerage and the mansion, the social occasions, or the funneling of state business. The two men came to share patronage of an intimate adviser—a link that would last all the way to the White House.

Lasater had given jobs to the children of a Clinton campaign official, and in 1984 he hired as his chief assistant a longtime Clinton associate, Patsy Thomasson, who had begun as an aide to Congressman Wilbur Mills in the 1970s and later became a close friend of state legislator and Lasater partner George "Butch" Locke. She had been named to the Arkansas Highway Commission by Governor Pryor and kept on by Clinton, and she reportedly continued to serve on that notoriously powerful body even as she worked for Dan Lasater. A self-described "yellow dog Democrat," Thomasson was a discreet, almost cryptic figure and was never to be charged in any of the crimes surrounding her employer. Thomasson was a frequent companion on Lasater's business and social flights, including a 1984 flight to Belize that came under investigation by the FBI, which was probing Lasater's attempted purchase of a suspected marijuana farm in that country. She ultimately became president or board member of various Lasater properties and subsidiaries, including Angel Fire, and in 1987 Lasater would give her an extraordinary seven-page durable power of attorney, granting her sweeping authority over his financial affairs after his conviction for drug distribution.

Again, even as she held positions with a convicted Lasater, Thomasson would go on to succeed Betsey Wright as executive director of the Arkansas Democratic Party. In 1993 Clinton quickly named her special assistant to the president and director of the Office of Administration in the White House, where she was one of the more obscure yet most powerful members of the Arkansas circle. It would be Patsy Thomasson who was among the first to enter the office of White House deputy counsel Vince Foster following his controversial death in July 1993—"in the middle of a 'cats and dogs' scramble," reported the *Wall Street Journal*, "to find the combination of Vince Foster's safe the night of his death." At the time her presence in the Foster affair seemed odd to many, but "only if you didn't know where she came from, and how," said an Arkansas politician.

In the meanwhile, the luck of her former employer, Dan Lasater, was to run out, in a sense, with his criminal indictment on federal drug charges in 1986. Up until then, though, the company's intriguing transactions seem to have been going full swing. In the summer of 1985 a county official named Dennis Patrick from a small town in Kentucky was contacted by a Lasater broker, an old school friend, who proposed to open an account for Patrick that would require no money from him yet would yield $20,000 a week at no risk. Seeming to make money at first, as Patrick told his story later, he duly followed instructions and arranged to deposit his profits automatically at a Little Rock bank. Meanwhile he enjoyed cordial, even warm relations with the brokerage. The trading volume in his account appeared to reach as high as $23.5 million in one transaction, though he never received the profits personally. After several weeks he grew suspicious when he was asked to sign several documents, and he asked his friend to stop trading. There followed a hiatus of months, and then Lasater and Company brought a lawsuit against him, claiming that he and the salesman, who had since been fired, had conspired to defraud the brokerage of some $86,000. But the suit was soon dropped—according to the company because Patrick had no money to justify the litigation, according to Patrick because he threatened a public airing.

In the welter of accusations, including ones about Patrick's own troubled business dealings in Kentucky, the episode remained murky, though some elements were telling. Before his falling-out with the brokerage, Patrick told a writer, he had been flown at Lasater's expense from London, Kentucky, to Angel Fire and had even gone dove hunting on the same Arkansas farm alleged to have been used for cash drops by Barry Seal. Examined by another bond broker, Patrick's trading records with Lasater and Company showed a total of some $50 million run through the account in less than six months, vast amounts of cash of unaccountable origin, the very definition of money laundering. Not least, the flush trades stopped early in 1986, just after Barry Seal was murdered.

That autumn Lasater was indicted on federal drug charges. A federal-state narcotics task force had been formed in Arkansas in 1985 after reports of blatant cocaine trafficking and use, especially in the Little Rock bond business, became what one officer called "overwhelming." Lasater was soon implicated by a torrent of informants' reports and formal statements. But almost from the beginning, the investigation followed what agents remembered as "unusual procedures." By his own account the lead state police investigator, J. N. DeLaughter, was ordered to give "only verbal reports on his investigative findings" and only to the state police commandant, Tommy Goodwin, who at least twice took DeLaughter's briefings on the nearly year-long probe while in Governor Clinton's private office. At the same time, Lasater was receiving reports on the inquiry from a source in the state police to whom he had made loans and given other favors.

Clinton would later claim that he learned of the Lasater probe only at the last moment in the fall of 1986. But not only had Goodwin received earlier briefings in the governor's office, the inquiry itself had been what investigators called "a spinoff of the Roger Clinton investigation," the files and testimony of which the governor and Roger's lawyers had followed closely. In any event, even with the Lasater inquiry at its height, Clinton lobbied heavily and successfully for a bond issue for a new state police communications system, an issue for which Lasater and Company would receive $750,000 in underwriting fees while its owner was under active investigation for multiple federal and state felonies. "Because they backed the right individual in Clinton," Butch Locke would tell the FBI, "Lasater and Company received the contract."

In mid-October 1986, with two of his lawyers present, Danny Ray Lasater himself was finally interviewed by local US attorney George Proctor, an FBI agent, and a Little Rock police detective, but none of the agents most familiar with the evidence. Recorded in the bureaucratic prose of the FBI, the result was a relatively perfunctory interrogation with no sustained questioning and a seeming lack of curiosity about the broker's dealings beyond his confessed recreational use of cocaine. "It was either a high dive or incredibly unprofessional, take your pick," said one law enforcement officer. With the interview and his indictment only days later, the investigation came to a premature halt. Though it was standard practice in drug cases, agents were enjoined from seizing any monies or property clearly associated with the cocaine, including Lasater's Lear jet. Most important, they never pursued the complex web of financial affairs that trailed off from Little Rock. When members of the powerful bond community in Little Rock grew worried that the Lasater indictments might go beyond the obvious charges of cocaine use to include money laundering, officials were said to have reassured them discreetly. "Somebody went out and told them not to sweat it, that there was no money laundering involved," said an IRS agent familiar with the investigation, "though we had tons of evidence for cases of just that." Inquiries into Lasater elsewhere fared no better. In 1989 a federal investigation into Angel Fire fell apart in an interagency jurisdictional dispute between Customs, the FBI, and the DEA.

Having testified to the Lasater grand jury, Roger Clinton would be named as an unindicted coconspirator in the charges against Danny Ray. Despite pleas by state and federal agents to pursue the leads suggested by the evidence already gathered, the prosecutors were ultimately no more curious about the millionaire's powerful friends than about his far-flung finances.

When a local journalist asked US Attorney George Proctor in October 1986 about any possible connections between Lasater and organized crime, Proctor responded quickly: "None there," he said tersely.

Questioned further by another reporter as to Clinton's "involvement" in the case, Proctor answered almost dismissively about the man who was among Lasater's most intimate associates. "No way," he told the reporter. A Carter appointee kept on by Reagan and Bush, George Proctor would become a ranking official in the Clinton administration, head of the Justice Department's Office of International Affairs, responsible for, among other things, narcotics matters.

Law enforcement officers were dismayed and angry at the stunted probe of Lasater. Whatever the limits or extent of Lasater's cocaine trafficking or the nature of his other dealings, most believed that beyond him the larger corruption in Little Rock and elsewhere pointed unmistakably to organized crime, not to mention the vast crimes of Mena—none of which would be pursued.

For his part, Bill Clinton had by now publicly distanced himself from the man to whom he had once been so close. "I feel very sick about it," he said at the time of Lasater's indictment, "and I'm sad about it because a person who supported me, who supported a lot of good causes in Arkansas and made a very great success in three careers has been devastated by getting involved in cocaine." Had he ever used cocaine? a reporter asked the governor at the time. "No," he said casually, "I'm not sure what it looked like if I saw it." Had he ever asked Dan Lasater about the rumored cocaine parties? "No," Clinton told the *Gazette,* "I never asked him about it. But I never would have had the occasion to ask him about it in a social setting."

Just before his indictment, Lasater sold his share in Lasater and Company to an associate of John Y. Brown and a partner in the brokerage, William D. McCord, who was later indicted on money laundering and gambling charges. Given "use immunity" in return for cooperation in other cases, Lasater was sentenced to only thirty months in prison, though he apparently never offered testimony in another major case. He served just six months in prison and four in a halfway house and would be pardoned by Clinton immediately after the 1990 gubernatorial election. The pardon allowed him to reacquire state-regulated business licenses and thus, as a prominent Arkansas attorney told the *Los Angeles Times,* was "worth big bucks to Lasater." By the 1992 race, however, the singular relationship between the two men had been virtually expunged. Bill Clinton and Danny Ray Lasater, the Clinton presidential campaign would claim, "didn't socialize."

◆   ◆   ◆

Clinton would continue to hear reports about Mena after 1986, though he apparently never again spoke openly about "Lasater's deal." L.D. Brown was not alone among the bodyguards in witnessing Clinton's reactions to stories of Mena. Joining the security unit in 1987, trooper Larry Patterson would testify later about frequent conversations among state policemen "that there was [*sic*] large quantities of drugs being flown into the Mena airport, large quantities of money, large quantities of guns, that there was an ongoing operation training foreign people in that area. That it was a CIA operation." At one point the mansion detail and state police headquarters buzzed with a story of how local and federal law enforcement officials had obtained a warrant and were about to conduct an important search at Intermountain Regional when they were called off by the state police commandant, Tommy Goodwin. "Do not under any circumstances execute that search warrant," Goodwin was said to have ordered.

A number of the discussions took place "in the presence of Governor Clinton," Patterson recalled. Yet, whether the subject was drugs, guns, guerrilla training, or an apparent cover-up, the state's chief executive would seem somehow detached and uncharacteristically reticent and uninquisitive. "He was just interested in what was, you know, what was going on. He had very little comment to make," the trooper would say. "He was just listening to what was being said." Patterson would also remember "verbatim," he testified, an intriguing conversation between Clinton and Goodwin as the two men rode in the governor's limousine. It was in 1991, when Attorney General Bryant and Congressman Alexander were speaking out on Mena and Clinton, on the verge of his presidential candidacy, was about to hold his lone press conference on the crimes. "Tommy, I want to know—what the hell is going on at Mena?" Clinton asked his police chief, using the present tense, as Patterson insisted he heard the dialogue. "Governor," he heard Goodwin answer, "I have been told by Senator Pryor and Senator Bumpers to stay out of Mena, Arkansas." But with that, according to Patterson, neither Clinton nor Goodwin had said another word on the subject—as if the federal usurpation of state police, the seeming involvement of two United States senators in suppressing investigation of widely discussed drug and arms smuggling, needed no further explanation.

Years later a retired investigator familiar with both the Lasater and the Mena files would reflect on what happened. "You know, I guess I never really knew what we were looking at until I read that part in Clinton's letter to the ROTC fellow. You know, the part about being corrupt and all of us being lost." The passage in Bill Clinton's letter to Colonel Holmes had been, he thought, all too prophetic. "I do not think our system of government is by definition corrupt, however dangerous and inadequate it has been in recent years," Clinton had written as a young man, adding in parenthesis, "The society may be corrupt, but that is not the same thing, and if that is true we are all finished anyway."

In a sequel sadly characteristic of the story, L. D. Brown's testimony under oath about flights with Seal and Clinton's telling response would be known to some in the media in the spring of 1996. In addition, new witnesses close to Seal confirmed that the smuggler spoke of flights with "this Arkansas state trooper." Yet, as for Welch, Duncan, and others, the revelation drew attacks on the unwanted messenger rather than sparking intensified scrutiny of the crimes of Mena. Though Brown had been the last and most reluctant of the bodyguards to tell what he knew, it would be the young police officer and his own scarred record in state police politics, including a Clinton smear, not Mena, that became the issue.

·20·

Little Rock to Washington
"We Saw in Them What We Wanted to Believe"

The Clintons' campaign for the presidency began in 1986.

His third reelection as governor that year was in some ways a rehearsal for the charges and responses of the 1992 campaign. Orval Faubus, the six-term, twice-defeated seventy-six-year-old former governor, was the opponent in the primary, running out of "spite," as *Arkansas Democrat* editor John Robert Starr saw it, because Clinton had fired him from the state office of veterans affairs at the urging of the *Gazette*. But Faubus, the old hill-country populist and segregationist, was upset also by Clinton's increasingly comfortable accommodation with the state's oppressive corporate powers, especially the secretly negotiated Grand Gulf settlement that left Arkansas ratepayers charged for 80 percent of AP&L's share in a nuclear plant that did not supply power to the state (all of it went to Louisiana). Clinton, the onetime putative utility critic and consumer advocate, was now discreetly supported by AP&L and refused to release his own files on Grand Gulf despite the clamor of consumer groups.

To many, the utility deal—more than any other episode—seemed to symbolize the forty-year-old governor's compromised career. For almost a year Clinton had been using corporate contributions and other campaign funds from a rich war chest in an advertising blitz to blame the federal government for utility hikes, to "soften the impact" of Grand Gulf, as Starr reported it. The preemptive effort stifled both the criticism and Faubus's primary challenge. The governor also attacked his relic opponent for abuses of power. In a twist few were likely to perceive, the same Clinton who used his troopers to hide his own excesses now denounced Faubus for exploiting the Arkansas State Police for his "personal and political purposes."

A florid Frank White was once again the opponent in the general election, sounding hypocritical in a blunted attack on Grand Gulf because of his own earlier support of the utility and captivity by monied interests. The campaign skirted genuine issues. When White learned relatively late that Dan Lasater was under investigation by a grand jury he began to attack Clinton for steering state bond business to the contributor and suspected "coke trafficker." Republican commercials played against a backdrop of what one account called Lasater and Company's "tony Louisiana Street headquarters." But there was no inkling of how close or intense the Clinton-Lasater relationship had actually been. White's characteristically refracted charges were easily swatted away. When the GOP candidate claimed that as governor he was briefed in 1982 about police suspicions of Lasater and that Clinton had to have known about them when he allowed state bond business to pour into the renegade brokerage, state police commandant Goodwin once again supported Clinton's denials, claiming he had seen no police files on Lasater prior to 1983. And when White pointed to the Rose Law Firm's handsome share of legal fees in connection with state bond work (Hillary's "conflict of interest"), Clinton and his regime would say accurately enough, as they did of Lasater's state largesse, that the generous fees had been spread over several firms. That, after all, was the way the system worked in Little Rock. White was only slinging mud at one of the finest, most respected women in the world, a model of rectitude, Clinton would say of his wife. "Remember, Frank," he taunted, "you're running for governor, not for First Lady."

Nonetheless, the relatively lame attacks touched raw nerves. When the media at a mid-September news conference questioned Clinton about his brother's appearance as a government witness before a grand jury and about the Clintons' Lasater ties in general, Hillary stood behind the reporters, listening in visible agitation. "There have been no charges filed. The grand jury's still convened," she interrupted peremptorily when Clinton was asked about Lasater's chauffeur Chuck Berry (though Berry had already been indicted). Afterward she angrily asked a journalist if Senator Pryor and Senator Bumpers, "who also received campaign funds from Lasater, were going to be questioned on their relationship with Lasater as her husband had been," the *Gazette* reported. "Mrs. Clinton continued for several minutes questioning the nature of inquiries that had been made to her husband

and lectured a reporter on the propriety of covering grand jury investigations." Though the First Lady's outburst was the talk of newsrooms and political offices, it had the effect of chilling further questions, and neither the local press nor White would come close to exposing the reality. Even Lasater, who made an iron rule of never talking to the media, suddenly appeared—after his indictment and only days before the election—to announce that he had also contributed to Frank White in 1980 and to flourish a "Dear Supporter" form letter from the GOP camp asking the broker for another donation in 1986.

In the richest campaign in state history, Clinton would raise more than $800,000 for the languid primary against Faubus and more than a million in the general. The money had come in part from the single-largest fund-raising event ever held in Arkansas, a $500-a-head gathering of the state's elite in the fall of 1985 that netted more than a half million dollars. He overwhelmed White four to one in recorded contributions, to say nothing of the inevitable "walking around" cash. As witnesses later told the Whitewater special prosecutor, it was in 1986 that corporate pilots and other discreet messengers began carrying to Clinton intermediaries unmarked envelopes stuffed with cash. "Lots and lots off the books that year in particular," said a prominent Democrat in White Heights.

In any case, the "books" themselves, their official list of contributors, again read like a who's who of Arkansas power old and new—the trucking giants; the timber conglomerates Georgia Pacific and Weyerhauser; the financial houses Drexel Burnham, Merrill Lynch, American Express, Smith Barney, and E. F. Hutton; Worthen Bank; TCBY Yogurt; various Stephens enterprises; and on through the roll, including the usual crowd of rich supporters like the Blairs. As it had before and would again, the cash obliterated the opposition and any serious questioning of records or ties. Clinton was "as surprised as anyone," Starr noted, when the public did not seem to take his opponents or their charges seriously. He would crush White with 63.9 percent of the vote, winning two and three to one in Little Rock's wealthiest precincts and, as usual, sweeping the African American precincts and running impressively throughout the poor white regions— what one observer termed a "red-neck, black-neck" coalition. "A clear, unambiguous, and almost stunning mandate," the elated governor would call it.

That September Clinton had solemnly assured concerned Arkansas voters that he would serve a full term as governor, that he had "removed himself from contention as a candidate for president" in 1988, as one account described the pledge made repeatedly during the race. Despite a late party on election night, however, he was up before dawn the next morning for a *Today Show* interview; and in a few days, with discreet touting and leaks from Little Rock and elsewhere, *Newsweek* was listing Bill Clinton as a likely contender for the White House. Secretly, the Clintons' race began even before the 1986 vote, with national scheduling already planned for the following winter and spring, leading to an announcement of candidacy in the early summer of 1987. "We knew if we got by good in 1986, we were off," said a statehouse aide.

Yet other secrets, other plans turned out to be far more decisive. The shadowy destruction of Democratic front-runner Gary Hart in the Donna Rice affair was to influence not only the Clintons' fate and the presidential election in 1988 but also the campaign of 1992 and the presidency that followed.

◆ ◆ ◆

Absorbed by the bid they had contemplated so long, Clinton dealt with the legislative session at the beginning of 1987 in what one observer called a "chaotic" manner, agreeing to seal from public scrutiny previously open tax records, flouting his own promises of open government, betraying black supporters on a Highway Commission appointment, signing a bill fastening the hold of the giant AP&L on Arkansas cities and towns—altogether moving from commitment to surrender with a carelessness that dismayed even the more cynical Clinton watchers among local press and politicians. "He's running out of friends," one legislator told the *Democrat*, characterizing him as "so consumed by running for president that he's just used and abused people to the point that he's lost his ability to influence."

As would be the case four years later, however, many in Arkansas could see an underlying caprice and shallowness in their outwardly impressive young governor yet proudly, heedlessly thrust him forward to lead the nation and to carry the same flaws of inconstancy and disarray into the White House. On March 13, 1987, a vacillating Dale Bumpers ruled himself out of the presidential race, removing Clinton's last apparent obstacle, though some believed the governor's ambition now so burning that he would run in defiance of convention even if the state's senior senator ran as well. With Bumpers gone, however, Clinton was endorsed for the White House by AP&L president Jerry Maulden, and the Democratic State Committee—including the many members who privately deplored the leader he had become and who had leaked bitter criticism of him—unanimously adopted a resolution urging him to seek the presidential nomination.

"Oh yes, I'd very much like to do it," the governor said in response, and his wife agreed. "I don't have any ambition for him other than what he has for himself," Hillary said in her own interviews. His purpose was simple, he told reporters. He wanted to bring to Washington what he had done in Little Rock. After all, he added, Arkansas was "a pretty good microcosm of the nation."

Beginning in February and March his pace was "frantic," as one observer described it, including a major speech in New Hampshire and visits to eighteen states, what the *Gazette* called "a convincing impression of a barnstorming candidate." There were constant meetings and phone calls around the nation to raise money, which quickly yielded nearly $3 million in pledges, much of it from the wealthy individuals and large corporations he had long cultivated outside the state, including Wall Street financial houses, as well as the Arkansas interests. Asked about campaign funds in a local television interview later that spring, the governor refused to reveal how much had been committed but smilingly said money would be "no barrier" to his running. As Clinton admitted, however, he would enter the race far from the obvious choice. The front-runner for the Democratic nomination was clearly Senator Gary Hart of Colorado, a former McGovern campaign manager and a nationally known, well-financed veteran of the 1984 race. He was receiving increasingly favorable publicity, had run well ahead of George Bush, the likely GOP nominee, in the polls, and already seemed to many an odds-on favorite to be the next president.

On March 27 Clinton went to Los Angeles for an exclusive dinner with television producer Norman Lear and other figures from the entertainment industry—"Hollyticking," as the process of currying and money seeking came to be known. By striking coincidence, however, among those dining with Clinton that evening was Don Henley, a former member of the Eagles rock band. The same night, across the continent in Miami, one of Henley's close friends, a young woman named Donna Rice, was boarding a yacht called the *Monkey Business* for a voyage that would change the course of American politics.

Within the next few weeks, the public would witness the swift destruction of Gary Hart's candidacy and potential presidency. Only days after his April 13 formal announcement for the White House, the senator was the object of media speculation about his alleged womanizing. Acting on what it claimed was an anonymous tip, the *Miami Herald* followed a woman to Washington, staked out a townhouse where she was visiting Hart, and on May 4, in a story that swept through the media nationwide, accused the front-runner of an illicit "relationship" with twenty-nine-year-old party girl Donna Rice of Miami. The next day it was confirmed that Hart had spent the weekend of March 27–29 aboard the *Monkey Business,* which his aide Billy Broadhurst had chartered for the candidate's relaxation after Hart attended a scheduled fund-raiser in South Miami. On Saturday the two men had taken an overnight trip to Bimini with Rice and her girlfriend.

In the wake of the later *Herald* story, compromising photos of the Bimini trip, including one showing Rice on the senator's lap, were sold to the tabloid press for six figures. And though Hart adamantly denied charges of adultery and seemed to be riding out the *Herald* story, which some reporters had begun to question, there was more. The *Washington Post* put the Hart campaign on notice that it had been given a private detective's report purporting to show the candidate's involvement with yet another woman in Washington. It was what many later saw as the paper's power play to force the candidate out of the race. Meanwhile, amid the blaring headlines and rumors, crucial sources of Hart campaign money and support were deserting him. On May 8, less than a month after he had declared as the clear favorite and only three days after the *Monkey Business* exposé, Hart withdrew.

As elements of the Hart drama began to emerge afterward, it was clear that his personality and habits had driven his fate to some extent. Yet there had been more to the politician's destruction than vulnerable psychology. Whatever his other strengths or weaknesses, Hart was no ordinary candidate to those in the inner recesses of power.

As a freshman senator he had been a key member of the celebrated Church committee investigating CIA abuses and specifically the agency's incessant links to organized crime. He had gone on to serve on the new Senate Intelligence Oversight Committee, where he continued to be known for advocating further investigation and exposure of the alliance between the mob and the US intelligence community. Hart would be a vocal critic of CIA covert operations in general. A leading opponent of the Nicaraguan Contra war, the senator had barely escaped what he and others believed to be an assassination plot in 1983 when he flew into Managua at the time of an extraordinary CIA-sponsored Contra air strike against the capital.

From 1984 to 1987 Hart was repeatedly on record voicing his skepticism about the official version of the assassination of President John F. Kennedy and promising that if elected president in 1988 he would order the opening of all CIA and other government files in question, looking in particular at the possible role of organized crime figures Santo Trafficante, John Roselli, and Sam Giancana in the Kennedy murder—the last two of whom had been killed during the Church committee inquiry. By the mid-1980s Hart was increasingly bold in exposing the "sleaze factor" in the Reagan administration, including the wider influence of the mob in Washington. According to someone familiar with a written record of the remark, Trafficante had said of Gary Hart, "We need to get rid of the son of a bitch."

Though it came too late to affect his fate, there would be still more evidence that Hart's fall was not what it seemed at the time. According to US Customs sources, one part of the setting of the episode had long been suspected of a role in drug running. Some of those involved in Hart's Miami-Bimini weekend turned out to have links to organized crime and cocaine trafficking and, in spiraling circles beyond, to crime bosses of the Jewish and Italian syndicates, who in turn possessed ties to the US intelligence community dating back to the Bay of Pigs and earlier.

Discrepancies were plain in the *Miami Herald*'s role in the affair as well. In the supposedly spontaneous call of the paper's public-spirited tipster there had been highly implausible detail about Hart's movements and phone records over the preceding period, intimate knowledge that should have prompted journalistic suspicion but that the paper apparently never questioned. In fact, as a subsequent independent investigation would show, Hart had been under surveillance by unknown parties for days and perhaps weeks before the weekend of March 27–29.

There were also reports of sensational videotapes of the *Monkey Business,* part of a professional surveillance of the vessel. Despite unexplained money, incriminating phone calls, and even evidence of a contract murder, most of the media had simply repeated the first trumpeted charges and reprinted the supplied photos, joined the clamor that forced the candidate from the race, and then moved on to the next story. There was no doubt that Hart inhabited the edge, but there was compelling evidence, too, that he had been pushed over it. And both self-inflicted and arranged, the ruin of Gary Hart would have historic impact on the Clintons.

Though Clinton continued to travel to a few dates in Washington and elsewhere after the headlines of May 4–8, for most of the next month the Hart scandal and withdrawal threw him and his campaign into a fearful paralysis. "What happened to Gary Hart scared the hell out of him," said one statehouse aide. "He just pulled back and shivered like it had been him," said another, "and of course with the women problem it could have been." Whereas only days before there had been a coy smugness about the cash he was raising and funds were "no barrier," reporters suddenly detected in Clinton a cautious ambivalence about both money and support and, in place of the almost boyish gleefulness of April, a studied indecision by the second week in May.

Returning from a trip in mid-June, he gave the waiting press in Little Rock a bleak assessment. "I can tell you there has been erosion," he said of his position, though never hinting at the real fear and vulnerability. The front-runner's withdrawal ought to have strengthened his chances considerably, but now he was the victim of circumstance and logistics. He had waited for Bumpers to pull out, he said, and perhaps the senator's indecision had made him too late. Since he had not yet formally declared, the former Hart aides and contributors Clinton had hoped to inherit were going instead to Massachusetts governor Michael Dukakis. "Clinton was thinking of all the reasons he normally would have waved aside," an aide remembered. "Inside he was still acting like he was going to run," said a friend, "but he was getting ready in June to bail out, making excuses because he was afraid he'd be the next candidate everybody would see sitting there grinning stupidly with a woman on his lap."

At midnight on June 30 Clinton called former Hart aide Raymond Strother in Washington to tell him, "Let's go." In early July the Clintons were reported to have bought a condominium for the Rodhams in Little Rock so the grandparents could care for seven-year-old Chelsea during the coming campaign. The national media and aides and backers from around the country were invited to what many believed would be an announcement of candidacy at a luncheon on July 15.

Most in the crowd of three hundred would be shocked. His eyes watery, Hillary at his side in obvious distress, Clinton said he had decided against a run because he wanted to spend more time with his daughter. He had promised himself "a long, long time ago if I was ever lucky enough to have a kid, my child would never grow up wondering who her father was." The decision had been a real "tug-of-war," he told the hushed, sniffling audience, but "I knew it wasn't my time." Fear of scrutiny of his personal life had not been a factor in his decision, he told them earnestly. "But I thought about it a lot and we debated it a lot." He had decided how he would handle questions about his personal life, but he would not discuss it further at this point "because I am not a candidate."

To loud applause he added, "For whatever it's worth, I'd still like to be president. And if I get another chance, I'll be 110 percent."

Behind closed doors at the mansion there had been another reality, genuine vacillation but a rather different "tug-of-war." According to three separate accounts, Clinton had been strangely undeterred by Hart's early, almost prohibitive lead. Much as he would four years later, he seemed to some uncharacteristically ready to settle for less than the top prize, perhaps the vice presidency or merely name recognition for another run in 1992. "He'd been itching to go for so long," said an associate. "I think he just wanted to jump in and see what happened." Hart's sudden removal in May might now have opened Clinton's way as he had never imagined—except for the fact that his personal excesses made him far more vulnerable than Hart.

If Clinton himself thought Hart had been set up by outside forces, aides who were with him much of the time never heard him say so in the restless days of talking and arguing leading up to his July 15 announcement. Whether or not Hart's removal surprised Bill Clinton, the manner in which it was done clearly sent a chill through the mansion in Little Rock. Suddenly a candidate's private life and philandering seemed susceptible to scrutiny as never before. While Clinton had long been immune in Arkansas—almost cavalier in the openness of some of his extramarital affairs—the rules seemed to be changing just as he was reaching for his ultimate ambition.

In an embarrassed, vain attempt to confront the issue, two of his closest backers met with him privately at the mansion in late June, while Hillary was gone. They carried a list of some of the women most widely known to have been involved with the governor since the late 1970s. It was a precursor of what would be called inside the 1992 campaign the "doomsday list," a later and longer enumeration of Clinton's affairs or other sexual episodes, with each woman assessed and action recommended according to her potential for exposure or betrayal. In the early summer of 1987, however, Clinton had been dismayed, and angry, at this first crude effort at the "damage control" for which his campaign later became famous.

"He didn't even recognize some of the names of women we knew he'd done," said one adviser. "He just got red in the face and waved his arms and said, 'Get this goddamned paper out of here. Hillary doesn't know any of this. What good is this goddamned paper?' " As if to make the advisers' point, there were soon stories gusting around Little Rock that the *Democrat* had what was called "a Hart-like exposé" of Clinton's womanizing ready for its front page on the Wednesday the governor announced. Though the paper had no such story then or later, "either in the works or in the can," as Oakley noted in a column, the rumor further sealed his decision.

About what happened next, accounts differed. In one version Clinton had finally raised the issue more explicitly than ever with his wife, who was obviously aware of the problem, if not its magnitude, and whose reaction was bitter. It was the "nadir of their marriage," Gail Sheehy reported. There was a "raging argument," according to an aide. "She was furious that he was so worried it would come out, that it couldn't be handled," said an adviser who saw them together at the time.

In yet another recollection, Clinton had simply told his wife that they could not run, that he was too "vulnerable," but they had not talked much more until after his withdrawal. "They had the real hashing-out after everybody went home," said a former aide.

In either case, Clinton had told friends and advisers that "I'm not ready for this," as one recalled, "and neither is Hillary." A handful in the July 15 audience knew that his teary remarks to the press were the usual political cover. He "could not face the prospect of the national media spreading rumors of his infidelities," one foreign journalist reported the governor's telling his closest supporters just before his announcement. Yet at the time both the local and the national media remained largely silent on Clinton's deeper motives, in effect crucially postponing any wider publicity on the issue of womanizing. The usually acerbic Oakley seemed relieved that he was not running for the White House and ready to take him at his word that he had done what was "best for himself and for his family," though she gently reminded readers of his personal frailty. "They were so caught up in the excitement about having a viable presidential contender from Arkansas," she wrote in words of lasting relevance, "that they forgot about the man in question."

Furious then or later, Hillary Rodham Clinton was outwardly stoic as usual when his indiscretions now cost them the chance for which she had worked so hard and sacrificed so much. She gave the media her own excuses. "As far as she was concerned," the *Gazette* noted in contradiction to most of what it had been reporting for weeks, "she had not wanted to launch another campaign at this time." There was a strange foreshadow of 1992 and the Clintons' famous *60 Minutes* appearance. "BY HER MAN," the *Democrat* captioned a photo of the First Lady wiping away a tear as her husband announced he would not run for president.

◆   ◆   ◆

Clinton would give an early endorsement to the relatively conservative Michael Dukakis for the 1988 campaign against Jesse Jackson and more reform-minded elements in the Democratic Party, many of them the remnant or spiritual legacy of the old McGovern forces. By several accounts, he even "coached" Dukakis in a more homey and earnest style and—as Republicans mounted one of the worst smear campaigns of the century, including the infamous Willie Horton ads playing on racism and fear of crime—in a more aggressive counterattack. But the taut, technocratic, privately acid and publicly diffident Massachusetts governor was a frustrating, eventually enraging pupil. "Dukakis drove him crazy, positively nuts," said one aide who watched the two men interact, the nominee largely ignoring Clinton's advice while the Southerner seethed in the conviction that he himself would have been a far better candidate. The disdain extended to their wives as well, Hillary Clinton privately deploring Kitty Dukakis's relative informality and self-effacement. "She thought Kitty had no fight in her," said a woman who heard the remarks, "and not the dignity or sense of real privacy to be a president's wife."

When Dukakis chose Clinton to give his nominating speech at the Atlanta convention, what should have been an impressive nationwide exposure turned into a cosmetic disaster for the Arkansas Governor. In a draft polished by Hillary, like all other important speeches, but then tampered with by the fratricidal Dukakis camp, Clinton droned on for what seemed endless minutes on prime-time television as the Omni house lights remained undimmed and undisciplined Dukakis delegates milled and murmured in utter distraction. It was an unprecedented humiliation for a Clinton who prided himself on his oratory and who was invariably deferred to both in Arkansas and around the country. All too aware of the debacle, he was apparently powerless to improvise to escape it; his voice grew "tinny" and "desperate," as one Arkansas reporter remembered, and his face typically "redder by the minute." When it was finally over, the crowd cheering his departure from the stage, the pride of Hope and Hot Springs had become the butt of jokes. "What a windbag," Johnny Carson remarked to his audience of millions. The surgeon general, he said, had approved Clinton as an over-the-counter sleep aid.

The Clintons were more furious than staff or friends had ever seen them. Dukakis was the "son of a bitch of the week," recalled one reporter, while for months afterward Clinton bitterly referred to the nominee in front of the troopers and other aides as "that little Greek motherfucker." Meantime, Hillary moved with customary resolve to retrieve the situation, summoning Betsey Wright to Atlanta to manage the aftermath and shrewdly telephoning Hollywood friends Harry Thomason and Linda Bloodworth-Thomason, Arkansans made good as sit-com producers. In hours Clinton had an invitation to be on Carson's show, where his self-deprecating performance and saxophone solo seemed to redeem him. The Thomasons threw a gala party afterward with a sign showing the White House and captioned "On the Road Again. Clinton '96." Some were not so sure. The Atlanta speech showed "the real Bill Clinton," thought *Gazette* reporter John Brummett, and had been damaging with "the big-money people in the Democratic Party."

As it was, Dukakis's forfeit of a seventeen-point poll lead and his decisive defeat by George Bush would mean more than any Clinton blunder; he would have a chance again in 1992, though the specter that drove him from the race still loomed. Hardly noticed amid the campaign, the Gridiron Club of Little Rock journalists and politicians put on a skit at a 1988 gathering that brought down the house. Members impersonating Gary Hart and Bill Clinton came on stage and sang a parody of a popular song, "To All the Girls We've Loved."

◆ ◆ ◆

As Clinton had hinted in his 1987 withdrawal, he and Hillary had already begun to formulate the tactics they would adopt to deal with the all too real potential for a sex scandal's erupting during a presidential campaign. He had thought it a "weakness" in Hart, aides remembered, that the senator seemed to equivocate over issues like a definition of adultery and appeared unprepared to lash back to discredit the attacks. Hart, who had formally and openly separated from his wife in 1979 and again in 1981, would admit to having seen women during the separations but otherwise refused to answer questions about infidelity. At the same time, no woman had come forward to accuse him, including Donna Rice.

With Hart's precedent and four years to prepare, Clinton's response would be more concerted and sophisticated, at least as staff and advisers saw it evolve between 1987 and the 1992 race. He might acknowledge having had "difficulties" in his marriage—"nodding humbly at the weakness of the flesh," as a Hot Springs friend put it caustically, "like a good Southern Baptist is supposed to do"—but dismiss them as all in the past. Unlike what they saw as a passive Lee Hart, Hillary would stand behind him with characteristic firmness. "She was never to play the poor little wife," said one adviser. They would also be prepared to strike back at any women accusers—"taking on the bitches," as one former staff member put it—including with private campaigns of "spin" to discredit them with the media and even pressures to silence them. Above all, however, Clinton would simply deny everything. Barring the most direct evidence—which advisers and others say he always assumed would never be available—he was sure the story could go no further. The governor, they remembered, had an almost mystical faith in the absence of photographs. "He felt it was probably those pictures that killed Hart, that and being sort of mealy-mouthed about the whole thing," one friend remembered. "If you could deny it over and over, the reporters would get tired sooner or later and go away to something else." As Clinton himself would tell one of the women, Gennifer Flowers, late in 1991, "If they ever hit you with it, just say no and go on. There's nothing they can do. . . . If everybody kinda hangs tough, they're just not going to do anything. They can't . . . if they don't have pictures."

Even given all the familiar reasons for discretion and concealment by the women themselves, there was no small potential for revelation. There had been far too many cases. As they eventually told their stories after he was elected president, the Arkansas trooper bodyguards and others would testify to Bill Clinton's extramarital relations with literally hundreds of women. "There would hardly be an opportunity he would let slip to have sex," a state police security guard told the London *Sunday Times* in 1994. Insistent denials by both Clinton and the woman in question would not always be a guarantee of erasing suspicion, even without photos. While one woman employee of an Arkansas utility continued to deny any relationship with the governor, for example, the *Los Angeles Times* unearthed partial phone records between 1989 and 1991 that showed Clinton telephoning her fifty-nine times at her home and office, placing eleven cellular calls to her residence on July 16, 1989, and, two months later, while on an official trip, making a ninety-four-minute call at 1:23 a.m. and another for eighteen minutes the next morning at 7:45. Clinton had been wrong when he talked about telephone evidence in a tape-recorded conversation with Gennifer Flowers in December 1991. Did she have phone records? he had asked her after she told him someone had broken into her apartment.

"Unh unh. I mean why would I? You . . . you usually call me, for that matter. And besides, who would know?" Flowers had answered. And Clinton, speaking from the mansion, had seemed to reassure himself: "Isn't that amazing? Well . . . I wouldn't care if they . . . you know, I, I . . . They may have my phone records on this computer here, but I don't think it. . . . That doesn't prove anything."

Though most of the eyewitness accounts would appear only after the 1992 election, the list of the future president's illicit affairs would be remarkably detailed, including more than twenty women who stepped forward or were otherwise publicly identified by the spring of 1994. Troopers would describe the wife of a prominent local judge, a Little Rock reporter, a former state employee, a cosmetics clerk at a Little Rock department store, and several others, including Flowers, whom Clinton had seen at intervals of two to three times a week in the course of relationships lasting anywhere from weeks to months to years. According to the British press, there had been a black woman who claimed, after more than a dozen visits by the future president, that Clinton was the father of her child. In the testimony, too, were the settings and circumstances—the flaunting of girlfriends in public, Clinton's slipping troopers cash to pay for gifts at Victoria's Secret in Little Rock's University Mall, the constant and often vain efforts to conceal movements from Hillary and the periodic scenes between Clinton and her, the numberless one-night stands with strangers in the state and beyond, oral sex in the dark parking lot of Chelsea's elementary school. "Later he told me that he had researched the subject in the Bible," trooper Larry Patterson told the *American Spectator,* "and oral sex isn't considered adultery." Some thought it all undeniably pathological. "What has emerged," Geordie Greig of the London *Sunday Times* wrote, "is a man with what would appear to be an almost psychotic inability to control his zipper."

From the first alarm and strategizing after the Hart episode in 1987, the response of the Clinton entourage had been to view the womanizing in an almost prudish way, fearing outright public rejection. "We were thinking how it was going to play in Jonesboro or Paragould," said one aide, "and of course we were thinking of Gary Hart." But the national public response in 1992 would prove apparently more lenient and worldly. When audiences in New Hampshire, New York, or California seemed ready to accept that a presidential candidate's private life—whatever his extramarital sexual habits and whether they credited his denials or not—had no bearing on his integrity as a leader, Clinton's aides regarded their strategy of simply stonewalling as vindicated.

Neither then nor later did many of those around Clinton reflect on the deeper meaning of the womanizing and what it said about other aspects of the man and leader.

At almost every turn in the history was an abuse of power and trust: the routine employment of the troopers to facilitate, stand guard, and cover up; the use of state cars and time and the sheer good name and prestige of the governor's office.

It was not that Clinton had governed and then made his sexual forays as part of some scrupulously separate private life. In part because of the furtive shadow play with Hillary, in part the product of his own insouciance and sense of entitlement, much of the philandering took place during the workday, on official trips, or around ceremonial or political functions. He had indulged a good deal of his relentless promiscuity *as* the government. Propositioning young women at county fairs or enticing state employees at conferences, he enjoyed much of his predatory privilege because he *was* the government.

There was also the issue of how much the illicit practices opened the governor and future president to blackmail or how much the gifts and other expenses, which could not be taken from any legitimate income that Hillary might notice, made him all the more dependent on his own "walking around" cash from backers. Equally telling was what it all revealed about his genuine attitude toward women. The repeated testimony of the troopers would show the undisguised Clinton rating women as objects, "ripe peaches," as he called them, "purely to be graded, purely to be chased, dominated, conquered," according to L. D. Brown. The governor had been predatory even toward one of the trooper's wives and toward another's mother-in-law.

There was a sharp demarcation between his two worlds, the public champion of equal rights naming women to high office and the seducer who preferred his partners without too much rival seriousness, rewarding substance only as part of the seduction. A young staff analyst for the National Governors' Association would remember Clinton's courting her not only by personal charm and flirtation but also by ardent support of her policy proposals. When she firmly rebuffed his advances one night at an NGA dance, however, he instantly lost interest in her ideas—"cut me and the policies dead the next day," she remembered. When a former Miss Arkansas, Sally Perdue, told of a four-month affair with Clinton that began not long after he returned to power in 1983, reports fixed on her colorful details of the governor parading around her apartment in one of her black nightgowns playing his saxophone, using cocaine. More significant were the circumstances of their breakup. When she told him she was thinking of running for mayor of Pine Bluff, Clinton bristled. "You'd—you'd better not run for mayor," he warned her, and the relationship ended in an angry argument. He was clearly upset that she had crossed a line, Perdue remembered. A "good ole boy," as she recalled him, he had wanted a "good little girl" as an intimate. "I don't think he really wanted me to be an independent thinker at that point," Perdue would say.

Fear of exposure notwithstanding, the behavior would continue through the election and transition. Among the troopers' stories would be a scene at the Little Rock airport as the president-elect and his wife left for Virginia and their inaugural procession into Washington. Hillary noticed a security guard escorting one of the women to the farewell ceremony and turned on him angrily. "What the fuck do you think you're doing?" she asked Larry Patterson, according to his account in the *American Spectator*. "I know who that whore is. I know what she's doing here. Get her out of here." In a reaction familiar to many aides, Clinton simply shrugged and the trooper took the woman back to the city. At the same juncture, having witnessed during the later days of the campaign and during the transition what some in Arkansas had seen for years, even the legendarily discreet Secret Service was shocked by the new occupants of the White House. According to reliable sources, some of the agents who had been in Little Rock filed an extraordinary warning with headquarters referring in old-fashioned terms to issues of "moral turpitude" involving the president-elect.

Even after the troopers' initial revelations in the *Los Angeles Times* and the *American Spectator* late in 1993, however, the issue would be all but marginalized by the mainstream media. "I'm not interested in Bill Clinton's sex life as governor of Arkansas," *New York Times* Washington bureau chief R. W. Apple told a British reporter. At the same time, longtime *Washington Post* journalist Mike Isikoff would find himself in a shouting match with editors who were refusing to publish even a portion of his meticulously researched investigative report on Paula Jones, who would later bring a sexual harassment lawsuit against the president. Jones's much-substantiated story of being propositioned by Clinton at the Excelsior Hotel in Little Rock on May 8, 1991, when she was a twenty-four-year-old Arkansas state employee, was typical of the situation in which many young women of her time and class found themselves during the Clinton era. Yet few episodes so starkly expressed the inherent sexism, class discrimination, and willful myopia of the Washington establishment as the Jones case. The media, national women's organizations, leaders throughout the Congress, and organized labor and other ostensibly progressive institutions alternately ignored, dismissed, or even belittled Jones and witnesses like her. The studied hypocrisy and insensitivity to the underlying issues of abuse of power and exploitation of women would be one more vivid example of the capital's culture of complicity.

◆ ◆ ◆

In the years leading to the 1992 election the Clintons would enjoy a similar tacit indifference and acceptance regarding the life and career that Hillary Clinton pursued.

There would be several sources—including a former US attorney, sometime aides, a number of lawyers, social friends, and many of the same troopers who testified about the governor's illicit acts—who described the First Lady's affair, dating to the mid-1980s, with Rose partner Vince Foster. A relationship evident in the semiprivate kisses and furtive squeezes at parties and dinners described by the security guards, it was also an intimate professional bond between two attorneys who worked together on some of their firm's most sensitive cases. Along with Webster Hubbell, they staged a veritable coup d'état to wrest control of the Rose firm in 1988. Many thought that the governor was well aware of the affair and ultimately accepted it as one more implicit bargain in their marriage. Clinton continued to treat Vince Foster as the close friend he had been since childhood in Hope, even entrusting him with some of the most crucial secrets of the 1992 campaign. "Bill knew, of course he knew," said a lawyer close to Foster who was familiar with them all. "But what the hell was *he* supposed to say to anybody about being faithful?"

To some, Hillary's relationship with Vince Foster, a tall, handsome, courtly figure who was widely respected in the Little Rock legal and business community, was an understandable and natural response to her husband's behavior. Foster was known to treat her with the dignity, respect, and abiding love she was missing in her marriage. "He adored her," said a fellow lawyer. Under other circumstances, it might have been one of those relationships that remained private and without any political relevance to the Clinton presidency. What set it apart was that, once in the White House, the Clintons would install the First Lady's confidant in one of the nation's most sensitive positions as deputy counsel to the president, where he would handle controversial matters stemming from their Arkansas past as well as highly classified presidential affairs.

"I cannot make this point to you too strongly," Foster told University of Arkansas Law School graduates in the spring of 1993 in his last public statement. "There is no victory, no advantage, no fee, no favor which is worth even a blemish on your reputation for intellect and integrity. . . . Dents to the reputation in the legal profession are irreparable." But the man whom the *Washington Post* would call the "integrity cop" in the Clinton White House was destined to die an unquiet death. According to the official inquiry, on a sultry July day Foster ate a hearty lunch from the White House mess at his desk, left the office at midday without explanation, and was found only hours later in a park overlooking the Potomac, a fatal gunshot wound through his mouth. Nothing else about the event would be without controversy: Foster's state of mind, the unaccountable debt he left at the White House credit union despite personal affluence, the Clinton papers on Whitewater and other matters that were in his office, which was entered soon after his death by Patsy Thomasson and other White House aides, and even whether he lost or actually gained weight in the weeks leading up to his death. Initially ruled a suicide, Foster's shooting would come under investigation by the Whitewater special prosecutor in 1995, an office that had not even been contemplated at the time of his death.

Whatever the circumstances of Foster's fate would eventually prove to be, he had been a man who knew many of the money secrets of both the campaign of 1992 and the Clinton presidency, just as he knew the secrets of the Rose firm and of Hillary Rodham Clinton's business and financial dealings over the previous decade, dealings that would become the subject of numerous investigations and would cast an even greater shadow over the White House than his death would.

◆　◆　◆

In the summer of 1990, in the midst of a bitter reelection campaign, the Clintons would publish a financial statement purporting to show their financial condition while in the governorship, though the figures went back only to 1980—discreetly short of Hillary's 1979 windfall in the commodity trades. Even at that, the numbers were surprising to many in Arkansas. Clinton had made only $35,000 a year as governor, and Hillary's income had risen from $46,000 to $98,000 yearly over the decade as a Rose partner. The couple's net worth at the end of 1989 was listed at more than a half million dollars, their total assets first claimed to be $418,692, then revised upward the next day to $614,094 because investment accounts had been left out of the initial statement. Their adjusted gross income had been well over $100,000 annually for most of the ten years, and in addition to their salaries, Hillary's director's fees from corporate boards, miscellaneous income, and capital gains had reached as high as $70,000 yearly by the late 1980s.

In one of the poorest states in the nation—its average annual income barely $19,000 and one in every five, or half a million people, living below the poverty line—the Clintons were relatively affluent. Dorothy Rodham need not have worried at their wedding fifteen years before that they were sacrificing "luxury and money," as she had put it, by "realizing their ideals" in running for office. As the record would show, Bill and Hillary Clinton were as committed to making money as to holding political power, and in many ways the two drives and results were so entwined as to be inseparable. It was an old and simple reciprocal in Arkansas and American politics. They had gained and held power in large measure because of their appreciation of money, and they had received much of their money because they were in power.

Their official financial statement in 1990 revealed little of the Clintons' real circumstances, the perquisites and favors that surrounded and mortgaged their political rise, and none of Hillary Clinton's steady, often tenacious acquisitiveness. By the end of the decade they were benefiting from a tax-paid household budget of over $800,000 a year, including a thousand dollars a week for food alone. By special legislative dispensation, Clinton was also receiving for purposes of retirement benefits three years' credit for every one served as governor and two for every one as attorney general, which would give him some thirty-eight years' worth of retirement benefits when he left office in 1993, as if he had been working at the top of state government in Arkansas since the age of eight.

But that was only the beginning of their wider advantages. From 1983 to 1988 Clinton obtained twelve bank loans from one bank totaling some $400,000, according to an exclusive Associated Press report—all of which were personally guaranteed by Clinton and arranged without security or collateral. By May 1995 the *Washington Post* would report that the Whitewater independent counsel was looking beyond the $400,000 into more than $800,000 in "campaign-related loans that a handful of Arkansas banks made to Clinton while he was governor." Though the Clintons would later claim that $300,000 of this borrowed money was used for elections, his official campaign contribution records would not reflect such donations or loans from the candidate and there would be no explanation for as much as $500,000 of the borrowed money. Apparently, much of this personal debt was eventually paid back by contributors, including $25,000 from TCBY, $15,000 from Tyson Foods, and $11,500 from the same Union Bank that had loaned them the $20,000 Whitewater down payment. (Spokesmen for Tyson and others later claimed they believed they were contributing to a fund for promoting education or other Clinton policies, as distinct from paying back personal debts or giving to a political campaign.) In the end, some suspected that what may have been nearly a million dollars constituted, as one called it, a Clinton "slush fund." How they spent the money would not be completely accounted for by 1996. Tax records showed that they never claimed it as income, though many in Arkansas believed that they obviously benefited personally from much of it. "It's still sitting out there in fiscal limbo," wrote author Martin Gross.

As Clinton was taking in $400,000 to $800,000 in unaccounted loans repaid by someone else over the late 1980s, Hillary was avidly pursuing her own opportunities in circumstances that would prove questionable as well. In 1983 she had put $2,014 into an investment group under David Watkins—a Hope native and Clinton loyalist whose Little Rock advertising firm produced many of the governor's political spots—to compete for a lucrative cellular-phone franchise in Little Rock. When their bid failed initially, Watkins took a loan—with Hillary Rodham Clinton personally guaranteeing $60,000 of it—to buy out the winner of the franchise. In 1988 the group sold the franchise to a large telecommunications firm for a profit of more than $2 million, and the First Lady received $45,998 on her original $2,014 investment. On the surface it seemed another fortunate venture, but Hillary Clinton had been no ordinary investor in the scheme and David Watkins no ordinary promoter.

As Larry Wallace, owner of the NBC affiliate in Little Rock and another partner in the group, later told a reporter, influence with the Federal Communications Commission had been assumed crucial to winning the franchise, and "Hillary's connection to the governor was thought to be a way of attracting the FCC." As for Watkins, according to a 1994 investigative report by *Business Week*, interviews with more than a dozen former associates and investors, as well as court documents and financial statements, showed what the magazine called "a man with a past," including "a trail of disappointed investors" and "a string of failed penny-stock companies from New York to Texas, hawking items from cruises to credit cards." Watkins's Amerinet was started in 1986 to market Visa cards, went public through a reverse merger with a Nevada shell company, and sank amid investor complaints of securities fraud and management plunder; a 1987 franchise cash-checking operation soon collapsed with more embittered investors; and elder-care franchises and ocean cruises floundered as well. "Many of Watkins's ventures," *Business Week* concluded, "flew below SEC radar."

Yet, as with Jim McDougal and others, the dealmaker's record was no deterrent to his relationship with the Clintons. Not long after Hillary's boon in the cellular-phone franchise, the governor named Watkins's father to the Arkansas Pollution Control and Ecology Commission, whose sweeping powers over Arkansas's air and water quality standards and land use policies made it one of the most prized preserves of the interests. By the early 1990s David Watkins was a millionaire despite his business history and the fate of the investors he recruited, and he in turn would help the Clinton presidential campaign arrange at the beginning of 1992 a candidacy-saving but highly controversial bridge loan of $3.5 million from the Stephens-controlled Worthen Bank. Equally important, as deputy manager and chief financial officer of the campaign, he also helped arrange around the same time a contract worth more than a million dollars designating his friends in Little Rock's World Wide Travel the campaign's travel agents. It proved a critical relationship, at least behind the scenes. At a crucial moment early in the 1992 race, when Bill Clinton was still reeling financially and politically from charges of infidelity and a second-place finish in the New Hampshire primary, World Wide would defer billing on enormous travel costs, allowing Clinton to pour scarce money into the pivotal Michigan and Illinois primaries. "Were it not for World Wide Travel here," Watkins would boast to *Travel Weekly* magazine, "the Arkansas governor may never have been in contention for the highest office in the land."

Named assistant to the president for management and administration in 1993, Watkins would go on to be a central figure in the Travelgate scandal, a furtive maneuver by Hillary and others in the first weeks of the Clinton presidency to replace the White House Travel Office with World Wide. In the resulting controversy, inquiry, and findings of shady practice, Watkins would be officially reprimanded by White House chief of staff and old friend Mack McLarty and taken to task by Congress for backdating personnel appointments and pay raises. Eventually he resigned when he was discovered using a presidential helicopter for a golf outing to Maryland's Eastern Shore.

Cellular-phone franchises were a common windfall for the politically connected during the 1980s. "The scandal isn't what's illegal, the scandal is what's legal," observed the *New Republic*'s "TRB." But the franchise episode was only one of many ways Hillary Clinton realized a financial advantage from her position. Seemingly oblivious or indifferent to the companies' practices, she would take and keep lucrative seats on the boards of numerous corporations. She was a $30,000-a-year director of Lafarge Corporation, the nation's second-largest cement producer, whose kilns were under official and private condemnation from Michigan to California for burning hundreds of millions of gallons of toxic waste. She was the first and sole woman on the board of Arkansas's giant Wal-Mart under a reactionary, authoritarian Sam Walton, known for his low wages, antiunion venom, sexism, and a company patriarchy that forbade employees to date one another without approval. She was a trustee of Little Rock's booming TCBY Yogurt, which paid Rose hundreds of thousands of dollars in fees and whose executives gave themselves pay raises and golden parachutes while shareholders filed a class-action lawsuit citing the corporation's "disdain for the truth." In the boardrooms of each, as among the Rose partners, as in other settings, she would not only fail to challenge the abuses petty and major but, by her very presence and prestige, lend support.

It was much the same in her more visible, noncorporate public roles during the late 1980s: chairing an ad hoc group of the American Bar Association on sexism in the legal profession, sitting on the board of the Children's Defense Fund, or, somewhat more behind the scenes, devising a desegregation scheme for the Little Rock federal court or a state government ethics reform proposal. She would be outwardly impressive in each yet, on closer examination, substantively vacant in the end. In the ABA review of what amounted to massive gender discrimination, "Clinton's tangible accomplishments," as one study of the review put it, "amounted to little more than a few reports and manuals and a lot of speeches." While she claimed the Children's Defense Fund as the very symbol of her commitment, policies on child welfare and foster care under the Clinton administration in Little Rock had produced a scandalous system of neglect, leading some of the groups Hillary Rodham had once supported to bring a scathing lawsuit against Bill Clinton. So, too, her recommendations on Pulaski County desegregation—still to be achieved nearly four decades after the US Supreme Court's *Brown* decision—would prove a convoluted political expedient, and her plan for governmental ethics reform in Arkansas, passed as well through her quietly felonious partner Webb Hubbell, managed to exempt the governor's office from critical accountability. "She was far less adept at making a difference in public policy than at making money," said one man who worked closely with her in Little Rock and elsewhere. The verdict of those who looked beyond the mere résumé went back to the bargain she had made long before. "No matter how accomplished and brilliant she is, or what she wants, or what she has done, or what she stands for," wrote Nina Martin after a 1993 investigation of the record, "in the end it is her husband's agenda—and career—that always comes first."

Meanwhile she continued to expand her financial portfolio. She would join Vince Foster and Hubbell in a private investment scheme in 1983 that made them rather than their spouses the beneficiaries; bought into oil-drilling partnerships for tax deductions; invested substantially in Value Partners, a prestigious White Heights investment pool; and in 1990–91 reportedly accepted $101,630 as a consultant to a New York State–funded commission on education and the economy. At home, at least, she could be persistent, even intimidating, in her reach. When she joined the board of the Southern Development Corporation, a consortium of local charities put together with state funds to make loans to the most needy, she soon lobbied for Rose to get the group's legal work, yielding some $150,000 in fees. "She just pitched a fit to get that retainer," said another member of the board.

Together the future president and First Lady seemed no less concerned about realizing the benefits of their own charity, taking nearly $200,000 off their taxes in charitable deductions over the 1980s, usually attaching a handwritten list itemizing their noncash contributions—$30 for three shower curtains, $5 for an electric razor, $40 for an old pair of Bill's running shoes, various amounts for discarded undershorts and shirts. By many accounts the grasping at opportunity was part of her fierce sense of sacrifice—and thus of self-justification. Hillary was said to be furious when their handler, Dickie Morris, told her at one point that many in hard-up Arkansas were likely to resent her putting in a swimming pool at the governor's mansion. "Her friends in the Heights had one, so why couldn't she?" said another adviser. "Why can't we lead the lives of normal people?" Hillary Rodham Clinton had demanded in an angry argument with the consultant.

◆   ◆   ◆

If the Clintons did well enough in the mansion, if they felt entitled to all their income, perquisites, and more, their portion was still only a relative scrap compared to the great fortunes their governance allowed a handful of the ultrawealthy to amass during the 1980s. "You have to remember that for political purposes there are really just two classes in this state—rich and dirt," a prominent Little Rock attorney would say. "The Clintons got their votes from the dirt and their money from the rich and saw themselves always as part of the money." By the early 1990s, as Clinton ended his dozen years as governor and readied himself to enter the White House, wealth and power were consolidated in Arkansas as never before.

Forbes called them the "undeniably formidable business juggernauts"—the "mind-boggling" concentrations of wealth and influence like Stephens, Wal-Mart, Tyson Foods, J. B. Hunt, Dillards, TCBY, and others, whose success "had everything to do with a no-holds-barred unfettered approach to free enterprise," as the magazine put it. "Be assured that when these entrepreneurial Arkansas capitalists want to talk, Bill Clinton is ready to listen."

Their arrogance and reach were legends in Little Rock and beyond. Confronted with a state supreme court decision that might have cramped his control, Witt Stephens, "Mr. Witt," as his kept governors and legislators respectfully knew him, was only momentarily annoyed. "Well, hell, we'll just change the law," he said and proceeded to do just that. Under his brother Jackson Stephens, the multibillion-dollar Stephens, Inc. continued to wield the same, almost perfunctory dominance during the Clinton years despite a facade of mutual distaste the financier and the politician found it expedient to present to the public. "Privately they had a very warm relationship," a Rose senior partner would say of Clinton and the Stephens clan and executives, whose interests Hillary and Vince Foster represented legally and who openly joined the Clinton contributor lists in 1990 and 1992, as well as moving to save his presidential candidacy with the Worthen Bank credit line.

If less subtle, it was much the same with poultry tycoon Don Tyson. From his Springdale headquarters, adorned with an executive suite that was a replica of the Oval Office (but with doorknobs in the shape of hen's eggs), and with Clinton confidante Jim Blair installed as house lawyer, Tyson disposed a multibillion-dollar empire of international scope. Like Wal-Mart, it was a gigantically profitable corporation of primitive paternalism. Norman Solomon wrote that the poultry industry in Arkansas "keeps its farmers in near indentured servitude . . . works its underpaid, frequently injured workers at an extraordinary pace . . . discharges half a million tons of chicken shit into Arkansas' rivers every year." The grizzled, hard-partying Tyson poured money into Clinton throughout the politician's career to preserve and extend the company's interest, including $12 million in state tax breaks and what Charles Lewis of the Center for Public Integrity called "laggard and unaggressive" enforcement of environmental regulations. Under Clinton, as before him, the chicken industry effectively made its own rules in Arkansas. Even the state inspection laboratory was controlled by poultry producers. "A series of unsentimental transactions," Michael Kelly described Don Tyson's view of American politics, "between those who need votes and those who have money."

Beneath the most enormous fortunes were dozens less vast or flamboyant, though many of the holders had similar views of social responsibility. The Dillard's department store chain was charged by its own employees with racial discrimination and was said to treat shareholders with what *Arkansas Business* magazine called "a big case of the Marie Antoinette syndrome ('Let them eat cake!')." Comparison to Bourbons was not idle. When the *Arkansas Times* early in 1992 began to profile "fat cats" in a state with a per capita yearly income of $14,629, those with less than $100 million net worth were well down the list. It was the fat cats' Arkansas in which Clinton came to power. It was theirs more than ever when he went on to Washington.

What Tyson and others saw as "unsentimental transactions" were far more than the permits or rate increases or random favors that defined special-interest influence in other states and even more than the over $400 million yearly in corporate tax exemptions, a fifth of the state's budget. Bought and sold was a political culture, a way of life for the two and a half million people of the state. It was not only that Clinton's government exercised no regulatory power worth the name. Utterly uncontested by the early 1980s, no longer even denounced in Arkansas's ritual verbal populism, the immense monied power shrouded every part of the state—finance, the job market, incomes, prices, institutions of all kinds, including educational institutions from grade schools, whose funding was hostage to the interest-controlled tax system, to colleges, where the new rich dictated as they donated.

If either of the Clintons had been troubled by that crude oligarchy, there was no sign in their continued silence and collusion. Over the decade after 1983, they enjoyed an unprecedented political dominance not only in the governor's enduring hold on the electorate but through some two thousand appointees to more than two hundred commissions and boards dispensing hundreds of millions and overseeing much of the economy. The Clinton "machine" was now unlike any other in Arkansas history, and many believed it the only administration strong enough to have taken on private power in the state. That was the paradox and the tragedy.

Afterward, among both supporters and critics there were differing explanations of the relative emptiness of Bill Clinton's record in Arkansas: that he was capricious and inconstant as a matter of personality and leadership style, that he often intended to do the right thing yet wanted to be liked even more and was unable or unwilling to confront the opposition or inertia of a backward legislature, that he was distracted by national ambition, that he spent too much time traveling or vacantly politicking or philandering, even that he was emotionally or intellectually unable to sustain the necessary concentration. Whatever the pattern of the moment, however, the common outcome in policy was submission to the interests. Of a dozen years of examples, none was more illustrative than the Arkansas Development Finance Authority's involvement in the Beverly nursing home scandal.

While giants like Tyson and Wal-Mart made their way as usual, Clinton's ADFA provided what *U.S. News* would call "pinstripe patronage" and "insider lending" for a number of smaller, less-known Arkansas companies whose chief distinction was often a tie to partners in the Rose firm, the owners' contributions to Clinton, or both. In the seven years after Rose-drafted legislation created it in 1985, ADFA issued bonds of more than $700 million and claimed to have created twenty-seven hundred jobs in Arkansas. But on closer examination, most of the new wages were well below the national standard, and the overall number of jobs was shockingly low compared to the ninety thousand produced by Orval Faubus's Arkansas Industrial Development Commission over nine years with no bonding power—all in a state where the unemployment rate remained nearly 8 percent and twenty-three counties had rates in the double digits, with some as high as nearly 19 percent. Instead, ADFA had been a bonanza for Lasater and Company as well as for Stephens, Goldman, Sachs, and other larger financial houses, who continued to underwrite millions in issues despite the competition of newer Clinton patrons. At least ADFA provided job security for the governor himself, his 1990 campaign receiving over $400,000 in contributions from those benefiting directly from the publicly guaranteed bonds.

Ostensibly for economic development, ADFA had the power literally to "create money," as one writer described it, though the creation went largely to the profit of solvent, credit-worthy companies who received loans well below market rates. There was virtually no legislative oversight or other public accountability, save for that provided by Governor Clinton himself, who appointed the ADFA board and personally approved every bond issue and major transaction from 1985 through 1992. Though there were later suspicions and even published accounts of ADFA's being used to launder millions in drug money, including some of Barry Seal's from Mena, the agency's official records did little to dispell the charges. When reporters began to look at ADFA seriously for the first time after Clinton's election to the presidency, it was plain that the agency had not exercised what many in the financial world regarded as "due diligence" in its bond issues, and even relevant documentation seemed to be missing or hidden. There were differing versions of exactly how many bond issues the authority had released and no clear accounting of precisely where the more than $700 million had come from or, for that matter, how it had all been spent. "ADFA had its own 'Don't ask, don't tell' policy," said a Little Rock broker.

What was visible was a burlesque of the incestuous world of Arkansas government and business. In the $2.75 million loan to POM, the thriving parking meter manufacturer and Pentagon contractor, Rose got its fee as ADFA's certifying attorney while Hubbell was counsel to POM. In two bond issues totaling $1.77 million for the Pine Bluff Warehouse Company, the trustee bank's vice president sat on the ADFA board; the bank's chief executive officer, the father of Rose partner William Kennedy III, sat on the board of the warehouse company; Stephens underwrote the bonds; and Rose handled the legal work. A $4.67 million loan went to Arkansas Freightways, whose largest outside stockholder was Stephens, who in turn underwrote the bonds, with Rose cocounsel on the issue and the trustee bank's executive vice president a Clinton appointee to the ADFA board. Cavalier practices extended well beyond Arkansas as well. In 1987 ADFA would suddenly borrow $5 million from a Japanese bank's Chicago branch to purchase stock in a Barbados reinsurance firm called Coral, all in a relatively risky and vague venture that was unquestioned by the Clinton regime in Little Rock but later prompted investigation by securities authorities in New York and Delaware as well as by the SEC.

Yet the most vivid portrait of ADFA would be in what Arkansas lawyers and others came to call the "Beverly operation." In the late 1980s one of the Stephens investments, a nursing home chain called Beverly Enterprises, was troubled by debt and the financial house, abetted by a Texas banker and the Rose firm, formed a nonprofit corporation to buy the nursing homes. The banker and underwriters would take millions in profits, Beverly would make millions in needed cash, and Rose and Stephens would realize their share—all because the deal was to be financed by tax-exempt state bonds. Early in 1989 they had executed the scheme to buy forty-one nursing homes in Iowa with $86 million in state bonds, a transaction an Iowa court would denounce four years later as using "a 'shell' nonprofit corporation . . . to make millions of dollars of excessive profits."

In September 1989 they were about to carry off a similar deal in Arkansas for the purchase of thirty-two nursing homes with $83 million in ADFA bonds, and as much as a half million dollars in fees to Rose. "The Beverly operation was one of the biggest contracts the firm had handled and was the subject of regular discussion among the partners," the London *Sunday Times* noted later. "It is inconceivable that Hillary Clinton did not know about the deal." Then, at the last moment, the deal collapsed when Attorney General Steve Clark claimed he had been offered $100,000 in campaign money as a thinly disguised bribe to drop his opposition to the Beverly bonds. Suddenly, if fleetingly, like Mena two years later, the affair and the usually obscure ADFA practices were front-page news in Little Rock, the Texas banker was challenging a state official to a fight, and Clinton "reluctantly stepped in and killed the transaction," as a team of British journalists described it afterward. "They tried to milk us like an old, full cow. It was wrong," the governor told reporters. "The more I study and the more I learn about it, the worse I feel." In his indignation he said nothing of ADFA's earlier agreement to the deal with his approval or of Rose's role. The partner who devised both the Iowa and the Arkansas schemes, William Kennedy III, would be named a counsel to the president in the Clinton White House.

As in Washington in the 1980s, the toll of such governance was not only in favor and enrichment but in negligence and suffering. Behind the claims of the Clinton presidential campaign in 1992, the sum of his actual policy record was stunning. An Arkansas that spent less than half as much on environmental protection as Mississippi and often allowed powerful interests to pollute at will would be rated last in the nation for the effectiveness of its environmental policies. In what the *Los Angeles Times* called "one of the nation's most regressive tax systems," Arkansas families earning less than $9,000 a year paid nearly four times more state tax proportionately than families making in excess of $600,000. The state's economy remained mired in what one observer called a "low-wage, low-skill trap," near the bottom of the nation, as it always had been, in average annual pay, income distribution, joblessness, and poverty. When the fanfare of education "reform" had died away, the state remained almost last in the United States in per capita expenditure for education, in the percentage of its students completing high school, in the proportion of its citizens with college degrees. While as governor and later as president Clinton spoke earnestly of welfare reform, Arkansas's own system was "flawed from start to finish" with inadequate child care, transportation, supervision, or jobs.

In those areas of government that required more detailed and sustained attention, among the more entrenched bureaucracies and stolid, corrupt institutions, the cost of the Clinton style and substance was still more evident. The scandalous system of child welfare and foster care that left dead and maimed children in its wake and provoked a class-action lawsuit in 1991, constituted what one witness called "a silence . . . and a stench one can't forget." The state systems of juvenile justice and adult corrections were nightmarish by several accounts. In health care, Arkansas remained among the worst in the nation—second in the country in teen pregnancy, plagued by scandal in its nursing homes, state hospitals, and mental-health programs in general, its infant mortality approaching Third World rates. At a 1989 conference Hillary Clinton, seated next to President Bush, made a point of complaining, justifiably, that US infant mortality overall left the nation far behind other wealthy societies, a fact Bush at first denied and later acknowledged. Campaign aides would tell the story as one more example of her strength and caring, yet at the same moment infant mortality among African Americans in Arkansas was twice the national average she had deplored with Bush.

Nowhere was the toll sharper than in the black community that gave its votes so fully and decisively to Bill Clinton. In the Delta's Lee County, one of the ten poorest counties in the nation and emblematic of the region, two-thirds of all children never graduated from high school. While black appointees came and went at the statehouse and powerful black bosses emerged in the Clinton machine, the African American community at large was at the juncture of what the *Economist* cataloged as the state's "dismal failures" in economic development and welfare. Discreet redlining by banks kept the state residentially segregated, while nearly three decades after Orval Faubus's historic confrontation at Little Rock Central, many Arkansas schools remained quietly separate and unequal. One of the worst districts, and last even to acknowledge what a 1988 class-action lawsuit called "widespread discrimination," was a place called Hope.

• ◆ •

With Dukakis's defeat in 1988, Clinton would spend more and more time traveling as the prelude to his presidential candidacy, much of the time at National Governors' Association meetings or in Washington with the Democratic Leadership Council he had helped found in 1985 to move the party more overtly to the right. Sessions of a few days deliberately designed to showcase the participating politicians, the settings put a premium on performances issue to issue and furthered his reputation as what the press would term a "policy wonk," a politician with an unusually avid grasp of governing problems and solutions.

Those inside the process knew how shallow and scattered the presentable young Arkansas governor could be, how marginal visiting politicians were to Washington despite their pretense, and how little they saw or understood of the genuine capital. "He and others would go up to the Hill and have these polite sessions with the leadership, who indulged them for appearances, and then think, 'This is big-league politics,' " said a senior staff member of the National Governors' Association who watched Clinton come to Washington over the 1980s. "I don't think he understood a damn thing about how Washington *really* worked." Another staff analyst thought Clinton's Washington trips "one long retreat where a lot of people who thought he'd run or might even be president told him what he wanted to hear and where he was too busy impressing them anyway to do a serious inventory of what was happening to Washington."

The result of it all would be plain in his presidency. A Clinton thought to be a successful governor of innovative policies would have few successes or truly new policies in the White House. A Clinton assumed to be a masterful politician would be thwarted and often baffled by the tribal politics of the national capital. Not least, a Clinton who spoke so much about the future and a changing world came from an Arkansas deliberately locked in the past, his major patrons not the corporations or figures of change but relics of paternalism and social-economic reaction. He would miss the cutting edge of business and corporate evolution in the America of the 1990s much as he missed the inner reality of the Washington he wanted so long to lead.

He returned to Arkansas for one more run for the governorship, promising yet again to serve out his term even as he honed themes and husbanded money for the 1992 presidential bid. It was in many ways a classic Arkansas race. For the first time since 1982 he had serious opposition in the primary. Briefly Jim Guy Tucker was again a rival, trying in vain to coax some of the state troopers to tell him their stories of Clinton's womanizing. Tucker eventually faded, then appeared later as lieutenant governor before succeeding Clinton. The more serious rival was young Attorney General Steve Clark, who enjoyed a brief wave of popularity in exposing the Beverly nursing home scheme and even led Clinton in the polls for a time.

But Clark was soon victim of his own scandal when the *Gazette* published an exposé of his expense accounts with a state credit card, including interviews with prominent figures whom Clark claimed to have entertained but who denied being with him. While Clark was clearly guilty of account padding and tens of thousands of dollars in excesses and while the *Gazette*'s reporter on the story, Ann Ferris, later claimed that "Mr. Clinton was merely the timely beneficiary of aggressive independent journalism," Steve Clark, like Gary Hart, was pushed. As onetime Clinton adviser and confidante Bert Dickey and others told the story later, the governor had been anxious about Clark's poll numbers. Clinton pressed for "somebody to take him down," as Dickey remembered him saying. "What can we get that's real good?" Clinton had asked. Records had been checked, calls made, the first tips given in a trail Clark obligingly provided by his own abuses, and a last local obstacle was eliminated.

In the primary he would face a patrician Tom McRae, a former Bumpers aide who had presided over the Winthrop Rockefeller Foundation with mounting dismay at Clinton policies. The idealistic, almost professorial McRae posed little threat and took only 40 percent of the primary vote—though not before Hillary, taking nothing for granted, staged one of her more dramatic interventions on behalf of her husband and their common future. A week before the primary election, McRae was holding a news conference at the capitol when he was visibly astonished to hear the First Lady shout out an interruption from the back of the hall. She had just been passing by, she would say later, when she heard McRae misrepresenting the facts and she could not resist stopping. Then a Hillary Clinton who was only passing by pulled from her purse a four-page statement refuting McRae with quoted passages from some of his own Rockefeller Foundation reports.

Meanwhile, as McRae tried to engage issues of economic policy or education, the old gothic Arkansas hovered on the edge of the campaign. That June Clinton denied parole to Wayne Dumond, a man wrongly accused in the 1984 rape of a Clinton relative in the Delta and imprisoned after being sodomized and castrated by local vigilantes. Behind the gruesome crimes was the story of a corrupt local sheriff who kept Dumond's testicles in a jar in his office and of a courthouse machine closely linked to the governor. There was also the unsolved mystery of two teenage boys, Kevin Ives and Don Henry, who were placed on railroad tracks to be run over by the northbound train on the Pulaski-Saline county line. Despite blatant bungling and cover-up by authorities, the crime would be linked to drugs, the murders of six figures implicated in the first killings, and allegedly to Mena. But those deeper politics of Arkansas would not intrude on the campaign.

Against former Stephens protégé and onetime Democrat Sheffield Nelson in the general election, Clinton was richly financed and clearly confident. Some thought it his best run. "He has an informed, thoughtful answer to virtually every question he is posed," wrote *Spectrum*'s Philip Martin on a swing with the candidate that he called "Riding with the Sun King." "He remembers names and faces. He tosses off facts, numbers, anecdotes, and rude rustic stories. He can be ruthless when aroused. . . . They reach out to him as though he were a faith healer, their confidence absolute, their eyes dancing. . . . He takes the microphone, and all the Walker Evans faces go rapt."

Still, he was vulnerable. In the last days Nelson ran a series of effective ads attacking Clinton taxes and spending, and when a last-minute Dickie Morris poll showed serious erosion in their sizable lead, Clinton panicked once more, calling wealthy friends, obtaining a $50,000 emergency loan from yet another friendly bank controlled by one of his highway commissioners, answering Nelson with his own flood of spots in the final days and hours. Using "palm cards" and voting booth strings in black precincts, busing voters in some areas from precinct to precinct with changes of shirts, handing out $30,000 in $100 bills just days before the balloting and free fried chicken at some polling places, he would win with 59 percent. A week after the election he pardoned Dan Lasater and began to take soundings for the presidential race. In Little Rock and in the countryside people seemed to take it all in stride, many not knowing, or not wanting to know. Former *Gazette* editor Max Brantley, a backer and friend, would look back at 1990 and all the races before and voice a kind of requiem for Arkansas that would soon apply to a nation. "We saw in them," he said of the Clintons, "what we wanted to believe."

◆　◆　◆

The surface chronology of his election began in May 1991, when Bill Clinton emerged at a carefully staged DLC convention in Cleveland as the best of six possible Democratic presidential contenders in a field stunted by calculations of George Bush's prohibitive lead in the race. Publicly and privately Clinton had used the event to mark out what would be called the "Bubba tactic" in his campaign, pointedly excluding Jesse Jackson from giving a policy address at the gathering of the corporate-funded group that Jackson called the "Southern White Boys Club."

By the autumn of 1991, suddenly Bush and the Republicans did not seem invulnerable. That November Clinton would begin to pull ahead of the field in New Hampshire and be "anointed" by the party hierarchy, as the *Economist* reported it, at a meeting of his fellow governors in Chicago. By the winter and spring of 1992 Clinton would finish second-place in New Hampshire and declare victory as "The Comeback Kid," and billionaire Ross Perot would declare his candidacy on a television talk show. Clinton would go on to sweep the March 10 Super Tuesday southern primaries and a week later the crucial Illinois and Michigan races, clinching the nomination in final primary victories over former California governor Jerry Brown.

Southerner and contemporary Senator Al Gore of Tennessee would be selected as his running mate by early July. Then, at the close of the Democratic Convention in New York, with Clinton and Gore surging ahead of Bush on a wave of celebrity, there would be the unpredictable Perot's sudden withdrawal from the race. The much-publicized Clinton-Gore bus tour through the Rust Belt, producing signs of genuine popular enthusiasm for the Democrats, would be followed in August by a chilling Republican Convention dominated by the religious and rightist minorities that had captured the party.

Into the fall Clinton would maintain a lead over Bush. With Perot back as an independent third candidate, however, the race would narrow in the last days. But on November 3, 1992, eighteen years after his first run as a losing yet launched young politician in the Ozarks, Bill Clinton would be elected president of the United States, though with only 43 percent of the popular vote.

Standing outside the old statehouse in Little Rock on election night, Clinton made a special appeal to Perot voters as well as his own, promising the "fundamental change" for which a clear majority voted, in what the president-elect called the "great mystery of American democracy." Yet what had happened behind the public facade of the race was less a "great mystery" than it was the banal result of the Clintons' machinations and the system.

The troopers would have no trouble recalling Labor Day, 1991, as the Clintons nervously prepared for his October announcement of formal candidacy. Early that morning, as Larry Patterson related the scene, Hillary had pulled out from the mansion in her blue Oldsmobile, only to return moments later, tires squealing. The guards ran out to her thinking "something was terribly wrong," as Patterson recalled. "Where's the goddamn fucking flag? I want the goddamn fucking flag up every fucking morning at fucking sunrise," she had screamed at them. "Such displays," the *American Spectator* noted dryly in publishing the account, "made Hillary by far the most unpopular member of the First Family."

It was obviously a very different impression than the apparently bright and articulate couple was now leaving around the country. Scarcely two weeks later the Clintons were in Washington for a specially arranged session of the "power breakfast" put on by *Christian Science Monitor* journalist Godfrey Sperling to bring politicians together with prominent Washington reporters for a supposedly more intimate conversation. The mutually understood subject of the meeting was what the *Gazette* called nimbly "The Question"—old and new rumors about the governor's womanizing. There was perfunctory talk of foreign policy, taxes, abortion, liberalism and conservatism, and eventually The Question. Would he take the advice of some Democrats "to settle conclusively the issue of your personal past"? After a pregnant pause Clinton broke the tension with what was supposed to be a small joke. "This is the sort of thing they were interested in in Rome when they were in decline too." Yes, his marriage had experienced "difficulties," he said with Hillary at his side. Then the carefully crafted and rehearsed statement that would be used often in the months ahead: "What you need to know about me is that we have been together for almost twenty years and have been married almost sixteen, and we are committed to our marriage and its obligations, to our child and to each other. We love each other very much. Like anybody that's been together twenty years, our relationship has not been perfect or free of difficulties. But we feel good about where we are. . . . And we intend to be together thirty or forty years from now regardless of whether I run for president or not. And I think that ought to be enough."

Two months later, in the wake of Harris Wofford's Senate victory in Pennsylvania, where Wofford had made an issue of health-care reform, Clinton met privately in Washington with outside advisers to discuss the issue. For two hours the governor and his campaign staff listened as Yale professor Ted Marmor advocated the Canadian single-payer system and Ron Pollack, a Washington lobbyist, pushed the managed care, or "play-or-pay," scheme of employer-paid coverage favored by much of the insurance and medical industry. "Ted, you win the argument," Clinton had said to Marmor, and then gestured toward Pollack. "But we're going to do what he says." Whatever its virtues, Clinton and his staff argued then and later, the Canadian system would only arouse Republican and industry charges of "socialized medicine" and jeopardize major industry contributions to the campaign. "The price of this preemptive concession was large," the *Washington Monthly* noted with understatement in recounting Marmor's story three years later.

The campaign would feature well-planned responses and predetermined "debates" like the health-care issue, but there would be a largely new Clinton staff. They included James Carville, a Baton Rouge native who was credited with engineering the Wofford upset and who cultivated his acid irreverence and lack of pretension. "I was really hired because Clinton didn't want to be the biggest redneck in the campaign," he would tell the press. With him was George Stephanopoulos, a former Dukakis aide who had joined the staff of House majority leader Richard Gephardt after the 1988 defeat; Paul Begala, who had worked with Carville in the Pennsylvania race; David Wilhelm, a former campaign aide to Senator Joe Biden and manager of Richard M. Daley's last two mayoral races in Chicago; Rahm Emanuel, another former Daley assistant; press secretary Dee Dee Myers, who had handled the media in a 1991 mayoral race in San Francisco; and others like them. Clinton's "extensive policy network" included figures from the DLC and the National Governors' Association, the "Rhodes gang" from his student days, influential lobbyists and Washington consultants, Wall Street backers (some who had been prominent in the Muskie, McGovern, or Mondale campaigns or the Carter administration), and not least Hillary Clinton's own circle, including Mickey Kantor, the formal chairman of the campaign. They would come from different precincts of the political or business establishment and Washington culture. But they would all have that governing orthodoxy and mentality in common, along with the obligatory, sometimes fierce loyalty to their candidate. "A pack of lies" and "a new low for American journalism," DLC adviser David Osborne would say of the Gennifer Flowers revelations on CNN. "I trust his integrity completely," Ira Magaziner, a business consultant who would direct health-care reform in the Clinton White House, assured the *National Journal.*

What they also had in common, however, was an oblivious ignorance of—or indifference to—the Clintons' Arkansas history. "I've had blind dates with women I've known more about than I know about

Clinton," Carville would finally explode in the spring of 1992, when the slow, fitful uncovering of Hillary Clinton's work at the Rose firm began. Some advisers, like Wall Street broker Roger Altman, who became deputy secretary of the Treasury and was soon embroiled in the Whitewater–Madison Guaranty scandal, would pay for what they did not know about Little Rock. Yet the members of the campaign staff, most of whom would join the White House staff, would largely be typical of the political retainers of the era, frequently serving politicians and the forces behind them without much independent awareness or judgment, accepting and perpetuating the culture by surrendering to it the integrity of their careers.

It was only after the convention that the famous "war room" took shape, and only then, too, that Carville was given firm day-to-day charge of the campaign. At one point the candidate had seemed to be flailing so ineptly that in desperation his handlers booked him on MTV and *Arsenio Hall* in an effort to fashion a new public image. For months there had been no clear lines of authority and confused, almost chaotic decision making. As in Arkansas, however, no frailty of candidate or organization would outweigh the sheer force of the money. Behind the scenes, it was utterly decisive at crucial moments— and the decision, as it were, was made in Arkansas. By January 1, 1992, thirty-one cents of every dollar raised in the pivotal early months of the presidential race—more than a million dollars—would come from Arkansas, most of it from the big interests the Clintons had furthered. The most lucrative fund-raiser in the Democratic primaries for any 1992 candidate would be "Winter Wonderland" at Little Rock's Excelsior Hotel, providing $900,000 in a single evening to make Bill Clinton president of the United States.

However scattered the rest of his campaign, the Clintons had planned the money strategically and with historic effect. The Worthen Bank line of credit from the Stephens empire would be established in early January, before any of the crises of the campaign were apparent. Altogether it would provide over $3.9 million in eleven installments, supposedly collateralized by federal matching funds—though there was a typical fast-and-loose quality to the borrowing, the first draw of a million made on March 4, only two days after campaign submissions to the FEC sufficient to cover the draft. In any event, the Worthen money would be there when the draft controversy and the Flowers story broke with their predictable numbing impact on fund-raising. Unlike Gary Hart in 1987, the Clintons would not be driven from the race by financial blackmail. And the early contributions that made possible the federal matching funds, and thus the razor's edge collateralizing of the Worthen loan, came largely from Arkansas and a relative handful of wealthy Clinton backers around the country. Altogether, less than twenty-three thousand donors would make a president. A study that summer by the *Los Angeles Times* established that the Stephens family and employees alone had given over $83,000 to the Clintons and that by the spring of 1992 the largest share of his financial support—some $2.6 million—would come from lawyers and lobbyists, with nearly another million from financial interests.

With World Wide Travel in Little Rock carrying the campaign's huge travel costs, Clinton would emerge from his second-place finish in New Hampshire not a questionable candidate with unresolved issues and flagging support but a front-runner with monied momentum. It would allow them to invest early and effectively in the determining Illinois and Michigan primaries. After Illinois and Michigan, the money began to come in again to the media-declared front-runner and likely nominee, though the Worthen money continued to finance the April 7 New York primary victory over Jerry Brown, a race fought in typical New York fashion with what participants on both sides would describe as "dirty politics" and what one Brown operative called "a good deal of money changing hands that never showed up on anybody's report." But dirty or not, New York was anticlimactic. Clinton's rivals had had no Worthen reserve, no comparable, long-cultivated bank of big contributors. In a sense, the race for the 1992 Democratic presidential nomination had been over before it started.

From the beginning he had renounced PAC money and used the corruption of campaign finance as one more issue in his "outsider's" run against Washington, even promising Common Cause and others early in the primaries that he would make reform of campaign spending an urgent priority in his administration. But the disavowal had been no disability with the Worthen money and other contributors, and after his nomination the so-called soft money had flooded into the campaign, close to $30 million of it from a list of nearly every major interest in the country. By summer the process was unabashed. For the New York convention the campaign would organize a special train on which lawyers and lobbyists could mingle with Democratic Party leaders and likely members of the new administration, the passengers paying $10,000 just to be on board, $25,000 to roam the train. "The journey promises to be memorable," said the campaign's promotional flyer. Traveling north through Baltimore, Philadelphia, and Trenton, the train retraced the route taken by J. P. Morgan in the age of the spoilsmen for similar purposes.

Only momentarily did Arkansas ghosts appear. Jerry Brown raised the issue of Hillary's conflict of interest at Rose and even Madison Guaranty, but there would be little media interest in an obscure past. "If somebody jumps on my wife, I'm going to jump them back," Clinton responded to Brown as he had earlier to Frank White and others, and there was scant coverage of Hillary's own initial response: "For goodness sake, you can't be a lawyer if you don't represent banks." For a moment both Tom Harkin and Brown had looked at the Mena suspicions, but that issue, too, remained out of public view. "I'll raise it if the major media break it first," Brown told aides. "The media will do it, Governor," one replied wearily, "if only you'll raise it."

As it was, Arkansas issues emerged in 1992 only by the Clintons' own choosing; otherwise they were concealed, sometimes by smear or coercion. At one of the most critical moments of his campaign, after the Flowers exposé and on the eve of the *60 Minutes* broadcast, Clinton had suddenly flown back to Little Rock to attend to the execution of Ricky Ray Rector, a severely brain-damaged black man convicted of the murder of a white police officer. So completely disoriented was Rector by the time of his scheduled execution that he regularly howled like an animal. "I'm gonna vote for him, gonna vote for Clinton," Rector would say in a thick mumble as he watched the television coverage of the Flowers affair, and he made a point of saving the dessert of his last meal to have the next day. "Never—or at least not in the recent history of presidential campaigns—has a contender for the nation's highest elective office stepped off the campaign trail to ensure the killing of a prisoner," wrote the *Houston Chronicle*. But Rector, the black killer of a white policeman, was not just any prisoner and a reeling Clinton was not just any contender. The governor would reject all pleas for clemency with what author Marshall Frady thought "the brutal clumsiness of an essential decency obsessed with larger purposes." But others were less sympathetic. "He had it in his power, and for all intents and purposes he killed a man for political purposes," said a lawyer and old friend from Hot Springs.

Much of the rest of the campaign would be directed not at making a point of his power and willingness to use it but at hiding its embarrassments. The Clintons summoned Betsey Wright to brief reporters on local Arkansas critics and seemingly trivial local issues and incidents. "I'll swear to God there were dossiers kept on anybody who said anything crossways of Clinton, and I don't know who did it, but a lot of folks got smeared real good with the reporters," said one Little Rock activist. "You'd talk to a reporter and they'd be ready to jump on a story and look into everything," remembered another, "and then they'd go down to [Clinton campaign] headquarters and come out thinking you ought to be in a straitjacket or jail or you were just dumb or vengeful. When they got through attacking people personally down there, it wasn't just the people who suffered, but real issues like Whitewater or funny money didn't have any credibility either." "Where's the info on Gennifer?" Hillary Clinton had asked Little Rock from a pay phone on the campaign trail when the story broke. The tactics of suppression were not limited to Arkansas, however, and were not always so genteel as providing discrediting information or spin for visiting reporters. The campaign soon hired a private detective to work on the "bimbo problem." Then, too, Sally Perdue would later tell of being approached by a Democratic functionary in Illinois and none too subtly warned that she might have her knees broken or worse if she continued to speak publicly about her relationship with Clinton. For their part, the professionals of the campaign would deny any knowledge of such practices, though Betsey Wright, gone to a lobbying job in Washington, would be enlisted again in 1994 and afterward to "explain" the instability or seamy motives of those, like the state troopers, who told their stories. It would be a mark of the Clinton White House to attack in open and secret the people who exposed its inhabitants and thus to evade, often successfully, the substance and truth of the charges, the issues themselves.

Protected for the time being from their past, however, the Clintons would enjoy their moment of triumph outside the old statehouse on election night. In the crowd were many who had been with them from the beginning, followers who believed in them or at least still saw, as Max Brantley would say, what they "wanted to believe." They had touched millions around the nation in the same way—a brilliant young couple appearing to represent the best of their generation, a seemingly enlightened and equal partnership in marriage, and, not least, the promise of a new beginning in a political system gone so painfully wrong. Bill Clinton had said it to a Philadelphia audience earlier that spring, and he spoke it there so earnestly, as he did in Arkansas over the past two decades, that his audience clung to the words: "We all have to change," he told them, promising sweeping reform and new leadership in Washington. "We all have to change."

Afterword

As the expectant Inauguration crowds soon discover, the Clinton presidency issues in disappointment for millions who welcomed it with such hope: The story of the new administration is neither its present nor future, but its past.

Both the Clinton regime and the Washington surrounding it are virtual parodies of the system so many voted to change. Pledging to install a government that "looks like America," his appointees represent nothing so much as the old Washington and an Arkansas that was its provincial replica. Though the new president begins with a few token gestures of promised reform, every major decision is captive to the oppression of the interests. His budgets remain hostage to the old myths and claimants. Almost immediately after taking office, Clinton goes behind closed doors to abandon his commitment to campaign finance reform, the essential precondition to all else in any struggle against Washington's misrule. The only major accomplishment he can claim after a year in office—passage of the North American Free Trade Agreement—is for a controversial treaty negotiated by his Republican predecessors, considered a betrayal by many who elected him.

Leaving the governing power of the K Street lobbyists unchallenged, the Clintons pay a historic price in the killing of their health insurance reform—in which they suffer a devastating defeat comprised of their own original compromises, the hubris and convolution of their pro-

467

posal, and, most of all, the massive power of industry interests they have made little effort to check or honestly expose.

Meanwhile, in 1993–1994, the majority of Democrats and minority of Republicans in the Congress continue to stifle authentic congressional reform, and the rest of Washington remains unchanged. When the Republicans seize control of both houses of Congress in the 1994 midterm elections—a low voter turnout ceding power to the zealous right-wing minority—their own so-called revolution only continues the tide of reaction from the 1980s, slashing at social programs and public purposes while maintaining and extending the customary fix and favor for the monied interests.

Halfway through the administration, the Clinton White House effectively abandons even the pretense of reform, and spends its time and energy combating the irrepressible ghosts of their Arkansas past. Once more Hillary Rodham Clinton responds to rejection and crisis by undergoing a series of cosmetic changes, adapting to whatever more modest role is prescribed by image handlers. Once again, Bill Clinton responds to his own failures and defeats by returning to what he has always been—the consummate salesman, practicing not the politics of substance but of self, like Arthur Miller's traveling man, like his own father, Bill Blythe, *"out there . . . riding on a smile."*

By the spring of 1996, scarcely three years in office, the Clintons are besieged on all sides by criminal and civil investigations. Not since Richard Nixon has a White House been so under suspicion for acts of wrongdoing both before and during the presidency. Some of the attacks, as always, are vacantly partisan. Others involve the most serious allegations ever leveled against a sitting president and First Lady. On the eve of their reelection campaign, the Clintons are under scrutiny by special prosecutors and federal grand juries, in civil and even criminal cases, from Little Rock and Mount Ida, Arkansas, to Washington, D.C. The subjects under investigation range from sexual exploitation and petty abuses of power, to bribery, obstruction of justice, financial corruption, and election fraud. Perhaps most historic, and most ominous, by the spring and summer of 1996 investigators from one congressional committee have begun to gather sworn testimony linking the president of the United States to drug money and organized crime.

For all that, however, the President and First Lady are clear favorites to be reelected. They are the lesser of evils in a contest with Republican rivals who are the worn epitome of the Washington system, and they remain unchallenged by their own Democratic Party equally bereft, corrupt, unable or unwilling to face itself. Neither their opponents nor supporters recognize the reality of these partners in power—that the Clintons are not merely symptomatic, but emblematic of the larger bipartisan system at its end-of-century dead end.

Acknowledgments

Two colleagues were incomparable inspiration and example. In intellect and spirit, the book's guardian angel has been my partner and co-author in a number of projects, the distinguished investigative journalist Sally Denton. Out of pure friendship and in a moment of personal trial herself, she gave without the asking one writer's inimitable gift to another—her own shining talent and commitment—informing, encouraging, editing from start to finish, standing by the book even when she stood alone. With the same devotion, a close friend and colleague in the national media who wishes to remain anonymous shared his singular insights, cheered me on, and made me believe anew in the integrity of political journalism. "Since we cannot expect much truth from our institutions," as Edward Abbey wrote, "we must expect it from our writers." This friend and Sally fulfill his promise.

Beyond, there are many others whose help was significant, though they in no way bear responsibility for what I did with it. They are listed alphabetically only but with much gratitude: Craig Barnes, Tom Blanton, Peter Bloch, Rodney Bowers, Max Brantley, Tristan Clum, Nancy Cook, John Crudell, Ken Cummins, Michael Dowd, Ambrose Evans-Pritchard, Bob Fink, John Floresku, Mike Gallagher, Jeff Gerth, Peggy Giltrow, Josh Goldstein, Felice Gonzales, Marcy Goodwin, Jim Grady, Laura Hagen, Ned Hall, John Hammer, Sy Hersh, Erika Holzer, Jim Hougan, Jennifer Howard, John Kear, Peter Klempay, Peter Kornbluh, Albert LaFarge, Mara Leveritt, Dennis Marker, Conrad Martin, Ian Masters, David McMichael and fellow members of the Association of

470

National Security Alumni, Robert S. Meloni, Dan Moldea, Jason Nelson, George D. Oleson, Mark Oswald, Greg Pleshaw, Zach Polett, Dr. Marge Prefontaine, Nick Pulaski, Janice and Terry Reed, Hilda Rush, Steve Schmidt, Jeff and Nancy Smith, Mark Swaney, and Stuart and Lee Udall.

I owe the usual inadequate thanks to librarians, of the Arkansas State Library, the University of Arkansas at Little Rock, the Arkansas *Democrat-Gazette,* and the University of New Mexico, as well as the public libraries of Little Rock, Hot Springs, and Chicago. Public interest groups were also vital: mainly Common Cause, the Center for Responsive Politics, Charles Lewis and his invaluable Center for Public Integrity, and the brave, vindicated Arkansas Committee at the University of Arkansas at Fayetteville.

Once again, my family gave me generous gifts: Kathy Morris helped interview in Washington and Little Rock and did an essential first analysis of many depressing files. David Hammer lent months of fine research in Washington. Zoe Hammer-Tomizuka and Ethan Morris ran down crucial documents and dispatches. My parents, Cathrine and Paul Morris, lovingly stood with me as always, even when my findings clashed with their enduring hope that the Democratic Party might be true to its name.

Finally, I have an incalculable debt to so many unnamed sources who shared not only experience and insight but also the example of their courage. The dark side of American politics was often discouraging, but there could be no abandoning this book once they gave me that trust. Their integrity is the redemption of this story.

Roger Morris
March 19, 1996

Sources and Notes

A principal resource for this book has been over a hundred interviews with sources whose knowledge and experience spanned the entire range of the lives and careers of Bill and Hillary Clinton, and who would answer my questions and tell their stories only on the condition of complete confidentiality. Several compelling reasons existed for their discretion. By the time I began interviewing for this book in the summer of 1993, many of those in Arkansas and elsewhere who had spoken on the record about the Clintons during the previous months had suffered what they described to me as severe reprisals in both personal and professional terms. Even those who might have been quoted in the *New York Times* or *Washington Post* only weeks or months before now refused to talk further without a guarantee of anonymity. Moreover, even those who had not yet experienced any consequences for their cooperation with a writer or reporter were clearly apprehensive about the potential power of a sitting president and his continuing reach into Arkansas years after his presidency. Not least, many of those who described to me embarrassing or arguably illicit or illegal acts were in some way parties to those acts themselves, and while willing to talk about the events for the sake of public knowledge were not ready to incriminate themselves by name. Finally, there was a large category of sources—many of them law enforcement officers and other government officials as well as employees of prominent businesses in Arkansas—who legitimately feared for their jobs and livelihoods if they were quoted on the record telling what they knew about the president of the

472

United States. The result is a regrettable but inevitable phenomenon in the attempt to write candidly about contemporary American politics—the unnamed source. At no point in the narrative, however, is an unidentified witness the sole or even main source for the point at hand. I have followed the historian's rule of requiring documentary support for every major assertion of fact or state of mind and at least two and usually three verifying sources for *any* quoted statement. In any case, that so many Americans are afraid to speak out publicly about what they know of American politics says far more about the subject of this book than about its sources.

Prologue

This narrative of the inauguration is drawn mainly from my own eyewitness notes; interviews with those present, including reporters covering the events; and stories in the *Washington Post, Washington Times, New York Times, Los Angeles Weekly, New Yorker,* and European press, in particular the *Economist* and the *Independent on Sunday.* Follow-up interviews were conducted with Charles Lewis and others quoted in various media accounts.

Page
3 "Cynics don't buy this": The diarist is Philip Hamburger in the *New Yorker,* January 27, 1993.
4 "chump change": *New York Times,* January 18, 1993.
5 "desperate for things to start working better": *Wall Street Journal,* January 20, 1993.
6 East St. Louis mayor: *Washington Post,* January 21, 1993.
7 "We need health and education": *New Yorker,* January 27, 1993.
9 "deliberate, and perhaps calculated, charm": *Independent,* January 24, 1993.
9 "Everybody knows where Arkansas is now": *Washington Post,* January 21, 1993.

1. Sikeston

The account of the life of Bill Blythe is based on extensive interviews with family members and former wives and their families, including Ola Hall, Vera Ramey, Judith Ritzenthaler, and Sharon Lee Pettijohn; several others of the Blythe, Clinton, and related families who wish to remain anonymous; and Mrs. John Lett and others in Sikeston who described the accident. Published sources include the *Washington Post,* June 20, 1993; *Fort Worth Star Telegram,* June 22, 1993; *People,* November 16, 1992, and September 13, 1993; *Sikeston Standard-Democrat,* February 20, 1992; *Kansas City Star,* August 7, 1993, and October 10, 1993; *National Enquirer,*

August 17, 1993; and relevant civil court records for Jackson County, Missouri; Pulaski County, Arkansas; and other locales.

15   local "boot heel" boys: *Sikeston Standard-Democrat,* January 20, 1992, and interview with Mrs. John Lett.

16   "somebody in a hurry": Interview with Mrs. John Lett.

19   "ladies' man": Interview with Vera Ramey.

19   "standing there by the jukebox": *Kansas City Star,* October 10, 1993.

21   Virginia Kelley's recollections: *People,* November 16, 1992, and September 13, 1993; Kelley, 33–69.

23   "you could just never tell": Confidential interview.

2. Hope

The portrait of Hope is cast from a number of interviews as well as published sources, including the WPA Writers' Program *Guide* to Arkansas in the 1930s, Kelley, the Dumas oral histories, files of *Spectrum* and *Southern Exposure,* and articles about the 1993 inauguration in the *New York Times, Washington Post, Maclean's, Time,* and other publications.

27   Virginia Kelley's recollections are mainly from her *Leading.*

28   "bright little orphan": *Time,* July 20, 1992.

29   "a streak in the Arkansas character": *Time,* July 20, 1992.

30   rigged crap table: Kelley, *Leading; Maclean's,* July 20, 1992, and November 16, 1992.

31   "stealing from himself" and Roger's business practices: Interviews with Roger Clinton's stepsons, Roy Murphy and George Murphy, and Kelley, 90.

31   "shacking up together": Confidential interview.

31   wild parties: Kelley, 84.

31   "Hempstead County Idiot": Kelley, 84.

31   "if you misbehaved": Dumas, 30.

31   lingerie on a clothesline: Kelley, 85.

32   "blackness inside her": Kelley, 86.

33   toy train: Kelley, 88.

33   "had no problems": Confidential interview.

33   Raymond drives to Hope: Kelley, 92, and confidential interviews.

33   Shooting incident and aftermath: Kelley, 92; *Maclean's,* July 20, 1992; *Time,* July 20, 1992; *People,* November 16, 1992.

33   speak to new father: Kelley, 171–72.

34   "racing up and down": Dumas, 27.

34   Miss Mary's: Dumas, 31–33, and confidential interviews.

34   Foster and Hervey Street homes: *Esquire,* November 1993; *New Yorker,* August 9, 1993; *Washington Post National Weekly Edition,* August 23–29, 1993.

35   recollections of Billy: Dumas and confidential interviews.

3. Hot Springs

This chapter is based principally on extensive and repeated interviews with Hot Springs natives and residents who knew the Clintons well or dealt with them. Most of these sources, including law enforcement officers, asked to remain confidential. Published sources include a singularly insightful report in *Maclean's*, July 20, 1992; feature articles in *People*, January 11, 1993, *Washington Post National Weekly Edition*, July 20–26, 1992, *Time*, July 20, 1992, *Philadelphia Inquirer*, March 8, 1992, and October 15, 1992; Gail Sheehy's groundbreaking profile in *Vanity Fair*, May 1992; and the files of *Spectrum*, *Spectrum Reader*, *Arkansas Gazette* and *Arkansas Democrat*. Books include in particular Scully, Dumas, Kelley, Abbott, Gallen, O'Clery, and Dee Brown.

36   images of Hot Springs: WPA *Guide; Spectrum Reader,* 145; D. Brown; *People,* November 16, 1993; Scully.

36   "field for quackery": *Maclean's,* July 20, 1992.

37   "liquor flowed . . . buy it here": *Maclean's,* July 20, 1992, and confidential interviews.

38   "pleasure tax": O'Clery, 16.

38   Roger Clinton in Hot Springs, Kelley, 95–100, and confidential interviews.

38   "Everybody knew": Confidential interview.

38   "rhinestone of corruption": O'Clery, 16.

39   "roughness and tackiness to it": Confidential interview.

39   "deconstructs and demolishes:" quoted O'Clery, 17.

39   Clinton family politics: Confidential interviews.

39   portrait of Raymond Clinton: Confidential interviews and Kelley, 96–97.

40   "ran some slot machines": *Maclean's,* July 20, 1992, and confidential interviews.

40   Ku Klux Klan, firebombing, and "A lot of us just knew": Confidential interviews.

40   Raymond the authoritarian: Kelley, 96.

40   "scoop up that boy": Confidential interview.

40   "a father figure": Oakley, 25.

40   "needs an Uncle Raymond": Confidential interview.

41   "If you wanted to get something done": Confidential interview.

41   Park Avenue house: Kelley, 102–105, 135.

42   Ramble, housekeepers, and Billy: Allen and Portis, 6, 19; *People,* November 16, 1992; *Washington Times,* January 20, 1993; *Philadelphia Inquirer,* October 15, 1992.

43   Rose Crane's recollections: Author's interview.

43   "such a handful": Confidential interview.

43   "if you use this": *People,* November 16, 1992.

44   Virginia in Hot Springs: Crane interview; *Washington Post,* January 26, 1992; Allen and Portis, 16; *Vanity Fair,* May 1992; *People,* November 16, 1992; *Spectrum,* June 10–16, 1992; and confidential interviews.

44   the Clintons' social life: Kelley, 107–10.

44   "woman as the real breadwinner": Confidential interview.
44   "very *powerful* woman": Crane interview.
45   "father, brother, and son": Kelley, 137.
45   images of Bill: Confidential interviews and *Washington Times,* January 20, 1992.
45   "Bill's reactions to Hot Springs's excesses": Kelley, 138; see also *Vanity Fair,* May 1992.
46   Roger Clinton's violence: Kelley, 94–161; *Philadelphia Inquirer,* October 15, 1992; and confidential interviews.
47   "bedlam": Kelley, 111.
47   Edith Cassidy's addiction: Kelley, 113–14.
47   "Bill's *real* father": Confidential interviews.
48   Roger's birth: Kelley, 123–25, and confidential interviews.
48   "Women who run around": Kelley, 125.
48   "pretty bad stuff": Confidential interview.
49   "she would handle it herself": Confidential interview.
49   police called: Kelley, 133ff.; confidential interviews; *Washington Post,* January 26, 1992.
49   Bill's confrontation: *Washington Post,* January 26, 1992; *Vanity Fair,* May 1992; Allen and Portis, 13ff.
49   "like a dog burying a bone": Confidential interview.
50   "lie automatically": Fick, 65.
50   "We can only guess": Confidential interview.
51   Skully Street house: Kelley, 145ff., and confidential interviews.
51   Bill's deposition: *Washington Post,* January 26, 1992.
51   "playing the role": Confidential interview.
52   "A real conversation": Kelley, 165.
52   "Imagine the feeling": Fick, 42.
52   "the real reason": *Time,* July 20, 1992.
52   name change: Garland County archives, June 12, 1962.
53   "Bubba! Bubba!": Kelley, 161.
53   "took me to St. Louis": *Vanity Fair,* May 1992.
54   "never really had a chance": Confidential interview.
54   "One of the biggest problems": *Philadelphia Inquirer,* October 15, 1992.
54   "He was a perfect kid": *Spectrum,* October 31–November 6, 1990.
55   "veil over his whole being": *Philadelphia Inquirer,* October 15, 1992.
55   Mackey: *Washington Times,* January 20, 1993.
55   school politics: Dumas, 36–39; Allen and Portis, 10ff.; Levin, 29–31.
55   "If you beat me": *Washington Times,* January 20, 1993.
56   "looked down on him": Confidential interview.
56   "risk his political future": Confidential interview.
56   "fat and rejected": Confidential interview.
56   "I was a fat boy": Author's interview with Ernest Dumas.
56   "the strikingly attractive": Kelley, 151.
57   "seemed to do all right": Kelley, 151.
57   "He always knew": Confidential interview.
57   Miller's textbook: Crane interview.
58   "the shrine": Confidential interviews.

58 "Virginia really belittled": Confidential interview.
59 Edith moves in: Kelley, 163.

4. Georgetown

Robert Sabbag's article in *Rolling Stone,* August 1993, was an especially useful memoir, as was Tom Campbell's reminiscence in Dumas. Like all others, this chapter also draws on confidential interviews. Background articles came from the *Washington Post* and *Washington Times.* D. Sams's portrait of Carroll Quigley in *Spectrum,* October 28–November 3, 1992, was particularly revealing.

60 "State Department bureaucrat's version": Confidential interview.
61 "A three-suit school": *Rolling Stone,* August 1993.
61 "They'll know what I'm doing": Levin, 39.
62 Georgetown student politics: *Rolling Stone,* August 1993; Dumas 43ff.; Levin, 38ff.; and confidential interviews.
64 Quigley: *Spectrum,* October 28–November 3, 1992; *Washington Post,* January 26, 1992.
67 "a pleasant vegetable": Starr, 50, 81–82.
67 Fulbright job: *Washington Times,* January 20, 1993; Levin, 55ff.; and confidential interviews.
70 "It wasn't Kennedy": Confidential interview.
70 "He revered Fulbright": Dumas, 47.
70 student council race: Levin, 49–51.
71 "my political enemies": Kelley, 165.
71 "It didn't hit me": Confidential interview.
73 Roger Clinton's illness: Kelley, 162–73.
74 "Of course I know": Kelley, 164–65.
75 "What a girl!": Kelley, 167–68.
75 "deepest, darkest prayer": Kelley, 170.
75 "Never have I been so sorry": Kelley, 175.
76 "If we learn the facts": Oakley, 56.
76 Washington riots: Levin, 56ff.; Dumas, 44ff.; *Washington Times,* January 20, 1993.
77 "never before paid much attention": Dumas, 50.
77 "an army brat": Dumas, 48.
77 "a kind of grazer": Confidential interview.

5. Oxford

Important published sources include Alessandra Stanley's insightful article on Frank Aller in the *New York Times Magazine,* November 22, 1992; *Time,* February 24, 1992, and April 6, 1992; *Washington Monthly,* December 1992; and Oakley, who cites an invaluable collection of interviews in the London press in 1992–93. The chapter also relies heavily on interviews with a number of Clinton contemporaries, most of whom requested anonymity. The account of Clinton's draft crisis is drawn from confidential interviews; published accounts in the *Los Angeles Times,* especially September 2, 1992, and the *Wall Street Journal,* especially February 6, 1992; and various reports in the *Washington Times.* Interviews on the issue of Clinton and the CIA were arranged in part through organizations of retired intelligence officers and other national security officials and included former ranking members of the CIA stations in London, Stockholm, Paris, and Moscow, as well as some who served at agency headquarters in Langley, Virginia, during the late 1960s and who were familiar with the Operation Chaos files.

79   "just a fluke": *Los Angeles Times,* September 2, 1992.

80   "grown a little embarrassed": Confidential interview.

80   "kind of cruel": Confidential interview.

81   Henry Britt account and other versions: *Los Angeles Times,* September 2, 1992, and confidential interviews.

83   voyage to UK: Levin, 65ff.; *Washington Times,* January 20, 1993.

84   "fluency and glibness" and other comments on Oxford: *Washington Monthly,* December 1992, and confidential interviews.

84   "as little or as much": Author's interview with Dell Martin.

84   Segal comments: *Washington Monthly,* December 1992.

85   "better in argument": *Sunday Times* (London), October 25, 1992.

85   "most comforting figure": *New York Times Magazine,* November 22, 1992.

86   "jotted down the day's names": *New York Times Magazine,* November 22, 1992.

86   "moved on before he had finished": *Sunday Times* (London), October 25, 1992.

86   Clinton with women: *Washington Times,* January 20, 1993.

86   "No one is going to believe": *Time,* July 20, 1992.

86   "You wouldn't understand": Kelley, 189.

86   Evans affair: Oakley, 68–69.

87   "Hush Puppies": *Washington Times,* January 20, 1993.

87   "overrated orgasm": Author's interview with Sara Maitland.

87   "big noisy parties": *New York Times Magazine,* November 22, 1992.

89   account of draft crisis: *Los Angeles Times,* September 2, 1992; *Wall Street Journal,* February 6, 1992; *New York Times Magazine,* November 22, 1992; *Time,* February 24, 1992, and April 6, 1992; *Boston Globe,* September 6, 1992; *Arkansas Gazette,* September 6, 1992; *Washington Post,* September 8, 1992; Oakley, 72–82; D. Brown, 14–25; Levin, 71ff.

92   Father McSorley: Quoted in Floyd Brown, 23–26.

92   "only observed": Allen and Portis, 28.

93   Clinton caution in antiwar demonstrations: Levin, 75–76, and confidential interviews.

93   "having it both ways": Martin interview.

93   Frank Aller: *New York Times Magazine,* November 22, 1992, and confidential interviews.

96   "If you look closely": Confidential interview.

96   "At the end of the day": *New York Times Magazine,* November 22, 1992.

96   Holmes letter and affidavit: Floyd Brown, 141–48; see also Allen and Portis, 199–202.

101 "loneliness seemed to engulf him": *New York Times Magazine,* November 22, 1992.

101 "networking and glad-handing": *Washington Post National Weekly Edition,* July 20–26, 1992.

102 Clinton and CIA: Confidential interviews.

6. Park Ridge

Background material on the Rodhams and Park Ridge was compiled from confidential interviews in the Chicago area and around the country, as well as from the biographies of Hillary Rodham Clinton by King, Radcliffe, and Warner. Periodical sources include Mara Leveritt's revealing article in the *Arkansas Times,* October 1989; files of *Hillary Clinton Quarterly,* 1993–1994; *People,* January 25, 1993; *New York,* January 20, 1992; *Washington Post National Weekly Edition,* July 12–18, 1993; *Washington Post,* January 19–21, 1993; *Family Circle,* May 18, 1993; *Washington Times,* January 20, 1993, and March 25, 1993; *Newsday,* January 10, 1993; *Albuquerque Tribune,* November 9, 1993; *Vanity Fair,* May 1992; *New York Times Magazine,* May 23, 1993; and the *Federal Writers' Project Illinois Guide* for 1946.

107 Howell and Rodham histories: *Washington Post,* January 19–21, 1993; biographies cited above; and confidential interviews.

109 "Frank Capra set": *Washington Post,* January 20, 1993.

109 "where Dick and Jane lived": Confidential interview.

110 descriptions of Park Ridge: *Federal Writers' Project Illinois;* confidential interviews.

110 "never knew any professionals": *Arkansas Times,* November 1989.

113 Hillary Rodham's childhood: *Vanity Fair,* May 1992, and confidential interviews; see also Warner, King, and Radcliffe; *Washington Post,* January 19, 1993.

114 "good investments": Confidential interviews.

114 "Making money": Confidential interviews.

114 "Mr. Reality Check," *Family Circle,* May 18, 1993.

114 "flop another potato": *People,* January 25, 1993.

114 "eat and sleep for free": Warner, 17.

114 "I was a quick learner": *Family Circle,* May 18, 1993.

115 "should have completed": *Albuquerque Tribune,* November 9, 1993, and *Washington Post,* January 19, 1993.

115 "unbreakable": Warner, 16.

115 "the real little Hillary was broken": Confidential interview.

116 "She had to put up with him": *Washington Post,* January 19, 1993.

116 "I was determined": *Family Circle,* May 18, 1993.

117 "Why can't she put on a little": *Family Circle,* May 18, 1993.

118 Sister Frigidaire: *Newsday,* January 10, 1993.

118 "always voted Republican": Confidential interview.

118 relationship with Donald Jones: Warner, 19ff.; *Washington Post,* January 19–21, 1993; *Newsday,* January 10, 1993, and confidential interviews.

122   "He thinks I'm a radical": Warner, 22.
123   "I just crawled": *Washington Post*, January 19, 1993.

7. Wellesley

This chapter draws on a number of confidential interviews with classmates and faculty at Wellesley and male friends at Harvard and other institutions, as well as on many of the same biographical and other sources indicated above for the Park Ridge chapter, particularly Radcliffe and Warner, and a series of 1992 articles in the *Philadelphia Inquirer*. The account of the Chicago convention riots is based on eyewitnesses, press reports, Hodgson, and Gitlin. Excerpts of Hillary's commencement speech were published in *Life*, June 20, 1969. The *Hillary Clinton Quarterly*, Fall 1993, provides interesting background on Hillary Rodham's undergraduate thesis and her views of Saul Alinsky.

124   "Women in those places": Confidential interview.
124   "all very rich": *Arkansas Times*, October 1989.
125   Jeff Shields and other young men: Warner, 29ff., and confidential interviews.
125   "as decadent as any upright Methodist": Radcliffe, 61.
126   "sentimental liberalism": Radcliffe, 63.
126   "I was testing me": Radcliffe, 69.
126   "Just because a person": Radcliffe, 63.
128   black armbands and King's murder: *Washington Post*, October 20, 1993, and confidential interviews.
128   "Individual consciences are fine": Radcliffe, 70.
128   "implement the change": Quoted in Radcliffe, 71.
128   "I can't believe it": Radcliffe, 72.
130   "Hillary and I just looked at each other": *Washington Post*, January 20, 1993.
131   difficulties at Wellesley: Warner, 41.
133   Alinsky: *Hillary Clinton Quarterly*, Fall 1993.
135   commencement speech: *Life*, June 20, 1969; *Washington Post*, January 20, 1993; Warner, 39ff.; *Washington Times*, January 20, 1993.
138   "Blind as a bat": *Washington Post*, January 20, 1993.

8. Yale I

Beyond confidential sources, principal published sources include the *Arkansas Times*, October 1989; Allen and Portis, King, Radcliffe, and Warner; the *Washington Post*, January 26, 1993; *Vanity Fair*, May 1992; *Time*, January 4, 1993; and contemporaneous accounts in the *New York Times* and the *Washington Post*.

139   impressions of Hillary at Yale: *Vanity Fair*, May 1992; *Washington Post*, January 20, 1993; Radcliffe, 87ff.
140   "whether we were selling out": Warner, 46.
140   "a radical and feminist only of sorts": Confidential interview.

140 "equal of men": Warner, 41.

140 "Not a lot in between": Confidential interview.

141 Bruck: *New Yorker,* May 30, 1994.

141 League speech: Radcliffe, 94–95.

143 Mondale hearings: *New York Times,* July 25, 1970.

143 "Nail your ass": Confidential interviews.

143 Bentsen: *New York Times,* July 22, 1970.

144 meeting Clinton: Warner, 53–56; Allen and Portis, 33ff.; *Vanity Fair,* May 1992.

145 "She certainly wasn't his first": Confidential interview.

145 "at the 'black table' ": Dumas, 54–55.

145 "somewhat casual": Dumas, 57.

146 "define himself as a politician": Dumas, 59.

146 impressions of Clinton: Levin, 86; Dumas, 60ff.; Warner, 57; *Vanity Fair,* May 1992; and confidential interviews.

146 "it tells volumes": Confidential interview.

146 "Let's face it": Confidential interview.

147 Clinton jobs: Allen and Portis, 32; Dumas, 56.

148 Duffey campaign: Confidential interviews.

149 "saw right past the charm": Warner, 53–55.

150 "had a bad day": *Vanity Fair,* May 1992.

150 "Come off it, Bill": Levin, 92.

150 "The best story I know": Quoted in Oakley, 68.

150 visit to Park Ridge: Warner, 59.

151 "women who dressed flossy": Confidential interview.

151 "if it isn't Hillary": Warner, 67–68.

151 "scraggly": Kelley, 190.

151 won't marry a beauty queen: *New York Times Magazine,* January 17, 1993; *Time,* January 4, 1993; Kelley, 191.

151 "She didn't particularly care for Arkansas": Confidential interview.

152 "cultural tension": Kelley, 191.

9. Yale II

This narrative draws on several confidential interviews with former staff members of the McGovern campaign, including some now working in the Clinton administration. Published sources include *Spectrum,* June 10, 1992; Allen and Portis; and the King, Radcliffe, and Warner biographies. Sources on Hillary Rodham's views on children's issues include *Harper's,* October 1992; *U.S. News and World Report,* August 31, 1992; *Time,* January 4, 1993; *Wall Street Journal,* September 16, 1992; *Los Angeles Times,* May 23, 1993; and *Village Voice,* January 28, 1993.

153 "It's a little too clear": Confidential interview.

154 Texas liberals: *Washington Post,* January 26, 1992, and January 20, 1993.

155 Wright's impressions of the Clintons: *Vanity Fair,* May 1992; Allen and Portis, 35; *Spectrum,* August 14–20, 1991.

158 "In a little while": Author present at the dinner.

159   "The glue holding it together": Confidential interview.

160   "Those who were willing": Confidential interview.

162   "Only trying to help": *Harper's,* October 1992.

164   recruitment by Doar: *Washington Post,* January 20, 1993; Radcliffe, 119ff.

165   Altshuler perspective: Radcliffe, 123–24; Warner, 71–74.

165   "She was sensitive": Confidential interview.

166   "We're so damned secretive": Remark heard by the author.

168   "already the Washington type": *Washington Post,* January 20, 1993.

168   "exciting jobs": Radcliffe, 135.

168   arrival at Clinton headquarters: Radcliffe, 137; King, 58; Levin, 114; Warner, 77–79; *Time,* January 4, 1993; and confidential interview.

10. Fayetteville

Sources for the 1974 race include confidential interviews with Clinton staff and supporters in the campaign, the files of the *Arkansas Gazette,* Arthur English's unpublished manuscript, Allen and Portis, the Dumas collection, and Levin. Accounts of the Clinton-Rodham relationship and wedding were compiled largely from confidential interviews with friends close to one or both of them; background material came from the *Philadelphia Inquirer* and *Washington Post;* the King, Radcliffe, and Warner biographies; Kelley; the May 1992 *Vanity Fair;* and other published sources.

170   "just posted his grades": Allen and Portis, 39.

170   Rudy Moore: Dumas, 85–95.

171   Hammerschmidt background: English manuscript; Dumas 86–87.

173   bank loan and Uncle Raymond: *Arkansas Gazette,* March 29, 1974, and May 22, 1974; Kelley 202–03; and confidential interviews.

174   Rose fund-raising: Confidential interviews and *Newsweek,* January 24, 1994.

174   "They did their part": Confidential interview.

175   "Money from the money folks": Confidential interview.

175   Whillock recollections: Dumas, 78–82.

176   "I was astonished": Dumas, 149.

177   "I hadn't displayed": Kelley, 199.

179   "We hope it's a good article": Allen and Portis, 45.

179   "These are the kind of people": Allen and Portis, 45.

180   "the most impressive": Allen and Portis, 50.

181   "He was red-faced scared": Confidential interview.

181   attempted suppression of Holmes letter: Confidential interviews and *Washington Post,* February 6, 1995.

183   "I *know* it was": Confidential interview.

185   Hillary and the Marines: *New York Times,* June 16, 1994.

187   "It was just a little": Warner, 89.

11. *Regnat Populus*

The Hattaway campaign is described in T. Harry Williams's *Huey Long*. The portrait of Arkansas politics draws on extensive interviews in Little Rock and around the state and, among published sources, on Blair and the Arthur English manuscript, as well as on Roy Reed's insightful essays in Dumas. The accounts of the 1976 and 1978 campaigns are based on confidential interviews with Clinton staff members and other observers, on the files of the *Arkansas Gazette* and *Arkansas Democrat*, and on useful background material in Starr, Oakley, and Beyle. The story of Hillary Rodham's joining the Rose firm and Rose's general background is drawn from interviews with former partners and associates of the law firm and with other attorneys in Arkansas and Washington, as well as on reports in the *American Lawyer*, July-August 1992; *Sunday Times* (London), February 13, 1994; and *Business Week*, May 24, 1993. As in the following chapters, Connie Bruck's article in the *New Yorker*, May 30, 1994, and Michael Kelly's piece in the *New York Times Magazine*, July 31, 1994, provided excellent background.

194   "to arouse into a full fury": Williams, 613.
194   "the worst American state": Quoted in Blair, 16.
194   "About five old men": Blair, 45.
195   "the nearest approach": Leland Duvall, *Arkansas: Colony and State* (Little Rock: Rose Publishing, 1973), 38.
197   "ARKLA didn't have to worry": Blair, 105.
198   Bumpers and Pryor history: Confidential interviews and author's interview with Ernest Dumas.
202   "It was a populism": English manuscript.
204   "The decision had been made": Confidential interview.
204   Rose firm traditions and history: Confidential interviews; *American Lawyer*, July-August 1992; and *Business Week*, May 24, 1993.
208   "separating means from ends": *Washington Post*, June 23, 1995.
208   "Virtually flawless": Dumas, 12.
210   "It was not a pretty sight": Confidential interview.
210   gas rate controversy: *Arkansas Gazette*, May 7, 1978, May 27, 1978, May 28, 1978, and especially May 21, 1978.
211   "He was *always* better": Dumas interview.
212   McDougal's background: *USA Today*, January 13, 1994, and March 30, 1994, and confidential interviews.

12. Little Rock I

This account of the first Clinton term in the governorship is based very much on confidential interviews with former staff members and supporters and with legislative and other sources in Little Rock. Johnston's *Public Policy* was especially useful for governance issues. Starr, Oakley, the files of the *Gazette*, Dumas, Beyle, Allen and Portis, Blair, Bruck's *New Yorker* piece, and David Maraniss's 1992 reporting in the *Washington Post* were also consulted. Sources on the commodity trades include especially the *Village Voice*, April 5, 1994; *USA Today*, March 30, 1994; *American Spectator*, August, 1994; and *National Review*, February 20, 1995.

218 "He was a punk kid": *New Yorker*, February 22, 1993.

223 "It was pure cannibalism": Confidential interview.

224 "It was like nailing people": Confidential interview.

224 "The truth is": Confidential interview.

226 "I'd never heard *anybody*": Confidential interview.

226 Hillary's temperament: Confidential interviews; *American Spectator*, January 1994 and April-May 1994.

227 Jim Blair's clients: *Martindale-Hubbell Law Directory* for the years 1975–80; *Village Voice*, April 5, 1994; *USA Today*, March 30, 1994.

229 "Like the Whitewater thing": Confidential interview.

229 Hillary's commodities trades: *Village Voice*, April 5, 1994; *American Spectator*, August 1994; *USA Today*, March 30, 1994; Bartley, passim; *National Review*, February 20, 1995; *Albuquerque Journal*, March 30, 1994.

233 "all the trappings": David L. Brandon, quoted in Bartley, 338.

233 "If this was such a rogue": Bartley, 374.

234 "There were too many big interests": Confidential interview.

235 "In Arkansas you remember everyone": Confidential interview.

236 "You have to understand": Confidential interview.

236 "It's a bitter pill": Confidential interview.

238 "Hillary was said": *New Yorker*, May 30, 1994.

238 "I think the truth is": Confidential interview.

240 "always thinking about his own future": Confidential interview.

243 "The man in this building": Dumas, 91.

243 "in search of a magic consensus": Dumas, 92.

244 Frank White: Dumas 99; *Arkansas Gazette*, November 2, 1980; and confidential interviews.

245 "The road construction companies": *Arkansas Gazette*, November 6, 1980.

248 "half-laughing, half-crying": Dumas, 67.

248 "He looked me right in the eye": Confidential interview.

13. Washington I

The setting of the inauguration and first months of the Reagan administration is drawn substantially from Haynes Johnson's brilliant *Sleepwalking through History* as well as from press reports. The postwar history of the two parties is largely my own interpretation, with quotations from my own experience, though informed by the books of Greider, Hodgson, Stern, Lapham, Smith, and Solomon. Articles of particular value appeared in *Mother Jones*, June 1990, July-August 1992, and March-April 1993, and in *Common Cause*, Winter 1992.

252 homeless on Capitol Hill: Johnson, 19–22.

258 Goldwater and the New Right: *New Yorker,* July 18, 1994; Greider, 275ff.; *Phoenix Gazette,* April 11, 1992.

259 "God help us": Confidential interview.

14. Little Rock II

The story of the comeback is based on detailed confidential interviews in Arkansas, including with several people who worked in and around the 1982 campaign. The published sources, however, are rich as well, including Starr, Oakley, the files of the *Arkansas Gazette,* Blair, Allen and Portis, Beyle, Radcliffe, the Bruck and Kelly pieces previously cited, and the Dumas collection.

269 Lindsey background: *Washington Post,* July 7, 1994, and confidential interviews.

272 "an extraordinarily appropriate reaction": *Reason,* November 1994.

272 Clinton's drug use: multiple confidential sources; *Sunday Telegraph* (London), July 17, 1994; *Washington Times,* April 14, 1992.

273 Betsey Wright joins staff: *Spectrum,* August 14–20, 1991; *Vanity Fair,* May 1992; *Philadelphia Inquirer,* October 15, 1992; *Arkansas Gazette,* November 7, 1982; Starr, 185; and confidential interviews.

275 Hillary's reaction to defeat: Confidential interviews; Radcliffe, 184–89; *Mother Jones,* November-December 1993; *Vanity Fair,* May 1992; *New Yorker,* May 30, 1994.

275 Clinton and newfound religion: Confidential interviews; Radcliffe, 191; Allen and Portis, 75–77; *Philadelphia Inquirer,* October 15, 1992; Dumas, 113; Beyle, 249.

276 "The Look": *Philadelphia Inquirer,* March 8, 1992.

277 Hillary's transformation: Confidential interviews and numerous published accounts, including *New Yorker,* May 30, 1994; Radcliffe, 187ff.; Warner, 113ff.; *Newsday,* January 10, 1993; *New York,* January 20, 1992.

279 "all his rich friends": Confidential interview.

284 "out of money": Starr, 187.

284 "went into overdrive": Starr, 187.

287 "he toyed with it": Author's interview with Ernest Dumas

288 "No matter how hard": Confidential interview.

288 "They were watching it like a prize fight": Confidential interview.

289 "They waved everything": Confidential interview with prominent African American attorney.

289 "He worked like a demon": *Arkansas Gazette,* November 4, 1992.

289 "More like beat-up": Confidential interview.

290 "It was a marvel of backtracking": Confidential interview; see also Blair, 94.

290 "admiring and fondling the antique guns": *Arkansas Gazette,* November 7, 1983.

15. Washington II

This relatively brief summary of the money tyranny derives largely from Stern, Phillips, and Greider and from several articles in *Public Citizen, Mother Jones, Common Cause,* and *Washington Monthly.* Interviews with Charles Lewis at the Center for Public Integrity and Josh Goldstein at the Center for Responsive Politics were invaluable. The toll on the nation has been vividly charted in Bartlett and Steele, Phillips, and Greider and in numerous articles in *Mother Jones, Public Citizen, U.S. News and World Report, In These Times, Washington Monthly,* the *Nation,* the *Washington Post,* the *New York Times,* and other periodicals.

294   Team 100: Records of Common Cause, Washington; see also *Common Cause,* August 1992 and Fall 1992.

296   "The politicians dress up: Lapham, 23.

301   decline of Democratic Party: *Mother Jones,* July-August 1992; *Washington Monthly,* July 1992; Greider, 90–103; *Common Cause,* April 1992 and August 1992; Stern, 31ff. and 198ff.; see also Karp and Lewis and *New Republic,* June 19, 1995.

302   decline of American jobs, decay of economy: see Bartlett and Steele, *America: What Went Wrong,* 18–20; see also Johnson 242–43 and 478; Greider, 284; *Nation,* February 1, 1993, and August 9–16, 1993; *Z,* February 1995; *Public Citizen,* January-February 1993; *New York Times,* June 25, 1995; *Utne Reader,* March-April 1994; *Washington Post National Weekly Edition,* April 25– May 1, 1994; *In These Times,* January 11, 1993, and July 26, 1993; Phillips, *Rich and Poor,* 15ff.

304   poverty statistics: *Nation,* April 21, 1991, March 23, 1992, and February 15, 1995; *New Republic,* November 23, 1992; *Los Angeles Times,* June 15, 1994; *Washington Post,* June 19, 1992; *Newsday,* February 11, 1995; *New York Times,* June 25, 1995; *Washington Post National Weekly Edition,* January 11–18, 1993, August 23–29, 1993, October 4–10, 1993, November 29–December 5, 1993, and March 21–27, 1994; *Journal of Population Economics,* August 1994; *Progressive,* June 1993; *In These Times,* November 30, 1992, and January 11, 1993; Phillips, *Rich and Poor,* 30–31, 35ff., and 254–55; Greider, 11–23; *Public Citizen,* January-February 1993; *National Journal,* May 4, 1991; *Common Cause,* Fall and Winter 1992.

16. Little Rock III

The narrative of Clinton's second term and his education reforms, the 1984 election, and Roger Clinton's drug conviction comes mainly from confidential interviews, against a backdrop based on the files of the *Gazette* and *Democrat,* Oakley, Allen and Portis, Dumas, Blair, and Starr. In addition to confidential interviews with law enforcement officers, prosecutors, and others, the Roger Clinton episode is derived from Kelley and Oakley. Fick describes the black-vote money in some detail, as does the *American Spectator,* December 1994. Special reports on the cocaine parties and visits to the mansion appeared in the London *Sunday Telegraph,* July 17, 1994, and the *Washington Times,* April 14, 1992.

308   "scam hot spot": *Arkansas Business,* September 12, 1988.

309   "the economy of plantations": Reel, 159.

311   IRS interest in Little Rock: *Arkansas Gazette,* November 4, 1990.

311   Little Rock drug scene: Arkansas State Police documents, August 4, 1982, August 21, 1986, September 11, 1986, September 22, 1986, October 2, 1986, and October 14, 1986; FBI memoranda, October 20–21, 1986; *Economist,* May 7, 1994; *Arkansas Gazette,* November 15, 1986; *Albuquerque Journal,* May 8, 1994, May 22, 1994, June 26, 1994, September 20, 1994; DEA documents, March 12, 1984, and September 8, 1986; *Sunday Telegraph* (London), July 17, 1994, and March 26, 1995.

313   used her political status: Confidential interviews and *Business Week,* May 16, 1994 (for franchise scheme, see chapter 20, below).

315   "It was very humble and watery": Confidential interview.

315   Inauguration: Beyle, 257; see also English manuscript and Starr, 191ff.

315   Maurice Smith: Oakley, 305.

316   "He knew it was popular": Confidential interview.

318   "most turbulent of their marriage": *Mother Jones,* November-December 1993.

319   politics of education reform: *New York Times,* April 1, 1992; *Arkansas Times,* February 1984; Allen and Portis, 83ff.; Blair, 349–50; Oakley, 275–89; Fick, 145–46; Starr, 195; Bartley, 464; and several confidential interviews.

320   stand by in studied silence: Confidential interviews; Oakley 289–91; Starr, 193–94; Warner, 128–30; *New Yorker,* May 30, 1994; *New York Times,* March 27, 1992.

321   "I don't think he's got a conscience": Fick, 145–46.

322   education reform and the Bubba factor: *Arkansas Times,* February 1984; *Mother Jones,* November-December 1993; Oakley, 290–92; Warner, 131; *Washington Post,* February 3, 1992, and March 28, 1992; *Philadelphia Inquirer,* October 15, 1992; Dumas, 114ff.

329   Roger Clinton drug case: *Sunday Telegraph* (London), July 17, 1994; *Washington Times,* March 25, 1992, April 4, 1992, April 14, 1992, September 27, 1994; Kelley, 245ff.; Floyd Brown, 57ff.; Allen and Portis, 103–04; *Arkansas Gazette,* September 18–19, 1986, October 9, 1986, October 30, 1986; Oakley, 296–300; Warner, 137; *Newsweek,* January 24, 1994; *Albuquerque Journal,* September 20, 1994; FBI memoranda, October 21, 1986; *Rocky Mountain News,* July 27, 1994; *Atlanta Journal and Constitution,* March 24, 1992; Auerbach, 16ff.; and numerous confidential interviews.

331   1984 campaign finances: Fick, 152–53.

333   "Within his eager earnestness": *New Yorker,* February 22, 1993.

333   Clinton and Highway Commission: Oakley, 306–08.

17. Washington III

This summary of the Washington institutions is based mainly on Peters, the files of the *Washington Monthly,* the *National Journal* and its *Hill People,* Jackley, Penny and Garrett, Greider, Birnbaum, Parry, Hertsgaard, Smith, and Lapham. Major sources also included *Public Citizen, Common Cause,* and the *Congressional Quarterly.*

336   Realities of Congress: In addition to Peters, Penny and Garrett, Jackley, and Greider, see *Mother Jones,* July-August, 1992, January-February 1993, and March-April 1993; *American Heritage,* April 1994; Stern, 3–22, 107–19, and 243ff.; *Common Cause,* August 1989, May 1990, and August 1991; "Who Owns Our Government?" *Listening to America with Bill Moyers,* PBS, April 7, 1992; *Nation,* December 5, 1994; *Washington Monthly,* October 1992 and January 1993.

342   Executive branch: Greider; Peters; *Public Citizen,* January 1993; *Washington Monthly,* July-August 1991, May 1992, November 1992, and January 1993; *Common Cause,* March 1990, August 1991, April 1992, and July 1992; *Mother Jones,* July-August 1992 and January-February 1993; *National Journal,* February 22, 1992, September 19, 1992, and November 21, 1992.

347   Washington lobbies: Birnbaum; Greider; Peters; Lapham; Phillips, *Arrogant Capital; Washington Monthly,* June 1992, July 1992, January 1993, and April 1993; *Common Cause,* May 1989, Fall 1992, and Winter 1992; *National Journal,* October 10, 1992, November 24, 1990, and December 15, 1990.

350   The media: Hertsgaard; Parry; *Washington Monthly,* March 1992; *New Yorker,* December 12, 1994; *Columbia Journalism Review,* March-April 1995; *Extra,* January-February, 1993 and January-February 1994; *Village Voice,* September 14, 1993; *Washington Monthly,* November 1994; and *Utne Reader*'s annual "Top Censored Stories," 1992–95; and numerous confidential interviews.

357   Culture of complicity: Greider, 115; Peters, xiii–xiv; *Public Citizen,* January 1993; *Mother Jones,* July-August 1992 and January-February 1993; *Washington Monthly,* March 1993; *Common Cause,* May 1989; Parry, 11 and 208–09; Karp, ixff.

18. Little Rock IV

Beyond repeated confidential interviews with federal investigators and others, principal published sources include Bartley, the *New Yorker,* January 17, 1994; the *American Spectator,* February and September 1994; *USA Today,* March 30, 1994; several articles in the *Washington Post* and *New York Times; Reader's Digest,* June 1994; *Los Angeles Times,* April 15, 1994; Gannett News Service, February 4, 1994; *People,* January 24, 1994; the *Times* (London), May 12, 1994; files of the House Banking Committee, including RTC and Rose firm documents; and the *Congressional Record,* March 24, 1994.

360 "The moral of that story": Confidential interview.

360 McDougal background: *People*, January 24, 1994; Oakley, 521–24.

360 "It was understood": Confidential interview.

361 Early Whitewater dealings: *Washington Post National Weekly Edition*, December 6–12, 1993, and December 27, 1993–January 2, 1994; *New York Times*, December 15, 1993, and March 25, 1994; *American Spectator*, February 1994; *Reader's Digest*, June 1994; *USA Today*, January 13, 1994; *New Yorker*, January 17, 1994; Gross, 73–89; *Los Angeles Times*, April 15, 1994; *National Review*, March 21, 1994.

364 "All that money": Confidential interview.

365 "neither . . . was booming": Oakley, 524.

365 "too many risky loans": *USA Today*, January 13, 1994; Gross, 115; *American Spectator*, February 1994.

366 "unsafe and unsound" and examination results: *American Spectator*, February 1994; *Washington Post National Weekly Edition*, December 6–12, 1993; and confidential interviews. See also Gross, 115ff., and *New Yorker*, January 17, 1994.

367 "not particularly unique": Confidential interview.

367 "a local sex celebrity": Confidential interview.

367 Susan was known to live: *People*, January 24, 1994.

367 "In their heyday": *Washington Post National Weekly Edition*, December 6–12, 1993.

367 "they just kept quiet": Confidential interviews.

368 "Pursuant to your discussions": Gross, 113, and RTC documents; see also *New York Times*, March 25, 1994, and *Congressional Record*, March 24, 1994.

368 "Hillary was the point person": Confidential interview.

368 Gold Mine Springs: *American Spectator*, February 1994.

369 "knew you had no recourse": Confidential interview.

370 Hillary's retainer: Confidential interviews; *Washington Post*, March 9, 1992, and March 12, 1992; *American Spectator*, February 1994; *New York Times*, December 15, 1993; *Harper's*, October 1994; *Business Week*, January 31, 1994.

371 "No one thought": Confidential interview.

372 Madison Guaranty fund-raiser: *New York Times*, December 15, 1993; *Washington Post National Weekly Edition*, December 6–12, 1993; Gross, 130–32; *American Spectator*, December 1994.

372 "phantom contributors": *New Yorker*, January 17, 1994.

372 "I guess you could say": Confidential interview.

372 "Whatever else it was": Confidential interview.

373 stock scheme: *New Yorker*, January 17, 1994; *New York Times*, March 25, 1994.

375 Frost suit: *Washington Post National Weekly Edition*, January 10–16, 1994; Bartley, 175; and confidential interviews.

375 "I need to know": RTC documents.

376 "tens of thousands": *Washington Post National Weekly Edition*, December 27, 1993–January 2, 1994.

376 "Any attempt to extract": Notes of conversation between RTC and senior criminal investigator L. Jean Lewis and FDIC attorney April Breslaw, February 2, 1994; RTC documents.

376 "Poor man's": Confidential interview.

376 typical Whitewater buyers and contracts: *Washington Post National Weekly Edition,* April 25–May 1, 1994.

378 "A feller could live off the land": *Washington Post National Weekly Edition,* December 27, 1993–January 2, 1994.

379 David Hale case: Confidential interviews; *Washington Post National Weekly Edition,* February 21–27, 1994; Gross, 117ff.; Bartley, 93ff. and 355; *American Spectator,* February 1994; *New Yorker,* January 17, 1994; Associated Press, July 18, 1994; *Albuquerque Tribune,* October 20, 1994; *Wall Street Journal,* September 26, 1994.

379 Castle Grande meeting: Associated Press, July 4, 1995.

383 "Let's close the place down": Gross, 120.

383 "Have you heard": *American Spectator,* February 1994.

384 International Paper and Great Southern: Gross, 119–21.

385 "off of old Jim": Confidential interview.

385 "but a footnote": Oakley, 527.

386 McDougal transcript: Associated Press, March 11, 1995.

386 "slightly around the bend": *USA Today,* March 30, 1994.

387 "People knew": Author's interview with Max Brantley.

387 "When the rip-off artists": Quoted in Bartley, 188.

387 "If you know": Lewis-Breslaw conversation cited above; RTC documents.

19. Little Rock and Mena

The documentation of this chapter begins with the 2,000-document personal papers of Barry Seal—cited below as Seal Papers—and extensive law enforcement files, including investigative memoranda of the IRS, FBI, US Customs, and Arkansas State Police; the "thesis" and diary of ASP investigator Russell Welch; and the congressional testimony of Welch and IRS agent William Duncan. Additional evidence comes from the sworn depositions in the federal court case of *Reed and Reed v. Young and Baker, et al.,* including the testimony of the following—most of whom are Arkansas State Police officials: Tommy Baker, John Bender, L. D. Brown, William Canino, John Chappelle, David Dillinger, William Duncan, Ricky Edwards, Lawrence Graves, James Jenkins, Melanie McGill, John Morrow, Larry Patterson, Terry and Janice Reed, David Sanders, Barry Spivey, Michelle Tudor, Russell Welch, Doug Williams, and Raymond "Buddy" Young. In addition to the voluminous official and sworn documentation, there are also a number of revealing published sources, including *Unclassified,* February-March 1992; *Nation,* February 10, 1992, February 24, 1992, March 23, 1992, April 6, 1992, May 4, 1992, and September 24, 1995; *Wall Street Journal,* June 29, 1994, and October 18, 1994; *Sarah McClendon's Washington Report,* March 9, 1991; *Boston Phoenix,* November 23, 1990; *Village Voice,* July 1, 1986, and April 14, 1992; *Texas Observer,* June 17, 1994; *American Spectator,* August 1995; various Jack Anderson syndicated "Washington Merry-Go-Round" columns; an account of Bill Holmes's story and testimony in *Grapevine* of Fayetteville, July 2, 1993; and a *CBS Evening News Special Report* produced by Michael Singer in March 1994.

Several books set the backdrop of the drug trade and official complicity in it, including *The Man Who Made It Snow* by Max Mermelstein; *Cocaine Politics: Drugs, Armies, and the CIA in Central America* by Peter Dale Scott and Jonathan Marshall; *The Big White Lie* by Michael Levine; *Out of Control* by Leslie Cockburn; *The Bluegrass Conspiracy* by Sally Denton; and *The Chronology* (National Security Archives).

The Lasater story is documented by interviews with confidential law enforcement sources, including two former US attorneys in the area; by FBI memoranda of October 20 and 21, 1986; and by Arkansas State Police investigative reports dating from 1984 to 1986 and correspondence from the Regional Organized Crime Information Center, Nashville, Tennessee. Published accounts include a series in the *Albuquerque Journal*, May 8, 1994, May 22, 1994, June 26, 1994, and September 20, 1994; *Newsweek*, January 24, 1994; *Economist*, May 7, 1994; *Washington Times*, December 20, 1993; *United Press International*, April 23, 1987; *Sunday Telegraph* (London), October 9, 1994; and *Louisville Courier Journal*, September 21, 1994.

389 Mena history: WPA Writers' Program *Guide*, 318–20.

390 notable exceptions: *Wall Street Journal*, June 29, 1994, July 25, 1994, and October 18, 1994; two "Eye on America" segments on *The CBS Evening News* aired in spring 1994.

391 "Full of fun": Gugliotta and Leen, 146.

391 "He didn't fly an airplane": Gugliotta and Leen, 146.

391 Case quietly dropped: Confidential interviews and Seal Papers.

391 "broker": Gugliotta and Leen, 149.

391 CIA operative both before and during: Seal Papers.

391 Children playing with money: Seal Papers.

392 "One must find": Seal Papers.

392 El Gordo: Gugliotta and Leen, 148, and Seal Papers.

392 invariable routine: Seal Papers, including videotapes of training exercises and actual drops.

392 "only the transport": Seal Papers and *Penthouse*, July 1995.

392 "between $3 billion and $5 billion": Letter of Louisiana Attorney General William J. Guste, Jr., to US Attorney General Edwin Meese, March 3, 1986.

393 "stacks of cash": Deposition of IRS agent William C. Duncan, June 21, 1991.

393 "bank officer went down the teller lines": Ibid.

393 hundreds of thousands washed through: Arkansas State Police files; IRS memoranda, 1984–85.

393 "magnet": *Arkansas Gazette*, November 4, 1990, and November 5, 1990.

393 largest cocaine smuggling operation: Interviews with numerous federal and state law enforcement officers; see also US Senate Subcommittee on Terrorism, Narcotics and International Operations Report, "Drugs, Law Enforcement and Foreign Policy," December 1988, 41, 121.

393 one channel: For the other aspects of Iran-Contra, see *The Chronology*, Cockburn, and Scott and Marshall.

393 Holmes case: *Grapevine*, (Fayetteville) July 2, 1993; *Washington County Observer* (Arkansas), June 30, 1994 and September 30, 1994; and author's interview with Holmes. Holmes's testimony was in a federal court trial in Fayetteville that concluded on September 10, 1993.

394   Mena tales: *In These Times,* February 12, 1992; *Arkansas Times,* May 12, 1992; *Village Voice,* April 14, 1992; "Now It Can be Told," April 13, 1992, and July 9, 1992; *Sunday Telegraph* (London) October 9, 1994, and March 26, 1995; and confidential interviews.

394   Seal aircraft links to CIA: FAA registrations, modification orders, Aircraft Owners and Pilots Association (AOPA) reports of title search, aircraft title insurance documents, bills of sale, promissory notes, transport insurance, FAA conveyance recordation notices, and other documents in author's possession (Seal Papers).

394     $750,000 for avionics: Welch thesis.

394   "works for Seal and cannot be touched": Confidential source; *Penthouse,* July 1995.

394   "told not to touch anything": Welch thesis.

394   Southern Tier: Confidential interviews with law enforcement and intelligence sources.

395   "fixed": Confidential interview.

395   Address book and financial contacts: Seal Papers.

395   "night depository": Reed and Cummings, 138–44.

395   "Seal knew them all": Confidential interview and investigative report in *Reed v. Young.*

395   "no limit on cooperation": Confidential interview.

395   Seal income and IRS jeopardy assessment: Seal Papers.

395   "CIA-DEA employment": Seal Papers.

396   Royale businesses: Seal Papers.

396   Quaaludes charge: Seal Papers; Shannon, 149–50; Gugliotta and Leen, 149–50.

396   "always smarter": Confidential interview.

396   dicker with the staff: Gugliotta and Leen, 149–50; Shannon, 149ff.

396   DEA informant number: Gugliotta and Leen, 151.

396     $800,000-a-year double agent: Seal Papers.

396   Sandinista sting operation: Gugliotta and Leen, 149–69; Shannon, 151–57; *The Chronology,* 288. See also Barry Seal's testimony to the President's Commission on Organized Crime, October 5, 1985.

396   Leak to *Washington Times: Washington Times,* July 17, 1984; Shannon 156–59.

396   "a world nearly devoid of rules": Seal Papers.

396   Camp's death: Confidential interviews; *Penthouse,* July 1995.

396   *Fat Lady* logs: Confidential interview.

397   Seal goes public: Confidential interviews; Gugliotta and Leen, 340; Shannon, 153–63; and Seal Papers.

397   "Every time Berri": Welch diary, August 27, 1985.

397   "allowed to smuggle what he wants": Welch diary, note on conversation with DEA agent Steve Lowrey, June 4, 1985.

397   Seal's murder: Mermelstein, 195–204, 216, 224, 265–68, 284, 287; Shannon, 160–63; Gugliotta and Leen, 168–69; and confidential interviews.

397   Reagan address: The broadcast was on March 15, 1986. The president said in part: "Every American parent will be outraged to learn that top Nicaraguan government officials are deeply involved in drug trafficking. There is no crime to which the Sandinistas will not stoop. This is an outlaw regime."

397 *Fat Lady* shot down: Cockburn, 214–31; *Penthouse,* July 1995; *The Chronology,* 505ff.

398 Linkage to Nevada test site: *Penthouse,* July 1995; *Las Vegas Sun,* October 6, 1986; and confidential interviews.

398 CIA agent's call to Bush's office: The call was from Felix Rodriguez to Bush aide Samuel Watson. See *The Chronology,* 505; *Washington Post,* December 16, 1986; *New York Times,* December 16, 1986.

398 "couldn't find a soul around Mena": Author's interview with William Holmes.

398 "new activity . . . an Australian business": *Penthouse,* July 1985; deposition of Russell Franklin Welch, June 21, 1991.

398 "something going on": Welch deposition, June 21, 1991.

398 "CIA or DEA operation": Arkansas State Police memorandum, August 25, 1987.

398 Missile system tested, etc.: *Wall Street Journal,* July 10, 1995.

398 "the CIA still has ongoing operations": IRS memorandum, October 8, 1991.

398 "rogue DEA operation": *Wall Street Journal,* July 10, 1995.

398 Duncan and Welch investigations: Depositions before Congressman Alexander and Arkansas Attorney General Bryant, June 21, 1991; *Wall Street Journal,* October 18, 1994; Welch diary; Arkansas State Police documents; IRS memoranda; and confidential interviews.

399 "sufficient for an indictment": Senate subcommittee report cited above, December 1988, 121.

400 "Mena tires of rumors": *Arkansas Gazette,* June 28, 1988.

400 Sheriff A. L. Hadaway: *Arkansas Gazette,* June 28, 1988; Hadaway letter to the Arkansas Committee, University of Arkansas, January 14, 1992.

400 Jack Anderson and Rodney Bowers: *San Francisco Chronicle,* March 1, 1989; *Arkansas Gazette,* December 14–17, 1987, and February 23, 1988.

400 appeal to Hammerschmidt: *Arkansas Gazette,* December 14, 1987; sworn testimony of Terry Capeheart to Sheriff A. L. Hadaway, FBI agent Tom Ross, ASP agent Russell Welch, and IRS agent William Duncan, April 30, 1986.

400 "federal umbrella": *Arkansas Gazette,* April 11, 1988.

400 Black's approach to Clinton: letter from Charles E. Black to the Arkansas Committee, January 13, 1992; *Unclassified,* March 1992.

401 "extinguish a raging forest fire by spitting on it:" Black letter.

401 "superiors": *New York Post,* July 28, 1995.

401 "shredding party": Deposition of Michelle Tudor, July 25, 1995.

401 Files "dismantled": Confidential interview; Tudor deposition.

401 ASP investigation: *New York Post,* July 28, 1995.

401 "why no one was prosecuted": letter from Arkansas Attorney General Winston Bryant to Lawrence Walsh, May 30, 1991.

402 "credible evidence": *Arkansas Gazette,* September 10, 1991.

402 "conspiracy of the grandest magnitude": *In These Times,* February 18, 1992.

402 Clinton press conference: *Arkansas Gazette,* September 11, 1991.

404 L. D. Brown's account: deposition of L. D. Brown in *Reed v. Young*, July 25, 1995; plaintiff's response to defendant's *Motion in Limine*, December 14, 1995; *Nation*, September 25, 1995; *American Spectator*, August 1995; and confidential interviews.

413 Arkansas National Guard: Confidential interview; *Nation*, May 4, 1992.

413 "Arkansas Traveler" honorifics: *Nation*, May 4, 1992.

413 "dumping grounds nobody else wanted": Confidential interviews.

413 Wackenhut: Confidential interviews; author's interview with Jim Hougan; *Arkansas Gazette*, March 20, 1986, July 31, 1987, August 7, 1987, April 17, 1988, and November 18, 1988; *Humanist*, March-April 1994. The corporation was linked to the old Church League of America, an ultraconservative group dating to the 1950s. The late Hal Hendrix, a Wackenhut executive vice president, was also a self-confessed CIA operative.

414 "trying to be the tough guy": Confidential interview.

414 "no position to say no": Confidential interview.

414 Removal of mansion logs: Confidential interview; *American Spectator*, January 1994.

414 "worried about the girls": Confidential interview; *American Spectator*, January 1994.

415 "closet Contra supporter": Confidential interview.

415 Quiet lobbying outside state: Confidential interviews.

415 Hillary, POM, and Seth Ward: Confidential interviews; *Nation*, April 6, 1992; *Village Voice*, April 14, 1992; *American Spectator*, June 1994. See also the Baker, Young, Sanders, and Edwards depositions in *Reed v. Young*.

417 Lasater background: Confidential interviews; *Economist*, May 7, 1994; *Newsweek*, January 24, 1994; *Washington Times*, December 20, 1992; *Albuquerque Journal*, May 8, 1994, May 22, 1994, June 26, 1994, September 20, 1994; FBI interrogation memoranda, October 21, 1986. See also Auerbach.

418 Sanctions against Lasater and Company: *Albuquerque Journal*, September 20, 1994; UPI, April 23, 1987; see also *Economist*, May 7, 1994, and *Newsweek*, January 24, 1994.

418 Clinton-Lasater intimacy: Spivey deposition, August 9, 1995, Brown deposition, July 25, 1995, Patterson deposition, March 8, 1995 in *Reed v. Young*; *Rocky Mountain News*, July 27, 1994; *Los Angeles Times*, March 24, 1992; Gannett News Service, February 4, 1994; confidential interviews.

419 Kentucky Derby trip: Spivey deposition, August 9, 1995; *Louisville Courier Journal*, September 21, 1994; Regional Organized Crime Information Center (Nashville); correspondence with Arkansas State Police, May 15, 1986; FBI memoranda of October 20–21, 1986.

420 Hillary keeps tabs: Confidential interview.

420 Lasater and Company state business: *Bond Buyer*, March 24, 1992; *Arkansas Gazette*, October 12, 1986; *Washington Times*, March 25, 1992, and September 27, 1994; *Atlanta Journal and Constitution*, March 24, 1992; *Los Angeles Times*, March 24, 1992.

421 Angel Fire: DEA memoranda and letters, January 19, 1989; US Customs Service investigative memorandum, January 19, 1991; *Albuquerque Journal*, May 8, 1994, and September 20, 1994.

421 "putting one in the boot": Arkansas State Police investigative memorandum, September 24, 1986.

421 Lasater and Madison Guaranty: *Washington Times,* February 16, 1994, and May 12, 1994; see also Gross, 148.

422 Patsy Thomasson: Confidential interviews; *Washington Times,* March 25, 1992, and December 20, 1993; *Albuquerque Journal,* May 8, 1994, May 22, 1994, June 26, 1994, and September 20, 1994. Lasater's durable power of attorney to Thomasson is dated March 11, 1987. A formal written request of the Clinton White House for Patsy Thomasson's résumé went unanswered despite repeated efforts.

423 Dennis Patrick: *Economist,* May 7, 1994; *Sunday Telegraph* (London), May 8, 1994; *Washington Times,* June 9, 1994; author's interview with Patrick.

423 Lasater investigation: Arkansas State Police investigative files and memoranda, including witness statements, August–October 1986; *Albuquerque Journal,* September 20, 1994; *Arkansas Gazette,* October 30, 1986 and March 24, 1992.

424 Lasater FBI statement: FBI memorandum, October 21, 1986.

424 Angel Fire investigation falls apart: DEA and Customs memoranda cited above; *Albuquerque Journal,* May 8, 1994.

425 Lasater indictment and Proctor statements: *Arkansas Gazette,* October 26–30, 1986, and November 15, 1986.

425 Clinton statements: *Arkansas Gazette,* September 18–19, 1986, and October 26–30, 1986.

425 Sequel and pardon: *Los Angeles Times,* March 24, 1992; *Washington Post,* March 3, 1994.

426 "large quantities of drugs": Patterson deposition in *Reed v. Young,* March 8, 1995; *Sunday Telegraph* (London), March 26, 1995.

426 "execute that search warrant": Patterson deposition, March 8, 1995.

426 "He was just interested": Patterson deposition, March 8, 1995.

426 "what the hell is going on at Mena?": Patterson deposition, March 8, 1995.

426 "I have been told": Patterson deposition, March 8, 1995.

427 "I guess I never really knew": Confidential interview.

20. Little Rock to Washington

Sources for the Hart episode include private manuscripts and files of my colleague investigative reporter Sally Denton; press accounts in the *Denver Post, Miami Herald,* and *Washington Post;* and a number of confidential interviews. The 1986 race is drawn chiefly from the *Gazette* and interviews. Sources for Clinton's withdrawal from the presidential race in 1987 include several confidential witnesses, the *Gazette,* and the *Democrat.* The issue of Clinton's extramarital relations has been discussed in several published sources, including the *Los Angeles Times,* December 21, 1993; *Sunday Times* (London), May 1, 1994, and May 8, 1994; *Sunday Telegraph* (London), January 23, 1994; *New York Times,* April 19, 1994; *American Spectator,* January 1994 and April-May 1994; *Albuquerque Tribune,* February 12, 1994; *Economist,* April 16, 1994; Edith Efron's landmark article in *Reason,* November 1994; and Michael Issikoff's controversial piece in the *Washington Post,* May 22, 1994.

Published sources on Clinton's "corporate culture" in Little Rock include L. J. Davis's much-noted article in the *New Republic,* April 4, 1994; *Sunday Times* (London), February 13, 1994; *Nation,* March 14, 1994; *Forbes,* May 11, 1992, and December 21, 1992; *Business Week,* May 24, 1993, and May 16, 1994; *Village Voice,* June 8, 1993; *Mother Jones,* November-December 1993; *Arkansas Times,* February 1992; Trimble, *American Spectator,* June 1994; *Southern Exposure,* Spring 1990, Winter 1990, Fall 1990, Winter 1991, and Summer 1991; the files of the *Arkansas Times* and *Spectrum;* and *Social Policy,* Spring 1993. Mara Leveritt's stunning article "The Boys on the Track," about the 1987 murders of Don Henry and Kevin Ives, appeared in the *Arkansas Times,* January 1992.

Sources on ADFA include *U.S. News and World Report,* July 6, 1992; *Arkansas Democrat,* June 7, 1988; *Washington Times,* April 10, 1992; and John Crudell's remarkable series in the *New York Post,* January 6, 23, and 30, and February 10, 1995.

The account of the 1992 campaign was drawn mainly from confidential interviews, with background in the *Washington Post,* the *New York Times,* and in Germond and Witcover. Marshall Frady's "Death in Arkansas," about the execution of Ricky Ray Rector, appeared in the *New Yorker,* February 22, 1993.

429   "personal and political purposes": *Arkansas Gazette,* April 30, 1986.

429   Lasater issue: Oakley, 330ff.; Starr, 202–04.

430   Hillary's outburst: *Arkansas Democrat-Gazette,* September 19, 1986.

430   "Dear Supporter": Oakley, 330–31.

430   1986 campaign money: *Arkansas Gazette,* September 18, 1986, and October 10, 1986; Starr, 201–02; Blair, 278, 282, and 354; Oakley, 325; and confidential interviews.

430   "as surprised as anyone": Starr, 200.

430   "red-neck, black-neck": Blair, 276.

431   "if we got by good": Confidential interviews.

431   "running out of friends": Oakley, 340.

431   endorsements: *Arkansas Gazette,* March 13, 1987, and April 15–16, 1987.

432   "pretty good microcosm": *Arkansas Gazette,* April 16, 1987.

432   dinner with Lear, Don Henley, and others: *Arkansas Gazette,* April 19, 1987.

433   Hart scandal and withdrawal: Confidential interviews with participants, journalists, and law enforcement officials; *Miami Herald,* May 4, 1987 and May 10, 1987; *Washington Post,* May 5–10, 1987; *Denver Post,* January 11–July 13, 1987; private files, interview notes, and manuscript of Sally Denton; *New York Times,* February 20, 1992. See also producer Charles Thompson's documentary for ABC's *20/20* on organized-crime connections in the Hart affair.

435   "scared the hell out of him": Confidential interviews.

435   "there has been erosion": *Arkansas Gazette,* June 18, 1987.

435   "with a woman on his lap": Confidential interview.

435   "Let's go": *Arkansas Gazette,* July 18, 1987.

435   decision not to run: Confidential interviews; *Arkansas Gazette,* June 19–August 17, 1987; Oakley, 346ff.; see also *Vanity Fair,* May 1992; O'Clery, 28ff. The "By Her Man" photograph appeared in the *Arkansas Democrat,* July 16, 1987.

438   Dukakis and 1988 campaign: Oakley, 361–63; *American Spectator,* January 1994 and April-May 1994; *Arkansas Gazette,* July 20, 1988; *Spectrum Reader,* 31; and confidential interviews.

439   womanizing: *Los Angeles Times,* December 21, 1993; *New York Times,* April 19, 1994; *Albuquerque Tribune,* February 12, 1994; *Sunday Times* (London), May 1, 1994, and May 8, 1994; *Sunday Telegraph* (London), January 23, 1994, and July 17, 1994; *Times* (London), December 23, 1993; *American Spectator,* January 1994, April-May 1994, August 1994, December 1994; *Washington Post,* February 6, 1992, and May 22, 1994; *Spectrum,* February 19–25, 1992; *Nation,* February 10, 1992; *Pittsburgh Tribune-Review,* November 14, 1994; *Reason,* November 1994; *Economist,* April 16, 1994; *Washington Post,* July 7, 1994; transcripts of Clinton–Gennifer Flowers conversations, Floyd Brown, 151–59; *Sally Jessy Raphael Show,* July 17, 1992 (appearance by Sally Perdue); Warner 110–11; Radcliffe, 186–87; Floyd Brown, 160ff.; Fick, 129–33, 191, and 204; *New Yorker,* May 30, 1994; extensive interviews with confidential sources. See also Flowers.

444   Vince Foster: *American Spectator,* January 1994, and April-May 1994; *American Lawyer,* July-August 1992; *Sunday Telegraph* (London), February 6, 1994; *Washington Post National Weekly Edition,* August 23–29, 1993; *New Yorker,* August 9, 1993; *Esquire,* November 1993; *National Enquirer,* August 10, 1993; *Village Voice,* August 3, 1993; *Economist,* February 12, 1994; *Hope Star* (Arkansas), July 20, 1993; *In These Times,* September 6, 1993; *New York Times,* August 13, 1993; *U.S. News and World Report,* August 23, 1993; and confidential interviews.

445   finances and income: *Arkansas Gazette-Democrat,* March 25, 1990, and July 25, 1990; *New York Times,* March 27, 1992, and December 15, 1993; Oakley, 366–70; Gross, 95–97, 98–99, 134–41, and 224–25; *Albuquerque Tribune,* May 1, 1993; *Washington Times,* January 12, 1996; *New York Times,* October 23, 1995.

447   Hillary's activities: *Mother Jones,* November-December, 1993; *New Yorker,* May 30, 1994; Warner, 139–41; *Arkansas Gazette,* April 13, 1986, October 19, 1986, May 6, 1987, May 7, 1989, May 22, 1989, August 12, 1990, July 24, 1990; *Forbes,* May 11, 1992; confidential interviews.

450   New York money: *New York Post,* January 11, 1996; *Washington Times,* January 12, 1996.

450   "just pitched a fit": Confidential interview.

450   tax deductions: *Albuquerque Tribune,* May 1, 1993; Gross, 224–25; *Arkansas Gazette,* February 2, 1991.

450   "Her friends in the Heights": Confidential interview.

450   "Why can't we": *New York Times,* October 23, 1995.

451   "rich and dirt": Confidential interview.

451   "ready to listen": *Forbes,* December 21, 1992.

451 Stephens, Tyson, et al: *Arkansas Times*, February, 1992; *Village Voice*, June 8, 1993, and August 3, 1993; *Sunday Telegraph* (London), October 9, 1994; *Forbes*, December 21, 1992; *Arkansas Business*, January 15, 1992, and April 4, 1994; *Nation*, August 17–24, 1992, and March 14, 1994; *Mother Jones*, November-December, 1993; *New York Times*, May 17, 1978, and April 26, 1993; *Washington Post National Weekly Edition*, March 21–27, 1994; *Newsweek*, January 24, 1994; *New Republic*, April 4, 1994, and April 24, 1994; *American Spectator*, October 1992; *Business Week*, September 14, 1992. See also Trimble; Schwartz; and Rosenberg.

452 Clinton "machine": *Spectrum*, November 7–13, 1990.

453 ADFA and Beverly: *Los Angeles Times*, June 29, 1992, and March 30–31, 1992; *Sunday Times* (London), February 13, 1995; *Des Moines Register*, June 13, 1993; *Barron's*, February 25, 1991; *Wall Street Journal*, February 1, 1993, February 8, 1993, February 9, 1993; *New York Post*, January 6, 1995, January 13, 1995, January 23, 1995, January 30, 1995, February 10, 1995; *Arkansas Gazette*, March 5, 1995; *Arkansas Democrat*, June 7, 1988; *Washington Times*, April 10, 1992; *U.S. News and World Report*, July 6, 1992; ADFA documents; investigative documents, State of Delaware, Department of Insurance, August 18, 1992; *New Republic*, April 4, 1994; Bartley, 19, 260; Oakley, 409–10.

455 the toll of governance: Corporation for Enterprise Development, *State Report Cards, 1993; Health Care Financing Review*, Summer 1992 (on infant mortality); *State Rankings, 1993; Arkansas Times*, November 1990; *Spectrum*, Spring 1990, Fall 1990, Winter 1990, Summer 1991; *Little Rock Free Press*, June 17–30, 1993; *Social Policy*, Spring 1993; *Government Executive*, January 1993; *New York Times*, March 14, 1992, March 15, 1992, March 27, 1992, April 1, 1992, April 2, 1992, April 4, 1992.

457 "policy wonk" and knowledge of Washington: Confidential interviews.

458 1990 campaign: English manuscript; *Spectrum*, October 31–November 6, 1990; Fick, 150, 165; *American Spectator*, April-May, 1994; Allen and Portis, 134–39; Oakley, 409–42; Warner, 153–54; *Arkansas Times*, January 28, 1992; Bartley, 379–82; and confidential interviews with candidates, staff, and others.

461 Sperling breakfast: *Arkansas Gazette*, September 17, 1991.

461 meeting on health reform: *Washington Monthly*, November 1994.

462 Clinton staff: *Newsweek*, April 11, 1994, and *National Journal*, May 9, 1992.

463 chaos and blunders: *Washington Post National Weekly Edition*, May 24–30, 1993.

463 campaign money: Federal Election Commission releases, March 1, 1993, and March 19, 1993; *Washington Times*, March 13, 1994; *Arkansas Business*, February 3, 1992, and April 4, 1994; *Los Angeles Times*, July 25, 1992; Common Cause memorandum, June 21, 1993; *Extra*, May-June 1994; *Village Voice*, July 14, 1992; *Economist*, November 7, 1992.

465 ghosts: Confidential interview.

465 execution of Ricky Ray Rector: *New Yorker*, November 22, 1993; confidential interviews.

465 "dossiers": Confidential interview.

466 "You'd talk to a reporter": Confidential interview.

466   Perdue threat: *Sunday Telegraph* (London), and confidential interview.
466   "We all have to change": *Philadelphia Inquirer,* March 8, 1992.

Periodicals

Albuquerque Journal, Albuquerque Tribune, American Journalism Review, American Lawyer, American Spectator, Arizona Republic, Arkansas Business, Arkansas Democrat, Arkansas Democrat-Gazette, Arkansas Gazette, Arkansas Times, Associated Press Wire Service, *Atlanta Journal and Constitution, Baltimore Sun, Bond Buyer, Boston Phoenix, Business Week, Columbia Journalism Review, Common Cause, Congressional Quarterly, Des Moines Register, Economist, Esquire, Extra, Forbes, Foreign Policy,* Gannett News Service, *Governing, Government Executive, Grapevine* (Fayetteville, Arkansas), *Guardian, Harper's, Hillary Clinton Quarterly, Hot Springs Sentinel Record, Houston Chronicle, In These Times, Kansas City Star, Lies of Our Times, Little Rock Free Press, Los Angeles Times, LA Weekly, Louisville Courier Journal, Maclean's, Sarah McClendon's Washington Report, Memphis Commercial-Appeal, Miami Herald, Money, Mother Jones, Nation, National Journal, National Review, New Republic, New Statesman and Society, New York, New Yorker, New York Post, New York Review of Books, New York Times, Newsweek, Parade, Penthouse, People, Pittsburgh Tribune-Review, Progressive, Public Citizen, Reader's Digest, Reason, Rocky Mountain News, Rolling Stone, Social Policy, Southern Exposure, Spectrum* (Little Rock), *Sunday Telegraph* (London), *Sunday Times* (London), *Thomson's International Banking Regulator, Time, Times* (London), *Unclassified, USA Today, U.S. News and World Report, Utne Reader, Vanity Fair, Village Voice, Wall Street Journal, Washington Monthly, Washington Post, Washington Spectator, Washington Times, Z.*

Documents

Arkansas State Government documents: letters, files
Arkansas State Police: investigative files and interviews
US Attorney, Little Rock: Memoranda and interrogation files
Federal Bureau of Investigation: interviews, files, and telexes
Drug Enforcement Agency: investigative interviews
Internal Revenue Service: investigative files and memoranda
Adler Berriman Seal, Private Papers
Resolution Trust Corporation: memoranda and investigative files
US Department of Justice: memoranda and files
Federal Election Commission: reports and records

Business and legal files, INSLAW, Inc.

Unpublished manuscript, Professor Arthur English, University of Arkansas at Little Rock

Reed and Reed v. Young, Baker, et al. legal files and deposition transcripts, etc.

Russell Welch, Diary and "Thesis"

Files and reports: Common Cause, Center for Public Integrity, Center for Responsive Politics

Select Bibliography

Abbott, Shirley. *The Bookmaker's Daughter: A Memory Unbound.* New York: Ticknor & Fields, 1992.

Allen, Charles F., and Jonathan Portis. *Bill Clinton: Comeback Kid.* New York: Carol Publishing Group, 1992.

Auerbach, Ann. *Wild Ride: The Rise and Tragic Fall of Calumet Farm, Inc., America's Premier Racing Dynasty.* New York: Henry Holt, 1994.

Bartlett, Donald L., and James B. Steele, *America: What Went Wrong.* New York: Simon & Schuster, 1992.

———. *America: Who Really Pays the Taxes?* New York: Simon & Schuster, 1994.

Bartley, Robert, ed. *Whitewater: A Journal Briefing.* New York: Dow Jones and Company, 1994.

Beyle, Thad, ed. *Gubernatorial Transitions: The 1983 and 1984 Elections.* Durham: Duke University Press, 1988.

Birnbaum, Jeffrey. *The Lobbyists.* New York: Random House, 1992.

Blair, Diane. *Arkansas Politics and Government.* Lincoln: University of Nebraska Press, 1988.

Brown, Dee. *The American Spa.* Little Rock: Rose Publishing, 1982.

Brown, Floyd. *Slick Willie.* Annapolis: Annapolis Publishing Company, 1992.

Brummett, John. *High Wire: From the Back Roads to the Beltway—the Education of Bill Clinton.* New York: Hyperion, 1995.

Byrne, Malcolm, et al., eds. *The Chronology: The Documented Day-by-Day Account of the Secret Military Assistance to Iran and the Contras.* New York: Warner Books, 1987.

Cockburn, Leslie. *Out of Control.* New York: Atlantic Monthly Press, 1987.

Corporation for Enterprise Development. *State Report Cards, 1993.* Washington, DC: Corporation for Enterprise Development, 1993.

Denton, Sally. *The Bluegrass Conspiracy: An Inside Story of Power, Greed, Drugs and Murder.* New York: Doubleday, 1990.

Drew, Elizabeth. *Finding His Voice: Clinton's Ambitious and Turbulent First Year.* New York: Simon & Schuster, 1994.

Dumas, Ernest, ed. *The Clintons of Arkansas.* Fayetteville: University of Arkansas Press, 1993.

Fick, Paul. *The Dysfunctional President: Inside the Mind of Bill Clinton.* New York: Carol Publishing Group, 1995.

Flowers, Gennifer. *Passion and Betrayal.* Delmar: Emery Dalton Books, 1995.

Gallen, David. *Bill Clinton As They Know Him.* New York: Gallen Publishers, 1994.

Germond, Jack, and Jules Witcover. *Mad As Hell: Revolt at the Ballot Box, 1992.* New York: Warner Books, 1993.

Gitlin, Todd. *The Sixties: Years of Hope, Days of Rage.* New York: Bantam Books, 1993.

Greider, William. *Who Will Tell the People?: The Betrayal of American Democracy.* New York: Simon & Schuster, 1992.

Gross, Martin L. *The Great Whitewater Fiasco: An American Tale of Money, Power and Politics.* New York: Ballantine Books, 1994.

Gugliotta, Guy, and Jeff Leen. *Kings of Cocaine: An Astonishing Story of Murder, Money and Corruption.* New York: Harper and Collins, 1990.

Hertsgaard, Mark. *On Bended Knee: The Press and the Reagan Presidency.* New York: Farrar, Straus & Giroux, 1988.

Hodgson, Godfrey. *America in Our Time: From World War II to Nixon—What Happened and Why.* New York: Random House, 1978.

Jackley, John L. *Hill Rat: Blowing the Lid Off Congress.* Washington, DC: Regnery, 1994.

Johnson, Haynes. *Sleepwalking Through History: America in the Reagan Years.* New York: Norton & Company, 1991.

Jones, Bill, et al., eds. *The Spectrum Reader.* Little Rock: August House, 1991.

Kelley, Virginia, with James Morgan. *Leading With My Heart.* New York: Simon & Schuster, 1994.

Key, V. O. *Southern Politics in State and Nation.* Knoxville: University of Tennessee Press, 1984.

King, Norman. *Hillary: Her True Story.* New York: Carol Publishing Group, 1993.

Lapham, Lewis. *The Wish for Kings.* New York: Grove Press, 1993.

Leonard, John. *The Last Innocent White Man in America.* New York: The New Press, 1993.

Levin, Robert. *Bill Clinton: The Inside Story.* New York: Shapolsky Publishers, 1992.

Levine, Michael. *The Big White Lie.* New York: Thunder's Mouth Press, 1994.

Lewis, Charles, Alejandro Benes, and Meredith O'Brien. *The Buying of the President.* New York: Avon Books, 1996.

Maraniss, David. *First in His Class: The Biography of Bill Clinton.* New York: Simon & Schuster, 1995.

Mermelstein, Max. *The Man Who Made it Snow.* New York: Simon & Schuster, 1990.

National Journal. *The Hill People, 1992.* Washington, DC: National Journal Press, 1992.

Oakley, Meredith. *On the Make: The Rise of Bill Clinton.* Washington, DC: Regnery Publishing, 1994.

O'Clery, Conor. *America: A Place Called Hope?* Dublin, Ireland: The O'Brien Press, 1993.

Parry, Robert. *Fooling America: How Washington Insiders Twist the Truth and Manufacture the Conventional Wisdom*. New York: Morrow, 1992.

Penny, Timothy J., and Major Garrett. *Common Cents*. New York: Little Brown, 1995.

Peters, Charles. *How Washington Really Works*. Reading, Mass.: Addison & Wesley, 1983.

Phillips, Kevin P. *The Politics of Rich and Poor: Wealth and the American Electorate in the Reagan Aftermath*. New York: Harper Collins, 1991.

———. *Boiling Point: Republicans, Democrats, and the Decline of Middle Class Prosperity*. New York: Harper Collins, 1993.

———. *Arrogant Capital: Washington, Wall Street and the Frustrations of American Politics*. New York: Little Brown, 1994.

Radcliffe, Donnie. *Hillary Rodham Clinton: A First Lady for Our Time*. New York: Warner Books, 1993.

Reed, Terry, and John Cummings. *Compromised: Clinton, Bush and the CIA*. New York: Shapolsky Publishers, 1994.

Reel, Guy. *Unequal Justice*. Buffalo: Prometheus Books, 1993.

Rosenberg, Leon. *Dillard's*. Fayetteville: University of Arkansas Press, 1988.

Rosenstiel, Tom. *Strange Bedfellows: How Television and the Presidential Candidates Changed American Politics, 1992*. New York: Hyperion, 1994.

Sanders, Keith, et al., eds. *Political Communication Yearbook, 1984*. Carbondale: Southern Illinois University Press, 1985.

Schwartz, Marvin. *Tyson*. Fayetteville: University of Arkansas Press, 1991.

Scott, Peter Dale, and Jonathan Marshall. *Cocaine Politics: Drugs, Armies and the CIA*. Berkeley: University of California Press, 1991.

Shannon, Elaine. *Desperados*. New York: NAL/Dutton, 1989.

Skully, Francis J., MD. *Hot Springs, Arkansas*. Privately published. Hot Springs, 1966.

Smith, Sam. *Shadows of Hope: A Freethinker's Guide to Politics in the Time of Clinton*. Bloomington: Indiana University Press, 1994.

Solomon, Norman. *False Hope: The Politics of Illusion in the Clinton Era*. Monroe, Maine: Common Courage Press, 1994.

Starr, John Robert. *Yellow Dogs and Dark Horses: Thirty Years on the Campaign Beat*. Little Rock: August House, 1987.

State Rankings, 1993: A Statistical View of the 50 United States. Lawrence, Kansas: Morgan Quitno Corp., 1993.

Statistical Abstract of the United States, 1993. Austin, Texas: Reference Press, Inc., 1993.

Stern, Philip. *The Best Congress Money Can Buy*. New York: Pantheon Books, 1988.

Trimble, Vince H. *Sam Walton: The Inside Story of America's Richest Man*. New York: Dutton, 1990.

Warner, Judith. *Hillary Clinton: The Inside Story*. New York: Penguin Books, 1993.

Work Projects Administration Writers' Program. *Arkansas: A Guide to the State*. New York: Hastings House, 1948.

Index

Abbott, Shirley, 39
Aboureszk, James, 342
Acheson, Dean, 69, 131
Acheson, Eleanor, 131, 135
African Americans, *see* blacks
Agnew, Spiro T., 137
agribusiness, 296, 299
Aid to Families with Dependent Children, 299
Air America, Inc., 394
Air Force, U.S., 88
Alexander, Bill, 400, 401–2, 403, 426
Alexander, Wanetta, 19–22
Alinsky, Saul, 119, 133–34
Allen, Charles, 90
Aller, Frank, 93–98, 101–2, 105
All Our Children (Keniston), 161
Altman, Roger, 10, 463
Altshuler, Fred, 165, 167–68
American Bar Association, 204, 377, 449
American Commonwealth, The (Bryce), 251
American Express, 430
American Legion Auxiliary, 55, 80
Boys State of, 57
American Spectator, 332, 441, 443, 461
Anderson, Jack, 400
Anderson, Sam, Jr., 329

Andreas, Dwayne, 262
Angel Fire ski resort, 421, 422, 423, 424
Angelou, Maya, 11
Anthony, Beryl, 220
antiwar movement, 66–67, 68, 76, 263
Operation Chaos and, 102–5
WJC and, 72, 91–93, 95, 97, 100
Apple, R. W., 443
Arkansas, 193–250, 268–91, 305–38, 359–457
amendment of governor's term in, 330
draft in, 79–82, 87–91, 95, 97, 100
economy of, 67, 195–96, 220–21, 241, 308–10, 319
fraud in, 183, 194, 196
government influence in, 218
health care in, 220, 456
HRC's dislike of, 151, 163, 177, 178, 226
interest groups and vested interests in, 197–99, 202, 218–21, 241, 313, 316–17, 319, 321
legislature of, 39, 197, 219, 221, 316, 320, 322, 364, 431
McGovern campaign in, 156–59
oligarchy of, 195–96, 204–5, 218, 452
politics in, 24, 29, 38, 39, 58, 67,

505

Arkansas (*cont.*)
68–69, 170–84, 193–200, 203–12, 215–19, 241, 264, 268, 271, 273–91, 322, 328, 329, 331–32, 333, 370, 371–72, 418, 422, 428–30, 457–59
poverty in, 25, 26, 28, 156–57, 173, 195, 196, 308–9, 310, 455
public-interest law in, 163
Third District of, 171–84
Arkansas, University of, 276, 334, 402
HRC's teaching at, 168–69, 184, 214
Legal Aid Clinic of, 184–85
ROTC at, 88–91, 95, 98–100, 104, 182, 209, 427
WJC's teaching at, 164, 168, 170, 199, 214
Arkansas Democrat, 183, 200, 216, 223–25, 248, 249, 282, 284, 286–87, 310, 315, 330, 428, 431
WJC's womanizing and, 437–38
Arkansas Development Finance Authority (ADFA), 310–11, 416, 421, 453–55
Arkansas Education Association (AEA), 283, 319
Arkansas Gazette, 92, 156, 157, 216, 219, 223–25, 330, 334, 365, 425, 432, 459, 461
gubernatorial campaigns and, 209, 212, 241, 244, 247, 248, 286–89, 290–91, 458
Mena operations and, 400
Arkansas-Louisiana Gas Company (ARKLA), 197–98, 210, 227, 288
Arkansas Power & Light (AP&L), 219, 221, 226, 241, 246, 288, 428, 431
Arkansas Times, 154, 195, 452
Armstrong, William S. (Bill), 81, 82, 87
Ashby, Kit, 72, 77
Ashley, Elizabeth, 418
Ashmore, Harry, 197
Associated Press, 245, 248, 446
AT&T, 268, 295–96
Atlanta Journal and Constitution, 298
Austin, J. Paul, 143

Bachman, Dru, 63, 64
Baker, James, 257, 346
Bankers Trust, 351
Banking Commission, Arkansas, 360, 365, 368
Bank of Cherry Valley, 333, 371
Bank of Credit and Commerce International (BCCI), 234, 311, 349
Bank of Kingston, 362, 363, 365
see also Madison Bank and Trust
Baptists, 42, 61, 275, 277
Barber, James David, 335–36
Bassett, Beverly, 371–75, 382, 383
Bassett, Woody, 250, 289, 372
Bastian, Walter, 72
Baum, Caroline, 231–33
Begala, Paul, 462
Benson, Elmer, 259
Bentsen, Lloyd, 143, 154, 262
Berry, Chuck, 429
Bersin, Alan, 140
Beverly Enterprises, 454–55
Beyond the Best Interests of the Child (Goldstein, Freud, and Solnit, eds.), 161
Biden, Joseph, 339, 462
Billingsley, Bob, 62
Birnbaum, Jeffrey, 348–49
Black, Charles, 400
Black Panthers, 140
blacks, 7, 11, 37, 80, 83, 145, 304–5, 322, 441, 456, 465
in Arkansas government, 198, 199, 331
campaign funds and, 332–33
as Cuban refugees, 241–42, 244–45
as Democrats, 4, 69
in Hope, 25–26, 28, 195
HRC's exposure to, 119–20, 126, 127
integration and, 42, 63, 83, 198, 449, 456
racism and, 196, 304–5, 340, 452
riots of, 77, 126, 128
WJC's reliance on, 196, 212, 284–85, 289, 290, 332–33

WJC's views on, 54, 63
Blair, Diane Divers Kincaid, 185, 229, 234, 248, 275, 276, 277, 288, 331
Blair, James B., 158, 185, 202, 249, 270, 277, 320, 451
  commodities trading and, 214, 227–35
  marriage of, 234
  Tyson Foods and, 227, 234
Bloodworth-Thomason, Linda, 439
Blythe, Lou, 16, 17, 22
Blythe, Sharron, 20, 22
Blythe, Virginia Dell Cassidy, *see* Kelley, Virginia Dell Cassidy
Blythe, Wanetta Alexander, 19–22
Blythe, William Jefferson, II (W. J.; Bill), 15–25, 47
  appearance of, 16, 19, 21, 22
  car accident of, 15–16, 22–23, 32, 54
  family background of, 16–17
  marriages and affairs of, 19–22
  Rodhams compared with, 107–9
  as traveling salesman, 17–20
  World War II and, 20, 21, 32
Blythe, William Jefferson, I (Willie), 16–17
Boland amendment, 393
bond market, bonds, 6, 310, 314, 423–24, 429, 455
Bone, Robert L. (Red), 227–35, 313
Bonhoeffer, Dietrich, 120
Bookmaker's Daughter, The (Abbott), 39
bootlegging, 30–31
Boston, Mass., 125, 127, 128
Bowen, Bill, 203
Bowers, Rodney, 400
Bowie, James, 24
Boyle, Peter, 375
Branch, Taylor, 154–55, 173
Brandeis University, 136–37
Branson, Johanna, 127–28
Brantley, Ellen, 164
Brantley, Max, 271, 387, 460, 466
Britt, Henry, 81, 82
Broadhurst, Billy, 433
Brooke, Edward, 135, 136

Brown, Dee, 37
Brown, Dwayne, 410, 411
Brown, Jerry, 249, 460, 464
Brown, John Y., 249, 417, 420, 425
Brown, Larry Douglass, 404–12, 419, 426, 442
Brown, Ron, 4
Bruck, Connie, 141, 149, 210, 238, 271, 277, 278
Brummett, John, 248, 290, 439
Bryan, William Jennings, 389
Bryant, Winston, 401–2, 403, 426
Buchanan, Pat, 258
Buick agencies, 29–32, 35, 39–40, 41
Bumpers, Dale, 156, 171, 184, 198–99, 202, 220, 227, 237, 269, 372, 426, 429
  in election of 1980, 242, 247
  election of 1988 and, 431, 435
Burros, Marian, 114
Bush, George, 3, 5, 8–9, 254, 256–58, 267, 312, 343, 345, 346, 407, 410, 456
  in election of 1988, 432, 439
  in election of 1992, 1, 5, 6, 9, 65, 100, 102, 104, 460
  federal debt under, 299–300, 303
  Hammerschmidt and, 172
  L. D. Brown and, 404
  Mena operations and, 396, 398, 400, 403, 405
  "Team 100" and, 294–95
Bush, Gordon, 6
Bush, Prescott, 256–57
Business Week, 447–48

Calero, Adolpho, 413
Calero, Mario, 413
Camp, Emile, 396
Campbell, Tom, 66, 70, 74
  on WJC at Georgetown, 62, 63, 67, 77
Capital Management Services, Inc., 379–81
Caplan, Tom, 66, 77
Capone, Al, 37, 39

Caraway, Hattie, 193–94, 234, 389
Carleton, Kearnie, 213
Carmichael, Stokely, 126
Caro, Robert, 260
Carson, Johnny, 438, 439
Carter, Jimmy, 206, 217, 252, 277
    Cuban refugees and, 241–42
    in election of 1976, 200–202, 239,
        264
    in election of 1980, 233, 236, 239,
        245, 264–65
    inflation and, 233, 236
Carville, James, 5, 462, 463
Cash, Clarence, 200
Cassidy, Edith Grisham, 26–27, 31–34,
        46, 58–59
    committed to asylum, 47, 59, 198
    death of, 75
    morphine addiction of, 47
    rages of, 26–27, 33, 47, 75
    Roger Sr. and, 31–32, 47
    WJC influenced by, 27, 32, 34
Cassidy, Eldridge, 26–29, 315
    grocery store of, 24, 26, 28–31
Cassidy, Virginia Dell, *see* Kelley,
    Virginia Dell Cassidy
Castro, Fidel, 118
Catcher in the Rye, The (Salinger), 120
Catholics, Catholic Church, 42, 61, 72,
        110
Central Intelligence Agency (CIA), 93,
        263, 312, 346, 356, 402–10, 426
    Hart and, 433, 434
    L. D. Brown and, 403–12
    Operation Chaos of, 102–5
    Seal and, 391–98, 403, 405, 407–10
    WJC's ties to, 102–5, 406–15
Chicago, Ill., 22, 107–11, 118, 119–20
    Democratic National Convention
        (1968) in, 129–31
Chicago Daily News, 134
Chicago Mercantile Exchange, 214,
        228, 230, 234, 235
Chicago Tribune, 110, 111, 229
child abuse, 26, 29, 46, 48–49, 51, 115

Children's Defense Fund, 164, 167,
        225, 449
children's rights, 160–63
Children's Rights (anthology), 160
child support, 21, 32
Christian Science Monitor, 461
Churchill, Winston, 16
Citizens Bank and Trust, 213, 371
Civil Rights Act (1964), 61
civil rights movement, 64, 66, 69, 76,
        119–20, 126, 128, 142, 196, 261
Civil War, U.S., 24, 357
Clark, Bill, 279
Clark, Steve, 455, 458
Clinton, Chelsea, 235, 237, 247, 282,
        289, 404, 435
Clinton, Hillary Rodham, 107–44,
        160–69, 184–89, 200–206, 225–39,
        258, 260–61, 442–50
    ambition of, 122, 141, 142, 149, 163,
        204, 225, 262, 275, 281
    appearance of, 116–17, 121, 139,
        140, 144, 151, 184, 188, 242, 277–
        78, 315, 334
    athletic skills of, 112, 113, 116, 140
    awards and honors of, 123, 330
    birth of, 109
    as camouflaged woman, 115–16,
        123, 137
    in Carter campaign, 200–202
    commencement speech of, 134–37,
        141, 149
    commodities trading of, 214–15,
        227–37
    competitiveness of, 117, 122, 123
    conflicts of interest of, 210–11, 309,
        429, 465
    Democratic shift of, 127, 129
    determination and endurance of,
        112, 115, 149, 186
    early jobs of, 116
    early political activities of, 121–22,
        125–31
    education of, 113, 116, 122–28, 130–
        44, 149–50, 155
    education policy and, 317–22

election of 1972 and, 154, 155, 157
election of 1988 and, 435–39
election of 1992 and, 439–40, 442–43, 461–66
on eve of inauguration, 2, 7, 443
extracurricular activities of, 112, 113, 116–21, 125
family background of, 107–18, 123, 161–62, 226
father's relationship with, 113–16, 121, 129, 135, 162, 229
feminism of, 134, 140, 163
finances of, 142, 204, 212–15, 224, 227–37, 269, 270–71, 274, 309, 313, 362–65, 368, 370, 383–88, 445–50
as First Lady, 167, 444
as First Lady of Arkansas, 117, 142, 220, 225–39, 242–46, 313–15, 317–22, 327–30, 334, 414–16, 429–30, 435–38, 444–50
Foster's affair with, 404, 414, 444–45
as Goldwater Girl, 122, 255
health care and, 220, 321
independence of, 115, 134, 139, 163–64, 237, 239, 242, 277
interviews of, 119, 125, 272, 432
J. Blair's role in enrichment of, 158, 214, 227–35
maiden name maintained by, 187, 188, 210, 225, 242, 244, 248
marriage of, 187–88
Mena operations and, 414–16
as Methodist, 113, 118–22, 125, 126, 143, 277
mother-in-law's relationship with, 48, 115, 187, 329
name change of, 245, 277, 282
postgraduate work of, 160–63
pregnancy and childbirth of, 235, 237
as reformer, 125, 126–27, 133, 142
as Republican, 122, 125, 127, 128–29, 255
at Rose Law Firm, 203–5, 210, 225–26, 233, 237, 269, 271, 289, 368,

373–75, 382, 415, 429, 444, 449–51, 465
Senate Migratory Labor Subcommittee and, 142–43
senior thesis of, 131–34
sexism experienced by, 134, 165, 185, 242
sexuality of, 117, 131, 140
speeches of, 134–37, 141–42, 144, 149
staff relations with, 225, 226
teaching of, 168–69, 184, 214
Vietnam War and, 125, 126, 127, 129, 135, 136, 139, 141–42
voter registration and, 154
Whitewater and, 212–14, 229, 234, 236, 309, 313, 362–65, 368, 375–78, 382–88
WJC compared with, 123, 149, 280–81
WJC criticized by, 149, 243, 274
WJC's complex relationship with, 163–64, 236–39, 243–44
WJC's defense of, 210–11
in WJC's early campaigns, 168–69, 173, 180, 182, 184, 186, 200, 210–12, 242–46, 248, 273–75, 277–82, 285–87, 289, 429–30, 458
WJC's fights and marital problems with, 47, 178, 237–39, 271, 274–75, 281, 285–86, 314, 318, 404, 437, 439, 441–44, 461
WJC's first meeting with, 144, 149
WJC's loss and comeback and, 268, 271–75, 277–82, 285–87, 289
WJC's love for, 149–52, 160, 163, 168, 186, 461
WJC's speeches edited by, 8, 438
in youth group, 118–21, 143
Clinton, Mr. (Roger Sr.'s father), 29
Clinton, Mrs. (Roger Sr.'s mother), 29, 40
Clinton, Raymond G., 29–31, 39–43, 50, 66, 69, 259
business interests of, 29, 39–40, 41, 58

Clinton, Raymond G. (*cont.*)
  political connections of, 41, 79–82,
    87, 97, 156, 205
  Roger Sr. aided and influenced by,
    29–30, 33, 35, 40, 41, 42
  WJC's campaigns and, 173, 174, 179,
    181, 182, 184, 199, 200, 207
  WJC's relationship with, 39, 40–41,
    67, 79–82, 123
Clinton, Roger, Sr., 29–42, 44, 46–53,
    178
  abusiveness of, 8, 30, 33, 40, 46–51,
    53, 73
  arrests of, 33, 49
  Buick agency of, 29–32, 35
  divorces of, 32, 33, 48–52, 73
  drinking and alcoholism of, 8, 30,
    32, 33, 40, 41, 46, 48, 49, 51, 53,
    56, 58, 73, 212–13, 323
  extramarital affairs of, 31, 48
  finances of, 31, 32, 41, 42
  gambling of, 30, 32, 44, 46, 53
  gun incidents and, 33, 49
  HRC and, 151, 177, 187
  illegal dealings of, 30
  legal custody of WJC denied to, 46
  marriages of, 31, 32
  Raymond's relationship with, 29–30,
    33, 35, 40, 41, 42
  Virginia's divorce from, 48–52, 73
  Virginia's remarriage to, 52–53, 73
  WJC's correspondence with, 73–74
  WJC's relationship with, 32–33, 40,
    46, 48–49, 51, 53, 73–75
Clinton, Roger Cassidy, 48, 52, 56–57,
    73, 75, 418, 420
  arrests of, 323
  band of, 10, 272
  drugs and, 272, 323–30
  indictment of, 327–30, 424
  Lasater probe and, 424, 425, 429
  WJC's gubernatorial campaigns and,
    206, 247, 328, 329
  WJC's relationship with, 43, 44, 52,
    53, 58, 73
  women supplied by, 324–25, 329

Clinton, Roy, 39
Clinton, Virginia Dell Cassidy, *see*
  Kelley, Virginia Dell Cassidy
Clinton, William Jefferson (Bill):
  ambition of, 28–29, 55–59, 61–63,
    70, 85, 90, 95, 146, 149, 150, 163,
    171, 248, 249, 262, 268, 313, 333,
    432
  anger of, 55, 56, 71, 74, 88, 151, 178,
    180, 286, 321, 383
  antiwar movement and, 72, 91–93,
    95, 97, 100, 102–5
  appearance of, 35, 43, 49, 56, 87,
    144, 145, 175, 218, 276
  Arkansas accent of, 63, 83, 145
  as attorney general, 104, 199–200,
    202–6, 210, 211, 237, 238
  awards and honors of, 57, 58, 75–76,
    77, 203, 330
  as Baptist, 42, 61, 275, 277
  birth of, 23
  in campaign of 1972, 101, 153–60,
    177, 181
  charm of, 9, 50, 55, 59, 71, 83, 86–
    87, 101, 144, 145, 149, 150, 164,
    171, 275
  childhood of, 8, 27–50
  CIA ties of, 102–5, 406–15
  conflicts of interest of, 210–11, 309–
    10
  congressional campaign of, 165,
    168–84, 186
  country boy image of, 63, 85, 87
  cover-up of, 327, 390, 400, 402–3,
    414
  dating and womanizing of, 56, 62,
    77, 83, 86–87, 94, 144–45, 147,
    149–51, 184, 186, 237–38, 249,
    269, 272, 274, 281, 314, 324–25,
    328, 404, 414, 436–37, 439–43, 461
  defeats of, 149, 183, 246–49, 268,
    271–75
  depressions of, 54, 71, 87–88, 96,
    250
  draft crisis of, 79–82, 87–91, 94–100,
    104–6, 139, 181, 209–10, 463

drug use of, 272, 325–26, 328, 442

eating habits of, 62, 147

education of, 34–35, 42, 43, 54, 57–72, 75–79, 82–90, 144–52, 155, 160; *see also* Georgetown University; Oxford University; Yale Law School

election of 1988 and, 431–32, 434–39

in election of 1992, 2, 4, 5, 6, 50, 64, 90, 100, 102, 155, 234, 269–70, 343–44, 428, 431, 436, 441, 444, 448, 455, 459–61; *see also* election of 1992

emotional crisis of, 268, 271–73

on eve of inauguration, 1–7, 442

family background of, 15–54, 226

finances of, 212–15, 224, 229, 237, 268–69, 313–14, 333–34, 359–60, 363, 368, 370–72, 376–78, 380, 383–88, 441, 442, 445–48

as Fulbright intern, 67–70, 358

as governor, 2, 47, 56, 185, 199, 215–27, 234–51, 269, 312–14, 367–73, 376–78, 380, 390, 400, 402–21, 424–32, 434–44

gubernatorial campaigns of, 205–12, 215, 241–50, 264, 268, 271, 273–91, 322, 328, 329, 332, 333, 370, 371–72, 418, 422, 428–30, 457–59

gubernatorial problems of, 217–21, 223–24, 241–43, 322, 333–34, 372

Hart scandal and, 434–37

houses purchased or built by, 187, 214, 234, 271

HRC's relationship with, *see* Clinton, Hillary Rodham

on inauguration day, 7–11

as Intermark director, 270–71

interviews of, 76, 79, 215, 248, 272, 333, 431

lack of commitment of, 63–64, 221–23

leadership pathology of, 321–22

in McGovern campaign, 101

mask of, 49–50, 53–56, 272–73

Mena operations and, 390, 400, 402–15, 419, 424–27

networking of, 59, 67, 85–86, 156, 172, 273, 331

pardons granted by, 312, 459

as peacemaker, 35, 42, 54, 73

physicals of, 82, 87, 88

political background of, 39, 41, 55, 57, 156

political comeback of, 250, 268–70, 271–85, 316–17, 418

political role models of, 39, 70

popularity of, 56, 71, 101, 105

press conferences of, 328, 402–3, 429–30

public remorse of, 271–72, 275–76, 280, 282, 283–84

racial attitudes of, 28, 54, 63

as reformer, 202–3, 219, 220, 271, 317–22, 466

Rhodes scholarship of, 75–76, 82–85; *see also* Oxford University

in ROTC, 63

saxophone playing of, 9, 45, 54, 83, 439, 442

school-years politics of, 55, 57, 61–62, 66, 67, 70–72, 74, 147–49

speeches of, 8, 10–11, 64, 66, 169, 175–76, 216, 239–40, 315, 438, 439

status seeking of, 226–27, 271

storytelling of, 63, 83, 144, 145, 150, 315

as surrogate parent, 45, 53

values and character of, 56–57

volunteer work of, 66, 76

Clinton White House, 358, 444–45, 448, 455, 466

decision making in, 47

Office of Administration in, 422

Coca-Cola, 143, 331

cocaine, 405, 411, 417, 423

at Little Rock parties, 147, 272, 311–12, 314, 325–26, 419, 425

Roger Jr. and, 272, 323–30

Seal and, 391–93, 400, 405, 409, 419

cold war, 16, 63–64, 93, 111, 118, 253, 255, 258–60, 302
Coleman, William, III, 145, 146, 147
Collier, Harold, 111, 128, 143
Colombia, drug dealing in, 392, 396
Columbia Lace Company, 107, 108
commodities trading, 214–15, 227–36
Common Cause, 295, 349, 464
Commonweal, 161
Compromised (Cummings), 416
Congress, U.S., 16, 91, 253, 261, 266, 336–42, 349, 393, 468
  bureaucracy of, 339
  corruption in, 340–42
  lack of turnover in, 298–99
  The Numbers and, 337–38
  pay raise of, 348
  see also House of Representatives, U.S.; Senate, U.S.
Conlin, Joseph, 105
Contras, 393–94, 397, 406, 408, 409, 412–13, 415, 433
  see also Iran-Contra scandal
Coolidge, Calvin, 252, 253, 256, 265, 300
corporations, 176, 220, 292, 301, 303, 451–55
  HRC's view of, 142, 224
  media controlled by, 350–51
  PACs of, 293–98, 336–38, 464
  taxes of, 265, 266–67, 287, 300, 301, 452
Corrado, Robert, 82
Cox, Archibald, 167
Crane, Rose, 43, 44, 49, 179
Crane, Stephen, 119
Crawford, Gabe, 30, 31, 32, 41, 42
  WJC's congressional campaign and, 173–74, 175, 179, 184
Crawford, Virginia, 32
crime, 6, 8, 304–5
  organized, 37, 38, 39, 58, 293, 312, 315, 331, 411, 417, 425, 434
Criner, Patty, 65, 175
Crockett, Davy, 24
Crudele, John, 401

Cuba, 63–64, 259
Cuban refugees, 241–42, 244–45, 247, 265, 391
cummings, e. e., 119
Cummings, John, 416
Customs, U.S., 391, 404, 421, 425, 434

Daley, Richard M., 118, 130, 462
Daniels, Charles, 104
Danner, John, 222, 243
death penalty, 185, 203, 211, 465
Deaver, Michael, 343
Defense Department, U.S., 72, 159, 242, 259, 297, 346, 349, 416
Defense Intelligence Agency, 392
DeLaughter, J. N., 423–24
Democratic-Farmer-Labor Party, 259
Democratic Leadership Council (DLC), 301, 457, 459, 462
Democratic midterm convention (1978), 239–40
Democratic National Convention:
  of 1968, 129–31
  of 1972, 157–58
  of 1980, 238, 239–40
  of 1988, 438, 439
  of 1992, 460
Democratic State Committee, 431–32
Democrats, Democratic Party, 23, 28, 64, 67–70, 111, 193–94, 251–55, 258–65, 275–76, 296–302, 341, 342, 345
  chairmanship of, 249
  decline of, 300–302
  in election of 1960, 118, 212–13, 264, 292–93
  in election of 1964, 122
  in election of 1966, 67
  in election of 1968, 68–69, 76, 127, 129–31, 153, 262
  in election of 1970, 148–49
  in election of 1972, 101, 153–60, 263
  in election of 1976, 199–202, 239–40, 264
  in election of 1978, 205–12, 215

in election of 1980, 233, 236, 239–
49, 265–66
in election of 1982, 249, 271, 273–
91, 364
in election of 1984, 143, 322, 328,
329, 332, 333, 370, 371–72
in election of 1986, 380–88, 422,
428–31
in election of 1988, 431–39, 457
in election of 1990, 457–59
in election of 1992, 2, 4, 5, 6, 50, 64,
90, 100, 102, 155, 235, 269–70,
343–44, 428, 431, 436, 441, 444,
448, 455, 459–66; *see also* election
of 1992
on eve of inauguration, 1–7
Mena operations and, 390, 400, 402–
16, 419, 424–27
New, 2, 149, 239, 264
Dewey, Tom, 254
Dickey, Bert, 321, 331–32, 458
Dillards, 451, 452
Doar, John, 164–67, 184
Dodd, Thomas, 148
Dole, Bob, 295, 297
draft:
race and class factors in, 79–80
in Vietnam War, 79–82, 87–92, 94–
100, 104–6, 139, 181, 209–10
Drexel Burnham, 430
Drug Enforcement Agency (DEA),
395–98, 402, 405, 412, 424
drugs, 6, 47, 58, 147, 302, 311–15, 323–
30, 434
Lasater's dealing in, 411, 421, 422–
25
Seal operation and, 389–93, 395–96,
400, 405, 408–10, 419, 422, 454
WJC's aversion to, 56
WJC's use of, 272, 325–26, 328
see also cocaine; marijuana
Duffey, Joseph P., 148, 153
Dugger, Ronnie, 300
Dukakis, Kitty, 438
Dukakis, Michael, 413, 435, 438–39,
457

Duke, David, 241
Duke University medical center, 73,
74–75
Dumas, Ernest, 212, 286
Dumond, Wayne, 458–59
Duncan, Bill, 398–99, 402
Dwire, Jeff, 48, 178, 179
Dylan, Bob, 118

Eagleburger, Lawrence, 346
Eagleton, Thomas, 234
Eakeley, Douglas, 101, 147
Eccles-Williams, Tamara, 86
Economist, 11, 267, 456, 460
Edelman, Marian Wright, 142,
164
Edelman, Peter, 142
education, 5–6, 7, 219, 304–5
federal aid to, 175
in Hot Springs, 42
school integration and, 42, 83, 198,
449, 456
WJC's policy for, 317–22, 333
Educational Standards Commission,
317–18
Edwards, E. David, 94, 95, 96, 173
E. F. Hutton, 430
Efron, Edith, 272
Ehrmann, Sarah, 123, 154, 168–69
Eisenhower, Dwight D., 111, 254, 257,
259, 354
election of 1992, 2, 322, 343–44, 428,
431, 444, 448, 455, 459–66
Betsey Wright's role in, 155
Bush in, 1, 5, 6, 9, 65, 100, 102, 104,
460
doomsday list in, 436, 441
fundraising in, 4, 311, 463, 464
Lindsey in, 269–70
Oxford years and, 102, 104
Perot in, 1, 5
Quigley and, 64, 65
WJC's childhood and, 50
WJC's ROTC exemption and, 90,
100
WJC's staff in, 462

elections:
  of 1860, 24
  of 1932, 194
  of 1960, 118, 212, 258, 264, 292–93
  of 1964, 122
  of 1966, 67
  of 1968, 68–69, 76, 127, 129–31, 153, 255, 293
  of 1970, 148–49
  of 1972, 101, 153–60, 263, 276, 293
  of 1974, 227
  of 1976, 199–202, 239, 255, 264–65
  of 1978, 205–12
  of 1980, 233, 236, 239–49, 256, 257, 265–66, 430
  of 1982, 249–50, 271, 273–91, 364
  of 1984, 143, 253, 322, 328, 329, 332, 333, 370, 371–72, 422
  of 1986, 380, 422, 428–31
  of 1988, 431–39, 457
  of 1990, 457–59
Ellis, Carolyn, 168
Ellis, Opal, 82, 88, 89
Ellis, Trice, Jr., 81, 82
El Salvador, 406, 415
Emanuel, Rahm, 462
Emerson, Thomas, 140
employment, *see* job loss; unemployment; wages
English, Art, 183, 202
Engstrom, Stephen, 327, 328
environment, 5, 220, 324, 452, 455
Equal Rights Amendment, 185
Erickson, Steve, 7
Ernst, Don, 322
Errand into the Wilderness (Miller), 57–58
Espy, Mike, 10
Esquire, 330
Evans, Sharon, 86
Evans-Pritchard, Ambrose, 325
Excelsior Hotel, 443, 463

Farmer-Laborism, 259–60
Fat Lady, 396, 397–98, 408

Faubus, Orval, 83, 147, 198, 199, 206, 237, 244, 453
  in election of 1986, 428–30
Fayetteville, Ark., 167–89, 202
  WJC's visit to, 88, 89, 96, 98, 100
  see also Arkansas, University of
Federal Bureau of Investigation (FBI), 293, 326, 390, 398, 401
  Lasater and, 412, 417, 419, 420, 422, 424
Federal Deposit Insurance Corporation (FDIC), 365, 366, 372, 375
Federal Home Loan Bank Board (FHLBB), 202, 214, 366, 369, 373, 382–83
Federal Savings and Loan Insurance Corporation, 383
feminism, 86–87, 134, 140, 163, 274
Fernung, John, 326
Ferris, Ann, 458
Fitzhugh, J. Michael, 399
Fletcher, John Gould, 197
Florida, 326–27, 395, 417
Flowers, Gennifer, 417, 440–41, 462, 463
Foley, Thomas, 296, 297
Forbes, 308, 451
Ford, Gerald R., 159, 201, 202, 254, 256, 262, 264
Fors, Henry, 104
Fort Chaffee, Ark., 240, 241, 244
Foster, Mr. (the Fascinator), 28, 34
Foster, Vincent, 10, 28, 34, 174, 220, 237, 450, 451
  death of, 422, 445
  HRC's affair with, 404, 414, 444–45
  in WJC's administration, 10, 444
Frady, Marshall, 333, 465
Franco, Francisco, 101
Fray, Paul, 181, 182
Freeman, Woody, 333
Freud, Anna, 160–61
Friends of Bill (FOBs), 9–10
Friends of Newt Gingrich, 297
Frost and Company, 374, 375
Frum, David, 299

Fulbright, J. William, 57, 72, 156, 171, 227, 259, 260, 261, 269
  McDougal and, 227, 360
  WJC's congressional campaign and, 170, 181
  WJC's draft notices and, 81–82, 89
  WJC's work for, 67–70, 96–97
fund-raising, 4, 59
  for attorney general campaign, 199–200
  for congressional campaign, 173, 174, 183–84
  for election of 1992, 4, 311, 463, 464
  for gubernatorial campaigns, 205, 206–7, 211–12, 245–46, 283, 288, 333–34, 370, 371–72, 418, 422, 430
  Madison Guaranty and, 370–72

gambling, 30, 32, 37–38, 44, 45, 46
gangsters, 37, 38, 39
Garland County, 51, 183
Gash, Adele, 19, 20
Gash, Henry Leon, 19
Gash, Minnie Faye, 20
General Electric, 268, 296, 350–51
General Motors, 29, 205
Gentry, Larry, 224, 249
Georgetown University:
  curriculum of, 60, 64–65
  Foreign Service School of, 57–72, 75–78
  R. Kennedy's visit to, 66
  ROTC at, 63
Georgia Pacific, 246, 430
Gephardt, Richard, 296, 462
Geren, Billy, 209
Gergen, David, 245, 343
Germond, Jack, 236
Gerth, Jeff, 229, 372, 385
Giancana, Sam, 434
Gingrich, Newt, 105, 296–99
Gitlin, Todd, 68, 92, 106, 112
Glaspeny, Michael, 179–80
Goldman, Sachs, 420, 453
Gold Mine Springs, 309, 368–69, 382
Goldstein, Joseph, 160–61

Goldwater, Barry, 122, 255, 258, 300
Goodwin, Tommy, 327–28, 411, 423–24, 426
GOPAC, 297, 298
Gore, Al, 460
Graham, Katharine, 10
Gramm, Phil, 105
Gramm-Rudman act, 266
Grand Gulf controversy, 219, 224, 316, 428
Great Britain:
  antiwar movement in, 92–93
  CIA operations in, 102–5
  see also Oxford University
Great Depression, 16–17, 25, 107, 108, 114, 267, 302
Great Southern Land Company, 360, 384–85
Greenberg, Paul, 320–21, 322, 331
Greer, Germaine, 86–87
Greider, William, 253, 355, 356
Greig, Geordie, 441
Griffee, Carol, 206
Grisham, Edith, see Cassidy, Edith Grisham
Grisham, Oren (Buddy), 28, 29, 39
Gross, Martin, 362, 371, 384–85, 447
gubernatorial campaigns:
  of 1978, 205–12, 215
  of 1980, 241–50, 264–65, 268
  of 1982, 271, 273–91
  of 1984, 322, 328, 329, 332, 333, 370, 371–72, 422
  of 1986, 380, 422, 428–30
  of 1990, 457–59
gun control, 211, 289–90

Hadaway, A. L., 400
Haig, Alexander, 345–46
Hale, David, 203, 379–81, 383–84
Hamilton, Alexander, 292
Hamilton, Barrett, Jr., 417
Hamilton, Jo, 61, 63
Hammerschmidt, John Paul, 171–72, 174, 175, 177, 180–84, 364, 400
Handley, Charles, 366

Harkin, Tom, 465
Harmon, John, 210, 211
Harp, William, 38
Harper's, 3, 36
Harriman, Pamela, 331
Harris, Fred, 201
Harris, Oren, 328, 329
Hart, Gary, 159, 263, 431–36, 439, 440, 441, 463
Hart, Lee, 440
Hasenfus, Eugene, 397–98
Hatfield-McGovern amendment, 148
Hawkins, Willard (Lefty), 88–89
Hayes, Peter, 101
health care and insurance, 5, 7, 305–6, 456, 461–62
national, 175, 321, 322
Heiden, Sherry, 110, 120
Henley, Don, 432
Henry, Ann, 188
Henry, Don, 459
Henry, Morris, 188
Herget, Richard, 288
Highway and Transportation Department, Arkansas, 245, 334, 360, 361
Highway Commission, Arkansas, 331, 333–34, 372, 422
Hill, Anita, 339
Hill Rats (Jackley), 339
Hodson, Philip, 86
Holmes, Eugene, 88, 89–90, 95–100, 209
WJC's letter to, 96–100, 106, 181–82, 209, 427
Holmes, William, 393–94, 398
Holt, J. Frank, 67, 156
Honduras, 408, 409, 411
Hoover, J. Edgar, 255
Hope, Ark., 2, 21–35, 42, 47
blacks in, 25–26, 28, 195
Buick agency in, 29–32, 35
corruption in, 30
gambling in, 30
segregation in, 28
Horton, Willie, 438
Hot Springs, Ark., 29–30, 31, 35–59

Bathhouse Row in, 36, 37, 66
blacks in, 37
corruption in, 30, 36–39
draft board of, 79, 81–82, 87–91, 95, 97, 100
economy of, 37, 58
gambling in, 32, 37–38, 44, 45, 46, 53
HRC's visit to, 151, 163
impoverished elderly in, 38–39
political reform in, 38, 58
prostitution in, 37, 38, 45, 58
WJC repelled by, 45
WJC's move to, 35
WJC's returns to, 66, 151
House of Representatives, U.S., 266, 296–99, 337–38, 341, 342
Banking Committee of, 375, 386
cost of running for, 292, 293
Judiciary Committee of, 164–67, 402, 403
Small Business Committee of, 230–31
WJC's campaign for, 165, 168–84, 186
Houston, Sam, 24
Houston Chronicle, 465
Howard, Ed, 182
Howell, Dorothy, *see* Rodham, Dorothy Howell
Hubbell, Webster, 10, 210, 237, 415–16, 421, 444, 449–50, 454
Humphrey, Hubert, 130, 131, 132, 153, 259–60, 262
Hutchinson, Asa, 329, 399, 401
Hyde, Henry, 111
Hyland, Denise, 62, 77

Immanuel Baptist Church, 275, 277
inflation, 233, 236
integration of schools, 42, 83, 198, 449, 456
Intermountain Regional Airport, 390, 392–93, 398, 400, 408, 409
Internal Revenue Service (IRS), 311, 312, 332, 363

Mena operations and, 390, 393, 395, 398–99, 402
International Paper, 384, 385
Iran-Contra scandal, 312, 393, 398–99, 400–403, 415
Isikoff, Mike, 443
Ives, Kevin, 459

Jackley, John, 339–40
Jackson, Cliff, 88–89
Jackson, Henry, 77
Jackson, Jesse, 438, 460
Jackson, Marlin, 363, 365, 367–68
Janske, Peggy, 55
Jaworski, Leon, 167
Jefferson, Thomas, 2, 292, 356
Jesuits, 60, 61, 66, 92
Jews, 42, 69, 110
job loss, 6, 302–3
John Birch Society, 111, 118
Johnson, Betsy, 129, 130
Johnson, Haynes, 254
Johnson, Jim, 67
Johnson, Lyndon B., 122, 129, 150, 260–61, 262, 338
    graduate study exemptions ended by, 80, 81
    presidential abdication of, 68, 76, 262
    Vietnam War and, 61, 76, 80, 81, 102, 132
    War on Poverty and, 61, 125, 131–34
Johnston, Phyllis, 222
Jones, Clinton, 182
Jones, Donald, 118–23, 131, 143, 236
    HRC's correspondence with, 122, 125, 126
Jones, Jimmie (Red), 279
Jones, Paula, 443
Jordan, Vernon, 141, 277
Justice Department, U.S., 38, 164, 370, 425
    Public Integrity office of, 324

Kalell, John, 62, 72

Kansas City, Mo., 19, 20, 21
Kantor, Mickey, 4, 202, 462
Karp, Walter, 251–52
Kasindorf, Martin, 134
Kell, George, 279
Kelley, Virginia Dell Cassidy, 21–24, 30–35, 38–53, 56–59, 102, 220
    appearance of, 21, 22, 43–44, 179
    drinking of, 31, 32, 43, 46, 53
    earnings of, 42, 44, 48, 50
    family background of, 26–27, 47
    gambling of, 32, 44, 46, 53, 75
    house purchased by, 50–51
    HRC compared with, 152
    HRC's correspondence with, 178–79
    HRC's relationship with, 48, 115, 187, 329
    on inauguration day, 8
    marital problems of, 33, 35, 46–53
    marriages of, 21, 32, 178
    memoirs of, 48, 52, 75
    as nurse, 21, 27, 43, 44, 45
    pregnancies and childbirths of, 22, 23, 24, 47–48
    on Raymond Clinton, 39, 40, 41
    Roger Jr.'s drug dealing and, 323, 326, 329–30
    WJC's college years and, 58–59, 61, 67, 86, 88, 100, 147, 151
    WJC's congressional campaign and, 173, 174, 179
    WJC's correspondence with, 74–75, 86
    WJC's gubernatorial campaigns and, 206, 212, 247
    WJC's relationship with, 8, 27, 43–46, 51, 52, 53, 58, 75, 177–78
    on WJC's relations with females, 48, 56, 151
Kelly, Michael, 451
Keniston, Kenneth, 161
Kennan, George, 16, 92
Kennedy, Bill, 10
Kennedy, Edward, 217, 239, 265
Kennedy, John F., 69, 262
    assassination of, 433–34

Kennedy, John F. (*cont.*)
  in election of 1960, 118, 212, 258, 264, 292–93
  WJC compared with, 57, 70
  WJC's meeting with, 57, 66, 260, 358
Kennedy, Joseph, 292–93
Kennedy, Robert F., 66, 68, 77–78, 130, 142, 164, 262
Kennedy, William, III, 454, 455
Kentucky, 417, 420, 422
Key, Christopher, 93
Key, V. O., 194
Khrushchev, Nikita, 93
Kierkegaard, Søren, 120
Kincaid, Diane Divers, *see* Blair, Diane Divers Kincaid
King, Martin Luther, Jr., 72, 126, 154
  assassination of, 68, 76, 128, 198, 262
  HRC's meeting of, 119–20
King, Norman, 113, 114
Kissinger, Henry, 346
Knowland, William, 255
Korean War, 97
Ku Klux Klan, 40, 241
Kuttner, Robert, 342

labor, 143, 160, 175
Laird, Melvin, 128–29
Lambert, Jimmy, 417, 420
Lapham, Lewis, 3, 296, 357
Lasater, Dan, 207, 324, 326–27, 328, 411–12, 416–26, 429, 459
  background of, 417
  drug dealing of, 411, 421, 422–26
  Frank White and, 429, 430
  HRC's dislike of, 420
  indictment of, 422–26
Lasater and Company, 310, 327, 420–25, 453
Lasch, Christopher, 162
Leach, Jim, 362
League of Women Voters, 141–42, 144
Lear, Norman, 432
Ledbetter, Brownie, 157–58, 163, 164, 281

Legal Services Corporation, 161, 202, 225, 277
Leonard, John, 352
Leopoulos, David, 45
Lett, John, 15
Leveritt, Mara, 125
Levine, Robert A., 132
Lewis, Charles, 4, 452
license costs, 221, 248, 280
Life, 137, 141
Lincoln, Abraham, 24
Lincoln Memorial, 2–3, 72, 76
Lindsay, John, 127
Lindsey, Bruce, 10, 269–70, 273
Little Rock, Ark., 67, 183, 202–5, 216–50, 268–91, 305–38, 359–88, 428–56, 465
  blacks in, 308
  cocaine parties in, 147, 272, 311–12, 314, 326, 419, 425
  corruption in, 38, 223, 309–15, 324, 331–32
  Democratic state convention (1972) in, 156
  integration crisis in, 42, 83, 198, 456
  political machine in, 193–94, 330–31, 452–53
  power elite of, 76, 163, 218, 309–10
lobbyists, 4, 347–50, 467
Locke, George (Butch), 422
Logan, Hillman, 363, 378
Long, Huey, 193–94, 389
Lorrance Heights, 384–87
Los Angeles Times, 79, 426, 440, 443, 455, 464

McCarthy, Eugene, 76, 127, 129, 130, 148, 260, 262
McCarthy, Joseph, 16, 257
McCarthyism, 261
McClellan, John, 41, 57, 171, 203, 205, 358
McCord, William D., 425
McCormack, Robert R., 110–11
McCoy, Jack, 272
McDougal, James (Diamond Jim), 55,

207, 212–15, 227, 309, 310, 334, 359–88, 415
background and personality of, 212–13, 360
FDIC investigation of, 365, 366, 372
Hale and, 379–81
HRC hired by, 370–71, 386
indictment of, 385
Madison Guaranty and, 309, 313, 364–76, 378–88
Whitewater and, 212–13, 270–71, 309, 355–80
McDougal, Susan (Hot Pants), 213, 214, 309, 364, 367, 370, 374, 376, 380–85, 387, 388
McGovern, George, 239
in election of 1972, 101, 153–60, 177, 263
Mackey, Johnnie Mae, 55, 57
McLarty, Thomas F., III (Mack), 34, 57, 203, 207–8, 210, 245, 249, 279, 288
McMath, Sid, 38, 317
McNamara, Brenning, 85–86
McRae, Tom, 458
McSorley, Richard, 92, 104
Madison Bank and Trust, 365, 367, 368
Madison Guaranty, 309, 313, 362–74, 378–88, 415, 462
audits of, 374, 375, 382–83
FDIC and, 365, 366
Lasater's ties to, 421–22
stock plan of, 373–74
Mafia, 293, 331
Magaziner, Ira, 137, 462
Maine East High School, 116, 122
Maine South High School, 116, 117, 122, 123, 255
Maitland, Sara, 86
Mamet, David, 310, 313
Mankiewicz, Frank, 158, 159
Maple Creek Farms, 309, 365, 381–82
Marafiote, Frank, 137
Maraniss, David, 208
marijuana, 272, 325, 391, 422
Marmor, Ted, 462

Marshall, Burke, 141, 146
Martin, Dell, 84, 93
Martin, Nina, 225, 318, 450
Martin, Philip, 459
Mathews, David, 180
Maulden, Jerry, 431
May, Elaine Tyler, 108, 112
Medicaid, 287, 305
Medicare, 305
Meese, Edwin, 392
Mena, Ark., 313, 389–416, 419, 422, 425–27
Mencken, H. L., 194
Merrill Lynch, 420, 430
Methodism, 108, 113, 118–22, 125, 277
Mexico, 188, 196, 268, 391
MI–5, 103
Miami Herald, 432–33, 434
Michel, Robert, 296
middle class, 258, 263, 266, 275, 344
shrinking of, 6, 305, 306
migrant labor, 143, 160
Miller, Arthur, 19, 468
Miller, Perry, 57–58
Milloy, Courtland, 4
Mills, Wilbur, 156, 188, 212, 422
Mintz, Morton, 351
Mississippi, 219, 455
Mississippi Delta, 25, 80, 309, 456
Missouri Pacific Railroad, 24, 28
Mitchell, George, 296
Mixner, David, 92
Modglin, Terry, 71
Mondale, Walter, 142–43, 160, 161, 259–60, 265
money laundering, 311, 312, 332, 393, 412, 422–25
Monkey Business, 432–33, 434
Moore, Alexis, 276
Moore, Rudy, Jr., 210, 222, 223, 278
WJC's congressional campaign and, 170–73, 175, 183
WJC's gubernatorial campaign and, 243, 247
Moore, Tom, 77
Morgan, J. P., 252, 256

Morris, Richard (Dickie), 207, 210, 212, 246, 450, 459
  WJC's political comeback and, 279–80, 282–83
Moscow, WJC's trip to, 100, 102, 104
murders, 6, 304–5, 315, 325
  of Seal, 390, 397–98, 400, 402, 422
Muskie, Edmund, 153, 154, 263
Myers, Dee Dee, 462

Nash, Robert, 332, 333
National Governors' Association (NGA), 217, 316, 442, 457
National Rifle Association (NRA), 290
national security, U.S., 346–47, 391, 395, 399, 414
Navy, U.S., 81, 82, 87, 88
Nelson, Sheffield, 385–86, 459
New Deal, 17, 23, 28, 158, 263, 301
New Democrats, 2, 149, 239, 264
New Republic, 449
Newsweek, 183, 431
New Yorker, 225, 375
New York Post, 401
New York Times, 11, 130, 215, 227, 228, 229, 244, 297, 303, 353, 370, 372, 385, 405, 443
Nicaragua, 415
  Sandinista regime in, 393, 396, 397, 406
Niebuhr, Reinhold, 120, 121
Niederhof, Victor, 231–33
Nixon, Richard M., 16, 87, 106, 142, 254, 255, 259, 260, 262, 264, 338
  death of, 167
  draft lottery and, 91, 92, 99
  in election of 1960, 118, 258
  in election of 1968, 127, 129, 262, 263, 293
  in election of 1972, 154, 156–59, 276, 293
  pardoning of, 264
  resignation of, 167, 176, 180
  Watergate and, 157, 158, 159, 164–67, 176, 177, 180
North, Oliver, 401

Nussbaum, Bernard, 10, 166–67

Oakley, Meredith, 104, 249, 310, 315, 320, 327, 329, 333, 365, 385, 437
Ochoa, Jorge, 392
Oldham, Chester, 15
Orwell, George, 354
Osborne, David, 462
Ouachita Mountains, 312–13, 389
  see also Mena, Ark.
Oxford University:
  image vs. reality at, 83–85
  tutorial system at, 83, 84
  WJC at, 82–90, 92–106

Park Ridge, Ill., 109–23, 254–55
  First United Methodist Church in, 113, 118–22
  HRC's visits to, 129, 150–51
  origins of, 109
  politics of, 110–11, 118, 122
  whiteness of, 110
  WJC's visit to, 150–51
Parks, Jane, 325
Patrick, Dennis, 422
Patterson, James N., 213
Patterson, Larry, 426, 441, 443, 461
Patton, Boggs, 349
Pelczynski, Zbigniew, 85
Pentecostals, 268
Perdue, Sally, WJC's affair with, 325, 442–43, 466
Perkins, Mary, 34
Perkins, Nanny, 34
Perot, Ross, in election of 1992, 1, 5, 460
Perry, Roger, 226
Peters, Charles, 347
Picasso, Pablo, 118, 119
Piercy, Jan, 115–16, 126, 127, 189
Pietrafasa, Nancy, 243
Podesta, Anthony, 148, 153
Pogue, Don, 147
Polet, Zach, 221
police, 130, 304–5, 312, 324, 326, 429

Mena operations and, 398, 401, 402, 403, 426–27
political action committees (PACs), 293–98, 336–38, 464
Pollack, Ron, 461–62
polls, 5, 6, 282, 288
POM, Inc. (Park on Meter), 415–16, 454
Portis, Jonathan, 90
poverty, 5–6, 119, 261, 266, 267, 300, 303–6
    in Arkansas, 25, 26, 28, 156, 173, 195, 196, 308–9, 310, 455
    of Blythe family, 16–17
    War on Poverty and, 61, 125, 131–34
    WJC's exposure to, 147
Powers, Mark, 229
pregnancy, teenage, 220, 304, 456
presidency, U.S., 342–44
    cost of running for, 292–93
Presley, Elvis, 2–3, 43
Priest, John W., 270
Proctor, George, 424, 425
Project Pursestrings, 148, 153
prostitution, 37, 38, 45, 58, 312, 314
Protestantism, 25, 108, 110, 258
    see also Baptists; Methodism
Pryor, Barbara, 188, 208, 237
Pryor, David, 171, 188, 198–99, 217, 237, 248, 269, 330, 422, 426, 429
    Senate campaign of, 205, 208, 212
Purcell, Joe, 283–86
Purvis, Joe, 34, 35, 46

Quaaludes, 396, 397
Quayle, Dan, 258
Quigley, Carroll, 64–65, 69, 70, 75, 305

racism, 196, 304–5, 340, 452
Radcliffe, Donnie, 126, 145, 166, 168, 188, 201, 268
railroads, 16, 24–26
Raphael, Robin, 85
Reagan, Ronald, 3, 5, 127, 176, 226, 252–58, 266–67, 299, 312, 343–44, 393, 399, 413, 434

in election of 1980, 233, 236, 241, 242, 244, 247, 256, 265, 266
in election of 1984, 252
federal debt under, 299–300, 303
real estate development, 212–14, 309, 313, 360–65
    see also Whitewater
Rector, Ricky Ray, 465
Reed, Terry, 401, 416
Reel, Guy, 309
Reeves, Richard, 260
Refco, Inc., 228, 230, 233–35, 236
Reich, Robert, 83, 94, 150
Remnick, David, 339
Republican Governors' Association, 244
Republican National Committee, 244
Republican National Convention:
    of 1964, 255
    of 1968, 129
    of 1980, 256
    of 1992, 460
Republicans, Republican Party, 3, 23, 88, 193–96, 226, 251–67, 270, 277, 296–303, 322, 333, 342, 345, 468
    in election of 1960, 118, 122, 258
    in election of 1968, 127, 128, 255, 262, 263, 293
    in election of 1970, 148
    in election of 1972, 154, 156–59, 276, 293
    in election of 1974, 171–72, 174, 175, 177, 180–84
    in election of 1976, 255
    in election of 1980, 231, 234, 238, 239, 242–46, 254, 255, 263
    in election of 1982, 285, 287–90
    in election of 1984, 253, 333
    in election of 1986, 429, 430
    in election of 1988, 432, 439
    in election of 1990, 458–59
    in election of 1992, 1, 4, 5, 6, 9, 65, 100, 102, 104
    HRC as, 122, 125, 127, 128–29, 255
    Mena operations and, 390, 393, 396, 398–99, 403

Republicans (*cont.*)
of Park Ridge, 111, 118
special interests and, 64
Resolution Trust Corporation, 295, 376
revenue sharing, 128–29
Rice, Donna, 431–33, 439
roads and highways, 220–21, 248, 279
Roberts, Joan, 286
Robinson, Tommy, 225–26, 331
Rockefeller, Nelson, 127, 129, 255
Rockefeller, Winthrop, 58, 88, 173, 198, 199, 237, 245
Rodham, Dorothy Howell, 107–10, 112–17, 135, 140, 435, 446
HRC's marriage and, 187, 188, 238
on Wellesley years, 123, 125, 131
WJC as viewed by, 150–51, 163
Rodham, Hillary, *see* Clinton, Hillary Rodham
Rodham, Hugh, Jr., 112–16, 135
Rodham, Hugh, Sr., 107–10, 113–16, 137, 180, 185, 188, 238, 435
HRC's relationship with, 113–16, 121, 129, 135, 162, 229
politics of, 118, 129
Rodham, Tony, 112, 114, 116, 135
Rodriguez, Maurice, 324
Rogers, Kris, 125, 127, 131
Roosevelt, Franklin D., 241, 299
Rose, Charlie, 353
Rose Law Firm, 76, 174, 214, 220, 310, 331, 453–55
HRC's job with, 203–5, 210, 225–26, 233, 237, 269, 271, 290, 368, 373–75, 382, 415–16, 429, 444, 449–51, 465
Roselli, John, 434
Rosenthal, Abe, 353
Rosenthal, Benjamin, 230, 233
ROTC, 63, 81, 87–91, 95, 98–100, 104, 182, 209, 427
Rule, Herbert, III, 204
Rush, Van, 88
Rusk, Dean, 69

Sabbag, Robert, 61, 63, 71–72, 78
Sacher, Fred, 298
Salinger, J. D., 120, 121
Salomon Brothers, 331
Sampson, Patsy, 131
Sandinistas, 393, 396, 397, 406
Satter, David, 95
savings and loan institutions (S&Ls), 296, 303, 309, 363, 364, 369–70, 373, 387
see also Madison Guaranty
Sawyer, Wallace (Buzz), 397
Schaffer, Archie, 372
Schechter, Alan, 131, 133, 134
Schenk, Brack, 34
Schlafly, Phyllis, 185
school integration, 42, 83, 198, 449, 456
Schwarzlose, Monroe, 243, 283
Scowcroft, Brent, 346
Seal, Adler Berriman (Barry), 389–403, 405, 407–10, 419, 422, 454
background of, 391
murder of, 390, 397–98, 400, 402, 422
Quaalude charges against, 396, 397
Seal, Debbie, 391
Securities Department, Arkansas, 360, 366, 367, 371–75
Segal, David, 84–85
segregation, 42
Senate, U.S., 57, 171, 193–94, 266, 277, 298, 299, 337, 341–42, 399
Church committee in, 433, 434
confirmation powers of, 338–39
cost of running for, 292, 293
Foreign Relations Committee of, 68, 72
Intelligence Oversight Committee of, 433
Judiciary Committee of, 339
Migratory Labor Subcommittee of, 142–43
WJC's job in, 67–70, 96–97
Serling, Rod, 118

sexism, 134, 165, 185, 242, 274, 340, 449
sex scandals, 263, 431–38, 439
sexual harassment, 238, 339, 443
Sheehy, Gail, 274
  on HRC, 125, 139, 144, 149, 186, 272, 437
  on WJC, 125, 144, 146, 149, 272, 437
Sherrill, Martha, 113, 117, 121, 127
Shields, Jeff, 125, 127, 131, 134
Shreveport, La., 20–21, 22, 27, 32
Simmons, Bill, 183, 245
Simon, Justin, 137
Simpson, Alan, 296
Singlaub, John, 413
60 Minutes, 437, 465
Slater, Rodney, 332
slot machines, 30, 37, 38, 40, 45
small business investment company (SBIC), 379–81
Smeeding, Timothy, 306
Smith, Ray, 156
Smith, Sam, 349, 351
Smith, Stephen, 156, 158, 220, 222, 243, 278, 362, 380
Smith, W. Maurice, 279, 283, 290, 315, 333–34, 371, 372
Smith, Barney, 430
Snider, Harold, 65, 66
Snodgrass, Jennie, 117
Soapes, Clyde, 377
Solnit, Albert, 161
Soloman, Norman, 301, 451
South Africa, 142, 234, 270
Southern Tier (Southern Arc), 394, 395, 400, 415
Soviet Union, 16, 253–54, 258, 304
  Cuba's relations with, 63–64
  WJC's trip to, 100, 102, 104
Spectrum, 459
Sperling, Godfrey, 461
Spivey, Barry, 418, 419, 420
spouse abuse, 26–27, 33
Springdale, Ark., 227–30
Staley, Carolyn, 55, 76, 280
Stanley, Alessandra, 87, 93, 94–95

Starr, John Robert, 223–24, 239, 272, 315, 316, 318, 319, 330, 332
  WJC's gubernatorial campaigns and, 206, 212, 248, 282, 284, 286–87, 291, 428, 430
State Department, U.S., 60, 346
"Statements of Information," 167
Stearns, Rick, 90–91, 92, 99, 100–101, 148, 153
  in McGovern campaign, 153, 157, 159
Steinbeck, John, 350
Steinfels, Margaret O'Brien, 161
Stenson, Bob, 117
Stephanopoulos, George, 462
Stephens, Inc., 67, 195, 198, 199, 200, 202, 448, 451, 453, 454, 464
  WJC's gubernatorial campaigns and, 206, 210, 234, 430
Stephens, Jackson, 202, 451
Stephens, Witt, 67, 451
Stern, Philip, 295
Stockman, David, 266
Stolz, J. Stephen, 270
Strauss, Robert, 336
Streisand, Barbra, 3
Strother, Raymond, 435
Stuart, Gilbert, 34
Sunday Times (London), 86, 440, 441, 455
Supreme Court, U.S., 211, 338–39, 449
Susman, Carolyn, 113

Talbott, Nelson Strobridge, III (Strobe), 90, 92, 93, 99, 414
  draft deferment of, 93, 95
taxes, 194, 198, 256, 455
  Carter and, 265, 266
  cigarette, 132
  of Clintons, 384–86, 447
  corporate, 265, 266–67, 287, 300, 301, 452
  education, 318–21
  exemptions from, 287, 294, 295–96, 452
  fuel, 220–21

taxes (*cont.*)
  pleasure, 38
  property, 203
  Reagan and, 266–67
  road, 248
  sales, 205, 207, 221, 320
  of Seal, 395–96
Taylor, Rev. Gardner, 7
TCBY Yogurt, 430, 447, 449, 451
Teagarden, Jack, 45
"Team 100," 294–95
television, 351, 353, 431, 437, 462, 463
Texas, 16–17, 22
  election of 1972 and, 154–55, 158
Thalheimer, Lee, 366, 371
Thomas, Dylan, 100
Thomas, Mike, 80
Thomason, Harry, 439
Thomasson, Patsy, 10, 422, 445
Tillich, Paul, 118, 120
timber companies, 220, 221, 222, 246
Time, 75, 90, 93
Tolliver, Michael, 400
Trafficante, Santo, 434
Tragedy and Hope (Quigley), 64
Travelgate scandal, 448
traveling salesmen, 17–20, 25, 29
trucking industry, 221, 227, 242, 248, 316
Truffaut, François, 118
Truman, Harry S., 16, 258, 299
Tucker, Jim Guy, 171, 188, 362, 372, 379, 458–59
  in election of 1982, 282–84
  Senate campaign of, 205, 208, 212
Tutwiler, Guy, 182
Tyson, Don, 228, 271, 451, 452
Tyson Foods, 10, 207, 214, 221, 227, 228, 235, 242, 248, 311, 316, 447, 451

Udall, Morris, 201
Umin, Steven, 168
unemployment, 6, 287
USA Today, 386
U.S. News & World Report, 453

utilities, 203, 205, 210, 219, 287, 316, 428

Vanity Fair, 272
Vapors, 44, 45, 58
Ventura, Michael, 341
Vietnam Moratorium Committee, 91–93
Vietnam War, 61, 66–69, 76, 77, 87–106, 122, 148, 261
  casualties in, 68, 69–70, 80, 87, 106
  Democratic convention (1968) and, 130
  draft and, 79–82, 87–92, 94–100, 104–6, 139, 181, 209–10
  election of 1972 and, 153, 157, 159, 160
  HRC and, 125, 126, 127, 129, 135, 136, 139, 141–42
  see also antiwar movement
Village Voice, 228
voter registration, 154

wages, 303, 304, 319, 344–45, 348
Wagner, Carl, 148, 153
Walker, Martin, 85
Wallace, George, 41, 262
Wallace, Larry, 447
Wall Street Journal, 5, 233, 299, 310, 348, 390, 398, 422
Wal-Mart, 311, 449, 451, 453
Walsh, Lawrence, 401–2
Walton, Sam, 449
Ward, Seth, 210, 415
Warner, Judith:
  on Dorothy Rodham, 110, 113, 131
  on HRC, 115, 122, 129, 131, 149, 168, 184, 280, 281, 328–29
  on WJC, 149, 280, 281, 329
War on Poverty, 61, 125, 131–34
Washington, D.C., 2–11, 57–79, 164–67, 251–67, 292–307, 335–36, 457, 466
  American Legion national assembly in, 57
  antiwar movement in, 91–92

Barber's view of, 335–36
bureaucracy in, 339–42, 344–47
eve of inauguration in, 2–7
HRC's internship in, 128–29
inauguration day in, 7–11
journalism and, 350–56
Little Rock compared with, 335, 358
lobbyists in, 4, 347–50, 467
riots in, 76–77
Washington, George, 34, 292
Washington Monthly, 462
Washington Post, 4, 9, 201, 208, 367, 376, 433, 443, 445, 446
Washington Research Project, 142
Washington Times, 396
Watergate, 157, 158, 159, 164–67, 176, 180, 203, 264, 293
Watkins, David, 10, 447–48
weapons, 5–6, 393–95, 397, 408
Webb, Kane, 313
Weicker, Lowell, 148
Welch, Russell, 398–99, 402
Weld, William, 85, 165
welfare, 300, 304, 456
Wellesley College:
  blacks at, 126, 127
  endowment of, 124
  HRC at, 123–28, 130–37
  HRC's commencement speech at, 134–37, 141, 149
  Internship Program of, 128–29
  rebellion at, 126–27, 128, 130
Wexler, Ann, 149, 153
Whillock, Carl, 172–73, 175, 184, 282
White, Clay, 40
White, Earline, 42
White, Frank, 244–50, 266, 271, 285, 287–88, 380, 418
  in election of 1986, 429, 430
White, Theodore H., 158
White House Travel Office, 448
Whitener, Freddy, 368–69
Whitewater, 212–14, 229, 234, 236, 270, 281, 309, 313, 360–66, 368, 371, 375–80, 382–88, 463
  advertising of, 376–77

Foster's death and, 445
  Lot 13 of, 362–64, 378
Whitewater Development Corporation, 384
Whitman, Walt, 357
Whitten, Jamie, 337
Wicker, Tom, 130
Wilhelm, David, 462
Wilhelmina, Queen of the Netherlands, 389
Williams, T. Harry, 194
Williams and Connolly, 168
Williamson, Tom, 83
Willis, Carroll, 332
Willkie, Wendell, 254
Wills, Garry, 29, 86, 95, 252
Wilson, Sharlene, 325–26
Wilson, William R., Jr., 327, 328
Wilson, Woodrow, 299
Wirges, Gene, 196
Wish for Kings, The (Lapham), 296
Witcover, Jules, 236
Wofford, Harris, 69, 462
women:
  in Arkansas government, 198, 199
  feminism and, 86–87, 134, 140, 163, 274
  sexism and, 134, 165, 185, 242, 274, 340, 449
  sexual harassment and, 238, 339, 443
  WJC's attitude toward, 274, 440–44
World War I, 299
World War II, 20, 21, 25, 32, 89, 97, 267, 299
World Wide Travel, 448, 464
Worley, David, 298–99
Worthen Bank, 364, 430, 448, 451, 464
Wright, George, 35
Wright, Jim, 297
Wright, Onie Elizabeth (Betsey), 155, 201, 315, 327, 367, 422, 439, 465–66
  in election of 1992, 155, 465
  WJC's gubernatorial campaigns and, 273–74, 280–84, 289–90, 332

Yale, University, Child Study Center of, 160–63
Yale Law School, 100, 139–50, 160, 164
   Barristers Union of, 149
   HRC's application to, 133, 134
   HRC's graduation from, 155
   rebellion at, 140–41
   WJC's application to, 96
Yale Review of Law and Social Action, 140
Young Democrats, 212